Social Media in Asia

Social Media in Asia

Co-editors:

Cui Litang
Xiamen University, Tan Kha Kee College

Michael H. Prosser
*University of Virginia and
Shanghai International Studies University*

Dignity Press
World Dignity University Press

Social Media in Asia, coedited by Cui Litang and Michael H. Prosser; offers a set of 20 scholarly essays, covering 14 countries in Asia and the Pacific-Rim, the first book to fully assess this critical aspect of Asia's media today, for the world's most populous region. Sixteen of the chapter authors are natives of the Asia-Pacific region and two are from Russia.

Published by Dignity Press
16 Northview Court
Lake Oswego, OR 97035, USA
www.dignitypress.org

Book design by Uli Spalthoff
Front cover map from http://commons.wikimedia.org/wiki/File:Map_of_Asia.svg by Cacahuate. The front cover features an arbitrary selection of logos from nine social media companies that are active in Asia. They are, in order of appearance from the top, Twitter, Facebook, YouTube, VKontakte, Sina Weibo, Happy Network, LinkedIn, Pinterest, TencentQQ. These social media companies and their respective logos are trademarks or registered trademarks in the U.S. and other countries. These and all other trademarks and logos featured in this book belong to their respective owners. All rights reserved.

Printed on paper from environmentally managed forestry:
http://www.lightningsource.com/chainofcustody

Book website: www.dignitypress.org/social-media-in-asia

ISBN 978-1-937570-36-1
Also available as EPUB: ISBN 978-1-937570-43-9
and Kindle eBook: ISBN 978-1-937570-44-6

Contents

To Brenda Cui Yan for her master's program at Peking University and all contributors to Social Media in Asia.

Cui Litang

To my daughter, Michelle Ann Epiphany Prosser-Levasseur, and her husband Roger Donald Levasseur, my son, Leo Michael Prosser, and my son, Louis Mark Prosser and his wife Bernadette Prosser.

Michael H. Prosser

Preface

Michael H. Prosser

University of Virginia, Charlottesville, Virginia,
and Shanghai International Studies University

While teaching at Yangzhou University in 2001–02, I had the opportunity to meet a younger faculty member, Cui Litang, who gave several very interesting lectures in my junior level mass media course. He also has since had media experiences at the Australian Broadcasting Corporation and Deutsche Welle, and twenty-seven years of experience in teaching EFL/ESL. As a multilingual translator, web author, developer, and podcaster, his translations and writings as a contributing author reflect his research interest both in linguistics and media. In 1995 he taught Chinese at Green River Community College in Washington State and was honored there as a "Cultural Ambassador." In my, Sharifzadeh's and Zhang's 2013 "Finding Cross-Cultural Common Ground", he wrote:

> *As a media person since a long time ago, I have always had extensive media exposure, the print as well as the electronic media, plus the Internet. But in 2001 I was still more of a radio guy than a TV person, spending many hours daily tuned to VOA, BBC and several other international broadcasters on the shortwave, sometimes feverishly during crises…*

"The media is the message" is what Marshall McLuhan says about the human–media relationship. And this has turned out very true in my survival efforts over the past decades. I have been using the media to navigate the world, from the magic soundsphere of the radio world, to the deluge of subscribed newspapers and magazines and to the imagery world of film and TV. So it's only natural for me to have developed a profound interest and insight in man and media which has paved the way for some intellectual and academic research later, drawing on resources, not only like that of my

personal media exposure, but also serious study and thinking…

I appreciated your invitation to me that year for a guest speech in your media class, which I felt, has piloted my first media class in my life, and triggered my total plunge into media study. Since then, with this turn of interest, I have witnessed some interesting changes in my intellectual thinking involving pragmatic linguistics and about man and media relations.

My published papers like "The Communication Convention and Functions of English Discourse Markers in Speech Communication" and "A Map Without Boundary: William Gibson's Cyberpunk Novel Neuromancer Reexamined" have manifested this significant change. About when I was going about launching my first course of "Let's Get to Know Mass Communication" at Shanghai Industry and Commerce Foreign Language College, I participated in a massive renovation program as an interior designer of Shanghai Municipal Situational Foreign Language and Experiencing Center which I have illustrated by presenting a brief communication history of English on the walls, all the way from Canterbury to the country in the New World.

In the meantime, as part of media practice, I have started to post regularly on:

- *facebook at http://www.facebook.com/people/Cui-Litang*
- *youtube at http://www.youtube.com/user/cuilitang*
- *flickr at http://www.flickr.com/photos/cuilitang, with media and communication related videos and photos.*

A better example of these is Bappa's Chinese New Year's Message at Shanghai Reman Factory of Caterpillar, when the General Manager, Bappa, a student of Global LT Chinese program delivered a message in Chinese to the factory. On top of that, my website "Let's Learn Chinese the e-way!" also serves the purpose of communication. The general situation of the mass media in the last decade since 2001 has seen changes within the status of the state media, as analyzed in my contributed writing "Wrangling the Media Market Place" to Prof. Li Mengyu and Prof. Michael Prosser's Communicating Interculturally [2012]…

Media technology has enormously proliferated over the past decades as embodied and manifested by the Internet, when we have not only seen a surge of netizens but also convergence of media toward mobile and personal, to that of the media prophecy of EPIC 2014 by Robin Sloan and Matt Thompson. China has benefited from recent decades of economic growth which has fed the media consumption on the Internet, and the growth of the Internet in the size of e-commerce, in the number of educational, organizational, governmental and personal portals have, in turn, fed the growth of the Internet and media in general. If this is to be accounted for by the favorable government policy, the sheer number of netizens shouts the story...Baidu has edged over Google as the No. 1 search engine in China, with 83.6% query share over 11.1% since fourth quarter of 2010. And Baidu seems to have emerged as the search engine of China. Among a few things that favor Baidu: fast search speed at local servers and free music downloads.

But since Baidu search results are filtered on government requirements, the chance of penetrating by western media is significantly curtailed.

(Cui Litang in: Prosser, Sharifzadeh, & Zhang, 2013,
Finding Cross-Cultural Common Ground, pp. 276–283).

Michael H. Prosser:

With an early strong interest in internationalization, at 22 I traveled by ship from Montreal to Liverpool, visiting twelve European countries for two months, attending an international student conference in southern Germany, and returning by air to the US. The following year, I returned to Europe, and made my first of five visits to Russia. When my children were small, we attended an interreligious conference at Oxford University and a communication conference at the University of Heidelberg. I had an opportunity eleven years later to attend a communication conference in Berlin, when I also visited Poland, Hungary, Czechoslovakia, and East Germany. I have attended conferences or have given lectures in Cambodia, Canada, China, England, Germany, Japan, India, Italy, Mexico, Peru, Russia, Singapore, South Korea, the Netherlands, and Sweden, leading to my increasing internationalization, first Europe-centered; then Afro-centered, and now Asia-centered.

During the 1980s, my personal intercultural experiences included being a host father to international high school exchange students from Sweden, Belgium, France, Spain, Brazil, and South Africa and to a refugee boy from El Salvador. From 1984 to 1986, I was President of the International Society for Intercultural Education, Training and Research. Two boys from Swaziland came to the US with me in 1991 for added education. From 1996 to 2001, three adult refugees from South Sudan lived witih me in Rochester, New York from 1996 to 2001.

Many of my university courses have emphasized intercultural communication, international and global media, and the United Nations. Additionally, I have had the rich opportunity for intercultural research or editorship with Cui Litang, Jun Lu, Li Mengyu, Zhang Shengyong, and L. Zhou from China; Nemi C. Jain and K.S. Sitaram from India; Mansoureh Sharifzadeh from Iran; and Muneo Yoshikawa from Japan. I taught twice in the 1970s at Canadian universities, offering the first intercultural communication course there in 1972 at Memorial University of Newfoundland. As a Fulbright Professor at the University of Swaziland in 1990–91, I initiated its communication major. Between 1995 and 2001, K.S. Sitaram and I chaired six Rochester Intercultural Conferences. Before 2001, I had taught 8800 students in American and Canadian universities, and from 2001-2011 I taught 2300 students at Yangzhou University, Beijing Language and Culture University, Shanghai International Studies University, and Ocean University of China. As the faculty advisor for 61 Life Long Learners, I participated in the University of Virginia/Institute for Shipboard Education Semester at Sea around the world study voyage in 2011.

The progression in my academic research moved rather naturally from international rhetoric and public discourse to intercultural and international communication and media, to social media, and thus leading to the rich contours of this book, Social Media in Asia, with essays by very diverse and talented authors. My academic interests in international social media developed over time. In my "Civic Discourse for the Third Millennium" series, 1998–2004, Lara B. Lengel's book on Social Media in Eastern Europe, Leo A. Gher and Hussein Y. Amin's book on the Middle

East (2000) and Richard Holt's book about Dialogue on the Internet (2004) are illustrative.

When I began to consider editing Social Media in Asia, based on our long term friendship, Cui's and my intercultural/international/global interests and experiences, and our shared enthusiasm in studying social media, inviting him as the first coeditor was an obviously excellent opportunity for our collaboration on this project. With much good advice, he has commented that many of the authors of essays in the book are exceptionally sharp in their understanding of the Asian media, and I certainly agree.

We especially wish to thank Dr. Uli Spalthoff from Dignity Press who has already wisely guided my, Mansoureh Sharifzadeh's, and Zhang Shengyong's 2013 book, Finding Cross-Cultural Common Ground, plus his colleagues in the Dignity Press and Human Dignity and Humiliation Studies Network, Dr. Evelin Lindner, a global citizen and Dr. Linda Hartling, Director of Dignity Press. Our thanks go also to all the excellent scholars whose essays appear in Social Media in Asia.

Charlottesville, Virginia
July 30, 2013

Introduction: A Cross-Cultural Perspective on Social Media in Asia

Michael H. Prosser
University of Virginia, Charlottesville, Virginia
and Shanghai International Studies University
(Corresponding author) prossermichael@gmail.com

Cui Litang
Tan Kha Kee College, Xiamen University, Xiamen, China
clitang@gmail.com

"Intercultural communication…should really be called Intercultural Relations, but isn't simply because of an accident of the way interdisciplinary fields are treated in the US."

L. Robert Kohls

"The medium, or process, of our time—electric technology is reshaping and restructuring patterns of social interdependence and every aspect of our personal life. It is forcing us to reconsider and re-evaluate practically every thought and action."

Marshall McLuhan

"It shouldn't be too much of a surprise that the Internet has evolved into a force strong enough to reflect the greatest hopes and fears of those who use it. After all, it was designed to withstand nuclear war, not just for the puny huffs and puffs of politicians and religious fanatics."

Denice Caruso

"The key is the Internet....The Internet is the heart of this new civilization, and telecommunications are the nervous system or circulatory system."

Carlos Slim Helu

"A further examination of how computer-based technologies have become more and more dynamic and much less controlled by political systems; recognizing, however, that the orderly and efficient development of telecommunications infrastructures in developing countries is necessary to keep pace with development with other sectors of economics."

Kenday Samuel Kamara

"Today, the Internet revolution has brought ever-changing business websites, inexpensive e-zines, blogging and social networking sites, such as My Space and Facebook—all of which are rapidly changing the way the world communicates. The proliferation of information technologies thus suggests a phenomenal progression in people-to-people communication and a decentralization of communication away from old vertical patterns of broadcasting systems."

Kenday Samuel Kamara

Abstract

Cultural dialogue, emphasizing similarities among cultures, and leading later to a focus on multiculturalism, universalism and global communication has long been identified as a major trend in the study and practice of intercultural communication. A second major trend also long identified is cultural criticism which emphasizes cultural critiques, leading to comparative or contrastive views of intercultural communication and an emphasis on cultural diversity, particularism and specific cultural identities. This introduction highlights both of these trends as well as the linguistic concept of functionalism (surveillance, interpretation, linkage, transmission of values, and cultural dimensions) as well as democratization as a means of analysis for constructing the social media in Asia.

Major facets also worthy of consideration include 1. The various types of social media prevalent in Asia; 2. Particular language use as related to social media; 3. Attitudes of the authors in various chapters related to social media; 4. The values espoused in various cultural settings in Asia in their own use or promotion of social media in their own countries; 5. The authors' critiques of social media usage, promotion, and control; and 6. Michael H. Prosser's and Cui Litang's perspectives of the cross-cultural trends seen in the book's chapters.

Our findings identify one third of the essays in the category of cross-cultural dialogue with two thirds of the chapters emphasizing cultural criticism and functional analysis.

Keywords: Asia, Cross-cultural trends, cultural dialogue, cultural criticism, cultural dimensions, functionalism, social media

Setting The Stage

L. Robert Kohls, one of the premier practitioners of intercultural communication, states:

> "Intercultural communication...should really be called Intercultural Relations, but isn't simply because of an accident of the way interdisciplinary fields are treated in the US. Anthropology, which is where the intercultural field began, and where we should be located, had it not been for the fact that in the mid-1960's, when the intercultural field had its beginnings, anthropology was so busy trying to establish itself as a science that they wanted nothing to do with such a practical application of their beloved science—so we were lucky that the schools of communication which were reestablishing themselves (out of what had been departments of speech or drama)... were willing to pull in 'Intercultural Communication' as well. We are grateful to the communication departments for giving us a home

base ..." *(Kohls, personal communication to Steve J. Kulich, January 2003, quoted in Kulich (2012).*

Renaldo Anderson, writing of the influence of Molefi Kete Asante, writes:

"Yet as a positive aspect of the advent of the social media revolution in relation to intercultural communication is how it is impacting personal relationships as Asante notes:"

"...human communication has really changed and the way we look at it today has a lot to do with the new media that we predicted but could never have imagined fully. Yes, media can and does influence intercultural communication and the real truth is that we have a world that is far smaller than it was and we are confronted everyday with changes in Libya, Egypt, Iraq, and other countries while we are sitting in our living rooms. This is the impact of media. I can be in another culture, interact on Skype with my friends in China, Nigeria, Japan, South Africa, and Singapore almost immediately. I can know something more of their cultures than I could a few years ago." *(Asante, 2011, quoted in Anderson, 2012)*

Cultural Dialogue and Cultural Criticism

In their early coedited book, Handbook of Intercultural Communication (1979), Molefi Kete Asante, Eileen Newmark, and Cecil Blake began by noting two trends at that time in the development of the study and practice of intercultural communication. The first, which they associated with Michael H. Prosser (Intercommunication among Nations and Peoples, 1973, and The Cultural Dialogue, 1978) emphasized this topic, cultural dialogue, which over time has led to the study of multiculturalism and global communication, stressing the similarities among cultural groups. This early and continuing study includes such variables as the definitions of intercultural communication, language and nonverbal patterns, perceptions, objective and subjective culture, attitudes, beliefs, values and world views. A major aspect of The Cultural Dialogue was one quarter of its text which paraphrased a cultural dialogue among four Americans and four Japanese, taking place as part of a bicultural Japanese and American research project in the summer of 1974 which was held in Nihonmatsu, Japan. Muneo Yoshikawa provided an introduction to the dialogue by commenting on his own intercultural experiences when he was living and teaching in Hawaii. Prosser's paraphrased dialogue itself demonstrated both the group findings of similarities between the two cultures, and the separating differences of culture, customs, and values.

D. Ray Heisey, former President of the International Association for Intercultural Communication, articulated a proposal for the study of intercultural communication in Hong Kong in 2001, claiming that inherently intercultural communication must include the dialogical process in order to have any validity. He offered four key points for this process in its study, teaching, practice, and research:

> 1. "...we purposefully select those texts that present differing views and interpretations of the data so that students can see that scholars differ and disagree on certain findings. This includes engaging in dialogue in teaching, including the students in the process. 2. Case studies involving individuals from different cultures provide an understanding of 'the creative mind at work' which grows out of an intellectual dialogue where the professor and student have different interpretations. 3. Case studies serve as useful examples of cultural dialogue as a teaching tool for students (such as the Chinese students) who may not have much real life experience with other cultures. More dialogue is needed both to understand the substance of such dialogue and case studies and the process of becoming intercultural in orientation for both teachers and students. 4. Let's try to engage a colleague who has a different perspective or is from a different culture to sound out our research questions, our research objectives, our research issues."

Heisey submits that

> "When we acknowledge the rule of transparency, we reach the conclusion of multi-dimensionality of intercultural communication. When we see the multidimensions of intercultural communication,

we are confronted with the second rule, which is interconnectedness"
(Heisey in Prosser, 2012, pp. 812–813).

K. S. Sitaram, who launched the first professional division for the study of intercultural communication and development at the International Communication Association in Minneapolis on May 6, 1970, was an avid supporter for the study and practice of intercultural dialogue in his journal articles and professional conference presentations as well as in his and Ray T. Cogdell's book, Foundations of Intercultural Communication (1976), and in his book Culture And Communication: A World View (1995). In his proposal to establish the Division of Intercultural and Development Communication for ICA, he argued:

> *"That intercultural communication "involves a communicator of one culture and an audience of another culture…. A person could be a communicator this moment and an audience the next, since the art of understanding and being understood goes on simultaneously. Intercultural communication could be studied both as an art and a process. This process involves these variables: mind, sense, and medium…. Intercultural communication takes place at cultural levels. The communicator and his audience interact as members of their cultures rather than as nations.*
> *Intercultural communication does not take place in a vacuum. It does take place in an environment, which could be intercultural, interethnic, or intra-cultural. It involves a communicator and audience of entirely different to slightly different cultures.*
> *Therefore, intercultural communication is the study of not only the art and the process of communication between cultures but also the many cultural variables that shape the art and affect the process."*
> *(1970: May 6, quoted in Prosser, 2012).*

Tapio Varis, former UNESCO Professor at the University of Tampere, Finland, commented in terms of Sitaram's influence:

> *"As Professor Sitaram has noted, in the early days of developing intercultural communication, as a field of study, we focused on studies of cultural similarities, positive imaging, cultural relativism, and generally convergence. The ideal of world peace has also figured more*

recently as a goal of intercultural communication. We have indeed traveled a long way from interculturalism to multiculturalism and from intercultural broadcasting to the information superhighway. We have grown more mature, teaching intercultural related areas, but technology is making the world ever more interconnected and global.... The time is now ripe for a new view of intercultural communication in the new media, digital communication, and the cultural environment" (1998, pp. xiii–xiv).

One of the 1990s books promoting cultural dialogue as a basic underpinning for the study of intercultural communication is Craig Storti's book, Cross-cultural Dialogues: 74 Brief Encounters with Cultural Difference (1994). Promotional materials for the book provide the following details:

"Culture affects everything we do: the simplest phrase can be so steeped in cultural context that even seemingly innocent exchanges between people are loaded with cultural differences waiting to expand into misunderstanding and tension. In response, Cross-Cultural Dialogues: 74 Brief Encounters with Cultural Difference offers a collection of 74 brief conversations between an American and people from other cultures, spanning nearly every major region of the world. Each dialogue is categorized as a social, workplace or business interaction and contains at least one breach of cultural norms, which the reader is then challenged to address. Even the most careful reader will be caught off guard by some of the dialogues' hidden subtleties. Storti is meticulous in his analysis of each dialogue, pinpointing not only the moment when the interaction goes wrong, but also identifying the cultural reasons behind each participant's point of view. Whether training others or adding to your own cultural awareness, Cross Cultural Dialogues is an excellent resource, encouraging readers to engage in the world and increase their multicultural understanding."

In Li Mengyu's and Michael Prosser's intercultural communication text book for Chinese students, Communicating Interculturally (2012), they have constructed eleven cultural dialogues between an imaginary class of Chinese students, and imaginary Professor Zhang, and Prosser as a real teacher. The first ten dialogues proceed the ten chapters (1. Culture, 2. Communication and Intercultural Communication, 3. Creating Our Own Cultural Stories, 4. Perceptions, Beliefs, World Views and Values, 5. Cultural Patterns and Cross-Cultural Value Orientations, 6. Verbal and Nonverbal Communication, 7. Contemporary Youth, 8. Cultural Media, 9. Intercultural Communication in Business, Training, and Education, and 10. Intercultural Theories and Research). There is also an epilogue, A Final Conversation: Think Globally and Act Locally. The chapter dialogues represent a wide variety of Chinese students and set the tone for the chapter materials which follow.

Jia Yuxun who writes the Foreword for Communicating Interculturally offers the following perspective relating to the dialogues:

> "As Professor Hui-ching Chang comments, these dialogues are both serious and light-hearted. There is considerable humor in the dialogues, and at the same time, serious teaching is also taking place as Professor Zhang and Michael Prosser speak authoritatively. Often, also the imaginary students, who actually represent a cross-section of the 2,200 Chinese students that Michael Prosser has taught in China, speak authoritatively with a wide array of topics covered in the different chapters. Some students are nationalistic, some are typically humorous, some are frivolous, and still others are very serious about their own goals and intercultural development."

Michael H. Prosser, Mansoureh Sharifzadeh's and Zhang Shengyong's book, Finding Cross-Cultural Common Ground (2013), has multiple essays relating to the concept of cultural dialogue, and also in some cases related to cultural criticism.

The second trend that Asante, Newmark, and Blake saw developing was that of cultural critiques, espoused by Edward C. Stewart, among others, and emphasizing cultural differences. Stewart argued that the major reason for studying intercultural communication came from understanding these cultural differences. He was the innovative and creative developer of the "Contrast American", who produced two of his most important works: "Contrast Culture Method (CCM) of Intercultural Training," and his book, "American Cultural Patterns: A Cross-Cultural Perspective"

(1971). Jacqueline Howell Wasilewski and Holly Siebert Kawakami write of Stewart,

> *Although this approach moves beyond simple contrasts to embrace similarities and the realization that differences are a matter of degree, later in his career Stewart focused more on adaptation, on dialectical, and contrasting forces (2012: November).*

This trend has subsequently developed more theories to test and has led to the broad study of identity, which Asante helped to develop through his studies of interracial communication, and later Afrocentrism. Still later studies investigated Latino culture, Asian culture broadly, and Chinese culture specifically. Two recent books emphasizing cultural criticism through the concept of identification include Dai's and Kulich's Identity and Intercultural Communication (1): Theoretical and Contextual Construction (2010) and Kulich's and Dai's Identity and Intercultural Communication (II): Conceptual and Conceptual Applications (2011). Additionally, Kenday Samuel Kamara's recent book, Online Collaborative Learning; Challenges and Opportunities for NGOs in Developing Countries (2013) offers both cultural critiques and the prospect for cultural dialogues among development NGOs in Africa, South Asia, North America, and Europe.

Perspectives, Paradigms and Prerogatives of Social Media in Asia

Cultural dialogue, or global dialogue (Cui, 2012), as a brush-pen expression for intercultural communication or cross-cultural communication, has evolved a long way, from communication studies, amid globalization as a result of unprecedentedly increasing contact, communication, commerce, exchange, participation, immigration and democratization on a global scale, with two distinct mission agendas both in academic study and social development, mainly through college programs of interdisciplinary orientation and organizational (government, incorporate and NGO) trainings, workshops and projects for development and enrichment.

As an interdisciplinary study, cultural dialogue stays focused on communication, but tethering around interdependent areas of anthropology, cultural studies, psychology and communication, seeking to understand "what we as humans have in common," and what underlines our universal and unique "ways of organizing and constructing knowledge" that were involved in shaping our "social relationships," inter-personal, inter-ethnic, and inter-cultural. A critical awareness of "social relationships," coupled with inter-cultural or cross-cultural norms or by following new models of conduct may strategically help to resolve "conflicts" in the global dialogue.

In his book The Cultural Dialogue, Prosser (1978) defined cultural dialogue respectively intercultural communication as "interpersonal communication on the individual level between members of distinctly different cultural groups" and cross-cultural communication as "the collective communication between cultural spokespersons of different cultural groups or between whole cultural groups." The distinction between intercultural communication and cross-cultural communication is meaningful, from the perspective of United States culture where he is from, and by the tradition of "explicit Western communication culture" versus "the implicit Eastern communication culture" (Prosser, 1978, p. 12), but it quickly was overridden by the more convenient term, intercultural communication, as communication in most instances by nature, is one-on-one and bi-lateral and in fact "all individuals are influenced by culture writ large, by our cultural civilization, by our cultural institutions, by the technological impacts upon our culture, by the political culture which surrounds us, by the cultural maximizers in our own culture, by the ethnocentric influences upon us as cultural beings, and by our own unique development" (Prosser 1978, p. 196).

Cultural dialogue, either as an intellectual pursuit and academic study, or as a developmental agenda, is proactive, constructive, engaging, participatory, collaborative, mission-critical, instrumental and often objective-oriented. It is macroscopic and implicit in approach.

Cultural criticism or cultural studies developed from the "Frankfurt School," drawing on resources and inspirations of the political economics of Karl Marx, for instance, "take a macro-analytic perspective that examines such concepts as ideology, culture, and politics as they relate to the role of media in society" (Dominick, 1999, p. 49), focusing on media ownership (emphasizing power relationships), the culture industry, culture myths, slanting toward, as James Carey, looking upon communication as a ritual, suggested that scholars should study "how communication creates, maintains and modifies culture" (Dominick, 1999, p. 52), in the communication ritual that "draws people together" and "represents a sharing of beliefs."

Another popular paradigm approach is functional analysis. Functional analysis, in contrast, is micro and explicit, holding that the media are best understood by examining how they are used. In social media, the use that audiences make of their interactions between them, and with the media makes a source of interest and significance.

Functional analysis has several advantages in approaching social media: First of all, it provides a definite and defined perspective from which the social media and interactions can be examined. Second, it helps to project concepts that are meaningful in framing and figuring out social media behavior and habit. And finally, it makes us aware of the diverse nature of motivations for social networking and gratifications provided by the social media.

According to functional analysis the media function comprises the following components:

1. The surveillance function, which is informational as well as empirical, with concern over credibility, media angst (over "air time or column inches," or "news-hole," for instance), and media presence/prominence versus status conferral.

2. The interpretation function is value-oriented, about the ultimate meaning and significance of events, specific information and ideas, as communicated on and by the social media, examining and predicting how "a transformative development of critical thinking that values multiple sources and accepts 'the social construction of reality," as identified in the chapter "Political Uses of Social Media in Kazakhstan" (Couper, Nurmanov and Adams) evolves on the social media.

3. The linkage function explores how social media enable people who are not directly connected across demographics to meet and join in a common experience of business or banner. According to an analysis of the linkage function, social media are capable of "public-making."

4. The transmission of values is believed to be a more subtle, slow, but nonetheless an important function of the media that has been pushed ahead and further expanded in the social media, not only allowing socialization (networking), but also consciously instilling values in the audience, or transmitting values by enforcing social norms and behavior among them, as Szu-Wei Chen expresses in the chapter "PTT: A Unique Social Media in Taiwan". This function may be countervailed by diverse and multiple sources of information, or curbed all together by efforts of gate-keeping, blocking or censorship, for instance.

5. The entertainment function is obvious and forms a brave new world on social media, to solicit audience as well as to serve both the audience and the advertisers. This is indicated in the chapter: "Cultural Values, Gender, and Chinese Young Adults in Using Social Media" by Qingwen Dong, Yun Wu, Xiaoting Gu, and Dale Dong.

Functional analysis transfers the paradigm to the uses-and-gratification model if there is a shift in position, with the scrutiny turning to a fourfold category system of: 1. cognition; 2. diversion; 3. social utility, and 4. withdrawal, as explained in Huan Chen's chapter "Chinese Consumers' Perception of Social Media; A Phenomenological Study".

"Cultural dimensions," constructed by Professor Geert Hofstede from his IBM research (Hofstede, 1991), is a more recent paradigm changer representing the latest research effort attempting to address and implement the concept of "cultural dimensions" data-crunched in the "cultural indexes," from different layers and levels of group, organizational and national cultures.

The "cultural dimensions" approach quantifies the cultural traits 1. Power Distance, 2. Individualism, 3. Masculinity, 4. Uncertainty Avoidance, 5. Long Term Orientation, and 6. Gratification and Indulgence. The approach is comprehensive, dynamically evolving, empirical and prominently data-driven (quantitative), involving social psychology, cross-cultural communication and international management. It has developed into a paradigm of its own right and an important theoretical framework for cross-cultural communication studies.

Social Media in Asia represents a potpourri of the major approaches and perspectives of cross-cultural and media studies, crossing over between the cultural dialogue, cultural criticism and functional studies, with frequent references to the "cultural dimensions." With descriptive, analytical, cross-cultural trends, and case studies, the various authors provide an up-to-date perspective on social media in Asia.

A quick thumb-through exploration will find one-third of all contributed essays in the category of cross-cultural dialogue, focusing on

- internationalization (Michael Prosser, Preface),
- interrelationships of social media and intercultural communication in Chapter 1, "Social Media, Communication and Culture; An Asian Perspective" by Haslett,
- global dialogue in chapter I, "Vox Populi—Vox Dei: In Search of the Common Golden Gates" by Cui Litang,
- cross-cultural communication, social networking, social relationships, public sphere, in chapter XII, "Mad Cow Blues: South Korea, Clay Shirky and the Digital Public Sphere" (Jarvis),
- democratization in chapter VI, "Political Uses of Social Media in Kazakhstan" by Couper, Nurmanov, and Adams,
- free speech in Chapter XIII, "Social Media and Protest—The Indian Spring" (Lucas) and Chapter XIV, "When Freedom Tweets; Social Media Invigorates India's Psyche of Free Speech" (Aikat),
- social media and civic activism in Chapter 15, "Community Broadcasting as a Predecessor of Social Media in Sri Lanka" (N'Weerasinghe),
- media and integrated national bicultural worldview, in Chapter XIX, "We Are All in the Same Waka; Key Concepts of Indigenous Maori Culture in the Contemporary New Zealand World View" (Nikolaeva).

The other two thirds are in the category of cultural criticism and functional studies,

- with various focuses and overlaps on social media interactions, social media motives, in Chapter VII, "Cultural Values, Gender, and Chinese Young Adults in Using Social Media" (Qingwen Dong, Wu, Gu, and Dale Dong),
- perception of social media in Chapter VIII, "Chinese Consumers' Perception of Social Media: A Phenomenological Study" (Huan Chen),
- the emerging role of social media in opinion making in Chapter IX, "PTT: Taiwan's Unique Social Media" (Szu-Wei Chen),

- social media in emergency management in Chapter X, "Can 140 Characters Save Your Life? Social Media in the Aftermath of the 3.11 Earthquake in Japan"(Kiuchi) and in Chapter XI, "Pray for Japan; Reinventing 'Japanese National Character' after the 2011 Tohoku Earthquake" (Abe),
- social media "glocalization" in Chapter XVI, "Content Analysis of Interactions between Global Brands and Their Publics on Global and Thai Brand Pages" (Waiyachote),
- media transformation in Chapter XVII, "The Transition from the Traditional to the New Social Network in Malaysia" (Chew and Tie),
- social media and Australia in "the Asian Century" in Chapter XVIII, "Australian Social Media Trends" (Harrison, Rintel and Mitchell).

We note in Cui Litang's essay "Vox Populi–Vox Dei: In Search for the Common Golden Gates", at 45% of the world's Internet distribution (28% in penetration versus population) and the evolving demographics of the social media, to over 700 million who speak seven of the most important Internet languages of English, Chinese, Arabic, Japanese, Korean, Russian and Indonesian, Asia has become an inevitable "residential support" near the top, for the emerging social media world community.

Social media as reemergence of the Internet in Asia has clearly followed the route of the mainstream media, congruent with their Internet distribution in all Asian countries and regions. The only exception is North Korea where the top domain name .kp for DPRK was created in September 2007 and broadband access has yet to be deployed for significant penetration.

Despite its low average Internet penetration of 28% compared to other world regions, Asia has a strong social media user base, with India, Indonesia, the Philippines, Thailand, Malaysia, Taiwan, and Japan leading the way on Facebook, and Twitter has found its prominence in Indonesia, Japan, India, Singapore, the Philippines, Malaysia, Thailand, China and South Korea, accounting for 37% of Twitter users in all languages.

The revealing documentary "Love affair between the Indonesians and the social media" (BBC, 2013; February 16,) showed trendy Indonesians wearing their hearts on their sleeves in a Twitter film and the crown they have earned for Jakarta as the "Twitter Capital." The soaring of Japanese as the most tweeted language in the world, only after English, has manifested the Japanese profound and obsessive fondness of Twitter for developing and maintaining the "kizune," with brevity and unclutteredness, reminiscent of the Japanese cultural essence of the haiku poetry, which perfectly serves an answer to the thoughtful question: "What Has Become of the Japanese on the Internet?" raised in the book with the same title, co-authored by Toru Nishigaki and Jonathan Louis, who assessed and described the initial impact of the Internet as "the arrival of the black boat."

Facebook, YouTube and Twitter have enjoyed significant prominence in Asia as the mainstream social media while they are joined, if not significantly challenged, over time, by a number of emerging variations and vernacularized versions of social media. In South Korea, a country having topped the world in Internet penetration and bandwidth, home to one of the world's largest blogging communities (second only to China), it is Cyworld that has reportedly attracted 18 million regular users. In Japan, it is Mixi that has shored up a sizable audience of its own at 15 million. In Taiwan, it is Wretch.cc and Pixnet that have rallied about 10 million in their social media audience. In Viet Nam, Zing has charted out a chunk of 15 million social media users. Put together, this fits into a model that trails the path of social media development in Asia, all along with the mainstream league of Facebook, YouTube and Twitter.

In the social media sector, by sheer numbers, China is home to the world's largest population of 1.3 billion and a netizenship of 590 million, nearly half of whom—over 300 million—are regular users and bloggers on the social media sites, Qzone, Renren, QQ, SinaWeibo, and Kaixin, among others, making it the world's largest social media cluster and an enormous consumer market for businesses and brands, with an estimated annual online transaction (2012) of 20 billion in CNY or about 3.2 billion in USD.

This is further corroborated in "A Cross-cultural Study of Social Media Access and Online Communication in India, Indonesia and the Philippines," by Brown and Fraser who illustrate social entrepreneurship as an emerging landscape on the Internet where both social capital and corporate social responsibility are being developed as new business and marketing tools and models, using new and accessible technologies. They further describe how "social media have eliminated most boundaries, giving even small companies and organizations access to many people with differing socio-demographic characteristics." and "social media profoundly changes the manner in which business is conducted and managed."

China, on top of all Asian countries and regions, has followed a unique strategy to develop the information industry and social media in particular, that could be best appreciated and described as a model of nationalization that China has apparently followed for development, albeit along an "obstacle course" (The Economist: 2013; April). It is characterized by a rapid growth under policy mitigation from administrative and legislative measures tailored to strengthen the centralization of the Internet.

This accounts for a drift and transition of social media mainstream away from the dominance of Facebook, YouTube and Twitter, which has characterized the development of social media in China and parts of Asia, reflecting aspects of cultural conflict and value judgment concerning technology, as elaborated by Couper, Nurmanov and Adams in "Political Uses of Social Media in Kazakhstan" who pinpoint the role of social media in political processes, as a political factor "between individuals and groups versus institutions to achieve political prominence," facilitating basic citizen involvement in politics, such as spreading opinions and information, which "culminated in a total Internet's impact on political processes and systems that goes beyond the ability of political actors to gathering and distributing information", also suggesting an evolutionary pressure for change in the culture of politics, "despite being currently constrained or overshadowed by government control."

If there is any indicative significance, the joint research 'A Cross-cultural Study of Social Media Access and Online Communication in India, Indonesia, and the Philippines' (Brown and Fraser) considers and discusses the obvious role that online communication and social media have to play in the dawning and fledgling democracies in many parts of Asia, however, as if being overpowered by an interest and concern over the boundless resources rather than on border-lined revolutions, scattered in online communication and on social media, the authors suggest future research of online communication and social media for political power and activism, in the discipline of national development.

The role of social media in democratization is further elaborated in "When Freedom Tweets: Social Media Invigorates India's Psyche of Free Speech" by Debashis Aikat who was once a journalist in India. Aikat argues "India's social media transform free speech" as "social media constituted a key aspect of the anti-corruption movement that mobilized millions in India in 2011. With its global audience, social media brought international focus to the anti-corruption movement, which ranked high in Time magazine's top 10 news stories in the world in 2011." In summing up the lessons and legacy of free speech and social media, Aikat concludes that "social media have enhanced India's media landscape by facilitating a more participatory networked population to gaining greater access to information, more opportunities to engage in civil society, and cultivate collective action," despite attempts of some Indian officials to "curb, control and censor media."

Inevitably, gate-keeping or censorship, either of which ultimately underpins a moral judgment about technology. In the East, the moralizing can be traced to the concept of "ti-yong" (essence vs. application) by Confucian philosopher, Xun Zi (312–230 BC), of the Warring States period (483–403 BC) and contributor of the One Hundred School thought, a philosophical concept once employed by Buddhists in the Song dynasty before transforming into a buzzword of the neo-Confucian reformers in the 19th century who envisioned the strengthening of China by practicing "ti-yong," that is to "maintain its own style of learning to keep the 'essence of society,' while at the same time using Western learning for 'practical application' in developing its infrastructure and economy" (Spencer, 1999. p. 225–226). In the West, moralizing has its origin in the "noumenon" or "thing-in-itself" (das Ding an sich) as opposed to phenomenon, in the philosophy of Immanuel Kant who claimed "that man, however, is not altogether excluded from the noumenal because practical reason—i.e., the capacity for acting as a moral agent—makes no sense unless a noumenal world is postulated in which freedom, God, and immortality abide." (Encyclopedia Britannica).

In the post-cyberpunk novel "The Diamond Age", Neal Stephenson attempts a literary and cartoonistic interpretation of the Chinese philosophical thinking of technology, through protagonist interrelations and conflict between the Source, the matter compiler, the Feed and the Seed, where "'yong' is the outer manifestation of something. 'ti' is the underlying essence. Technology is a yong associated with a particular ti." The Seed is technology rooted in the Chinese ti, by which the Chinese have lived for five thousand years. (Stephenson, p. 457) The Seed represents a hierarchy that was to be destructed by the Feed which came in from Atlantis, from Japan, when the rice no longer came from the farm but from the matter compiler, the Source, which deranged the filial relationships between virtue, the root and wealth, the result—as "under the Western ti, wealth comes not from virtue but from cleverness." (Stephenson, p. 458). This has culminated in and constituted a typical Western insight into the Chinese thinking of technology ever since the Qing Dynasty that has affected the Western outlook on the technical development in China.

Conclusion

Social Media in Asia expresses and embodies the value orientations of various authors and cultures in their attempt to find out "how do social media transform who we are?" through investigations into "the effects and utilities of social media," which are found as mostly descriptive, culturally specific, and thus objective, and at some point prescriptive and forward-thinking, with various degrees of enthusiasm, especially in view of the role that the social media have to play in ongoing development and democratization.

We notice that the surveys and studies in Social Media in Asia have identified and elaborated on the social media trends in the sustained growth of online communication and development of social media and social networking in the Asian countries, and found them in line with findings of the leading literature in the media research, regardless of national or categorical differences and discrepancies.

Many findings in Social Media in Asia have been comprehensive and even profound, despite inevitable limitations of providing "a snapshot of a dynamic phenomenon" (Huan Chen). Nevertheless significant insight is gained, with theoretical as well as managerial implications that may be constructive and instrumental to future development of social media.

We recognize the fact that social media have emerged in the fourth wave of media development, along with the computers and the Internet, experiencing "the evolution of a universal interconnected network of audio, video, and electronic text communications that will blur the distinction between interpersonal and mass communications and between public and private communication" (Neuman, cited in Croteau and Hoynes 2003, p. 322). This "mass media symbiosis" or media convergence is made possible by the digital technologies, where the convergence of new methods of communication with new technologies shifts the model of mass communication, and radically reshapes the ways we interact and communicate with one another.

We feel that the emergence and evolvement of social media have provided us with alternative means and opportunities of communication, and new perspectives from which to think about communication, representing the latest round of human efforts in search for resources and opportunities in an increasingly global world. The enormous and dynamic resources made available by the evolving technology have pre-reinvented and morphed into the emerging social media whose impact has just started to be felt and fathomed in Asia. As suggested in Social Media in Asia, "communication technologies represent opportunities for cultural breakthroughs as well as technical ones." (Schmidt and Cohen, p. 5). Though a number of questions remain difficult to answer, pending the drastic changes on the media scene, regarding accurate prediction of the definite future of the new media, the future and evolution of the old media. For instance, how and how much will newspapers, radio, and television have to change in transition, in order to co-exist and compete with the new media in their onslaught? Much less are we able to predict "our future selves," "the future of identity," "the future of conflict, combat and intervention" and "the future of reconstruction" (Schmidt and Cohen, 2013). Internet architects Robert E. Kahn and Vinton G. Cerf have this to say, in an attempt to explain what the Internet is and what makes it work:

> "Over the past century and a half, important technological developments have created a global environment that is drawing the people of the world closer and closer together. During the industrial revolution, we learned to put motors to work to magnify human and animal muscle power. In the new Information Age, we are learning to magnify brainpower by putting the power of computation wherever we need it, and to provide information services on a global basis. Computer resources are infinitely flexible tools; networked

together, they allow us to generate, exchange, share and manipulate information in an uncountable number of ways. The Internet, as an integrating force, has melded the technology of communications and computing to provide instant connectivity and global information services to all its users at very low cost."

If this is indicative of or presages future development of the media, the Internet architects thoughtfully suggest that "the success of the Internet in society as a whole will depend less on technology than on the larger economic and social concerns that are at the heart of every major advance," suggesting that "the Internet is no exception, except that its potential and reach are perhaps as broad as any that have come before."

We believe this is exactly where cross-cultural dialogue (global dialogue) comes in, in our attempt to achieve an integral and more truthful understanding of the social media experiences, in order to address the angst, tensions, contradictions and paradoxes of the social media in its current form pending its viral development, and in order to help accommodate cultural breakthroughs (Schmidt and Cohen, 2013), and maybe to provide new communication technologies.

References

Anderson, R. (2012: November). Molefi Kete Asante: The Afrocentric idea and the cultural turn to intercultural communication studies. In M. H. Prosser and S. J. Kulich (Eds.) Special issue: Early American pioneers of intercultural communication. *International Journal of Intercultural Relations, Vol.36*(6), pp. 760–769.

Asante, M. K. (2011, personal communication to R. Anderson). In R. Anderson. Molefi Kete Asante: The Afrocentric idea and the cultural turn to intercultural communication studies, in M. H Prosser and S. J. Kulich (Eds.) (2012: November). Special issue: Early American pioneers of intercultural communication. *International Journal of Intercultural Relations, Vol. 36*(6). pp. 760–769.

Asante, M. K., Newmark, E., and Blake, C. (Eds.) (1979). *Handbook of Intercultural Communication*. Beverly Hills, CA; Sage.

Bond, M. H. (2007). Fashioning a new psychology of the Chinese people: Insights from developments in cross-cultural psychology. In S. J. Kulich and M. H. Prosser (Eds.). *Intercultural perspectives on Chinese communication*. Shanghai, China: Shanghai Foreign Language Education Press.

Cui, L. (2012). Wrangling the media market. In M. Li and M. H. Prosser. *Communicating Interculturally*. Beijing, China: Higher Education Press.

Dominick, J. (1999). *The Dynamics of Mass Communication. Second edition*. Boston, MA: McGraw Hill.

Economist, The (2013; April).

Encyclopedia Britannica. http://global.britannica.com/EBchecked/topic/420847/noumenon

Heisey, D. R. (2012). A dialog proposal, International Association for Intercultural Communication Studies Conference, Hong Kong, quoted by M. H. Prosser (2012: November). D. Ray Heisey: Having lived life abundantly, "time is running out," in M. H. Prosser and S. J. Kulich (Eds.), Special Issue: Early American pioneers of intercultural communication. *International Journal of Intercultural Relations, Vol. 36*(6), pp. 810–822.

Hwang, Kwang-Kuo (2007). The development of indigenous social psychology in Confucian society. In S. J. Kulich and M. H. Prosser (Eds.). *Intercultural perspectives on Chinese communication*. Shanghai, China: Shanghai Foreign Language Education Press.

Jia, Y. (2012). Foreword. In M. Li and M. H. Prosser, *Communicating Interculturally*. Beijing, China: Higher Education Press.

Kamara, K. S. (2013). *Online Collaborative Learning: Challenges and Opportunities for NGOs in Developing Countries*. Lake Oswego, OR: Dignity Press.

Kohls, L. R. (2012: November). Message to S. J. Kulich. In M. H. Prosser and S.J. Kulich, Special issue: Early American pioneers of intercultural communication. *International Journal of Intercultural Relations, Vol. 36(6), pp. 744–759.*

Li. M. and Prosser, M. H. (in press). *Chinese communicating interculturally.* Lake Oswego, OR, USA: Dignity Press.

Li, M. and Prosser, M. H. (2012). *Communicating interculturally.* Beijing, China: Higher Education Press.

Nishigaki, T. and Louis, J. ( ). What has become of the Japanese on the Internet? [publication details unavailable].

Prosser, M. H. (1978, 1985, 1989). *The cultural dialogue: An introduction to intercultural communication.* (Boston, MA): Houghton Mifflin. (Washington, D.C.). SIETAR International. Translated into Japanese, Roichi Okabe, 1982, Tokyo, Japan: Toko University Press; translated into Chinese, He Daokuan, 2013: Peking University Press.

Prosser, M. H. (2007). One world, one dream: Harmonizing society through intercultural communication: A prelude to China intercultural communication studies. In S. J. Kulich and M. H. Prosser (Eds.). *Intercultural perspectives on Chinese communication.* Shanghai, China: Shanghai Foreign Language Education Press.

Prosser, M. H. (2012: November). K. S. Sitaram, an early interculturalist: Founding the field May 6, 1970. In M. H. Prosser and S. J. Kulich (Eds.) Special issue: Early American pioneers of intercultural communication, *International Journal of Intercultural Relations, Vol. 36(6).* pp. 857-868.

Prosser, M. H. (2012). Universal human rights as cultural values: A historical perspective. In S. J. Kulich, M. H. Prosser, and Weng, L. (Eds.). *Value frameworks at the theoretical crossroads of culture: Intercultural research, Vol. 4.* Shanghai, China: Shanghai Foreign Language Education Press.

Prosser, M. H., Sharifzadeh, M., and Zhang S. (Eds.) (2013). *Finding Cross-Cultural Common Ground.* Lake Oswego, OR: Dignity Press.

Schmidt, E. and Cohen, J. (2013). *The New Digital Age: Reshaping the Future of People, Nations and Business.* London, UK; John Murray Publishers.

Sitaram, K. S. (1970: May 6). *Intercultural communication: The what and why of it.* Unpublished paper given to International Communication Association Board of Directors to create Division V: Intercultural and Development Division. Minneapolis, MN: International Communication Association.

Sitaram, K. S. (1995). *Culture and Communication: A World View.* New York, NY: McGraw Hill.

Sitaram, K. S. and Cogdell, R. T. (1976). *The Foundations of Intercultural Communication.* Columbus, OH. Charles E. Merrill Publishing Co.

Spencer. J. (1999). *Search For Modern China.* Second edition. New York, NY: Norton.

Stephenson, N. (1996). *The Diamond Age.* A Batman Spectra Book. USA and Canada.

Stewart, E. C. (1971). *American Cultural Patterns: A Cross-Cultural Perspective.* Chicago, IL: Intercultural Press.

Storti, C. (1994). *Cross-Cultural Dialogues: 74 Brief Encounters With Cultural Difference.* Yarmouth, MN: Intercultural Press.

Varis, T. (1998). Foreword. In K. S. Sitaram and M. H. Prosser (Eds.) *Civic discourse: Multiculturalism, cultural diversity, and global communication.* Stanford, CT. Ablex.

Wasilewski, J. H. and Kawakami, H. S. (2012: November). Edward C. Stewart: Cultural dynamics pioneer. in M. H. Prosser and S. J. Kulich (Eds.). Special issue: Early American pioneers of intercultural communication. *International Journal of Intercultural Relations. Vol. 36*(6). pp. 869–884.

PART ONE:
CROSS-CULTURAL SOCIAL MEDIA STUDIES IN ASIA

I.   Vox Populi—Vox Dei:
In Search of the Common Golden Gates

Cui Litang

Xiamen University, Tan Kha Kee College, Xiamen, China
clitang@gmail.com

Abstract

This essay attempts to elaborate the ultimate purpose of language and communication is universal solidarity, metaphorically through an ever-going global dialogue in spite of disruptive inventions of culture and civilization. The author believes that human communication is a revelation of shared intentionality and common humanities, upon which global solidarity will rest. And social media as expression and manifestation of the human ideal for solidarity are now experiencing in Asia a sea change and exciting developments on the way toward the future.

Keywords: language, communication, global solidarity, social media, Asia

1. A Dream of Millenniums

Philosophical sage of ancient China, Lao Tzu (571–471 BC), glamorized distantly in some general notion, with the romantic appeal as a forerunner of Christ, propounded in Tao De Ching (Book of the Way):

Let there be a small state with few people,
where military devices find no use;

Let the people look solemnly upon death,
and banish the thought of moving elsewhere.
They may have carts and boats,
but there is no reason to ride them;
They may have armor and weapons,
but they have no reason to display them.
Let the people go back to tying knots to keep records.
Let their food be savory,
their clothes beautiful,
their customs pleasurable,
their dwellings secure.
Though they may gaze across at a neighboring state, and hear the
sounds of its dogs and chickens,
The people will never travel back and forth, till they die of old age.

(Chapter 80: Tao De Ching, translated by Victor H. Mair)

This idyllic utopia of primordial morals and prescribed life scenes, free from disruptive "inventions of culture and civilization" (Rousseau, 28 June 1712–2 July 1778) not only did not exist, either in "the Iron Age historical power" of the Maurya Empire (322–185 BC) of India or in the fledgling Empire of Zhou (1046–256 BC) of China, but also soon got trotted down and traversed over, first by the couriers and then by an elaborate postal system of high efficiency that later Confucius (551–479 BC) made reference to by exalting "the influence of the righteous travels faster than a royal edict by post-station service"(Encyclopedia Britannica, http://global.britannica.com/EBchecked/topic/472092/postal-system/15437/China).

Marshall McLuhan contributed the extraordinary expansion of time space and increased flow of information, to writing, the new dimension of communication, the concrete manifestation and embodiment of human speech:

"The goose quill put an end to talk. It abolished mystery; it gave architecture and towns; it brought roads and armies, bureaucracy. It was the basic metaphor with which the cycle of civilization began, the step from the dark into the light of the mind. The hand that filled the parchment page built a city." (McLuhan, 1996, p. 48)

In McLuhan's hypothesis, speech made a "social charter" of the mind "bog", "boundless, directionless, horizonless and in the dark," (McLuhan, 1996, p. 48) and writing, the monument emerged after it, bridged the acoustic mental space and the visual dimension, manifesting the embryonic and emerging human communication "grounded in fundamentally cooperative, even shared, intentions" (Tomasello, 2008, Jacket inside), serving the purpose in the entire process of human survival, ultimately towards enlightenment of the mind, as soul-searched and chanted in a heartily-felt way by the English poet Alfred Lord Tennyson (In Memoriam A.H.H, 1849, Canto 54):

"So runs my dream, but what am I?
An infant crying in the night
An infant crying for the light
And with no language but a cry."

In the "Cave of Forgotten Dreams" (Herzog, 2010), the Chauvet-Pont-d'Arc cave in southern France, the dwelling of what could be one of the earliest social media sites in pre-writing history, from the Upper Paleolithic (Later Stone Age) periods (32,000–25, 000 years ago), our pre-history ancestors created hundreds of "ritual" and "shamanic" animal paintings, one batch at a time, 500 years apart, at different stages of a long time passage, recapturing and revealing a universal human intention and dream.

The emergence of writing created the scribes and a new social division, made new inventions like printing a reality, unprecedentedly extending the width and breadth, as well as permanence, of contact and reach in propagating ideas and disseminating information, and this, in addition to the roving troubadours and roaming minstrels bringing entertainment and teachings to distant villages, in a process that Armand Mattelart called "the domestication of communication flows and society movement." (Mattelart, 2000)

In the documented history the spread of human civilization and ideals of the Western tradition, conveying and propagating ideas and wishes, started from the Code of Hammurabi spelled the end of "savage human existence" and "primitive tribalism of pre-civilization," identified, reaffirmed, and spread the earliest tenets of universal freedom and individual rights. The

Hebrew Torah laid the foundation of the Holy Bible. The rise of Grecian city-states conceived the concept of *cosmopolite* (citizen of the world). In its footsteps, the Roman Empire turned to build a *humanitas*, focused on developing a cultivated and educated society, drawing on inspirations from Greek philanthropia. In the process, a paradigmatic *universal bond for global solidarity* (Mattelart, 2000) was thus created and augmented in all possible expressions.

The first millennium saw the dawn and rise of faith, in both the Old Testament and Qu'ran that preached brotherhood, love of one's neighbor as well as human potential for virtue and moral equality, justice, tolerance and solidarity. Burgeoning expressions and attempts at bonding across cultures and boundaries were only disrupted by crusaders' expeditions and incidences of violent religious persecutions.

The Renaissance nurtured, revived and embodied the humanistic ideals of the Magna Carta (the Great Charter, 1215) and envisioned a *Utopia* (Thomas More, 1516) of free education and freedom from religious and economic oppression, brewing the dawn of the Enlightenment in a dynamic and comprehensive cultural dialogue chanting universal humanities and shared destiny, in a prelude to spurts in science, bursts of revolutions and the arrival of mercantilism and entrepreneurialism.

The Reformation and the Great Awakenings that eventually led up to the Enlightenment and modernity divided and refined the human sphere, breaking up the "moral monopoly" (from the Church) and bringing in values that "emphasized the capacity of the human mind to construct its own present and future, and means of communication" (Osborne, ABC, Lines of Communication, 2000, Program One: Contact), to that, in the spirit of "if there is something you know, communicate it. If there is something you don't know, search for it."

The Enlightenment came at the dawn of the Age of Discovery prior to industrialization that navigated and charted the unknown territories in the can-do Zeitgeist—"if there is more of the world, they will conquer it,"—paved the way for discovery of the New World, pilgrimage, colonization and eventually saw its culmination in the Bill of Rights and founding of the United States of America, a democracy believed to have been built upon the bedrock of the Western civilization with inspirations from the two-millennia-old Confucian ethic, and the great Eastern civilizations of China and India that advocated citizens' rights for peace and security as well as the universal role of government in cultivating and endorsing economic and moral welfare.

If the emergence and rise of language were an ultimate revelation of human *shared intentionality* and *collaborative nature* of communication, projecting a particular *psychological infra-structure* (Grice & Tomasello, 2008), then it had certainly contributed enormously to knitting fibers of great ideals onto the tapestry of human civilization, unfolding on the forever extending horizon in the dawning brave new world.

With the drafting of the Declaration of Independence, the ideal of freedom and democracy became an institutionalized and internalized dream and ambition, and the document, a permanent embodiment of the pursuit and its universal significance of the call for a global dialogue.

Access to ideas and information, and indeed participation of individuals in social, cultural, political and economical affairs became a universal practice and habit, with the emergence of the public sphere that took shape pending the Enlightenment (Kellner, undated) and underwent the global structural transformations thereafter, as language and communication continued to evolve and reemerge as the steering media in the increasingly global village that would prompt *communicative action* (Habermas), as presaged by Marshal McLuhan (1996, p. 8):

> *The medium, or process, of our time—electric technology—is reshaping and restructuring patterns of social interdependence and every aspect of our personal life. It is forcing us to reconsider and reevaluate practically every thought, every action, and every institution formerly taken for granted.*

And in *The Medium is the Message*, McLuhan continued:

> *The older training of observation has become quite irrelevant in this new time, because it is based on psychological responses and concepts conditioned by the former technology—mechanization. Innumerable confusions and a profound feeling of despair invariably emerge in periods of great technological and cultural transitions. Our 'Age of Anxiety' is, in great part, the result of trying to do today's job with yesterday's tools—with yesterday's concepts.*

The social angst came from disruptions of the upcoming *steering media* and revealed an inconvenient truth that commercial, cultural and institutional power excluded a genuine and meaningful participation and interaction that the public sphere and the steering media meant to conjure. So apprehended *The Medium is the Message*: "Our time is a time for crossing barriers, for erasing old categories—for probing around" such that Michael H. Prosser, pioneer of Intercultural Communication Studies ponderously and warmly heralded "if we have indeed created ourselves by building cultural structures, those cultural structures and barriers are developed within and between cultures by our ability to communicate." (Prosser, 1978, p. 15)

2. A Long Way Towards Solidarity

This message enunciated a resonant outcry, and a long call for *international solidarity through cross-cultural communication*, in a genuine dialog, more than for a different version of what it is to be naturally human (McHoul, 2000), a magnificent ordeal that media technology like the telephone had come a long way to endorse, with instant access to one another, by crossing the existing social hierarchies, with a logic of inclusiveness (Poster, 2000), following the tap of *the first definite pulsation of the real nervous system of the world* (Poster, 2000).

This warm message came at a time when Michael Prosser experienced a shift in his global excursions for *internationalization* (Prosser, see Preface) in nearly 70 countries, "from earlier Europe-centric and then Afro-central, to Asia-oriented, embarking on a life long journey in a genuine cultural dialogue between the West and the East."

The global excursions made by Prosser and many other intellectuals, artists, teachers, students, and other professionals, have not only fostered and fortified internationalization in their own intercultural experiences and personal development, but also nurtured along the way, in close contact, ideas of internationalization and awareness of international solidarity beyond barriers of linguistic and cultural differences. Meanwhile, these excursions and encounters have helped to instill a global consciousness in peoples and populations, especially those living and confined to, behind the "Iron Curtain" and the "Bamboo Curtain," for a time, denied of travel, migration or simply, contact and information of this virtue.

The Internet boom on a global scale generated a new wave of international exchanges and excursions, which were joined, among others, by Dave Chapman, on the US task force spearheading the Internet development in the Asia Pacific. Chapman, from Yale University, a former Silicon Valley hardy boy, a techie and suits, currently multi-tasking as technical consultant and adviser to the US Government and campaigner for the US Congress in District 18, California, delivered one of the earliest and probably the most comprehensive lectures about the Internet, of any China missions at that time, with a message he thoughtfully shared in presaging the future development of China. Chapman unprecedentedly noted that China traced a route of drastic development over the past thousands of years, through three distinctive stages: the Grand Canal era, starting from the Spring and Autumn Warring States (771–476 BC), the era of railway network of the recent century, and the era of the Internet and information super-highway that was about to take off, in the mid 1990s, when the birth of the brainchild already was announced, and the building blocks were quickly falling into places.

This came to the shore of China, incidentally a few months after my return to China from my early international excursions as a visiting lecturer at Green River Community College, in Washington State, at a location close to the Boeing Field and the Microsoft Campus, where I conducted a credit course of Chinese and Chinese culture in a lecture series entitled "Cross-cultural Communication: What Does it Mean to the Westerners and the Chinese." And through my participation, thankfully, I had the opportunity for a genuine hands-on experience with the Internet which I considered a very rewarding learning experience and my first term in the computer network, when it was only a notion in most of China, and meager access was only available on an experimental basis between several major universities in Beijing.

During my first encounter with the Internet at GRCC, I learned to project students' academic records from an Apple, retrieve e-mail messages and data from the PINE system on a Windows-based computer, send and retrieve voice mails from the office shared with Professor Bruce Haulman and our colleague Pamela.

My interest in the workings of the computer and the Internet was greatly encouraged and enhanced when Professor Haulman dug out a first generation IBM-compatible from his garage and sat it on my desktop for me to tap, click and clink away with, which truly opened up for me, as I felt, an entirely new alternative way of work and interactions. This was in the primary school year of homepages in the US, the year of cyberspace, and a few months away from the milestone release of the Windows 95 operating system.

The long Japanese-American dialogue initiated by Michael H. Prosser in *The Cultural Dialogue* (1978) which has been translated into Japanese (1982) and Chinese (2013), and followed by numerous excursions and encounters, half a world apart, across national and cultural boundaries, has been sustained and rendered to grow on the Internet.

The proliferation of the Internet in Asia and the impact of wiring up the largest continent of the world (now 45% of world's Internet users), has been enormous, in that it has brought free flow of information on the way, lifting the watergate across borderlines and boundaries, over a land of nearly 1/3 of the world surface, home to roughly 2/3 (4.2 billion) of the worlds' population, whose demographics including speaking 33% (2322) of the world's languages and cultures that "have no term for communication separate from *language* and no term for *culture* separate from *nation* and no term at all for *intercultural communication* (Prosser, 1978). This was at a time of the Asian financial crisis, in countries with a juncture of issues relating to democratization and development. However, the Internet was yet to experience its growth, doldrums of development, the dot-com bubble and the technology meltdown before its reinvention in the form of social media that would continue its miraculous myth through deeper and dynamic transformations it has triggered off, in cultures and contexts where it is pervasively embedded, and in every possible social and human aspect, dimension and beyond.

3. A Social Media Manifestation

It all started with Facebook, though BBS is often credited as the prototype of the Internet and today's social media. The BBS or Bulletin Board System was born in the early 1970s and really boomed in late 1980s when the personal computer and the modem became widely accessible. With a PC, a phone line and a modem, BBS extended and transformed the genuine human dialogue over a distance, with a full visual dimension and experience, previously not accessible, neither by voice nor the Morse code system. For the first time people were able to talk to one another by writing and reading remotely, via the Sysop, the BBS operator which provided a hub relaying the text messages. While the Sysop was reminiscent of the ancient scribe who was often privileged by possessing the writing, the BBS was democratic rather than exclusive in nature and in operation. BBS became a paradigm changer in how we kept up communication over a distance.

From an evolutionary perspective, BBS may have been a precursor of social media, prior to the web, though social media is typically described as *the web of the web*, the *next web*, or defined as *a group of Internet-based applications that build on the ideological and technological foundations of Web 2.0* (Kaplan and Haenlein, 2010).

Sir Tim Berners-Lee, web visionary and inventor of the World Wide Web, challenged the viral concept of Web 2.0 (and Web 3.0, for that matter), describing it as jargon, for the simple fact that his original vision of the Web was "a collaborative medium, a place where we (could) all meet and read and write" (BBC), indicating that he didn't believe that Web 2.0 (or the future Web 3.0) could be substantially different from prior web technologies. This sense of continuity embodied in the emerging social media has also been expressed by numerous former Sysops in Jason Scott's "The BBS Documentary" (2005), which treated BBS as a source of innovations, the social media de jure, rather than a passing fad or a source of nostalgia.

This gives Facebook a privileged status (as a pioneer of social media) of a crystal-ball into the development and future of social media, while Facebook in its current morph has strongly manifested social media's reach, accessibility, usability, immediacy and permanence. With worldwide users exceeding 1 billion (2012), of whom 169 million (54% of the US population) are found in its home country, and another 100 million plus in Asia and the rest elsewhere—excluding yet another 20,000 or so accounts being deleted on a daily basis for security maintenance, Facebook has reportedly caused traffic flow higher than Google. When put side by side with Google, to be examined for comparative advantages, it is Facebook's enormous user base and its integration with 1 million sites, it is believed, that would be a game changer.

The way that Facebook operates as a social network, can be described by the notion of "six degrees of separation, "a shrinking world built upon a chain of 'a friend of a friend' in a maximum of six steps", or better yet by the classic Westley-MacLean Conceptual Model of Mass Communication "which are between events, advocates, channel and the behavior roles" (Westley & MacLean, 1999, p. 23), a communicative and interactive running environment, the web that provides applications, tool-kits and innovative features for creating a page or group, launching or/and joining an event, or feeding and growing the social networks.

Facebook might have fulfilled the role of a collaborative medium and a market niche made possible by the information technology, at a time (2004) described as "it was the best of times, it was the worst of times." (Sloan & Thompson, EPIC 2014) of the Internet media, when the whole world was anxiously waiting for the next big thing after Google which was rapidly growing into a media empire in search, news, location service, online advertizing and its controversial book digitalization ambition— Chrome and Android were still some years away. This happened to be a time of haunting memories of 9/11 and heydays of the war on two fronts, a turn of events that for a time reversed, challenged and changed the way the American audience kept informed and indeed even the way that they viewed the news events, as citizen journalism continued to flourish, for instance, in CNN's Fan Zone, predecessor of the very popular CNN iReport, where the audience had started to report, or *snap and share.*

In a country that cherishes both oral as well as visual culture, the emergence of YouTube in February, 2005, was embraced as a necessary addition to the Americans' profound visual culture and persistent TV habit. A Pew study indicated that TV, ahead of the Internet, surpasses newspaper and radio for news), and in a timely fashion, as a catalyst to wider deployment of Internet connectivity and bandwidth. With as many as 65,000 new videos being uploaded with 100 million views on a daily basis, YouTube has rapidly surged as the most visited site only behind Google and Facebook. Its acquisition in 2006 at a staggering price of 1.5 billion USD by Google not only has opened a revolving door to the fledging Internet video streaming culture, popularly adopted by the news and government organizations, campaigners, businesses, social groups and individuals, but also, despite issues of copyright infringement, it has catalyzed the development of YouTube video streaming into an "embedded solution" to the creation of communities and forums based on spontaneous, democratic and creative participation and sharing, before its rise as the largest video site, according to Alexa, on the web, and the fourth largest on the Internet, with 5 billion video streams every month which is 40% of all videos online.

This staged a great talk and walk onto the web the American way, with an extended visual dimension, which in March 2006 was joined by and orchestrated in the chitchat chirps of Twitter, a web-based portal for exchanging text messages with no more than 140 characters. Twitter operates on exchanges of short bursts of inconsequential information posted by the Twitter users and their followers, under #hashtags and @ usernames which can be seen as a means of categorization, either by following up what's happening now or else. For leads and links, Twitter has created a unique URL shortening service that allows secure onsite backtracking, review, reading and re-tweeting (re-posting), exclusively available to Twitter users.

Twitter's simplicity, instance, unclutteredness, mobility and reach have made it a huge success, resulting in a blowup of 175 million daily tweets, surging accounts, especially those of top state officials, dignitaries, celebrities and activists. According to research and analysis heads of state of 125 countries, a great number of leading politicians, cardinals, the pope, missionaries and other religious workers, have Twitter accounts and followers all across the world.

Twitter's popularity as a mouth and messenger was hailed by Sir Tim Berners-Lee when he tweeted live at the opening ceremony of the 2012 London Olympic Games: "This is for everyone!". A similar message was communicated by William Gibson, cyberpunk novelist and creator of the term "cyberspace", in a Wired interview, when he proclaimed "I am a natural born Twitter machine."

Twitter was selected as the Word of the Year 2009, and Twitter has seen its prominence as an emerging source of the public sphere and political power, in Iranian and Italian elections, in the Wikileaks, Occupy Wall Street, the Arab Spring, and in the Indian Spring movements (Barn, 2013). Twitter has emerged as a mission-critical social media during rescue operations after major disasters. In the 2010 Haitian Earthquake, US Twitter texting raised $11 million for Haiti, and in the 2011 Japan earthquake and tsunami, Twitter played out the indispensable lifeline for disseminating and documenting, blow by blow, piece by piece, the devastation of an unprecedented disaster. Numerous Twitter stories have revealed the Japanese desperate and tenacious endeavors in evacuation and rescue, in reconstructing the human bondage, *kizuna* (Prosser, 1978) in the earthquake and tsunami devastation. Of all social media postings in the 2011 Japan earthquake, tsunami, and nuclear disaster, Twitter alone accounted for an enormous 180 million tweets (NHK Big Data Project, 2013), that are now being analyzed for invaluable data and information that will reveal the moment of truth during and after the devastation, in terms of geo-location and evacuation movement, which believably will contribute to minimizing death tolls and casualties in unpredicted disastrous devastations. Anthropologist David H. Slater et al. (2012) suggested that:

> "3/11 was the first natural disaster fully experienced through the social media", which primarily greatly helped as well when thirty-two American charity organizations opened up a prompt channel of charity support on Facebook and Twitter, raising a donation of over $163 million within two weeks after the quake and tsunami, which would be impossible "if social media were not readily available" (Kiuchi, 2013).

Indeed, a global dialogue and a universal human bond, started in the perfect world, sustained and expanded by the Internet, has now been taken further by social media (represented by mainstream Facebook, YouTube and Twitter), with new and more accessible means of expression and creativity, tremendous resources and opportunities.

At 45% of the world's Internet users (27.5% of population) and the evolving demographics of the social media, to the tune of over 700 million who speak the seven most important Internet languages English, Chinese, Arabic, Japanese, Korean, Russian and Indonesian, Asia has become an indispensable residential support near the top, for the social media world community.

Social media emergence in Asia has clearly traced the route of the mainstream media congruent with Internet use in all Asian countries and regions, except in North Korea where the top domain name .kp was created in September 2007 and broadband has yet to be deployed.

Despite low average Internet penetration of 28%,, Asia has dominated the social media landscape in a unique demographic, with India, Indonesia, the Philippines, Thailand, Malaysia, Taiwan, and Japan leading the way on Facebook, and Twitter has found its prominence in Indonesia, Japan, India, Singapore, the Philippines, Malaysia, Thailand, China and South Korea, accounting for 37% of the Twitter world in all languages.

The revealing "love affair between the Indonesians and the social media" (BBC, February 16th,) has seen trendy Indonesians wearing their hearts on their sleeve in a Twitter film and the crown they have owned for Jakarta as *the Twitter Capital*. The soaring status of Japanese as the most tweeted language in the world only after English has manifested the Japanese profound and obsessive fondness of Twitter for developing and maintaining the *kizune*, with brevity and unclutteredness, reminiscent of the Japanese cultural essence of the haiku poetry, which perfectly serves an answer to the thoughtful question: "What Has Become of the Japanese on the Internet", raised in the book with the same title, co-authored by Toru Nishigaki and Jonathan Louis, who assessed and described the initial impact of the Internet as "the arrival of the black boat."

Facebook, YouTube and Twitter have made significant prominence in Asia as the mainstream social media while they are joined, if not significantly challenged, over time, by a number of emerging variations and vernacularized versions of social media. In South Korea, a country having topped the world in Internet penetration and bandwidth. Home to the world's largest blogging communities (second only to China), it is Cyworld that has reportedly streaming away 18 million regular users. In Japan, it is Mixi that has shored up a sizable audience of its own at 15 million. In

Taiwan, Wretched.net and Pixnet.net have rallied about 10 million social media users. In Viet Nam, Zing has charted out a chunk of 15 million social media users. Put together this fits into a model that trails the path of social media development in Asia, all along with the mainstream league of Facebook, YouTube and Twitter.

China, on top of all Asian countries and regions, has rolled out a different landscape, and unique in that regard, of the information industry and social media in particular, that could be best appreciated and described as a model of nationalization that China has apparently followed for development, albeit along an "obstacle course" (The Economist, April 2013) characterized by a rapid growth under the policy mitigation from administrative and legislative measures gnarred to strengthen the centralization of the Internet.

While the Chinese government has always been diplomatic and matter-of-fact for that matter, regarding allegations of the Internet censorship and in recent times cyber-espionage, several events leading up to the release of China's first white paper on the Internet in June 2010 would help to illustrate and put into perspective China's nationalization model out of growing concerns over the Internet's proliferation as an unprecedentedly new media, where "more than one million IP addresses in China were controlled from overseas, 42,000 websites were distorted by hackers" and computer crime cases rose up to 48,000 (China White Paper on the Internet, June, 2010).

The release of China's first white paper on the Internet was immediately followed up by comments and discussions in Western media that saw it as "a reiteration of need for censorship" and a declaration for China's *national Internet sovereignty*, an idea believed to be at odds with the fundamental concept of the Internet, and as well, with the ideal of *global Internet sovereignty* inspired by the 1996 *Declaration of Independence of Cyberspace*, in which John Perry Barlow, American poet, essayist, and cyber-libertarian, enthused: "Governments of the Industrial World, you weary giants of flesh and steel, I come from Cyberspace, the new home of mind. On behalf of the future, I ask you of the past to leave us alone. You are not welcome among us. You have no sovereignty where we gather."

The cyber-libertarian ideal undoubtedly had its source in the same line of thinking in Western cultural tradition, as propounded by Benjamin Constant (1767–1830) who believed that "there is a part of human existence that necessarily remains individual and independent, and by right beyond all political jurisdictions. Sovereignty exists only in a limited and relative way" (Powers, Freedom of Speech: the History of an Idea, 2011, p. 151).

When translated into a real life situation, in the context either devoid of or deviant from the Western cultural tradition and habit, it would be hardly justified or appropriate to put a national Internet policy along with the cyber-libertarian ideal for scrutiny, and in so doing, conveniently suggest infringement on the Internet "sovereignty," national versus global, when such universal sovereignty was either non-existent or inadequate to curb crimes and controls.

The China-Google confrontation over Google hacking allegations and Google's discontent with China-imposed censorship in early 2010 eventually led to Google's withdrawal from China's search market, and clearly "pointed to two different watersheds and value orientations" (Cui, 2012) over the sovereignty and a severe lack of sovereignty as a result, culminated in clashes between national interests, that of China as reflected in its position, and that of the US as reflected in its diplomatic stance, allegedly surrogated by Google.

Nevertheless, in the absence of Google from China's search market, Baidu has quickly edged over Google as the number one search engine in China, by 84% search queries over Google's 11% share in the fourth quarter of 2010. Among what favored Baidu's rise as the search engine of China and the world were fast search speed made possible from Baidu's local servers and free music downloads. (Cui, in Prosser, Sharifzadeh, & Zhang, 2013, pp. 276–283).

China is home to the world's largest population of 1.3 billion and a netizenship of 590 million, nearly half of whom, over 300 million, are regular users and bloggers on social media sites. Qzone, Renren, QQ, SinaWeibo, and Kaixin, among others, build the world's largest social media cluster and an enormous consumer chunk for businesses and brands, with an estimated annual online transactions (2012) to the tune of 20 billion CNY or about 3.2 billion USD.

This accounts for a phenomenal *movement to the web* in China, whether trenchant or transient, from a finite brick and mortar world, to the infinite cyberspace, considering that the social media have been nascent and a very recent phenomenon of interactions and transactions, even among Internet-savvy netizens.

In China, the drift and transition of social media, from the dominance of Facebook, YouTube and Twitter, started with *Fanfou* (literally "have you eaten" in English translation, an acronymic classic version of the popular Chinese greeting "chile ma"), which is believed to be the very first Chinese social media site, modeled on Twitter, launched as early as May, 2007, but then suspended two years later, before the bewildered gradually building audience had an opportunity to think about the social media site's destiny. The suspension lasted for 505 days before Fanfou came back on the web, when the early mover found it had already been overtaken by, and trailed behind several other, then novice social media sites, among others, Kaixin, SinaWeibo, Qzone and Renren, to name just a few.

A broader perspective would trace social media's seemingly bumpy road of development in China to early 2002, apparently under "protectionism" (Chovanec, 2009), first with alleged censorship of Google search queries in China, and later alleged curtailing access to Facebook (July, 2008), YouTube (March, 2009) and Twitter (June, 2009), reportedly for Internet security concerns and amid China's gigantic efforts in building its e-government. In the aftermath, the universally embedded and integrated social media widgets on all mainstream websites either ended up displaying a blank-out or a 404 error message, and consequently there has emerged in China, an elaborated cyber-culture, popularly called "climbing the firewall," among a few tech-savvy netizens, social media elites and experts for maintaining an "iffy" access on VPN, to the mainstream sites allegedly blocked by the *Great Firewall of China*, famously known as the GFW.

By 2013, trailing behind Facebook, YouTube and Twitter in major social media markets outside of China, QQ (Qzone) has surged as the largest social media site in China, claiming quality service for 637 million active users across the world, with a worth of 11 billion USD in monetary value. SinaWeibo ranks the second at a worth of 3.9 billion USD, followed by Tencent Weibo at 3.5 billion USD of worth. Unfortunately despite a steady and healthy growth, the Internet's lack of universal sovereignty and clashes of interests in its culmination, as illustrated earlier, has repeatedly taken a toll within other national borders as well, sometimes in drastic junctures of events and issues.

The infamous "Facebook arrest" of a 21-year-old girl graduate and her Facebook friend in India on November 18th, 2012, for posting and "liking" a message that questioned the shutdown of Mumbai for the funeral of a powerful politician ("Every day thousands of people die, but still the world moves on. Today, Mumbai shuts down out of fear, not out of respect"), according to Professor Ravinder Barn it revealed the vulnerability of India despite its advances as a liberalizing society and invigorated economy (WSJ, 2013: January 9), in freedom of speech and Internet legislation, underlining a wider range of broader issues of "overall infrastructures of inefficiency, corruption and patriarchy" that had allowed incidents of this nature to happen and repeat, which was further illustrated by the brutal rape and murder of the 23-year-old Indian student, mid-December, 2012, in New Delhi and "a national grief and outrage" expressed in what was described as "the Indian Spring" (Barn, 2013), a series of massive protests, both on the streets as well as on the social media, that triggered off "a new movement and an awakening to demand action, fairness, gender equality and above all safety for girls and women of India."

Another intriguing story of social media growing pains in Asia, indicative of Internet sovereignty being at odds between national interests and freedom of speech, was experienced in the Republic of Kazakhstan. Land-locked, with 4.5 percent of its territory under lease to Russia, and time-warped in nearly 3000 year history of West-East conversation and commerce along the Silk Road, Kazakhstan arguably is the largest fledgling democracy in Central Asia after the breakup of the Soviet Union, a country on its way to democratization with the media still being morphed in ownership, transparency, media censorship and press freedom. Kazakhstan, with a Internet penetration above Asian average, has staged a number of significant events that, on one hand, culminated in the "social media diffusion of political expression" that "might help create a discursive environment for more official and institutional political activities" (Couper, Nurmanov, & Adams, 2013), and on the other hand, witnessed the government's revealing complex dilemma in attempting to strike a balance between appeasing "a discourse of dissatisfaction" and polish an image of "a mostly western-style open society" in the international community, either by "overt and direct control", "by selectively blocking" "objectionable" sites, or by "more intricate and less-overt means of making inaccessible sites," with a control mechanism, "in favor of the governmental priorities and efforts."

Social media in Asia have obviously traced an "adoption model" (DeLeo, 2013), characterized by tethering around and circumventing "the ideological and technological foundations" (Kaplan & Haenlein, 2010) on which social media operate, and consequently created a conundrum, at the social and cultural level, which was found to be paradoxical, unjustified and counter-Zeitgeist in view of social media's viral development, when its role and impact have already seen manifestation in the major turn of events in recent history.

This social media conundrum was puzzling and mythical, and at some point, serving as a testimony to the concept and reality that "communication between people is a fragile thing, and high technology is only one of many factors that make it more difficult." (Dominick, 1999). Bearing this in mind, we recognize the difficulty in attempt to assess issues regarding prediction of the ultimate future of the social media, pending drastic developments, for instance, in the first place, what changes will have to take place in a supposed transition, in order to maintain the global dialogue and keep up the universal bondage towards universal solidarity, and without disrupting the existing order? And if social media are remote versions of the "cultural product" of the democratic ideal, how can they be made to grow in full swing, to get universalized and internalized across the national and cultural boundaries, by tiding over a driven industry that would forever seek innovations, by managing a keen academia who would continue to experience digital divide, and by appeasing a public who would still be devastated by communication breakdowns and disruptions?

However we understand and therefore we are confident that the difficulty or obstacle is temporary and transitional in a long process of development and democratization, communication breakdown and disruptions are only exceptional and may even be accidental in a millennium-long global dialogue, as Asia has already reemerged from the major crises and continued to benefit multi-dimensionally from development of the Internet and now social media.

Social Media in Asia is a reflection and celebration of this development either in the spirit of the millennium-long international solidarity or by the current Zeitgeist of globalization, focusing on the social media, as the Internet landscape continues to extend, sometimes, become mapped and chartered by national and cultural boundaries, sometimes by no borderlines at all, amid unanimous efforts by the governments, institutions, organizations, businesses and individuals in developing and reaping ROI (Return of Investment) of social entrepreneurship, social capital, CSR (Corporate Social Responsibility) and eventually the public sphere as a powerful mover in the democratization process, and ultimately toward what Pierre Teilhard de Chardin (1881 – 1955) called the "golden gates to the super human future for all people all together" (Cui, 2005, Pope, 2004), and hopefully "for the good of the infinite, or immortal universal environment" and ultimately "to protect the continuity of an immortal soul." (Cui, 2013: April; Pope, 2004).

References

Barn, R.(2013). The Indian Spring. Retrieved from: http://www. huffingtonpost.co.uk/professor-ravinder-barn/india-social-media-and-protest_b_2430194.html

China White Paper on Internet (June, 2010). Retrieved from: http:// www.china.org.cn/government/whitepaper/node_7093508.htm

Couper, J., Nurmanov, A. & Adams, T. L. (2014). Political uses of social media in Kazakhstan. In L. Cui, M. H. Prosser (Eds.). *Social Media in Asia*. Lake Oswego, USA: Dignity Press.

Cui, L. (2005). A map without boundaries: William Gibson's neuromancer reexamined. *Shanghai Industry & Commerce Foreign Language College Teaching and Research*, Issue 2, 2005, (ISBN 988-98935-1-7)

Cui, L. (2012). Wrangling the media market place, pp. 196–19. In Li Mengyu and M. H. Prosser. *Communicating Interculturally*. Beijing, China: Higher Education Press.

Cui, L. (2013). Michael H. Prosser, Public Conversation interview on professional, cultural and personal topics with Cui Litang, Shanghai, China. In M. H.Prosser, M. Sharifzadeh, & S. Zhang (Eds.). *Finding cross-cultural common ground* (pp.276–283). Lake Oswego, OR: Dignity Press.

Chovanec, P. (2009). Retrieved from http://chovanec.wordpress. com/2009/12

DeLeo, M. (2013). Retrieved from: http://www.socialmediaexplorer. com/social-media-measurement/tools-process-and-culture-oh-my/

Dominick, R. J. (1999). *The dynamics of mass communication*, 6th Edition, New York, NY: McGraw-Hill College.

Encyclopedia Britannica. Postal system in China. Retrieved from: http:// global.britannica.com/EBchecked/topic/472092/postal- system/15437/China

Kaplan, A. M., Haenlein, M. (2010). Users of the world, unite! The challenges and opportunities of social media. *Business Horizons* p. 61. Retrieved from: http://www.sciencedirect.com/science/article/ pii/S0007681309001232

Kellner, D. (undated). Habermas, the public sphere, and democracy: A critical intervention. Retrieved from: http://pages.gseis.ucla.edu/ faculty/kellner/papers/habermas

Mattelart, A. (2000). Program one: Contact, lines of communication, ABC.

McLuhan, M. (1967). The medium is the message, p. 48, San Francisco, CA, USA: Hardwired.

McHoul (2000): Program two: Hi-Tech, lines of communication, ABC, Australia.

Nishigaki, T. & Louis, J. (2001): What has become the Japanese on the Internet? Tokyo, Japan: Iwanami.

NHK (April, 2013). The big data project.

Osborne, G. (2000). Program one: Contact, lines of communication, ABC.

Pope, R. (2004). Science-Art and global human survival technology, Murwillumbah, NSW, Australia: Science-Art Research Center.

Poster, M. (2000). Program two: Hi-Tech, lines of communication, ABC.

Powers, E. (2011). Freedom of speech: The history of an idea, p .151. Retrieved from: http://zh.scribd.com/doc/68736242/Freedom-of-Speech-The-History-of-an-Idea

Prosser, M. H. (1985). *The cultural dialogue.* Washington, DC: SIETAR International, p. 15.

The Economist (2013: April).

Tomasello, M. (2008). *Origins of human communication*, Jacket inside, Cambridge, MA: London, UK: The MIT Press.

The Wall Street Journal (2013: January 9).

II. Social Media, Communication and Culture: An Asian Perspective

Beth Bonniwell Haslett

Department of Communication, University of Delaware,
Newark, Delaware
bjh@udel.edu

Abstract

With developments in communication technology and transportation, globalization is part of our daily lives. As Giddens (1984) notes, our relationships have become distanciated where we can simultaneously be "here and there, and now and then." We also have unprecedented speed in the changes we experience.

Computer-mediated communication (CMC) has changed the way in which we communicate. We live in an evolving, multimodal digital environment that shapes and integrates our daily lives. Although our early communicative experiences are face-to-face (F2F), that quickly changes to incorporate face-to-device communication (F2D). Through social media, we are able to extend our relationships across time and space, through skype, instant messaging, Facebook, Twitter, cell phones and other forms of mediated communication. Social network sites (SNS) are used not only for relationship development, but also for news, education, political activism, and entertainment. I shall explore some of the interrelationships of the social media and intercultural communication, focusing on these issues in Asia.

Keywords: Asia, uses of social media, culture, change, globalization

1. Introduction

Social media influence our view of the world and our view of culture. Culture is no longer a matter of place, or space, but rooted in identity. Immigration, diaspora and the worldwide movement of people have blurred the traditional definitions of culture. We gain a significant amount of knowledge about other lifestyles from CMC—through news channels, Facebook, YouTube and other mediated channels.

As we acknowledge the changes mediated communication has brought in communication itself as well as in our understanding of culture, we can also chart the cultural influences on the way in which social media is used. Thus, the influences of social media, culture and communication are intertwined with one another.

Communication and culture have always been intimately intertwined. Broadly defined, culture represents a shared set of beliefs and social practices among a group. Communication is essential for such beliefs and practices to be shared. Thus, communication is critical for the development and maintenance of culture; culture, in turn, shapes communication, including verbal, nonverbal and mediated forms of communication. Given social and economic changes wrought through advances in transportation and communication, a re-examination of the nature of culture and communication, and their interrelationships, with recognition of the importance of social media in these processes, seems necessary. In a recent article, Chen (2012) suggests that new media and intercultural communication mutually impact one another in terms of (1) cultural influences on the development of new media; (2) the influence of media on cultural/social identity, and (3) new media influencing intercultural communication. Similarly, Zhang and Prosser (2012) also point out that international and intercultural communication will be influenced by the traditional and modernizing high-tech societies in East Asia, most notably in China.

In what follows, I shall explore some of the interrelationships of the social media and intercultural communication, focusing on these issues in Asia. I begin with a brief overview of the sociohistorical context in which social media is embedded, and then move into a discussion of social media. In discussing social media, I will discuss the impact of social media on culture, how social media have changed communication, the interrelationships of media, culture and communication and finally, suggest some considerations for future research.

2. The Sociohistorical Context of Social Media

The theory of structurational interaction (Haslett, 2012a) provides a very useful theoretical framework for examining some of these changes. Structurational interaction synthesizes the work of two world-renowned social theorists, Anthony Giddens and Erving Goffman. Both focus on social order: Giddens analyzes social order generally, as in social systems or cultures, while Goffman analyzes the interaction order—how people develop and sustain communication. As such, structurational interaction (SI) provides a comprehensive analytic framework for examining culture (a type of social system) and communication (the interaction order). In particular, Giddens' theoretical orientation looks at cultural changes across time while Goffman was among the first scholars to focus on both verbal and nonverbal communication. Giddens, in particular, reflects upon the influence of mediated forms of communication and its social and cultural impact.

According to Giddens, social structure and agency are intertwined and manifest through interaction. Giddens relies on Goffman's concept of the interaction order (1974, 1983a, b) as a foundation for creating, maintaining and extending social systems, like institutions and cultures. Goffman's work provides a very cogent analysis of face-to-face (F2F) interaction, and the presentation of self in everyday encounters. Goffman's interaction model details the multi-modal nature of interpersonal communication, especially in the presentation of self and identity (Haslett, 2012a). Through synthesizing their perspectives, a very rich analysis of identity and distanciated relationships is possible, moving from the interpersonal bases of identity to mediated influences on identity.

In modernity, Giddens argued that the pace of change is so rapid and global that it is "discontinuous" with prior changes. First, there is time-space distanciation: in traditional civilizations "systems of time and space are still closely connected with place. Time-reckoning never becomes completely separate from 'where' one is, while space remains infused with characteristics of localized milieux. In circumstances of modernity, time and space become 'emptied out' and distinguished from one another. The 'emptying' of time has priority in this process, because control of time, through abstract time-regulation, permits the coordination of activities across space" (Giddens, 1990b, pp. 306). Computer-mediated communication, of course, makes possible and facilitates this time-space distanciation.

Secondly, social systems are disembedded, where social interaction and relations are "lifted out of" local contexts of interaction. For example, banking and food production may have been local where now it is global. The separation of time and space is essential for disembedding, and "disembedded activities promote a massive increase in time-space distanciation" (Ibid.). Through CMC, we also disembed and re-embed social relationships, identities and information (Haslett, 2012a, b).

Finally, there is the reflexivity of modernity, which Giddens argues goes beyond ordinary human reflexivity (i.e., keeping in touch with what is going on). As Giddens notes, "In conditions of modernity, social practices are constantly examined and reformed in terms of novel information about their nature—in a process which has no intrinsic end-point" (Ibid., pp. 306–307). Through continuous evaluation of social practices in the light of new information, more uncertainty and risk is created. Ontological security becomes more fragile, with knowledge being questioned and human action being subjected to increasing reflexivity (Giddens, 1990, 1991). CMC provides a significant increase in information from a wide variety of sources.

With the standardization of time and space, we possess a world-wide frame of action and experience. Giddens sees "media and communications as having a fundamental role because most of the institutions we now associate with globalization would not be possible" without them (Rantanen, 2005, p. 68). As Giddens observes "communications has become the driving force of successive waves of transformation of human society…the simplest meaning of globalization is interdependence. We have started to be much more dependent on other people than ever before, and part of the reason is that we are constantly in communication with them all" (Rantanen, 2005, p. 73, emphasis mine). Thus, social contexts are now global and distanciated in both time and space. Giddens points out that "Distant events may become as familiar or more so, than proximate influences, and integrated into the frameworks of personal experience" (1991, p. 189).

Through transportation and telecommunication, culture and knowledge is no longer localized in time or space. Media, in all their forms, provide increased knowledge about the world, both past and present. As such, we are presented with a wide variety of lifestyles; shared beliefs and values may extend across individuals and groups dispersed throughout the world. This new sociohistoric context appears to require a reframing of models of culture and communication.

3. Social Media

The increasing expansion and evolution of new social media requires a brief overview of their diversity. In 2010, Ogilvy's social media team did a fairly comprehensive analysis of social media in China. The range of social media channels included online trade, online music, professional and corporate SNSs, message boards, blogging and micro-blogging, mobile chat and instant messaging, wikis and various sharing platforms for video and photos. This is a brief illustration of the variety of Internet social media available, not only in Asia but throughout the world.

In a very short span of time, social media channels have increased dramatically and new forms and use continue to develop. For the purposes of this chapter, I will exclude professional corporate sites and concentrate on how people use the social media, focusing primarily on SNSs (social network sites). boyd and Ellison (2008) defined SNSs as web-based services that allow individuals to construct public or semi-public profiles within a service; list others with whom they wish to connect, and view/traverse their connections and those of others in the service. The limits and use of a service varies across social network sites. Since the first SNS in 1997 was launched, hundreds more have been launched including professionally oriented sites, such as LinkedIn, and various sharing SNSs, such a Flickr, FaceBook and YouTube.

Before we begin looking at social media in Asia more specifically, we need to briefly survey the penetration of social media in Asian countries. Asia is viewed as the most rapidly growing market for social media, given its population and opportunities for growth. Popular SNSs in the Asian-Pacific area include Renren (China), Cyworld (South Korea) and Mixi (Japan). Approximately two-thirds of active Internet users have managed their profiles and over 71% have visited friends' SNSs (Universal McCann, 2009). High growth in Asian SNSs was also found by comScore (2008).

Facebook has substantial penetration in Asian countries, with Hong Kong, South Korea and Singapore all having 50% percent of the population using that particular social media (We Are Social, January, 2012). Statistics show that more than 25% of Facebook users are from Asia, and English, Indonesian, and Chinese are among the top ten languages on Facebook (Crampton, n.d.). In China, Sina Weibo, with 300 million users, and Tencent's Weibo, also with about 300 million users, are also important social network platforms; in Japan, Twitter is the most popular platform (Kemp, 2012).

By 2015, it is anticipated that India will have more Facebook members than the U.S.: the challenge, of course, will be how Facebook can monetize this usage and gain needed revenue (Panjam, 2012; see also, Saeki, 2012). Overall, Facebook users in the major Asian countries total approximately 90 million, while Qzone (China) has a network of 531 million and CyWorld (South Korea) has an 18 million member network. So we must keep in mind both media penetration and media member numbers. World-wide, SNSs are "essential ways in which people stay in touch" (Mussell, 2012). As he points out, Facebook claims 800 million to one billion active users; Twitter has over 100 million and YouTube claims 3 billion views per day.

Corporate presence in social media channels in quite strong. Across Asian countries, most corporations (from 60–99%, except for Singapore, Taiwan and the Philippines) use micro-blogs and social networks in addition to their own corporate blogs (Econsultancy, 2011).

Although mobile phones are usually not considered part of social media because of their limited connection, usually between two individuals, nevertheless they are now a major connector to the Internet. Due to space considerations I will not discuss mobile phones, but we need to think about their importance in terms of access to the Internet. For example, in 2005, only 20% of the population in Indonesia had mobile phones, in less than five years, 50% of the population has mobile phones (Crampton, 2011). And with advances in mobile phone technology, costs associated with connecting to the Internet will decrease and thus widen the pool of individuals able to connect with the Internet from multiple locations. More research connecting cellphones and their mediated as well as face-to-face implications needs to be done (see, for example, Garcia-Montes, Caballero-Munoz & Perez-Alvarez, 2006; Humphreys, 2006; Qiu, 2010).

With this broad context in mind, we now turn to discuss how media transforms culture. Over human history, communication has played an important role in how societies develop and change, and influence our perspectives on culture(s).

4. Social Media and Culture

Shifting views of culture. Scholarly views of culture have traditionally associated culture with nation-states, but with globalization and the flow of information and immigration increasing worldwide, that perspective may no longer be satisfactory. Giddens notes that "With the advent of cultures having writing, there develops the phenomenon of location in time, allowing quite different modes of organization... A society in which there are records, used to systematize social relations across time and space, is inevitably structurally different from a purely oral culture" (1987, pp. 147–148). In addition, cultures that have differential access to various forms of CMC may also strongly differ from one another in their social practices, their social organization and their potential for surveillance.

Giddens suggested that societies (cultures) need to share a way of communication (usually language(s)); a way of life/values; control over a territory and its resources; and to maintain a group identity. Through distanciation of time and space, the global has become local and the local global, and thus cultures may not be limited to nation-state boundaries. We may commit to a group or community, although we are not co-present with other group members. Although I believe we must move beyond the *control over territory* as a definition of culture, clearly it is still a vital issue as we witness continual conflicts over territories.

Identification with and commitment to a group seems essential for a culture. As such, it seems reasonable to assume that shared beliefs might be a fundamental condition for culture. And modern telecommunication systems have been essential in forming and maintaining those commitments. As van Dijck (2009) notes, "Media use was and still is strongly defined by evolving group identities, as individual viewers tie in their personal taste and lifestyles with shared 'mediated' experiences" (p. 44). Culture and identity appear to move beyond face-to-face (F2F) interpersonal connections, and increasingly incorporate the influence of others distanciated in time and space. (For a fuller discussion of these issues, see Haslett, 2012a). Internet connections, using SNSs or other public forums, seems particularly important in maintaining cultural connections for diasporic communities—"grounded in local and national spaces but sustained in global networks.... Many of the public diasporic spaces on the Internet are sustained around ideologies and practices of participation in transnational communities and multiethnic societies" (Georgiou, 2006, pp. 131–132).

For Giddens, "the level of time-space distinction introduced by high modernity is so extensive that, for the first time in human history, 'self' and 'society' are interrelated in a global milieu" (McPhee, 1998, p. 32). The increasing range of lifestyle choices, the more open and multiple contexts of action, and varied sources of authority provide agents with daily choices for constructing a narrative of identity (Giddens, 1990, 1991). Social systems exist through the continuity of social practices and its structure may be characterized as *position-practice* relations. "A social position involves the specification of a definite 'identity' within a network of social relations, that identity, however, being a 'category' to which a particular range of normative sanctions is relevant" (Giddens, 1984, p. 83). Social positions are thus social identities and people are also positioned differently within different cultures, contexts and groups. As Hargittai (2010) notes, even controlling for Internet skills, access and experience, those with more privileged backgrounds (i.e., social positions) use the Internet in more varied and sophisticated ways. Also, gender, race and ethnicity, and parental education levels are related to SNSs use as well as the user's experience and autonomy influence SNS usage (Hargittai, 2008).

In brief, social positioning incorporates a wide range of influences which extend beyond any individual's own life span. Social positioning reflects one's own body-life activities as well as social relations with others. These activities and relationships are contextualized within time-space and within a specific sociohistorical moment and culture. One's identities are formed and re-formed within and across social positions, reflecting both local and global influences over one's life span. Within this world of distanciated relationships and world wide connectivity, one's identity is influenced by both F2F relationships as well as mediated relationships and sources of information. Shared beliefs are present in groups ranging from nation-states to groups sharing ethnicity, age, gender, educational level, and so forth. Indeed, one's identity reflects movement through complex social structures in global cultural systems (Giddens, 1984). We next explore social media and identity in more detail.

5. Social Media and Identity.

It is in this globalized, distanciated world, in which cultures (social systems) are viewed as nation-states as well as representing social groups categorized by age, gender, religion, education and so forth, that identities are negotiated. The role of communication, both mediated (CMC) and face to face (F2F), is central to the development of the self as well as for the development of social systems. Hybridity is a term used to describe a "state of culture in transnational movements constituted by flows of people, goods, communication, ideas, technologies, finance, and more" (Lee, Kim & Min, 2009). Chen (2012), for example, has explored ways in which new media have altered our perceptions of cultural/social identity and altered intercultural communication processes.

Because many of our experiences are mediated, we need to "appreciate the subtleties and complexities of different modes of experience available to human beings in conditions of modernity" and be aware of the qualitative differences across different types of mediation (Tomlinson, 1997, p. 123).

The different affordances of communication technologies provide different opportunities for personal identity and cultural identification. The term "prosumer" has been used to identify "how users' agency hovers between the bipolar categories of producer versus consumer, and of professional versus consumer" (van Dijck, 2009). A study among adult Singaporeans indicated that the Internet did not promote or displace other media use (Lee, Tan & Hameed).

Shifting sources of identification are provided by mediated communication. The range of communication media is itself daunting, ranging from search engines like Google and Yahoo, to MUDs (Multi-User Dungeons), MOOs (MUDs, Object-Oriented) and SNSs. In our discussion of culture and social media, we should note several qualifiers at the outset. First, access to a variety of communication technologies is a function of economic wealth or social position (i.e., having sufficient infrastructure to support communication technology—as captured by the idea of the 'digital divide') (Pan, Yan, Jing & Zheng, 2011). Differences in relative wealth, for example, can be seen in the unequal coverage of websites across countries by major search engines (Vaughan & Zhang, 2007) or differential access to mobile phones (Burrell, 2010). Second, political attitudes shape the use of communication technologies (i.e., what type of access do governments allow as, for example, in the recent controversy between Google and the Chinese government). With these caveats in mind, we can examine the ways in which social media and culture influence one another, ranging from direct expression of one's identity online to the development of relationships online to the affordances offered by different SNSs.

6. Expressing or Creating Identity Online

Identity may be directly expressed online in SNSs. Liu (2008) argues that users' statements of interests (in music, movies, books, etc.) operate as an expression of identity. Four types of expressive identity statements—taste performances—were identified: those conveying prestige, differentiation, authenticity, and theatrical persona. Such cultural signs express who we are and differentiate among users. Prestige and differentiation were the two

Social Media, Communication and Culture: An Asian Perspective

most important types of taste statements, with authenticity and theatrical persona as secondary qualities. Taste statements also connect users with groups expressing the same interests and thus express identification with that group. Siles' analysis of blogging (2012) found that bloggers often form their self-identities on the web through online diaries, statements of personal interests and viewpoints. Schwammlein and Woodzicki (2012) examined reasons for participating in online communities, distinguishing between common-bond orientations or common-identity orientations. Those having common-identity orientations focused on the qualities they shared with community members and generally, community members manage their self-presentation in line with personal goals.

7. Online Relationship Development.

Yum and Hara (2006) explored the influence of self-disclosure on relationship development across Korea, Japan and the United States. These cultures varied in their perceptions of the relationship between self-disclosure and trust. In online relationships, self-disclosure and trust were positively related for U.S. participants, inversely related for the Koreans and a nonfactor for the Japanese. Across all cultures, greater self-disclosure was associated with greater love, liking, commitment and a willingness to adjust their communication style to match that of their partners. Results indicated that people have confidence in cyberspace relationships and use cyberspace to substantively enhance their F2F relationships.

Similarly, Ma (1996) found that misperceptions and misinterpretations surrounded the use of self-disclosure on CMC by North Americans and East Asians. As Yum and Hara commented, in Ma's study, "East Asians indeed felt that they crossed their typical cultural constraints and engaged in greater self-disclosure. However, North Americans still perceive that their East Asian partners were indirect and did not self-disclose sufficiently, while East Asians felt that their North American partners were overexplicit and rude" (2006, p. 148). Yum and Hara conclude that when participants from high-context and low-context cultures interact, more attention to face (identity) concerns may be needed to prevent misunderstanding. In fact, Chen (1995) suggests that cultural patterns in communication might strongly influence self-disclosure in terms of its breadth and depth. Timing and social positioning might also influence decisions about self-disclosure and vary across cultures.

The Internet has also been viewed as increasing the cosmopoliteness of users (that is, such users have a greater interest in other cultures, more tolerance of other cultures, more cultural knowledge, more cultural diversity in media content, more diversity in interpersonal networks, etc.) (Jeffres. Atkin, Bracken & Neuendorf, 2004). Their results, although exploratory, suggest that cosmopolitanites use the Internet for seek out information, control their access to mediated content and gather timely information. Technology access and Internet access was significantly related to the cosmopolitan dimensions of diversity of interests, appreciation of different cultures, knowledge of different cultures, knowledge of current events, cultural diversity of media content and diversity of interpersonal networks. These findings suggest that media users who have cosmopolitan tendencies actively use the Internet to further their knowledge of cultures. As the authors note, however, this may not translate into cross-cultural understanding. One of the values of this study is in its theoretical development of the concept of cosmopolitanism and its relationship to social media.

8. Cultural Influences on Social Media.

The affordances of the various websites will also influence the capacity of users to form relationships (Donath, Karahalios & Viegas, 1999; Hutchby, 2001). Interestingly, cultural cognition theory, proposed by Faiola and Matei (2006) examines the influence of Web designers' cultural cognitive styles and its impact on user responses. Web users performed information-seeking tasks faster when using websites designed by a native of their culture. Segev, Ahituv and Barzilai-Nahon (2007) found that culture influenced the local homepages of MSN and Yahoo!—MSN revealed more cultural heterogeneity and localization of content and form than did Yahoo!. They also note that "differences in website form and content reflect a variety of cultural attributes" (p. 1271). Barnett and Sung (2005) found that nation-state culture was significantly related to Internet network centrality and its overall structure. Wurz (2006) argued that high context cultures used graphic elements and indirect messages extensively while low-context cultures were more static and direct in their messages. Such differences are considered aspects of cultural marking (colors, graphical density, etc.) (Callahan, 2006; Cyr, Bonanni, Bowes & Ilsever, 2006). A comparative analysis of U.S. and South Korean websites found that South Korean websites oriented toward high-context and polychronic time-management websites (Kim, Coyle & Gould, 2009). Thus, culture (viewed as nation states) already seem to subtly influence the way in which information is presented in CMC (see also Hermeking, 2005).

A fascinating study by Gevorgyan and Manucharova (2009) contrasted responses to and uses of social media by Chinese and North American students. Those cultures were chosen to contrast the collectivist/ individualist and power distance differences between the two cultures. Their study sampled favorite websites (the top ten) for attractiveness of design and layout characteristics. Chinese participants responded most favorably to websites emphasizing collectivist features whereas North Americans responded most favorably to individualistic features in web design. Those participants with a "relatively strong sense of ethnic identity had particularly strong reactions to culture consistent design features" (p. 403). Thus, culture plus strong ethnic identification influence judgments of web design. They concluded the global websites need to be adapted to specific cultures and increasingly this means adapting to particular Asian cultures, not just to a regional block characterized as South East Asian. The driving motivation behind this, of course, will undoubtedly be consumer consumption pressure.

As we have seen, social media have influenced our views of culture and emphasizes culture primarily as an identification with a particular group or community. Social media have also influenced how identity is expressed online and how online relationships develop. In addition, the affordances of various social media influence how users approach the social media. In many ways, social media have altered cultures and yet display cultural values as used in various social media (i.e., preferences for one's cultural values in website design). While social media have profoundly influenced culture as well as reflected cultural practices, social media have also profoundly altered communicative practices. It is to these issues we now turn.

9. Social Media and Communication

Various telecommunication devices have created new spatial-temporal conditions of human contact (referred to as face-to-device communication, F2D, or more generally, CMC) (Giddens, 1984; Meyerowitz, 1995; Tomlinson, 1997). Through inventions from the telegraph to instant messaging, in mediated communication, especially electronic communication, there has been a "tearing space away from place" (Giddens, 1990). Zhao pointed out that mediated communication extends human perception as well as the zone of operation (opening up a secondary zone of operation), and time becomes somewhat "elastic" because of varying times taken to respond to messages. "New technologies such as blogs, wikis, massively multiplayer online games, social networking technologies and video- and music-dissemination technologies have rapidly spread, by means of the Internet, each with additional, new literacy forms and functions that are reshaped by social practices (Coiro, Knobel, Lankshear & Leu, 2008, p. 5). Twitter is commonly used to update users' current status (Java, Song, Finn & Tseng, 2007). Twitter also, because of its brevity, shapes the way in which it can be used—and there is debate as to whether ongoing, instantaneous coverage of unfolding events by citizens represents citizens acting as journalists (Murthy, 2011). Journalistic practices in China have been altered through the use of hyperlinks, videos and tweets, because such devices enhance the interactivity between journalists and readers (Gao & Martin-Kratzer, 2011).

When two or more "worlds within mediated reach" coincide, a new connection is forged, termed "telecopresence." When people are in a situation of telecopresence, they are simultaneously in two meaning streams—one in real time and real space (geospace), and the other in real time, but distanciated space (cyberspace). As Zhao (2004) notes,

> *The full conditions of telecopresence, therefore, consist in a situation in which individuals, though not mutually present in the same physical locale, are in each other's electronic proximity and capable of maintaining simultaneous contact with one another through the mediation of an electronic communications network.... The term "telecopresence" thus captures the essence of the emergent condition of human interaction that brings distant people temporally together in cyberspace. (pp. 98–99)*

Donath (2008) suggests that SNSs may provide a *social supernet*; however asks if individuals will find the costs of these connections to outweigh the benefits (the major draw of *ceaseless novelty*) (p. 267). Her essay is a fascinating discussion of the different affordances of various SNSs and their ability to establish trust, identity and cooperation. Facebook users in Singapore was primarily used it to maintain relationships (Hew & Cheung, 2012). Bloggers tend to write for their interpersonal connections to family and friends, and more extroverted and self-disclosive bloggers have larger and more strong-tie social networks (Stefanone & Jang, 2008).

In brief, social media offer many new ways to communicate, and presents new challenges, both technical and social, for users. While social media present new forms of communication, what is the nature of the connections formed online and how do they compare with connections formed offline? Research tends to suggest that the lines may be blurred between online and offline (F2F) communication as individuals themselves express themselves and connect with others in both ways. SNSs are used to express emotions, resolve conflicts and express identity—apparently the full range of communicative functions in F2F interactions.

10. Affective Expression

A fascinating study by Kim and Yun (2008) explored the influence of Cyworld on relationships among Koreans. They found a tension between offline and online interactions. As they concluded, "Cyworld users routinely negotiate multiple dialectical tensions that are created in the online world, transferred from face-to-face contexts, or imposed by interpersonal principles that relate to Korea's collectivist culture" (p. 298). Minihompies (private sections on one's site that have access controlled by the site creator) functioned as a forum for private thoughts and self reflections which were free from distressing social contexts. Interviewees referred to them as "another me." A minihompy thus provided a place for exchanging and expressing elaborate emotional communication—lacking in F2F interpersonal interactions. Users could express regrets, their thoughts on an ongoing conflict or deeply felt sentiments. The importance of yon (a predestined close relationship, like that of family or regionalism) could be extended to special online buddies called ilchons (some of which may be fabricated). What is especially noteworthy in this study is the online expression of emotions that usually were not expressed F2F and the use of the minihompy for identity construction and maintenance of close offline relationships in a fashion consistent with Korean communicative norms.

In addition, cying (maintaining social networks) also connected people with others as well as providing a place for self-reflection. Their study found that "Cyworld's design features and functions encourage users to transcend the high-context communication of Korean culture by offering an alternative channel for elaborate and emotional communication, which fosters the reframing of relational issues offline" (Kim & Yun, 2008, p. 298). In addition, the capacity to elaborate on complex ideas was also provided. They conclude that "For Cyworld users, the system represents an aspect of reality itself, inseparable from their "real" lives, because it is within those spaces that users search for and construct their true identities. Communication technologies seem to create a new space that represents neither, but rather exists somewhere in-between. The nature of this luminal space changes constantly, shaped by social uses of communication technologies (including SNSs)" (2008, p. 314). Hjorth and Kim (2011) also found that social media, especially cell phones, created an affective space in which to share feelings after the recent, devastating Japanese earthquake. As they note, in Japan, "camera-phones and social media ... are playing a significant role in producing affective cultures" (p. 196). Gender also plays a significant role in the use of mobile media (Hjorth, 2009).

Socioemotional and interpersonal connections are found in CMC as well as face-to-face communication. Park (2008) found that politeness and face-work was used in CMC and such devices, both textual and graphic, help signal this. Westbrook (2007) found that expressions of informality, such as humor, self-disclosure and appeals to group identity, made the CMC interaction viewed as more positive. A fascinating study of communicative differences, conducted in South Korea, contrasted the use of various social media, such as email, instant messenger, mobile phone and SMS with F2F communication (Kim, Kim, Park & Rice, 2007). Students favored IM, SMS, and mobile phones while homemakers favored mobile phones and organizational workers favored email. They also found that mobile phones reinforced strong social ties while text-based CMC media explored expanded relationships with weak ties. Face-to-face communication was valued equally across respondents and fostered close relationships. Interestingly, in using Wikipedia in a Singapore classroom, students were reluctant to edit one another's work for fear of causing others to "lose face": an illustration of cultural values in online communication (Young, 2010).

11. Developing and Maintaining Relationships.

Relationship development has also been examined in CMC. An intriguing study by Rabby (2007) examined how relationships began and developed (whether via CMC or F2F) and whether or not this influenced relational commitment. Subjects were divided into four groups: those meeting for the first time online include the virtuals (who continue to meet online) and the Pinocchios (who now meet offline, F2F). Those who first met offline include the cyber emigrants (who now meet online) and real worlders (who continue to meet offline, F2F). Rabby suggests that the boundaries between offline and online may be somewhat fuzzy because, on occasion, an offline relationship may use online interaction and vise versa. However, the groupings represent predominant trends for F2F or mediated interaction. Rabby found that when commitment is high, relationships are strong across all groups: "the strength of the relationship can transcend the medium" (p. 333). Because relationships will increasingly blend both offline and online interactions, this seems to be an important area of research, particularly in light of users' mobility and global social networks. Wellman (1997) found that online relationships are strong when they are voluntary and focus on a common interest. Others have indicated that their best friends are in their online relationships (Turkle, 2011).

12. Social Media and Social Capital.

Social capital refers to the connections people form through CMC. Putnam (2000) suggests that social capital can be bridging capital (connections via social networks that are wide ranging and provide new information and new resources). In contrast, bonding social capital are ties formed with individuals, such as friends or family, that provide emotional and substantive support—these are in-depth relationships. Massively multiplayer online games (MMOs) provide an opportunity to engage with others and form bridging social capital (while not providing in-depth relational connections, exposing people to a variety of worldviews) (Steinkuehler & Williams, 2006). Facebook friends were found to provide social capital such as improved mental and physical health, and improved psychological well-being (Johnston, Tanner, Lalla & Kawalski, 2011). Ji, et al, (2010) found cultural differences in bridging and bonding social capital: South Koreans and Chinese use SNSs for expert advice (bridging social capital) while users in the U.S. used them primarily for communicative purposes (bonding social capital).

Furthermore, Skoric and Kwan (2012), in a study of Singaporean youths, found a positive relationship between online social capital and intensity of Facebook use. Civic gaming was related to online bridging while MMO play build online bonding social capital. Offline bonding social capital and education were significant predictors of online bonding social capital. This study, as have others, link online behaviors with offline relationships; thus, the lines between online and offline behaviors is frequently blurred (also see Vergeer, Lim & Park, 2011). They suggest that "MMOs provide new alternative venues of informal public life and facilitate communication between people of diverse backgrounds" and that "SNSs represent important technological tools for the creation and maintenance of cross-cutting social ties" (p. 480).

Steinkuehler and Williams (2006) argue that both bridging and bonding social capital are socially important. Greenhow and Robelia (2009) found that SNSs provided social support, facilitated social learning and demonstrated complex, creative activities as well as strengthening both weak and strong personal ties.

In Singapore, online social capital facilitated political participation in both online and offline circumstances (Skoric, Ying & Ng, 2009). In particular, they found that bridging capital is related to online, but not offline, political participation; bonding capital was related to offline social capital. And according to a Shanghai survey (Zhou, 2011), an individual's sense of social positions in society were influenced by new media adoption and use. However, opportunities for access and participation were also limited by resources, utility values and literacy levels that impacted people's Internet use. Thus social media is embedded in systems of social stratification (see also Wong, 2001), and may also help perpetuate such stratification. The degree to which the Internet can be used as a site of political activism and how effective the Internet can be in terms of mobilizing action is a widely contested issue: among the issues discussed are the potential for such action (Tang & Yang, 2011); are alternative media used to express dissent and mobilize (Smeltzer & Keddy, 2010); the penetration/participation paradox (George, 2005); the restricted communicative environment (Zhong, 2012) and the users' responsiveness to social change (Special issue on South Asian media in the Noughties, *Contemporary South Asia*, 18, 2010).

Asian international students in South Korea used the Internet to maintain and strengthen close ties with family and friends, but also used media to gain information, familiarize themselves with South Korean SNSs (the Hallyu effect) and to further their own personal interests (Kim, Yun & Yoon, 2009). Asian-Pacific students, in the U.S., used SNSs to maintain contacts with friends and family at home, while also gaining more information about the U.S. in other SNSs (Phua & Jin, 2011). With regard to their home countries, intensity of SNS usage was related to bridging social capital, while collective self-esteem and social identification (with their home country or with the U.S.) had the strongest association with bonding social capital. When measuring self-construal and SNSs use, Kim, Kim and Nam (2010) found that people with interdependent self-construal with motivations to use SNS experience satisfaction with SNS use. In addition, because of cultural hybridity, scholars need to be sensitive to the social context in which interaction occurs as those contexts will impact what particular values might be relevant in that context (Lee, Kim & Min, 2009).

What is the social capital of friends on SNSs? And what are the implications of publicly acknowledging one's friendship circle? A thoughtful article by danah boyd (2006) suggests that friendship brings a sense of community into SNSs and that participants are able to express themselves in personal and cultural terms. She suggests that "What differentiates social network sites from other computer-mediated communication sites is the feature that allows participants to articulate and publicly display their relations to others in the system.... When users are surfing social network sites, they can hop from one profile to another through a chain of friendship" (p. 7).

Friending is influenced by pre-existing social norms as well as the technological affordances of the medium being used. She notes that searchability, replicability, persistence and invisible audiences are all characteristics of SNSs. Importantly, boyd notes that friendship is viewed differently by different cultures and different social contexts will also frame friendship. Some users want to build up a larger number of "friends", including false and make-believe friends (i.e., fakesters), so, at first glance, it may be difficult to discern what level of intimacy is represented (for example, acquaintances, colleagues, BFFs/best friends forever). From a research perspective, boyd suggests that friending is "a modeling of one aspect of participants' social worlds and that model is evaluated in other contexts.... It is critical that we watch what people are doing and understand why their choices make sense to them" (p. 27). This underscores the importance of culturally sensitive research in this area, such as that of Kim and Yun, 2008.

13. Third Places

Third places are viewed as neutral territories where people are free to enter, leave and are under no social obligations, like being a host (Oldenburg, 1999). Such places are defined as: neutral; accessible and accommodating; conversation and interaction are the main focus of activity; social status has no effect; the atmosphere is playful; there are people who participate regularly; the place is not pretentious and people treat third places like home (welcoming and in which one is at ease). Steinkuehler and Williams (2006) argue that online games and SNSs provide such third places. Third places may also provide important social connections which individuals may be reluctant to pursue in F2F contact: as Oldenburg argues, a regular in third places "enjoys a richness of human contact that is denied the timid, the bigoted, the pretentious, and others who choose to insulate themselves from human variety" (2006, p. 45).

14. Factors Influencing the Adoption of SNSs.

There are multiple factors influencing the choice of SNSs. In a study of Singaporean adults, two categories of adopters (Continuers and Discontinuers) and non-adopters (Potentials and Resistors) were analyzed (Lin, Chiu & Lim, 2012). Adopters use SNSs and continue to use them; discontinuers used, but then discontinued use; potentials are likely to try within a year, and the resistors were those who have not used and are not likely to use SNSs. Continuers, adopters and potentials perceived SNSs as popular among their networks, and thus were positively disposed to use and continue using them. Three qualities of SNSs—their relative advantage, compatibility and limited complexity—influenced decisions to use SNSs. Age was an important predictor of adoption and use, with younger adults being early adopters. The authors suggest looking into media qualities and personal characteristics as influences on SNS use. Another study by Bradtzeag (2012), following SNS users over a three year period, found that high users of SNSs scored more highly on several social capital dimensions—bridging capital, number of acquaintances and face-to-face interaction.

Thus, as we have seen, social media have influenced our views on culture as well our view of communication and communicative practices. In turn, social media, culture and communication have more complex, dynamic interrelationships. Social media views cultures as locations in which identities are formed, whether F2F or via social media. Social media provide us with more information about others, other lifestyles and other world views. This exposure alters our perspectives. Our communicative practices also change as we extend F2F interaction to telecopresence, and increasingly, our lives blend online and offline interactions. We express our identities and form relationships in both communicative contexts. Despite the promise and challenge of SNSs, they also present us with some critical issues in need of further discussion. It is to these issues we now turn. Full discussion of these critical concerns is beyond the scope of this chapter, but we need to be cognizant of some of these issues in our scholarship.

15. Critical Issues in Social Media

Privacy

One critical issue is that of privacy, given the personal information being presented and shared via SNSs. Lange (2008) found that YouTube users had nuanced views of privacy in that some behavior was "publicly private" (identities were revealed, but restricted to a few viewers) to "privately public" (widely accessible, but privacy of the creator was protected). Participants displayed considerable technical knowledge in terms of manipulating various functions of YouTube for controlling access to video content. Concerns also emerge because youth may be unaware of risks when revealing information on the Internet and of their vulnerability to stalking and surveillance. Raynes-Goldie (2010) argues that different groups define privacy differently and these nuances need to be more fully understood. As she noted, "younger Facebook users mean something different when they speak about privacy and in turn manage that privacy in different or unfamiliar ways" (p. 12). Despite the presence of gossip, phishing, hacking, data mining and use of data by third parties, many students continue to use Facebook and believe that these intrusions are likely to be experienced by others (Debatin & Lovejoy, 2009). Yet another dimension of privacy is the use of the Internet for surveillance of individuals and groups deemed to be terrorists, or others presenting security risks: as Werbin (2011) notes that because 'dataveillance' is collected by dispersed and uncoordinated individuals and machines, errors may creep in with very serious consequences.

Government, Civil Society and Social Media.

This concern underlies much of the use and penetration by SNSs. Some express concern over the effectiveness and efficiency of ICTs and balancing that against governmental and societal needs (Low, 1996). Yet others have discussed the complex challenges posed by government limitations of the Internet, for both citizens and a central government (see, for example, Zhang & Stening, 2010, for a discussion of issues about social media in China). E-government has been examined in order to see if transparency and participation have been altered by information and communication technologies (ICTs) and social media (Bertot, Jaeger & Grimes, 2010). Considerable attention has also been given to the use of SNSs for political activism (Christensen, 2011). Others have critically examined the research on media and politics and called for more research in this area, given the rapidly changing Asian context (Lo & Wei, 2010; Wei, 2009).

The Need for More Nuanced, Sophisticated Research

Especially in SNSs, and social media generally, there is a need for more complex research tools, including multiple types of methods and for multimodal investigations (Norris, 2005, Pauwels, 2012). Information is presented visually, using photos and videos, as well as text. In order to capture this richness, multimodal methods seem to be an important research technique to use. Goffman's detailed analyses of F2F interaction has been applied to online interactions and would appear to be a very useful analytic tool.

For example, cultural influences extended to Facebook photographs. East Asians, from collectivist societies, tended to de-emphasize their faces whereas North Americans tended to have their faces as a focal point and had less context (Huang & Park, 2012). Thai participants in a popular website (pantip.com) used politeness forms in offline encounters as practices most appropriate for online communication (Hongladarom & Hongladarom, 2005). Yuan (2011) also points out a need for scholarship that investigates multiple uses of mediated sources with an eye toward looking at how people blend and mix their media sources.

In an innovative study of online social capital, Vergeer, Lim and Park (2011) demonstrate the use of hyperlink network analysis and semantic network analysis to assess online communicative practices. Another interesting research approach is taken by Miller (2010) in which he connects the Facebook practices of Trinidadians to their cultural contexts.

Advertising research also points at the need for more culturally-nuanced websites and more complex models of culture (Hermeking, 2006). Some very interesting cultural studies of SNSs, websites and corporate web pages are being conducted with an eye towards assessing what advertising message appeals attract what types of audience (see, for example, Akar & Topcu, 2011; Chang, 2012; Lee & Choi, 2006; Yin, 1998). People using the Internet may be subject to pop-up ads and other mediated advertising, and while these studies explore cultural differences it may be problematic to assume that these differences transfer to other uses. Nevertheless, such advertising studies provide very useful insights into cultural practices on SNSs.

Becoming Asia-centric

This calls for more control of the production and distribution of social media by Asian countries. Iwabuchi (2010) noted that while East Asian production of media and its consumption of media should increasingly become de-Westernized, more attention needs to be paid to the unevenness, inequities, and structural differences in media development in Asia as well (see also Shim, 2006).

We need a very rich, nuanced view of culture(s), and must carefully guard against "essentializing culture (Ess & Sudweeks, 2006). Many scholars are now incorporating ethnic identity and within culture (as nation-states) variables. Communication models should also become increasingly diverse and move away from Westernized conceptualizations.

As we have seen, new media also involve new media literacy that is shaped by social practices (Greenhow & Robelia, 2009). In addition, new forms of collective action are becoming more multi-layered and heterogeneous because more complex and diverse networks can be developed, no longer driven by single source (Constantinides, 2012). As Baym and boyd (2012) argue, socially-mediated publicness is "an ever-shifting process throughout which people juggle blurred boundaries, multi-layered audiences, individual attributes, the specifics of systems that they use, and the contexts of their use" (p. 328). To this, we might add, culture as an important variable to study—as identity and nation-state—as a factor that influences all aspects of the evolving, shifting processes constituting social media and its use.

References

Akar, E. & Topcu, B. (2011). An examination of the factors influencing consumers' attitudes toward social media marketing. *Journal of Internet Commerce, 10*, 35–67.

Barnett, G., & Sung, E. (2005). Culture and the structure of the international hyperlink network. *Journal of Computer-Mediated Communication, 11* (1), article 11. http://jcmc.indiana.edu/vol11/issue1/barnett.html.

Baym, N., & boyd, d. (2012). Socially mediated publicness: An introduction. *Journal of Broadcasting & Electronic Media, 56*, 320–329.

Bertot, J., Jaeger, P. & Grimes, J. (2010). Using ICTs to create a culture of transparency: E-government and social media as openness and anti-corruption tools for societies. *Government Information Quarterly, 27*, 264–271.

boyd, d. (2006: December). Friends, Friendsters, and Top 8: Writing community into being on social network sites. *First Monday, 11, 12.*

boyd, d., & Ellison, N. (2008). Social network sites: Definition, history and scholarship. *Journal of Computer-Mediated Communication, 13* (1), article 11.

Brandtzaeg, P. (2012). Social networking sites: Their users and social implication—a longitudinal study. *Journal of Computer-Mediated Communication, 17,* 467–478,

Burrell, J. (2010). Evaluating shared access: Social equality and the circulation of mobile phones in rural Uganda. *Journal of Computer-Mediated Communication, 15* (20.

Callahan, E. (2006). Cultural similarities and differences in the design of university websites. *Journal of Computer-Mediated Communication, 11* (1), article 12.

Chang, C. (2012). How people tell an ad story: Western vs. Asian styles. *Asian Journal of Communication, 22,* 235–252.

Chen, G. M. (1995). Differences in self-disclosure patterns among Americans versus Chinese: A comparative study. *Journal of Cross-Cultural Psychology, 26,* 84–91.

Christiansen, C. (2011). Twitter revolutions? Addressing social media and dissent.*The Communication Review, 14,* 155–157.

Coiro, J., Knobel, M., Lankshear, C. & Leu, D. (2008). Central issues in new literacies and new literacies research. In J. Coiro, M. Knobel, C. Lankshear and D. Leu (Eds.*), Handbook of research on new literacies.* New York, NY: Lawrence Erlbaum Associates.

Constantinides, P. (2012). The development and consequences of new information Infrastructures: The case of mashup platforms. *Media, Culture & Society, 34,* 606–622.

Couldry, N. (2010). Theorising media as practice. *Social Semiotics, 14,* 115–132.

Crampton, T. (n.d.). *Facebook Asian Stats Infographic.* http://www. thomascrampton.com/facebook/facebook-asia-states-infographic.

Crampton, T. (n.d.). *Facebook's Top 10 Languages*. http://www.thomascrampton.com/facebook/facebook-indonesia.

Crampton, T. (2011). *Teens now drive Indonesia's mobile phone market*. http://thomascrampton.com/indonesias/mobile-phone-market.

Cyr, D., Bonnani, C., Bowes, J. & Ilsever, J. (2005). Beyond trust: Website design preferences across cultures. *Journal of Global Information Management, 13* (4), 24–52.

Debatin, B., & Lovejoy, J. (2009). Facebook and online privacy: Attitudes, behaviors, and unintended consequences. *Journal of Computer-Mediated Communication, 15*, 83–108.

Donath, J., Karahalios, K. & Viegas, F. (1999). Visualizing conversation. *Journal of Computer-Mediated Communication, 4* (4), 0.

Donath, J. (2008). Signals in social supernets. *Journal of Computer-Mediated Communication, 13*, 231–251.

Econsultancy. (2011). *Corporate use of social media channels by market-2011*. http://econsultancy.com/de/blog/8674-social-media-in-asia-understanding-the-numbers.

Ess, C., & Sudweeks, F. (2006). Culture and computer-mediated communication: Toward new understandings. *Journal of Computer-Mediated Communication, 11*, 179–191.

Faiola, A. & Matei, S. (2006). Cultural cognitive style and web design: Beyond a behavioral inquiry into computer-mediated communication. *Journal of Computer-Mediated Communication, 11*, 375–394.

Gao, F. & Martin-Kratzer, R. (2011). New scheme of communication: An exploratory study of interactivity and multimedia use in Chinese j-blogs and the implications. *Asian Journal of Communication, 21*, 69–83.

Garcia-Munoz, J., Caballero-Munoz, D. & Perez-Alvarez, M. (2006). Changes in the self resulting from the use of mobile phones. *Media, Culture & Society, 28*, 67–82.

George, C. (2005). The Internet's political impact and the penetration/ participation paradox in Malaysia and Singapore. *Media, Culture & Society, 27,* 903–920.

Georgiou, M. (2006). Diasporic communities online: A bottom-up experience of transnationalism. In K. Sarikakas & D. Thussu (Eds.), *Ideologies of the Internet.* Cresskill, NJ: Hampton Press, Inc.

Gevorgyan, G., & Manucharova, N. (2009). Does culturally adapted online communication work? A study of American and Chinese Internet users' attitudes and preferences toward culturally customized web design elements. *Journal of Computer-Mediated Communication, 14,* 393–413.

Giddens, A. (1984). *The constitution of society.* Berkeley, CA: University of California Press.

Giddens, A. (1987). *Social theory and modern sociology.* Cambridge, MA: Polity Press.

Giddens, A. (1990). *The consequences of modernity.* Cambridge, MA: Polity Press.

Giddens, A. (1991). *Modernity and self-identity.* Cambridge, MA: Polity Press.

Goffman, E. (1974). *Frame analysis.* New York, NY: Basic Books.

Goffman, E. (1983a). The interaction order. *American Sociological Review, 48,* 1–17.

Goffman, E. (1983b). Felicity's condition. *American Journal of Sociology, 9*(1), 1–53.

Greenhow, C., & Robelia, B. (2009). Old communication, new literacies: Social network sites as social learning resources. *Journal of Computer-Mediated Communication, 14,* 1130–1161.

Hargittai, E. (2010). Digital na(t)ives? Variation in Internet skills and uses among members of the "net generation." *Sociological Inquiry, 80,* 92–113.

Hargittai, E. (2008). Whose space? Differences among users and non-users of social network sites. *Journal of Computer-Mediated Communication, 13*, 276–297.

Haslett, B. (2012a). *Communicating and organizing: Toward a theory of structurational interaction.* New York, NY: Taylor Francis.

Haslett, B. (2012b). A structurational interaction approach to investigating culture, identity and mediated communication. In P. Cheoung, J. Martin & L. Macfayden (Eds.), *New media and intercultural communication: Identity, community and politics.* New York, NY: Peter Lang.

Hermeking, M. (2006). Culture and Internet consumption: Contributions from cross-cultural marketing and advertising research. *Journal of Computer-Mediated Communication, 11*, 192–216.

Hew, K., & Cheung, W. (2012). Use of Facebook: a case study of Singapore students' experience. *Asian Pacific Journal of Education, 32*, 181–196.

Hjorth, L. (2009). *Mobile media in the Asia-Pacific: Gender and the art of being mobile.* New York, NY: Routledge.

Hjorth, L, & Kim, H. (2011). Good grief: the role of social mobile media in the 3.11 earthquake disaster in Japan. *Digital Creativity, 22*, 187–199.

Hongladarom, K. & Hongladarom, S. (2005). Politeness in Thai computer-mediated communication. In R. Lakoff & S. Ide (Eds.), *Broadening the horizon of linguistic politeness.* Philadelphia, PA: John Benjamins.

Huang, C., & Park, D. (2012). Cultural influences on Facebook photographs. *International Journal of Psychology, 1*, 1–10. DOI:10.10 80/00207594.2011.649285

Humphreys, L. (2006). Cellphones in public: social interactions in a wireless era. *New Media & Society, 17*, 810–833.

Hutchby, I. (2001). *Conversation and technology.* Cambridge, MA: Polity.

Iwabuchi, K. (2010). Globalization, East Asian media cultures and their publics. *Asian Journal of Communication, 20,* 197–212.

Java, A., Song, X., Finn, T. & Tseng, B. (2007). Why we twitter: Understanding microblogging usage and communities. *Proceedings of the 9th WebKDD and 1st SNA-KDD workshop* on Web mining and social network analysis, pp. 56–65.

Jeffres, L., Atkin, D., Bracken, C., & Neuendorf, K. (2004). Cosmopoliteness in the Internet age. Journal of Computer-Mediated Communication, 10, article 2, November, 2004.

Ji, Y., Hwangbo, H., Yi, J., Rau, P., Fang, X.W., & Ling, C. (2010). The influence of cultural differences on the use of social network services and the formation of social capital. *International Journal of Human-Computer Interaction, 26,* 1100–1121.

Johnston, K., Tanner, M., Lalla, N. & Kawalski, D. (2011). Social capital: The benefit of Facebook 'friends.' *Behavior & Information Technology, 1,* 1–13.

Kemp. S. (2012: May). *Social Network Users in Asia.* Cited on http://wearsocial.net.blog/2012/05/social-network-users-in-asia-2012.

Kim, H., Coyle, J. & Gould, S. (2009). Collectivist and individualistic influences on website design in South Korea and the U.S.: A cross-cultural content analysis. *Journal of Computer-Mediated Communication, 14,* 581–601.

Kim, J., Kim, M. & Nam, Y. (2010). An analysis of self-construals, motivations, Facebook use, and user satisfaction. *International Journal of Human-Computer Interaction. 26,* 1077–1099.

Kim, H., Kim, G., Park, H. & Rice, R. (1997). Configurations of relationships in different media: FtF, Email, instant messenger, mobile phone, and SMS. *Journal of Computer-Mediated Communication, 12,* 1183–1207.

Kim, K., & Yun, H. (2008). Crying for me, crying for us: Relational dialectics in a Korean social network Site. *Journal of Computer-Mediated Communication, 13,* 298–318.

Kim, K., Yun, H. & Yoon, Y. (2009). The Internet as a facilitator of cultural hybridization and interpersonal relationship management for Asian international students in South Korea. *Asian Journal of Communication, 19,* 152–169.

Lange, P. (2008). Publicly private and privately public: Social networking on YouTube. *Journal of Computer-Mediated Communication, 13,* 361–380.

Lee, W. & Choi, S. (2006). The role of horizontal and vertical individualism and collectivism in online consumers' responses toward persuasive communication on the web. *Journal of Computer-Mediated Communication, 11,* 317–336.

Lee, H., Kim, J. & Min, E. (2009). Hybridization of reality: re-imagining the communication environment in South Korea. *Asian Journal of Communication, 19,* 133–136.

Lee, W., Tan, T. & Hameed, S. (2006). Polychronicity, the Internet, and the mass media: A Singapore study. *Journal of Computer-Mediated Communication, 11,* 300–316.

Lin, T., Chiu, V. & Lim, W. (2011). Factors affecting the adoption of social network sites: Examining four adopter categories of Singapore's working adults. *Asian Journal of Communication, 21,* 221–242.

Liu, H. (2008). Social network profiles as taste performances. *Journal of Computer-Mediated Communication, 13,* 252–275.

Lo, V., & Wei, R. (2010). New media and political communication in Asia: A Critical assessment of research on media and politics, 1988–2008. *Asian Journal of Communication, 20,* 264–275.

Low, L. (1996). Social and economic issues in an information society: A Southeast Asian perspective. *Asian Journal of Communication, 6,* 1–17.

Ma, R. (1996). Computer-mediated conversations as a new dimension of intercultural communication between East Asian and North American college students. In S. Herring (Ed.), *Computer-mediated communication: Linguistic, social and cross-cultural perspectives*. Amsterdam, The Netherlands: John Benjamins.

McPhee, R. (1998). Giddens' conception of personal relationships and its relevance to communication theory. In R. Conville & L. Rogers (Eds.), *Personal relationships and communication* (pp. 83–106). Thousand Oaks, CA: Sage.

Miller, D. (2011). *Tales from Facebook*. Cambridge, MA: Polity Press.

Murthy, D. (2011). Twitter: Microphone for the masses? *Media, Culture & Society, 33*, 779–789.

Mussell, J. (2012). Social media. *Journal of Victorian Culture*, 2012, article 1.

Norris, S. (2005). Discourse in action: Introducing mediated discourse analysis. New York, NY: Routledge.

Ogilvy. (2010). Infographic: China's Social Media Evolution. Cited in http://www.thomascrampton.com/china/china-social-media-evolution.

Oldenburg, R. (1999). The great good place: Cafes, coffee shops, community centers, beauty parlors, general stores, bars, hangouts, and how they get you through the day. New York, NY: Marlowe & Company.

Pan, Z, Yan, W., Jing, G. & Zheng, J. (2011). Exploring structured inequality in Internet use behavior. *Asian Journal of Communication, 21*, 116–132.

Panjam, A. (2012). *Facebook's India challenge*. Cited on http://www.thomascrampton.com/india/facebooks-india-challenge.

Park, J. (2008). Linguistic politeness and face-work in computer-mediated communication, Part 1: A theoretical framework. *Journal of the American Society for Information Science and Technology, 59*, 2051–2059.

Pauwels, L. (2012). A multimodal framework for analyzing websites as cultural expressions. *Journal of Computer-Mediated Communication, 17,* 247–265.

Phua, J., & Jin, S. (2011). 'Finding a home away from home': The use of social networking sites by Asia-Pacific students in the United States for bridging and bonding social capital. *Asian Journal of Communication, 21,* 504–519.

Putnam, R. (2000). *Bowling alone: The collapse and revival of American community.* New York, NY: Simon & Schuster.

Qiu, J. (2010). Mobile communication research in Asia: changing technological and intellectual geopolitics. *Asian Journal of Communication, 20,* 213–229.

Rabby, M. (2007). Relational maintenance and the influence of commitment in online and offline relationships. *Communication Studies, 58,* 315–337.

Rantanen, T. (2005). Giddens and the 'G-word': An interview with Anthony Giddens. *Global Media and Communications, 1,* 63–77.

Raynes-Goldie, K. (2010: January 4). Aliases, creeping and wall clearing: Understanding privacy in the age of facebook. *First Monday, 15,* 1.

Saeki, J. (2012). *Facebook in Asia Infographic by AFP.* Cited in http://www.thomascrampton.com/ facebook/facebook-asia-infographic.

Schwammlein, E., & Woodzicki, K. (2012). What to tell about me? Self-presentation in oonline communities. *Journal of Computer-Mediated Communication, 17,* 387–407.

Segev, E., Ahituv, N. & Barzilai-Nahon, K. (2007). Mapping diversities and tracing trends of cultural homogeneity/heterogeneity in cyberspace. *Journal of Computer-Mediated Communication, 12,* 1269–1297.

Shim, D. (2006). Hybridity and the rise of Korean popular culture in Asia. *Media, Culture & Society, 28,* 25–44.

Siles, I. (2012). Web technologies of the self: The arising of the "blogger" identity. *Journal of Computer-Mediated Communication, 17*, 408–421.

Skoric, M., & Kwan, E. (2011). Platforms for mediated sociability and online social capital: The role of Facebook and massively multiplayer online games. *Asian Journal of Communication, 21*, 467–484.

Skoric, M., Ying, D. & Ng. Y. (2009). Bowling online, not alone: Online social capital and political participation in Singapore. *Journal of Computer-Mediated Communication, 14*, 414–433.

Smeltzer, S. & Keddy, D. (2010). Won't you be my (political) friend? The changing Face(book) of socio-political contestation in Malaysia. *Canadian Journal of Development Studies, 30*, 421–440.

Stefanone, M., & Jang, C. (2008). Writing for friends and family: The interpersonal nature of blogs. Journal of Computer-Mediated Communication, 13, 123–140.

Steinkuehler, C., & Williams, D. (2006). Where everybody knows your (screen) name: Online games as "third places." *Journal of Computer-Mediated Communication, 11*, 885–909.

Tang, L. & Yang, P. (2011). Symbolic power and the Internet: The power of a 'horse'. *Media, Culture & Society, 33*, 675–691.

Tomlinson, J. (1997). A phenomenology of globalization? Giddens on global modernity. In C. Bryant and D. Jary (Eds.), *Anthony Giddens: Critical assessments, vol. 4* (pp. 116–136). New York, NY: Routledge.

Turkle, S. (2011). *Alone together: Why we expect more from technology and less from each other.* New York, NY: Basic Books.

Universal McCann (2009). Power to the people report, Wave 4. Cited in http://oedb.org/ilibrarian/universal-mccann-social-media-study-wave-4/

van Dijck, J. (2009). Users like you? Theorizing agency in user-generated content. *Media, Culture & Society, 31*, 41–58.

Vaughan, L. & Zhang, Y. (2007). Equal representation by search engines? A comparison of websites across countries and domains. *Journal of Computer-Mediated Communication, 12,* 888–909.

Vergeer, M., Lim, Y. & Park, H. (2011). Mediated relations: new methods to study online social capital. *Asian Journal of Communication, 21,* 430–449.

We Are Social. (2012). *Social media in Asia: understanding the numbers, posted by L. Richards. Econsultancy.com.*

Wei, R. (2009). The state of new media technology research in China: A review and critique. *Asian Journal of Communication, 19,* 116–127.

Wellman, B. (1997). An electronic group is virtually a social network. In S. Kiesler (Ed.), *Culture of the Internet.* Hillsdale, NJ: Lawrence Erlbaum.

Werbin, K. (2011). Spookipedia: Intelligence, social media and biopolitics. *Media, Culture & Society, 33,* 1254–1265.

Westbrook, L. (2007). Chat reference communication patterns and implications: Applying politeness theory. *Journal of Documentation, 63,* 638–658.

Wong, L. (2001).The Internet and social change in Asia. *Peace Review: A Journal of Social Justice, 13,* 381–387.

Wurtz, E. (2006). A cross-cultural analysis of websites from high-context cultures and low-context cultures. *Journal of Computer-Mediated Communication, 11,* article 13.

Yin, J. (1998). Selling to the middle kingdom: Culture is the key. *Asian Journal of Communication, 8,* 41–69.

Young, J. (2010). In wired Singapore classrooms, cultures clash over web 2.0. *The Chronicle of Higher Education, 57* (4) (September, 7, 2010).

Yuan, El (2011). News consumption across multiple media platforms. *Information, Communication & Society, 14,* 998–1016.

Yum, Y. & Hara, K. (2006). Computer-mediated relationship development: A cross-cultural comparison. *Journal of Computer-Mediated Communication, 11*, 133–152.

Zang, M., & Stening, B. (2010). China 2.0: The transformation of an emerging superpower...and the new opportunities. New York, NY: Wiley and Sons (Asia).

Zhang, S. & Prosser, M. (2012). Globalization, Asian modernity, values and Chinese civil society. *China Media Research, 8*, 18–25.

Zhao, S. (2004). Consociated contemporaries as an emergent realm of the lifeworld: Extending Schutz's phenomenological analysis to cyberspace. *Human Studies, 27*, 91–105.

Zhong, Y. (2012). *The Chinese Internet. Journal of International Communication, 18*, 19–31.

Zhou, B. (2011). New media use and subjective social status. *Asian Journal of Communication, 21*, 133–149.

III.   Social Media in China, Hong Kong, and Taiwan: A Cross-Cultural Comparison

Richard Holt

Department of Communication, Northern Illinois University,
DeKalb, Illinois
Corresponding Author: richholt@niu.edu

and Hui-ching Chang

Department of Communication, University of Illinois at Chicago,
Chicago, Illinois
Huiching2006@gmail.com

Abstract

This chapter examines the current climate of social media in three Chinese cultures: China, Hong Kong, and Taiwan. The current presence and usage of social media is described for each culture and the cultures are delineated in terms of Hofstede's five dimensions of culture (power distance [PDI], individualism [IDV], masculine-feminine [MAS], uncertainty avoidance [UAI], and long-term orientation [LTO]). Usage data and dimension profile are combined with a literature survey to provide insight into the possible effects of culture on social media use, and vice versa. It is concluded that this combination results in valuable lessons to guide future research on social media.

Keywords: Social media, Hofstede dimensions, China, Hong Kong, Taiwan

1. Introduction: The Ethereal World of Social Media

Like much of what is discussed with respect to the Internet and the World Wide Web, the idea of social media, in all its burgeoning impact, is a difficult set of concepts to wrap one's mind around, especially in light of the role played by rapid technological innovation, where today's startling innovation may be next year's antiquated "dinosaur." Following Kaplan and Haenlein (2010), we assume social media are "...a group of Internet-based applications that build on the ideological and technological foundations of Web 2.0, and that allow the creation and exchange of user generated content" (p. 61).

As is well known, Web 2.0, a term coined, some say, in 1999 by Tim O'Reilly (O'Reilly, 2005), refers to a (purportedly) new vision of the World Wide Web as a domain where content and applications "are no longer created and published by individuals, but instead are continuously modified by all users in a participatory and collaborative fashion" (Kaplan & Haenlein, pp. 61–62). Web resources that qualify under O'Reilly's definition are not so easy to identify, as they burst into (and/or fade out of) existence frequently and develop much more quickly than the ability to analyze them (Beer & Burrows, 2007). Web 2.0 tools include search engines, encyclopedias, video and photo sharing, blogs, content communities, collaborative projects, virtual game worlds, virtual communities, and social networking (or network) sites (SNSs) accessible through microcomputers, cell phones, PDAs, and MP3 players, among others (Huang, Chan, & Hyder, 2010; Lin, Le, Khalil, & Cheng, 2012).

When identifying what counts as social media worldwide, it is easy to "round up the usual suspects"—Facebook, Twitter, Wikipedia, YouTube, and so on (Beer & Burrows, 2007). In particular, SNSs are the dominant, most influential and widely recognized form of social media, whose widespread diffusion has been "deemed an important revolution in the Internet after Google" (Chang & Zhu, 2011). SNSs, according to boyd and Ellison (2008) are "web-based services that allow individuals to (1) construct a public or semi-public profile within a bounded system, (2) articulate a list of other users with whom they share a connection, and (3) view and traverse their list of connections and those made by others within the system" (p. 211).

Beginning with the 1997 launch of SixDegrees.com, which combined available features of creating profiles and list friends (the site closed in 2000), many other SNSs proliferated and/or became popular worldwide, such as QQ, Cyworld, LunarStorm, Skyrock, AsianAvenue, MiGente, BlackPlanet, Friendster, MySpace, Facebook, LinkedIn, and the newest star, Pinterest, among others (boyd & Ellison, 2008). Some claim worldwide popularity while others serve members of a specific geographic location. The culture/country of a site's origin may also be different from where the site will become popular.

Websites focusing on media sharing, such as YouTube, Flickr, and Last.FM, and blogging services as well, have followed suit to begin augmenting SNS functionality (boyd & Ellison, 2008; Yu, Asur, & Huberman, 2011). Microblogging, such as on Twitter, Plurk, and Weibo (microblog), for example, allows users to send brief text updates and/or micromedia such as photos or audio clips, which can, in turn, be forwarded to others. By allowing timely dissemination of information, microblogging is seen as having the power to exchange ideas and interests for specific communities in a scientific context (Huang et al., 2010).

These social media differ in their target audiences and focus, as well as in available communication tools such as mobile connectivity, blogging, audio- and video-sharing for participants (boyd & Ellison, 2008; Yu et al., 2011). Media users become "prosumers"—producing consumers and professional consumers—who can read, cite, and share information (Chu, 2010). The popularity of SNSs can be confirmed through the following statistics: 20% of Internet time on personal computers, and 30% on mobile phones, are spent on SNSs. Also, as mobile technology continues to advance, more people access SNSs more through mobile devices than personal computers. Across both platforms, application usage accounts for more than a third of social networking time (Nielsen, 2012).

These configurations allow hundreds of millions of participants to generate enormous post content online and connect with others. For example, on many large SNSs such as Facebook, participants communicate with those in their extended social networks by uploading their profiles and allowing others to access them according to site regulations and user discretion (boyd & Ellison, 2008; Tse, 2008). SNSs become sites for identity performance, serving as an anchor point of conversation with others

(Tse, 2008). They make visible or solidify pre-existing social networks, or build new ones with acquaintances as well as strangers who share similar interests, even if only temporarily.

It is worth noting that, while SNSs are designed to be accessible through public display of profiles, many attract homogeneous populations initially and end up segregating themselves in ways similar to segregation processes in society. Hence, while weak ties may increase, strong ties may not increase substantially (boyd & Ellison, 2008; Tse, 2008):

The rise of SNSs indicates a shift in the organization of online communities. While websites dedicated to communities of interest still exist and prosper, SNSs are primarily organized around people, not interests. Early public online communities such as Usenet and public discussion forums were structured by topics or according to topical hierarchies, but social network sites are structured as personal (or "egocentric") networks, with the individual at the center of their own community. (boyd & Ellison, 2008, p. 219)

Whether interest-based or extending an individual's existing connections, SNSs change the way people connect with each other and redefine the character of their communities. Aside from individuals, SNSs can also be utilized by groups and organizations to manage and extend their memberships. They are at the forefront of public relations for both individuals and special interest groups. Companies market their products on such sites, and governments utilize them to communicate with citizens and help mobilize a civil society.

2. Social Media, Culture, and Society

Unique cultural configurations and patterns of social media use may lead to different preferences and expectations. Asian social media are especially interesting. By actual figures of use and popular stereotype as well, members of East Asian cultures are closely associated with the explosion of "new Internet technologies" such as SNSs (Nielsen, 2012; Zhang, 2010).

Facebook, for example, has 80% of its users residing outside the United States, with about 25% in Asia (Alhabash, Park, Kononova, Chiang, & Wise, 2012), though local social media presence (such as China's Renren [Facebook of China] and Taiwan's Wretch) has also been very strong (Wee, 2011). Also, in accessing SNSs through personal computers, while people in the Asia-Pacific region do not differ much from users in Europe, Middle East/Africa, and Latin America, they have the largest percentage of users accessing SNSs through mobile phones (59% as compared to 33%, 48%, and 33%, respectively), and through tablet computers (28% as compared to 8%, 10%, and 6%). They are also more likely to buy products based on social media websites/online reviews than people in other regions of the world (Nielsen, 2012). As for their usage patterns, Qiu, Lin, and Leung (2012) contend that, compared to Americans, Asian-based SNSs tend to have tighter social relationships, practice indirect communication, and perform less open self-disclosure. Their online cultures seem to correspond to national cultures.

Configuration of social media in specific countries/cultures involves a complex interplay of cultural as well as political factors, though some may argue that what counts as politics is itself cultural. Kuzma (2010), for example, found that most Asian governments utilize SNSs to disseminate information, education, and promote tourism. Use of social media is also subject to individual government restriction (such as China's Weibo, a microblog). As Yu (2007) puts it, "This entertainment and consumption pattern of Internet use at the micro, individual level is often put side by side with a control model at the macro (level)" (p. 423). Regardless of specific platforms utilized by members of a given culture, the fact that social media allow users free exchange of information not only raises issues about identity, privacy, and the blurring of boundaries between the personal and the public, but also impinges upon civic participation (Holt, 2004, p. 333) and even influences political stability.

This chapter explores the comparative role of social media in three Chinese cultures—China, Hong Kong, and Taiwan—and suggests some approaches from which to scaffold future studies. With its fast-growing economy since economic liberation in 1978, China, or the People's Republic of China (PRC), has been seen as the new powerhouse, continuing authoritarian rule under the Chinese Communist Party, but with a market-oriented economy. Hong Kong has been a special administrative region of China since emerging from British rule in 1997, and has since traveled a rocky path in facing political and economic crisis, epitomized in the July 1, 2003 protest, when half a million people protested the regulations of Basic Law Article 23, the "National Security Bill" (Leung, 2008). As for Taiwan, despite its economic success and democratization, its political identity (the Republic of China [ROC]) vis-à-vis the PRC remains contested (Chang & Holt, 2007; Huang & Li, 2010), especially since it became isolated from the international society when the United Nations moved to recognize the People's Republic of China in 1971. While sharing some Chinese cultural commonalities/traditions, the three political entities also have traversed their distinctive cultural and political histories, and each has forged its own idiosyncratic spaces for social media.

It is possible to bring out and begin to correlate some cultural understandings with respect to social media. Though a variety of issues concerning social media can be explored, past SNS research has explored topics such as impression management, friendship performance, networks and network structure, online/offline connections, and privacy issues that confront a "networked social world" (boyd & Ellison, 2008). In this study, we rely upon established measures of culture such as Hofstede's (1980) dimensions (Dimensions, 2012) to guide our analysis on aspects of relationships and community development vis-à-vis social media in the three cultures.

3. Culture Profiles: Brief Portraits of Three Cultures

As a preferred way to describe cultures, one of the most widely applied is the cultural dimension scheme of Geert Hofstede in his groundbreaking work, *Culture's Consequences* (Hofstede, 1980, 1983). In his original research, Hofstede used an extensive matched-sample attitude survey of the employees of the same multinational company in the world's forty largest countries, deriving four dimensions said to describe anthropological domains handled differently depending on the social context in which they are found. These four dimensions are: (1) power distance index

(PDI), the extent to which the less powerful accept and expect that power is distributed unequally; (2) individualism (IDV) versus collectivism, the degree to which individuals are integrated into groups; (3) uncertainty avoidance index (UAI), a society's tolerance for uncertainty and ambiguity; and (4) masculinity (MAS) versus femininity, the distribution of emotional roles between the genders.

Following work by Michael Harris Bond, who used a survey developed in collaboration with Chinese respondents and colleagues, and data collected from additional countries, there was added a fifth dimension in 1991, long-term orientation (LTO), also originally known as "Confucian dynamism" because of its grounding in Confucian philosophy (Hofstede & Bond, 1988). This fifth dimension, controversial in part due to its appropriation (some say "mis"-appropriation [Fang, 2003]) of Confucian philosophy, is prominent in all three of the target cultures. As will be clear in the comparisons, one of the target cultures (China) registers a markedly higher LTO score, affording some opportunity to think of the reasons why and how higher LTO might impact practices and structures of SNSs.

China

According to Hofstede's dimensions, Chinese society comprises hardworking, resourceful members (a somewhat high MAS score of 60) who are more interested in the concerns of the group rather the individual (low IDV score of 20) and hence show markedly different attitudes toward those of ingroups (warm and accepting) and outgroups (cold and distant) (Eberhard, 1971). People in this culture would be expected to be pragmatic, flexible, and adaptable (low score of 30 on UAI, revealing less of a need to render life circumstances subject to control [less uncertainty] and a higher tolerance for ambiguity). The Chinese are strongly interested in long-term societal goals (very high LTO score of 118) and thus its members tend to have a high degree of perseverance toward the achievement of enduring and abiding aims and objectives. At the same time, they accept the inequality of people of differing social status in society (high PDI of 80).

Hong Kong

Regarding Hong Kong, one finds some of the same propensities (for a chart comparing the scores of the three target cultures, see Figure 1). Although not quite as high as China's, Hong Kong's PDI of 68 also shows a society where inequality in social roles is acknowledged and tolerated. That this score is somewhat lower may be a residual effect of Hong Kong's status as a former British colony from 1945 to 1997 (the PDI of the United Kingdom is 35, along with a very high IDV score of 89).

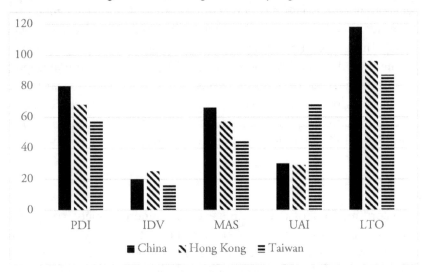

Figure 1. Comparison of China, Hong Kong, and Taiwan on Hofstede's Dimensions of Culture (Dimensions, 2012).

Hong Kong's status as a former British crown colony from 1945 to 1997 (the United Kingdom's PDI is 35, along with a very high IDV of 89). Hong Kong's IDV of 25 is close to China's 20, marking it too as a collectivistic culture where group interests are given precedence over those of individuals. With a 57 MAS, Hong Kong again falls very close to the score for China (60) denoting a somewhat masculist culture, that is, oriented toward success and the hard work needed to attain it. The flexibility and pragmatism of people in Hong Kong society are confirmed by the low UAI of 29 (almost identical to China's 30) indicating a higher tolerance for ambiguity and uncertainty. Although its LTO measure (96) is less than China's remarkably high 118, it is still very high, denoting a society strongly oriented to a more extended view of the future than a culture whose interests focus more on the shorter term (such as the United States, which scores 29). The similarities in dimension scores are what one might expect, given that Hong Kong and China share many cultural characteristics and, since 1997, a common top-level government.

Taiwan

Though not radically so, Taiwan's cultural dimension profile is different. For one thing, Taiwan measures 45 on the MAS dimension, meaning it is classified as a feminine, rather than a masculine, society, showing inclination toward achieving consensus, solidarity, and a system which prefers solving conflict by conciliation and negotiation. In more feminine societies, ambition and achievement often are subordinated to attaining wellbeing. Another difference is that its UAI score is far higher (at 69, more than twice China's and Hong Kong's), denoting a tendency to place less value on unorthodox notions and behavior. Codes of conduct in such cultures tend to be more inflexible and innovation less sought after. On the PDI, Taiwan scores a bit more like Hong Kong (58, as compared to 68), though not as high as China's 80. That Taiwan registers a bit lower on accepting inequality may reflect its continuing movement toward democracy, with corresponding awareness that the bonds of social status need not necessarily be something one has to live with. Like the other two, Taiwan has a pronouncedly longer-term orientation (LTO score of 87), roughly in the range of Hong Kong's 96, but well below China's 118. With an IDV score of only 18, Taiwan measures even more collectivist than either Hong Kong (25) or China (20), denoting its society as one in which loyalty is paramount, even to the extent of overriding other cultural precepts.

Summary

Although in applying Hofstede's dimensions one must be cautious (for one thing, the surveys grounding these dimensions were obtained in exclusively organizational environments), one may yet draw some tentative points of comparison to aid in comparative research.

First, the consistency and stability of Hofstede's dimensions confirm that China and Hong Kong are closely linked, especially with respect to IDV and UAI, and China noticeably higher in three other dimensions (PDI, MAS, and LTO). Hong Kong appears to retain strong elements of its period of rule by Britain (thus lower PDI and comparable MAS, matched against China, with a UAI score lower than for Taiwan), undergirded by strong traditions from its Chinese origins (thus higher LTO, though less than China, due perhaps to China's tradition of exerting firmer control over planning, situated in markedly collectivistic society [very low IDV score]).

Second, in some ways Taiwan is the "odd one out" in this triad. With higher UAI and lower MAS scores, Taiwanese are described as less ambitious (lower MAS) and a little more fearful (with higher UAI, less tolerant of ambiguity and uncertainty). Such qualities may likely be partially driven by the uncertainty Taiwan experiences as it seeks to establish its identity in a turbulent political landscape (Chang & Holt, 2007). In response to China's claim to "own" Taiwan, the majority of Taiwanese choose not to tackle the issue—they prefer "maintaining the status quo" and "butong budu" ("no unification [with China] and no [Taiwan's] independence").

Keeping in mind both the strong similarity in the dimensions of the three target cultures (most noticeably on IDV, and also in the same general range for PDI and LTO), as well as the distinctions just noted, we turn now to a discussion of what these cultural similarities and differences might mean in the use of social media by people in these cultures. For each culture, we start with a portrait of its Internet profile, then move to discuss, specifically, social media, followed by analysis utilizing Hofstede's dimensions. As this proceeds, one should note the interesting fact that all three share the same rank order in social media use: video-watching; reading and writing blogs, social networking, and photo-sharing (Wee, 2011).

4. Social Media in China

Internet Profile

According to *World Factbook* (Central Intelligence Agency, 2012a), China has 20.6 million Internet hosts (a "host" being any computer directly connected to the Internet), which, as of 2012, was fifth largest in the world; and 389 million Internet users (as of 2009). The number of total Internet users increased to 564 million by the end of 2012, with 51 million new "'netizens" and a 42% penetration rate, though considerably different for rural areas as compared to urban centers and cities (CNNIC, 2013).

While growth rate of its netizens has stabilized somewhat, China has seen a rapid growth in mobile users. Those accessing the Internet through mobile devices increased from 69.3% to 74.5%, with 420 million mobile netizens and an annual growth rate of 18.1%. Since 2012, the mobile device has become users' first choice, surpassing the desktop in accessing the Internet. This also explains why Internet access in Internet bars and school computer rooms has declined, as 91.7% of netizen access the Internet at home (CNNIC, 2013).

One characteristic of China claiming immediate attention is the tight control the PRC government exercises over the Internet (Kuzma, 2010). In 2003, the "Great Firewall of China" went into operation, allowing the government to block Internet sites and monitor its users. In June 2009, on the twentieth anniversary of Tiananmen Square, Facebook and Twitter were permanently blocked, and even domestic social networking sites temporarily limited. As China worries that 'Netizens will disrupt the society's stability, "...censorship is a constant presence in China, in subtle and not-so-subtle form... [State authorities] block websites, scan content for keywords, and hire people to steer online discussions in directions favorable to the state" (Canaves, 2011, p. 76).

While technologically savvy users may "climb" the "Great Firewall" to get access to these SNSs, circumvention tools do not automatically change people's behavior (Jiang, 2010), especially since most seem satisfied with substitute services, such as Renren, Youku, Baidu, and QQ. Self-censorship by Internet companies and by individuals for fear of losing their licenses or being arrested, and many other patent forms of censorship, such as hiring people to shape public discourse, is likely to continue to keep state control from being subverted (Canaves, 2011).

Jiang (2010) contends that China practices an "authoritarian informationalism," with an emphasis on collective socioeconomic justice backed up by the public's belief in the existing political institutions' legitimacy and consent to its moral authority: "...the Web is not something inherently emancipating but an intermediary that can be configured and regulated in an ad hoc manner" (Jiang, 2010, p. 75); hence, the state's claim to the right to control the Internet. China's policies are made possible by five major areas of legitimacy promotion: the economy; nationalism; ideology; culture; and governance, i.e., economic development and promotion of nationalism, together with appropriating Confucianism to help promote social order and responsibility, and the acceptance of hierarchy. It is a state-centered approach and an Internet development and regulatory model that combine elements of capitalism, authoritarianism, and Confucianism (p. 72). It is simultaneously state-led and market-driven (Yu, 2007).

There are indications that the Chinese government's grip on the Internet (and with it acceptance of unequal status) is hardly absolute. For example, in July 2009, in the wake of ethnic conflict in Xinjiang province that left some 200 dead (Jacobs, 2009), China was said to have been capable of shutting down the Internet, yet did not, opting to "use their force sparingly since this prevents a new generation of Internet users from discovering the numerous ways netizens have figured out to thwart their efforts" (Tuinstra, 2009), a development which would thereby have augmented the cadre of the "technologically savvy" who appear to be the only ones capable of breaching China's "Great Firewall" (Canaves, 2011).

Social Media Landscape

China's social media landscape thrives under its unique cultural and political contexts, which are "...strikingly different from the one most Western users inhabit" (Cavanes, 2011, p. 76), and hence different from those in Hong Kong and Taiwan. Overall, cyberspace is dominated by urban students aged 18-30, who utilize BBS (Bulletin Board System); blogs; microblogs; and SNSs to share information and exchange ideas (Yu et al.,

2011). Various surveys have found that Chinese are more likely to blog and share content, and spend more time on SNSs, than Americans; spend more time online; and express a sense of being able to live more fully in cyberspace (Canaves, 2011; Men & Tsai, 2013).

Popular foreign SNSs such as Facebook, YouTube, and Twitter, have been replaced with "home-grown," Chinese-language-only substitutes like Renren, Youku, and Weibo, among others. Lukoff (2011b) notes, "Despite government regulations that make the Internet an 'invisible birdcage,' Chinese social networks have just enough space to fly...Just don't attempt to directly port your 'global' Facebook strategy here."

Though it may be challenging to get accurate figures on SNS usage—varying statistics are available from different agencies at varying times—China's social networking landscape is no doubt "diverse and thriving" (Lukoff, 2011a). According to China Internet Watch (March 12, 2012), social network users (and penetration rate) moved from 256.5 million (50%) in 2011, to 307.5 million (54%) in 2012, 366.2 million (59%) in 2013, and 414.5 million (63%) in 2014, with QZone (Tencent), Tencent Weibo, Sina Weibo, Renren, and Kaixin001.com as its five top sites. Lukoff's (2011a) top five replaces Tencent Weibo with Pengyou. Among non-microblogs, Qzone is a nickname SNS, the others real-name. CNNIC (2013) found Renren and Pengyou to be the two largest SNSs in China.

Research on Chinese use pattern of SNSs produces conflicting results. Compared to their American counterparts, Jackson and Wang (2013) found Chinese to spend less time on SNSs, to consider them less important, and to have fewer SNS friends. Chu and Choi (2010), however, reported Chinese to spend more time on SNSs, and to have less extensive network—i.e., fewer strong ties and fewer weak ties—than Americans, though the two groups did not differ in extending weak ties. That Chinese collective cultural orientation places emphasis on family, friends and one's own groups may result in users wishing to invest more in "real world" than online relationships (Jackson & Wang, 2013), or it could mean people want to spend more time online to obtain a sense of belonging (Chu & Choi, 2010). Regardless, Qiu et al. (2012) found that Chinese students perceive Renren culture as more collectivistic than Facebook's. Moreover, they perform more benevolent in-group sharing in the Renren than the Facebook community.

Also noteworthy is that SINA, the largest web portal in China, launched Sina Weibo in August 2009 after Twitter and its leading clone Fanfou—established in 2007, launching China's weibo era—had been blocked a month earlier (Biao, 2012; Yu et al., 2011). Since then, microblogs have exploded—309 million Weibo users (54.7% of all 'Netizens) by the end of 2012, an astonishing increase of 58.73 million users in just one year. Among these, 202 million (65.6%) are mobile Weibo users (CNNIC, 2013), with Sina Weibo as China's most influential microblogging site (Biao, 2012). Lukoff (2011b) claims, "You don't understand China social media if you don't understand Sina Weibo."

There are more than fifty million active users per day, with about 10 million newly registered users per month. Blending Twitter and Facebook (Men & Tsai, 2013), Weibo is used almost entirely by people in China, and in Chinese, a language that, despite text limits of 140 words, can convey a whole story better than the English language under the same constraints (Canaves, 2011; Yu et al., 2011). Following Sina Weibo, "With the establishment of aggregate gateway microblogs...vertical gateway microblogs, news microblogs, e-commerce microblogs, SNS microblogs, and independent microblogs websites, China formally entered into the Weibo era" (Biao, 2012).

By incorporating social media features such as uploading photos and videos and allowing for comments (as compared to Twitter's text and link only), and creating a "conversational feel" by allowing users to tack messages onto previous posts by using the "forward" (or "re-Tweet") function, and with an added group function showing users online, Weibo has become a major platform for young people to gather information and make friends, and has encouraged the growth of social networks. Related to this is the fact that a significant portion of posts are re-Tweets of media content such as jokes, images, and videos to illustrate and share more trivial contents, as compared to Twitter's messages, which tend to have more to do with current global events and less with re-Tweets (Canaves, 2011; Yu et al., 2011).

Central to our discussion of social media in China is the Chinese blogosphere, a creative textual-visual-audio set of practices that has altered culture with its "grassroots spirit": "Some function as personal online diaries; others function as social forums and part of a wider network of social media...blogging represents a new way of living" (Yu, 2007, p. 425). As media contents have come to be produced by participants, people have moved from "what media do to people" to "what people do to media," with consumption becoming "central to the cultural production of a symbolic order of everyday life and politics" (p. 427).

Aside from expressing oneself and making connections in private realms, social media also enables civic participation. New media have become "a new venue for individuals to exercise citizenship, not through overt resistance, but through a process of re-subjectification via mediated expression, social interaction, and circulation of their own media stories" (Yu, 2007, p. 424). This is evident in blogging, which does not "challenge the mainstream culture (be it political or business), but rather deconstructs it through playful (mis)use (and often juxtaposition) of the available resources" (p. 429), even if participants seldom admit its subversive nature. In addition, users have utilized SNSs as "an effective manhunt tool to identify, expose, and chastise the misconducts and crimes of social wrongdoers" (Men & Tsai, 2013, p. 14).

Overt activism is also possible—while the government still sets boundaries for political discourse, Chinese citizens do join public dialogue online to challenge the status quo (Harp, Bachmann, & Guo, 2012). Not surprisingly, compared to Americans, activists in China assign greater importance to social media in promoting debate; in usefulness for communicating with journalists; and in fundraising. On the other hand, they are less concerned with posting links about their works, announcements, and news (Harp et al., 2012). Social media provide sites where activism may be initiated or promoted, and function less as platforms for message exchange.

Yang (2009) calls this a "communication revolution" that can help build "unofficial democracy." Social media sites have become China's primary forum for protests and activism; in particular, with an estimated 100 millions posts per day, Weibo poses a challenge to censorship (Canaves, 2011). This is aided by mobile technology: by end of June 2012, 170 million people blogged from cell phones (Biao, 2012). "The combined use of microblogs and cell phones is an extension of online interactive behaviour that allows netizens to maintain a shifting linearity" (p. 31). Even prohibited SNSs, such as Twitter, continue to be used by a mindful individuals or activists in human rights and citizen participation (Biao, 2012), as "Web 2.0 changed the face of social movements and became an effective tool for promoting democracy on the global scale" (p. 31).

Nonetheless, rather than closing down social media and inciting underground resistance, it might be seen as better to closely monitor public forms of dissent, and even use these for public discourse (Canaves, 2011), especially since the government may not be able to directly delete Twitter feeds due to some technical features (Biao, 2012). Still keeping to tight censorship and a watchful eye, the Chinese government has become more sophisticated in managing its SNSs. The see-saw struggle between the Chinese government and its social media netizens continues.

Application of Hofstede's Dimensions

China's control over social media can be partially explained by its power distance (PDI), representing how comfortable people in a society are with inequalities in status. In China, it may on the surface seem as if users and controllers of the Internet occupy unequal roles in the social enactment of Internet activities. That China's PDI score is higher than either Hong Kong's or Taiwan's suggests that its landscape for social media use encompasses a system in which both controllers and consumers see governmental control of the Internet as a fact of life, and, unable to gain access to SNSs like Facebook, resort instead to microblogs like Sina Weibo (Yu et al., 2011) or to its own brand, Renren. Internet producers, consumers, users, and promoters (roles which constantly merge and overlap in Web 2.0) seem to all accept that they deal with a form of communication in which status of enactors is inherently unequal.

This cultural precept is further endorsed by China's high collectivistic orientation, where the group's welfare takes precedence over that of the individual. Note how the State Council expresses its "authoritarian informationalism" (Jiang, 2010) in the White Paper on Chinese Internet policy, "The Internet in China" (2010), first of its kind to formalize Internet policy:

To build, utilize and administer the Internet well is an issue that concerns national economic prosperity and development, state security and social harmony, state sovereignty and dignity, and the basic interests of the people.

The government has a basic policy regarding the Internet: active use, scientific development, law-based administration and ensured security. The Chinese government has...endeavored to create a healthy and harmonious Internet environment, and build an Internet that is more reliable, useful and conducive to economic and social development. (p. 2)

Yet because of the wide-ranging nature of the Internet, whose practitioners generally have little regard either for national borders (Perritt, 1998) or conventional social roles, this apparent unanimity in China's attitude toward SNSs and the social status of those who play roles in their propagation cannot be presumed. Indeed, simply the explosive growth of microblogs as an answer to government restrictions on world-renowned SNS "players" such as Facebook proves that when Chinese want to engage something they think useful, a "workaround" will be found—perhaps an expression of a low UAI that prompts them to seek novel and creative approaches to solve problems at hand. Coverage of the Xinjian conflict, mentioned earlier, is just one of many instances demonstrating that the presumed acceptance of social inequality, through which the Chinese government allegedly enforces its will, is increasingly difficult to defend.

The other point to note about China is its remarkably high LTO score (118), easily highest in the world. This is not surprising since LTO was added to the original dimensions to distinguish between Western and Eastern thinking and was based on the precepts of Confucian thought said to form the basis of Chinese societies (Fan, 2000). A characteristic of high-LTO cultures is that, instead of being normative in their thinking (concerned with absolute truth), they consider truth to be governed by factors related more to moment and context, which leads them to adapt and take the "long view" in which perseverance and careful management of resources take priority, as through investment and thrift. There is also great concern for relationships appropriately ordered by status (and note how this trait fits well with high PDI) and the importance of shame as a social mechanism to regulate society.

Despite the seeming transience of SNSs and their products, there is some evidence that users, especially when observed over time, rely upon them to cement long-term relationships and a view of life seemingly correlated with higher LTO. The concept of social capital, "...the benefits accruing to individuals or families by virtue of their ties with others" (Portes, 2000,

p. 2), is one sociological mechanism that might clarify thinking about China's high LTO in relation to SNS users (Ellison, Steinfield & Lamp, 2007; Lackaff, Lim, Kwon, Tripoli, & Stefanone, 2009; Steinfield, Ellison, & Lamp, 2008). Chang and Zhu (2011), addressing pre- and post-adoption of SNSs in China, for example, observed

SNS is unique in being able to help users maintain social capital...With longer use and connecting with more old friends, the core value of SNS, social value, is manifested. Therefore, connecting with old friends replaces entertainment in motivating users to continue using SNS. (p. 1847)

The connection between social capital and high LTO may rest in what is most important in a Chinese society, namely, cultivation, through guanxi (relations), of access to needed resources (Chang & Holt, 1991). Guanxi also resonates well with collectivist cultural values, in which one is intimately connected to his/her networks, perhaps a reason why China has experienced exponential success with SNSs. Drawing the connection between human resources "in real life" and on SNSs, Lin et al. (2012) found social capital to be "the construct that describes potential cumulated resources and benefits embedded in the relationships with other people, such as emotional support, useful information, or financial aid assistance" (p. 422). Obviously—with the exception of financial aid—the elements of social capital are abundant on SNSs, which makes them particularly appropriate as factors in the thinking of those in a high-LTO culture. As an added indicator, of course, navigating the Internet and engaging in "hands-on" impression management on SNSs are excellent examples of the kind of flexible and pragmatic activity said to be found in high-LTO cultures (Dimensions, 2012).

5. Social Media in Hong Kong

Internet Profiles

As one of the most densely populated living spaces in the world—7.1 million people occupying 1104 square kilometers—Hong Kong has one of the world's most sophisticated telecommunications market. As China's Special Administrative Region (or HKSAR), Hong Kong functions under its common law framework, with its macro-economic guiding principles of "big market, small government" and "market leads, government facilitates." Liberalized since the 1990s, Hong Kong's telecommunication sectors comprise one of the most competitive markets in the world (International Telecommunication Union, 2011). This does not mean Hong Kong operates entirely independently; under CEPA (Closer Economic Partnership Arrangement, signed in 2003), HKSAR (with its free economy) and the Central People's government (with its planned economy) agree to further liberalize services and promote economic cooperation (Fung, 2010).

The Factbook (CIA, 2012b) reports that Hong Kong has 870,041 Internet hosts (as of 2012, forty-eighth largest in the world) and 4.873 million Internet users (as of 2009, forty-seventh largest in the world). Hong Kong reached a household broadband penetration rate of 77.8% (not including dial-up access) by January 2009 and increased to 86.1% by November 2012; mobile subscription penetration rate also increased from 163.1% by March 2009 to 229.6% by November 2012. While in 2009 there were 7,987 public Wi-Fi access points, by January 2013 that number more than doubled to 18,736 (Chu, 2009; OFCA, 2013a).

Social Media Landscape

Hong Kong's social media landscape is more similar to Taiwan than China. In line with many countries in the world, for example, its popular SNSs include Facebook, Twitter, and so on, along with its local Xanga.com. Facebook has been the most popular SNS with a total of 4.034 million subscribers (56% of the population) by the end of 2012, as compared with Taiwan's 13.240 million (57%) and China's 633 thousand (0.00047%) (Internet World Stats, 2013).

Since Facebook allows its users to post messages, the popularity of Facebook and its cost-effectiveness may explain the reduced number of short message services. For 2013 Valentine's Day, for example, there was a 54% reduction in instant messages sent, and a 44% reduction in messages received, as compared to the previous year (OFCA, 2013b).

Tse's (2008) ethnographic study shows that the majority of people interviewed never made new friends on Facebook, and even those who did said that making new friends is not their main purpose in visiting the site. Similar to Taiwanese users who use the verb "play" (wan) to express their engagement with Facebook, Tse's respondents found Facebook convenient, trustworthy, and cost-effective in expressing oneself and getting connected with others. It is seen as fun and practical, as friends and acquaintance comprise one's social capital in ways that may prove useful in the future.

As for characteristics of people visiting SNSs, Leung and Lee's (2012) survey of adolescents between 9 and 19 found that Internet addicts tend to be low-income family males not confident in accessing information from multiple resources, though they are technologically savvy and frequent visitors to SNSs, and participants in online games. Such incidences provide opportunities for strangers to be connected, even if just on the surface, as they focus on some specific issues or interests. Chu's (2010) survey of high school students, however, shows that they are more passive consumers than active prosumers. They go online for entertainment and to get information and news; nevertheless, they are not familiar with information management tools, and seldom share videos. Of course, these SNS user patterns and characteristics may be different for college students.

Whether it is Facebook or weblog, social media allow people to express their identity. Lin and Tong (2009) analyzed messages posted on a discussion forum for the popular Korean hit, Dae Jang Geum, finding Hong Kong viewers' identities to be unstable, ambivalent, and contradictory. While these confirm traditional Chinese values, they also seem to stigmatize mainland Chinese as outsiders associated with the underclass and cultural inferiority. This ambivalence captures the uncertainty of Hong Kong residents since returning to China's control in 1997.

Aside from the more personal implications, from a macro perspective, the Internet also plays an important role in Hong Kong's democracy movement: "... Web 2.0 technology ... supports a loose and uncoordinated form of participation.... Social and political actions, gatherings, and demonstrations are being organized online, via blogs, through Facebook, by email circulations, and the like." (Fung, 2010, p. 190). Leung (2008) contends that the 2003 protest sparked Hong Kong's "Internet activism": social media not only helps in scrutinizing the government, it becomes a new mobilizing power, allows for discussion and information-sharing, and provides social networking platforms. The event has helped civil associations and citizen participation to flourish (Leung, 2008).

Chu (2009), analyzing the popularity of a cell-phone videotaped incident, "Bus Uncle," in 2006, claims that sites such as YouTube take on a role as public space, playground, and cultural public sphere. That video's popularity must be examined through the lens of post-1997 Hong Kong, when pressure of uncertainty and sense of unsettledness provide fertile ground for emotional release by attending to, and expanding the range of, offerings such as "mash-ups" to the original video. Similarly, in 2007, a social movement was initiated online to conserve a public pier (Fung, 2010).

Hong Kong's government has also actively utilized social networking applications. For example, the Environmental Protection Department supports recycling and encourages its users to exchange second-hand items (Fung, 2010).

Application of Hofstede's Dimensions

Apart from the salient difference noted previously (that international SNSs not seen elsewhere in China are seen in Hong Kong), one finds it more challenging to distinguish the cultural foundations of Hong Kong's SNS practice from those of China, as the governance of Hong Kong, which includes Internet infrastructure, rests with PRC's central government. Moreover, a great many SNS resources are used in common by both China and Hong Kong (as well as Taiwan and others in East Asia).

To determine whether Hong Kong's cultural profile permits identification of clear anomalies that might lead us toward understanding its distinctive SNS use (as with the PDI and LTO scores of China), one can again note that Hong Kong exceeds the scores of the other two targets only in one area: a 25 on IDV, compared with China's 20 and Taiwan's 17.

Part of Hong Kong's slightly higher IDV is likely actualized not only by cultural precept, but practice: regardless of where this greater individualism comes from (Great Britain or elsewhere), Hong Kong is treated differently by China with respect to access to the Internet, with more allowance for individual deviations from that which regulates others. Thus, in terms of business and commercial concerns, Hong Kong's greater latitude in using social media would be expected to correlate with a more elevated IDV score, though not exaggeratedly so, since the foundations of its culture are still firmly tied to presumed collectivism arising from its Confucian roots.

SNSs are an interesting form of communication, one in which numerous highly individualistic activities are performed by users, such as making decisions about what to post (videos, photographs, links, and so on); how precisely to respond to acts of communication directed toward the site; how to accommodate parameters of the site to accomplish all this; and so on. At the same time, use and maintenance of SNSs require collaborative behavior to actualize understandings about what is appropriate, both on sites in general (conforming to rules of computer usage) and any given user's site, or "friends'"s sites, in particular. These latter behaviors are more in line with presumed indicators of collectivism, specifically with respect to human dependence on others.

Therefore, the most important thing about Hong Kong's IDV score may be what it does not show, namely, that despite the influence of British rule (for one very important thing, its official languages are both English and Chinese, not Mandarin Chinese as in China and Taiwan), its IDV is not significantly higher than either of the other two targets. Given the large Chinese national population (95%, according to the Factbook [CIA, 2012b]), for all its modernity and technologically advanced state, Hong Kong's roots in "classic" Chinese culture are strong and deep.

The lack of a markedly distinguishing anomalous dimensional characteristic for Hong Kong may in fact be the point at which one can begin to think about its place in SNS usage vis-à-vis China and Taiwan. Particularly relevant to IDV is privacy, a social psychological concept that has proved enormously important in thinking about SNSs and which has received some scholarly attention (see, among many others, Fogel & Nehmad, 2009 and Gross & Acquisti, 2005). Rosenblum (2007) notes,

Specifically, Milberg et al. proposed that citizens in high "individualism" countries would exhibit higher levels of concern for information privacy. They based their assertion on prior work that found that a societal norm, associated with countries that strongly value individualism is the belief that everyone has the right to a private life, while in countries for which individualism is of lower importance there is more an acceptance of organizational practices that will intrude into one's private life. (p. 40)

Different concern for information privacy can be observed in a study comparing self-reports of SNS behavior by users in France (high IDV) and Hong Kong (low IDV). Tsoi and Chen (2011) found that although both groups were "averagely" concerned about privacy on the Internet (and tended to use higher settings in configuring privacy settings), Hong Kong users rated significantly more positive on three measures: they felt "more comfortable in giving personal info [sic] on SNS"; "perceived higher control in specifying and updating their profiles"; and "rated more positively that their privacy is protected on the site" (p. 459). Perhaps Hong Kong users demand less information privacy, and feel more comfortable and trusting about the site's protection of their privacy.

Paradoxically, such findings may also indicate that, far from supporting the common stereotype of the collectivistic society as one that excludes outsiders, tends to support the image of Hong Kong residents as inhabiting a center of worldwide culture, and not a culture where "the same strong ties of solidarity that help members of a group accomplish goals often enable it to exclude outsiders and dissenters..." (Silver, Scott, & Kazepov, 2010, p. 462). This effect can be felt in many facets of Hong Kong life, but in a kind of structurational linkage (Giddens, 1984), behavior on SNSs may both support and encourage, while at the same time benefit from, a faith in the legitimacy of their effort, and an assumed protection of privacy, between users and those with whom they interact via SNSs. Whether this insight extends to other social media demands further investigation.

6. Social Media in Taiwan

Internet Profile

Compared with China and its political restrictions, Taiwan's profile presents a very different appearance. The Factbook (Central Intelligence Agency, 2012c) asserts that Taiwan has 6.3 million Internet hosts (as of

2012, eighteenth largest in the world). It had 17.5 million Internet users by the end of 2012, with an Internet penetration rate of 75% (Internet World Stats, 2013). Taiwan ranked sixth in the 2010-2011 Networked Readiness Index (FIND, 2011).

As for mobile phones, there are 29 million subscriptions—i.e., 124 subscriptions per 100 residents—and mobile Internet subscriptions totaled 21 million by the end of 2011 (FIND, 2012). InsightXplorer's survey from December 2012 showed the percentage of people obtaining access to wireless Internet through cell phones is 91%, with 52% using notebooks and 38% for tablets.

Given the wide range of information available through the Internet, Taiwan has implemented a rating system similar to that for television. The Government Information Office of the Executive Yuan promulgated Regulations for the Rating of Internet Content on April 26, 2004, as authorized by The Protection of Children and Youths Welfare and Rights Act. Also established was the Taiwan Internet Content Rating Promotion Foundation on January 7, 2005. With revision of the Act, the Regulations were no longer legitimate and were abolished by the National Communications Commission (NCC) on May 16, 2012, with a new private foundation, Taiwan Internet Watch Foundation, to be established to continue to help observe Internet contents.

Also worthy of note is PTT.CC (telnet://ptt.cc/), Taiwan's largest Bulletin Board System (BBS), founded in 1995. Since 2000, it has become the largest BBS both in Taiwan and the Chinese-speaking world, registering over 1.5 million users and an average of one million visitors per day, with over 150,000 users online simultaneously during peak hours. Though utilizing "old fashioned" technology, this online forum is actively used by college-educated young people, with over 20,000 boards on different topics, and more than 20,000 articles and 500,000 comments posted each day. It has added two branch sites: Ptt2 (in 2000) to provide a similar system and Ptt3 (in 2004) in America for overseas Taiwanese students (H.-J. Chang, 2009; PTT Bulletin Board System, 2012).

These systems allow users to post messages on personal issues as well as commenting on current events, providing a platform allowing individuals to share information and ideas. Also implemented has been an article recommendation and criticism process in 2002 (PTT Bulletin Board

System, 2012) to indicate the importance of discussed issues. This may challenge the higher-contexted patterns of communication that people in Taiwan have seen (H.-J. Chang, 2009). Following every step of technological advancement, clubs or other associations built upon shared interests become possible. The system also provides video and other services (ptt. cc/index.video.html), making it more similar to a typical social network site. The board generates significant social impact when topics and issues are enthusiastically discussed on PTT, which journalists monitor to report updates (PTT Bulletin Board System, 2012).

Social Media Landscape

Facebook, YouTube, Yahoo Taiwan's Wretch, and Pixnet are some of the most popular SNSs in Taiwan (Alexa, 2013, February 28). SNSs have been used by more than 75% of Taiwan's population, and Facebook (Chinese language interface) has outperformed Taiwan's homegrown sites, ranking first in usage frequency (Alhabash et al., 2012). As for microblogs, most popular in Taiwan are Plurk and Twitter. Taiwanese increased from 19% of Plurk users in April 2009, to 35% in July 2009 (Huang et al., 2010), though Wretch's digu and Pixnet's suisuinian are also popular and Sina Weibo has made inroads to Taiwan. As Silvio (2007) puts it, "...in postindustrial societies like Taiwan, new media technologies, despite their foreign origins, are not merely 'appropriated,' but come to be seen as emerging from local aesthetics and local needs" (p. 287).

Initially SNSs did not claim much attention, until visitors started to play online games. Facebook launched its Mandarin Chinese version in June 2008, and its success came in 2009, following rollout of the game application, "Happy Farm." People visited Facebook to play the game so much, that it encouraged software companies to develop new games, so much so that the government and many companies actually had to ban employees from accessing Facebook during work hours (Lin et al., 2012). Lin et al.'s 2012 survey of 400 workers showed that for 60% of users, the most frequently used function was gaming. Taiwanese interest in gaming has continued long after the popularity of "Happy Farm."

Alhabash et al.'s (2012) survey of 4,346 participants shows that 78% spend less than an hour daily on Facebook, and 63% reported that 30%

or fewer of friends on Facebook are those with whom they have daily encounters. Results also show that the best predictor of Facebook intensity was the motivation to use it for status updates, whereas the best predictor for content-generation behavior was the motivation to view and share photographs. Taiwan's social media, for Facebook at least, appear to be used less to solidify existing ties than to create new ones or to sustain remote ties.

Taiwan's homegrown site, Wretch.cc, the third most visited SNS after Facebook and YouTube (Alexa, 2013, February 28), presents a different scenario. Established in 1995, Wretch, with its Chinese name xuming xiaozhan (nameless small stop), began by providing blog and album services, and has popularized blogging as Taiwan's major social networking activity. Now its portal also includes video-sharing; jiutuan (finding and forming groups for specific purposes such as shopping, travel, activity, etc.); and digu (minor complaints, similar to the function of a micro-blog). Users comprise a large portion of young people who post and comment on self-portraits online; specifically, Wretch Album is famous for its collection of "beautiful chicks" photos (Wang, 2010).

Pixnet (Chinese name, pikebang, the state of ruffian guests), the next most popular site, is similar to Wretch in offering a variety of functions, with 78% of its audience located in Taiwan as compared to Wretch's 87% (Alexa, 2013, February 28, 2013). These sites allow individuals to write blogs and post photos, as well as to engage in a variety of social activities and current affairs in the various communities in which they find themselves and share interests with strangers. They integrate personal and public seamlessly in a light-hearted, somewhat entertainment-oriented mode.

As elements in a civil society, in addition to solidifying existing ties and making new connections, whether in personal or public domains, Taiwan's social media end up affecting society, particularly as many "villagers" (xiangmin, users of social media) form opinions and even inspire action. This becomes the basis upon which issues confronting society may be addressed. Not surprisingly for a democratic society, political candidates have used blogs, especially during elections.

Moreover, these mechanisms can be used to address specific problems or social ills, as in examples where they have been used as an effective disaster management tool; these distributed, decentralized technologies have empowered the public to more effectively share information and experiences (Huang et al., 2010). In August 2009, typhoon Morakot devastated Taiwan. The government's ineffective Central Response System prompted Internet users from the Association of Digital Culture Taiwan to establish an unofficial Morakot Online Disaster Report Center (http://typhoon.adct.org.tw/) to aid in the crisis—gathering and exchanging pertinent information—which was eventually integrated into the local government's communication system. The site also provided assistance to other popular SNSs, such as Twitter http://twitter.com/TaiwanFloods or Plurk http://www.plurk.com/floods, aiding rescuers. The map service provided by Google also helped identify affected locations. In addition, people use micro-blogs to share information and compile data; for example, first aid needs were reported directly on the government's official Plurk. These SNSs also served as a platform in the gathering of resources; distribution of supplies; and promotion of volunteer efforts (Huang et al., 2010). Their success led Huang et al. (2010) to call for more political support to develop a disaster response system based on the social network framework.

Application of Hofstede's Dimensions

Having identified Taiwan as the "odd one out," it might prove a bit easier to build a speculative scaffold about its SNS usage and trajectories along which such insight might take future researchers. Referring to Figure 1, two characteristics distinguishing Taiwan from the other targets claim attention. First, Taiwan's MAS score (45) is lower than either China's 66 or Hong Kong's 57 (Hofstede classifies Taiwan as "feminine," Hong Kong as "somewhat masculine" and China simply as "masculine" [Dimensions, 2012]). Second, on the UAI measure, Taiwan (with a 69) is significantly higher than China and Hong Kong (30 and 29, respectively).

What role do cultural qualities measured by MAS and UAI play in the use of SNSs? It is thought that lower MAS describes a culture as emphasizing stereotypically "feminine" qualities such as relationships and quality of life, as compared to masculine cultures emphasizing competitiveness, ambition, power, and materialism. More precisely, the MAS dimension refers to the distribution of emotional roles between genders, so that in feminine cultures gender roles are less dramatically sex typed and women and men are more likely to have the same values of modesty and caring. As to UAI, if one associates fearlessness with stereotypical masculinity, then it is hardly surprising that a less masculine culture might also evidence greater fear about an uncertain future (higher UAI), and this is precisely the situation with Taiwan.

With respect to how the first of these cultural qualities, MAS, emerge in practices relating to SNSs, evidence is harder to find, perhaps because as far back as 1984 Hofstede faulted the relative lack of work on the MAS dimension, calling for an increase in research related to it (Hofstede, 1984, p. 199). Indeed, one influential article on the dimensions and Internet regulation (Yang, 2007) mentions MAS effects only in passing, while devoting entire sections to the effects of IDV, PDI, and UAI. Nevertheless, since the MAS is fairly specific about what behaviors are encompassed in feminine and masculine cultures, one can relate these to practices in participating in SNSs. Writing about Internet design (for what is the construction and maintenance of a page on Facebook or similar SNSs but a design activity?), Cook and Finlayson (2005) note, "Low MAS cultures tend to de-emphasize traditional male and female stereotypes... Low MAS Website designs include promotions of cooperation and support rather than competitiveness and using poetic and pleasing aesthetics as a means of motivation" (p. 18).

One would expect, then, to see less evidence of competition and more evidence of cooperation in Taiwan use of social media, and there are several indications of this in the literature. Ko (2012) notes,

> *Currently, 53.4% of bloggers in Taiwan publish "journal-type" blogs, including family journals, love journals, student journals, and work journals (InsightXplorer 2007). Bloggers share their lives with others by voluntarily writing or posting their thoughts. This behavior of sharing their inner feelings, experiences, or information with others in journal-type blogs is called self-disclosure (Lines 64-69).*

In Taiwan, at least, there is a significant presence. 'Netizens in Taiwan write blogs to present themselves in both words and photos and to solidify or extend their connections. They also mobilize themselves through social media when there is legitimate cause for action and they want their voices heard. However, unlike China where the Internet is actively monitored by the government, Taiwan's netizens have these varying channels for them to engage the society. Social media, for them, is indeed primarily for the purpose of being social and seems to fit well with their predilections toward greater collectivism and greater avoidance of uncertainty.

7. Conclusion

The massive growth in research on social media seems to have paralleled actual user growth in social media. With a large and growing body of scholarly literature on the three target cultures, our analysis is necessarily limited and selective and best viewed as moments in an ongoing scholarly conversation. We offer three tentative suggestions about future research in social media in Chinese cultures.

First, future researchers should avoid subscribing to too-general conclusions about how members of "Chinese culture" use social media in the same or similar ways. A presumed "cultural characteristic" such as IDV or LTO gets worked out in idiosyncratic ways, depending upon specific sociohistorical circumstances. For example, in the face of presumed acceptance of unequal power distribution in China, we find numerous examples of Netizens and prosumers managing to get their social media work done despite seemingly intransigent government opposition. A premature subscription to assumed cultural characteristics might lead the inquirer to overlook creative ways in which people in China operate via social media—whether their behaviors are original or prompted—to counteract the effect of the dimensions they presumably operate under. Chinese who use Sina Weibo, for example, seem highly individualistic (not low IDV) and unwilling to accept their "place" in the hierarchy (not high PDI).

Secondly, researchers need to pay close attention to the governmental or state infrastructures in which prosumers of social media function. Government regulations function not simply to provide "bricks and mortar" infrastructure, but to either reinforce or discourage (through numerous and often invisible regulatory mechanisms) Chinese cultural norms under whose influence social media take shape and evolve. Because social media involve sharing and discovery of personal information about oneself and others, such an intimate activity can be easily taken to be functioning primarily according to the individual user's private predilections. Our findings show that, quite in conflict with measures that invoke personal partiality, like IDV or PDI, the supposed private cultural predispositions of social media users are encompassed and strongly influenced by what happens in the public sphere, as can be observed in the different approaches taken by China and the other two. Researchers in social media would therefore do well to begin their investigations with a thorough account of how the public sphere constrains and actualizes social media use.

Finally, Hofstede's dimensions (or other classificatory schemes) can be more fruitfully conceived as generative metaphors (metaphors that provoke insight due to unusual comparisons [Schön, 1978]) than as definitive variables. The dimensions help get us "into" questions of culture and media use; but more than a simple correlation between dimensions and social media use as illustrated by the three Chinese cultures, culture and new media are interconnected, at times mutually influencing or acting in conflict with each other on multiple fronts, as people constantly negotiate and integrate new media culture into their everyday culture overseen by their governments. This scenario becomes even more complex when we take into account that some SNSs are globally popular while others are locally specific, necessitating a multi-cultural orientation on the part of users, as one mingles with others on manifold platforms simultaneously (Qiu et al., 2012), making it difficult to draw boundaries between Asians and non-Asians, or even between Asians themselves. The study of social media is still in its formative phases (and because things change so quickly that one sometimes despairs of technology ever slowing down enough to formulate a perspective on it), there are many opportunities for inquiry that permit us to take advantage of rapid flare-ups of insight in this briskly emerging field.

References

Alexa (2013, Feb. 8). *Top sites in Taiwan.* Accessed from http://www. alexa.com/topsites/countries/TW

Alhabash, S., Park, H., Kononova, A., Chiang, Y.-H., & Wise, K. (2012). Exploring the motivations of Facebook use in Taiwan. *Cyberpsychology, Behavior, and Social Networking, 15*(6), 304–311. doi:10.1089/cyber.2011.0611

Beer, D., & Burrows, R. (2007). Sociology and, of and in Web 2.0: Some initial considerations. *Sociological Research Online, 12*(5), 17.

Biao, T. (2012). Rights defence (weiquan), microblogs (weibo), and the surrounding gaze (weiguan). *China Perspectives, 3*, 29–41.

boyd, d., & Ellison, N. B. (2008). Social network sites: Definition, history, and scholarship. *Journal of Computer Mediated Communication, 13*, 210–230.

Canaves, S. (2011). China's social networking problem. *IEEE Spectrum, 48*(6), 74–77.

Central Intelligence Agency. (2012a). *World Factbook—China.* Retrieved December 9, 2012, from https://www.cia.gov/library/publications/ the-world-factbook/geos/ch.html.

Central Intelligence Agency. (2012b). *World Factbook—Hong Kong.* Retrieved December 10, 2012, https://www.cia.gov/library/ publications/the-world-factbook/geos/hk.html.

Central Intelligence Agency. (2012c*). World Factbook—Taiwan.* Retrieved December 10, 2012, from https://www.cia.gov/library/ publications/the-world-factbook/geos/tw.html.

Chang, H.-C., & Holt, R. (1991). More than relationship: Chinese and the principle of kuan-hsi. *Communication Quarterly, 39*(9), 251–271.

Chang, H.-C., & Holt, R. H. (2007). Symbols in conflict: Taiwan (Taiwan) and zhongguo (China) in Taiwan's identity politics. *Nationalism and Ethnic Politics, 13*(1), 129–165.

Chang, H.-J. (2009). Online supportive interactions: Using a network approach to examine communication patterns within a psychosis social support group in Taiwan. *Journal of the American Society for Information Science and Technology, 60*(7), 1504–1518.

Chang, Y. P., & Zhu, D. H. (2011). Understanding social networking sites adoption in China: A comparison of pre-adoption and post-adoption. *Computers in Human Behavior, 27*(5), 1840–1848.

China Internet Watch (2013). Social Network Users in China 2011–2014. Retrieved February 17, 2013, from http://www.chinainternetwatch.com/1403/social-network-users-in-china-2011-2014-chart/

China Internet Network Information Center [CNNIC]. (Jan. 16, 2013). *CNNIC Released the 31st Statistical Report on Internet.* Retrieved Jan. 20, 2013 from: http://www1.cnnic.cn/AU/MediaC/rdxw/2012nrd/201301/t20130116_38529.htm

Chu, D. (2009). Collective behavior in YouTube: a case study of 'Bus Uncle' online videos. *Asian Journal of Communication, 19*(3), 337–353.

Chu, D. (2010, January 30). In search of prosumption: Youth and the new media in Hong Kong. *First Monday* [Online], 15(2).

Chu, S. C., & Choi, S. M. (2010). Social capital and self-presentation on social networking sites: A comparative study of Chinese and American young generations. *Chinese Journal of Communication, 3,* 402–420

Cook, J., & Finlayson, M. (2005). The impact of cultural diversity on website design. *SAM Advanced Management Journal, 70*(3), 15–24.

Dimensions (2012). *The Hofstede Centre.* Retrieved December 27, 2012, from http://geert-hofstede.com/dimensions.html.

Eberhard, W. (1971). On three principles of Chinese social structure. In W. Eberhard (Ed.), *Moral and social values of the Chinese: Collected essays* (pp. 1–14). Taipei, Taiwan: Ch'eng-wen Publishing Company.

Ellison, N.B., Steinfeld, C., & Lampe, C. (2007). The benefits of Facebook "friends": Social capital and college students' use of online social network sites. *Journal of Computer-Mediated Communication, 12*, 1143–1168.

Fan, Y. (2000). A classification of Chinese culture. *Cross Cultural Management: An International Journal, 7*(2), 3–10.

Fang, T. (2003). A critique of Hofstede's fifth national culture dimension. *International Journal of Cross Cultural Management, 3*(3), 347–368.

FIND [Foreseeing Innovative New Digiservices]. (2012, Oct. 24). *Observation on Mobile Internet in Taiwan: 2011 Q4.* Accessed February 5, 2013 from http://www.find.org.tw/eng/news.asp?msgid=544&subjectid=4&pos=0

Fogel, J., & Nehmad, E. (2009). Internet social network communities: Risk taking, trust, and privacy concerns. *Computers in Human Behavior, 25*(1), 153–160.

Fung, J. Y.-c. (2010). '.hk' Hong Kong. *Digital Review of Asia Pacific 2009–2010*, 182–191.

Giddens, A. (1984). The constitution of society: *Outline of the theory of structuration.* Cambridge, UK: Polity Press.

Gross, R., & Acquisti, A. (2005, November). Information revelation and privacy in online social networks. In *Proceedings of the 2005 ACM workshop on privacy in the electronic society (pp. 71–80).* ACM.

Harp, D., Bachmann, I., & Guo, L. (2012). The whole online world is watching: Profiling social networking sites and activists in China, Latin America, and the United States. *International Journal of Communication, 6*, 298–321.

Hofstede, G. (1980). *Culture's consequences.* Beverly Hills, CA: Sage.

Hofstede, G. (1983). National cultures revisited. *Behavior Science Research, 18*, 285–305.

Hofstede, G. (1984). *Culture's consequences (abr. ed.).* Beverly Hills, CA: Sage.

Hofstede, G., & Bond, M. H. (1988). The Confucius connection: From cultural roots to economic growth. *Organizational dynamics, 16*(4), 4–21.

Holt, R. (2004). *Dialogue on the Internet—Language, civic identity, and computer-mediated communication.* Westport, CT. Praeger.

Huang, C.-M., Chan, E., & Hyder, A. A. (2010). Web 2.0 and Internet social networking: A new tool for disaster management? – Lessons from Taiwan. *BMC Medical Informatics and Decision Making, 10,* 57.

Huang, J., & Li, X. (2010). *Inseparable separation: The making of China's Taiwan policy.* River Edge, NJ: World Scientific.

Hwang, J. M., Cheong, P. H., & Feeley, T. H. (2009). Being young and feeling blue in Taiwan: Examining adolescent depressive mood and online and offline activities. *New Media & Society, 11*(7), 1101–1121.

International Telecommunication Union (2011). *Hong Kong China: Some valuable pointers.* Accessed Feb. 23, 2013 from http://www.itu.int/net/itunews/issues/2011/07/29.aspx

The Internet in China (June 8, 2010). *State Council Information Office of the People's Republic of China.* Accessed Jan. 20, 2013 from http://www.scio.gov.cn/zxbd/wz/201006/t667385.htm

Internet World Stats (2013). *Asia Internet use, population data and Facebook statistics.* Accessed Feb. 23, 2013, from http://www.internetworldstats.com/stats3.htm

Jackson, L. A., & Wang, J.-l. (2013). Cultural differences in social networking site use: A comparative study of China and the United States. *Computers in Human Behavior, 29,* 910–921.

Jacobs, A. (July 15, 2009). At a factory, the spark for China's violence. *New York Times,* July 15, 2009, Retrieved February 6, 2012, from: http://www.nytimes.com/2009/07/16/world/asia/16china.html

Jiang, M. (2010). Authoritarian Informationalism: China's approach to Internet sovereignty. SAIS *Review of International Affairs, 30*(2), 71–89.

Kaplan, A. M., & Haenlein, M. (2010). Users of the world, unite! The challenges and opportunities of social media. *Business Horizons, 53*(1), 59–68.

Ko, H.-C. (2012). The determinants of continuous use of social networking sites. *Electronic Communication Research and Applications.* Retrieved January 11, 2013, from: http://dx.doi.org/10.1016/j. elerap.2012.11.002

Kuzma, J. (2010). Asian government usage of Web 2.0 social media. *European Journal of ePractice, 9,* 1–13.

Lackaff, D., Lim, D., Kwon, K.H., Tripoli, A., & Stefanone, M. A. (2009). Resource mobilization on social network sites. Paper presented at the Annual Conference of the National Communication Association. Chicago, IL, USA

Leung, D. K.-k. (2008). Internet radio and democratic citizenship: An experience of Hong Kong. Paper presented at the Annual Meeting of the International Communication Association, Montreal, Canada.

Leung, L., & Lee, P. S. N. (2012). Impact of Internet literacy, Internet addiction symptoms, and Internet activities on academic performance. *Social Science Computer Review, 30*(4), 403–418.

Lin, A., & Tong, A. (2009). Constructing cultural self and other in the Internet discussion of a Korean historical TV drama. *Journal of Asian Pacific Communication, 19*(2), 289–312.

Lin, J. H., Peng, W., Kim, M., Kim, S. Y., & LaRose, R. (2012). Social networking and adjustments among international students. *New Media & Society, 14*(3), 421–440.

Lin, J. Y.-C., Le, A. N. H., Khalil, S., & Cheng, J. M.-S. (2012). Social media usage and work values: The example of Facebook in Taiwan. *Social Behavior and Personality, 40*(2), 195–200.

Lukoff, K. (March 8, 2011a). China's top 15 social networks. *Techrice.* Retrieved December 16, 2012, from http://techrice.com/2011/03/08/ chinas-top-15-social-networks/

Lukoff, K. (March 18, 2011b). What makes China's top 4 social networks tick? *Mashable.* Retrieved February 27, 2013, from http://mashable.com/2011/03/18/china-top-social-network/

Men, L. R., & Tsai, W.-h. S. (2013). Beyond liking or following: Understanding public engagement on social networking sites in China. *Public Relations Review, 39,* 13–22.

Nielsen (2012). State of the media: The social media report 2012. Downloaded February 22, 2013 from http://www.nielsen.com/us/en/insights/reports-downloads/2012/state-of-the-media-the-social-media-report-2012.html

Office of the Communications Authority [OFCA]. (2013a). *Key communications statistics.* Retrieved Feb. 18, 2013 from http://www.ofca.gov.hk/en/media_focus/data_statistics/key_stat/index.html

Office of the Communications Authority [OFCA]. (2013b). *SMS Statistics1 for Special Dates.* Retrieved Feb. 18, 2013 from http://www.ofca.gov.hk/en/media_focus/data_statistics/key_stat/index.html

O'Reilly, T. (2005). *What is Web 2.0.: Design patterns and business models for the next generation of software.* Retrieved December 15, 2012, from http://oreilly.com/web2/archive/what-is-web-20.html

Perritt, Jr., H. H. (1998). The Internet as a threat to sovereignty? Thoughts on the Internet's role in strengthening national and global governance. *Indiana Journal of Global Legal Studies, 5*(2), 423–442.

Portes, A. (2000, March). The two meanings of social capital. *Sociological Forum, 15*(1), 1–12.

PTT Bulletin Board System (2012. Dec. 2). *Wikipedia.* Accessed February 8, 2013 from http://en.wikipedia.org/wiki/PTT_Bulletin_Board_System.

Qiu, L., Lin, H., Leung, A. K.-Y. (2012). Cultural differences and switching of in-group sharing behavior between an American (Facebook) and a Chinese (Renren) social networking site. *Journal of Cross-Cultural Psychology, 44*(1), 106–121.

Rosenblum, D. (2007). What anyone can know: The privacy risks of social networking sites. *Security & Privacy, IEEE, 5*(3), 40–49.

Schön, D. (1978). Generative metaphor: A perspective on problem setting in social policy. In A. Ortony (Ed.), *Metaphor and thought* (pp. 137–163). Cambridge: Cambridge University Press.

Silver, H., Scott, A., & Kazepov, Y. (2010). Participation in urban contention and deliberation. *International Journal of Urban and Regional Research, 34*.3, 453–477.

Silvio, T. (2007). Remediation and local globalizations: How Taiwan's "digital video knights-errant puppetry" writes the history of the new media in Chinese. *Cultural Anthropology, 22*(2), 285–313.

Steinfield C., Ellison, N. B., & Lampe, C. (2008). Social capital, self-esteem, and use of online social network sites: A longitudinal analysis. *Journal of Applied Developmental Psychology 29*(6): 434–445.

Tse, H.-M. (2008). An ethnography of social network in cyberspace: The Facebook phenomenon. *The Hong Kong Anthropologist, 2*, 53–77.

Tsoi, H. K., & Chen, L. (2011, October). From privacy concern to uses of social network sites: A cultural comparison via user survey. In: *Privacy, Security, Risk and Trust* (passat), 2011 IEEE International Conference on Privacy, Security, Risk, and Trust, and IEEE International Conference on Social Computing (pp. 457–464). IEEE.

Tuinstra, F. (2009). Internet censorship: The myth, oft told, and the reality. *Nieman Reports, 63*(3), 51.

Wang, Y.-H. (2010). Teenage girls' views and practices of "sexy" self-portraits in a Taiwanese social networking site. Interactions: *Studies in Communication & Culture, 2*(3), 209–224. Doi: 10.1386/iscc.2.3.209_1

Wee, W. (2011). Social media in Asia [Infographic]. *TECHINASIA.* Retrieved February 20, 2013 from www.techinasia.com/social-media-in-asia/

Yang, K. C. C. (2007). A comparative study of Internet regulatory policies in the Greater China Region: Emerging regulatory models and issues in China, Hong-Kong SAR, and Taiwan. *Telematics and Informatics, 24*(1), 30–40.

Yang, G. (2009). *The power of the Internet in China: Citizen activism online*. New York, NY: Columbia University Press.

Yu, H. (2007). Blogging everyday life in Chinese Internet culture. *Asian Studies Review, 31,* 423–433.

Yu, L., Asur, S., & Huberman, B. A. (2011). *What trends in Chinese social media. arXiv:1107.3522* [cs.CY]. Retrieved January 2, 2013, from http://arxiv.org/pdf/1107.3522.

Zhang, Q. (2010). Asian Americans beyond the model minority stereotype: The nerdy and left out. *Journal of International and Intercultural Communication, 3*(1), 20–37.

IV.   A Cross-Cultural Study of Social Media Access and Online Communication in India, Indonesia, and the Philippines

William J. Brown

Department of Strategic Communication & Journalism, School of Communication and the Arts, Regent University, Virginia Beach, VA 23464
Corresponding email: willbro@regent.edu

Benson P. Fraser

School of Communication and the Arts, Regent University,
Virginia Beach, VA 23464
Email: bensfra@regent.edu

Abstract

The use of social media and online communication is growing rapidly throughout Asia. In particular, India, Indonesia, and the Philippines have experienced rapid growth in the diffusion of new communication technology. In this chapter we present the results of a two-year investigation of online and social media access in these three nations. The results confirm that from 2011 to 2012, India, Indonesia, and the Philippines all experienced substantial growth in the use of the Internet for social interaction, personal development, and business. Implications of these findings for future social media development in Asia are discussed.

Keywords: social media access, online communication, India, Indonesia, The Philippines

1. Literature Review

In recent years the development of the Internet and social network sites (SNSs) such as Facebook, YouTube, Twitter, etc. have changed the way people communicate both within nations and within communities. The increasing number of individuals using the Internet and SNS sites has drawn both academic and industry researchers into a plethora of studies examining the use and influence of online communication. The purpose of this chapter is to examine major trends in the literature of these emergent phenomena in three nations in an effort to summarize existent scholarship that investigates online communication and SNSs.

For the purposes of this study, we have identified four major trends in research of online communication and SNSs in Asia. Firstly, there are numerous studies that examine the business and marketing uses of online technology and SNSs. Secondly, given the recent use of online communication by political activists to change political power structures, there has been valuable research assessing the use of online communication and social media for political power and social activism. Thirdly, and closely allied to the political use of online communication and SNSs, there are a number of studies that examine the use of online communication and SNSs for development. Fourthly, there are a number of researchers studying the use of online communication and SNSs for religious purposes. We shall now briefly review important studies in each of these areas. Although there are a number of other facets of online communication research that could be examined, for example, impression management and friendship performance, network structure, bridging online and offline social networks, and privacy, to name a few (boyd & Ellison, 2008), these studies are usually limited to SNSs use and are not seen as central to this study.

Business

It is apparent that the Internet has helped individuals connect based on shared interests, political views, common language, shared religious beliefs and national identities. Understandably, this fact has not been lost on businesses and organizations wanting to connect with customers regarding their products and services. Possibly the greatest number of studies conducted in regard to the use of online communication and SNSs is in the area of business and marketing. Stephan (2012) observed that "tools of social media are becoming the most prevalent venues for online content sharing and creation worldwide" (p. 163). She adopts Benedict Anderson's concept of the "imagined communities" of nations as analogous to the imagined member communities related to social networks in order to discuss "social network in post-1977 Indonesia and the Philippines" (Stephan, 2012, p. 164). Her discussion outlines how an economic crisis led individuals in the economic communities of both Indonesia and the Philippines to embrace Internet technology. Furthermore, she theorizes that the adoption of social media across geographical boundaries ultimately led to the shift from nation-building to online community-building. This shift, if confirmed by future research, has profound implications for how these countries conduct economic activities.

Rattle (2010) suggests that computer technology may lower operational costs and transform businesses into more profitable arrangements worldwide (pp. 89–100). However, whatever the promise these technologies bring, there are also risks involved in their use. He states that "in every situation, it seems, where web-based technologies can be used for sustainable purposes, counterintuitive uses or results also exist that can be, and are, used to serve less than ideal objectives or generate unanticipated consequences" (Rattle, 2010, p. ix). The manner in which business is conducted and managed profoundly changes as participation in online communication and SNSs increases, providing venues for almost instantaneously creating and sharing content. For example, Stephan (2012) points out that "both the manner in which online social interaction of individuals and groups is targeted through behavioral tracking and use of resulting data ultimately can affect the way diverse groups of people perceive and interact with each other" (p. 188). This, of course, has profound effects on both national and international economic activity— not to mention the impact on nation building.

With regard to electronic shopping, Lin (2007) explains that "consumers have been drawn to teleshopping, either on- or offline, for both utilitarian as well as hedonic motives" (p. 215). Utilitarian advantages of shopping online, including saving time, time flexibility, reduced physical effort, reduced aggravation and less impulsive buying, were identified as reasons for online buying. On the other hand, hedonistic motives were viewed as psychological gratifications—by fulfilling people's needs for excitement, stimulation, pleasure, relaxation, parasocial interaction and/or companionship—often through the use of interesting and attractive images, graphics, sounds, and videos" (Lin, 2007, p. 215). It is likely that this form of mediated-marketing of products will continue to expand globally.

Marketing and business practices are changing as more of the world engages in online economic activities (World Internet Users Statistics Usage, 2012). In India, "consumers are getting smarter," suggests Vinay (2012), as online consumers in India shop globally with the advantage of more control and influence than when they were limited to offline buying. This, he suggests, was brought about by the "tremendous growth of online retail in India" (Vinay, 2012, p. 384). As "Asia's business elite are turning to social media for news in increasing numbers" (Tan & Bateman, 2012, p. 54) new opportunities and challenges emerge. For example, Otremba (2012) identifies Filipinos as among the most active users of Facebook, although this has not yet translated into a large amount of business activity (p. 57). Our purpose here is to point out that there are a great number of studies examining the role of Internet technology in business and marketing and that there is need for further research in this area.

Social Relations and Identification

Increasingly, scholars are beginning to understand that despite the use of online technology for business and marketing, it is that the social and personal use of online technology is most prevalent—even in developing countries. Kim (2008, p. 1), for example, sees the media as central to everyday life. He asserts that everyday life in Asia is under the domain of both the economic and material as well as cultural and symbolic resources influenced by the media. He states that, "new media technologies such as the Internet are embedded in and continuous with other social spaces, happening not just within a virtual world that is somehow disconnected from the everyday, but within mundane social structures and relations that they may transform but cannot escape" (Kim, 2008, p. 6). The emerging mobile technologies give "rise to new contingencies for subjectivity, alternative ways of presenting gender, emotion, sociality as well as a performative space to negotiate online and offline identity" (Kim, 2008, p. 16). Furthermore, Kim (2008, p. 1) asserts that online media in particular are central to Asian transformation in the age of globalization. Media culture, he suggests, "is creating new connections, new desires and threats, and the identities of people are being reworked at individual, national, regional and global levels" (Kim, 2008, p. 1).

Bakker and Sádaba (2008) advise that media technologies are used in a "social context and have to fulfill existing needs" (p. 88). Furthermore, they believe that existing technology is better explained by looking at the user rather than the technology itself. Therefore they find value in the uses and gratifications approach to media use. They suggest that "it would be very hard to argue that the Internet has not affected the way in which people work, study and look for information or communicate with others" (Bakker & Sádaba, 2008, p. 86). Again we see that Internet technologies influence and may help organize our social life. Perhaps, too, it plays a significant role in our identity formation.

Caplan, Perse and Gennaria (2007) reviewed studies on the use of computer-mediated communication technologies (such as instant messaging, e-mail, and chat rooms) in a social context (pp. 39–58). They found that computer-mediated communication (CMC) allowed for "greater flexibility in self-presentation" while at the same time providing a "greater opportunity to fabricate, exaggerate, or intensify more positive aspects of oneself to others online" (Caplan, Perse, & Gennaria, 2007, p. 48). Also, they reported that "participants in FtF [face-to-face] conversations exhibit a smaller proportion of direct question-asking, self-disclosure statements, and politeness strategies then those in CMC interactions, suggesting that effective FtF communication demands greater communicative flexibility and creativity then CMC interactions" (Caplan, Perse, & Gennaria, 2007, p. 49). Finally, CMC users have the opportunity to receive and give social support in an anonymous fashion.

Another such study that takes a rather negative view of Western influence through the Internet concerns the use of media of all types to promote Western sports in Asia. Rowe and Gilmour (2010) argue that "Asia has become a prime target for the expansionary strategies of some of the world's most powerful professional sports league, teams, and media conglomerates" (p. 1530). These scholars claim that this assault by such sports organizations as the National Basketball Association (NBA) "crowd out" domestic Asian professional sport (Gilmour, 2010, p. 1530). While Rowe and Gilmour do not identify online media as the sole culprit in this endeavor, they clearly see all Western sports as a predominant product of modernity and all Western media corporations as engaged in disseminating and branding its products to Asia. This situation, they believe, "presents a clear barrier to the development of sports within Asia" (Rowe & Gilmour, 2010, p. 1543). The obvious implication is that "sports culture in Asia still primarily revolves around imported consumption" which is promoted by all types of media. Now we will turn our attention to the use of online and SNSs for political purposes.

Political Communication

Perhaps no other research area of online communication and SNSs has developed so swiftly in recent years as the use of this technology for political and social change. The promise that people can raise their voice against perceived elements within one's community or country against elements harming their culture is seductive and infusive. One study that represents these efforts is Mahajan's (2009) analysis of online communication in India. Specifically, he assesses how social networking can be used to enable people to connect with others and promote a worthy cause "despite the hindrances of distance and time" (Mahajan, 2009, p. 135). However, he cautions that social networking can be used to promote negative effects which may degrade a culture. Online communication and SNSs can be used for beneficial social and political purposes but their influence may detrimentally alter everyday life and the social or political systems within a country.

A number of other authors discuss the role of online communication and SNSs in tackling larger political issues such as the use of the Internet by activists (Bennett, 2003; Chattopadhyay, 2011; Joseph, 2012; Shirky, 2011; Wong, 2001). Scholars such as Shirky (2011) argue for the use of social media in fostering freedom of speech and "de-emphasize anti-censorship tools, particularly those aimed at specific regimes" (2011, p. 40). Although he cautions that progress toward freedom of speech and the benefits of social media will be slow in developing countries, he sees potential long-term benefits by taking an environmental view rather than an instrumental view of social media use (Shirky, 2011, p. 41). However, using these new technologies for political and social activism may not have the immediate success people hope for but may well lead to disappointment—at least in the short run.

There seems to be a consensus expressed by many scholars, articulated by Joseph (2012), who states that "the need for caution in promoting social media as an instrument of progressive political change must be acknowledged" (p. 187). For example, she advises that "there is no doubt that Internet-based technology can be used to track and profile dissidents, just as it can be used to promote the views of those dissidents. Good and bad ideas can be spread, and one cannot guarantee that the former will prevail" (Joseph, 2012, p. 187). There is no doubt that "social media in its various forms have created an unprecedented global public space that vastly increases and amplifies the number of accessible voices and connections in all parts of the world" (Joseph, 2012, p. 187). However, there are no guarantees that the powerbrokers of any culture might not take control of these platforms and challenge the potential freedoms now enjoyed by so many. In fact, some countries are "adopting proactive approaches to contesting cyberspace but supplementing long-established filtering, censorship, and surveillance techniques with more aggressive measures, including cyber-attacks on dissident websites" (Gershman, 2012, p. xiii). Many governments are trying to quiet the liberating potential of cyberspace within their political and physical borders.

Joyce (2010, p. 209) argues that there is not enough "foundational knowledge" of ICTs for political use, especially in the area of digital activism. She argues that in order for "digital activists to succeed in using digital tools in contests against the forces of oppression and injustice, those practices must continually increase in effectiveness" (Joyce, 2010, p. 209). What seems clear is that more strategic knowledge is needed in order for the sustained use of digital media for politically beneficial purposes.

Development Communication

Closely observing the use of online communication and SNSs for political and social power are scholars and professionals who are studying the role of online communication and SNSs for development. Obviously, many of the issues that we have discussed overlap with one another, but this is especially true with the present topic. These scholars are concerned with the use of online communication and social media for various uses in development; however, it is difficult to discern the difference between activism and political power and issues of development and hegemony (Ali, 2011; Choudhury, 2011; Iwabuchi, 2010a; Iwabuchi, 2010b; Mazzarella, 2010, Sonwalker, 2001).

Bakker and Sádaba (2008) point out that "many developing countries are already in a situation where the majority of the population uses the Internet on a daily basis" (p. 98). Furthermore they argue that "younger people use the Internet more, and there is also a distinct income gap" (Bakker and Sádaba, 2008, p. 98) between users and nonusers. Clearly there are those who now believe that the Internet and social media are uniquely positioned to make a substantial contribution to development and social change.

In discussing the power of social media in development, Ali (2011) cannot refrain from mentioning the fall of Egypt's president, Hosni Mubarak, who desperately attempted to contain the demonstrations by "shutting off the Internet for five days…which cost Egypt an estimated $90 million and outraged the international community" and "demonstrates the incredible power of social media" (p. 185). Clearly politics and development often work together. Ali (2011) encourages the use of social media for development as so many others have done. However, he also cautions us to see the various ways in which social media can be misused in development efforts.

The use of new communication technology for personal growth and development spans across many different kinds of online behavior. In many nations of Asia as in much of the world, communication technology has "become increasingly central to daily life" (Woodier, 2008, p. 2). New entertainment products and information services flow across national borders on a continual basis (Woodier, 2008, p. 3). In particular, social media have eliminated most boundaries, giving even small companies and organizations access to many people with differing socio-demographic characteristics (Spry, 2010, p. 1). This bodes well for Asia's future economic development in the communication technology and services sector.

Religious Uses

Now we will turn to scholars who are studying religion and the social media. Cheong et al. (2009) examined how protestant organizations in Singapore used new media to communicate their religious messages online. They found that churches throughout Asia are linking to Singapore churches to access information (p. 27). In this way religious information, images and rituals are communicated across national borders and leapfrog over educational barriers. In a follow-up study, Cheong, Huang, and Poon (2011) conducted in-depth interviews with Protestant pastors in Singapore. They concluded that competition from Internet access delocalized their epistemic authority and allowed pastors to develop "new competencies as strategic arbiters of religious expertise and knowledge" (p. 938).

Hjarvard (2006) found that media not only support existing interests in spiritual issues, but also encourage further religious discussion by raising important questions. His study explores how popular media symbols draw interest to religious themes, providing a theoretical framework for understanding how media work as agents of religious change. The potential dramatic effects on religious practices in Asia are profoundly influenced by online communication. Meyer (2011) argues that "the negotiation of newly available media technologies is a key to the transformation of religion" (p. 23). Although the study of media use in the shaping of religion in modern society "has generally been overlooked in the mainstream sociology of religion" (Lövheim, 2011, p. 153), there is a great opportunity now to explore how online communication is diffusing new religious beliefs and practices in rapidly developing Asian nations like India, Indonesia, and the Philippines.

National Differences

National comparisons of online communication and social networking are difficult to make when perusing the academic literature. Most media studies are conducted within a single country or geographical region, making cross-cultural comparisons difficult. Differing measures and questions used in different studies do not allow country by country comparisons except for certain variables such as media access and content. There are a few important tendencies in the three nations we are studying that should be noted.

First, the Philippines is regarded as a social networking capital of the world, boasting the most active users on social networking sites such as Facebook, Twitter, and Multiply (Otremba, 2012, p. 57). Social media networks in the Philippines are well-developed venues for not only civic engagement, but also the development of interpersonal relationships through greater affective personalization (Hjorth & Arnold, 2011). In addition to online communication for relational development, e-commerce and the use of social networks for business purposes have been rapidly growing in the Philippines (Alampay, 2008).

Second, since the passing of Suharto's leadership, new media in Indonesia have been integrated more thoroughly into commerce, resulting in a "convergence between information technology, entertainment and education" that has resulted in "new businesses that power media growth" (Ida, 2011, p. 13). Media companies are now heavily intertwined with government and political processes in much of Asia. Social networking is expanding rapidly across the many islands of Indonesia. One of the growing online behaviors among Indonesians is blogging. The Indonesian blogosphere has made important contributions to social media and is expanding its influence on social and political culture (Kumar et al., 2009).

Our third observation is that India is experiencing similar online media growth as its own infrastructure continues to expand its communication technology capabilities. University students in India are particularly prodigious in their use of social networking websites for social and interpersonal purposes (Agarwal & Mital, 2009). Businesses across the globe are making profitable use of online websites such as Wikipedia, YouTube, Facebook, Twitter, and Second Life (Kaplan & Haenlein, 2010), and Indian companies are no exception. The immense size of India's population coupled with its expanding Internet literacy will undoubtedly make India a global leader in the new information societies that emerge from developing nations. With the rapid potential growth of online media use in India, Indonesia, and the Philippines in mind, we will now present the research questions that guide our present study.

2. Research Questions

As explained earlier, the purpose of our study is to conduct a comparative analysis of the online and social networking access of Internet users in India, Indonesia, and the Philippines over a two-year period. Our exploration of online communication and social media access in these three Asian nations focuses on four major areas of study. First, we explore two ways in which people interact socially online—through sharing videos and through social networking. Our first research question is:

RQ1. How much do Internet users in India, Indonesia, and the Philippines access the Internet to interact socially?

Two measures of social interaction are assessed in our study. First, we asked respondents how often they share videos with others through the Internet. Second, we asked respondents how often they use social networking websites.

The second area of exploration in this study focuses on using the Internet for personal development, conceived of as multiple behaviors that describe how individuals seek out information and entertainment to satisfy their own personal growth needs. Our second research question is:

RQ2. How much do Internet users in India, Indonesia, and the Philippines access the Internet for personal development?

Our study assesses five measures of online access for personal development: obtaining news and information, obtaining religious content, accessing educational programs, listening to or downloading music, and listening to radio programs.

The third area of research focus pertains to how Internet users in India, Indonesia, and the Philippines explore business uses of the Internet. The following research question is posed:

RQ3. How much do Internet users in India, Indonesia, and the Philippines access the Internet for business purposes?

Two measures of business use were created in our study: making charitable contributions online and shopping online.

Finally, the literature review reveals that the use of online communication and social networking by women has been of particular interest to many scholars. We therefore explored potential gender differences with the following research question:

RQ4. *Is the online behavior of women different than men in these three countries?*

Due to the two-year timeframe of our study, embedded in each research question is an assessment of changes that might have occurred from one year to the next. Therefore, each of these areas of study will be compared both across the three nations and within each nation.

3. Methodology

National survey studies for each country were designed in consultation with a research team that was employed and trained in each country. Each 6 to 8-member research team had an experienced project coordinator who helped to develop a national research plan. The survey was created collaboratively with each project coordinator who then had the survey translated into one or more primary languages spoken in each region. The data collection plan was designed to obtain data in a financial center, government center, and cultural center of each country. We also asked country coordinators to choose cities and regions to collect data where people with different religious affiliations, languages, and cultural identities lived. Surveys were then created for each country with the same survey questions but with different response options to create diverse samples in commercial and cultural centers of each nation that could be compared directly.

Survey data were collected in a total of 20 major cities for this study: Delhi, Dehradun, Chandigarh, Guntur, Hyderabad, Kolkata, Lucknow, Ludhiana, Mumbai, Pune, and Vizag in India; Bandung, Jakarta, Makassar, Medan, Surabaya, and Yogyakarta in Indonesia; and Metro Manila, Cebu, and Davao in the Philippines. The sample sizes for each location averaged from 500 to 600 respondents, with generally larger sample sizes in India. All survey coordinators followed a stratified random sampling data collection technique. Respondents were selected randomly within targeted demographics in order to obtain a representative sample of people who lived in that city or region. In 2011, 4,316 completed surveys were gathered in five cities of India, 3,026 completed surveys were gathered in six cities of Indonesia, and 1,707 completed interviews were gathered in three cities in the Philippines, for a total sample size of 9,049. In 2012, 3,056 people were interviewed in India, 2007 people were interviewed in Indonesia, and 1,731 were interviewed in the Philippines, making the total sample size 6,794. These sample sizes are provided in Table 1.

Procedures and Sampling

First, survey coordinators were asked to choose from 3 to 6 cities in their country, depending on its size, that represented a diversity of people groups and regions. In every country each country coordinator developed a research plan that was approved before data collection could begin.

Random sampling procedures were used to insure that the best possible information was collected within the various settings. Survey coordinators were asked to balance the demographic characteristics of their respondents the best they could to match the general demographic characteristics of the population. Special attention was given to age and religious affiliation. All interviews were conducted face-to-face in public settings. Those interviewed were representative of the variety of Internet users in the urban areas of each country. By design, no particular religious group, ethnic or cultural group, age group (of those 10 and older), or any other demographic characteristic were excluded from the study. Likewise, no particular group was purposefully oversampled.

Survey participants were randomly selected in parks, shopping areas, train and bus stations, school campuses and playgrounds, residential neighborhoods, and other public venues. Sampling was stratified to obtain representative numbers of men and women in each age group according to the U.S. Census Bureau's International Data Base. Appropriate interview strategies were used to reduce tendencies toward social desirability and other response biases. Random sampling procedures were implemented in each venue where interviews were conducted.

Research Instrument

The survey questionnaire was designed on the basis of McGuire's (2001) model of the hierarchy of media effects identified as "output persuasion steps" (p. 32). The measures of online media and social networking access are part of a much larger multi-national research project on media consumption of religious content. The survey includes ten measures of online media use, including video sharing, social networking, news and information, religious content, music, radio, financial contributions, educational programs and online shopping. The survey also includes nine demographic measures: gender, education, primary language, age, marital status, number of children living at home, family income, religious heritage, and religious practice. All survey questionnaires were translated into the most common languages spoken in each of the regions where data were collected and were pre-tested before they were finalized.

4. Results

Results will be presented in the order of the research questions posed. All of our research questions explored online behavior; therefore, the results presented here are based on the subset of Internet users in each sample, which ranged from 37.4 percent to 51.6 percent in 2011 and from 44.9 percent to 59.4 percent in 2012 (see Table 2).

Social Interaction

The first research question explored how much Internet users in India, Indonesia, and the Philippines accessed the Internet to interact socially, focusing on video sharing and social networking. All three nations experienced a substantial increase in video sharing and social networking. In India, the percentage of Internet users sharing videos rose from 19.6

percent in 2011 to 48.7 percent in 2012 (see Table 3), and the percentage of Internet users who engaged in social networking dramatically increased from 31.4 percent in 2011 to 74.8 percent in 2012 (see Table 4). In addition, the frequency of interacting socially online also increased as shown in Tables 3 and 4. The finding that in 2012, 43.6 percent of the online users in the sample engaged in social networking in India at least 7 or more times per week; and another 21.4 percent engaged in social networking from 1 to 6 times per week, is remarkable (see Table 4).

Similar findings for increasing in online social interaction were found in Indonesia and the Philippines. Video sharing increased in Indonesia from 19.2 percent to 30.8 percent from 2011 to 2012 and social networking increased from 44.0 percent to 82.4 percent over the same time period. In the Philippines, video sharing increased from 29.1 percent to 53.5 percent and social networking increased from 51.7 percent to 94.0 percent from 2011 to 2012. Again, our finding that 94 percent of the online respondents in the Philippines reported involvement in social networking shows the extraordinary diffusion of social networking behavior.

Personal Development

The second research question explored how Internet users in India, Indonesia, and the Philippines are accessing online websites for personal development. All five measures of Internet use for personal development showed increases from 2011 to 2012. Internet users in India, Indonesia, and the Philippines increased their access to news and information (a 24.9 percent increase for Indians, a 33.5 percent increase for Indonesians, and a 54.4 percent increase for Filipinos), as shown in Table 5. They also increased their use of online websites for religious content. Indonesians increased their online religious website access by 3.9 percent, Indians by 17.9 percent, and Filipinos by 29.0 percent, from 2011 to 2012 (see Table 6). Accessing online educational programs also increased during the same time period, from 16.3 percent to 32.1 percent in India; from 11.4 percent to 12.4 percent in Indonesia; and from 17.4 percent to 29.5 percent in the Philippines (see Table 7).

Some of the strongest increases are seen for downloading and listening to music online. Among Filipino online users, 27.7 percent reported using the Internet for this purpose in 2011 and 71.4 percent reported using the Internet to access music in 2012, a dramatic increase. Indian Internet users also increased their online access to music, from 26.3 percent in 2011 to 59.1 percent in 2012 (see Table 8). Likewise, online users in Indonesia increased access to online music from 19.7 percent in 2011 to 27 percent in 2012.

The last measure of personal development use of the Internet, listening to radio programs, increased moderately in India (from 5.3 percent to 13.6 percent), decreased marginally in Indonesia (from 5.4 percent to 3.2 percent), and increased strongly in the Philippines (from 7.8 percent to 38.2 percent) from 2011 to 2012. Despite our focus in urban areas, a substantial number of people (more than one-third of the Filipinos who are online) are accessing radio programming online (see Table 9). In summary, all five measures demonstrate online users in India, Indonesia, and the Philippines are increasing their use of the Internet for personal development.

Online Business Use

The fourth research question explores the business uses of the Internet. We focused on assessing two specific behaviors: making financial contributions online and shopping online. Given that our respondents primarily lived in developing regions of the world, we did not expect to find many individuals doing financial transactions over the Internet. Our expectations were correct; however, as with other online uses, online business use is increasing in two of the three nations we surveyed. Making online charitable contributions increased from 3.9 percent to 12.4 percent in India, decreased from 2.6 percent to 1.9 percent in Indonesia, and increased from 0.8 percent to 9.0 percent in the Philippines, from 2011 to 2012. These results are provided in Table 10.

Online shopping increased in all three nations from 2011 to 2012. The Philippines experienced more than a seven-fold increase, from 1.6 percent to 11.7 percent from 2011 to 2012. Indonesia, which had the highest online shopping use of the Internet, more than tripled online shopping from 6.3 percent in 2011 to 20.8 percent in 2012. India nearly doubled its use of websites for online shopping, from 11.3 percent to 20.0 percent from 2011 to 2012. All three countries are clearly expanding their business use of the Internet. These results are provided in Table 11.

Gender Differences

The last research question explored gender differences in online communication in terms of how men and women use the Internet for various purposes. Results provide some interesting distinctions. Statistical comparisons in these three nations were made by conducting T-Tests with SAS (2004). In India, for 2011, there was only one significant difference in online use between men and women. On a scale of 0 to 3, with 0 indicating no use of online radio programs and 3 indicating daily use of online radio programs, women exhibited greater consumption of online radio programming (M = 0.16, SD = 0.62) than did men (M = 0.09, SD = 0.46) (t(3231) = 4.1, p < .001). In 2012, four differences were found. On the same 0 to 3 scale, women were engaged in more social networking (M = 1.91, SD = 1.18) than men (M = 1.78, SD = 1.26) (t(1367) = 2.0, p < .05); women gave more online financial contributions (M = 0.33, SD = 0.82) than men (M = 0.20, SD = 0.66) (t(1041) = 2.1, p < .01); and women did more online shopping (M = 0.45, SD = 0.90) than men (M = 0.31, SD = 0.78) (t(1089) = 2.9, p < .01). Regarding accessing online radio programming, men were more engaged in that activity (M = 0.31, SD = 0.81) than women (M = 0.23, SD = 0.68) (t(1310) = 2.1, p < .05).

In Indonesia, there was one significant difference between men and women's online behavior in 2011. On a scale of 0 to 3, with 0 indicating no use of online video sharing and 3 indicating daily online video sharing, Indonesian men shared videos more (M = 0.45, SD = 0.92) than did women (M = 0.34, SD = 0.83) (t(3008) = 3.4, p < .001). In 2012, no differences were found between men and women in all nine online media use measures.

In the Philippines, the 2011 data revealed one difference between men and women. Men were more likely to listen to or download music online (M = 0.68, SD = 1.08) than women (M = 0.52, SD = 0.97) on a 0 to 3 scale, with 0 indicating no use of the Internet to listen to or download music and 3 indicating daily use of the Internet for these activities (t(829) = 2.4, p < .05). The 2012 data from the Philippines revealed four gender differences in online behavior. First, women engaged in more social networking online (M = 2.09, SD = 0.78) than men (M = 1.95, SD = 0.99) on a 0 to 3 scale, with 0 indicating no use of the Internet for social networking and 3 indicating daily use of the Internet for social networking (t(901) = 2.4, p < .05).

On three other online behaviors, Filipino men were more active than Filipino women. Men were more likely to listen to or download music online (M = 1.53, SD = 1.2) than women (M = 1.20, SD = 1.15) (t(826) = 4.0, p < .001); men were more likely to access radio programs online (M = 0.91, SD = 1.18) than women (M = 0.53, SD = 0.97) (t(744) = 4.9, p < .001); and men were more likely to access educational programs online (M = 0.71, SD = 1.16) than women (M = 0.51, SD = 0.96) (t(701) = 2.5, p < .05).

5. Discussion

Results of our study demonstrate the rapid growth of online communication access and use in India, Indonesia, and the Philippines. We did not anticipate the high frequencies of online communication and social networking that we found. Our data indicate that once people do get online in these three nations, they quickly find multiple uses for the Internet and readily engage the Internet for social interaction, personal development, and business. The marked increases that we found between 2011 and 2012 shows how quickly the media landscape is changing in many nations in Asia. We were especially intrigued by the daily use of the Internet in India, Indonesia, and the Philippines for so many different kinds of activities. Social interaction through the use of social networking websites is clearly one of the primary categories of online activities that is emerging in many Asian nations. More than any other activity, we found that online media consumers use the Internet to connect and communicate and share information with others. The growth of Internet access in all three of these countries will continue to fuel their growing information societies, which will take them beyond the status of developing nations.

Our findings confirm recent studies of the rapid expansion of online communication in developing nations of Asia. It is clear that these three nations are growing exponentially in their online media use, which eventually will positively impact the education and productivity of their populations. Women in particular seemed to be engaged in many types of online communication behavior as much as men. We found comparatively few differences between men and women. The potential use of social networking sites by women for greater participation in decision-making, leadership roles and empowerment needs much more focused attention in future research in these three nations.

In addition, future studies need to continue to explore how online behavior is being used toward both personal and national development. As noted at the beginning of our chapter, much of the research of online social networking has focused on political involvement. Indeed, both the political and economic implications of our study warrant future research. For example, what effect do the interlocking business and political social networks in Indonesia have on the unfair collusion of government and business leaders that are detrimental to overall economic development? Do the close interpersonal relationships between political leaders and entrepreneurs in the Philippines enhance or detract from the greater vision of national development that lifts the majority of the population out of poverty? Likewise, will India's growing online community create an economic surge that will 'lift all boats,' or will the lower castes continue to be disadvantaged? These are important questions for scholars to explore regarding the implications of the great expansion of online communication in Asia.

Finally, we note that comparatively little attention has been given to the role of online communication in the religious life of the peoples of Asia. This may be due in part to the tendencies for Western scholars to overlook and underestimate the important integration of religion, media, and culture and their combined effects on individuals, communities, and nations. Religious beliefs are fundamental to the way in which people interact with each other, conduct business, involve themselves in political processes, and negotiate shared values and social norms. The dominant religious worldviews of Hinduism, Buddhism, Islam, and Christianity are all interacting in India, Indonesia, and the Philippines and it is critical that a better understanding and peaceful co-existence of these religious worlds be promoted through online communication. The need is particularly great for intercultural communication scholars to expand their research into a greater exploration of the religious dimensions of social networking and online communication.

A growing number of online users in India, Indonesia, and the Philippines will undoubtedly provide more opportunities for political involvement and entrepreneurial activities of any individual who can learn basic computer skills and gain access to the Internet. These two requirements may still pose a high threshold to cross for the millions of impoverished families who live in rural areas. However, these limitations are decreasing as online access is expanding. The potential of online communication to expand political, social and economic involvement of more and more people could substantively enhance the quality of life among the peoples of Asia. We hope our study of online communication in these three Asian nations has contributed to a better understanding of the dynamic changes that are now taking place.

References

Ali, A. H. (2011). The power of social media in developing nations: New tools for closing the global digital divide and beyond. Harvard Human Rights Journal, 24, 185–220. Retrieved from http://harvardhrj.com/wp-content/uploads/2009/09/185-220.pdf

Agarwal, S., & Mital, M. (2009). An exploratory study of Indian university students' use of social networking websites: Implications for the workplace. Business Communication Quarterly, 72(1), 105–110. doi: 10.1177/1080569908330379

Alampay, E. A. (2008). Filipino entrepreneurs on the Internet: When social networking websites meet mobile commerce. Science Technology & Society, 13, 211–231. doi: 10.1177/097172180801300203

Bakker, P. & Sádaba, C. (2008). The impact of the Internet on users. In Kung, L., Picard, R. G. & Towse R. (Eds.), The Internet and the mass media (pp. 86–101). Thousand Oaks, CA: Sage Publications Ltd.

Bennett, W. L. (2003). New media power: The Internet and global activism. In N. Couldry & J. Curran (Eds.), Contenting media power, (pp. 20–35). New Your, NY: Rowman and Littlefield.

boyd, d. m. & Ellison, N. B. (2008). Social network sites: Definition, history, and scholarship.Journal of Computer-Mediated Communication, 13, 210–230. doi: 10.1111/j.1083-6101.2007.00393.x

Caplan, S. E., Perse, E. M. & and Gennaria, J. E. (2007). Computer-Mediated technology and social Interaction. In C. A. Lin & D. J. Atkin (Eds.), Communication technology and social change: Theory and implications (pp.39–58). Mahwah, NJ: Lawrence Erlbaum Associates, Inc., Publishers.

Chattopadhyay, S. (2011). Online activism for a heterogeneous time: The pink Chaddi Campaign and the social media in India. Proteus: A journal of ideas, 27(1), 63–67.

Cheong, P. H., Huang, S. & Poon, J. P. H. (2011). Religious communication and epistemic authority of leaders in wired faith organizations. Journal of Communication, 61, 938–958. doi: 10.1111/j.1460-2466.2011.01579.x

Cheong, P. H., Poon, J. P. H., Huang, S. & Casas, I. (2009). The Internet highway and religious communities: Mapping and contesting spaces in religion-online. The Information Society, 25(5), 291–302.

Choudhury, P. S. (2011, December). Media in development communication. Global Media

Journal-Indian Edition, 2(2), Retrieved from http://www.caluniv.ac.in/ Global%20mdia%20journal/Winter%20Issue%20December%20 2011%20Commentaries/C5%20Sen%20Choudhury.pdf

Gershman, C. (2012). Forward. In R. Deibert, J. Palfrey, R. Rohozinski, and J. Zittrain (Eds.), Access contested: Security, Identity, and Resistance in Asian Cyberspace (pp. xiii–xv). Cambridge, MA: The MIT Press.

Hjarvard, S. (2006). The mediatization of religion: A theory of the media as an agent of religious change. Paper presented to the 5th International Conference on Media, Religion and Culture: Mediating Religion in the Context of Multicultural Tension. Sweden, 6–9 July, 2006. http://mrc-metwork.media.ku.dk

Hjorth, L., & Arnold, M. (2011). The personal and the political: Social networking in Manila. International Journal of Learning and Media, 3(1), 29-39. doi: 10.1162/ijlm_a_00059

Ida, R. (2011). Reorganisation of media power in post-authoritarian Indonesia: Ownership, power and influence of local media entrepreneurs. In K. Sen & D. T. Hill (Eds.), Politics and the media in twenty-first century (pp. 13–25). New York, NY: Routledge.

Iwabuchi, K. (2010a). De-Westernization and the governance of global cultural connectivity: adialogic approach to East Asian media cultures. Postcolonial Studies, 13, 403–419. doi: 10.1080/13688790.2010.518349

Iwabuchi, K. (2010b). Globalization, East Asian media cultures and their publics. Asian Journalof Communication, 20(2), 197–212. doi: 10.1080/012929981003693385

Joseph, S. (2012). Social media, political change, and human rights. Boston College International and Comparative law Review, 35, 145–188.

Joyce, M. (2010) Conclusion: Building the future of digital activism. In M. Joyce (Ed.), Digital activism decoded: The new mechanics of change (pp. 209–216). New York: NY: Idebate Press.

Kaplan, A. M., & Haenlein, M. (2010). Users of the world, unite! The challenges and opportunities of social media. Business Horizons, 53(1), 59–68.

Kim, Y. (2008). Introduction: The media and Asian transformations. In Y. Kim (Ed.), Media consumption and everyday life in Asia (pp. 1–24). New York, NY: Routledge.

Kumar, S., Agarwal, N., Lim, M., & Liu, H. (2009). Mapping socio-cultural dynamics in Indonesian blogosphere. Paper presented to the 3rd International Conference on Computational Cultural Dynamics of the Association for the Advancement of Artificial Intelligence. Retrieved from http://www.aaai.org/ocs/index.php/ICCCD/ICCCD09/paper/viewFile/1019/3317

Lin, C. A. (2007). Interactive media technology and electronic shopping. In C. A. Lin & D. J. Atkin (Eds.), Communication technology and social change: Theory and implications (pp.203–222). Mahwah, NJ: Lawrence Erlbaum Associates, Inc., Publishers.

Lövheim, M. (2011). Mediatisation and religion: A critical appraisal. Culture and Religion: An Interdisciplinary Journal, 12, 153–166. doi: 10.1080/14755610.2011.579738

Mahajan, P. (2009). Use of social networking in a linguistically and culturally rich India. The International Information & Library Review, 41, 129–136. doi: 10.1016/j.iilr.2009.07.004

Mazzarella, S. (2010). Beautiful balloon: The digital divide and the charisma of new media in India. American Ethnologist, 37, 783–804. doi: 10.1111/j.1548-1425-2010.01285.x

McGuire, W. J. (2001). Input and output variables currently promising for constructing persuasive communications. In R. E. Rice & C. K. Atkin (Eds.), Public communication campaigns (3rd ed.) (pp. 22–48). Thousand Oaks, CA: Sage Publications.

Meyer, B. (2011). Mediation and immediacy: Sensational forms, semiotic ideologies and the question of medium. Social Anthropology, 19(1), 23–39. doi: 10.1111/j.1469-8676.2010.00137.x

Otremba, J. (2012, August). Social media report: Philippines the social capital. Campaign Asia-Pacific, p. 57.

Rattle, R. (2010). Computing our way to paradise? New York, NY: Rowman & Littlefield Publishers, Inc.

Rowe, D. & Gilmour, C. (2010). Sport, media, and consumption in Asia: A merchandised milieu. American Behavioral Scientist, 53, 1530–1548. doi: 10.1177/0002764210368083

SAS (2004). SAS 9.0. Cary, NC: SAS Institute Inc.

Shirky, C. (2011). The political power of social media. Foreign Affairs, 90, 28–41.

Sonwalker, P. (2001). India: Makings of little cultural/media imperialism? International Communication Gazette, 63, 505–519. dio: 10.1177/0016549201063006003

Spry, D. (2010). In Routledge media, culture and social change in Asia. [On-line]. Retrieved from http://0-his.ebscohost.com.library.regent. edu/eds/delivery?sid=a42c.

Stephan, S. H. (2012). Datamining for gold: Social media and social capital in a pro-national global market. Northern Kentucky Law Review, 39(2), 163–188.

Tan, E. & Bateman, N. (2012, October). Asia sees surge in digital consumption. Campaign Asia-Pacific, p. 54. http://0-ehis.ebscohost. com.library.regent.edu/eds/delivery?sid=fa4b4

Vinay, J. (2012). The new marketing renaissance: Paradigm shift in social networks.International Journal of Engineering & Management Sciences, 3, 384–386. Doi: 10.1037/0278-6133.24.2.225

Woodier, J. (2008). Media and political change in Southeast Asia: Karaoke culture and the evolution of personality politics. Northampton, MA: Edward Elgar Publishing, Inc.

Wong, L. (2001). The Internet and social change in Asia. Peace Review, 13, 381–387. doi:10.1080/13668800120079090

World Internet Users Statistics Usage and World Population Stats, Internet World Stats (2012, June). Retrieved from http://www.internetworldstats.com/stats.html

Table 1

Sample Sizes and Locations

Year	Country	City No.	Cities	Sample Size
2011	India	1	Delhi	1000
2011	India	2	Mumbai	526
2011	India	3	Chandigarh	995
2011	India	4	Dehradun	813
2011	India	5	Vizag	982
2011	Indonesia	1	Jakarta	521
2011	Indonesia	2	Bandung	497
2011	Indonesia	3	Surabaya	502
2011	Indonesia	4	Medan	503
2011	Indonesia	5	Makassar	505
2011	Indonesia	6	Yogyakarta	498
2011	Philippines	1	Manila	701
2011	Philippines	2	Cebu	504
2011	Philippines	3	Davao	502
2012	India	1	Lucknow	600
2012	India	2	Pune	585
2012	India	3	Ludhiana	200
2012	India	4	Kolkata	469
2012	India	5	Hyderabad	602
2012	India	6	Guntur	600
2012	Indonesia	1	Jakarta	504
2012	Indonesia	2	Medan	500
2012	Indonesia	3	Makassar	503
2012	Indonesia	4	Surabaya	500
2012	Philippines	1	Manila	533
2012	Philippines	2	Davao	675
2012	Philippines	3	Cebu	523

Table 2

Percentage of the Sample Accessing the Internet

Country	2011	2012	Change
India	37.4%	44.9%	+ 7.5%
Indonesia	44.0%	58.2%	+ 14.2%
Philippines	51.6%	59.4%	+7.8%

Table 3

Respondents' Frequency of Sharing Videos via the Internet

Country	Frequency of Use	2011	2012	Change
India	7 or more times/week	8.9%	20.4%	+ 11.5%
	1-6 times per week	6.7%	19.5%	+ 12.8%
	Less than once/week	4.0%	8.8%	+4.8%
	never	80.4%	51.3%	
Indonesia	7 or more times/week	6.7%	12.0%	+5.3%
	1-6 times per week	7.2%	9.9%	+2.7%
	Less than once/week	5.3%	8.9%	+3.6%
	never	80.8%	69.2%	
Philippines	7 or more times/week	11.1%	13.5%	+2.4%
	1-6 times per week	15.9%	20.0%	+4.1%
	Less than once/week	2.1%	20.0%	+ 17.9%
	never	70.9%	46.5%	

Table 4

Respondents' Frequency of Using Social Networking Websites

Country	Frequency of Use	2011	2012	Change
India	7 or more times/week	19.6%	43.6%	+ 24.0%
	1-6 times per week	9.1%	21.4%	+ 12.3%
	Less than once/week	2.7%	9.8%	+7.1%
	never	68.6%	25.2%	
Indonesia	7 or more times/week	26.7%	48.0%	+ 21.3%
	1-6 times per week	12.9%	19.7%	+6.8%
	Less than once/week	4.4%	14.7%	+ 10.3%
	never	56.0%	17.6%	
Philippines	7 or more times/week	21.9%	31.2%	+9.3%
	1-6 times per week	26.5%	46.9%	+ 20.4%
	Less than once/week	3.3%	15.9%	+ 12.6%
	never	48.3%	6.0%	

Table 5

Respondents' Frequency of Accessing News and Information on the Internet

Country	Frequency of Use	2011	2012	Change
India	7 or more times/week	10.9%	17.1%	+6.2%
	1-6 times per week	7.6%	16.3%	+8.7%
	Less than once/week	2.7%	12.7%	+ 10.0%
	never	78.8%	53.9%	
Indonesia	7 or more times/week	16.1%	30.8%	+ 14.7%
	1-6 times per week	9.6%	18.3%	+8.7%
	Less than once/week	4.0%	14.1%	+ 10.1%
	never	70.3%	36.8%	
Philippines	7 or more times/week	4.5%	22.7%	+ 18.2%
	1-6 times per week	5.9%	21.9%	+ 16.0%
	Less than once/week	1.7%	21.9%	+ 20.2%
	never	87.9%	33.5%	

Table 6
Respondents' Frequency of Accessing Religious Content on the Internet

Country	Frequency of Use	2011	2012	Change
India	7 or more times/week	2.6%	8.7%	+6.1%
	1-6 times per week	3.9%	8.1%	+4.2%
	Less than once/week	3.0%	10.6%	+7.6%
	never	90.5%	72.6%	
Indonesia	7 or more times/week	4.4%	5.6%	+1.2%
	1-6 times per week	3.9%	3.7%	- 0.2%
	Less than once/week	3.3%	6.2%	+2.9%
	never	88.4%	84.5%	
Philippines	7 or more times/week	2.5%	12.0%	+9.5%
	1-6 times per week	4.0%	8.4%	+4.4%
	Less than once/week	2.7%	21.9%	+ 19.2%
	never	90.8%	61.5%	

Table 7
Respondents' Frequency of Accessing Educational Programs on the Internet

Country	Frequency of Use	2011	2012	Change
India	7 or more times/week	6.6%	11.7%	+ 5.1%
	1-6 times per week	6.1%	9.0%	+ 2.9%
	Less than once/week	3.6%	11.4%	+ 7.8%
	never	83.7%	67.9%	
Indonesia	7 or more times/week	4.0%	5.2%	+1.2%
	1-6 times per week	3.9%	3.9%	+0.0%
	Less than once/week	3.5%	3.3%	- 0.2%
	never	88.6%	87.6%	
Philippines	7 or more times/week	5.3%	11.4%	+6.1%
	1-6 times per week	10.5%	12.1%	+1.6%
	Less than once/week	1.6%	6.0%	+4.4%
	never	82.6%	70.5%	

Table 8

Respondents' Frequency of Listening to and Downloading Music on the Internet

Country	Frequency of Use	2011	2012	Change
India	7 or more times/week	16.3%	24.3%	+8.0%
	1-6 times per week	7.4%	21.6%	+ 14.2%
	Less than once/week	2.6%	13.2%	+ 10.6%
	never	73.7%	40.9%	
Indonesia	7 or more times/week	10.4%	12.5%	+2.1%
	1-6 times per week	6.2%	7.6%	+1.4%
	Less than once/week	3.1%	6.9%	+3.8%
	never	80.3%	73.0%	
Philippines	7 or more times/week	8.5%	23.3%	+ 14.8%
	1-6 times per week	13.6%	20.8%	+7.2%
	Less than once/week	5.6%	27.3%	+ 21.7%
	never	72.3%	28.6%	

Table 9

Respondents' Frequency of Listening to Radio Programs on the Internet

Country	Frequency of Use	2011	2012	Change
India	7 or more times/week	2.5%	5.0%	+ 2.5%
	1-6 times per week	1.6%	4.2%	+ 2.6%
	Less than once/week	1.2%	4.4%	+ 3.2%
	never	94.7%	86.4%	
Indonesia	7 or more times/week	2.9%	1.4%	-1.5%
	1-6 times per week	1.2%	0.9%	-0.3%
	Less than once/week	1.3%	0.9%	-0.4%
	never	94.6%	96.8%	
Philippines	7 or more times/week	3.8%	13.9%	+ 10.1%
	1-6 times per week	3.2%	11.9%	+8.7%
	Less than once/week	0.8%	12.3%	+ 11.5%
	never	92.2%	61.8%	

Table 10

Respondents' Frequency of Making Online Charitable Contributions

Country	Frequency of Use	2011	2012	Change
India	7 or more times/week	1.1%	4.4%	+ 3.3%
	1-6 times per week	0.9%	4.4%	+ 3.5%
	Less than once/week	1.9%	3.6%	+ 1.7%
	never	96.1%	87.6%	
Indonesia	7 or more times/week	1.7%	0.9%	- 0.8%
	1-6 times per week	0.1%	0.3%	+0.2%
	Less than once/week	0.8%	0.7%	- 0.1%
	never	97.4%	98.1%	
Philippines	7 or more times/week	0.1%	2.1%	+2.0%
	1-6 times per week	0.7%	3.8%	+3.1%
	Less than once/week	0.0%	3.1%	+3.1%
	never	99.2%	91.0%	

Table 11

Respondents' Frequency of Shopping Online

Country	Frequency of Use	2011	2012	Change
India	7 or more times/week	3.0%	6.1%	+ 3.1%
	1-6 times per week	2.4%	4.8%	+ 2.4%
	Less than once/week	5.9%	9.1%	+ 3.2%
	Never	88.7%	80.0%	
Indonesia	7 or more times/week	2.2%	9.0%	+6.8%
	1-6 times per week	0.8%	4.7%	+3.9%
	Less than once/week	3.3%	7.1%	+3.8%
	Never	93.7%	79.2%	
Philippines	7 or more times/week	0.4%	5.0%	+4.6%
	1-6 times per week	0.4%	1.7%	+1.3%
	Less than once/week	0.8%	5.0%	+4.2%
	Never	98.4%	88.3%	

V. A Pilot Study of Social Media and Intercultural Communication Experience of Chinese and Japanese Students in Russia

Maria Lebedko

Department of Linguistics and Intercultural Communication,
Far Eastern Federal University (FEFU), Russia
mlebedko@yanex.ru
[The project was supported by the Scientific Fund of FEFU]

Abstract

The chapter explores the experience of 4 international graduate students from China and Japan seeking for Master's degree in the Russian language and culture from a large university in the Russian Far East. The present day situation in the world is characterized by two very important influential processes: globalization and social media. The first process induced mobility which led to substantial growth of various culture contacts; the second process induced a new kind of communication. The focus in the chapter is directed to the study of "classical" categories of intercultural communication (culture shock and its stages, values, stereotypes, and acculturation/adaptation) and the way social networks impacted on these categories, and the role of social media in the intercultural communication. This chapter, first, examines the categories as part of constituents of intercultural communication and then proceeds to research the impact of social media on intercultural communication.

Keywords: Intercultural communication, culture shock, values, stereotypes, social media, acculturation/adaptation

1. Introduction

With the unprecedented range of globalization processes, the number of contacts across cultures has dramatically increased, which entailed exuberant growth of scholars' involvement into the issues of intercultural communication (IC), an unusual phenomenal spread of new social media embracing the whole world. These two processes predetermined new kinds of contact and new ways of communication. Despite the existence of intercultural contacts since ancient times (let me remind intercultural 'pioneers' of their time: Alexander the Great, Christopher Columbus, Genghis Khan, etc.), IC is still a relatively young interdisciplinary scholarly field presently characterized by various searches of better ways of intercultural communication. One may say that there is a search for paradigm shifts: from descriptive, to systematic to cognitive to discourse to synergetic to memetic approaches (Gu, 2009; Zinchenko, Zusman, & Kirnoze, 2007) and to the newest one "Intercultural New Media Studies" introduced by Shuter (2012, p. 220).

The second process mentioned above is social networking (sometimes also called Web 2.0., which is disputable but accepted by some authors), that had a special phenomenon which has significantly impacted on networked societies all over the world, and which recently called into being a new generation that is known under several synonyms: Generation Y, N Gen (network generation), generation D (digital generation), millenials. These people were born in the "computer epoch" (http://www.wordspy.com/ categories/ demographics.asp); they all grew on the Internet technologies. A brief glance at the characteristics of this generation confirms that they are different. According to Cheese (2008), Generation Y are "top young performers," "highly technological savvy," "relationship-oriented," "uses a wide range of media and technology to connect with others," "[j]ob-[h] opping," "hungry … for knowledge," "have fun at work" (paragraphs 3, 10, 11, 13). The interaction of interlocutors is presently based on the Internet, mobile Internet, text messaging, blogs, and social networking, which dramatically changed the attitude to communication and became a turning point for intercultural communication in general (Pfister & Soliz, 2011).

Despite this deep interest in Internet technologies and networking, there are voices of dissatisfaction, a phenomenon called social network fatigue. Why? Interlocutors create many accounts, they have to maintain networking sites (some of which are just useless) and try to live an active social life on the Web, but due to the lack of time, many of them feel frustrated and experience mental exhaustion (http://www.wordspy.com/words/socialnetworkingfatigue.asp). According to McFedries (as cited in Tossell, 2007), Tossell recognized that even young people of the network generation are suffering from 'social network fatigue' because an online identity is being required over and over again. Though much of the debate has focused on the issue of social network fatigue, the interest towards social media has recently grown so much that the current situation may be called revolutionary as Shuter stated (2012).

This pilot study starts from the investigation of "classical" categories (intercultural communication, culture shock, values, stereotypes, acculturation/adaptation) in the traditional way. No matter how well prepared for different cultural encounters a person can be, moving to a different culture is almost always accompanied, on one hand, with many amazing, extraordinary events and, on the other hand, misunderstandings and failures in intercultural communication. Cognizing a new culture individuals unconsciously keep on to the concepts, mental structures based on their experience acquired during primary socialization in their own country. Going through the process of secondary socialization, a person often applies own, well known cultural behavioral patterns, values, traditions, etc. that do not coincide with the new culture, which leads to communication failures. Multiple causes of the malfunction, disappointments, nostalgia, etc. to mention just a few, accompany sojourners in their new environment. Newcomers go through stages of culture shock before they achieve acculturation/adaptation (bicultural) stage and interiorize the new culture.

Regarding these two phenomena (IC in our globalized world and social media era) as tightly connected, the goals were set to monitor graduate students' progress in a form of questions: 1) Do you use social media and if yes, name them, please. 2) How often do you 'speak' with your friends? 3) How helpful were social media for your study? 4) What role did social networking play to you in the process of communication?" To achieve these goals the traditional key concepts and new social media had been examined.

In this pilot study, I focused on three constructs: IC, fundamentals of culture categories and social networking. The study first shortly examined the key concept notions in light of the theories. Secondly, it proceeded to administer the questionnaire to elicit the graduate students' understanding of the intercultural categories. Thirdly, the research examined the influence of social networking on IC and its categories.

2. Theoretical Background: Defining the Key Concepts

Intercultural Communication

Intercultural communication has been conceptualized in so many various ways that it would be difficult to cover all definitions. Let me give some examples of IC conceptualization: interpersonal interaction between members of various groups differing from each other by knowledge, behavioral models shared by all the members of those groups (Geertz, 1973). Samovar, Porter and Stefani (2000) conceptualized IC as "communication between people whose cultural perception and symbol systems are distinct enough to alter the communication event" (p. 48). Ishii (2006) regarded IC as culturally interconnected cognitive, affective and behavioral processes characterized by the exchange of verbal and nonverbal messages between interlocutors who have different frames of reference. In the present research, IC is understood as a multifaceted interdisciplinary scholarly field that integrates cognitive, affective, axiological, cultural, and behavioral patterns interacting in communicative acts between two individuals belonging to different cultures (interpersonal communication) or communicative acts between groups belonging to diverse cultural contexts (intercultural communication). IC is the process of exchanges of messages, which are performed either directly through linguistic (verbal) and body language (nonverbal/corporeal) or indirectly as a computer mediated communication, through Internet messages, blogs, networks, etc.

IC is dynamic, which is underscored by diverse cognitive processes which serve as a basis for humans' cognition, conceptualization, categorization and processing their own experience storing it in their individual and collective unconsciousness in a form of various mental structures. One may say that such cognitive processes as asymmetrical perception, cognitive bewilderment, cognitive dissonance, generalization, anchoring, etc. serve not only as a platform for IC, but also create dynamism. Summing up, since the time cognitive approach emerged, IC was often analyzed within the framework of cognitive theories.

Culture Shock

Since Oberg's notion of "culture shock" (1954) that was first called "occupational disease" was introduced to IC, the concept has received a lot of controversial definitions. Some authors regarded the concept of "culture shock" as "culture fatigue," that was considered more accurate because this idea expressed what was actually happening to sojourners or immigrants cognizing an entirely new culture (Levine, Buxter, & McNulty, 1987; Seeley, 1994; Seelye & Seelye-James, 1996). According Seelye & Seelye-James (as cited in Tyler, 1987), Tyler preferred such concepts as "self-discovery shock," "role shock," or "transition shock," to the widely spread "culture shock." Seelye (1994) would rather use "culture clash" to underscore possible communication failures. According to Seelye (as cited in Wasilevski, 1992), Wasilevski considered the term "culture shock" as hyperbolic referring to common culture fatigue of all the people entering a new culture. Levine et al. (1987) consider culture fatigue natural; it accompanies the process of adaptation. Kohls (1984) argues specifically in favor of imminence of culture shock: "There is no vaccination... for one malady you are likely to encounter—culture shock. In all probability, the doctor who gave you your other shots wouldn't even have been able to talk intelligently about it" (p. 18). Definitions vary, for example, for Ting-Toomey (1999) "Culture shock refers to the transitional process in which an individual perceives threats to her or his well-being in a culturally new environment. In this unfamiliar environment, the individual's identity appears to be stripped of all protection." (p. 245). Kohls' (1984) definition of culture shock sounds as follows:

> *"Culture Shock" is the term used to describe the more pronounced reactions to the psychological disorientation most people experience*

when they move for an extended period of time into a culture markedly different from their own. It can cause intense discomfort, often accompanied by hyper-irritability, bitterness, resentment, homesickness, and depression. In some cases distinct physical symptoms of psychosomatic illness occur (p.63).

Various synonyms of culture shock underscore its contradiction: on the one hand, the nature of culture shock is disputable, but on the other hand, it is inevitable. Nobody is immune to culture shock. The culture shock structurally consists of several stages (from three to eight). I have chosen the four stages (honeymoon. crisis, recovery, and acculturation/adaptation) as prevailing in numerous researches and more convenient for the students' understanding.

Values

The hierarchy of values is the result of long-lasting cognitive process and axiological attitude towards an object, relationship, image, etc. by the subject who interiorizes this or that value later. Barrett (1961) postulates that "values lie at the core of life and human action" (p. 1). Kluckhohn (1961) hypothesized that "[a] value is a selective orientation toward experience, implying deep commitment or repudiation, which influences the ordering of "choices" between possible alternatives in action. These orientations may be cognitive and expressed verbally or merely inferable from recurrent trends in behavior" (p. 18). The typology of values depends on scholarly fields and scholars attitude. Most researchers investigating values accept the following typology: vital (values referring to the quality of life, etc.); social (values related to the status, work, family, etc.); political (values oriented to freedom of speech, law, order, etc.); moral (values reflecting friendship, love, honor, etc.); religious (values based on the belief in God, savior, church, etc.); ethical (values connected with beauty, ideal, style, etc.) to mention just a few. So, I understand a value as a cognitive mental concept that appeared on the basis of experience and evaluated by a person since it can meet his/her needs and wishes. One cannot equate needs and wishes with values, which are significantly different. Values "do not arise solely out of an immediate situation and the satisfaction of needs and primary drives." (Kluckhohn, 1961, p. 18). Individuals can have specific personal values because all people are unique. At the same time individuals keep values as different mental structures in collective unconsciousness, which creates various world views. But values can also belong to a culture where most people share the same values.

Stereotypes

Stereotypes are defined in several ways: they can be seen as pictures in one's head (Lippmann, 1922), discrete cognitive units, as unique perceptual experiences (Adler, 1993; Kohls, 1984), as broader categories about groups of people (Stewart & Bennett, 1991), as forms of social perception (Stewart & Bennett, 1991), or as comprehensive belief systems, or sets of cognitions, held by the members of one social group about the members of another social group (Elligan, 2008). In discourse approach stereotyping is regarded as ideological statements (Scollon & Scollon, 2000). In cognitive terms, stereotypes are regarded as a normal process of categorization: it is only natural for people to categorize and classify objects in the environment, inanimate nature, wildlife and people (Brislin, 1993; Pinker, 2003; Stewart & Bennett, 1991; Ting-Toomey, 1999). "People share a stereotype, project it to all the members of a category..." (Pinker, 2009, p. 126). The paradox of this situation lies in the truth of some stereotypes and at the same time in the danger for stereotyped people. The peril of discrimination is extremely large for racial and ethnic groups. The controversy of stereotyping is in its strong bias of stereotypical assumptions, which is due to different world views and culturally specific perception. Psychologically and physiologically, perception is basic in forming our world view, but at the same time our world views are not the result of pure perception (Piaget, 1998). Perception (along with other factors) has a crucial place in a long chain from the environment to the consciousness (Robinson, 1997). Social perception of people may lead to stereotyping. In the cognitive theory of stereotyping, the idea of a special psychological mechanism was found: "one rule-based categorizer can block out those associations and make deductions" (Pinker, 2003, p. 203).

Social Media

Social-media networks as a special phenomenon have significantly changed the world's landscape. The interaction of interlocutors is presently based on the Internet, mobile Internet, mobile phones, and various social media, which have dramatically changed the attitude to communication and became a turning point for IC in general. Social media substantially impacted on networked societies in many countries with China presently booming. Chinese have created social-media platforms with distinctive characteristics, but at the same time these platforms also have some similarity to widely spread social-networking sites like Facebook, Twitter, or YouTube. For example, Qzone has some features close to MySpace; Sina Weibo (meaning Chinese "Microblogging") has traits of Facebook and Twitter. Renren (meaning "people") has similar functions as Facebook. "Chinese consumers follow the same decision-making journey as their peers in other countries, and the basic rules for engaging with them effectively are reassuringly familiar" (Chiu, Ip & Silverman, 2012, paragraph 1). More and more often, social networks are applied as an instrument in education, including home education (http://www.familyeducation.ru/; http://www.mouse.org/?gclid=CJL76_ xrQCFcl8c Aod4XcAjg). According to Suthiwartnarueput and Wasanasomsithi (2012), application of Facebook as a social networking instrument brought very good results in English grammar and writing and significantly enhanced the students' language competence. Sawyer and Chen (2012) reported interesting results of social media impact on intercultural adaptation among international students who overcame adjustment challenges, became aware of stereotypes, and integrated into the host culture, still feeling tight connection with the home culture.

Social media are very popular in advertizing and marketing; new horizons are promised to appear in 2013: "As you are planning for 2013, your business will find itself facing questions concerning the social impact of your business and brand" (Kallas, 2013, paragraph 2). Social media were more often used for political goals, especially since 2003 onwards. For example, due to social media 'colorful revolutions' took place. Pfister and Soliz (2011) enumerate several of them e.g., "Rose (Georgia, 2003), Orange (Ukraine, 2004–2005), Saffron (Burma, 2007), Green (Iran, 2009), and Jasmine (Tunisia, 2011)" (p. 246). Pfister and Soliz (2011) suggest that "these revolutions were not only televised but blogged, photographed, videoed, and, later, twittered" (p. 247). The authors draw attention to the role of computer mediated protests which fueled "intercultural communication on a world-historic scale" (p. 247).

Some authors reconsider IC in light of networking. Thus, Pfister and Soliz (2011) drew attention to changes in IC caused by social networking. The authors give four interconnected arguments to illustrate their idea: "(1) producing new public fora capable of (2) hosting rich, multimodal "spaces" of contact on (3) a scale of many-to-many communication that (4) challenges traditional modes of representation" (p. 246). Shuter (2012) succinctly outlined the present day cause of intercultural transformations all over the world: these are new media which have triggered contacts of people from different cultures. The researcher specifically captured attention to the changes from "face-to-face encounters" to instantaneous "communication with others regardless of geo-political boundaries, time, or space" (p. 219). Shuter (2012) pronounced these amplitudinous changes 'the revolution' and further introduced "Intercultural New Media Studies (INMS)" as a new field with the goal to explore "the intersection between ICT's and intercultural communication" (p. 220).

3. Methods

Participants

Participants were 4 international students pursuing the Master's degree in the Russian language and culture at a large university in Eastern Russia. According to the curriculum, the course "Introduction to the theory of Intercultural communication" was included among other disciplines. Demographically, their age ranged from 23 to 24; there were one male and three females. Three of them were Chinese and one was Japanese. As the teacher/researcher of the course, I invited the graduate students to participate in the pilot study. I promised the students to keep their names anonymous; nobody else except the teacher could know their names. The graduate students gave their oral consent to participate in this study. For this purpose, the names were alphabetically and numerically coded. Anonymity induced students to be open and to give direct answers.

Questionnaire Design and Administration

This pilot study employed a designed written questionnaire which focused on the phenomenon of culture shock and intercultural categories (values, stereotypes, acculturation/adaptation, and social media). The goal was to see if the participants experienced culture shock on various stages or not, and to observe whether the graduate students' progress was impacted by social-media or not. For this purpose, the students were asked to answer questions concerning their feelings relative to the stages of culture shock. Then the participants focused on their values compared to the Russian ones and described their perception of images of people from neighboring countries in general (Russian, Japanese, and Chinese); my purpose was to elicit their stereotypes. The next procedure concentrated on the way the graduate students used social media, networks, how often they spoke with their "friends," and how helpful social media were for their progress in the Russian language and culture and if, in their opinion, there were any intercultural changes. In mid-term (semester), the questionnaire was administered in the classroom to enhance the questionnaire return. The participants were allocated 90 minutes for their answers.

4. Results

Experiencing Culture Shock

Theoretically, the numbers of stages of culture shock significantly vary (from three to eight stages). When asked if they experienced culture shock all the graduate students admitted that they did experience culture shock arriving to Russia. The results of how the students went through the stages are in the table below.

Table 1: Going through the stages of culture shock

Culture shock stages	A1	B2	C3	D4
Honeymoon	+	+	+	+
Crisis	+	+	+	+
Recovery	+	+	+	-
Adaptation	+	+	+	-

Going through all the stages one can follow the graduate students' experience, learning and overcoming challenges.

The Honeymoon Stage

Let us see what the students' perceptions and feelings were at specific stages. What were their feelings at the Honeymoon stage? All the four students went through this stage. The sojourners experienced various feelings in the target country, which is seen as follows in the students' writing.

Student A1:
Before I came to Russia, I thought that this was one of the most beautiful countries. I thought about it only positively. I was not disappointed coming to Russia though the customs, behavior and some other things were quite different and sometimes unexpected. But I was happy.

Student B2:
I am so glad to be in Russia where I dreamed to study the language. I would like to know much more about Russian cultural customs.

Student C3:
I intend to do business in Russia and am glad to be here. I am "swallowing" everything around me, people in the streets, parks, and a lot of automobiles. I am so excited. Social nets are very important in modern world. They are inalienable part both of communication between friends, relatives, acquaintances and business partners. I use Facebook to speak

English with my friends all over the world. I like LiveJournal it helps me to practice Russian. What I like about the social media is that there are serious topics that are discussed, for example, education and business. I am going to be a businessman when I graduate from the university and will do business with Russian companies and I have to know life, culture, the way they do business.

Student D4:

Russia is an interesting country. I like some things, but I hate when people ask me about something and I cannot answer. I wish I knew Russian. Sometimes I feel lonely and miss home. I had expected quite different conditions in the dorm.

Crisis Stage

All four students went through the crisis stage with different results. The degree of their perception and feelings significantly differed: students A1, B2, and C3 could overcome the 'strange' phenomena, contrary to student D4. It was difficult for them to understand the reason why they were homesick, though at the beginning they liked being in the host country. Despite their low mood, homesickness and misunderstandings, the three participants stayed in Russia, which was impossible for student D4. The students shared their feelings about the first weeks in a new culture, a new city, a new university.

Student A1:

I felt lonely, missed my family and I would like to see my friends and I wanted to talk with them. I could not eat the food, which was so different from ours. I was glad when I knew that there were many cafes serving Chinese and Japanese food. I hope to get accustomed to the Russian food soon. The language is so different from ours, though took Russian classes at home. I like to hear how it sounds and intensively learn it. I felt as if I had lost something.

Student B2:

I was so happy the first days here, but now I'd like to be at home just for a day or two and then back. The language is a great challenge but I like to learn it; it is beautiful.

Student C3:

My first feeling when I came to the city of about a million people I was surprised to find out that there were not so many people in the streets, but there were too many cars. I noticed that people crossed the street (not equipped with traffic lights) without watching if there were cars or not; I was afraid to behave like this and had to stand and wait when all the cars go, but sometimes it was an endless stream of cars... Very strange!

Student D4:

Strange language; strange people; strange food; everybody is ineffective in Russia. I want to go home.

Recovery Stage

The recovery stage was overcome by all three graduate students when minor problems (shopping, transportation etc.) did not represent trouble any more. The culture of a host country becomes much clearer. One more factor was helpful – a better knowledge of the Russian language. The difference in conceptualization of the environment and "strange" behavior ("help" that was forbidden in China to give a ready answer at the exams to a person who asked about; in Russia, it is also forbidden, but some students do it) kept on surprising the three students. For example, student C3 was astounded when he was invited to a picnic. These cases are given below.

Student A1:

We were taking an exam last semester and I was sitting near a Russian graduate student who turned and asked for "help." By it the student meant to give an answer to what he failed to know. I think this is just laziness and I am not going to encourage it.

Student B2:

I came to my Russian friend and asked him to borrow his jacket because I was going to invite my girl-friend to a party. My friend said he cannot lend it to me. Next time we sat in the classroom and I took his small drinking water bottle and drank the water, he was surprised and did not even touch the bottle any more. The Russians are greedy, I thought.

Student C3:

I dressed up wearing my best white suit and black shirt and was shocked that the Russian students wore jeans as if we were going to pick up potatoes in the fields. I asked why they wore jeans. We are going to have some rest… they explained to me and I felt better… But next time when I was invited to an official meeting I noticed that the Russians wore clean and beautiful suits.

Acculturation/Adaptation Stage

Acculturation, also called adaptation and biculturalism, is defined as "full recovery with presupposed ability to function in two cultures with confidence" (Kohls, 1984, p. 67). Or as "…the process of becoming adapted to a new culture. A reorganization of thinking and feeling, not to mention communication, is necessary." (Brown, 1994, p. 33). In other models, this stage is known as Citizen. (Acton & Walker de Felix, 1994). This is the final, most important stage for sojourners since at this stage a person either uses highly restricted pidgin language or reaches the "acculturation threshold" (Acton & Walker de Felix, 1994, p.21), interiorizes and accepts a new culture, becomes almost bicultural. Still other investigators claim that sojourners keep on undergoing frustration and depression that is why the fourth stage is recognized by them as Further Culture Shock, or Mental Isolation stage. Archer (1991) assumed that visitors at this stage feel "disdain and anger against the host culture… self-doubt… resentment over loss of status… disappointment in oneself and/or the host culture" (p. 20).

Moving to a different culture is always accompanied, on one hand, with many amazing, extraordinary encounters and, on the other hand, with misunderstandings and failures in intercultural communication. Sojourners have to undergo a universal process of acculturation to the target culture. Understood as the gradual adaptation to a new culture through cognitive processes, acculturation is a highly complicated cognitive phenomenon.

Comparing Values

Individuals keep values as mental structures in collective unconsciousness, which creates various world views. The students were asked to juxtapose the Russian values with their own. Their answers are given in Table 2 which provides contrasting perception of the same values.

Comparing Russian values and their own ones the three students evaluated them both positively and negatively. For example, all three sojourners were unanimous about the value of hospitality in Russia ranking it rather highly. The two students evaluated the "love of dogs" also very positively. As for the attitude to work, time, money and vodka, the students evaluated them as highly negative.

Table 2: Comparing Values

Russian Values	Student A1	Student B2	Student C3
Work	Japanese are more industrious/ hard-working, Russians are not very industrious	Russians do not experience stress; in China, each person treats work diligently; many people work from morning to night	There is a great competitiveness among people instead of the joy of life like in Russia
Time	In Japan there is a phrase: "Russian Time." Japanese always come on time.	Russians are a little bit late. Chinese come a little bit earlier or on time.	Time is perceived more indifferently by Russians than Chinese. Russians are sometimes late.
Hospitality	Russians are more hospitable than Japanese. Russians like to invite people to their homes. The hosts cook a lot of food.	Hospitality is very high; Chinese do not like to invite people to their home, they prefer to meet at restaurants.	Whenever guests come, the hosts will treat guests with very tasty food.
Money	not mentioned	Russians prefer to receive the salary and immediately spend it.	Chinese receive the salary and keep it in the bank for th e future.

continued...

Russian Values	Student A1	Student B2	Student C3
Vodka	All Russians like vodka, but Japanese do not like to drink.	Russians like vodka, which became a symbol of Russia. In the streets I see a lot of drunkards. In China, I have never seen such situation, maybe there is, but not a lot.	To drink much beer or vodka is harmful for the health that is the reason that Russia males' longevity is so short. In China people do not drink so much.
Love of dogs	not mentioned	Russians think that the dog is a friend of a human being. I am touched to see such attitude. I am thankful to those babushkas who love the life. In China there are restaurants where the cooks prepare very tasty dog meat. I wish to see our babushkas who like Russian babushkas would take the dogs out in the streets of C hina."	Russians love animals, I often saw elderly women feeding homeless dogs.

continued...

Russian Values	Student A1	Student B2	Student C3
Family	not mentioned	For Russians family is a priority in their life but work and studies is less important; for Chinese family is less important because if we do not have work it will be difficult to build up a happy family, to take commitments.	Russian marriages are based on love, they ignore social borders. But Chinese definitely take other factors into consideration except pure love. Because life is not a fairy tale, but a reality, it means that one cannot keep love without other things.

Graduate Students' Stereotypes

Most students had some images about the country they were going to enter. These images were stereotypes, as a rule, which are difficult to overcome. The students' stereotypical perceptions are given in the table on the next page.

Table 3 Speaking about Hetero-stereotypes

Hetero-stereo-types	Student A1	Student B2	Student C3
All Russians like vodka	All Russians like vodka.	Russians drink alcohol even in the streets.	It's a symbol of Russia.
Cold	It is always cold.	There is no summer in Russia.	not mentioned
Look intimi-dating	not mentioned	Intimidating appea-rance, they never smile.	Russians do not smile to strangers, but if they meet an acquaintance they smile.
Russians are always sad	Always sad.	not mentioned	As it seen in fiction, Russians are always sorrow-ful and lamentable.

Though stereotypes can be positive, neutral, and negative, the graduate students' perception of hetero-stereotypes (perception of "others") was preferably negative: "All Russians like vodka" (A1); Russians drink alcohol even in the streets (B2); "It's [vodka] a symbol of Russia" (C3).

Table 4: Speaking about Auto-stereotypes

Auto-stereo-types	Student A1	Student B2	Student C3
Hard-working	Japanese are hardworking.	Chinese are hardworking.	Chinese work day and night.

continued...

Auto-stereo-types	Student A1	Student B2	Student C3
Modest	Japanese are modest.	Chinese are always polite and always say hello to teachers even if they do know them personally or see for the first time.	[no answer given]
Obeying women	Japanese women always obey men.	Chinese marriage can be without love.	There are marriages of convenience in China.
Samurai's soul	Samurai's soul still exists.	not mentioned	not mentioned
Vodka	Some Japanese like to drink sake but nobody drinks it in the streets.	Chinese males drink beer or vodka for the purpose of communication.	When Chinese drink vodka they go to a café.

The auto-stereotypes are mostly positive: Japanese are hardworking (A1), Chinese are hardworking (B2), and Chinese work day and night (C3).

The Usage and Significance of Social Networks

The assignment was to answer the questions 1) Do you use social media and if yes, name them, please? 2) How often do you 'speak' with your friends? 3) How helpful social media were for your study? 4) What role did social networking play for you in the process of communication?

Student A1:

Most often I use Facebook, I think this is the most popular network. But I also use Russian nets (vKontakte and Odnoklassniki) to learn Russian language and culture. I talk with my friends rather often but usually not for practical contacts (such as home tasks, schedules, for example), but for sharing some ideas, thoughts. Sometimes special incidents in daily life which is not likely to happen often. Each time I felt that my Russian was becoming better and better. I started understanding Russian character, their values, and customs.

I did not even think that I stereotyped; I believed that all Russians liked vodka, and after getting acquainted with other students, visiting their family, I understood that it was a stereotype. But most useful was communication on the net, first, I exchanged opinions on Facebook, then I used vKontakte and Odnoklassniki. And it was very useful for my major and getting rid of stereotypes. My friends live everywhere in the world but most of them live in Japan (as I'm a Japanese). I usually upload my "status" both in English and Japanese, since about half of my friends are not Japanese and understand only English (and some other languages). Social nets are very important in modern world. They are part both of communication between friends, relatives, acquaintances and business partners.

Student B2:

I communicate with my friends, acquaintances living in different countries in the world (China, Russia, Japan, Korea, and Germany). It takes a lot of time! I usually use Russian, as this is my major, to speak with Russians living in Russia and abroad, we discuss the problems not only about the Russian language but also about life in Russia and customs and behavioral patterns. I also use Chinese network Renren (initially created specifically to the students) to talk to my Chinese friends at home and abroad. Sometimes I talk in English.

The networking helped me polishing the Russian language acquiring new vocabulary which I like a lot because I learnt slang words (I don't think that teachers could let me learn slang words). Communicating through networking sites showed me different sides of the Russian culture. I talked over the love of dogs in Russia with my Chinese friends, but they tried to avoid this topic.

Stereotypes? I did not realize that some images I had before coming to Russia and during some time spent there were stereotypes. When we discussed stereotypes in class, I started thinking about them. I have a lot of friends on the net and communicate with friends in China, Russia, Japan,

Korea, and Germany using Chinese, Russian and English. I was surprised how many stereotypes I used to have!

I usually use Facebook but more often I use Livejournal which is more useful for me because this has a Russian version. I feel free to say whatever I want and like that most interlocutors speak under nicks, which gives the opportunity to speak openly and discuss any problem directly. Social media helped orient in Russian culture. I was too shy at the beginning to ask somebody to help, addressing the net helped with acculturation.

Student C3:

I talk with my "friends." But there is one phenomenon that there is no clear definition or understanding who is real friend and who is not in social net. I use Facebook to speak English with my friends all over the world. My friends live all over the world. Even in neighbor room. I like LiveJournal, it helps me to practice Russian. I speak with my Russian friend on FB and I know it better and better. This helps me to practice my Russian and I learn expressions I met for the first time. If there is no time to talk with friends [face to face] it is good to talk in net. Now I understand what people in the street speak. Chinese friends in Chinese, my native language.

"I had so many stereotypes about Russians and now they are gone. I understood that stereotypes exist not only in the physical world, but online too, as I read on the net."

What I like about the social media is that there are serious topics that are discussed, for example, education and business. I am going to be a businessman when I graduate from the university and will do business with Russian companies and I have to know life, culture, and the way they do business.

5. Discussion and Conclusion

The goal of this pilot study was to identify and analyze the experience of international graduate students (Chinese and Japanese) in the acculturation/adaptation process and the way social networks impacted their progress. Central to this perspective was interaction of culture shock (with four stages, including acculturation/adaptation) and social media.

The pilot study started from the "classic model" of culture shock with the four stages. The tentative analysis of graduate students' responses to the new culture was almost "classical": all of them experienced culture shock of various degrees gradually going through the stages. For example, Student D4's culture shock was very serious, D4 could not overcome the new culture and had to leave. Student C3 experienced culture shock and cognitive dissonance (Festinger, 1999): what C3 conceptualized as a "proper" behavior for picnicking being dressed up while Russian students conceptualized the same thing in contrasting terms. The culture shock of picnicking was a blend of cognitive (cognizing a new culture was very difficult and the student started thinking that it was a very strange attitude of Russians to their rest. C3's surprise lessened when Russian students explained that they wear comfortable clothing for picnics), affective (C3 was highly agitated and depressed), cultural (C3 could not fully understand Russian culture at this stage), axiological (C3 evaluated the way Russian people spent their weekends and compared with the Chinese culture), and behavioral (new behavior patterns of wearing the proper clothes).

Discussing Interaction of Social Media and Intercultural Categories: The Impact of Social Media on Culture Shock

The Honeymoon Stage

What were the students' feelings at the Honeymoon stage? At this stage, the affective aspect prevailed: all four students went through it. Thus, student A1 wrote in the questionnaire: "Before I came to Russia, I thought that this was one of the most beautiful countries. I thought about [it] only positively;" student B2 was happy to be in the target culture: "I am so glad to be in Russia where I dreamed to study the language;" student C3 was very excited: "I intend to do business in Russia and am glad to be here." It was found that the affective aspect correlated with the content of the Honeymoon stage: the sojourns were euphoric, elated, enthusiastic, and were interested in learning the new host culture. But student D4's response was out of this highly positive frames: admitting some interest in a new culture, D4 hesitated in the evaluation of it, which can be seen in the following: "I like some things, but I hate when people ask me about something and I cannot answer ... Sometimes I feel lonely and miss home. I had expected quite different conditions in the dorm. Student D4 was less enthusiastic than the rest of the group, could not properly understand what was wrong; was disappointed with the dormitory, could not answer the questions asked by other people of the target country; avoided contacts with Russian people and wrote that there was a great need in learning Russian. When questioned on the use of social media, the students answered "yes" and named popular networks: Facebook and Renren (Chinese network, initially created specifically for the students).

Crisis Stage

All of the students went through the crisis stage also known as Culture Shock, proper (Lebedko, 2002) experiencing 'classical' feelings (frustration, a physical and psychological response; nervousness, homesickness, withdrawal, an attempt to only see friends from their own countries; loss of some competences, such as the ability to work effectively, etc.). The environment was quite different from their own due to contrast in perception, as known from Humboldt's work (1984). This stage is regarded as the most difficult one when sojourns lose their enthusiasm due to the differences in cultures.

The three students (A1, B2, and C3) could overcome the crisis stage; attended classes and worked hard, though they were uncomfortable: student A1 wrote: "I felt lonely, missed my family... could not eat the food;" student B2 wanted "to be at home just for a day or two and then back;" "I was surprised to find out that there were not so many people in the streets..." However, student D4 could not go out of the personal crisis: one of the reasons was the difficulty of the Russian language and "strange" culture. The crisis of student D4 was very serious followed by missing classes, unexpected weeping, irritability, stereotyping of all the Russians (everybody is ineffective in Russia). Finally, D4 dropped out from the Master's degree program and had to return back home.

The use of social media at the crisis stage had widened compared to the honeymoon stage: graduate students added three Russian networks to Facebook and Renren: Facebook, Renren (Chinese network), vKontakte [in contact], Odnoklassniki [Classmates], Livejournal [live journal]. The graduate students employed social media for various reasons: to enhance their Russian ("I like LiveJournal it helps me to practice Russian"); to chat and speak with friends ("I use Facebook to speak English with my friends all over the world."); to get some moral support from home ("I also use Chinese network Renren to talk to my Chinese friends at home and abroad.").

Student A1 employed Facebook as the most popular network and also used "vKontakte" "Russian nets to learn Russian language and culture." The student was very positive and started learning Russian from what could be found on the net in addition to classroom learning. A1 was highly motivated at the crisis stage. Student B2 often used not only Russian social networks to learn the language better (Livejournal), but also Chinese network Renren (initially created specifically for the students) to talk to Chinese friends at home and abroad. "Sometimes I talk in English (Facebook)." B2 was very active and shared the news in three languages. Student C3 complained: I talk with my "friends." But there is one phenomenon that there is no clear definition or understanding who is real friend and who is not in social net. C3 asked the question about the word "friend" that presently connotes something vague and blurred: the student was right to ask that question "who is real friend and who is not in social net?" When people communicate on the net they sometimes speak under nicknames and interlocutors do not know who they are: this is one more reason to redefine this term. It is interesting to find the same idea that correlates with another study (Sawyer & Chen, 2012) discussing ambiguity of the term "friend" and pointing to an acquisition of a different connotation.

Recovery Stage

The recovery stage, sometimes called Adjustment/Initial adjustment/ Gradual adjustment, is characterized by gradual growth of self-reliance and self-confidence, feelings of hopefulness and ability to perform well.

Minor problems-- shopping, transportation etc. do not represent trouble any more. The culture of a host country becomes much clearer, sojourners start interpreting subtle cultural clues and regarding it as normal. One more factor was helpful—a better knowledge of the Russian language, which gave the opportunity to ask Russian friends questions about this or that 'strange' behavior of the Russian people.

Answering the question "How often do you 'speak' with your friends?" student A1 stated that it happens rather often, but they shared ideas and not home tasks. B2 underscored that communicating with so many friends and acquaintances in many countries (China, Russia, Japan, Korea, and Germany) takes a lot of time but it is worth doing. C3 was also rather talkative with the friends who "live all over the world. Even in neighbor room." As one can see from this example, the notions of space, distance, remote cities are acquiring new connotations. The world is "shrinking"? N generation perceive the world quite differently be it the whole world or an adjoining room.

Acculturation/Adaptation Stage

This is the stage at which sojourners reach "acculturation threshold" (Acton & Walker de Felix, 1994, p. 21), interiorize and accept a new culture, and become almost bicultural. At the Acculturation/Adaptation stage, the three students felt rather comfortable and functioning well in the Russian culture. It was important for the students to accept this new culture in order to be functional interculturally in both cultures.

The answers to the question "How helpful were social media for your study?" revealed their ability to speak Russian and understand Russian culture. Their Russian was significantly improved; they learned a lot about Russian culture, could express themselves. The following citation from their answers confirm it. Student A1 used "Russian nets (vKontakte and Odnoklassniki) to learn Russian language and culture" along with Facebook. Student B2 considered that "The networking helped me polishing the Russian language acquiring new vocabulary which I like a lot because I learnt slang words (I don't think that teachers could let me learn slang words)." Student C3 used LiveJournal (it is mainly in Russian) and said it helped to speak Russian adding "I learn expressions I met for the first time" which shows the feelings of good command of the language. C3 is proud to "understand what people in the street speak."

The inference here is as follows: the concept of "culture shock" is an inalienable part of culture cognition; practically each person goes through those stages before reaching the adaptation and bilingualism stage. Three students in this pilot study went through all the stages and overcame culture shock. Judging from their answers, they became bicultural.

The Impact of Social Media on Values

The analysis of Russian values compared with the graduate students' respective cultures showed various conceptualizations in contacting cultures: for example, in their view, work is of greater value for Japanese and Chinese than for Russians. Generalization led Student C3 to believe that all Russians are lazy, they do not value work. Recognizing the difference, I regard culture as a continuum at both ends of which are contrasting values (for some people, work is not so important, but for many others work is in the first place, and these people toil devotedly day and night. The value time is contrasting: A1 wrote that the Japanese conceptualized Russian attitude toward time as Russian time with conceptual signs of more relaxed time; for example, being late for the meeting is not a great "sin". Affective and behavioral components of attitudes to different values showed that after having lived in Russia for two years student B2 would rather prefer the Russian value "love of dogs". In the student's voice citation: "Russians think that the dog is a friend of a human being. I am touched to see such attitude. I am thankful to those babushkas who love the life. In China there are restaurants where the cooks prepare very tasty dog meat. I wish to see our babushkas who like Russian babushkas would take the dogs out in the streets of China." We see that the student interiorized this Russian value; it shows affective mode, a highly emotional reaction of the student. The Russian value Hospitality was regarded as more positive than in their respective cultures. Student A1 wrote: "Russians like to invite people to their homes. The hosts cook a lot of food; but Japanese do not like to invite people to their home, they prefer to meet at restaurants." Student B2 was also positive emotionally writing: "Hospitality is very high" and C3 wrote:

"Whenever guests come, the hosts will treat them with very tasty food."
They appreciated the Russian value hospitality.

The value time contrast is based on a cultural factor: A1 could not
understand why Russian people are very often late for classes and meetings
and wrote that Japanese conceptualize Russian attitude toward time as
Russian time. In this context time can be regarded as having conceptual
signs of 'more relaxed time'; for example, being late for the meeting is
not a great sin in Russian high-context culture, which means that the
time is not so seriously treated. This Russian value is regarded as negative
by B2 ("Russians are a little bit late.") and C3 ("Time is perceived more
indifferently by Russians that Chinese."). All three graduate students agreed
in their evaluation of this value. One more value, vodka, was viewed as
negative: A1 contrasted Russian and Japanese attitude to vodka saying
"All Russians like vodka, but Japanese do not like to drink"; B2 considered
vodka "a symbol of Russia" and was unpleasantly surprised: "In the streets,
I see a lot of drunkards." C3 reminded "to drink much beer or vodka
is harmful" and concluded his morality: "that is the reason that Russia
males' longevity is also short," adding that "In China, people do not drink
so much." Other values, money and family, were also compared with
their own cultures: B2 and C3 unanimously contrasted the value money:
"Russians prefer to receive the salary and immediately spend it;" "Chinese
receive the salary and keep it in the bank for the future." B2 presumed
that "For Russians family is a priority in their life but work and studies is
less important; for Chinese, family is less important…" C3 underscored
that "Russian marriages are based on love, they ignore social borders. But
Chinese definitely take other factors into consideration except pure love…"

Juxtaposing the values the students distinguished the differences between
Russian and their own cultures, which helped them to understand both
their own culture and the Russian culture. They accepted some values
and rejected other values. The result of this comparison was deeper
understanding of values.

The following question was asked with the purpose of eliciting the way
the international graduate students perceive, apply and regard social
media: 4) What role, for you personally, did social networking played in
the process of communication? Answering this question, A1 considered
that the social media were very helpful for her personally because due to

speaking with friends on Facebook and two Russian social nets (vKontakte and Odnoklassniki), "Each time I felt that my Russian was becoming better and better. I started understanding Russian character, their values, customs." Communicating with friends on the net A1 polished not only Russian, but also English, which became an international language in the world. B2 acknowledged the impact of social nets: "Communicating through networking sites showed me different sides of the Russian culture." As for the values, cognizing a new culture B2 interiorized the love to animals and expressed it with great emotions: "in China, there are restaurants where the cooks prepare very tasty dog meat. I wish to see our babushkas who like Russian babushkas would take the dogs out in the streets of China." B2 shared this idea with the friends in China using Chinese network Renren: "I talked over the love of dogs in Russia with my Chinese friends, but they tried to avoid this topic." We do not know a clear answer. Student C3 also mentioned this value: "Russians love animals, I often saw elderly women feeding homeless dogs." C3's emotions were not so explicit to say if it was accepted or not. The reaction might be negative, because values are not accepted when somebody offers them, a person has to evaluate it before he or she accepts it. But at least we saw the change of attitude toward the dogs.

To sum up, values are presently treated differently under the impact of social media. The major factor of influence is that values now are more dynamic due to the exchange of ideas. They are shared by bloggers from various communities. Tentative analysis of the values in this pilot study demonstrated the acceptance of such Russian values as hospitality, love of animals (dogs). Values are becoming less stable, I think.

The Impact of Social Media on Stereotypes

The controversy of stereotyping is in its strong bias of stereotypical assumptions, which is due to different world views and culturally specific perception. The international graduate students from China and Japan arrived to Russia with many stereotypes strengthened by the cognitive process of "anchoring," that is determined as dependence on one trait or a piece of information (the "anchor"). Speaking about hetero-stereotypes, student A1 asserted that "All Russians like vodka"; B2 affirmed: "Russians drink alcohol even in the streets." C3 argued: "Vodka is a symbol of Russia." In these unanimous answers one can clearly see anchoring in the phrases above. In the case we are discussing, the stable stereotype of the Russians is that they drink vodka all days long. This is the obvious case of anticipation categories, prejudices, and overgeneralization, which accompany selective perception. Hetero-stereotypes are usually negative. For example, two students A1 and B2 stereotyped about the climate in Russia: "It is always cold" in Russia and "There is no summer in Russia." One student (B2) categorized Russians as intimidating: "Intimidating appearance, they never smile. C2 experienced cognitive dissonance, mental conflict in a situation when new information is not compatible or contradicts to the interlocutor's assumptions about the self and the world. But C3 correctly objected to him explaining that "Russians do not smile to strangers, but if they meet an acquaintance they smile." Two students categorized Russians as being "always sad" (A1); the second student referred to the same categorization but the stereotype was taken from fiction: As it is seen in fiction, Russians are always sorrowful and lamentable (C3).

At the same time, almost all auto-stereotypes are highly positive: in A1, B2 and C3's views, "Japanese are hardworking," "Chinese are hardworking" and "Chinese work day and night." Among auto-stereotypes there are as follows "Japanese are modest" (A1); "Chinese are always polite" (B2). "Japanese women always obey men" (A1). "There are marriages of convenience in China." These auto-stereotypes about themselves are characterized by overgeneralization; the graduate students ignored differences among individuals.

The question was asked about the role of social network platforms and how useful they were in the process of communication? Student A1 admitted believing in stereotypes: "I did not even think that I stereotyped; I believed that all Russians liked vodka, and after getting acquainted with other students, visiting their families, I understood that it was a stereotype." A1 dwelt on the role of social media: "But most useful was communication on the net, first, I exchanged opinions on Facebook, then I used vKontakte and Odnoklassniki. And it was very useful for my major and getting rid of stereotypes." B2 wrote about the experience of using social media: "Communicating through networking sites showed me different sides of the Russian culture." In B2's views, stereotypes were something too far from real life: "Stereotypes? I did not realize that some images I had before coming to Russia and during some time spent there were stereotypes. When we discussed stereotypes in class, I started thinking about them. I have a lot of friends on the net and communicate with friends in China, Russia, Japan, Korea, and Germany using Chinese, Russian and English. I was surprised how many stereotypes I used to have!" C3 was very laconic this time: "I had so many stereotypes about Russians and now they are gone." C3 added: "I understood that stereotypes exist not only in the physical world, but online too, as I read on the net."

Social media impacted on graduate students' stereotypes: all of them did not treat them seriously, did not pay much attention until the class focused on stereotypes, found friends, visited their friends' homes, and addressed the social media. The realization of this highly controversial category of stereotypes, awareness of the role of networking sites regarding stereotypes was beneficial for graduate students; they all considered that stereotypes were gone.

An additional question was asked about graduate students' perception of social media in general. Student A1: "Social nets are very important in modern world. They are part both of communication between friends, relatives, acquaintances and business partners." Student B2 explained that "social media helped orient in Russian culture; I was too shy at the beginning to ask somebody to help; addressing the net helped with acculturation." Student C3 responded as the follows: "What I like about the social media is that there are serious topics that are discussed, for example, education and business. I am going to be a businessman when I graduate from the university I will do business with Russian companies and I have to know life, culture, the way they do business." C3 was highly motivated and was planning his future business and took all the opportunities including social media.

This tentative analysis of intercultural categories from the social media perspective brought out a number of key findings that have been presented in the pilot study. First, students addressed social media less at the honeymoon stage (Facebook and Renren), gradually widening social networking: vKontakte [in contact], Odnoklassniki [Classmates], Livejournal [live journal] at recovery and acculturation stages. Second, they pointed out that speaking with friends on the nets was supporting in their cultural failures; stated the enhancement of the Russian language. Third, the students accepted some values (hospitality, love of dogs) and rejected others (attitude of Russians to time, alcohol, and work). Fourth, values were impacted by social media: values now are more dynamic. Values are shared by bloggers from various communities. Fifth, the three students became bicultural thanks to social media (could understand even street talk, knew slang words, etc.). Sixth, the word "friend" connotes something vague and blurred (C3: "who is real friend and who is not in social net?"). Seventh, social media along with discussion of stereotypes in class, acquaintance with the Russian friends and visiting their homes deeply impacted on stereotypes (nobody of them treated stereotypes seriously). Eighth, the graduate students more deeply understood the role of social media.

The limitations of the pilot research were the following: a small number of international graduate students who participated in this survey. A larger number of participants could have broadened the results of the interaction of "classical" categories of intercultural communication and new social media. A larger research could bring more reliable results of social media study. For further research the interview and reflection on the interaction will be applied.

References

Acton, W. & Walker de Felix, J. (1994). Acculturation and mind. In J. M. Valdes, (ed.). *Culture bound. Bridging the cultural gap in language teaching.* Cambridge, UK: Cambridge University Press. Pp. 20-32.

Adler, S. (1993). *Multicultural communication skills in the classroom.* Boston, MA: Allyn & Bacon.

Archer, C. M. (1991). *Living strangers in the USA: Communicating beyond culture.* Englewood Cliffs, N.J.: Prentice Hall Regents.

Barrett, D. N. (1961). Value problems and present contributions. In D.N. Barrett (ed.). *Values in America.* South Bend, IN.: University of Notre Dame Press.

Brislin, R. (1993). *Understanding culture's influence on behavior.* Fort Worth, T: Harcourt Brace College Publishers.

Brown, H. D. (1994). Learning a second language. In J. M. Valdes, ed. *Culture bound. Bridging the cultural gap in language teaching.* Cambridge, UK: Cambridge university press, pp. 33–48.

Cheese, P. (2008). Netting the Net Generation. *Businessweek.com.* Retrieved from http://www.businessweek.com/managing/ content/ mar2008/

Chiu, C., Ip, C. & Silverman, A. (2012). Understanding social media in China. Retrieved from http://www.mckinseyquarterly.com/ Understanding_social_media_in_China_2961

Chiu, C., Lin, D. & Silverman, A. (2012). China's social-media boom. McKinsey & Company survey.

Education. Retrieved from: http://www.familyeducation.ru/

Elligan, D. (2008). Stereotypes. In *Encyclopedia of race, ethnicity, and society.* Retrieved from http://sage-ereference.com/ethnicity/ Article_n532.html

Festinger, L. (1999). *Teoriya kognitivnogo dissonansa [The theory of cognitive dissonance].* Saint Petersburg, Russia: Yuventa.

Geertz, C. (1973). *The interpretation of cultures.* New York, NY: Basic Books.

Generation Y retrieved from: http://www.wordspy.com/categories/ demographics.asp

Gu, J. (2009). Theorizing about intercultural communication: Dynamic semiotic and memetic approaches to intercultural communication (a commentary). In Guo-Ming Chen & D. R. Heisey (Eds.). *Intercultural communication research,* 109–115. Beijing: Higher Education Press. v. 1.

Home education. Retrieved from: http://www.mouse.org/?gclid=CJL76_ xrQCFcl8cAod4XcAjg

Hong, Y.-Y., Chiu, C.-Y. (2001). Toward a paradigm shift: from cross-cultural differences in social cognition to social-cognitive mediation of cultural differences. *Social Cognition, Vol. 19* No.3., pp.181–96. Retrieved from: http://cat.inist.fr/?aModele=affichen&cps: dt=1098 953

Humboldt, W. (1984). *Izbrannye trudy v lingvisticheskikh issledovaniyakh [A selection of works in linguistic studies].* Moscow, Russia: Progress.

Ishii, S. (2006). Complementing contemporary intercultural communication research with East Asian socio-cultural perspectives and practices. *China Media Research.* # *2*(1), pp. 13–20.

Kallas, P. (2013). Dreamgrow social media & Internet marketing. Retrieved from http://www.dreamgrow.com/

Kluckhohn, C. (1961). The study of values. In D. Barrett (ed.). *Values in America.* South Bend, IN: University of Notre Dame Press.

Kohls, L. R. (1984*). Survival kit for overseas living.* Yarmouth, ME: Intercultural Press.

Lebedko, M. (2002). *Culture bumps: Overcoming misunderstandings in cross-cultural communication.* Khabarovsk, Russia: DV.IIYA Press.

Levine, D. R., Buxter, J. & McNulty, P. (1987). *The culture puzzle: Cross-cultural communication for English as a second language.* Englewood Cliffs, NJ: Prentice Hall Regents.

Lippmann, W. (1922). *Public opinion.* New York, NY: MacMillan.

McFedries, P. (2013). *Social networking fatigue. The word lover's guide to new words.* 1995-2013, Paul McFedries and Logophilia Limited. Retrieved from: http://www.wordspy.com/words/socialnetworkingfatigue.asp

Moore, J. R. (2006). Shattering stereotypes: A lesson plan for improving student attitudes and behavior towards minority groups. *The Social Studies (ERIC Accession # EJ744210),* pp. 35–39.

Oberg, K. (1954). *Culture shock.* Indianapolis, IN. Bobbs-Merrill Reprint Series in the Social Sciences. A-329.

Pfister, D. S. & Soliz, J. (2011). (Re)Conceptualizing intercultural communication in a networked society. *Journal of International and Intercultural Communication* 4:4. pp. 246–251.
doi: 10.1080/17513057.2011.598043

Piaget, J. (1998). Skhemy deistviia i usvoienie yazyka. [Schemes of activities and learning language]. In *Semiotics.* Blagoveschensk, Russia: I. A. Boduen de Kurtene BGK.

Pinker, S. (2003). *The blanks: The modern denial of human nature.* New York: NY Penguin Books.

Pinker, S. (2009). *How the mind works.* New York, NY: W.W. Norton & Company.

Robinson, E. A. (1997). The cognitive foundations of pragmatic principles: Implications for theories of linguistic and cognitive representation. In: Y. Nuyts & E. Pederson (eds.). *Language and conceptualization.* Cambridge, UK: Cambridge University Press, pp. 262–263

Samovar, L., Porter, R. & Stefani, L. (2000*). Communication between cultures.* Singapore: Reprint: Thompson Learning Asia and Foreign Language Teaching and Research Press.

Sawyer, R. & Chen, G.M. (2012). The impact of new social media on intercultural adaptation. In J. Radwańska-Williams and L. Lam, (eds). *Intercultural communication studies*, xxi: 2, pp. 151–169.

Scollon, R. & Scollon, S.W. (2000). *Intercultural communication: A discourse approach.* Beijing, China: Foreign Language Teaching and Research Press.

Seelye, H. N. (1994). *Teaching culture strategies for foreign language educators.* Skokie, IL. NTC

Seelye, H. N. & Seelye-James, A. (1996). *Culture Clash: Managing Multicultural World.* Lincolnwood, IL: NTC Business Books.

Shuter, R. (2012: November).Intercultural new media studies: The next frontier in intercultural communication. *Journal of Intercultural Communication Research.Vol. 41*, No. 3, pp. 219–237.

Stewart, E. & Bennett, M. (1991). *American cultural patterns*. Yarmouth, ME: Intercultural Press, Inc.

Suthiwartnarueput, T. & Wasanasomsithi, P. (2012) Effects of using Facebook as a medium for discussions of English grammar and writing of low-intermediate EFL students. *Electronic Journal of Foreign Language Teaching, Vol. 9*, No. 2, pp. 194–214.

Ting-Toomey, S. (1999). *Communicating across cultures*. New York, NY: The Guilford Press.

Zinchenko, V., Zusman, V. & Kirnoze. (2007). Mezhkul'turnaya Kommunikatsiia. Ot Sistemnogo Podkhoda k Sinergeticheskoi Paradigme. [*Intercultural communication. From systematic approach to synergetic paradigm*]. Moscow, Russia: Flinta: Nauka.

Part Two:
Central Asia

VI.   Political Uses of Social Media in Kazakhstan

John L. Couper
Journalism Department, KIMEP University, Almaty, Kazakhstan
Corresponding author: couperjohn@hotmail.com

Adil Nurmanov
Journalism Department,
International Information Technology University, Almaty, Kazakhstan
adil.nurmakov@gmail.com

Tyrone L. Adams
Jeddah College of Advertising,
Jeddah, Saudi Arabia
leemanadams@gmail.com

Abstract

Social media are becoming a central part of political power. This study surveys and analyzes how blogs, twitter, forums and other media are used by governmental, opposition, religious, and non-partisan groups in Kazakhstan, a relatively stable, ethnically-diverse and prosperous Central Asian nation. Despite some degree of media diversity, mass media and Internet systems are owned or controlled by the ruling party, a centralized government-constrained technology corporation, and/or wealthy individuals. Opposition parties are permitted but have little political power. Press freedom is limited. The Internet is used by about half of the population, and social media are popular, especially among young people and community groups. Many sites are monitored by official agencies, often in the name of preventing terrorism, and the government supports several official or controlled websites. Officeholders are encouraged to offer social media sites, a few of which are popular. Some private blogs are also widely read. Some civil society groups have a web presence, and many journalists have blogs. Several popular sites have been blocked or restricted, but official control over websites has become less overt and more sophisticated. A dramatic use of social media was during violent protests in a western, oil-producing region, when briefly the only local news sources were government-sponsored private blogs. Laws allow a circumscribed degree of Internet freedom, though not all legal freedoms are enforced. Recent laws have, if anything, further restricted online access by equating the Internet with regulated traditional media. The importance of political social media, including unbalanced struggles between governmental and opposition information, is likely to increase.

Keywords: social media, political communication, Kazakhstan, Internet regulation, opposition sites, blogs

1. Introduction

If a key source of political power is communication, this source has shifted very quickly toward social media. Communication channels such as twitter, Facebook, blogs, and other new media are reshaping the needs and capacities to communicate political messages. For example, many analysts credit the skillful use of social media as a major factor in the two most recent presidential elections, and a reason for the election success of Barack Obama (Wortham, J., 2012; Greengard, S. 2009).

In some cases, political groups or candidates have used the social media to gain leverage. In other cases, such as the Arab Spring (Alsayyad, 2012), online networks were used to counteract officially controlled media networks. Asia, including Central Asia, is also experiencing communication evolution at the pace of revolution.

This case study analyzes current political factors of social media, explaining the current situation, placing it into historical context, and extrapolating from the comments of many specialists in the field to suggest future trends in how social media might develop in the near future and beyond.

2. Background: The Republic of Kazakhstan

The world's largest landlocked country, with one of its lowest population densities, Kazakhstan has 15.5 million people, or less than six people per square kilometer. Most of its population lives along the southern strip that borders Turkmenistan and Uzbekistan, or in urban areas scattered around the country. As a result of many centuries of migration and population movements during the Soviet period, Kazakhstan has a wide number of ethnicities. Its population is currently dominated by ethnic Kazakhs (63.1%), with a substantial minority of Russians (23.7%), Uzbeks (2.9%) Ukrainians (2.1%) and Uygurs (1.4%) (CIA Factbook). The religious affiliation is Muslim 47%, Russian Orthodox 44%, Protestant 2%, other 7% (CIA Factbook). The influence and intensity of religion remains weak in general, although Islamic religious and social activities have grown significantly in recent years.

In the smaller cities and villages, the dominant language is Kazakh, the language that official policy strongly encourages. However, in practice the main language of commerce, education, science, and political dialogue is Russian. The use of English as a way to facilitate international interaction is being enthusiastically accepted by citizens across the country. The nation spends only 2.8% of its GDP on education, placing it 137th in the world, but literacy levels are 99.5 (CIA Factbook).

Part of the group of five post-Soviet nations of Central Asia, Kazakhstan has national and regional elections. Its economic center is Almaty, which was also the political center until 2011 when an exploding new capital was built in the northern city that was renamed Astana ("Capital" in the Kazakh language).

Kazakhstan has a wealth of natural resources, especially oil, gas, coal, uranium, and other minerals. Compared to Western nations the distribution of wealth is uneven, but is still far above that of other nations in Central Asia. Buoyed by extractive industries and agriculture, its economy is healthy, with an estimated GDP growth rate of 7.3%, 25th in the world (CIA Factbook).

Although Kazakhstan is more progressive socially and politically than the other Central Asian regions, Transparency International's Corruption Perceptions Index lists it as 120th among 182 countries; The World Bank's Worldwide Governance Indicators label Kazakhstan's levels of political participation, accountability, the rule of law, quality of regulations, and government efficiency as "poor" (World Bank WBI, 2012).

Inheriting the transportation and communication infrastructure of the Soviet Union, and with large recent investments, both are relatively well served within Kazakhstan. Still, among international organizations, the region has consistently low rankings in press freedom and transparency. Mass media facilities are almost totally owned by the Government, although some opposition and several independent news sources exist, both in print and broadcast. Government subsidies of "independent" news organizations, and vague threats that encourage self-censorship, make it impossible for most international organizations to consider the media open and free (democracy web, 2012).

Controls over the media are more than official: most mass media have direct ties to leading political and economic individuals. Disclosure of the true ownership of media vehicles is not required, but is often hidden behind front organizations. In effect, the ability of the media to challenge the established political and commercial interests is very limited, and professional journalists often comment that any reporting that does not suit the agenda of the publisher rarely reaches the page or the television screen.

But media are being transformed by the Internet. In the words of one young journalist, "Google changed everything." It is possible to see the Internet as the modern extension of the region's 2,500 year history as the hub of the "Silk Road." The Internet in Kazakhstan is very widely available and used, although in smaller towns and villages the bandwidth and cost reduce its function. The Internet penetration rate increased by 60 percent during 2010–11, up from a 0.7 percent rate in 2000 to more than 53 percent (8.6 million users) by the end of 2011 and a 60 percent growth against 2010, according to official figures, which some critics considered inflated (FOTN 2012).

With the economy's strength, and government encouragement and investment, the commercial development of the Internet has been dramatic. With its widely-dispersed population, the Internet has quickly become a key way for citizens to learn about and discuss social and political issues. The proportion of people who use the Internet at home, via WiFi and on mobile applications have increased. Although there are several Internet providers, by law Kazakhstan's main Internet provider KazakhTelecom controls much of the national network, meaning that it can quietly but firmly support government goals (FOTN 2012).

During 2011, controls over Internet access steadily increased, with more filtering of websites, new or renewed blocks on blog sites, increased surveillance at Internet cafés, and some physical assaults on bloggers and online journalists. Statements by officials suggest that this increase will continue and deepen (FOTN 2012).

Because of blocked web applications, political censorship, and the arrest of bloggers, Freedom House evaluates Kazakhstan's press freedom as "Not Free" overall and its Internet freedom "Partly Free." With higher numbers representing greater freedom, the nation's "Obstacles to Access" score is now 15 out of 25, "Limits on Content" 23 out of 35, and "Violations of User Rights" 20 out of 40 (FOTN 2012).

One of the most popular ".kz" sites is the multi-modal "nur.kz", which has a number of blog and discussion areas. Another popular blog site is Yvision.kz, which is primarily in the Russian language and is said to have more than 60,000 users. This somewhat basic but complex portal has news and a large, popular blog area that users consider more credible because of its independence.

Below the presidential level, politics in Kazakhstan is relatively open and pluralistic. Some opposition parties put up candidates in elections, and (with the notable exception of any direct criticism of the president or his family) a degree of lower-level media criticism of officials is accepted and even appreciated as information useful to the ruling party. Although opposition and independent candidates cannot achieve electoral results that allow serious challenges to the Nur Otan party, the Internet, and especially social networking sites, offer a still-limited but lively interchange of political information and ideas.

3. The Role of Social Media in Political Processes

In one way, the emergence of social media as an important political factor merely continues the long term and evolving struggle between individuals and groups versus institutions to achieve political prominence. In the recent past, mass communication was overwhelmingly owned or controlled by the existing political powers; individuals, small groups and social movements had to insert themselves into the current political structure before they could change it. Although this pattern continues, in some regions and nations more than others, the rise of Internet discourse seems to have bypassed most older channels of information flow and has taken most traditional political institutions by surprise.

The interactivity of the Internet, along with widespread access, play major roles in facilitating basic citizen involvement in politics, such as spreading opinions and information. The capacity of the Internet, in particular social media, to inform, coalesce, and mobilize citizens is striking and unprecedented. One example is an environmental group that used the social media to spark protests again a development project (Protect Ak-Zhailau!, 2012). Of course, as the plethora of hate group sites around the world demonstrates, this capacity is not always societally beneficial.

The Internet's impact on political processes and systems goes beyond the ability of political actors to gather and distribute information. In this sense, a complexity of Kazakhstan's political and online systems might make it an instructive exemplar in how the political use of social media can lead to influential interactions.

4. The Landscape of Kazakhstani Social Media

As in most relatively-developed areas of the world, social media have become a central form of communication, especially for young people. Internet penetration is now estimated as at least 45 percent (FOTN 2012). The nation's first major Internet email and social media providers were based in Russia, especially Mail.ru, but more Kazakhstani portals and sites are opening. The most popular social media sites in Kazakhstan are

Facebook and twitter, while popularity of social media areas of a very popular Russian version of Facebook—vKontakte—is increasing. Culture, activities, entertainment, and personal recounting, as well as political commentaries, now dominate the social experience.

Many mainstream media institutions are reluctant to fully use social media beyond including forums on their websites, though the blogosphere is full of journalists who appreciate the chance to express themselves more freely, if to a (usually) very limited audience. Many young journalists argue, however, that online and social-media news has a double effect on traditional media: they draw away audiences but allow easy fact-checking and perspective-balancing by audiences. This might encourage a kind of professionalism in media industries that are considered, almost universally, as woefully and increasingly unprofessional.

Most social media content, however, is not political; many sites that are political were created by small opposition and independent parties. Blogs are the most popular route for individuals to make political statements. The Internet, with its low cost and easy communication, is especially valuable for civil society groups such as humanitarian and non-sectarian organizations, which tend to be more active and often more professional than political groups. For example, an increasing number of grassroots charity and youth groups depend on social media to attract, inform and mobilize members.

This civil use, outside of traditional communication, suggests an evolutionary pressure for change in the culture of politics—its terms and expressions—that springs from the ability of the Internet to engender and disseminate critical and analytical thinking.

Most Internet users in Kazakhstan, especially within social media, are accustomed to 404 error messages that indicate sites blocked by the government, although the vast majority of sites are freely available. Overt and direct control has always been used to shut down websites that the government found objectionable (Central Asia: censorship and control of the Internet and other new media, 2011).

The most famous such case was Russia-based LiveJournal, at the time the most popular blog platform. It was controversially blocked by the main ISPs (Kazakhtelecom and Nursat) from October 2008 to November 2010 after officials declared that it could be used by the President's ex-son-in-law and critic Rakhat Aliyev (Nurmakov, 2010). The site was opened for about a year, along with another Russia-based social networking site Liveinternet.ru, and although the latter site has since been unblocked, LiveJournal remains inaccessible to most Kazakhstanis. The popular blog hosting platforms Blogger.com and Wordpress have been periodically and selectively filtered, usually explained as preventing the growth of religious extremism (FOTN 2012).

In recent years, government agencies have also developed additional and less-overt technological ways to make sites inaccessible. The ability to control online materials without clear government involvement is important because of ongoing official efforts to counteract the widespread international perception that Kazakhstan's media and Internet landscapes are heavily constrained in ways that benefit the government. In effect, the government tries to balance its efforts to allow and encourage online usage against its efforts to minimize a discourse of dissatisfaction, yet against its need to be seen as a mostly western-style open society.

As mentioned above, the government's most common rationale for control of the Internet is the threat of radical Islamic groups. Interest in Islam remains much weaker in Kazakhstan than in some other nations, but has apparently been increasing. Certainly, some homegrown groups, as well as others based in neighboring Uzbekistan, call publicly for changing the basis of Kazakhstani society to Sharia law. A number of military actions and incursions by small Muslim groups that are increasing clearly concern the government, with about a dozen such incursions in 2011. Islamic groups have little online presence; the most notable exception is "Soldiers of Caliphate", the site of an international, recently-deregistered Islamic group.

Attitudes on social sites toward Islam are much more mixed than conventional news coverage. For example, the three most recent comments about the Caliphate group and recent financial disputes, posted on the centralasiaonline discussion area and accessed in November, 2012, show the diversity of views and underscore the capacity of social media to disseminate short, varied opinions on controversial topics.

April 23, 2012 @ 01:04:40PM ("Gamul"): "These are soldiers of caliphate, they are real, they exist, and you will never understand it."

January 29, 2012 @ 08:01:46PM ("Kannat"): "Soldiers of the Caliphate have no faith. They work off the money they borrowed for themselves, their families and businesses, and failed to repay."

January 29, 2012 @ 01:01:36PM (anonymous): "It was a setup by secret services to start a crackdown and fight the opposition. Terrorists never engage in small intimidation tricks, such as blowing up a trash can, then killing a lone bandit. The NSC needs it to obtain additional funding for alleged secret agents. The money is unaccounted for."

At present, the online presence of militant Islamic activists is very rare, so presumably their activities are mostly interpersonal. It is impossible to know to what extent this absence comes from the success of the government efforts, and to what extent it reflects the small and fractured characteristics of such groups. One London-based Islamic group is very critical of Kazakhstani policies (IHRC, 2012) but few other sites show open animosity.

Restrictions proposed and imposed by authorities have shifted from a focus on religious extremism to general "Internet aggression." The increased number of documents with unclear concepts and definitions but unpredictably applied and increasingly harsh penalties suggests a clear pattern of central control and uncertainty that increases pressures for self-censorship.

YouTube, an extremely popular destination for young Kazakhs, and Facebook, are not blocked – presumably because their popularity, the small proportion of antigovernment material, and their use by government officials themselves, argues against blocking. Without doubt, any government attempts to block these sites would be met with tremendous resistance that would probably far outweigh any benefits from increased control.

5. Personal Use of Social Media

Social media have become an integral part of communication across much of Kazakhstan, especially among more urban, educated, and young users. A substantial proportion of professional Kazakhstan journalists now use the social media to express ideas and opinions "horizontally" to other users and bypass traditional, government-constrained, mass media. Largely because of its importance for the elites, Russian is the most common language of social media content; this incidentally increases the international access of blogs and other online materials, whether cultural, social or political.

Predictably, the proportion of Kazakhstanis who consider traditional media as their main source of news is decreasing across the population-- dramatically so among young people. Although many use online news versions of print news, most now say that their preferred source of news is social media, including forums and blogs such as vlast.com. Across the country, newspapers and television news are still popular, but the widespread perception that the quality of mainstream news has dropped, as well as the increased options of online news and increased technical capacities (such as high-speed Internet), create pressure on the viability of traditional news organizations in Kazakhstan as in most other nations.

At the same time, however, the stream of specifically political social media sites and content is much less than the volume of personal and entertainment information. A number of new platforms attempt to attract audiences, including some produced by the government. One news portal that is particularly popular – technically independent but under strong government influence – is Tengrinews.kz. It offers a wide range of content, extensive news reports, and areas for blogs and discussions. It is popular because of the speed of posting and updating news, and its very active comments areas.

Political blogs are some of the most popular online political materials, especially among young Internet users; these are often well written and stimulating, although few pretend to be objective in the conventional journalistic sense. On the other hand, only the most naïve news consumers believe that there is much objectivity or balance in traditional news sites.

Two blogs that are currently popular are Aidashov.yvision.kz and Sadenka.yvision.kz. Most such blogs are in Russian, but a number of Kazkakh language blogs, (such as askaraktobe.wordpress.com and tamshi. wordpress.com) offer a more nationally-targeted perspective on events. These tend to offer either quick responses to current events or essays on trends and policies. Their social function, of linking individuals and groups to each other and to the rest of the world, is strong and increasing.

Most political blogs offer, with varying degrees of hostility, criticism of the government. This is inevitable in a system that offers little scope for dissent in traditional mainstream media. On the other hand, in conjunction with the dramatic increase of Internet's role in national communication, these blogs show the potential for media that is diffused, difficult to control, and offers a staple of information resources.

6. Government Use of Social Media

Kazakhstan's government has shown a revealing trajectory of attitudes and actions toward social media. During the early years of Facebook, blogs, forums and similar platforms, Government leaders showed little understanding of the nature or potential of social media. A few government leaders are considered more technocratic and Internet-aware, such as Askar Zhumagaliev, Minister of Transport and Communications, and Kuanyshbek Yessekeyev, head of Kazakhtelecom. Beyond the adoption by individuals of social media and Internet technologies, the government puts considerable resources into monitoring new and existing sites for content that it considers negative or dangerous (opennet.net, 2010).

According to Freedom House, new technologies now permit more selective blocking (FOTN 2012). The government of Kazakhstan, in parallel with trying to minimize critical content without antagonizing international agencies such as the European Union, has become increasingly adept at responding to unwelcome online content, and is also working on several fronts to become a dominant force in the social media directly (on official sites) and indirectly (by sponsoring nominally independent sites).

Virtually everyone interested in Kazakhstan social media credits Karim Masimov with leading the way for officials to tap into the Internet. While most officials in the government had little or no sense of the social media, in 2005 Masimov grasped the potential of effectively reaching young people around the country. At about the same time that LiveJournal was blocked, as Prime Minister he opened a government portal that quickly became popular. He became interested in video blogs and took on an active role in twitter, tweeting on the books he was reading and reflecting on official trips. His tweets became popular for their small windows into the attitudes and actions of a high government official.

The sites included clear attempts at PR. A few Internet-savvy leaders managed to present themselves as human beings and inspired considerable online feedback. However, many of these leaders soon abandoned the efforts to keep up these accounts, including Masimov, who for unexplained reasons has stopped tweeting.

During 2010, government offices and officials were effectively forced to create what were called blogs on government and personal activities. However, instead they operated like traditional complaint books, with only rare updates or interactions. At most, citizens could only post a comment and wait for a response.

Suddenly, under Masimov's leadership, the government began to treat social media as a way to directly reach, educate and influence citizens. Ministers, mayors, and levels of government official were soon "respectfully required" to produce official blogs of their own. The established rejection by Internet users of any sites that are not kept up to date seriously limited interest in most of these site. Essentially, most officials were unable to fully comprehend and take advantage of the interactivity and immediacy of the sites. The quality of official sites depended on the individual abilities of their authors, which were often quite weak. Despite such limitations of the content, government appreciation for the potential of the Internet and especially social media increased, jumpstarting active governmental involvement in the Internet.

This represented a tectonic shift in the attitudes and actions of officials who had mostly been trained in Soviet style stonewalling and information control. The idea of trying to appeal to citizens, often on personal level, was a small but significant cultural revolution. Various institutions, both governmental and commercial, began to invite prominent bloggers and unregistered online publications to media events, treating social media as a parallel way to reach new groups of citizens.

In the end of 2007, the government unveiled its large site, e-Gov. It now has an estimated 544,000 pages viewed monthly, with about 151,000 monthly visits (urlmetrics, 2012).

In effect, this fully fledged platform includes news, access to documents, the content of regulations, information about government services, blogs, and more. Although these have limited citizen involvement, the site is a widely-used resource for many Kazakhstanis since it provides information and forms that is much easier for many Kazakhstanis to get than visiting state offices.

To supplement the substantial traditional online news sites, and to offer an alternative to banned and filtered sites, the government has created a special location for blogs by officials: blogs.egov.kz. This Kazakh-language site has blogs by more than 30 officials and demonstrates increasing government efforts to not only control social media it considers objectionable, but also to offer its own versions.

Zhussupova (2012) analyzed the use of social media, specifically twitter, by 18 government officials, measuring the numbers of followers, requests and retweets to quantitatively investigate the personal and professional factors that officials use, and which aspects lead to the strongest response from twitter users. The author found that, although personal and trend-related (i.e., predictive) content led to the strongest response from readers, officials often emphasized a "protocol style of public communication." However, she found that most officials try to diversify their content and increase the number of subject lines in order to attract the most interest. The most popular tweets remain those by Karim Massimov, although Erlan Karin, Executive Secretary of the "Nur Otan" party, deputy Murat Abenov and Member of Parliament Mukhtar Tinikeyev also are very popular. These confirm the observation that online presence and success depend on individual interest and skill.

Hoping to reverse the current flow of Internet content—which is currently overwhelmingly into Kazakhstan from outside—both government and pro-government business interests have added new platforms that they hope will attract an increasing number of young people. These often mix public and private funding. For example, the government invests public funds into commercial projects managed by private entities, including the national search engine Kaz.kz, and a national video-hosting site at Kaztube.kz. Some observers criticize this use of tax revenues with little apparent public value, and worry that such funding distorts the competitive marketplace for social-media startups.

On the other hand, some investments support the growth of the Internet: JSC Kazakhtelecom has eliminated charges for internal traffic free, and domestic hosting is cheap or even cost-free.

Beyond sites and social media content, government officials and ministries have become better able to deal with the qualities of the Internet that eluded most of them in the past. Rather than wait several days or more before responding to events online, government agencies are often now quick to "spin" the government position when events arise. During 2011, more official sites became proactive in anticipating the activities of other groups in order to dominate the news agenda as much as possible.

An especially sophisticated government use of the social media as news occurred during the most severe challenge to the government since Independence. In late 2011, workers in the important Western oilfields at Zhanaozen began a strike for better conditions and pay. Rather than trying to control coverage by mainstream media, the government closed down all news access to the area for almost the whole of December 16. twitter was specifically blocked. After the riots were suppressed, access to the area was given to most media, including foreign journalists, but the government encouraged a group of young, nominally independent bloggers to post their own reports on the events. Their blogs did not include antigovernment information or interpretation, or challenge government claims that the striking workers were lazy or externally directed.

7. Opposition and Independent Use of Social Media

Many opposition and independent groups depend on the Internet, and especially social media, to communicate with members and the world. For example, members of Yvision coined the term "yvizhenka": a series of offline meetings of bloggers that have been held since 2009 (FOTN).

The government of Kazakhstan realizes that it cannot completely eliminate dissent and challenges. Compared to capital-heavy traditional news organizations, Internet news and social media sites offer tremendous scope for information that questions, contradicts, challenges or simply offers an alternative to official statements. Such sites have very mixed technical and journalistic qualities. Many are very simple and descriptive, some are complex and well designed, but all hope to become established among young citizens.

Two factors discourage the creation and production of non-governmental social media and other online alternatives. One factor is the possibility that the site could be blocked, temporarily or permanently, by KazakhTelecom JSC, which controls much of the traffic within Kazakhs; it is officially independent but effectively government-dominated. This organization is specifically constrained to carry out court decisions, which are alone authorized to block online content, and does not have the authority to decide censorship cases by itself.

The second, related, factor is self-censorship that arises in an environment in which the government rarely but decisively uses its power to shut down undesired sites. During 2012, 12 sites were blocked by the government with the claim that they were detrimental to the stability of society.

The tenor of political use of social media changed substantially between the presidential elections of 2010 and the parliamentary elections of 2011. Since there is no serious opposition to the reelection of President Nazarbayev—indeed, the law now names him as "Leader of the Nation" with the right to run for the presidency without term limits. This specifically outlaws criticism and serious challenges, which results in very narrow and shallow interest among voters in the presidential elections. Before the presidential election, both government and opposition Internet sites were very scattered and unsophisticated.

However, since it is possible (though very difficult) for independent or opposition candidates to run for office, and desirable for them to establish themselves for long-term value, the period leading up to the 2011 parliamentary elections saw a dramatic expansion in the quality and quantity of nongovernment political sites. In fact, the logistical barriers and pro-government tendencies of traditional media meant that the Internet became the primary focus of candidates who could not benefit from membership in the ruling Nur Otan party.

Because of massive constraints on electoral success by campaigns with such traditional media as TV ads and billboards, the online efforts of independent and opposition parties shifted from earning votes to creating awareness and establishing credibility. The goal appeared to be creating bona fides as independent candidates, with at least partial platforms and statements suggesting their ability to be true alternatives, at least in the future. These politicians often used personal social media accounts to promote their political careers.

These efforts do not always meet with clear success. Serizhhan Mambetalin was leader of the environmental party Rukhaniyat ("Spirituality") which quickly turned into a strongly nationalist party on the eve of the elections. Mambetalin, also a business columnist, had a popular personal blog on the Internet. During 2010–11 this blog not only proposed information and conclusions that opposed the government, emphasizing environmental issues, but during the campaign began harshly criticizing the Nazarbayev regime with claims that were often controversial claims and language that many found offensive. The party used Facebook to attract and mobilize members. This social-network writing attracted many followers, partly for sensationalistic reasons, and increased his fame. It also alienated some readers and eventually helped fuel a government ban of the party from the list of alternative parties allowed to compete in the elections.

In many ways, independent and opposition groups, like the government, are trying to discover, create and adapt to a new medium that is itself constantly reinvented under their feet. Such groups are learning how to make the best use of a medium that represents their best opportunity to get their messages out when the power and economic structures are largely arrayed against them. It is widely assumed that these groups look to sites in other countries, especially Russia, to improve skills and gain ideas they can use in their own sites. There is limited capacity to pursue change through conventional activism, and Kazakhstani political dynamics subtly work against it. For example, when one group used social media to attract nearly 300 supporters to a rally in early 2012, the meeting was deemed illegal and its organizers were arrested. Subsequent rallies brought together fewer and fewer people until their demonstrations and group actions stopped entirely.

Limitations on effective political use of nongovernmental social media to become better known and trusted include technical skills, but mostly reflect limited awareness of options, a limited grasp of effective public relations techniques, and a culture that, until fairly recently, was extremely top-down, paternalistic and domineering.

One dramatic use of the social media was not related to opposition groups, and indeed had a source that continues to be unknown, though many suspect that it was secretly created by government groups. In early 2012, a YouTube video showed three young men who seemed to be confessing to terrorist activities, then advised viewers not to follow in their footsteps. This video, apparently recorded in a prison cell, was very widely shared and viewed, both on social media and in newscasts. Because of its message and unknown origins, as well as the uncertain authenticity of the "stars", many Kazkakhs still wonder if this video was a clever misinformation effort by the government or some other group.

8. The Legal Environment of the Internet and Social Media

Since its creation as an independent state, Kazakhstan has boasted of its relatively progressive and transparent constitution and laws. Without doubt Kazakhstan leads the region in laws that explicitly guarantee an open flow of information. However, such laws are easier to write than to enforce, and most legal organizations conclude that even the statutory guarantees of free media are being cut back by a series of regressive laws. This is especially, and increasingly, true of Internet regulation.

For example, in October 2012, opposition leader Vladimir Kozlov was sentenced to seven-and-a-half years in prison on a number of charges. These included "inciting social discord" online, which has been called "a vague and overbroad criminal charge that is incompatible with international human rights law" (humanrightswatch, 2012).

A succession of laws and regulations by national agencies, which have been reorganized many times, has placed the Internet under the auspices of two new ministries, and which had been effectively treated as an independent category of information – in the same category as traditional mass media, which is subject to centralized monitoring and regulation (kazpravda, 2012). According to Zhandos Umiraliyev, official representative of the General Prosecutor's Office, "The Prosecutor's Office is taking steps to halt operation of certain websites spreading extremist and religious information and propagating terrorism and distributing other information forbidden by law. Measures have been taken, websites propagating terrorism and religious extremism have been closed down." (50 foreign extremists, 2011).

The ability of government bodies to block websites from foreign countries has been codified and enforced; although the law requires such filtering to occur only after specific court decisions, this requirement is often ignored. Within Kazakhstan, the website of a vocal and popular weekly newspaper, Respublika, was blocked for most of 2011, a move that is generally considered a response to its criticisms but also to its use of social networks to broaden the audience of its articles. Government sources and leaders of Kazakh telecom deny censorship, instead blaming technical errors within the newspaper itself.

In 2012, a court case was mounted jointly against several news and social media sites, including Respublika and Vzglyad, implementing the government report that equates Internet sites as a single media outlet (newskaz.ru, 2012).

A government working paper that might lead to a law regulating the Internet was passed in November 2011. The "Concept of Information Security until 2016" explicitly addresses what it calls the "growing role and influence of global mass media and communication tools on economic, political and social situation" with their potential "wide use of social networks and blogs by the Kazakhstani population creates possibilities for their utilization with the aim of deliberate influence on internally political situation against national interests of the Republic of Kazakhstan" such as "destructive content" and "political extremism." Such regulations and vague wording are seen as encouragement for all content providers and ISPs to restrict any content that is not clearly congenial to the Astana government, and as discouragement for blogs and other Internet content producers.

Efforts to close websites to fight terrorism and religious extremism is led by an agency called The Governmental Agency for Religious Affairs, which claims that nearly 3,000 extremist websites threaten the country. There is no doubt that some groups want to turn Kazakhstan into an Islamic Republic; much less clear is their ability to have much impact, and the capacity of current laws to short-circuit such efforts.

The law in 2009 equated Internet sites with traditional media outlets. A document produced in December 2011 contains rules that were not adopted by the parliament, but which in force because they are promoted by the ruling government. The primary current special regulation over Internet content was issued on December 30, 2011 (zakon.kz, 2012). This requires those who manage services, such as Internet cafés, to monitor the websites used by customers in what it calls "electronic journals." It also specifically prohibits "anonymizer" and similar techniques used to circumvent government controls.

9. Trends in the Political Uses of Social Media

The key historical trends in the political role of social media include the rapid spread and integration of the Internet, and especially social media, into communication channels across the country. Young Kazakhstanis in particular have enthusiastically embraced the social media as their primary source of information and opportunity for self-expression. Over time, most political groups are becoming more competent at using the social media to reach their goals, although this competence is not evenly apparent across the groups and still seems to depend mostly on individual motivation and learning. The government has demonstrated two clear priorities: the first is to use Internet and social media options as fully as possible to protect and retrench its political dominance; the second is to encourage Internet use in general, while using legal and technical means to restrict any aspects that it considers a challenge to the status quo.

10. Trends in Social Media Use within Kazakhstan

First, it is clear that the penetration and significance for citizens' social media will only increase. Second, given recent legal patterns, the government is likely to continue to bring the Internet in general, and social media in particular, under increased control, both legally and informally.

At the same time, the government will try to make its own use of the Internet more sophisticated, attractive, and effective. The Internet seems more likely to support political movements than to serve as their main focal point. The actual presence and importance of social media and Internet sites by radical Islamic groups will probably remain noticeable but marginal. Groups are likely to attempt to circumvent official controls over the social media, with only partial success.

Despite the official promise of the free flow of information in Kazakhstan, limitations operate on several levels that have decreased and further controlled the range of information that can be disseminated. In other words, an important trend in the freedom of Internet information has been an increase in restrictions on it. At the same time, the government accepts the value of pluralistic information flow in principle as an economic necessity, and works hard to find some balance that allows information flow while meeting its own political perspectives and purposes.

One important and intensifying trend is that information can now crisscross the country at a speed that is difficult for institutional structures to deal with. Although the government has learned to be more proactive and efficient in dealing with online and social media information, Internet users in Kazakhstan, like those in other countries, are also becoming better at circumventing attempts at control.

Although many political actors in Kazakhstan have been slow to grasp the communication implications of social media, they are now upgrading their technological and communication skillsets in ways that seem certain to continue.

Within the relatively rigid constraints of institution building in Kazakhstan, traditional social movements and activism (such as party-building and lobbying) are possible but very difficult to develop. The Internet makes conventional institutional changes less necessary. Online information flow is leading not only to the exchange of specific information and ideas, but also to a transformative development of critical thinking that values multiple sources and accepts "the social construction of reality." On a practical level, this means that many young people—certainly the educated and resourced elite—feel free to gather information from any available source and repackage it in any way that makes sense to them. This emerging attitude is very difficult for any institution to control, although the success of some pro-government websites and social media hubs suggests efforts by the government to effectively address changes in information attitudes among its young citizens. Of course, it is impossible to predict the results of this interacting dynamic, although it is easy to predict its continuation.

Given recent official efforts to control online systems and information, but also given widespread resentment and resistance to those efforts, a great deal depends on the process of transition toward a post-Nazarbayev government. Many citizens admit that they are holding their political breaths while the struggles for both power and acceptance of pluralism plays out in Astana and across the country—physically, institutionally, and informationally. The social media influence political factors by allowing an increasing proportion of the population to learn and decide about the meanings and impacts of events, and respond to them to some degree. While this has very limited impact on the individual level, the cumulative effect could be substantial.

Clearly, the network-building power of social media is likely to play an important role in Kazakhstani politics. The bigger question is how other factors will respond to this role, resulting for example in open and effective discussions of power. Political reform, our analysis concludes, could either move toward openness and collaboration or toward further restraint. A great deal depends on the further acceptance by government leaders of pluralistic perspectives, which in the recent past is not very apparent.

The impact of social media does not, of course, only benefit society. Destructive groups take advantage of its near-anonymity. Soviet leaders, like other leaders today, presented their subjectivity as unchallengeable objectivity. Many young Kazakhstanis accept that this older approach to news is being replaced by the social media's tendency toward reduced, if multi-sourced, information with increased opinionation. Kazakhstanis report that difficulties in evaluating the factuality of facts, along with the ease of posting them, is already leading to a general suspicion of information and increased acceptance of personal views as a form of information. This results in an odd twist, apparent across the online world, in which opinion is seen as more credible than fact.

11. Conclusions

While the future politics of the social media are impossible to predict, it seems likely that the Internet, and especially social media, will serve a political role that can best be described as organic and cultural, rather than a role based on institutions. In other words, the social media will probably continue to broaden and open up political discourse, which in Kazakhstan is currently constrained or overshadowed by government control. The social media's diffusion of political expression might help create a discursive environment that later leads to more official and institutional political activities. However, for now, control mechanisms (at any level above the individual) favor government priorities and efforts.

The authors conclude that the combination of institutional constraint and relative informational opportunity will lead to change that is primarily cultural and attitudinal. In other words, the globalized, relativized creation and spread of ideas via the Internet is already changing the nation's cultures and assumptions. Government leaders will rightly try to decide the future role of the Internet in Kazakhstan; these decisions will in turn shape their efforts to address the nation's online domain in which ideas are created and spread and public opinion is formed. Thus, to an extent that would have been inconceivable only a generation ago, rapid change in the social and political context represent a kind of democracy of conclusions that will, depending on the responses by those in power, help to shape Kazakhstan's democracy of institutions and actions.

References

Alsayyad, N. (2012). The virtual square. *Harvard International Review; Vol. 34*. Issue 1, pp. 58-63.

Central Asia: censorship and control of the Internet and other new media. (2011, November). Retrieved from http://www.chrono-tm. org/en/wp-content/uploads/ENG-Internet-briefing-paper-Nov-2011.pdf

CIA Factbook (2012). Retrieved from https://www.cia.gov/library/publications/the-world-factbook/geos/kz.html.

Democracyweb (2012). Retrieved from http://www.democracyweb.org/accountability/kazakhstan.php *E-gov* (2012).

FOTN (2012). Retrieved from http://www.freedomhouse.org/reports

Greengard, S. (2009: February). The First Internet president. *Communications of the ACM. Vol. 52* Issue 2, pp. 16-18.

Human rights watch. Retrieved from http://www.hrw.org/europecentral-asia/kazakhstan

IHRC (2012). Retrieved from http://www.ihrc.org.uk/show.php?id=650

Kazpravda (2012). Retrieved from http://kazpravda.kz/_pdf/jan12/200112law.pdf, accessed January 24, 2012.

Newskaz (2012). Retrieved from http://newskaz.ru/incidents/20121123/4339913.html

Newskaz.ru (2012). http://newskaz.ru/incidents/20121123/4339913.html. Retrieved November 26, 2012.

Nurmakov, A. (2010). Kazakhstan: Livejournal Unblocked After 2 Years of Filtering. Retrieved from http://globalvoicesonline.org/2010/11/17/kazakhstan-livejournal-unblocked-after-2-years-of-filtering/

Opennet.net (2012). Retrieved from opennet.net: http://opennet.net/research/profiles/kazakhstan

Protect Ak-Zhailau! Retrieved from http://k-zh.kz

Urlmetrics (2012). Retrieved from http://urlmetrics.co.uk/www.egov.kz

Worldbank wgi (2012). Retrieved from http://info.worldbank.org/governance/wgi/index.asp

zakon.kz (2012). Retrieved from http://www.zakon.kz/4469529-v-Internet-kluby-teper budut-puskat.html

Zhussupova, K. (2012). *Analysis of the Kazakhstani Government officials'*
presence on twitter. Unpublished Master's Thesis. KIMEP University,
Almaty, Kaakhstan.

Further Reading:

Abramov, V. (2012). Pravitel'stvo Kazakhstana v cifrah (The Government of Kazakhstan in figures). Retrieved from http://vlast.
kz/?art=863

Barker M. (2007) Conform or reform? Social movements and the mass
media. *Fifth-Estat**e Online - International Journal of Radical Mass*
Media Criticism, 2, retrieved from http://www.fifth-estate-online.co.
uk/criticsm/conformorreformsocialmovements.html

Bimendin, A. (2011). Kolichestvo pol'zovatelei interneta v kazakhstane
viroslo do 6,7 mln chelovek (The number of Internet users in
Kazakhstan has grown to 6.7 million). Retrieved from
http://www.inform.kz/rus/article/2416684

Central Asia: censorship and control of the Internet and other new
media (2011). Retrieved from http://www.chrono-tm.org/en/wp-
content/uploads/ENG-Internet-briefing-paper-Nov-2011.pdf

Grant, W. J., Moon, B., & Grant, J. B. (2010). Digital dialogue?
Australian politicians' use of the social network tool twitter.
Australian Journal of Political Science, 45(4), 579-604.

Gumarova, C. (2012). Kolichestvo ne znazhit kachestvo, no nadezhda na
buduschee est' (The quantity does not mean quality, but there is
hope for the future.). Retrieved from http://www.profit.kz/
articles/1736-Kolichestvo-ne-znachit-kachestvo-no-nadezhdi-na-
buduschee-u-Kazneta-est/

Hendricks, J. A., & Denton, R. E. (eds.) (2010). *Communicator-in-chief:*
How Barack Obama used new media technology to win the White
House. Lanham, MD: Lexington Books.

Institute of Political Solutions (2011). Social mood in main cities of Kazakhstan, analysis of the results of monitoring from June 5-10, 2011, (pp. 5-7). Retrieved from http://www.ipr.kz/projects/2/6/28#.UI-er2fqdY0.

Isabayeva, S. (n.d.). Setevaya demokratiya nastupaet. Retrieved from http://www.kazrus.kz/index.php?ab=news&$or=politika&&news=14032011101942

IMF Country Report No. 11/151, (2011). Retrieved from http://www.imf.org/external/pubs/ft/scr/2011/cr11151.pdf. (p.17).

Kazakhskih chinovnikov obyazali zavesti blogi (Kazakhstani officials were obliged to open blogs). (2009). Retrieved from http://meta.kz/novosti/kazakhstan/69318- kazakhskikh-chinovnikov-objazali-zavesti-blogi.html

Kazakhskie politiki v twitter. Massimov i drugie (Kazakhstani officials in twitter. Massimov and others). (2011). Retrieved from http://www.nashaagasha.org/actual/kazaxstanskie-politiki-v-twitter-masimov-i-drugie/

Klandermans, B. (1984). Mobilization and participation: social-psychological expansions of resource mobilization theory, *American Sociological Review, 49,* 5 (pp. 583-600).

Klandermans, B. (1997*) The Social Psychology of Protest.* Oxford, UK: Blackwell.

Masimov's twitter one of the best in Astana . (2011). Retrieved from http://en.tengrinews.kz/Internet/5711/

McCarthy, J. D., McPhail, J. D., Smith, J., and Crishock, L. J. (1998). Electronic and print media representations of Washington, D.C. demonstration, 1982 and 1991: A demography of description bias. In D. Rucht, R. Koopmans and F. Neidhardt (eds) *Acts of Dissent: New Developments in the Study of Protest,* Oxford, UK: Rowman & Littlefield.

The New York Times (http://www.nytimes.com/interactive/2012/10/08/technology/campaign-social-media.html

Obama, B. (2009). *Transparency and open government. Memorandum for the heads of executive departments and agencies.* Retrieved from White House website: http://www.whitehouse.gov/the_press_office/ TransparencyandOpenGovernment

Oficial'nye blogi chinovnikov ne interesny chitatelyam (Official's blogs are not interested for readers). (2011, July 1). Retrieved from http:// www.profit.kz/news/7402-Oficialnie-blogi-chinovnikov-ne-interesni-chitatelyam/

Oliver, P. E., & Maney, G. M. (2000: September). Political processes and local newspaper coverage of protest events: From selection bias to triadic unteractions. *American Journal of Sociology, 106* (2) 463–505.

Oliver, P. E., & Myers, D. J. (1999). How events enter the public sphere: Conflict, location, and sponsorship in local newspaper coverage of public events. *American Journal of Sociology, 105*, 38–87.

Papacharissi, Z. (2002). The virtual sphere: the Internet as a public sphere. *New Media & Society, 4*(1), 9–27. Retrieved from http:// www.cblt.soton.ac.uk/multimedia/PDFs/The% 20virtual sphere.pdf

Pochemu rossiyskie chinovniki vibrali dlya obscheniya twitter: Experty (Why have Russian officials chosen twitter for communication?) (2012). Retrieved from http://www.iarex.ru/news/30965.html

Razvitie e-gov v Kazakhstane tormozit electronnya podpis' (The electronic signature inhibits the development of e-gov in Kazakhstan). (2011). Retrieved from http://prodengi.kz/lenta/ razvitie_egov_v_kazahstane_tormozit_elektronnaya_podpis/

Robertson, S. P., Vatrapub, R. K., & Medinaa, R. (2010). Off the wall political discourse: Facebook use in the 2008 U.S. presidential election. *Information Polity 15*, 11–31.

Rudenko, A. (2012). Insighttrends research 2012 US presidential campaign: the first "social-media" presidential election ever. Retrieved from http://popsop.com/59456

Sniderman, Z. (2011). How governments are using social media for better & for worse. Retrieved from http://mashable.com/2011/07/25/ government-social-media/

Snow, D. A., E. Burke R., Jr., Worden, S.K., & Benford, R.D.. (1986). Frame alignment processes, micromobilization and movement participation. *American Sociological Review 51*(4): 546–481.

Turner, R.. (1996). The moral issue in collective behavior and collective action. *Mobilization: An International Journal* 1:1–16.

Tyler, T.R. & Smith, H.J. (1998). Social justice and social movements. In D.T. Gilbert and S.T. Fiske (eds), *Handbook of social psychology, 4th ed.* New York, NY: McGraw-Hill.

Ubayasiri, K. (2006). Internet and the public sphere: A glimpse of YouTube. *eJournalist, 6*(2), Retrieved from http:// ejournalist.com. au/v6n2/ubayasiri622.pdf

Viner, K. (2009). Internet has changed foreign policy for ever, says Gordon Brown. *The Guardian*. Retrieved from http://www.guardian. co.uk/politics/2009/jun/19/gordon-brown-Internet-foreign-policy

Web browser that bypasses big brother a Kazakh hit (2010). Reuters.

Retrieved from http://www.reuters.com/article/2010/04/13/us-kazakhstan-Internet-browser-idUSTRE63C37N20100413.

Zhizn' 2.0. fenomen social'nyh setei (Life 2.0. the phenomenon of social networks). (2010). Retrieved from http://ipr.kz/kipr/3/1/33

PART THREE:
EAST ASIA

VII. Cultural Values, Gender and Chinese Young Adults in Using Social Media*

Qingwen Dong

Department of Communication, University of the Pacific,
Stockton, California
Corresponding Author: qdong@pacific.edu

Yun Wu

Department of Communication, University of the Pacific,
Stockton, California
familmaggie@hotmail.com

Xiaoting Gu

Department of Communication, University of the Pacific,
Stockton, California
X_gu1@u.pacific.edu

and Dale Dong

Department of Communication, University of the Pacific,
Stockton, California
Ddong19@pacific.edu

Abstract

Based on a cross-sectional survey of 416 Chinese young adults, this study examined the impact of cultural values and gender on why college students use the Chinese social networking site, Renren. This study found that interdependent self-construal can predict four motives for Chinese young adults to use Renren: socialization, entertainment, self-status seeking and information seeking. The study also found that male and female respondents significantly differ in information seeking and self-status seeking; with male adults being higher in self-status seeking and female adults higher in information seeking. Limitations and suggestions for future research are provided.

Keywords: social media, Chinese social networking, Renren, cultural values & gender

1. Introduction

As one of the most dominant products of the Internet, social media have transformed both local and global communication significantly in the past decade. Scholars suggested the Internet, along with high-speed connections, affordable technology and the availability of news programs, changed the way we communicate (Rice & Haythornthwaite, 2007) and changed our cultural values (Zhang & Prosser, 2012). They pointed out Internet characteristics such as interactivity and digital content allow communication to flow nearly unrestricted (Dong, Day, & Deol, 2010). Thus, individuals, young people in particular, have learned to depend heavily on social media for socialization and entertainment.

Social media have existed since the very beginning of the Internet, but mostly as Bulletin Board Systems where people could post messages on various topics and wait for others to respond. It was MySpace in 2003 that popularized social media with its easy-to-use blogging platform and the ability to share music and videos among users. YouTube was established two years later, allowing individuals to share videos online. It was followed by the creation of Facebook in 2006, a social media site that allows users to share music, videos, photos, blogs, news stories and play interactive games on a virtual platform. Facebook has more than 1 billion users today, making it the most popular social media platform in the world. Overall, Social Media has penetrated life in the United States in ways not foreseen a decade ago, as two-thirds of all adults in the United States now use social media, and nearly half of all adults say they check a social media account at least once a day (Madden & Zickuhr, 2011). The functions of social media are hardly comprehended because they have dramatically altered the way we communicate, define the media, and interact with individuals and the media. The emerging dependency of individuals on social media for information, entertainment and persuasion has started changing our beliefs, values and behaviors. As a result, a new world order has begun to emerge due to these communication technologies and globalization agents (Zhang & Prosser, 2012).

Because of its dynamic functions and power, many countries have competed with the United States, launching their own social networking site (SNS) allowing governments to offer an online experience that is closer to their citizens while also still presenting a Facebook-type of experience. For example, in Japan, the most popular social networking site is called "Mixi." Mixi currently has more than 20 million users but is only available to those who have a Japanese cell-phone number. Foreigners who do not currently reside in Japan are not allowed to browse the site. In China, Renren is one of the leading social networking sites. There is, however, limited literature on Chinese social media, therefore it is critical for this study to fill the gap. This study examines why Chinese young adults use social media, and how they are affected by their cultural values and gender while interacting with the social media.

2. Literature Review: Chinese Social Media and Renren

In 1994 China's social media was born with online forums. It moved into instant messaging in 1999, according to Chiu, Ip and Silverman (2012). In 2004, blogging emerged, followed by social-networking, provided by Renren. Five years later, Sina Weibo was launched with micro-blogging with multimedia (Chiu et al., 2012). The study indicated that Jiepang started its service in 2010 with function and service similar to Foursquare's.

China's social media market is quite different from its counterpart in the Western countries (Crampton, 2011). Crampton said that although Facebook, twitter and YouTube are restricted in China, the Chinese equivalents are booming. Research said that there are more than 513 million Internet users in China, which is more than double the number in the United States (Chiu et al., 2012). According to Crampton, several factors help drive Chinese to social media: "These include rural-to-urban migration that has separated families, the loneliness of the one-child generation, and a distrust of information from government-controlled media" (p. 29).

Renren is the leading SNS in China. It had more than 160 million registered users in 2010, and was expected to surpass 170 million users in 2011. Much like Facebook, Renren, is a profile-based SNS that initially was used by Chinese college students, who continue to make up the majority of users. Overseas university students, high school students, and white-collar workers are the other primary users.

Renren offers similar services as Facebook. Users can design their own profile pages with a variety of choices offered free by Renren; it allows mobile browsing and desktop browsing; and it allows third-party applications such as social games and e-commerce features. Unlike Facebook, Renren allows more flexibility in design, thus giving a more unique user experience than Facebook. Among all the features of Renren, online currency and social games like Happy Farm are two of the more popular features of the SNS. At a glimpse, Renren appears to be a copycat of Facebook, but analytically it is a hybrid SNS that takes advantage of the U.S. original while adding new features that transform it into a Chinese-value oriented model.

Key Motives in Using Social Media

According to Urista, Dong, and Day (2010), individuals have five motivations to use social media such as Facebook or MySpace, including "efficient communication," "convenient communication," "curiosity about others," "popularity," and "relationship formation and reinforcement" (p. 221). Ray (2007) summarized that "the websites (SNS) fulfill entertainment, information exchange, surveillance, diversion and social utility functions simultaneously." Since Renren and Facebook have shared many similarities in technology, user characteristics, and application, the current study adopted motivation measurement developed by Ray's study (2007). The motivation categories include socialization, information seeking, entertainment and self-status seeking.

Socialization refers to maintaining existing social ties and being able to reconnect with friends from the past as social gratifications (Ellison,

Steinfield, & Lampe, 2007). Kim, Sohn and Choi (2011) suggested that Eastern people seem to give more weight to social support regarding the use of SNS. Kujath (2011) found some users tend to rely on Facebook and MySpace for interpersonal communication more than face-to-face interaction, adding that SNS interaction is an extension to off-line connection. In that study, socialization motivation includes maintaining and developing online connections, gaining social support, and helping group members.

As measurement time was short, not every aspect of each motivation could be determined. As for the motivation of information seeking, studies showed that Internet use is driven more by informational and interactive motives (Eun, Yoon, & Jae, 2005). As for the case of Renren, academic information, career development information, products/services, and facts about the society were included in the investigation. Entertainment refers to the time spent on Renren to gratify needs of happiness, excitement, and novelty. Self-status seeking included peer pressure, perceptions of coolness, usefulness to other group members, group sharing inclinations, high expectations on one's own posts, and sharing aspects of one's life to friends.

Cultural Values and Cultural Influence on Renren Use

Hofstede (2001) was one of the leading scholars to study cultural values. He initially identified four major cultural dimensions - power distance, individualism and collectivism, masculinity and femininity and uncertainty avoidance. He later added another dimension to illustrate that some cultures tend to be long term oriented, such as China, while other cultures tend to be short term oriented, such as the United States.

In 2007, Hofstede articulated value differences between business leaders of China and the United States. According to him, the Chinese values included respecting ethical norms; patriotism, national pride; power; honor, face reputation; and responsibility towards society. The American values focused on growth of the business, personal wealth, this year's profits, power and staying within the law.

Sitaram (1995) pointed out some major differences between people in the East and West. He said that people in the East tend to perceive highly those values including authority, benevolence and loving care for family members. People in the West tend to view highly the values including competitiveness, aggressiveness, challenges to authority and political differences. Dong, Day and Cao (2008) found that with the strengthening Chinese economy, the Chinese people tend to develop more hedonistic values such as paying more attention to image instead of function.

Researchers believe that language and cultural values change shape and affect each other (Lu & Chen, 2011). Language plays an important role in shaping individuals' cultural values while cultural values also help create and enhance individuals' symbolic social exchange. With fast social media development, it is interesting to see how culture plays a role in affecting Chinese young adults' use of SNS. Intercultural communication scholars often focus on a number of cultural constructs when investigating cultural influence in a global context: individualism and collectivism, low context and high context, independent self-construal and interdependent self-construal. Markus and Kitayama (1991) suggested that the perspective of independent self-construal views an individual as an independent entity with a focus on individual feelings, cognitions and motivations. They suggested that the perspective of interdependent self-construal views an individual as an interdependent entity with an emphasis on conformity and relationships with others.

Hall (1976) developed the concept of high and low context in intercultural communication. He explained that individuals who use high context communication tend to find the information in a physical context or internalized in communicators' minds. While people who use low context communication tend to put the information of communication into the message itself. Hofstede (2001) helped define both conceptual and operational definitions of individualism and collectivism which are critical to understanding of cultural differences. He emphasized that the dimension of individualism and collectivism can be viewed as a relationship between individuals and collectivity in a society. These cultural values significantly shape people's beliefs, values and behaviors. Gudykunst and Ting-Toomey (1998) indicated that people from individualistic countries tend to use low context with a direct and explicit communication style while people from collectivistic countries tend to use high context with an indirect and implicit communication style. Intercultural communication researchers believe that people from highly individualistic societies also have independent self-construals while people from collectivistic societies have interdependent self-construals. It is expected that these different self-construals will affect individual's social media use.

Gender Differences

Gender plays an important roles in adopting technology. From the telephone to the mobile phone, computer to the Internet, males and females use technologies for different purposes and in various ways. With historical analogues, it is very likely that SNS can shape and be shaped by the different gender of their users.

Joinson (2008) found that, in general, women use more SNS than men. Moreover, female participants in a multi-stage study conducted in 2007 scored higher on scales for social connection and posting of photographs. In Thelwall's study (2008) focusing on using MySpace, found that both genders have more female friends than male friends and all members tend to choose more female friends in their Top 8 list. In Thelwall's later study (2009) on homophily in MySpace, pointed out that women are simply more effective at using social network sites because they are able to control positive emotion.

Men and women use the Internet differently, although females play more important roles in the digital world. Women use it as a productivity tool while men are primarily engaged in downloading software, experimenting with new technology, and using it as a form of entertainment. Studies suggest that digital mainstream and social networking sites are central to women's Internet experience.

Studies indicated that nearly 56 percent of adult women said they used the Internet to stay in touch with people, compared to 46 percent of adult men (Dong, Wu, and Gu, 2011). When looking specifically at the social networking category, it becomes even clearer how important this activity is for women online. In North America, 9 out of 10 female Internet users visited a social network site in April 2010. Globally, women spent an average of 16 percent of their online time on social networks in April 2010, compared to only 12 percent for men. The increase over the past year showed the growing importance of social networking sites to women's online experience. Research suggests the gender impact on social network use and its experience tends to have a significant impact on social interaction and individual development.

It is expected that gender may have an impact on people using SNS. Men and women use online social networking sites at different rates and for different purposes. Since research for gender difference in Chinese social networking sites is limited, almost all aforementioned research was conducted in the United States. SNS in China may not be exactly the same as those in the United States, but some of the approaches will be valid ways to analyze the research question.

Based on the review of literature on intercultural communication, gender, and Chinese social media usage, this study suggests that there is a significant impact of cultural values and gender on Chinese young adults in using social media. Therefore, two research questions are proposed as follows:

RQ 1: What is the impact of independent and interdependent self-construal on motivating Chinese young adults to use Renren?

RQ 2: How do Chinese male and female young adults differ in using Renren?

3. Methods

Sample and Procedures

A total of 529 questionnaires were distributed with a response rate at 94.5%. However, some data were excluded because of data quality concern. The final data set came to 416. A four-section questionnaire was used in the study. The questionnaire was translated from English to Chinese by the researcher and overviewed by another Chinese graduate student to make sure accurate and appropriate information was conveyed to the participants. It was distributed in two waves: an electronic-version survey—using SurveyMonkey—and paper-version survey to college students in Southern and Northern China. The questionnaire was constructed according to the tailored design method (Dillman, 2000). Such interference factors as color indication, and unnecessary photo insertions were avoided. The design of the electronic questionnaire strictly follows the principle that a participant would not get any indication from the survey designer simply because of the appearance of web survey. Links to the survey were sent to the participants through e-mails. Participants could complete the survey when they had Internet access.

In the second wave, questionnaires were distributed to college students at a university in Southern China as well as to undergraduates of a university in Northern China. Convenience sampling was used and group-administered surveys were conducted in class.

Measurement

The first section in the questionnaire included 10 major services that Renren provides. Participants were required to rate their level of agreement with each specific service, including posting photos, writing articles about oneself, reading text-only articles, updating status, sharing music, watching videos, playing mini-games with friends, reading articles which have illustrations, finding information on celebrities, and finding professional organizations.

The second section listed 20 statements adopted from a study (Ray, 2007) about Renren use. Participants were asked to rate their level of agreement with specific reasons for using Renren, including socializing (e.g., to get peer support from others), entertainment (e.g., to kill time when I have nothing else to do), self-status seeking (e.g., because I feel peer pressure to participate), and information seeking (e.g., to get academic information or do research).

The third section was constructed to investigate participants' self-construal. The measurement was adapted from Gudykunst et al. (1996). The 10 statements of measuring self-construal included, "feeling emotionally connected with others is an important part of my self-definition," "My family and close relatives are important to who I am," "I often consult my close friends for advice before acting," etc. Participants were asked about their level of agreement (4, strongly agree; 1, strongly disagree.) on all 10 statements. The fourth section is about demographic information of participants, including gender, age, years using Renren, and frequency of usage.

Data Analysis

Collected data were entered manually into Microsoft Excel. Statistical Package for Social Sciences (SPSS) was used to analyze the data. First, a descriptive statisticical analysis was conducted to get demographic information of the participants. Reliability test and regression analysis were utilized for answering research question 1. Then, Chi-square analysis and t-test were used for answering research question 2.

4. Results

Demographic Information

The average age of the sample was 19.41 (SD=1.39). The sample was comprised of 183 (44%) male and 233 (56%) female. 197 students (47.4%) had their social media accounts for one year, 87 (20.9%) had the accounts for two years and 67 (16.1%) had accounts for three years. Of the respondents, 100 (24%) frequent users logged in multiple times a day, with 75 (18%) logging in everyday, and 65 (15.6%) logging in every two or three days, and 64 (15.4%) logging in once a week. There were 112 (26.9%) who were inactive users and logged in once a month or seldom used Renren.

Research Questions

The first research question of the study is: "What is the impact of independent and interdependent self-construal on motivating Chinese young adults to use Renren?" In order to answer this question, two statistical tests were conducted. First, a Pearson correlation analysis was run among the four motivation variables along with independent and interdependent self-construal (see Table 1 for details). Results showed that

Table 1: Means, Standard Deviation, Correlation, and Reliabilities

Variables	Means	SD	1	2	3	4	5	6
1. Interdependent Self-construal	3.08	.53	(.63)					
2. Independent Self-construal	3.28	.49	.46**	(.63)				
3. Socialization	3.53	.62	.37**	.23**	(.77)			
4. Entertainment	3.47	.74	.31**	.23**	.44**	(.71)		
5, Self-status Seeking	3.01	.67	.30**	.11*	.57**	.39**	(.71)	
6. Information Seeking	3.27	0.88	.18**	.09	.45**	.29**	.43**	(.88)

Note: N= 416. Reliability estimates, in parentheses, are alpha coefficients.
*P<.05
**P<.01

interdependent self-construal was significantly positively correlated with each of the four motivation variables, while independent self-construal variable was significantly positively correlated with all but information seeking.

In order to examine predicating power of two self-construal concepts for the four motives of using Renren, multiple stepwise regression analysis was conducted. In each of the four tests (Tables 2-5), the dependent variable was socialization, entertainment, self-status seeking and information seeking respectively and predicating variables included independent and interdependent self-construal, frequency logging on Renren, and years in using Renren.

Table 2: Regression Analysis of Variables Predicting for Socialization (Stepwise Regression Analysis)

Predicting Variables	B	SE	t	Beta
Interdependent Self-construal	.45	.05	8.37	.385**
Age	-.05	.02	-2.53	-.12*

Note: Dependent variable=socialization; N= 416;
adjusted multiple R2=.14

Table 3: Regression Analysis of Variables Predicting for Entertainment (Stepwise Regression Analysis)

Predicting Variables	B	SE	t	Beta
Interdependent Self-construal	.31	.07	4.39	.23**
Independent Self-construal	.16	.08	2.10	.11*
Frequency of log on Renren	.12	.02	5.25	.24*

Note: Dependent variable=Entertainment;N=416;
adjusted multiple R2=.16

Table 4: Regression Analysis of Variables Predicting for Self-Status Seeking (Stepwise Regression Analysis)

Predicting Variables	B	SE	t	Beta
Interdependent Self-construal	.38	.06	6.20	.30**
Age	-.05	.02	-2.10	-.13*
Frequency of log on Renren	.05	.02	2.30	.11*
Gender	-.18	.07	-2.74	-.13**

Note: Dependent variable=self-status seeking; N= 416; adjusted multiple R2=.11

Parallel to correlation analysis, interdependent self-construal had a consistent predicting power for each of the motivation variables including socialization, entertainment, self-status seeking and information seeking. Only in entertainment motive, independent self-construal had a significant predicting power. Other interesting findings included that age was a variable which negatively predicted self-status seeking, information seeking, and socialization; frequency of logging on Renren could predict entertainment and self-status seeking, and years in using Renren negatively predicted information seeking.

Table 5: Regression Analysis of Variables Predicting for Information Seeking (Stepwise Regression Analysis)

Predicting Variables	B	SE	t	Beta
Interdependent Self-construal	.39	.08	4.91	.24**
Age	-.09	.03	-3.10	-.15**
Years in Using Renren	-.15	.04	-3.93	-.19**

Note: Dependent variable=information seeking; N= 416; adjusted multiple R2=.16

The regression analysis showed that Chinese young adults were still driven by their interdependent self-construal to use Renren to socialize, be entertained, seek information and self-status. This result suggested that collective cultural values motivate individuals to use the social media site. Independent self-construal predicted for entertainment only, which suggested that being entertained tends to be individual needs oriented. The independent self-construal failed to predict socialization, self-status seeking and information seeking.

The second research question is: How do Chinese male and female young adults differ in using Renren? The first aspect of this research question refers to how gender may affect frequency of logging on the social media. Chi-square results on Table 6 showed that males and females were significantly different on the frequency of logging on Renren ($x2 =$ 9.85, df = 4, n = 416, p< 0.05). Females tend to log on Renren more often than males; 26% females logged on Renren several times a day, while 21% males did so.

Table 6: Chi-Square Analysis of Frequency of Log on Renren among Males and Females

| Variable | n | Gender | | $\chi2$ | p |
		Males	Females		
Frequency of log on Renren				9.85	0.043
Several times a day	100	39	61		
Once a day	75	28	47		
Once every two to three days	66	28	37		
Once a week	64	25	39		
Once a month or seldom	112	63	49		
Totals	416	183	233		

The second aspect of gender impact in using Renren is how Chinese male and female have different purposes of using Renren. A t-test was conducted to exam research question two. Table 7 showed that males were statistically significantly different from females on information seeking (t= -2.32, p<.05) and self-status seeking (t= 2.01, p < .05).

Table 7 Comparison of Males and Females on Motives of Using Renren (N = 183 males and 234 females)

Variable	M	SD	T	df	p
Information Seeking			-2.32	414	0.021*
Males	3.15	0.97			
Females	3.36	0.79			
Self-status Seeking			2.01	414	0.045*
Males	3.09	0.70			
Females	2.95	0.65			
Entertainment			-1.13	414	0.259
Males	3.42	0.73			
Females	3.51	0.75			
Socializing			-0.16	414	0.873
Males	3.52	0.66			
Females	3.53	0.58			

*p< .05

An inspection of the means of the two groups indicated that the mean of information seeking for female (M = 3.36) is significantly higher than the score (M = 3.15) for males, however the average score of self-status seeking for females (M = 2.95) is significantly lower than the mean score (M = 3.09) for males. Males did not differ significantly from females in entertainment and socialization.

6. Discussion

This is an exploratory study, focusing on how the cultural and gender factors affect Chinese young adults using Renren. It is evident that the Chinese economy has changed dramatically over the past 33 years, from a government controlled economy to a market oriented economy, from closed society to a more open society, from a third world country economy to the 2nd largest economic power in the world. All these economic changes are hardly seen in individual cultural value changes as the study showed. This study suggested that the interdependent self-construal is still dominating young adults' minds in terms of motivating them to use social networking site Renren. More important, the high economic development shapes young people's capitalist beliefs, values, and attitudes. People are expected to become more independent and individualistic. It was anticipated that this independent self-construal may have some more predicting power among the Chinese young people's minds. However, the results showed that the Chinese young adults are still influenced by the interdependent self-construal, which is the primary driving force for individuals to use the social networking site.

Secondly, the correlation results also suggest that independent self-construal does significantly correlate with all three motivations, except for information seeking. This finding indicates that although the interdependent self-construal remains the dominating driving force, independent self-construal also has a significant relationship with three motivation factors of using the social media site.

Thirdly, the variable of age tends to significantly negatively predict socialization, self-status and information seeking. The older individuals become, the less they want to use Renren to socialize, seek self-status and information.

Finally, the results show that gender did play an important role in Chinese college students' use of social networking sites. Most studies conducted in the United States show that females are more active in social media use than males. Chinese female college students also tend to use Renren more often than males. As for the motivations of using Renren, male users and female users are significantly different in information-seeking and self-status seeking. However, they are not significantly different in entertainment and socialization. Both genders use social networking sites to satisfy their socializing and entertaining needs. At the same time, women use Renren to find interesting and useful information. Men appear to focus more on self-status when using social networking sites than women. It is reasonable to assume that females are more protective to their personal information, and they tend to disclose less information about themselves. They simply look for information on social networking sites.

These results contribute to the cumulative body of knowledge and also verify the existing knowledge from previous literature. However, this study also has several limitations. Most participants are from southern and northern parts of China, especially large cities, limiting the representation of other places like small towns or other rural areas in China. Moreover, the scope in designing the questionnaire is also limited. Finally, this study used a convenient sampling which poses constraints in representativeness of the target population.

Future research could be developed in several directions. First, how other demographic information such as differences in heavy users vs light users in consuming SNS. Second, a longitudinal study could be conducted to see a gradual change of users when using the same SNS. Third, people may use different SNS for different purposes. For example, twitter users focus on information seeking and Facebook users focus on contacting friends. Fourth, an in-depth interview approach could be effective to better understand why people use social media.

*An earlier version of the paper was presented at the International Communication Association Annual Conference in Boston, MA, May 2011. The paper later was published (2012) in *Asian Pacific Journal of Human Communication, Vol, 15.*

References

Chiu, C., Ip, C., and Silverman, A. (2012). Understanding social media in China. *The McKinsey Quarterly*, 2, 78-81.

Crampton, T. (2011). Social media in China: The same, but different. *The China Business Review.* Retrieved from http://www. thomascrampton.com/china/social-media-china-business-review/

Dillman, D. A. (2000). *Tailored design of mail and other self-administered surveys.* New York, NY : Wiley-Interscience.

Dong, D., Day, D. K., and Cao, X. (2008). Consumer cultural value changes reflected through ads in a Chinese English language magazine: Beijing Review. In Q. Dong (Eds), *Readings in communication research methods.* San Diego, CA: University Readers.

Dong, Q., Day, D. D. & Deol, R. (2010). Resonant message and powerful media: Analysis of the success of the Obama presidential campaign. In H. Harris, K., Moffitt, K., & C. Squires, (Eds). *The Obama Effect: Multidisciplinary Renderings of the 2008 Campaign.* New York: NY: SUNY Press.

Dong, Q., Wu, Y., & Gu, X. (2011, May). *The Impact of culture and gender on Chinese young adults in using social networking site (Renren/Xiaonei).* Paper presented at International Communication Association Annual Conference in Boston, MA.

Ellison, N. B., Steinfield, C., & Lampe, C. (2007). The benefits of Facebook "Friends:" Social capital and college students' use of online social network sites. *Journal of Computer-Mediated Communication, 12*(4), 1143–1168.

Eun-A, P., Yoon, J. K., & Jae H. K. (2005). Why do they go to movie sites?: Motives and Activities of Internet Movie Site Users. Paper presented at International Communication Association Annual Conference, New York City, NY.

Gudykunst, W. B., Mtsumoto, Y., Ting-Toomey, S., Nishida, T., Kim, K.S., & Heyman, S. (1996). The influence of cultural individualism-collectivism, self construals, and individual values on communication styles across cultures. *Human Communication Research, 22,* 510–543.

Gudykunst, W. B., & Ting-Toomey, S. (1988). *Culture and interpersonal communication.* Newbury Park, CA: Sage.

Hall, E. T. (1976). *Beyond culture.* New York, NY: Double Day.

Hofstede, G. (2001). *Culture's consequences: Comparing values, behaviors, institutions, and organizations across nations (2nd Ed.).* Thousand Oaks, CA: Sage.

Joinson, A. N. (2008). "Looking at", "looking up" or "keeping up with" people? Motives and uses of Facebook. In Proceeding of the Twenty-Sixth Annual SIGCHI Conference on Human Factors in Computing Systems, 1027–1036.

Kim, Y., Sohn, D., & Choi, S. (2011). Cultural difference in motivations for using social network sites: A comparative study of American and Korean college students. *Computers in Human Behavior, 27*(1), 365–372.

Kujath, C. L. (2011). Facebook and MySpace: Complement or Substitute for Face-to-Face Interaction? CyberPsychology, *Behavior & Social Networking, 14*(1/2), 75–78. doi:10.1089/cyber.2009.0311

Lu, X. & Chen, G. (2011). Language change and value orientations in Chinese culture. *China Media Research, 7*(3), 56-63.

Madden, M. & Zickuhr, K. (2011). 65% of online adults use social networking sites. *Pew Internet & American Life Project.* Retrieved January 24, 2012 from http://www.pewinternet.org/Reports/2011/Social-Networking-Sites/Overview/Findings.aspx

Markus, R. H., & Kitayama, S. (1991). Culture and the Self: Implications for Cognition, Emotion, and Motivation. *Psychological Review, 98*(2), 224–253.

Ray, M. (2007). Needs, motives, and behaviors in computer-mediated communication: An inductive exploration of social networking websites. Paper presented at International Communication Association Annual Conference, San Francisco, CA.

Rice, R. & Haythornthwaite, C. (2007). Perspectives on Internet use: Access, involvement and interaction, In L.A. Lievrouw,. & S. Livingstone, S (Eds) *The Handbook of New Media, 92*–113. Thousand Oaks, CA: Sage Publications.

Sitaram, K. S. (1995) *Communication and culture: A world view.* New York: McGraw Hill.

Thelwall, M. (2008). Social networks, gender and friending: An analysis of MySpace member profiles. *Journal of the American Society for Information Science and Technology 59* (8), 1321–1330.

Thelwall, M. (2009). Homophily in MySpace. *Journal of the American Society for Information Science and Technology, 60* (2), 219–231.

Urista, M., Dong, Q., & Day, D. K. (2010). Explaining why young adults use MySpace and Facebook through uses and gratifications theory. *Human Communication, 12,* 215–229.

Zhang, S. & Prosser, M. H. (2012). Globalization, Asian modernity, values, and Chinese civil society. *China Media Research, 8,* (2), 18–25.

VIII.   Chinese Consumers' Perception of Social Media: A Phenomenological Study

Huan Chen

Department of Communication, The Behrend College,
The Pennsylvania State University at Erie, Pennsylvania
Huanchen.orange@gmail.com

Abstract

This chapter discusses Chinese consumers' perception of social media. Specifically, by using the phenomenological approach, the chapter focuses on Chinese consumers' understanding and interpretation of a popular social network site (SSN): Happy Network. The findings revealed that the shared meanings of the Happy Network were interdependent with participants' interpretations of time, fun, need to belong, social interactions, and information, shaped by and reflective of their social role as white-collar professionals and the cultural characteristics of contemporary Chinese society. Specifically, participants' understanding of the Happy Network entailed five dialectic relations: in control/controlled by, dependent/independent, public/private, intimate/distant, and personal/social.

Keywords: Social network site (SNS), China, Happy Network, phenomenological study

1. Introduction

During her lunch break, a young office worker logs onto a Chinese social network Website, "开心网" (Happy Network). She changes her status to "struggling" and checks the status of her friends, writing short comments in response to a few. Then she quickly browses new posts, after which she plays some online games, including parking war, trading friends, Happy Farm, Happy Restaurant, and Super Tycoon. Suddenly, her phone rings. She stops playing games, immediately picks up the phone, and resumes her work.

This typical scenario describes Chinese professionals' experiences, during their daily work, with Happy Network, a newly launched Chinese social network site (SNS). As U.S. SNSs, such as Facebook, MySpace, Friendster, and Twitter, have grown increasingly popular worldwide (boyd & Ellison, 2007; Donath & boyd, 2004; Tong et al., 2007), sites have launched in different regions to attract local users. For example, the most popular SNSs in specific cultural regions include Orkut in India, Mixi in Japan, LunaStorm in Sweden, Bebo in the United Kingdom, Friendster in Southern Asia, hi5 in Portugal and Latin America, and Cyworld in Korea (Cardon, 2009; Kim & Yun, 2007).

China has the largest Internet population in the world (Riegner, 2008; Zeng, Huang, & Dou, 2009). According to the China Internet Network Information Center (CNNIC, 2012), at the end of 2011, Chinese SNS users reached 244 million, approximately half of all Chinese Internet users (47.6%). Compared with general Chinese Internet users, users of Chinese SNSs have relatively more education, earn higher incomes, and are younger, which means social network sites are an attractive medium for marketers and advertisers (Zeng, Huang, & Dou 2009).

One of the most popular SNSs in China, Happy Network, was launched in April 2008 (Cao, 2008). Currently, it has more than more 60 million registered users ("Binhao Cheng", 2009), approximately half of which are urban, white-collar professionals. These Chinese urban white-collar professionals have significant buying power (Iresearch, 2007). Although they account for only 1% of the urban population, their disposable income constitutes 10% of all disposable income of this population. According to the CEO of Happy Network, at the end of last year, its advertising income thus reached $7 million per month, and more than $23 million have been invested as venture capital ("Binhao Chang," 2009).

This study aims to advance understanding of Chinese SNSs and their users by exploring the socially constructed meanings of social network sites among urban, white-collar, professional users, which should offer meaningful insights for marketers who want to communicate with Chinese consumers through this medium. Specifically, this study considers how urban white-collar professional users of Chinese social network sites perceive, understand, and interpret SNSs by investigating the newly launched Happy Network (www.kaxin001.com).

The Social Network Site: Happy Network

The Chinese government maintains relatively strict control over information flow on the Internet (Hu, 2010). Some popular SNSs, such as Facebook, are not available in mainland China. This strict control has offered Chinese program developers an opportunity to design and build their own versions of Chinese SNS. Since 2007, various Chinese SNSs have copied Facebook's methods, including Xiaonei (changed name to Renren in 2009), Hainei, 51.com, and Happy Network. Accordingly, SNSs have become more popular among Chinese Internet users; currently, more than 1,000 Chinese SNSs have been established. The most successful of these include Renren, Happy Network, and Shiji Jiayuan, which focus on social life, white-collar professionals, and dating, respectively (Zhao, 2009).

Since launching in April 2008 (Cao, 2008), Happy Network (www. kaixin001.com) reached a ranking of 1,300 among all global Websites in July 2008, but by April 2009, had moved up to 118, surpassing "校内网"(www.xiaonei.com), the largest SNS in China (Li, 2008a) as the top Chinese SNS and the most popular social network site among Chinese white-collar professionals.

Some experts have claimed that the Happy Network is the best Chinese imitator of Facebook (Xie, 2008b), though it differs in two ways: First, Happy Network focuses on a different user group. The foundational users of Facebook were college students while the first users of Happy Network were urban, white-collar professionals (Xie, 2008b).

Second, Happy Network focuses on web games. During its early developmental stage, the most popular games were "Trading Friends" and "Parking War" (Cao, 2008; Li, 2008a). However, like Facebok, the site allows users to change their personal status, store and share photos and music, write and share blogs, exchange short messages, send gifts, test themselves, launch polls or reports, and so forth. These functions are activated through various modules embedded in the website, which are updated and augmented regularly. As of January 2012, more than 30 modules covered diverse social and interactive functions. In addition, the site offers a platform for users to look for friends through its people search function (www.kaixin001.com).

2. Literature Review

Previous research on SNSs has explored diverse topics, including impression management (boyd, 2007; Donath & boyd, 2004; Walther et al., 2008), network structure (Acar, 2008; Donath, 2007; Zywica & Danowski, 2008), online/offline connections (Donath & boyd, 2004; Hargittai, 2007), privacy issues (Ibrahim, 2008; Lewis, Kanfman, & Christakis, 2008), niche communities (Byrne, 2007; McCabe, 2009; Mellin, 2008), motivations for using social network sites (Gangadharbatla, 2008), and specific types of social networks (Humphreys 2007; Wildermuth & Vogl-Bauer, 2007). Despite the variety of this content, most research on SNSs has focused on U.S.-based Websites and English-speaking populations (Kim & Yun, 2007). Fewer studies examine SNSs in other regions.

Motivations for Using SNSs

In a study of college students' attitude toward and willingness to join SNSs, Gangadharbatla (2008) suggests that Internet self-efficacy, need to belong, and collective self-esteem have positive effects on attitudes toward SNSs. In a similar study, Barker (2009) reveals that social identity gratifications and social compensation motivate older adolescents to use SNSs. Communication with peer group members is the most important motivation, and collective self-esteem relates positively to SNS usage.

SNSs in Other Countries and Regions

Two studies examine social network sites and users in other cultural regions. By interviewing 49 users of Cyworld, the most popular social network site in Korea, Kim and Yun (2007) reveal a relational dialectic that results from the desire to manage preexisting interpersonal relationships and self-representations. To participants, Cyworld is not an independent and technological cyberworld but rather an interdependent social world that buffers or transforms real-world relational issues. Agarwal and Mital (2009) survey 427 business school students in India and find that they use SNSs not only for leisure and personal socialization but also as a platform for more meaningful and serious deliberations, such as job hunting.

Chinese SNSs and Users

Zeng, Huang, and Dou (2009) examine the impacts of social identity and group norms on community users' group intentions to accept advertising in online social networking communities and find positive relationships in both cases. When users consider community advertising more relevant to the theme of the community and congruent with their social identities, they deem that advertising more valuable and display more favorable behavioral responses to it.

Chu and Choi (2009) find that younger Chinese consumers spend significant time on selected social network sites and have relatively positive attitudes toward those sites. Bridging social capital is an important motive for Chinese youth who use SNSs. In addition, their self-presentation strategies include competence, supplication, and ingratiation. Chinese youth also seem to engage in electronic word of mouth (eWOM) through social network sites.

Research Question

Previous literature makes clear that academic research on Chinese SNSs lags behind practices. Although a few studies have examined different aspects of Chinese SNSs and introduced several interesting theoretical perspectives, they have all been designed to test and confirm researchers' theoretical assumptions rather than focusing on users' experiences and interpretations. To gain a deeper understanding of Chinese SNSs, it is necessary to access the users' realities and reveal their lived meanings of the SNSs. This study therefore explores what are the lived meanings among Chinese, urban, white-collar, professional users in relation to Happy Network (www.kaixin001.com). As its overarching research question, this study considers how Chinese urban white-collar professional users make sense of SNSs. Specifically, this study explores users' motivations, activities, feelings, experiences, and attitudes toward the SNS to reveal the realities and socially constructed meanings of SNSs.

3. Methodology

The target population of the study are Chinese urban white-collar professional users of Happy Network. In the current study, urban white-collar professionals are broadly defined as educated adults who work in professional and nonmanual occupations with a middle-level (3000 yuan or $452 per month) or higher income (iResearch, 2010).

The theoretical perspective guiding the study is phenomenological, using in-depth interviews to collect data. All interviews were conducted face-to-face within the settings that were comfortable and natural for the participants. Based on participants' preferences, interview settings included office conference rooms, coffee shops, and restaurants. For participants' convenience, most of the interviews were conducted either during lunch breaks (12:00 pm – 2:00 pm) or in the evenings (6: 00 pm – 10: 00 pm). Each interview lasted about 30 to 75 minutes. To provide an accurate record of participants' comments, the interviews were audio recorded and transcribed in Chinese, then translated into English.

Before interviewing participants, a bracketing interview was conducted to make explicit the presuppositions and biases the investigator brings to the research situation. Through the bracketing interview, the investigator became conscious of her prejudgments, biases, preconceived ideas, and attitudes toward the SSN. As a result, when she interviewed her participants, she was conscious of her prepositions and attempted to focus on her participants' experiences with a fresh eye.

Purposive sampling and snow-balling sampling guided recruitment of participants. The criterion for sufficient sampling is saturation, that is, the point at which no new concepts and themes emerge (Corbin & Strauss,

2008). In total, 26 white-collar professionals from Beijing and Shanghai participated in this research. Among these participants, 11 were men and 15 were women, whose ages ranged from 24 to 33 years. All participants had some college-level education and had a variety of job titles, including insurance broker, marketing manager, customer service staff, salesman, engineer, journalist, PR consultant, head-hunting consultant, and IT technician. Their annual incomes ranged from 40,000 yuan ($6,021) to 500,000 yuan($75,258). All participants had the experience of exchanging virtual gifts and/or playing one or more social games in Happy Network (see Table 1).

Data analysis of the study followed the principle of phenomenological reduction (Moustakas, 1994). The first step of phenomenological reduction is horizonalization, which means putting the immediate phenomena on a level plane, without assuming an initial hierarchy of "reality" (Ihde, 1986). In order to do this, the researcher took extensive notes when she was conducting the interviews, listened to each interview twice, and intensively read each transcript three times to catch every detail and variation. The second step of phenomenological reduction is to delimit the invariant horizons or meaning units. In this stage, the primary job of the researcher was to identify and compare repeated or similar words, phrases, and sentences appearing in each transcript. Generally, 20 to 30 meaning units were generated in every transcript. The next step that the researcher took was to cluster the invariant constituents into themes. During this phase, the researcher focused on the internal relationships and structures of the meaning units and grouped them into appropriate themes.

Different research paradigms demand different evaluative criteria. Rather than validity and reliability for quantitative research, the criteria evaluation of qualitative research paradigms focuses on different aspects. Generally, "credibility," "transferability," "dependability," and "conformability" are the most important evaluative criteria for qualitative research (Hirschman 1986; Miles and Huberman, 1984; Lincoln & Cuba, 1985). Credibility refers to the reconstruction of multiple realities, credible to the constructors of the original multiple realities. In other words, credibility means authentic representations of participant's social experiences. Transferability means study findings fit within contexts outside the study situation. In other words, transferability is achieved when the findings have applicability to another setting, to theory, to practice, or to future research. Dependability refers to minimization of idiosyncrasies in interpretation. It suggests that multiple human investigators should draw similar interpretations regarding a specific phenomenon. Conformability refers to the extent to which biases, motivations, interests, or perspectives of the inquirer influence interpretation. However, the interpretation generated by the researcher is not assumed to be disinterested or value-free but is expected to be supportable from the data as gathered by the inquirer and to represent a logical set of conclusions given the reasoning he or she employed during the interaction.

Several steps were taken to ensure the quality of research. First, both Chinese and English versions of the data analysis reports were provided to some participants to ensure that the findings represented their perspectives and understanding. Second, during the entire study, the researcher constantly reflected on her own assumptions, beliefs, and biases, especially in comparison with participants' realities, to confirm that the interpretations reflected the participants' views, rather than her own. Third, peer debriefing and external auditors (Creswell & Miller, 2000) also ensured the quality of the analysis. Finally, this researcher observed one of the most important criteria for evaluating the quality of a phenomenological study is to make sure that each theme is evidenced by the words of the participants themselves (Graves, 2006). This is accomplished by presenting participants' own words and original expressions when reporting thematic findings. Such emic, inference-free descriptions render more information and provide readers a basis for "accepting, rejecting, or modifying an investigator's conclusion" (Haley 1996, p. 26).

4. Findings

As Figure 1 shows, the shared meanings of Happy Network were interdependent with participants' interpretations of time, fun, need to belong, social interactions, and information. Specifically, they expressed understandings of Happy Network through five dialectic relations: in control/controlled by, dependent/independent, public/private, intimate/ distant, and personal/social.

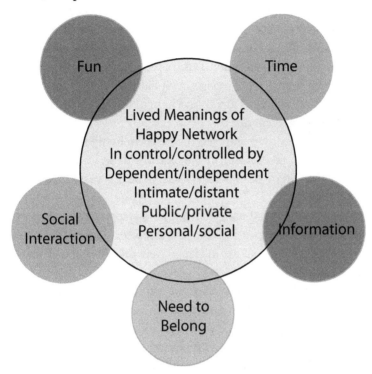

Figure 1: The General Meanings of Happy Network

Frame of Reference: Five Dimensions

The Time Dimension

Participants in the current study consistently showed their consciousness of time. The time dimension is closely related to participants' social role as white-collar professionals. On the one hand, as busy white-collar workers living in the "fast-paced working environment", these participants reported that Happy Network saves them time by helping them find information quickly, manage their social relationships efficiently, and entertain themselves and their friends flexibly. On the other hand, however, to some participants, playing social games wastes too much time. As a result, they "stop playing games in Happy Network".

Happy Garden is relatively entertaining. It does not occupy too much of my time. As white-collar professionals, we are working at office. We couldn't play games all the time. ... If I am not busy, I will log onto Happy Network at 10:00 a.m. Even when I don't play games, I still open the website because there are a lot of reposts. ... If I am too busy, I will close the website. If I am not too busy, I am always hanging on the website (Jenny, female, 28, marketing, Shanghai).

Urban city life is busy. Everyone has his/her own living space. We don't have time to see each face to face in the real world. So we communicate with each other in Happy Network (Wilson, male, 29, insurance broker, Beijing).

I have played Parking War, Living Together, and Happy Garden. However, I was tired of them later and felt that it wasted too much of my time. Therefore, I stopped playing games in Happy Network (Zara, female, owner of an online store, Beijing).

This theme partially signals Chinese white-collar professionals' "time syndrome" (Xiao, 2006). As noted above, Chinese white-collar professionals work longer hours, take fewer holidays and vacations, and suffer higher degrees of anxiety and pressure compared with white-collar professionals in Western countries (Xiao, 2006; Xie, 2008a). Consequently, these SNS users are highly sensitive to time and are eager to manage their limited time. In their fast-paced transitional society, alienated from both agricultural and industrial civilizations (Shi, 2009), they define time as a limited resource, which can either be squandered or saved by participating in Happy Network.

The Fun Dimension

Fun is another important element of the constructed meanings of Happy Network. Participants used different words to express this feeling, such as interesting, playful, happy, and entertaining. Seeking fun for themselves and entertaining their friends were two important motivations:

I have fun in Happy Network. ... I also make fun of others, such as I would like to issue tickets on my friends' cars. That's it (Laura, female, 24, data analyst, Shanghai).

Then, I felt that playing games with my friends makes me very happy. It is actually like its name – Happy Network (laugh) (Nancy, female, 28, graphic designer, Shanghai).

Happy Network is pretty good. It makes my life more colorful (Zara, female, owner of an online store, Beijing).

If I found something interesting in Happy Network, I would share with my friends through reposts (Sofia, 26, female, PR account executive, Beijing).

As Holt (2005) has indicated, play is an important aspect of consuming. Similar to baseball spectators, the participants in this study engage in two types of play in the context of the SNS: communing, in which they share mutually felt experiences with others, and socializing, in which they use experiential practices to entertain each other. Participants' pursuit of fun in Happy Network also reflects the characteristics of communication in contemporary China. According to Zhang (2009), industrialization and informationization have pushed China into an era of leisure communication, in which media help audiences improve the quality of their leisure activities. One indicator of this era is a blurred boundary between work and leisure, as represented by white-collar professionals who intentionally integrate their work and leisure activities in the SNS.

The Need to Belong Dimension

People need relationships characterized by both regular contact and ongoing bonding in their social lives (Baumeister & Leary, 1995). The need to belong motivated participants to initiate, participate, develop, and sustain their activities in Happy Network. The SNS offers them a platform to connect with others regularly and build a sense of belongingness:

All my friends registered for Happy Network. So I also registered. Now everyday when I go back to my home, after I open QQ and MSN, I will open Happy Network to read reposts and check my friends' statuses (Sunny, 27, female, group purchase staff, Shanghai).

I felt that at that time Happy Network was popular among my friends. If I didn't use Happy Network, I would be out. For example, (before I registered Happy Network), many of my friends asked me "Hi, you haven't joined Happy Network? You are too outdated" (Laura, female, 24, data analyst, Shanghai).

Do you know? When we played crazily about Happy Network, we talked about the games even in the elevator. We would ask each other "Hi, what cars have you bought?" I also heard that other people were discussing parking issues and stealing vegetables. ... I felt that everyone around me was playing Happy Network. When I logged onto Happy Network, I found that everyone was online (Nancy, female, 28, graphic designer, Shanghai).

Chinese urban white-collar professionals are a special social group in contemporary Chinese society. They are a newly emerging social class with relatively high education and income, and they greatly contribute to societal development through their knowledge, skills, and taxes (Yu, 2005). However, because they frequently change jobs and move to different places, it is hard for them to build belongingness through local communities. Thus, white-collar professionals often use the Internet to unite and build their collective social identity (Zhang & Lei, 2009). The SNS offers an ideal place for white-collar professionals to address their need to belong and establish their social identity through multiple services (Gangadharbatla, 2008). As the quotes indicate, Happy Network serves as a conversational resource and communicative platform that allows members to enact their sense of belonging to a group.

The Social Interaction Dimension

Participants discussed their Happy Network experiences in the context of social interactions. For participants, social interactions occurred at multiple levels, involving both online and offline communication and activities.

> *Another thing is social interaction. For example, some of my classmates or friends posted photos. I would like to make comments on those photos. Some of my classmates and friends like taking photos and they post their photos periodically. Sometimes I made comments on their photos. Sometimes I asked them their recent statuses, such as whether or not they buy new lens and things like that. Then we could start our conversation from a photo. It is like this (Serendipity, male, 28, engineer, Shanghai).*

> *It (Happy Network) influences my offline life. For example, many of my online friends are living in my neighborhood. Someone cooked a good dish and posted the photo in Happy Network. We all praised him or her about the dish, which make our relationships become more harmonious. Or they may post their kids' photos and we comment on those photos. It is like that we care for each other through the Internet. How to say, sometimes it is hard to express those through face-to-face communication, telephone, or messaging because these things are related to your social community. For example, you couldn't' send messages to everyone and tell them that you cook a good dish. So it is useful to communicate such stuff through Happy Network (Yilian, female, 31, patent attorney, Beijing).*

Just as Facebook is an important channel for college students in the United States to create and maintain social capital through bridging, bonding, and maintaining social relationships with multiple social interactions (Ellison, Steinfield, & Lampe, 2007), Happy Network performs a similar function for white-collar professional participants, to form and maintain their social capital through online social interactions that connect both online and offline social relationships.

The Information Dimension

According to the participants, Happy Network has become an important channel by which they assess a variety of information, such as recent news about friends and society, hot issues, public opinions, popular trends, tips of daily lives, and so forth. In this sense, Happy Network is a multifunctional information provider, which satisfies diverse information needs.

> *Yes, their statuses including whether or not they upload new photos or repost some funny posts. It is probably a channel for gathering information ... and to know their living environments. ... (I would like to read) on the one hand, funny reposts. On the other hand, because reposts are related to personal interests, there is lots of useful information, such as how to operate Excel or PPT or some useful data. I will save these data to use as resources. Most information is entertaining or the most popular stuff in the current society, for example, the world cup. There are many "world cup" related topics. In fact, in the contemporary environment of the Internet, everyone is the producer of content. You can assess a variety of weird thoughts or creative ideas. ... Yes, all (materials) are the original stuff created by the Internet users, through which you can know diverse social phenomena. In addition to propaganda of government, those national affairs and news, you can find real voices from grassroots (in Happy Network). Because they originated from grassroots, these contents are mostly jokes or funny stuffs. But behind the jokes and funny stuffs, you will see social realities or popular trends, which are reflective of the Internet users' mentality and attitude. ... I feel that currently the Internet users who post messages are those who have some education but are relatively vulnerable in the society. They are not the people who control the mainstream discourse. Therefore, they want to express their emotions and dissatisfactions through Internet (Tom, male, 33, vice manager, Beijing).*

Frame of Reference Themes to the Key Dialectics

The five dimensions described above intertwine and form the reference framework for participants to interpret their SNS experiences. Although the five dimensions demonstrate participants' basic understandings of SNS, these themes don't reflect all the tensions and contradictions existing in the data. Throughout the interviews, participants displayed complicated and paradoxical feelings toward the Happy Network. In order to fully capture the lived meanings of the SNS, the researcher further uncovered five interpretative themes. Specifically, the lived meanings of Happy Network are reflected in the five key dialectics: being in control/controlled by, dependent/independent, public/private, intimate/distant, and personal/social.

Being in Control/Controlled by

The participants' feelings of being in control of or controlled by the SNS were demonstrated in various dimensions of their experiences on Happy Network. Specifically, they expressed the feeling of being in control in terms of their perception of self-control and control of social relationships. As white-collar professionals, self-discipline is important for them to survive in their fast-paced and highly competitive working environment. In an unstable and dynamically transforming society, individual Chinese people also consciously or unconsciously seek self-control to secure their personal safety and development (Li, 2008b). The participants derive a sense of self-control from controlling their time, information, and entertainment:

> *The most important thing is speed. You can quickly check changes of your friends' statuses, such as what he or she has done recently, what they have played, any progress on their work and studies? You can also read some funny reposts at the earliest time. Its communication speed is faster than traditional news websites and BBS websites. In addition, it saves your time for selecting news and information because news that many people repost and comment must be the hottest issues happened recently (Steven, male, 30, IT technician, Shanghai).*

*Each time I stay in Happy Network for about half an hour. I log onto
it several times during my working hours. I mainly play games with
my friends for entertainment and relaxation because the games can
be stopped at any time (Sherry, female, 28, art editor, Beijing).*

In addition, the participants said that they are able to control their
social relations through Happy Network with more ease than relationship
management in the real world. Traditional Chinese culture emphasizes
human ethics and relationships (Wang, 1996). In traditional Chinese
society, all relationships are built on family and generate from family
members, which traditionally has made them relatively easy to maintain
and manage. However, in modern China, industrialization, modernization,
and informationization have induced a series of societal changes that
have fundamentally changed Chinese people's relationships. The scope of
relationships is much broader, the relationships are more heterogeneous,
and there is a greater sense of alienation (Zhang & Pan, 2009). Various
real-world obstacles make managing and maintaining relationships harder
for modern Chinese people. In particular, urban white-collar professionals'
high mobility and fast-paced work rhythm make relationships especially
hard (Liao, 2009). However, in the virtual world, Happy Network empowers
white-collar professional participants to overcome these restrictions and
manage their relationships through multiple communicative and social
functions:

*I felt that some functions of Happy Network helped me to reconnect
with my previous classmates including those who are studying
abroad. Em, for example, I reconnected with a high school classmate
through Happy Network and met her in a small party several days
ago. We haven't seen each other for 14 years. I felt very happy (Tresor,
female, 28, manager of a toy company, Shanghai).*

*I felt that it (Happy Network) facilitates social interaction among
people. For example, it is hard for friends or family members,
especially in big cities in contemporary China to have a dinner
together because everyone is busy. However, in Happy Network, we
can maintain our relationships through virtual caring for each other
(Victor, male, 25, PR account executive, Shanghai).*

> *I consider Happy Network as a two-dimensional cell phone. ...*
> *Sometimes its communication is better than cell phone or instant*
> *message tools such as QQ and MSN. For example, if I want to talk to*
> *someone online but don't know what to say, I can send a gift to him*
> *or her as a signal. It is better than messaging "Hello" to him or her.*
> *If she or he sees the gift and thinks of something to say, she or he will*
> *send messages back to me and then we can start our conversation.*
> *If she or he doesn't know what to say or is too busy to communicate,*
> *he or she can just receive the gift or send a gift back to me. It can*
> *reduce some embarrassment between me and my friends (Wilson,*
> *male, 29, insurance broker, Beijing).*

The feeling of being controlled mainly emerges from online game experiences. Unlike online games, Happy Network's games require that participants devote some time every day to each game. Although the games are simple, they are oriented toward the long run, designed to keep users in Happy Network. The games control the participants by controlling their time. As previously discussed, these white-collar professionals are sensitive to time (Shi, 2009), and when the participants realize the manipulation, they often take actions to regain their freedom:

> *Em, I felt that to speak objectively, the games of Happy Network*
> *are all time consuming. ... When I first played Happy Restaurant, I*
> *was crazy about this game. I would make a dish in the morning and*
> *another in the afternoon. I counted how much time left for me to log*
> *onto Happy Network again (to cook). After a while, I felt it was not*
> *necessary. Em, I felt that I shouldn't' waste too much time on games.*
> *So I quit playing the games (Sofia, 26, PR account executive, Beijing).*

As demonstrated across the whole group, experienced game players felt that their preexisting gaming knowledge and skills were not useful when playing Happy Network games. They thus felt restricted by the games. In other words, the games alienated experienced players by limiting their ability to demonstrate their knowledge and skills, which violated their sense of personal achievement. Because most Chinese urban white-collar professionals consider their personal feelings and self-actualization important with regard to evaluations of their experiences (Pan, 1999), they feel that Happy Network should find a better balance between ease and difficulty in designing its games.

> *To tell you the truth, for people who play online games, all web games in Happy Network are not so interesting. Therefore, for me, I don't feel that they are very fun. … The first difference between web games and online games is that the vision effect is different. Almost all online games have 3D version with different scenes. In addition, tasks of online games are much harder than those in web games. Moreover, each online game has a storyline. Web games in Happy Network are too easy. … To me, Happy Network is a platform of socialization rather than a platform of playing games (Jenny, female, 28, marketing, Shanghai).*

> *I don't consider any game in Happy Network interesting. According to me, I play these games only for freshness without persistency, that is, why I should continue to play these games. For some large MMORPG online games, I can gradually improve my rankings. With the highest ranking, I can ultimately beat everyone in the virtual world. However, for those small games in Happy Network, such as Trading Friends, it is fun in that you can buy your friends either rewarding or punishing them. In the Parking War, you try to find a parking lot and buy good cars to compare to your friends'. … I felt that they are too simple (Tom, male, 33, vice manager, Beijing).*

Being Dependent/Independent

The participants indicated both feelings of dependence and independence with regard to Happy Network. Internet users depend on the Internet for information, entertainment, convenience, and social interaction, and similarly, Happy Network users depend on the site to gain information, entertain themselves and others, and communicate and socialize. Thus, Happy Network has become embedded in participants' everyday experiences as a "habitual behavior" and an "addiction."

If I turn on my computer, I will log onto Happy Network no matter whether I check it or not. It has become my habitual behavior (Sunny, 27, female, group purchase staff, Shanghai).

Every day, I spend half of my time on Happy Network. … If it is counted by hour, I spend more than 12 hours on Happy Network each day. I have to admit that I am addicted to it (Wilson, male, 29, insurance broker, Beijing).

Even as participants expressed dependence on Happy Network, they demonstrated efforts to become independent of it. For example, they might log onto Happy Network less, stop playing online games altogether, or use other communicative channels. The participants mainly chose to seek more independence from Happy Network because they felt it waste of time or became fatigued to it:

Recently, I only stay in Happy Network about half of an hour every day to check my friends' statuses and read reposts. I don't play games anymore because first the games are lacking creative ideas, and most importantly I don't have time to play those games (Nelson, male, 26, head-hunting consultant, Shanghai).

At the beginning, I played several games in Happy Network but I currently don't play games because it wastes too much time and I am tired of those games (Samantha, female, 32, art editor, Beijing).

Being Public/Private

The participants' interpretations of Happy Network are intertwined with their sense of public and private space. According to the participants, Happy Network does not distinguish a clear boundary between public and private spaces. It could be described as a private-public or public-private platform. Unlike a general public webpage, the webpage of each user is not accessible to everyone; generally only the friends of users may browse their personal webpages. Thus, each personal webpage on Happy Network is constructed as a private area in a public space. This characteristic greatly shapes the participants' experiences with Happy Network:

> *I don't add strangers in my Happy Network because I often upload some photos in it. I don't want strangers to see my photos. I consider it as my private space. … Communications in QQ and MSN are between two people. The content is only known by the two of us. However, in Happy Network, if someone posts some photos of their vacations, we all can see and comment on them. So he or she doesn't need to tell people one by one. Once he or she posts something, he or she actually shares with all friends (Sunny, 27, female, group purchase staff, Shanghai).*

> *I feel that if I don't want my friends to know something, I would not post it in Happy Network. Even I write diaries in Happy Network, generally I just want to convey some information or I'd like to write some trivia things, such as comments of soccer games. But for some more private things, like my mood, especially my work, I would not write that stuff in Happy Network.… It is after all a public space (Gemini, female, 28, journalist, Shanghai).*

Being Intimate/Distant

Contradictory feelings of being intimate and distant arise from participants' perceptions of the closeness of their relationships on Happy Network. Happy Network allows participants to categorize their friends according to five types: most intimate friends, old friends (including previous classmates and colleagues), new friends (current social relations), friends' friends, and strangers. In traditional Chinese society, all relationships are extensions of relations within the family, and family-based relationships are simple, intimate, and stable (Zhang & Pan, 2009). Because all relationships extend from the family, the degrees of closeness across the different relationships are fairly clear. However, in contemporary Chinese society, the constant differentiation in social structures, innovations of communication technology, and the mobility of social groups have expanded and complicated Chinese people's social relationships, so that they are more fluid. The degrees of intimacy in relationships also has become fuzzy and ambiguous (Wang 1996). The acceleration of the pace of life and sense that time is scarce give modern Chinese people less time to cultivate their relationships, further blurring the degrees of closeness and distance that traditionally distinguished different relationships.

Because the virtual communities tend to lack the complexity and restrictions of the real world, people's social relationships tend to be simple and differentiated. As in traditional Chinese society, the closeness and distance of social relationships becomes salient online. The clarification and distinction of relationships on Happy Network allows its participants to reconstruct a sense of intimacy in this online space. Their feelings of intimacy and distance not only determine their communication and socialization strategies on Happy Network but also influence their offline social relations. Happy Network thus facilitates communications with old friends most, but has less impact on the offline social interactions that participants maintain with their most intimate or distant friends. In this sense, Happy Network transcends the online versus offline boundary and becomes a crucial medium that connects and integrates online with offline social relationships:

Regarding friends on other websites, you may know each other through the Internet but may not meet each other face to face. But in Happy Network, most online friends are your friends (in the real world), previous classmates, or friends' friends. Generally, you won't add someone who you totally don't know except some celebrities. ... Therefore, Happy Network is communicative platform for acquaintance (Frank, male, 28, customer service staff, Shanghai).

For my closest friends, I would like to make comments on their photos or statuses; for my general friends, usually I just browse their photos and read their statuses without making comments unless those photos were really interesting or something really intrigued me. ... I send gifts to my friends depending on closeness and age. If she or he is close to me and similar to my age, I would send her a set of swimming suit and him a package of condom (Gemini, female, 28, journalist, Shanghai).

Happy Network creates a topic for us to communicate about in the real world. I reconnected with many previous classmates through Happy Network. When we hang out to eat dinner or drink coffee, Happy Network became our conversational topic because we haven't seen each other for many years. There is a gap between us. We have to find something that both of us are familiar with to talk. Then we talked about things like who posted something in Happy Network and what I wrote in Happy Network. … I feel that Happy Network facilitates my communication and socialization with my old friends by making us know better about each others' current lives, but not the most intimate and unfamiliar friends (Tresor, female, 28, manager of a toy company, Shanghai).

Being Personal/Social

The participants' understanding of Happy Network is also expressed through their negotiation of personal and social identities on the site. According to Brewer (1991), personal identity is the individual self, denoting characteristics that differentiate one person from others within a given social context. Social identities are categorizations of the self into inclusive social units that depersonalize the self-concept, so that "I" becomes "we." As noted above, participants engage in multiple activities on Happy Network, such as updating their status, messaging, writing diaries, sharing music, commenting, and playing games. Through these activities, they express their personal characteristics and styles to signal and reinforce who they are as individuals. As some participants mention, their restaurants on Happy Network represent their "personal styles." Belk (1988) conceptualizes possessions as extended selves that reflect consumers' identities. In the current study, participants' personal pages on Happy Network could be considered representations of their extended selves, opportunities to construct and reinforce their senses of style, and thus, their personal selves. Meanwhile, the emphasis on personal identity among the participants also reflects the growing sense of individualism among contemporary Chinese (Lin 2001), especially among Chinese youth (Zhang & Shavitt, 2003).

Generally, multiple identities coexist in a specific context (Brewer, 1991). When participants express their personal identity on Happy Network, they also construct their social identities. Social identities on the Internet are changing, multiple, and fluid (Liu, 2009). In a virtual community, people can constantly construct and change social identities to satisfy their various needs and depict themselves from multiple perspectives. For example, the participants gained different life experiences through constructions of different social identities on Happy Network.

I felt that Happy Restaurant has many things in it. You can adjust and arrange these things by yourself at any time. You won't want them to be similar to others'. You have your own ideas. It is a way to show your personal style (Frank, male, 28, customer service staff, Shanghai).

You know, nowadays young people like to expose themselves, showing their personal stuff and displaying their uniqueness and personality. Happy Network is a platform for you to see others and be seen by others including both people you know and those you don't know. So I believe that everyone wants to post his/her coolest photos in Happy Network (Phoenix, male, 30, tourism manager, Beijing).

I feel that many users of Happy Network were born in 82 or 83. We are receptive to new things, like communicating gossip, are a little bit crazy, would like to complain, and are either critical youth or unconcerned citizens (Gemini, female, 28, journalist, Shanghai).

In Happy Network, we can have different life experiences from the real world. We can steal other people's vegetables, occupy other people's parking lots, buy large houses and luxury cars, and trade stocks. ... In other words, we can do whatever we want to do in the virtual world (Nancy, female, 28, graphic designer, Shanghai).

5. Discussion

The current study has explored the lived meanings of SNSs among Chinese, white-collar professionals. The emergent themes of this study reveal that participants' understanding and interpretations of SNS are multidimensional, dialectical, dynamic, and colorful, shaped by and reflective of their social role as white-collar professionals and the cultural characteristics of contemporary Chinese society. At the individual level, the pursuit of freedom and the liberation of the individual is the foundation for participants' experience of SNSs. In their everyday experiences, the participants actively and constantly seek freedom of control, time, communication, socialization, information, and entertainment, through which they extricate themselves from the multiple restrictions they face in the real world and obtain liberation. At the collective level, returning to Chinese traditional culture is an overarching theme that organizes participants' social experiences of SNSs. In their daily practices, the participants consciously or unconsciously fight against and overcome the alienation and isolation caused by industrialization and modernization. Through communications and social interactions on the SNS, they show their appreciation of traditional virtues that are lacking in contemporary Chinese society and collectively build a quasi-family community that highlights traditional Chinese culture. The current study thus has both theoretical and managerial implications.

Theoretical Implications

Theoretically, this study provides an active audience perspective on media. The reality of the SNS is clearly a joint construction by the media producer and individual users. The tension between user freedom and producer control is evidenced in the dialects uncovered in participants' experiences with Happy Network SNS, especially in relation to the limits of SNS use. Participants integrated the SNS into their total spectrum of communication and relationship building/maintenance tools.

Culturally, a major function of the SNS is to counter the increased alienation and isolation of young Chinese white-collar workers, which is interesting in light of Marxist critiques of Western capitalism. According to Marx, (Tucker, 1978), one of the problems of Western capitalism is its negative impact on individual workers, in terms of their alienation and isolation from the results of their labors and one another. Yet in China, demands on white-collar workers are even greater than those in Western cultures (Shi, 2009). The negative impacts of alienation are being felt by workers, even in this Marx-inspired culture. The SNSs help counteract this alienation and create a new way to connect and share.

A distinct feature of the participants' behaviors on Happy Network is sharing (Belk 2010, p. 717), a fundamental consumer behavior that differs from commodity exchange and gift giving, because sharing transcends the concept of ownership to emphasize nonreciprocal activities and tends to be "a communal act that links us to others." The participants engaged in sharing in multiple ways on Happy Network. Traditionally, Chinese society and culture is family-centric (Zhang & Pan, 2009). Sharing within and outside the family is typical (Hofstede, 2001). However, modernization, and especially materialism, has induced dramatic changes in Chinese society and indirectly transformed Chinese culture. To a degree, sharing as a traditional virtue has lost its prestigious status in modern Chinese people's value system. However, the emergence of SNSs offers a virtual space for Chinese people to return to traditional culture and construct a quasi-family community that emphasizes sharing.

Marketing and advertising literature studies product-facilitated community building closely, specifically in the context of brand communities. Happy Network SNS is similar to a brand community, in that it is a product that facilitates community. Like brand communities, Happy Network exhibits at least three traditional markers of community: shared consciousness, rituals and traditions, and a sense of moral responsibility (Muniz & O'Guinn, 2001). Similarly, this study demonstrates that a SNS can be a cocreation of value for users and operators; Happy Network is a user collective that exhibits "community-like qualities, as understood in sociology, and address[es] identity, meaning, and status-related concerns for participants. Such collectives provide value to their members through emergent participatory actions of multiple kinds and that consumer collectives are the site of much values creation" (Schau, Muniz, & Arnould 2009, p. 30).

Unlike brand communities that have arisen organically though, such as the Disney or Harley-Davidson groups that rely on the enthusiasm of the product's users, creating community is the main function of the SNS. In the context of this SNS, some Chinese users refer to themselves as "the brand," especially in discussing the difference between managing their private and social identities. Such use of the term "brand" supports Gabbott and Jevons's (2009) observation that brand is a theoretically diverse concept. The SNS thus is a tool through which a brand community can be created by sharing, whether that brand is an individual user or a product/service. The use of social networks also is one of the value-creation practices identified by Schau, Muniz, and Arnould (2009) in their analysis of brand community research.

Managerial Implications

Previous research has shown that on online community media platforms, when the community regards advertising as relevant to the theme of the community and congruent with their social identities, users (online community members) deem it more valuable and display more favorable behavioral responses to it (Zeng, Huang, & Dou, 2009). This study's exploration of the functions of Happy Network in the everyday lives of Chinese white-collar workers further suggests that for marketing communication to be relevant, it should support or facilitate uses of the community.

If the community builds and facilitates relationships, marketing communication should share that function. For example, games are an important way that Happy Network users build relationships and share, so marketers could work with game creators to incorporate real brands as gifts or other items to share through the games. These placements should be relevant to the game's theme. Other options for marketers might be to position marketing communication as a way for users to exercise control, have fun, and belong.

Because Happy Network appeared as an integrated, routine part of users' daily lives, marketers clearly can build message frequency among a habitual user base. However, this study also offers a warning to marketers: Users limit themselves to specific communication tactics on SNSs. For example, if users believed that the SNS controlled their time rather than facilitated their ability to control time, they expressed backlash against the site. Marketers want to build communication that creates longer-term engagement, as obtained by other functions of SNS like games, but they need to understand there are limits to users' willingness to participate.

6. Limitations and Further Research

Similar to most studies, this research is a snapshot in time of a dynamic phenomenon. A chronological tracking of the shared meanings of SNSs among Chinese urban white-collar professional users of SNSs would enhance the degree of cultural depth offered by the analysis. Participants' interpretations of SNSs may shift with their personal accumulated experiences. In addition, their interpretations are culturally contextualized and bound to be dynamic, changing as cultural meanings shift. Longitudinal data could provide additional insights into the interpersonal dynamics and micro-cultural characteristics of users' life worlds (Muniz & Schau, 2007).

This study focuses on urban white-collar professional users—one of the most important groups of users of Chinese SNSs. Although the findings reflect contextualized understandings of SNSs among these users, the complexity and dynamics of this group means that the collected data cannot reveal whether the unique meanings of SNSs emerge for subgroups within this or other groups. For example, white-collar professionals from small cities may have different interpretations and emphasize different aspects of Chinese SNSs than those from the metropolitan areas. Furthermore, as Chinese SNSs gain popularity and penetrate different socioeconomic layers within Chinese society, their structure has become more diverse. Studies designed to explore the dynamics and variations among subgroups of Chinese SNSs users should enrich understanding of this particular phenomenon.

Finally, this study investigates a specific social network site. In the life worlds of the participants, the meaning of a social network site is relatively broadly constructed, and various types of social network sites exist in their realities. Therefore, another possible research direction would be to examine socially constructed meanings of other types of SNSs or compare different types to offer further insights.

References

Acar, A (2008). Antecedents and consequences of online social networking behavior: The case of Facebook. *Journal of Website Promotion, 3*, 62–83.

Agarwal, S., & Mital, M. (2009). An exploratory study of Indian university students' use of social networking sites: Implications for workplace. *Business Communication Quarterly, 72*, 105–110.

Barker, V. (2009). Older adolescents' motivations for social network site use: The influence of gender, group identity, and collective self-esteem. *CyberPsychology &Behavior, 12* (2), 209–213.

Baumeister, R. F., & Leary, M. R. (1995). The need to belong: Desire for interpersonal attachments as a fundamental human motivation. *Psychological Bulletin, 117*, 497–529.

Belk, R. W. (1988). Possessions and the extended self. *Journal of Consumer Research, 15*, 139–168.

Belk, R. W. (2010). Sharing. *Journal of Consumer Research, 36*, 715–734.

boyd, d. (2007). Why youth (heart) social network sites: The role of networked publics in teenage social life. In D. Buckingham, ed. MacArthur Foundation Series on Digital-Youth, Identity, and Digital Media, Cambridge, MA: MIT Press.

boyd, d. & Ellison, N. (2007). Social network sites: Definition, history, and scholarship. *Journal of Computer-Mediated Communication, 13*, 210–230.

Brewer, M. B. (1991). The social self: On being the same and different at the same time. *Personality and Social Psychology Bulletin, 17* (5), 475–482.

Byrne, D. N. (2007). Public discourse, community concerns, and civic engagement: Exploring black social networking traditions on blackplanet.com. *Journal of Computer-Mediated Communication, 13,* 319–340.

Cao, M. (2008, September 12). Revelation of Happy Online: No private office and ¥9000 monthly salary for its founder. *Oriental Morning Post,* Retrieved from http://tech.sina.com.cn/i/2008-09-12/05522453139.shtml

Cardon, P. W. (2009). Online social networks. *Business Communication Quarterly, 72,* 96–98.

Cheng, B.: The users of Happy Network have reached 60 million with 200,000 new users every day. (2009, October 26). Retrieved from http://tech.163.com/09/1026/22/5MJ96KJL000915BF.html

Chu, S., & Choi, S. M. (2009). Use of social network sites among Chinese young generations. *Proceedings of AAA Asian-Pacific Conference,* 50–57.

CNNIC (2012). Chinese netizens' usage of social network websites. Retrieved from http://www.cnnic.cn/hlwfzyj/hlwxzbg/sqbg/201209/P020120903424883977032.pdf.

Corbin, J., & Strauss, A. (2008). *Basics of Qualitative Research (3d ed.).* Thousand Oaks, CA: Sage.

Creswell, J. W. (2003). *Research design: Qualitative, quantitative, and mixed methods approaches (2d ed.).* Thousand Oaks, CA: Sage.

Creswell, J.W. & Miller, D. L. (2000). Determining validity in qualitative research. *Theory Into Practice, 39* (3), 124–130.

Delorme, D., & Reid, L. N. (1999). Moviegoers' experiences and interpretations of brands in films revisited. *Journal of Advertising, 28* (2), 71–95.

Donath, J. (2007). Signals in social supernets. *Journal of Computer-Mediated Communication,13,* 231–251.

Donath, J. & boyd, d. (2004). Public displays of connection. *BT Technology Journal, 22,* 71–82.

Ellison, N. B., Steinfield, C., & Lampe, C. (2007). The benefits of Facebook friends: Social capital and college students' use of online social network sites. *Journal of Computer-Mediated Communication, 12,* 1143–1168.

Gabbott, M., & Jevons, C. (2009). Brand community in search of theory: An endless spiral of ambiguity. *Marketing Theory, 9* (1), 119–122.

Gangadharbatla, H. (2008). Facebook me: Collective self-esteem, need to belong, and Internet self-efficacy as predictors of the iGeneration's attitudes toward social networking sites. *Journal of Interactive Advertising, 8* (2), Retrieved from http://www.jiad.org/article100.

Gould, S. J., & Gupta, P. B. (2006). Come on down how consumers view game shows and products placed in them. *Journal of Advertising, 35* (1), 65–81.

Gurwitsch, A. (1974). *Phenomenology and the theory of science.* Evanston, IL: Northwestern University Press.

Hargittai, E. (2007). Whose space? Differences among users and non-users of social network sites. *Journal of Computer-Mediated Communication, 13,* 276–297.

Haley, E. (1996). Exploring the construct of organization as source: consumers' understandings of organizational sponsorship of advocacy advertising. *Journal of Advertising, 25,* 21–35.

Hirschman, E. C., & Thompson, C. J. (1997). Why media matter: Toward a richer understanding of consumers' relationships with advertising and mass media. *Journal of Advertising, 26* (Spring), 43–60.

Hofstede, G. (2001). *Culture's consequences: Comparing values, behaviors, institutions andorganizations across nations (2nd ed).* Thousand Oaks, CA: Sage.

Holt, D. B. (1995). How consumers consume: A typology of consumption practices. *Journal of Consumer Research, 22* (June), 1–16.

Hu, H. L. (2010). The political economy of governing Isps in China: Perspectives of net neutrality and vertical integration. *The China Quarterly, 203,* 11–24.

Humphreys, L (2007). Mobile social networks and social practice: A case study of dodgeball. *Journal of Computer-Mediated Communication, 13,* 341–360.

Ibrahim, Y. (2008). The new risk communities: Social networking sites and risk. *MPC, 4,* 245–253.

In 2007 China's online community advertising market size is 410 million yuan (2008, April 7). Retrieved from www.cnad.com/html/Article/2008/.../20080407153644722.shtml

Iresearch.com (2007*). White collar netizen research report.* Retrieved from http://irs.iresearch.com.cn/consulting/online_users/Free.asp?id=968

Kim, K., & Yun, H. (2007). Cying for me, cying for us: Relational dialectics in a Korean social network site. *Journal of Computer-Mediated Communication, 13,* 298–318.

Lewis, K., Kanfman, J., & Christakis, N. (2008). The taste for privacy: An analysis of college student privacy settings in an online social network. *Journal of Computer-Mediated Communication, 14,* 79–100.

Li, J. (2008a, December 18). Happy Network founders—Binghao Cheng: High and low profiles. *Entrepreneur China.* Retrieved from http://money.163.com/08/1218/07/4TE90761002524SC.html

Li, Y. (2008b), 30 years of reform and opening: Chinese societal changes. Beijing, China: Chinese Encyclopedia Publication.

Liao, Lan (2009). White-collar workers' psychological problems, *Bei Fang Jing Mao, 7,* 121–123.

Lin, C. A. (2001). Cultural values reflected in Chinese and American television advertising. *Journal of Advertising, 30* (4), 83–94.

Liu, Y. (2009). Media identity: Explanation of media identity and construction of Internet identity. Xinwen Jizhe, 3, Retrieved from http://media.people.com.cn/GB/137684/8958785.html

McCabe, J. (2009). Resisting alienation: The social construction of Internet communities supporting eating disorders. *Communication Studies, 60,* 1–16.

McCracken, G. (1988). *The long interview.* Newbury Park, CA: Sage.

Mellin, M. (2008). The female vampire community of online social networks: Virtual celebrity and mini communities: Initial thoughts. *MCP, 4,* 254–258.

Muniz, A. M., Jr., & O'Guinn, T. (2001). Brand community. *Journal of Consumer Research, 27* (4), 412–432.

Muniz, A.M., O'Guinn, T., & Schau, H. J. (2007). Vigilante marketing and consumer-created communications. *Journal of Advertising, 36,* 35–50.

Pan, Y. (1999). White-collar worker and social structure. *Social Science Research, 3,* 21–26.

Riegner, C. (2008). Wired China: The power of the world's largest Internet population. *Journal of Advertising Research, 48* (4), 496–505.

Schau, H. J., Muniz Jr., A. M., & Arnould, E. J. (2009). How brand community practices create value. *Journal of Marketing, 73* (5), 30–51.

Shi, W. (2009). *Cultural criticism on white-collar professionals high pressure of work.* Retrieved from http://www.chinaelections.org/NewsInfo.asp?NewsID=148861

Tang, X. (2004). Literature on Chinese white-collar research. *Qin Nian Xue Yan Jiu, 70* (3), 28–31.

Tong, S. T., Der Heide, B. V., Langwell, L., & Walther, J. W. (2007). Too much of a good thing? The relationship between number of friends and interpersonal impressions on Facebook. *Journal of Computer-Mediated Communication, 13,* 531–549.

Tucker, R. C. (1978). *The Marx-Engels Reader (2nd ed.).* New York, NY: W. W. Norton & Company.

Walther, J. B., Heide, V. B., Kim, S., Westerman, D., & Tong, S. (2008). The role of friends' appearance and behavior on valuations of individuals on Facebook: Are we known by the company we keep? *Human Communication Research, 34,* 28–49.

Wang, S. (1996). Primary level of Chinese relationships and societal change. *Management World, 3,* Retrieved from http://www.usc.cuhk.edu.hk/wk_wzdetails.asp?id=4306

Wildermuth, S. M., & Vogl-Bauer, S. (2007). We met on the net: Exploring the perceptions of online romantic relationship participants. *Southern Communication Journal, 72,* 211–227.

Xiao, F. (2006, August 11). *Chinese white-collar's working load is the highest around the world.* Retrieved from http://www.39.net/focus/jkjd/195579.html.

Xie, B. (2008a). Multimodal computer-mediated communication and social support among older Chinese Internet users. *Journal of Computer-Mediated Communication, 13* (3), 728–750.

Xie, P. (2008b: September 4,). How long can the Happy Network be happy? *Southern Weekly,* Retrieved from http://www.infzm.com/content/16815/1

Yu, F. (2004*). Chinese middle class and their consumer culture.* Retrieved from http://www.xslx.com/htm/jjlc/lljj/2004-12-07-17882.htm

Zeng, F., Huang, L., & Dou, W. (2009). Social factors in users perceptions and responses to advertising in online social networking communities. *Journal of Interactive Advertising, 10* (1)

Zhang, L. (2009). Leisure communication in the era of industrialization and informatization. *Modern Communication, 6,* Retrieved from http://academic.mediachina.net/article.php?id=6317

Zhang, J., & Pan, C. (2009). *Why did the relationships of urban communities alienate?* Retrieved from http://paper.jyb.cn/zgjyb/html/2009-03/28/content_7283.htm

Zhang, J., & Shavitt, S. (2003). Cultural values in advertising to the Chinese X-generation. *Journal of Advertising, 32* (1), 23–33.

Zhang, W., & Lei, K. (2009). The new city immigrations' social identity structure. *Social Science Research, 4,* 1–28.

Zhao, H. (2009). SNS, the pioneer broke up of traditional advertising pattern," *AD Panorama,* 123–124.

Zywica, J., & Danawski, J. (2008). The faces of Facebookers: Investigating social enhancement and social compensation hypotheses: predicting Facebook and online popularity from sociability and self-esteem, and mapping meanings of popularity with semantic networks. *Journal of Computer-Mediated Communication, 14,* 1–34.

Appendix

see next pages

Table 1: Profile of Participants

Pseudonym	Age	Gender	Location	Occupation	Education	Experience with Happy Network
Laura	24	Female	Shanghai	Data analyst	BS	1 year 5 months
Frank	28	Male	Shanghai	Customer service staff	AA	1 year 10 months
Sunny	27	Female	Shanghai	Group purchase staff	MS	1 year
Tresor	28	Female	Shanghai	Manager of a Toy company	BA	1 year 8 months
Jenny	28	Female	Shanghai	Marketing	BS	1 year 10 months
Serendipity	28	Male	Shanghai	Engineer	MS	1 year 2 months
Steven	29	Male	Shanghai	IT technician	AA	2 year and 2 months
Candy	31	Female	Shanghai	HR staff	BA	2 years
Nelson	26	Male	Shanghai	Head-hunting consultant	BA	1 year 11 months
Tony	33	Male	Shanghai	Copy writer	BA	2 years 1 month
Gemini	28	Female	Shanghai	Journalist	BA	2 years 2 months
Louiett	27	Female	Shanghai	Teacher	MA	1 year 5 months
Victor	25	Male	Shanghai	PR account executive	BA	1 year 2 months
Nancy	28	Female	Shanghai	Graphic designer	BA	1 year
Tom	33	Male	Beijing	Vice manager	BA	2 years and 4 months
Wilson	29	Male	Beijing	Insurance broker	BS	1year 9 months
Yilian	31	Female	Beijing	Patent attorney	BS	1 year and 8 moths
Judy	32	Female	Beijing	PR consultant	BA	2 years
Zara	29	Female	Beijing	Owner of an online Store	BA	1 year 7 months

Table 1 (continued): Profile of Participants

Pseudonym	Age	Gender	Location	Occupation	Education	Experience with Happy Network
Slater	29	Male	Beijing	Communication technician	BS	1 year 10 months
Samantha	32	Female	Beijing	Art editor	BA	1 year 8 months
Maggie	31	Female	Beijing	Accountant	BA	1 year 10 months
Sherry	28	Female	Beijing	Art editor	BA	1 year 6 months
Phoenix	30	Male	Beijing	Tourism manager	AA	1 year
Sofia	26	Female	Beijing	PR account executive	BA	1 year 6 months
Gondi	33	Male	Beijing	Salesman	BA	1 year 7 months

IX.   PTT: Taiwan's Unique Social Media

Szu-Wei Chen

Department of Communication and Creative Arts,
Purdue University, Calumet, Indiana
Chris55520@gmail.com

Abstract

This chapter introduces PTT, the unique and influential social media in Taiwan. The discussions begin with a definition of what PTT is, followed by an explanation of the importance and social location of PTT. The mass media in Taiwan frequently report stories about PTT and cites PTT users' opinions as information sources. This is thought to be a crucial factor that affects PTT users' perception and behavior. Several actual social events are used to illustrate the relationships between PTT, the mass media, and the society in Taiwan. This chapter also analyzes the social justice phenomenon on PTT, which is one of the most controversial issues PTT has raised in the past years. The users' social identities, communication styles, social support transactions will also be discussed.

Keywords: PTT, BBS, social media, social justice, social support

1. Introduction

In the last decade, social media have been a popular research topic in academia and has become one of the major social trends around the world. Taiwan is also not an exception to this worldwide trend. Like in many other countries, Facebook, the leading social networking site developed in the United States, has triumphed over most of the social media in Taiwan and begun to dominate the market since 2009. However, a unique social media platform did not fade away after the challenges brought by Facebook. More importantly, this economically sound non-profit platform is still growing in popularity and social influence. It is a virtual space, but the impacts are undoubtedly real. In Taiwan, it represents the power and wisdom of the crowd as well as the controversies revolved around social justice and the freedom of speech. It has triggered a multitude of newsworthy social phenomena and has invited dramatic attention from academia, mass media and the public. It is PTT, an acronym of *professional technology temple*, and arguably, the most influential virtual community and one of the most popular social media in Taiwan.

This chapter will take a critical view of PTT's importance, the discussions and debates it raises, and the effects it has on individuals and the society in Taiwan. Both empirical and theoretical studies will be utilized to describe how PTT connects individuals and the society in Taiwan. Specifically, this chapter will (1) introduce PTT's history and features and explicate how PTT differs from other leading social media, (2) cite actual social events to illustrate how PTT uniquely affects the cultural, political, and media development in Taiwan, and (3) examine individuals' use and misuse/abuse of PTT, including how individuals use PTT to acquire social support, form online persona, exchange information, trespass on personal privacy, execute social justice and launch relevant activities. Suggestions and questions for guiding future research will also be discussed.

2. Old Technology in the New Media Environment

Different from most of the leading social media, PTT was constructed based on traditional telnet technology, which has long been seen outdated, especially in this new media age. However, arguably, this purely text-based technology was one of the most important features that made PTT unique from other World Wide Websites. Because PTT contains text only, the information processing and operation speed is faster than websites that embed multiple images and animated functions. The faster processing speed can be particularly important under certain circumstances.

For example, in 2009, Typhoon Morakot attacked Taiwan and caused damage to many cities. At that point, PTT users created an information exchange center on PTT and the speed of information update was faster than the official typhoon information center created by the government. Moreover, in comparison to the leading social networking sites, a text-only environment offers the users more control over their anonymity.

With the control of anonymity, or at least pseudonymity (Wallace, 1999), individuals with diverse backgrounds and concerns can voice their opinions or seek out assistance without worries of the presence of their appearance or other identifiable information (Bacard, 1995). Similarly, because of the embedded anonymity, PTT seems to have higher possibility than other social media to become a non-hierarchical sphere (Soon & Kluver, 2007). This phenomenon was also viewed as an indirect drive to make PTT a place where numerous anonymous individuals implement their virtual justice. This point will be discussed in the following sections.

On the other hand, although one might argue that users of common social networking sites are still given power to customize their anonymity and privacy settings, it should be noted that maintaining complete anonymity on these social networking sites is a much more difficult job than one would assume. There are several reasons. First, a major goal of these social networking sites is to require or encourage people to use their real names, display their real and identifiable photos as well as share their personal stories. Second, even though typically a person needs to be a friend of another person in order to view each other's personal information and identification, the fact is that it is not uncommon to see that people acquire information about a person through that person's connections and activities with his or her friends without actually being a friend of that person. Consequently, even though a person chooses not to make personal information public, people may still be able to see it through that person's interactions with other people. Nowadays the Internet does not necessarily provide the users anonymity; social media's multi-layer connectivity functions (i.e., reaching a person through that person's friend's friend's friend's...) is challenging how much anonymity and privacy one can have. Things have dramatically changed since Peter Steiner drew his world famous cartoon "On the Internet, nobody knows you're a dog" on the New Yorker in 1993. In today's social media environment, it may not be hard to tell it is a "dog" behind the screen.

With regard to the ownership and management, PTT is currently owned by the largest national university in Taiwan and operated and maintained by the students of the institution. This fact indicates that PTT, unlike most of other social media, has better ability to separate from corporate intrusion and commercial interests. Notably, because of PTT's educational affiliation, it is inevitably monitored by the Ministry of Education of Taiwan. In other words, although PTT can do away with business and various profit-relevant factors, technically, it is still under governmental control, at least to some extent. In fact, although the spirit of PTT is to advocate the freedom of speech, it has received notices from the government asking the users to self-regulate their expressions of opinion. PTT users have accused this governmental control of being an example of the white terror.

PTT is an electronic bulletin board system (BBS) but it is not just a static online bulletin board for the users to post and reply messages. In addition to the basic features of a bulletin board, PTT serves as a multifunctional platform that enables the users to construct a public personal profile, exchange emails, engage in individual and group instant messaging, create discussion boards and form sub-communities, raise virtual pets, participate in online dating, and play various online games. PTT is widely used for information exchange and relationship creation and maintenance among Taiwanese young adults whose average age is about 21 years old (Chang, Ho, & Huang, 2008). Before moving on to further discuss the importance of PTT and its social impacts in Taiwan, a question needs to be addressed: is PTT a type of social media?

According to boyd and Ellison (2007), social network sites are defined to be a web-based service where users can create profiles within the system, reveal a friend list or a contact list on the profile, and visit and view these friend lists. By definition, PTT is not a typical social network site. First of all, PTT is not a website. Secondly, although PTT users can create personal profiles and friend lists, it is unusual to see PTT users make the lists public or traverse other users' connections. However, whether PTT can be considered a form of social media is another story. PTT should be deemed as a social media platform because a great deal of users heavily utilize PTT for social purposes, including searching for new relationships, maintaining and reinforcing existing relationships, forming supportive and other types interactive communities. Hence, the only component missing from boyd and Ellison's definition is the presence of the friend lists. However, although in the past many social network sites required the users to present their friend lists to everyone or at least to their "friends", currently most of these sites have eliminated this requirement. Further, observational research shows that after this option was available, many users have chosen not to make their friend or contact lists visible. More importantly, considering the features, functions, and the role in the Taiwan society, regardless of previous definitions of social network or social networking sites, PTT should be seen as an influential and unique social media service in Taiwan.

3. PTT in Taiwan

The importance of PTT is rapidly increasing because it has not only enjoyed remarkable popularity among young adults but also attracted attention from most of the mainstream mass media in Taiwan. Although there are numerous examples, the present chapter uses an article published by a major Taiwanese newspaper a few years ago to illustrate the relationships between PTT and mass media in Taiwan. The paragraph below is an excerpt of the article:

> *When the female anchor accidentally spoke out: "He will never return that money back to our society...sh**!" The public was shocked by this unexpected and inappropriate statement in a primetime news program. "espanol": "she was not professional at all.", "nakoru": "that was a big joke of the media industry." However, some users tried to support this female anchor. "ianlin45": "I agreed with her" (China Times, 2008).*

One might ask who these people in the quotation marks were. These combinations of letters, such as "espanol", are online IDs (identifications) created by registered PTT users. It is noteworthy that many Taiwanese mainstream mass media, such as television, newspaper, and magazines, regularly monitor and observe PTT in order to acquire news topics and information of current social trends. Subsequently, the mass media would report both the stories they found on PTT and the comments produced by PTT users back to the public. It should be clarified that PTT users are part of the crowd; they are not special authorities. Nonetheless, because of the media attention, the public opinions on PTT become more powerful than they are thought to be. Accordingly, the users' perception of their heightened opinion impact may be a catalyst that facilitates their motivation of executing vigilante justice. On the other hand, the reason of selecting this news article from 2008 is because it clearly articulates the "names" of the anonymous individuals on PTT. Since that year, those online IDs were frequently cited by journalists and appeared on multiple mass media outlets. The importance of source credibility seemed to be overlooked, and it should be taken into account with regard to news reporting.

In addition, this phenomenon also raised a concern of power. Why do newspaper readers or television viewers need to care about the opinions from a specific group of anonymous online individuals (i.e., PTT users)? How are these online opinions selected? Should it be acceptable that journalists exclusively report opinions they obtain from PTT? If it is a necessary need that journalists acquire online opinions for news production, how about other online platforms? Moreover, recent observations show that many newspapers and television news programs do not specifically mention the online IDs anymore. Instead, they utilize a general term "people on the Internet" when they attempt to refer to some online opinions although the source is PTT. This usage is highly biased because PTT users certainly are unable to represent all Internet users in Taiwan. This usage is also misleading because common mass audiences might presume that there is broad consensus of opinion on the Internet. Mass media are thought to be the major force that provides PTT extra power. However, the relationships between traditional mass media and PTT are more complex than this. Although the attention from mass media increases PTT's importance and the opinion visibility, many PTT users in fact oppose the intrusion of mass media and possess resistant positions against the dominant ideologies embedded in and conveyed by the mass media. The following example provides an illustration.

In 2005, PTT appeared on one of the major newspapers as headline news. This is the earliest event that pointed out the need of investigating the relationships between PTT and the mass media in Taiwan (Liu, 2008). This event invited a multitude of discussions, criticisms, and debates from various aspects of the Taiwan society including mass media and academia. This event began from a PTT user's post on a discussion board accusing his girlfriend cheating on him. Many PTT users who saw this post actually went to search for the pictures of the girl and her new boyfriend. After the author noticed that his story has become a popular topic among many PTT users, he soon posted another article explaining that the previous article was just a product of emotion, and he did not have actual evidence about the infidelity. However, it was too late. A journalist has made this story become national headline news and many other journalists started to conduct follow-up investigations. This event that originally existed just on the Internet has become extremely public and had tremendous impact on all the characters involved.

Whether mass media have the right to report everything they found online without further verification has been widely discussed. Most of PTT users claimed that mass media should not interfere with their freedom of speech and condemned mass media's ignorance of the latent rules on PTT. The original article was posted on a discussion board designed specifically for emotional release. In line with the purpose, one can post any complaint or emotional words even when the stories are fabricated. This was probably why PTT users believe that mass media should not force a random event on PTT to go through the cruel scrutiny of public eyes. However, ironically, although the majority of PTT users dislike and disagree with mass media's intrusion into their territory, after this event, many PTT users have learned the fact that mass media frequently monitor the things happening on PTT and started to enjoy and use this media attention. Many users started to include a sentence that "invites" journalists to report their stories when they post an article. Journalists' reliance on PTT for news stories was also a good example of the impact of backpack journalism (Stovall, 2011) in the digital age. There is an interdependent relationship between PTT and the mass media in Taiwan; the members are dependent on each other to grow in popularity, importance, and influence (Ball-Rokeach and DeFleur, 1976). This interdependence also plays a mediating role between the individuals and society in Taiwan. In other words, both PTT and the mass media become an in-between component that affects and is being affected by the individuals and society (See Figure 1).

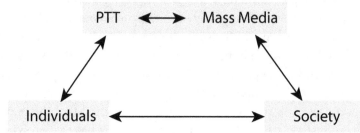

Figure 1: Interrelationships among PTT, Mass Media, Individuals, and Society in Taiwan

The attention from mass media not only made PTT receive public attention but also had significant effects on the users' communication styles and patterns. Analyzing how PTT users communicate on this unique social media sphere is critical to understanding the debates and controversies revolved around PTT as well as how the users utilize or misuse PTT's power to execute social justice. Therefore, the following two sections will introduce certain communication phenomena and how they could affect the individuals and society in Taiwan.

A Reduced-Cues Environment

As discussed earlier, perhaps the most important feature that makes PTT especially different from most of the leading social network sites is the control of anonymity. Greater anonymity also represents the absence of multiple common social cues, such as names, appearance, age, gender, race, and so forth. Indeed, typically PTT users do not reveal their personal identifiable information, although they have the ability to do so. Many early studies have examined the effects of reduced cues on quality of communication on the Internet (e.g., Baron, 1984; Kiesler, Siegel, & McGuire, 1984; Sproull & Kiesler, 1991; Walther, 1992). The researchers indicated that because of lacking the reference of certain usual cues existed in the physical context, it is expected to take a longer time to generate mutual understanding and reach consensus. This claim may be true on PTT because it is an open place where everyone can voice opinions. On the other hand, although a number of social cues that normally appear in face-to-face communication may be missing, this would not necessarily make online communication "cold". As Baym (2010) suggested, "people show feeling and immediacy, have fun, and build and reinforce social structures even in the leanest of text-only media" (p. 59). Individuals can still find ways of expressing emotion and affection, such as adding certain emoticons (Anderson, 2005), changing the structure of words (e.g., using boldface, upper-lettering), and using different punctuation and abbreviations (Herring, 2001). Importantly, because these cues are not naturally embedded in communication, the intention and behavior of including these cues also indicate one's effort, and the effort can inform others that he or she is interested in them (O'Sullivan et al., 2004). It should be noted that the inclusion of these cues is unable to make online communication equivalent to communication in the physical context; they are just different. By the same token, one should not see the difference between online and offline communication as a simple dichotomy of good and bad. Either communication mode could work well depending on numerous situational, demographic, psychographic, and sociographic factors. Although PTT is a text-only virtual environment and it may not be the most efficient place for decision-making, the communication is filled with all kinds of emotions and vivid interactions.

Certain individuals in the society (e.g., teachers, parents) have always had worries regarding whether use of Instant Messaging (IM), mobile phone texting, and social media would lead to deterioration of writing ability. For example, on Twitter, there is a 140 characters limitation for each tweet. To comply with this rule, people may distort sentence structures and use many non-standard abbreviations. Constantly producing only short sentences like tweets and status updates without appropriate use of grammar may impair people's ability to think and organize long and complex articles. Yet these types of worries may be hyperbolic. First, little empirical research has found support for the concern (e.g., Baron & Ling, 2003; Baron, 2008). Second, there are different kinds of social media. PTT, in fact, has a very different spirit regarding writing when compared with many leading social media. PTT strongly encourages users not to use non-standard languages and slams and sets up certain rules prohibiting posts that are not long enough. Moreover, with many cues that help convey missing information, writing is a key element of communicating on PTT. According to this rationale, use of PTT, unlike using other social media, is expected to improve writing ability rather than hurting it. Although anecdotal experiences and observations show that there seem to be some negative issues with younger generation's writing, use of social media and other digital communication technologies should not be viewed as the major cause. A possibility is that the worldwide cultural societal trend is gradually moving from formality to casualness, and it has affected writing across different media (Baron, 2008).

Communication on PTT

The discussion above has indicated that anonymous writing, which is still loaded with feelings and emotions, is the major means of how PTT users communicate with each other. In comparison to other leading social media where users tend to be relatively identifiable, there is a potential issue attached to the anonymous communication on PTT. That is, anonymity, a lack of social cues that could help regulate language use and behavior, can make individuals become meaner or more aggressive than how they behave in the face-to-face context (Joinson, 1998; Preece & Ghozati, 2001). Indeed, it is not difficult to imagine the heightened hostility in communication when the interactants' identity information is nearly untraceable. On PTT, it is common to see harsh comments and opinions, even geared toward articles that are fairly neutral and innocuous in nature. Yet, before continuing to depict PTT as a hostile and unfriendly environment, it should be noted that individuals still form caring and mutually helpful relationships and provide and seek out multiple types of social support in spite of all the aggressive opinions and flaming within PTT.

In addition to anonymity that disguises one's social identities, some scholars argued that a reason that causes hostile communication pattern on the Internet is a lack of social norms that govern behaviors and motivate politeness (Rice, 1989; Sproull & Kiesler, 1991). However, again, it is too far-fetched to claim that all online spheres are the same. PTT is by no means a norm-free medium. In contrast, PTT users have created a system of strong and unique norms. More importantly, in line with a perspective developed by Lea and his colleagues (1992), the aforementioned hostility and aggressiveness on PTT are believed to be closely related to its unique norms, as opposed to the viewpoint of lacking norms. PTT "members" frequently utilize these PTT norms to distinguish themselves from other PTT users and guests and condemn them for their ignorance about the embedded rules on PTT. The observed hostility and harsh opinions may be partially due to this phenomenon. This phenomenon is also consistent with what social identity theory (Tajfel & Turner, 1986) has suggested: individuals are motivated to construct and reinforce their social identities by observing their in-group members as well as by comparing with and showing how they differ from or stand out from the out-group members. Because of the intention to protect the PTT social norms and embody and intensify the "membership", plus the cover of anonymity, it seems reasonable to see many PTT users adopting the hostile communication style.

It is worth noting that not all PTT users utilize this kind of communication style to show their group identity and maintain the group norms. According to Chen (2010a), PTT users can be categorized into three major types—PTT fans, PTT anti-fans, and PTT non-fans. Borrowing knowledge from Gary's (2003) typology, PTT fans are defined as

> the users who regularly use PTT and strongly identify the ideologies and positions of PTT. For example, in an online interview, a college-age PTT fan said: "People are just too outdated if they don't use PTT. They don't understand how strong and powerful this BBS is. We almost can see PTT's power is everywhere and this power comes from the solidarity of all the PTT residents. The residents I met on PTT are all very nice. I felt really happy that I am part of them..." (Chen, 2010a).

As seen above, PTT fans also specifically label themselves as the "residents" of PTT. As mentioned earlier, this label is not the only way they use to indicate how they are different from other PTT users. Flaming, other aggressive languages, and a number of specific PTT jargons are often used by PTT fans to demonstrate their knowledge and familiarity about PTT use as well as their resident status:

"I really want to clarify a point here. That is, not every registered PTT user can be seen as a PTT resident. Everybody with a valid email account can register on PTT. Even though you don't register, it does not mean that you cannot be a PTT user. People can use PTT as a guest, which means that they do not need to provide any personal information to PTT, but of course, some functions will be restricted. However, PTT residents are very different from those common users and guests. If you have had some experience reading the articles and conversations on PTT, you would notice that there are a lot of jargons. And real PTT residents frequently and largely use these special terms to communicate on PTT. Although there are no official rules or criteria to define who would be a PTT resident, once one sees the conversations or he or she has an opportunity to actually talk with people on PTT, it is not at all difficult to tell who is a PTT inhabitant and who is just a common user" (Chen, 2010a).

This interview excerpt also implies that there is a learning curve. On the other hand, with regard to PTT anti-fans, although they are also regular PTT users, they often do not agree with the rules and spirit of PTT. Instead, PTT anti-fans have apparent dislike or other negative perceptions toward PTT. Importantly, they also often hold an oppositional position against PTT fans/residents' beliefs and behaviors. PTT anti-fans do care about things that happen on PTT, but they believe that PTT is in need of further changes or even revolution for a better future:

"Although I use PTT, I don't feel it is necessary to become a resident, and I actually don't like people to call me a PTT resident. I do not want people to think in this way because I feel many people and the society interpret this term very negatively. In addition, I especially don't like the conversions those residents produced on PTT. Those conversations are usually mean and impolite. And that is why I really don't like PTT because it hurts many people in many ways" (Chen, 2010a).

Both PTT fans and anti-fans refer to the users who are highly involved in PTT. Different from these two user types, PTT non-fans are so-called "light users" who use PTT in an occasional manner and typically choose not to actively post articles or responses. They are considered latent users or lurkers who tend not to participate in any "flaming wars" on PTT although they still use PTT for informational, social networking, and recreational purposes.

Virtual Justice

Contrary to PTT non-fans, both PTT fans and anti-fans invest more time, emotion, and effort in PTT but with different targets and focuses. PTT anti-fans' main target is PTT fans: they use this BBS on a regular basis but disagree with the ways PTT fans communicate and dislike the general atmosphere in PTT. However, earlier discussions already mentioned that both PTT anti-fans and fans have a tendency to use PTT as a platform to form arguments that are against dominant media and governmental ideologies. For example:

> "... Although in the modern society we have much more channels and options to voice our opinions than before, I will still say it doesn't mean much if we just simply talk on our blogs or on some other electronic discussion boards. The reason is obvious—because not so many people would really care about what you say. So you are still powerless. However, things started to change after PTT began to draw incredible attention from many mass media and the whole society. The story that I post today probably could be seen on seven o'clock news later. Why? It's because of the influence of PTT. I feel our voice becomes more powerful and influential. I feel we become a kind of social justice to discuss many problems in society. I even feel we are doing a better job of watching the government than are those politicians. Because of PTT, I think the small power from numerous PTT residents could aggregate to make a huge impact on the whole society" (Chen, 2010a).

This interview excerpt indicates that PTT users have confidence in their power. Notably, this confidence is not only related to the PTT community itself, the networks of the users, but also related to the mass media's frequent surveillance. With this confidence, many PTT users believe that they are capable of serving as a more objective "fourth estate" (in comparison to the mass media) to monitor the government. Moreover, they believe that the existence of PTT forces the mass media to face further public surveillance as well. This phenomenon can seem positive because it is thought to be in accord with the spirit of democracy and to facilitate the power redistribution in the Taiwan society.

However, PTT users' (especially PTT residents/fans) awareness of their opinion power has caused some problems in Taiwan. An issue that raised a multitude of debates and discussions is about how certain PTT users execute vigilante justice based on their own standards and definitions of social justice. The social justice mentioned here is slightly different from how the term "social justice" is commonly defined. In academia, social justice refers to a concept that discusses the importance of equality, power, and rights across diverse social components (e.g., majority versus minority, dominant versus marginal, developed versus developing or underdeveloped) and how social change or movement can help through certain strategies (Wilkins, 2012, 2008). With regard to PTT users, they often launch activities for social justice at micro levels; put differently, they often focus on certain individual targets rather than social groups. Because of the perception of the power and responsibility to unite and fight against inequalities and form resistance to dominant power and advocate social justice, some PTT users have misunderstood the role they should play and the limitation of their power. Consequently, in addition to the mainstream media, governmental, or societal power, PTT users also target the users who violate the PTT social norms or certain unknown individuals in society.

For instance, as an example of backpack or citizen journalism, PTT users often share information and stories about what they deem as inequality or events in need of further justice. However, indeed, most of the users are not professionally trained journalists, and oftentimes they do not have sufficient resources for reporting bigger news stories. As a result, many PTT users frequently just post and share individual affairs and other minor events. Yet this does not diminish their intention and desire of executing social justice. Similar to one of the previous examples, it is not uncommon to see a story with regard to infidelity in romantic relationships. PTT users often organize certain "social justice" actions to help the individual who is portrayed as a "victim" in the relationship. The actions include revealing the "cheater's" identity information, such as real name, phone number, work and home address, photos, and even a detailed history of the person. PTT users' intensive search for personal information has been extremely and mysteriously powerful. However, arguably, there tends to be no exactly right and wrong answers in a common relationship. Moreover, it should be seen as inappropriate to launch any "public punishment" without further verification of the truth of the event; simply relying on the opinions and accusations is biased and dangerous.

Further, even when an obvious fact of which side is right and which side is wrong is present, whether PTT users have the right to launch their private punishment is highly questionable. PTT users' social justice makes it possible that everybody could become like a character in the famous O. J. Simpson trial in 1995. Once a person violates what PPT users believe to be social norms, all personal and private information surrounding that person could be easily brought to light if the event or action is noticed by PTT users. In addition to all the possible "muckraking" actions, the subsequent torrent of ferocious and ruthless verbal abuse PTT users may produce should not be ignored. Sometimes verbal attacks could be more serious and harmful than the presence of factual information. Notably, as PTT evolves, this virtual justice that was supposed to exist only in the cyber world now has made a real impact in the physical context. There have been several incidents that PTT users met together in the offline world and went on to execute self-arbitrated justice. To reduce the harm caused by PTT and to rebuild social order, setting up a number of effective rules to regulate this virtual power is a task of top priority in Taiwan.

As noted earlier, the phenomena that certain PTT users misuse the power of PTT as well as the mean and aggressive verbal and non-verbal acts are the things that PTT anti-fans feel unwilling to tolerate:

> "... *However, I really think those residents should have never ever done those things, such as criticizing people and the government without any objective evaluation and appropriate evidence. I really don't think they would have lots of these sorts of mean comments in their real-world lives. They just become aggressive on PTT. I think that is because they are hiding behind the screen. Oftentimes their perspectives are extremely biased and sometimes unreasonable. Isn't it because they think they don't have to be responsible for their*

talking? Because of all that, they seem to argue and complain about everything. And because now many mass media have provided them extra power, I feel they are already disturbing the societal harmony" (Chen, 2010a).

PTT's power can be described as a double-edged sword. Although it can impose some pressure to the users and hurt individuals in many ways, at the same time it provides the users a sense of security. Some examples are like the facts that PTT users could receive a great deal of social support in a relatively short period of time:

> *"Be honest, I don't know any other way that can also help me to get a lot of help within a few hours. I cannot call fifty people to ask everybody, one by one, to ask whether anybody could help me. But because of PTT, many many online strangers suddenly become my helpful friends. The power of this online networking is much stronger than my real-world interpersonal network. I may not know those online people, but they do provide great helps. For example, when I needed to go to Taipei and asked for a ride on PTT, I even received more than thirty mails in two hours saying that they can help for free. Can you do this in two hours without PTT's help?" (Chen, 2010a).*

When PTT users suffer difficulties or inequalities, they always have a place to disclose their stories and a group of people to turn to, regardless of their gender, age, and socioeconomic status. Compared to face-to-face contexts, PTT also offers the users the ability to transcend the limitations of time and distance (Braithwaite, Waldron, & Finn, 1999; Wellman, 2001); that is, individuals are allowed to seek out and provide social support anytime and anywhere. Further, in addition to the attention from other PTT users, their stories may also catch the mass media's eyes. If the mass media choose to report the stories to the public, more social support that helps cope with the difficulty could appear. With the high popularity, PTT has become an important place where individuals engage in social support transactions, in addition to their offline face-to-face interactions. The next section will further examine PTT as a platform for seeking out, receiving, and providing social support.

PTT and Social Support

Social support has been a popular research topic across multiple disciplines. More importantly, it has been well documented that social support has many beneficial effects on individuals, both psychologically and physically. For example, research has found that social support can improve individuals' general immune system (Jemmot & Locke, 1984), repress salivary free cortisol levels (Heinrichs et al., 2003), increase life expectancy for women with breast cancer and help better manage with chronic illness (Goldsmith & Brashers, 2008). In addition, social support could also facilitate behaviors that have positive effects on health, such as seeking out medical support, or averting people from unhealthy behavioral patterns, such as smoking or consuming alcohol (e.g., Krantz, Grunberg, & Baum, 1985; Wills, 1983). It should be noted that many positive effects were found when the research measured individuals' perceived availability of social support. Interestingly, a great deal of studies have indicated actual receipt of social support either produced no help or worsened the situation such as increasing the stress levels (e.g., Barrera, 1986; Bolger, et al., 1996, 2000; Dunkel-Schetter & Bennett, 1990). A possible speculation of why actual social support receipt often could not function well is because there are multiple risks involved in face-to-face social support interactions. PTT, one of the most important social media platforms in Taiwan, may have the ability to help alleviate and improve a number of risks that could affect the quality and effects of social support.

For example, in face-to-face contexts, social support could work ineffectively or backfire if the social support provider violates the interpersonal boundaries set by the support recipient (Afifi & Guerrero, 1998; Petronio & Jones, 2006; Petronio, Jones, & Morr, 2003). On PTT, the users not only enjoy better privacy settings but also have the ability to opt out of the interaction whenever they feel uncomfortable or stressful.

Moreover, if the social support does not match with the support seeker's needs, social support may not help either. That is, if a support seeker is in need of emotional support, the provision of informational support may not be helpful. Research indeed has indicated that even people from one's close relationships (e.g., family members and close friends) often do not provide appropriate social support (e.g., La Gaipa, 1990; Brashers, Neidig,

& Goldsmith, 2004). Although it can be reasonably expected that most of these individuals do want to provide the right support to the people they care about, oftentimes they are incapable of doing so because of a lack of experiences or expertise about a specific stress or health issue. PTT can help this issue because it is an open computer-mediated platform where individuals can assess diverse information produced by other individuals with different backgrounds and expertise (Wright, 2002). Accordingly, the likelihood of obtaining appropriate social support would increase. Similarly, it would also be more likely and easier for a person with a specific need to find individuals who are suffering or have suffered similar problems. Indeed, PTT contains a myriad of different boards that are designed specifically for individuals to seek out and provide social support, such as a psychiatry discussion board and a plastic surgery discussion board (Chang, Ho, & Huang, 2008). Notably, the phenomena of social support exchange do not necessarily happen on those discussion boards that emphasize a relatively sensitive topic or a specific disease. Research reveals that individuals do report perceived social support from general PTT use, as discussed later in this section.

In addition to the control of interpersonal boundaries and access to diverse information and individuals, seeking out social support on PTT requires relatively less responsibility to reciprocate. It is common to see that people feel obligated to reciprocate, at least to some degree, in face-to-face social support transactions. Importantly, research has shown that dearth of reciprocity could result in negative interpersonal consequences (Albrecht & Goldsmith, 2003; Chesler & Barbarin, 1984). An even worse scenario would be when a support receiver feels a need to reciprocate, but he or she does not have the ability to do so. Extra stress could be added onto the original stress.

Further, when individuals are experiencing stress or difficulties, it is likely that they are also experiencing certain negative feelings, such as shame, disgrace, and embarrassment. These feelings are commonly referred to as stigma (e.g., Wright & Bell, 2003), and stigma often becomes an obstruction that discourages individuals' social support seeking behaviors (Cluck, & Cline, 1986). Anonymity can play an important and helpful role here. If a social support interaction does not require presence of one's appearance and other identifiable information, one can still activate self-disclosure and social support seeking even with these negative feelings. As discussed earlier, different from most of the leading social networking sites, PTT is a relatively anonymous Internet platform. In comparison to using other social media like Facebook, PTT provides a "safer" environment where the users can engage in "low-risk discussion with high-risk topics" (Adelman, Parks, & Albrecht, 1987, p. 33).

According to the aforementioned advantages of how PTT can facilitate social support processes, it is assumed that many individuals would rely on this social media for social support. A cross-sectional survey research specifically examining PTT's users' dependency on PTT, and their perceived online social support found that PTT users with higher PTT dependency reported significantly higher perceived online social support (Chen, 2010b). It should be noted that the concept "dependency" used in the study was different from "Internet addiction" developed by Young (1998). Similar to drug addiction and alcohol addiction, Internet addiction was defined and understood as a pathological symptom which denotes certain negative meanings. In comparison, the dependency concept was more active and positive because it referred to individuals' perception of usefulness with regard to using PTT in their everyday lives. The study also found that PTT users with higher PTT dependency reported lower levels of perceived offline social support. This finding indicated that PTT users who are highly dependent on PTT may be more likely to choose PTT to gratify their social support needs over communication channels in the physical contexts.

Based on these findings, it seems reasonable to conceive that perceived online social support would negatively relate to the levels of offline support. However, this relationship was not supported by the data. This statistically non-significant result was still important because it revealed that individuals have the opportunities to obtain social support from both online and offline environments. Yet for those users who perceived PTT to be an exceptionally useful medium, perhaps the PTT fans/residents as mentioned earlier, using PTT is obviously a better choice for social support seeking and gaining.

Certain gender differences were also found on PTT. For example, male PTT users reported that they spent about six hours a day using PTT, but female users reported only two and a half hours of PTT use on an average day (Chen, 2010b). Chang, Ho, and Huang's (2008) content analysis revealed that female PTT users tended to mix network social support with informational social support, whereas male PTT users largely provide only informational social support. The research also hypothesized that female users might be more likely to use non-verbal symbols to express emotions while exchanging social support than male users. This assumption has been supported by a number of empirical studies (e.g., Wolf, 2000). However, this hypothesis was not supported by the analysis.

Last but not least, intercultural difference should be considered. It has been widely acknowledged that different cultural backgrounds and value orientations could lead to different interaction needs and goals. Accordingly, it is also expected that individuals may prefer different approaches or communication channels to satisfy their social support needs. Anonymous social media, such as PTT, are thought to be particularly important to individuals in collectivist cultures. Research has indicated that explicitly disclosing weakness or stress and seeking out social support is often seen as behavior of disrupting group harmony in collectivist cultures (Wellenkamp, 1995). Contrary to collectivism, individualist cultures are inclined to encourage individuals to express difficulties and distress and actively ask for sympathy and social support (Burleson & Mortenson, 2003). In addition, observational research shows that individuals in the collectivist cultures are also less likely to use counseling services, seek out help from psychiatrists, or join face-to-face supportive discussion groups. Taken together, PTT can have the ability to become a convenient and helpful alternative to face-to-face communication for social support. It should be noted that the discussions in this section by no means attempt to downplay the value of face-to-face social support. Instead, the point is to emphasize the importance of certain individual differences and situational factors and to examine how these factors could affect individuals' choices of where to seek out and provide social support.

8. Conclusion

Although PTT is based on relatively old technologies, it has opened up its own territory in the new media environment. It has created important phenomena in Taiwan and has attracted tremendous social and media attention. It has been amazingly helpful as well as incredibly harmful. New regulations should be established to administer this social platform. A balance between personal privacy and social justice needs to be reached. More discussions about the relationships between PTT and mass media in Taiwan are also needed. Further research should further investigate these issues revolved around PTT. PTT is a unique social entity in Taiwan. PTT is still in a process of evolving because it is always transforming with the society.

References

Adelman, M. B., Parks, M. R., & Albrecht, T. L. (1987). Beyond close relationships: Support in weak ties. In T. L. Albrecht & M. B. Adelman (Eds.), *Communicating social support* (pp. 126–147). Newbury Park, CA: Sage.

Afifi, W. A., & Guerrero, L. K. (1998). Motivations underlying topic avoidance in close relationships. *Communication Quarterly, 46*, 231–249.

Albrecht, T. L., & Goldsmith, D. J. (2003). Social support, social networks, and health. In T. Thompson, A. M. Dorsey, K. I. Miller, & R. Parrott (Eds.), *Handbook of health communication* (pp. 263–284). Mahwah, NJ: Lawrence Erlbaum Associates, Inc

Anderson, J. Q. (2005). *Imaging the Internet.* Lanham, MA: Rowman & Littlefield.

Baccard, A. (1995). *The computer privacy handbook: A practical guide to e-mail encryption, data protection, and PGP privacy software.* Berkeley, CA: Peachpit.

Ball-Rokeach, S. J., & DeFleur, M. L. (1976). A dependency model of mass media effects. *Communication Research, 3*, 3–21.

Baron, N. S. (1984). Computer mediated communication as a force in language change. *Visible Language, 18*, 118–141.

Baron, N. S., & Ling, R. (October, 2003). *IM and SMS: A linguistic comparison.* Paper presented at Association of Internet Researchers Conference: Internet Research 4.0, Toronto, Canada.

Barrera Jr., M. (1986). Distinctions between social support concepts, measures, and models. *American Journal of Community Psychology, 14*, 413–445.

Baym, N. K. (2010). *Personal connections in the digital age.* Malden, MA: Polity Press.

Bolger, N., Foster, M., Vinokur, A. D., & Ng, R. (1996). Close relationships and adjustment to a life crisis: The case of breast cancer. *Journal of Personality and Social Psychology, 70*, 283–294.

Bolger, N., Zuckerman, A., & Kessler, R. C. (2000). Invisible support and adjustment to stress. *Journal of Personality and Social Psychology, 79*, 953–961.

boyd, d. m., & Ellison, N. B. (2007). Social network sites: Definition, history, and scholarship. *Journal of Computer-Mediated Communication, 13*(1). Retrieved from http://jcmc.indiana.edu/vol13/issue1/boyd.ellison.html

Braithwaite, D. O., Waldron, V. R., & Finn, J. (1999). Communication of social support in computer-mediated groups for persons with disabilities. *Health Communication, 11*, 123–151.

Brashers, D. E., Neidig, J. L., & Goldsmith, D. A. (2004). Social support and the management of uncertainty for people living with HIV or AIDS. *Health Communication, 16*, 305–331.

Burleson, B. R., & Mortenson, S. R. (2003). Exploring cultural differences in evaluations of emotional support behaviors: Exploring the mediating influence of value systems and interaction goals. *Communication Research, 30*, 113–146.

Chang, H. J., Ho, M. H., & Huang, C. J. (2008). 線上社會支持類型探討: 以PTT精神疾病版集整形美容版為例. [Typology of Online Social Support: A Study of Bulletin Board System in Taiwan]. *Mass Communication Research, 94*, 61–105. (in Chinese)

Chen, S.-W. (2010a, November*). Bridging Individuals and the Society: How Fans, Anti-Fans, and Non-Fans Interact with Taiwan's Largest Virtual Community.* Paper presented at the annual conference of the National Communication Association, San Francisco, California.

Chen, S.-W. (2010b, November*). Internet Dependency and Social Support: How Taiwanese College Students Obtain Social Support from the Largest Virtual Community in Taiwan.* Paper presented at the annual conference of the National Communication Association, San Francisco, California.

Chesler, M. A., & Barbarin, O. A. (1984). Difficulties of providing help in a crisis: relationships between parents of children with cancer and their friends. *Journal of Social issues, 40*, 113–134.

Cluck, G. G., & Cline, R. J. (1986). The circle of others: Self-help groups for the bereaved. *Communication Quarterly, 34*, 306–325.

Dunkel-Schetter, C., & Bennett, T. L. (1990). Differentiating the cognitive and behavioral aspects of social support. In B. R. Sarason, I. G. Sarason, & G. R. Pierce (Eds.), *Social support: An interactional view* (pp. 267–296). New York: Wiley.

Giles, H., & Noels, K. (1998). Communication accommodation in intercultural encounters. In J. Martin, T. Nakayama, & L. Flores (Eds.), *Readings in cultural contexts* (pp. 139–149). Mountain View, CA: Mayfield.

Giles, H., & Powesland, P. F. (1975). *Speech style and social evaluation.* London, UK: Academic Press.

Goldsmith, D. J., & Brashers, D. E. (2008). Communication matters: Developing and testing social support interventions. *Communication Monographs, 75*, 320–330.

Gray, J. (2003). New audiences, new textualities: Anti-fans and non-fans. *International Journal of Cultural Studies, 6*, 64–81.

Heinrichs, M., Baumgartner, T., Kirschbaum, C. & Ehlert, U. (2003). Social support and oxytocin interact to suppress cortisol and subjective responses to psychosocial stress. *Biological Psychiatry, 54,* 1389–1398.

Herring, S. (2001). Computer-mediated discourse. In D. Schiffrin, D. Tannen & H. E. Hamiton (Eds.), *The handbook of discourse analysis.* Malden, MA: Blackwell.

Jemmot, J. B., III, & Locke, S. E. (1984). Psychosocial factors, immunologic mediation, and human susceptibility to infectious diseases: how much do we know? *Psychological Bulletin, 95,* 78–108.

Joinson, A. (1998). Causes and implications of disinhibited behavior on the Internet. In J. Gackenbach (Ed.), *Psychology and the Internet: intrapersonal, interpersonal, and transpersonal implications* (pp. 43–60). San Diego: Academic Press.

Kiesler, S., Siegel, J., & McGuire, T. W. (1984). Social psychological aspect of computer-mediated communication. *American Psychologist, 39,* 1123–1134.

Krantz, D. S., Grunberg, N. E., & Baum, A. (1985). Health psychology. *Annual Review of Psychology, 36,* 349–383.

La Gaipa, J. J. (1990). The negative effects of informal social support systems. In S. Duck & R. C. Silver (Eds.), *Personal relationships and social support* (pp. 122–139). London: Sage.

Lea, M., O'Shea, T., Fung, P., & Spears, R. (1992). Flaming in computer-mediated communication: Observations, explanations, implications. In M. Lea (Ed.), *Contexts of Computer-Mediated Communication.* London, UK: Harvester Wheatsheaf.

Liu, H. W. (2008). 網際網路公共領域角色的反思: 以東海劈腿事件與鴻海打壓新聞自由事件為例. [Rethinking the role of public sphere on the Internet: A phenomenological perspective]. *Mass Communication Research, 97,* 45–81.

O'Sullivan, P. B., Hunt, S., & Lippert, L. (2004). Mediated immediacy: A language of affiliation in a technological age. *Journal of Language and Social Psychology, 23,* 464–490.

Petronio, S., & Jones, S. S. (2006). When "friendly advice" becomes privacy dilemma for pregnant couples: Applying CPM theory. In R. West & L. Turner (Eds.), *Family Communication: A reference of theory and research* (pp. 201–208). Thousand Oaks, CA: Sage.

Petronio, S., Jones, S. S., & Morr, M. (2003). Family privacy dilemmas: A communication privacy management perspective. In L. Frey (Ed.), *Bona fide groups* (pp. 23–56). Mahwah, NJ: Erlbaum.

Preece, J. J., & Ghozati, K. (2001). Experiencing empathy on-line. In R. E. Rice & J. E. Katz (Eds.), *The Internet and health communication: Experiences and expectations* (pp. 237–260). Thousand Oaks, CA: Sage.

Rice, R. E. (1989). Issues and concepts in research on computer-mediated communication systems. In J. A. Anderson (Ed.), *Communication Yearbook Volume 12.* Newbury Park, CA: Sage.

Soon, C. & Kluver, R. (2007). The Internet and Online Political Communities in Singapore. *Asian Journal of Communication, 17,* 246–265.

Sproull, L., & Kiesler, S. (1991). *Connections: New ways of working in the network organization.* Cambridge, MA: MIT Press.

Stovall, J. G. (2011). *Writing for the Mass Media. (8th ed.).* Boston: Pearson.

Tajfel, H. & Turner, J. C. (1986). The social identity theory of inter-group behavior. In S. Worchel and L. W. Austin (Eds.), *Psychology of Intergroup Relations.* Chicago, IL: Nelson-Hall.

Walther, J. B. (1992). Interpersonal effects in computer-mediated interaction. *Communication Research, 20,* 473–501.

Wallace, P. (1999). *The psychology of the Internet.* Cambridge, UK: Cambridge University.

Wellenkamp, J. C. (1995). Everyday conceptions of distress. In J. A. Russell, J. M. Fernandez-Dols, A. S. R. Manstead, & J. C. Wellenkamp (Ed.), *Everyday conceptions of emotion* (pp. 267–280). Dordrecht, The Netherlands: Kluwer.

Wellman, B. (2001). Computer networks as social networks. *Science, 293*, 2031–2034.

Wilkins, K. (2008). Development communication. In W. Donsbach (ed.), *The International encyclopedia of communication.* London, UK: Wiley-Blackwell.

Wilkins, K. (2012). Advocacy Communication. In S. Melkote (ed.), *Development Communication in Directed Social Change: A Reappraisal of Theories and Approaches.* Singapore: AMIC.

Wills, T. A. (1983). Social comparison in coping and help-seeking. In B. M. DePaulo, A. Nadler, & J. D. Fisher (Eds.), *New direction in helping: Vol. 2. Helpseeking* (pp. 109–141). New York, NY: Academic Press.

Wolf, A. (2000). Emotional expression online: Gender differences in emoticon use. *CyberPsychology & Behavior, 3*(5), 827–833.

Wright, K. (2002). Social support within an on-line cancer community: an assessment of emotional support, perceptions of advantages and disadvantages, and motives for using the community from a communication perspective. *Journal of Applied Communication Research, 30,* 195–209.

Wright, K., & Bell, S. B. (2003). Health-related support groups on the Internet: Linking empirical findings to social support and computer-mediated theory. *Journal of Health Psychology, 8,* 39–54.

Young, K.S. (1998). Internet addiction: The emergence of a new clinical disorder. *CyberPsychology & Behavior, 1,* 237–244.

PART FOUR:
NORTH-EAST ASIA

X.   Can 140 Characters Save Your Life? Social Media in the Aftermath of the 3.11 Earthquake in Japan

Yuya Kiuchi

Department of Writing, Rhetoric, and American Culture,
Michigan State University, East Lansing, Michigan
kuchiyu@msu.edu

Abstract

Social media played a significant role in the aftermath of the Great East Japan Earthquake as victims and their family members tried to ascertain their safety, survivors shared information about evacuation information, authorities located survivors, and the rest of the world partook in disaster relief efforts. Although wireless communication networks were shut down or slow immediately after the tremor hit the northern half of the country, they recovered relatively quickly. Victims used Twitter, Facebook, Mixi, and other social media sites as reliable means to keep in touch with relatives and update them with the latest information. Emergency numbers and information including tsunami alerts were also shared. Many victims found on Twitter where they could find water and food, for example. International organizations of various size collected funds and materials via social media to donate to victims. Despite shortcomings including inaccurate rumors, "slacktivism," and a lack of long-lasting measures to help victims, the experience of the earthquake reflected the effectiveness of social media in emergency management especially during the first most chaotic days and weeks following the earthquake.

Keywords: Japan, social media, earthquake

1. Introduction: Can 140 Characters Save Your Life?

When a natural disaster disrupts the lives of hundreds, thousands, or even millions, the value of social capital and network becomes evident. Victims share information and food. Neighbors check on each other. Volunteers gather to help those in need. When an affected resident is alienated from others physically or psychologically, they are exposed to a higher risk of suffering from psychological anguish (Ouyama, Nakamura, Suda, & Someya, 2012). Putnam (2000) explains that social networks matter to achieve both "private good" and "public good." In the age of digital networks, "organized reciprocity" and "civic solidarity" happen via social media technology (Putnam, 1995; Ikeda & Richey, 2005). Experiences from recent disasters and their aftermath have shown that social media have become an integral part of social capital and networks on which those that are affected rely. After the Great East Japan Earthquake on March 11, 2011 which killed over 15,000 people and left close to 3,000 missing to this day (National Police, 2012), social media played a vital role in maintaining the existing social network, minimizing the disruption of social capital, and creating new communities for affected residents.

The social media-related experiences from the 3.11 Earthquake call for better understanding of social media use value by various individuals, questions and concerns raised by the experience, and the continuing role that social media play as many people remain displaced. Social media use value can be judged in two ways: how much social media were used, and what kind of benefits social media brought to the users. Reluctance to use social media came from those who were concerned about their privacy, those who felt social media lacked authentic human relationships, and others who preferred traditional modes of social networking. In general, however, resistance to social media use was limited. As social media played significant roles in the aftermath of the earthquake, they also raised concerns about dissemination of non-factual information, digital divide, short-term slacktivism, and others.

This type of use value analysis is especially relevant within the current scholarly context that has examined the meaning of social media and their increasing role in numerous global events during the past several years. On the one hand, Sherry Turkle (1984; 1995) has questioned what human identities and relationships would mean in the age of digital technology. She showed before the age of today's social media, technology had already affected the way we interacted with others. Benedict Anderson (1983) suggested that we have moved to a world where communities were "imagined." Resonating with Marshall McLuhan and Bruce Powers (1989), Arjun Appadurai (1996) argued that geographical locations no longer mattered. Robert Putnam (2000) was cautious. He questioned if modern society was losing a sense of true community. Putnam (2003) shortly after suggested that there still was a hope to revive a sense of community. Turkle (2011) most recently argued that we now live in the world where we are alone even though we may be physically together. A lingering question, therefore, has been whether social media could allow us to have authentic communication with others. The matter is all the more challenging when there is an emergency.

On the other hand, however, recent global events have proven that social media indeed serve as a useful communication tool especially during a state of emergency. James D. White and King-Wa Fu (2012) suggested that social media were a significant part of crisis communication during both Hurricane Katrina in 2005 and the Sichuan Earthquake in China in 2008. Dave Yates and Scott Paquette (2011) reached a similar conclusion that social media worked as a wide knowledge base after the 2010 Haitian earthquake. What further struck some Japanese citizens was an article written by Hiroyasu Ichikawa (2011), published in Gendai Business on March 2, 2011, only nine days prior to the earthquake. In this article, Ichikawa explained that although Japanese media had looked at social media in the context of the Arab Spring, they could also function well when there was a natural disaster. He used the example of the earthquake in Christchurch, New Zealand, that killed over 180 people. He reported that social media, including Twitter, became very useful for affected individuals. Furthermore, he stated that Japan, as a country with constant threats of major earthquakes should consider how best to use social media during seismic emergencies. These abundant examples of social media turning into a meaningful way of creating circles of cooperation and support show that Anderson's concept may in fact be materializing.

Basic Facts about the Earthquake

The 2011 Tohoku Earthquake, or officially named "the 2011 off the Pacific Coast of Tohoku Earthquake [Tohoku-chiho Taiheiyo Oki Jishin]" happened at 2:46 pm local time on March 11, 2011, registering magnitude 9. Japan Metrological Agency and the U.S. Department of Interior's U.S. Geological Survey stated that it was the largest recorded earthquake of the nation (JMA, 2011a; USGS, 2011a). It was also the fourth largest earthquake in the world since 1900 (USGS, n.d.). Its epicenter located approximately 24 km below ground was only 130 km away from the Ojika Peninsula (JMA, 2011b). The damage by the earthquake was further devastating by tsunami tidal waves that recorded over nine meters in height and ran up to the ground as high as 38.2 meters from the sea level (JMA, 2011a; "Daishinsai," 2011).

The latest figure issued by the National Police Agency of Japan states that as of November 7, 2012, 15,873 people were killed, 6,114 people were injured, and 2,768 people were missing over a year and a half later. Over 1.2 million houses and buildings were destroyed or damaged (2012). Japan Press Network reported that it was the most devastating disaster in Japan after the World War II ("Higashi Nijon," 2011). Because of the quake, tsunami, and aftershocks, the World Bank estimated the total economic loss to be about $235 billion (Kim, 2011). The Japanese government's Reconstruction Agency (2011) similarly estimated that the recovery will cost at least $280 billion.

2. Social Media Usage

Since Hurricane Katrina in 2005, using social media has become a common behavior after a natural disaster. Social media are now the "go-to medium during times of crisis for victims, news and relief aid" (Green, 2011). Although Japan suffered from another major earthquake in the Kansai area in 1995, it was at a different time. Studying the seismic disaster of Kobe, Meg Neggers (1995) characterized the Internet as a lifeline. She wrote, "While Japanese telephone lines became flooded with calls, bringing telephone communication to a halt, the Net became a reliable communication line into Japan" (Para. 2). The disaster of 2011 was an incident in which not just the Internet but also social media became a reliable communication method. Tucker (2011) discusses that "[t]here are already more than 200 million cell phones with either photo or movie capability. It's a function we use for leisure, shooting video of our pets or our friends' stupid skateboard tricks. But, in a disaster, combined with the right social network and pointed in the right direction, this enormous global web of cameras takes on considerable value."

Social media users, in general, consider this new form of media to be a useful communication tool during emergencies. Hjorth and Kim (2012) correctly assessed that social media "did impact upon how [people] experienced the situation" after the earthquake (p. 187). According to Japan's Ministry of Internal Affairs and Communications (MIAC, 2011), 43% of Japan's population used social media. About 60% of social media users are on multiple social network sites such as Mixi, and Facebook. Of the same sample, 55% use blogs. 50% are Twitter users. Approximately 36.5 million Japanese people used their cellular phone to access information about the earthquake and tsunami. This was equivalent of 36% of the entire mobile population in the country. Similarly, 72% of them went online via their phone, 26% watched television or video, 24% received text- or email-based alerts, and 6% used cell phone application ("Television," 2011). A report (Green, 2011) cites Mashable's statistics that although there were only 1,200 tweets per minute about an hour after the earthquake, the number went up to thousands per second within a few hours. Many of these tweets contain #prayforJapan, #earthquake, and #tsunami as hashtags.

IMJ Mobile (2011) revealed that after the earthquake, many of its 932 respondents considered Facebook and Twitter as a means to share and obtain information after a disaster. For example, only 15% of Twitter users listed emergency communication as a reason to start using the microblogging service before the earthquake. After March 11, 2011, however, 39% of respondents answered so. Similarly, while 14% of Facebook users considered the site to be a useful information source before March 11, 21.9% considered so after. 79% of Twitter users and 62% of Facebook users stated that social media were "useful" or "somewhat useful" during the aftermath or the earthquake. These numbers were also reflected in the answers to the question whether or not they would recommend these social media to others. A post-earthquake survey discovered that 57% of Twitter users and 43% of Facebook users would recommend respective social media site to their non-user friends and family members because of their applicable use as a means for emergency communication.

The use value of social media can be analyzed for three distinctive groups of users. The first consists of direct victims. From hurricanes to earthquakes, survivors are often displaced, and find themselves without not only their personal possessions but even a sense of community and other basic needs in life such as food and electricity. When they gain access to social media either at a community center or on their fingertips after the restoration of mobile networks, they are able to learn which evacuation sites have basic necessities, where to post their whereabouts so their relatives would be assured of their safety, and other services. Therefore, social media connect not just victims with each other, but also victims and those who are indirectly affected, or the second group of social media users. When telephone and cable networks are disrupted, it can be extremely difficult to reach family members via phone calls or text messages. After an earthquake registered 6.7 on the Richter Scale in Hawaii in October 2006, Verizon reported that it witnessed 250% increase in call volume ("Quake Emphasizes," 2006). Such a surge can easily overtake networks. Therefore, it is often important that social media such as Facebook and Twitter serve as an online bulletin board where information can be posted for others to retrieve when networks are functioning. The last group of participants to social media at the time of a disaster includes governmental bodies from the national level to the local municipal levels. Furthermore, social media is used to disseminate information regarding evacuation, food supply, and other vital news from and to the affected regions.

Social Media Use by Affected Individuals

Being able to reaffirm the presence of social networks or a sense of community is particularly important at a time of emergency because "social support may serve as a buffer against the potentially harmful effect of life events" (Lin et al., 1985). In times of emergency, "people help each other before they are supported or replaced by government entities" (Shellong,

2008, p. 226). Social media allow these people and citizen-driven support systems to flourish. Many victims of the earthquake report that they started using social media immediately after the first tremor was over, even though power and landlines had been disrupted.

Weathernews Inc., a Japanese privately-owned metrological information provider, surveyed 37,279 victims of the earthquake between March 14 and 16, 2011. The survey outcome (2011) revealed a particular strength of social media in getting in touch with family and friends to confirm their safety. For those affected by the earthquake, on average, it took them four hours and nine minutes until they were able to reconnect with others. Those that used social media, however, were able to reach their family and friends in two hours and fifty-six minutes. As Table 1 shows, the advantage of social media was apparent.

Table 1: Average Time It Took to Reconnect with Family and Friends in the Affected Areas

Media	Time
Public Phone	5 hours and 46 minutes
Landline Phone	4 hours and 35 minutes
Mobile Phone	3 hours and 25 minutes
Texts	3 hours and 11 minutes
E-Mail	4 hours and 25 minutes
Online Bulletin Board	4 hours and 24 minutes
Social Media	2 hours and 56 minutes

Adapted from Higashi Nihon Dai Shinsai Chousa Chousa Kekka [East Japan Great Earthquake Survey Result] by Weathernews, 2011.

Weathernews also reports that many victims evacuated while gathering information via social media. Anecdotal episodes reflect their use of mobile devices and social media networks in order to learn where to escape, and to find out about conditions of roads and facilities.

For many, social media permitted them to share safety information about themselves with others. Agile Media Network (2011) calls this style of information sharing "pull format." To communicate one's safety via telephone or texts requires individualized communication. With Twitter and other social media, victims could post safety information of themselves so that others could simply "pull" that information from websites when needed or possible. Social media have become a locus of information hub. This is similar to what happened with the Haiti earthquake in 2010. Google launched "Person Finder" for those who sought information about missing victims. The site currently contains over 300,000 names (Green, 2011). Shitsuyuki (2012) explained that 32% of Twitter users that responded to the survey conducted by the Nihon Housou Kyoukai, Japan's government-run broadcasting station, used the site to check for the safety of family and friends.

Those who were directly affected by the earthquake used Twitter the most to obtain information about utilities such as electricity, gas, water, and phone. Half of the respondents in NHK's survey (Shitsuyuki, 2011) used Twitter for this purpose. A resident of Fukushima Prefecture in his 30s stated, "I used my cell phone's one-segment service to watch NHK and my smart phone to access Mixi to learn about the size of the earthquake and the safety of my friends. Mixi was particularly useful because in its local Iwaki community section, I saw many entries written based on a first-hand account about where I could get drinking water, which stores and gas stations were open, how severely each community had been damaged, and so on" (pp. 362–363). A woman in her 30s from Aomori Prefecture used #hachinohe to let other Twitter users know that the store where she was making purchases was still open. She also learned which gas stations were open from Twitter.

For many, Twitter also offered emotional relief. One female respondent from Iwate Prefecture answered that she felt that people all over the country were thinking about the victims of the quake. She continued, "On Twitter, I learned about support provided by other countries and saw how much the Self Defense Forces were assisting us. I also learned that many users were encouraging others not to waste power or to share merchandize at stores with others. Each of these short messages made me happy" (Shitsuyuki, 2012, p. 364). This woman's comment reflects different values that social media had for victims. Twitter's information is practical, on the one hand. When there are only a handful of stores open with food on the shelf, it is vital that such information is shared with those in need. Additionally, social media helped make customers aware that there are more people in need and making purchases in moderation will help more customers. On the other hand, social media disseminated words of support. Although they may not bring food or reconstruction funds to the affected regions, the sense of support was welcomed by those affected by the disaster.

Social Media Use by the General Public

Approximately two weeks after the earthquake, Nomura Research Institute (2011a) released a study on the use of various media to access information regarding the disaster. On March 19 and 20, the Institute surveyed 3,224 Internet users between the ages of 20 and 59. The survey was conducted in the Kanto Region where the nation's capital exists and where approximately a third of the national population resides. In this survey, social media ranked as the seventh most popular source of information. Nomura's study shows that 81% of the respondents considered NHK to be a trustworthy source. Similarly, 57% stated that other television stations provide useful information. Yahoo!, Google, and other web portal sites ranked third with 43%. Newspapers followed in fourth with 36%. Online information provided by national and local governments was fifth with 23%. Just above social media were online newspapers with 19%. This outcome confirms that social media play a significant role for those trying to acquire information about the earthquake.

Another comprehensive survey also showed a similar trend of social media serving as an alternative source of information. Japan Marketing Agency (2011) conducted an online survey on March 24 and 25, 2011, with an 800-respondent sample including residents of the Kanto and Kansai Regions, between the ages of 15 and 59. In this survey, 8% of respondents stated that they considered social media networks as their information source. Although this figure was smaller than Nomura Research Institute's findings, it nonetheless showed that social media were the most popular source of information among other personal media, such as text messages, email, and others.

Social media's significance in the mind of the Japanese climbed higher a year after. Another survey by the Japan Marketing Agency (2012) revealed that 27% of respondents considered social network sites to be useful information sources during an earthquake. Although the popularity of radio and television remained strong, it is significant that a quarter of the people sampled agreed that social media were more informational than newspapers, information provided by local municipalities, word of mouth, and other means of communication. As expected, 35% of males between the ages of 15 and 29 and 40% of female counterparts stated that social media would be helpful. About 20% of those over 50 years old, nonetheless agreed.

The aforementioned survey report by Weathernews also showed that social media were the quickest means of communication to get in touch with affected family members and friends. While the national average time it took to reach an affected individual was three hours and fifteen minutes, social media users only had to spend an hour and fifty-nine minutes. Table 2 attests the fact that while social media reconnected victims, their family, and friends in less than two hours on average, no other means of communication was able to do so in less than three hours. The advantage of social media is clear in this domain, as well.

Table 2: Average Time It Took to Reconnect with Family and Friends in Japan

Media	Time
Public Phone	3 hours and 49 minutes
Landline Phone	3 hours and 29 minutes
Mobile Phone	3 hours and 40 minutes
Texts	3 hours and 4 minutes
E-Mail	3 hours and 5 minutes
Online Bulletin Board	3 hours and 38 minutes
Social Media	1 hour and 59 minutes

Adapted from Higashi Nihon Dai Shinsai Chousa Chousa Kekka [East Japan Great Earthquake Survey Result] by Weathernews, 2011.

NHK's survey (Shitsuyuki, 2012) shows that those who lived outside of the most severely hit areas used social media to gain information about aftershocks, damages caused by earthquakes and tidal waves, and the accident at the Fukushima Dai Ichi Nuclear Power Plant.

Table 3: Information Users Obtained from Twitter

Content	Directly Affected Victims	Indirectly Affected Victims
Utilities	50%	25%
Safety of Others	32%	32%
Aftershock Info	32%	36%
Damage Info	27%	30%
Nuclear Plant	23%	33%
Evacuation Site	17%	17%
Volunteering	11%	15%

Adapted from Higashi nihon daishinsai hisaisha wa media wo donoyouni riyou shitanoka [How did victims of the Great East Japan Earthquake use media]. NHK housou bunka kenkyujo nenpou 2012 [NHK broadcasting culture research center annual report 2012] by Shitsuyuki, 2012.

Table 3 reveals that in many categories, there is a clear distinction in the purpose of Twitter use between those that were directly affected by the quake and those that were indirectly affected.

Collaboration was another key concept of social media use by the general public. Various wiki sites were launched to establish a portal where the name lists of those at evacuation sites were shared, where news on aftershocks were accumulated, or art-inclined users submitted their socially-responsible advertisements calling for donation and volunteer activities. Infographics, YouTube clips and other artistic works were made based on some tweets. For example, when there was a shortage of food and commodities, an infographic explained that twelve rolls of toilet paper would help about 1,000 victims. A loaf of bread would help an entire family. These messages were designed to prevent some from monopolizing a limited supply of commodities (Agile Media Network, 2011).

On Facebook, Pray for Japan's nulti-language translation project gathered volunteers who would translate various news articles and information into ten different languages. One of the translation projects stated the following:

A young lady was hollering at the media staff who came to report damages in Ishimaki. Thinking that she was calling for help, the media staff went over to where she was and met several locals evacuated from their homes handing out hot coffee. "You guys are working hard too. Have some coffee." They have enough things to worry about themselves. Japanese are such wonderful people.

Another story was about a small boy:

There was a small boy with a snack bar waiting for his turn in a checkout line at a local convenience store. When it was his turn, he saw a donation box. After a few seconds of thinking, he put the money he had in his hand in the donation box and put away his snack bar. The check-out lady's voice was trembling as she said, "thank you," to the boy.

Although some of the translation was low in quality and anecdotal in nature, it nonetheless demonstrated the collaborative potential over social media (Agile Media Network, 2011). This project turned out to be a successful one especially for the non-Japanese speaking population who were directly or indirectly affected by the quake (Agile Media Network, 2011).

Social Media Use by Governing Bodies

Nomura Research Institute (2011b) reported that there was a sharp increase in the number of local and national government bodies that signed up for social media accounts after the earthquake. In March 2011, right before the quake, there were 121 government-related Twitter accounts. The number increased to 148 by April 4, and to over 190 by the end of May 2011. The Prime Minister's office opened its Twitter account designed only for emergency information on March 13, 2011. Three days later, the office opened a separate account for general information sharing purposes. On March 17, 2012, TEPCO, the company that owned the nuclear power plant in Fukushima, opened its account, attracting over 260 thousand followers in a matter of a few weeks (Agile Media Network, 2011). NRI states that "social media not only strengthen the means of communication from the local government to its residents but also enable frequent communication." Hayashi (2011a) explains that Japan's cabinet's Twitter account that was opened after the earthquake captured approximately 300,000 followers within 2 weeks. Some municipal governments saw an increase of their followers by over thirty times.

Due to this sudden increase in local governments' interests in social media, the Cabinet Secretariat of Japan (2011) released a document to alert some of the risks associated with the use of social media. The primary concern of the Japanese government was the possibility of fake accounts. Yuasa (2011a; 2011b) agreed with this concern. In reality, at the end of 2009, then-Prime Minister Yukio Hatoyama learned that there was a fake account that pretended to be his official Twitter outlet (Yuasa, 2011b; 2011c). Since any individual can theoretically pretend to hold an official account for a governmental body, the Cabinet encouraged local governments to establish their own strong presence as an authentic information source. One way to do so was to create a link to official accounts on their official websites. Should there be a fake account, it was also recommended that such information shared widely so that general users would be more aware of it.

Hayashi (2011b) introduces another solution that the Ministry of Economy, Trade, and Industry has developed in cooperation with CGM Marketing. This firm runs a website called twinavi. It is a site that not only describes how to use Twitter for various purposes but also shares top news popular on Twitter. The joint effort between the public and private sectors has enabled an account authentication system so that users could know which Twitter account is the authentic one and which ones might be a fake account.

Less than three weeks after this notice was issued, the Office of Information Technology of the Prime Minister of Japan and His Cabinet (2011) released a report to summarize the examples of governmental social media use. It showed that there were mainly three ways in which the government communicated to the Japanese public through Twitter. The first was to simply share messages. The Fire and Disaster Management Agency, for example, suggested that since the public transportation systems were disrupted, hurrying home could cause secondary casualties. This message, sent on March 11, encouraged office workers to remain where it was most safe, especially with the imminent risks of aftershocks. Similarly, the Agency notified its followers that the evacuation instruction around the Fukushima Daiichi Nuclear Power Plant was expanded from 3 kilometer radius to 10 kilometer radius on March 12. The Ministry of Health and Labor also communicated that the aforementioned rumor on Twitter about the chemical rain was false, through its social network.

The Ministry of Economy, Trade and Industry used Twitter to update its followers on the latest information added to its website. On April 3, for example, it updated its website to let victims of the earthquake know which gas stations were open. Similarly, the Ministry of Internal Affairs and Communications notified its followers that it had added a special link on its website that will lead visitors to a portal website where they could find a list of donation opportunities. This second type of social media use by government agencies was to keep their followers informed of website updates (Office of Information Technology, 2011).

The last purpose of social media use was to share the content from announcements and press conferences. The cabinet frequently alerted its followers right before it started its scheduled conferences. It also tweeted comments and statements by the Chief Cabinet Secretary. When there was a question about the danger of staying in close proximity to someone who had been exposed to the radioactive explosion, especially among those who were planning to welcome victims who had been displaced, the Cabinet notified that the evacuation had taken place early enough that living with such victims would not cause any secondary radioactive exposure (Office of Information technology, 2011).

Japan's government was also careful about the format of digital information sharing. The Office of Information Technology (2011) described that much of the information was shared both as a web page for computers and a web page for mobile devices such as cell phones. The Local Authorities Systems Development Center advised municipal governments not to rely on PDF, especially to share a scanned document. The LASDEC recommended that JPEG would be a more optimal file type because of its versatility. Similarly, HTML was considered more useful than PDF pages.

Harumichi Yuasa (2011a; 2011b), a professor at the Institute of Information Security in Japan, questions some of the fundamental values of social media use for governments. First, he argues that tweets are nothing more than an utterance. This means that information sent via Twitter is nothing different from a casual comment made by a public official, which would not constitute public documents. Although public officials and offices are still held accountable for their Twitter content, Yuasa claims that tweets are fundamentally different from official documents. Furthermore, according to the Japanese law, an administrative document can only be considered official when the means of communication such as paper or electromagnetic records is owned by the government. Since the governmental bodies do not own Twitter or its tweets, what is uttered in such an environment would not be considered official, unless their drafts are saved on their computer. He explains that unlike in the U.S. where the U.S. Government Accountability Office had previously addressed its concerns about social media in relation to the Federal Record Act of 1950, privacy protection, Federal Information Security Management Act, and Freedom of Information Act, Japan lagged behind in establishing policies regarding governmental social media use. It is clear that tweets are public documents to be archived in the U.S., but there is no consensus on the matter in Japan.

Social Media Use for Volunteering and Fundraising

Unlike in 1995 when a large earthquake hit Kobe, social media brought like-minded people together and allowed them to organize volunteering and fundraising projects. National Public Radio's John Burnett explains that the limited number of volunteers after the quake was partially because many individuals were uncertain how to participate in humanitarian activities. In 2011, however, many Japanese used Mixi and other social media to ask victims how they could help. Many residents in the affected region, in return, made honest answers discussing what is needed ("Japanese Youth," 2011). As Banet-Weiser (2012) characterizes, with social media, "activism is as easy as a swipe of your credit card." McQueen (2011) reported that within two weeks after the earthquake, thirty-two American charity organizations donated over $163 million. There are critical views on this type of activism. While sending $5 or $10 is a helpful effort, it falls short of what activism truly means. The questions about so-called slacktivism will be discussed later. However, it is undeniable that many who decided to volunteer or donate money to help the victims of the earthquake would not have done so if social media were not readily available.

As stated before, social media made donation easier. It is not only easier than sending a check to an organization but also easier than having to make a phone call. Spencer Green (2011) wrote:

> *People looking to contribute $10 to the cause can do so by texting REDCROSS to 90999, or for those of us inclined to dabble in Facebook games, gamers can donate through Cityville, FrontierVille, Farmville or contribute to Zynga's efforts to raise $2 million for Save the Children's Japan Earthquake Tsunami Emergency Fund. There is also a Red Cross Facebook campaign. In short, there really are plenty of available channels that were unavailable only as recently as 2005.*

Green's reference to 2005, obviously, compares the earthquake to Hurricane Katrina. Although social media played a significant part in information dissemination in New Orleans, there is no question that there had been an exponential growth in various means to donate funds to affected individuals or organizations.

One of the Facebook games through which gamers could donate money was a game called, Car Town, which had attracted 7.5 million active users. The basics of the game are straightforward. Users collect virtual cars and customize them so that they can have their dream garage. Once they establish their collection of cars, they race against their friends to see who has the fastest car. In this process, instead of buying a new car, they could buy, with their in-game currency, a Red Cross ambulance. The profit went to the donation. Furthermore, users can send their ambulance to the "Help Japan" mission to make further donations ("Cie Games," 2011).

Over nine months after the earthquake, SONY Corporation of American encouraged the global community to share messages with those in Japan on its website, "Message to Japan." This was a part of the company's RESTART Japan initiative that stemmed from the joint efforts between SONY and Save the Children Japan. SONY, as the organizer of the public viewing events of the FIFA Club World Cup Japan 2011, stated that the submitted messages would be displayed at the viewing sites in the earthquake-hit areas, including Iwate, Miyagi, and Fukushima Prefectures. SONY invited local youth soccer players, those who continued to live in temporary housing, and any others in the affected areas to watch the final match of the tournament on its 250-inch screen. On the one hand, it clearly was a smart marketing scheme. SONY prepared an area where guests could play its games and watch animations. But on the other hand, it was an example of a corporate effort to use social media to maintain extended social networks in Japan. Although this initiative did not include any financial donation, it was meant to remind people in the Tohoku region that they were in many people's thoughts ("SONY Corporation," 2011).

Downsides of Social Media during Emergency

Despite Japanese's reliance on and use of social media during the aftermath of the earthquake, the experience also revealed the weaknesses and downsides of this new communication tool. Although Nomura (2011a) showed that 13% of respondents agreed that they trust information shared on social media by users more than they used to before the earthquake, 9% also said that they trusted social media less. While this number is significantly smaller than an increasing distrust in governments (29%) or private television stations (14%), it nonetheless suggests that social media contain their own shortcomings.

Ogawa (2011) argues that social media might have lost their trust from some because of its ability to share information to a wider audience. He suggests that many Twitter users, for example, retweeted information without checking its reliability. Consequently, as much as helpful information was shared, misleading and nonfactual information was also shared widely. Nomura Research Institute (2011a) agrees with this assessment. Agile Media Network (2011), for example, introduced an example of "chemical rain." Due to the earthquake, Cosmo Oil's refinery in Chiba Prefecture exploded. Numerous tweets were made to alert those in the neighborhood, according to one of the tweets, within 20 kilometers, that harmful substances will fall with rain. Some claimed that the alert was announced by the Ministry of Health, Labour, and Welfare. These tweets also asked for retweets to disseminate this information about health hazard as widely as possible. Consequently, both Cosmo Oil and news outlets issued that the tank that exploded contained liquefied petroleum gas, not a harmful substance to humans not on site.

A similar flow of rumors dealt with the shortage of power. Although it was true that the eastern half of Japan was under pressure to use less electricity upon the explosion of a nuclear power plant in Fukushima, the incident led Twitter users in the west half of the country to stop using excess power so that Kansai Electric Power and other power companies could send electricity to the eastern area. Many of these messages stated that it was a request shared by a friend that worked in the industry to add more credibility. Although these tweets began only a day after the earthquake, most likely made out of the general willingness to help out the victims, it added more confusion to the chaotic status in the country (Agile Media Network, 2011).

This is why Ogawa claims that Facebook was more suitable and helpful for many victims. Unlike Twitter, Facebook does not have a real-time update function that displays all the available updates. The site allows its users to filter what information to obtain and only certain information shows up in the News Feed. As a result, Facebook proved itself to be resistant to the risk of panic. Ogawa (2011) summarizes that right after the earthquake, many visited Twitter. But once some time has passed, users visited Facebook to sort out available information and examined the quality of information.

The quality of information on social media was not the only concern. Access to social media can potentially be a matter of life and death. This new form of digital divide is a life divide. Having access to social media meant knowing where to go to get food. Not having access to social media means spending a night without food. For others, Yokoyama (2011) explains that it was a matter of prolonged uncertainty. Since the many of the earthquake-stricken communities had suffered from an outflow of younger generations to Tokyo and other urban areas, many of the affected individuals were older residents who were less likely to be social media users. As a result, much of the older population remained unreachable for an extended period of time. The same was true with children and housewives who also tended to be non-social media users.

Kitabayashi (2011) explains that within 30 minutes after the earthquake, Twitter started showing tweets discouraging others to use landlines so that emergency calls could be made without maxing out the telephone line capabilities and encouraged them to use the Internet to check for the whereabouts of affected individuals. He remembers that he was immediately able to get in touch with his friends, whereas he was unable to reach his parents who were non-social media users. Later, he learned that they kept calling him via public phones and emailing him, and they were unable to reach him.

Even if someone had a social media account or had some experience of using online resources, many of these casual online users felt frustrations. Shitsuyuki (2011) summarizes that those who were not used to searching for and obtaining information and news from online sources were unable to access information that they were looking for. A female in her thirties mentioned that her brother and his family lived in the Hachinohe region that was affected by the tsunami. Since television news program did not share much about Hachinohe, she went online to find the status quo of the area, only to find as little information as she had found in the first place. A male respondent in his thirties from Iwate Prefecture tried to find out which gas stations were open in his neighborhood. He explained that he, however, ended up relying more on walking around town asking his friends for information.

This gap in familiarity to online resources, in general, ended up with two different ways of social media use. The first group included experienced social media users who were receiving constant updates via their mobile device. They set up their social media account so that they would automatically keep up with the latest development. The second group included less-experienced people that looked up information as they needed. Although this approach frequently fulfilled their needs, constantly staying updated by social media was beyond their imagination (Shitsuyuki, 2011).

Much of the digital divide was age-dependent. More than 50% of media users between the ages of 13 and 34 ranked mobile phones as a very important source of information, higher than any other age group. 78% of those between 35 and 44 years old stated that the Internet was very important, highest of all age groups. 90% of those between 55 and 64 year olds and 91% of those 65 years old and older said that television were very important. 75% of the former group and 78% of the latter group stated so about radio ("Television," 2011)

As mentioned above, many charity efforts were made through social media. Charity scams, however, were also present. This phenomenon was not unique to the 3.11 earthquake in Japan, the same happened with the earthquake in Haiti and New Zealand. McQueen (2011) wrote,

> *"Some of the email solicitations and social-network postings contain attachments or links that infect computers with malware designed to steal personal information for identity fraud.... Others solicit cash, PayPal or credit-card contributions for nonexistent charities" (p. 8).*

On the one hand, text message-based donation efforts primarily led by the Red Cross raised over $4 million in the U.S. within two weeks after the earthquake. On the other hand, during the same period, there were over 44,000 reports of fraudulent activities related to the earthquake donations.

One of the revelations about the Japanese society in the aftermath of the earthquake was that despite common assumptions, Japanese youth continue to be engaged. A Japanese interviewee during an NPR program denied that Japanese youth were apathetic. He said, "Ah no, no, no, no, no. That's a lie. Many people are really concerned about the Fukushima. So they really want to work as volunteer" ("Japanese Youth," 2011). This is a point that Don Tapscott (2008) had previously made. He argued that there had been a misunderstanding that youth today were apolitical and did not care about social issues. He, however, suggested that volunteer participation is on a rise. Youth pursued not just financial success, but also more holistic success by making responsible life choices.

This sense of engagement was not limited to youth. By the end of 2011, the Japanese word, kizuna, or "bond" became the kanji of the year. The annual event by the Kanji Aptitude Testing Institution selected this character to reflect the post-earthquake sentiment shared among many people in Japan ("Japanese Public," 2011). Kizuna represents social networks and capital whose importance many Japanese began to remember during the aftermath of the earthquake.

4. Conclusion

The earthquake of 2011 revealed that social media represented the third phase in digital networks. The Nomura Research Institute (2011b) analyzed that the first phase involved a network of computers of which many users took advantage. Although various forms of communication were made possible through networks of computers, it was nonetheless limited to networks of hardware. When the Internet became popular, it enabled networks of documents. This is the context in which the Great Earthquake of Kansai happened in 1995. As Neggers (1995) discussed, the Internet allowed victims and the general public to share information on websites. In 2011, social media, as networks of people, enabled closer and tighter communication. From the networks of computers to documents, then to humans, digital technology has evolved. This is how social media played significant roles during the emergency after the earthquake in the Tohoku region.

Nomura Research Institute (2011b) characterizes social media as "new public media." Of course, there is no doubt that social media are private in many ways. What the earthquake revealed, however, was that social media could also serve as a very public means of communication. Individual users sent information out to the world just as a major network newscaster would. Cell phones and other mobile devices kept the world up to date. Information was virally shared. As boyd and Ellison (2008) discussed, social media help "articulate and make [social networks] visible" (p. 211). Furthermore, Haythornthwaite (2005) explained that social media tend to reflect "latent ties" that share common interests offline. In the case of the aftermath of the 3.11 earthquake, the offline common denominator, evidently, was the disaster. Social media played an effective role in generating connections with latent ties.

In order to take advantage of the evident use value that social media had, two distinct efforts are necessary. First, as various statistics on the credibility of media suggested, many social media users continue to question how trustworthy information on social media might be. Not only is it difficult to authenticate the source of information, the traditional idea of authoritative information source is in question. The Japan Marketing Agency (2011) reported that even though 66% of respondents answered that social media was useful because of its speed, over 20% questioned if they are receiving accurate news. Devising a way to ascertain credibility of digital information is vital, especially in an emergency situation.

Second, the digital divide continues to be a significant issue. Now that social media have clearly demonstrated their strength during emergency, emergency preparedness should include signing up for social media and learning how to use them when needed. IMJ Mobile (2011) reported that within a few weeks after the earthquake, 40% of new users that signed up for a social media account did so because their family or friends' encouragement and recommendation. 23% more respondents stated after the earthquake that Twitter would be useful during emergency. 8% answered so about Facebook. This is just another case of the Japanese public becoming increasingly aware of the potential of social media during emergency.

Just as social media did not make the Arab Spring happen, they did not make communication among direct and indirect victims and other parties happen. Social media simply reflected existing social capital and networks of Japan. It is, nonetheless, noteworthy that this new form of technology allowed people in various situations to establish a sense of imagined communities, or kizuna. What Raymond Williams (1983) called "mobile privatization," or being "physically within the home and yet, simultaneously, be electronically transported to other places" (Hjorth & Kim, 2012, p. 188). This sense of ready access to the information and situations away from one's home—or temporary home—is a significant achievement that social media displayed during the aftermath of the earthquake. Social media do not replace social capital and network. But they enrich and reinforce existing ties that could easily be broken and disrupted by a disaster.

References

Agile Media Network. (2011). *Higashi nihon dai shinsai de kangaeru social media no yakuwari [The role of social media in the aftermath of the Great East Japan Earthquake]*. Retrieved from http://www.slideshare.net/tokuriki/-7424749

Anderson, B. *(1983). Imagined communities.* New York, NY: Verso

Appadurai, A. (1996). *Modernity at large: Cultural dimensions of globalization.* Minneapolis, MN: University of Minnesota Press

Banet-Weiser, S. (2012). *Authentic TM: The politics of ambivalence in a brand culture.* New York, NY: New York University Press

boyd, d.m., & Ellison, N. (2008). Social network sites: Definition, history, and scholarship. *Journal of computer-mediated communication, 13,* 210–230.

Cabinet Secretariat of Japan (2011, April 5). *Kuni chihou koukyou dantai nado koukyou kikan ni okeru minkan social media wo katsuyou shita jouhou hasshin ni tsuite no shishin [Guidance for information release using private social media services for national and municipal government bodies].* Retrieved from http://www.meti.go.jp/press/2011/04/20110405005/20110405005-2.pdf

Cie games: Players of Facebook game 'Car Town' can help Japan disaster relied by purchasing limited-edition Red Cross ambulance. (2011. April 9). *Marketing Weekly News.* Retrieved from http://www.verticalnews.com

Daishinsai no tsunami Mityako de 38.9m [Miyako recorded run-up wave of 38.9m after the Great Earthquake]. (2011, Apr. 15). *Yomiuri Shimbun.* Retrieved from http://www.yomiuri.co.jp

Granovetter, M. S. (1973). The strength of weak ties. *American journal of sociology, 78*(6), 1360–1380

Green, S. (2011, March 31). Japan, and the critical three ways social media plays during crisis. *PR Newswire.* Retrieved from http://www.prnewswire.com

Hayashi, M. (2011a). Shinsai go no ICT e no *kitai [Expectations for the ICT after the earthquake] [Electronic mailing list message].* Retrieved from http://www.jpc-net.jp/cisi/mailmag/m169_pa6.html

Hayashi, M. (2011b). Seifu ni yoru social media no katsuyou shishin to ninshou kansoka to korekara [Social media use by the government, simplification of authentication, and the future]. [Web log comment]. Retrieved from http://blogs.itmedia.co.jp/business20/2011/04/post-cd36.html

Haythornthwaite, C. (2005). Social networks and Internet connectivity effects. *Information, Communication and Society, 8*(2), 125–147.

Higashi Nihon Dai Jishin no shisha 6911 nin [Death toll at 6911 after the Great Eastern Japan Earthquake]. (2011, Mar 19). *47 News.* Retrieved from http://www.47news.jp

Hjorth, L., & Kim, K.H.Y. (2011). Good grief: The role of social mobile media in the 3.11 earthquake disaster in Japan. *Digital Creativity 22*(3): 187–199.

Ichikawa H. (2011). New Zealand jishin ni miru saigaiji ni life line to naru social media katsuyou hou towa [Learning from the earthquake in New Zealand to use social media as a lifeline during disasters]. *Gendai Business [Modern Business].* Retrieved from http://www.gendai.ismedia.jp/articles/print/2176

Ikeda, K., & Richey, S.E. (2005). Japanese network capital: The impact of social networks on Japanese political participation. Political behavior, 27(3), 239–260. doi: 10.1007/s11109-005-5512-0

IMJ Mobile. (2011, April 4*). Shinsai ni tomonau Twitter Facebook riyou jittai ni kansuru chousa [Survey on Twitter and Facebook usage in the context of the earthquake].* Retrieved from http://www.imjmobile. co.jp/news/file/pdf/report/imjm20110404_2.pdf

Japan Marketing Agency. (2011). *Shinsai go seikatsu ishiki chousa [Post-earthquake survey on lifestyle trends].* Retrieved from http://www.jma-net.com/files/shinsai02.pdf

Japan Marketing Agency. (2012) *Shinsai ichinen go seikatsu ishiki chousa [Survey on lifestyle trends a year after the earthquake].* Retrieved from http://www.jmra-net.or.jp/pdf/document/membership/release/jma20120629_1.pdf

Japan Metrological Agency. (2011a). *Jishin kazan geppou [Monthly newsletter on earthquakes and volcanos].* Retrieved from http://www. seisvol.kishou.go.jp/eq/gaikyo/monthly201103/20110311_tohoku_1 .pdf

Japan Metrological Agency. (2011b*). Heisei 23 nen touhoku chiho taiheiyou oki jishin ni tsuite: Dai 14 hou [On the 2011 off the Pacific Coast of Tohoku Earthquake: Report 14]*. Retrieved from http://www.jma.go.jp/jma/press/1103/13a/201103130900.html

"Japanese public chooses 'kizuna' as kanji of 2011." (2011. December 23). *BBC*. Retrieved from http://www.bbc.co.uk/news/world-asia-16321999

"Japanese youth step up in earthquake aftermath." (2011. April 12). *All things considered*. Washington, D.C.: National Public Radio. Retrieved from http://www.npr.org

Kim, V. (2011, Mar. 21). Japan damage could reach $235 billion, World Bank estimates. *Los Angeles Times*. Retrieved from http://www.latimes.com

Kitabayashi, T. (2011, March 18). *Jishin kara mananda social media kakusa [Social media divide as learned from the earthquake]. [Web log comment]*. Retrieved from http://infomationbook.blog136.fc2.com/blog-entry-106.html

Lin, N., Worlfel, M., & Light, S. (1985). The buffering effect of social support subsequent to an important life event. *Health and Social Behavior, 26*(3), 247–263.

McLuhan, M., & Powers, B. (1989). *The global village: Transformations in world life and media in the 21st century*. New York, NY: Oxford University Press

McQueen, M.P. (2011, April 2). The new basics: Japan scams spread. *Wall Street Journal*. Retrieved from www.wsj.com

Ministry of Internal Affairs and Communications. (2011). *Heisei 23 nendo ban jouhou tsuushin hakusho [2011 Information communication white paper]*. Retrieved from http://www.soumu.go.jp/johotsusintokei/whitepaper/ja/h23/html/nc232310.html

National Police Agency of Japan. (2012). *Damage situations and police countermeasures associated with 2011 Tohoku district – off the Pacific Ocean Earthquake*. Retrieved from http://www.npa.go.jp/archive/keibi/biki/higaijokyo_e.pdf

Neggers, M. (1995). Kobe earthquake on the Internet. *Cost Engineering, 37*(8), 17–18

Nomura Research Institute (2011a). *Shinsai ni tomonau sesshoku doukou ni kansuru chousa wo jisshi [Conducting a survey project on the media usage trend after the earthquake].* Retrieved from http://www.nri.co.jp/news/2011/110329.html

Nomura Research Institute (2011b). *Jichitai no social media katsuyou to sono shihyou [Applications and guidance for social media use by municipal governments].* Retrieved from http://www.nri.co.jp/publicity/mediaforum/2011/pdf/forum159.pdf

Office of Information Technology. The prime minister of Japan and his cabinet. (2011. April 25). *Seifu kikan ni okeru shinsai ni taiou shita gyousei jouhou no koukai teikyou nado no torikumi jirei ni tsuite [Examples of administrative information release regarding the earthquake by governmental bodies].* Retrieved from http://www .kantei.go.jp/jp/singi/it2/denshigyousei/dai14/siryou1.pdf

Ogawa, H. (2011). *Shinsai kara manabu social media no yakuwari [Lessons learned from the earthquake about the role of social media].* Retrieved from http://www.mdn.co.jp/di/newstopics/17638

Oyama, M., Nakamura, K., Suda, Y., & Someya, T. (2012). Social network disruption as a major factor associated with psychological distress 3 years after the 2004 Niigata-Chuetsu earthquake in Japan. *Environmental Health and Preventive Medicine, 17*, 118–123. doi: 10.1007/s12199-011-225-y

Putnam, R. (1995). Bowling alone: America's declining social capital. Journal of Democracy, 6(1), 65–78

Putnam, R. (2000). *Bowling alone: The collapse and revival of American community.* New York, NY: Simon and Schuster

Putnam, R. (2003). *Better together: Restoring the American community.* New York, NY: Simon and Schuster

Quake emphasizes value of text messages in emergencies: Verizon wireless network returns to full strength for Hawaii residents within 19 hours. (2006, Oct. 16). *PR Newswire*. Retrieved from http://ezproxy.msu.edu/login?url=http://search.proquest.com/docview/453906615?accountid=12598

Reconstruction Agency. (2011). *Higashi Nihon Daishinsai kara no fukkou no kihon houshin [Basic policies for the recovery from the East Japan Great Earthquake]*. Retrieved from http://www.reconstruction.go.jp/topics/doc/20110729houshin.pdf

Shellong, A.R.M. (2008). Government 2,0: An exploratory study of social networking services in Japanese local government. *Transforming government: People, process and policy, 2*(4), 225–242. doi: 10.1108/17506160810917936

Shitsuyuki, F. (2012). Higashi nihon daishinsai hisaisha wa media wo donoyouni riyou shitanoka [How did victims of the Great East Japan Earthquake use media]. *NHK housou bunka kenkyujo nenpou 2012 [NHK broadcasting culture research center annual report 2012]*. Retrieved from http://www.nhk.or.jp/bunken/research/title/year/2012/pdf/005-10.pdf

SONY Corporation of America: Share a message of support with the people of Japan this holiday season through Sony's 'Message to Japan' website. (2011. December 30). *Entertainment newsweekly*. Retrieved from http://www.verticalnews.com

Tapscott, D. (2008). *Grown up digital: How the net generation is changing your world*. New York, NY: McGraw Hill.

Television and fixed Internet found to be most important information sources in Japan following earthquake and tsunami. (2011. June 8). *Targeted News Service.*
Retrieved from http://www.targtednewsservice.com

Tucker, P. (2011, November/December). Lost and found in Japan. *The Futurist, 45*(6), 16–23.

Turkle, S. (1984). *The second self: Computers and the human spirit*. New York, NY: Simon and Schuster

Turkle, S. (1995). *Life on the screen: Identity in the age of the Internet.* New York, NY: Simon and Schuster,

Turkle, S. (2011). *Alone together: Why we expect more from technology and less from each other.* New York, NY: Basic Books

US Department of the Interior. U.S. Geological Survey. (2011a, March 14). *USGS Updates Magnitude of Japan's 2011 Tohoku Earthquake to 9.0.* Retrieved from http://www.usgs.gov/newsroom/article.asp?ID=2727

US Department of the Interior. U.S. Geological Survey. (n.d.). *Magnitude 8 and greater earthquakes since 1900.* Retrieved from http://earthquake.usgs.gov/earthquakes/eqarchives/year/mag8/magnitude8_1900_mag.php

Weathernews. (2011). *Higashi nihon dai shinsai chousa chousa kekka [East Japan Great Earthquake Survey Result].* Retrieved from http://weathernews.jp/ip/info/tsunami_enquete2_4.html

White, J.D., & Fu, K. (2012). Who do you trust? Comparing people-centered communications in disaster situations in the United States and China. *Journal of Comparative Policy Analysis, 14*(2), 126. doi: 10.1080/13876988.2012.664688

Williams, R. (1983). Mobile privatization. In P. du Gay, S. Hall, J. Lanes, H. Mackay, & K. Negus (eds.), *Doing cultural studies: The story of the SONY Walkman.* London: Sage.

Yates, D. & Paquette, S. (2011). Emergency knowledge management and social media technologies: A case study of the 2010 Haitian earthquake. *International Journal of Information Management, 31*(1), 6–13. doi: 10.1002/14504701243

Yokoyama, S. (2011). *Daishinsai de akiraka ni natta social media kakusa [Social media divide as revealed by the earthquake].* Retrieved from http://summit.ismedia.jp/articles/-/495

Yuasa, H. (2011a). *Seifu jichitai no social media riyou to jouhou koukai [Use of social media by the central and municipal governments and information sharing].* Retrieved from http://in-law.jp/archive/taikai/2011/kobetsu2-2-slide.pdf

Yuasa, H. (2011b). *Seifu jichitai no social media riyou to jouhou koukai [Use of social media by the central and municipal governments and information sharing]*. Retrieved from
http://in-law.jp/archive/taikai/2011/kobetsu2-2-resume.pdf

Yuasa, H. (2011c). *Seifu ga hasshin suru social media jouhou no houteki chii [Legality of information shared by the government via social media]*.
Retrieved from http://lab.iisec.ac.jp/~yuasa/docs/yuasa-110615.pdf

XI. "Pray for Japan": Reinventing "Japanese National Character" after the 2011 Tohoku Earthquake, Tsunami, and Nuclear Crisis

Yasuhito Abe

Annenberg School of Communication and Journalism,
University of Southern California, Los Angeles, California
yasuhito@usc.edu

Abstract

The 2011 Tohoku Earthquake, Tsunami, and Nuclear Crisis appears to be an unprecedented disaster if one takes a look at the role of social media in the triple disasters that devastated northeastern Japan. This chapter examines how people talked about their personal experiences following the triple disasters, how they situated them in history, and, as a consequence, how they contributed to the construction of "Japanese national character" by harnessing Twitter. Once the concept of national character is discussed, this chapter draws on Raymond Williams's distinction between television as technology and television as a cultural form to gain the perspectives of tweets as social practice. Then, the Discourse-Historical Approach, proposed by Martin Reisigl and Ruth Wodak, is taken to investigate a corpus of messages posted to Twitter represented by the website titled "Pray for Japan." Finally, this chapter analyzes how tweets interacted with each other in order to construct Japanese national character in the wake of the triple disasters.

Keywords: Japan, social media, earthquake, tsunami, nuclear disaster, national character, Twitter

1. Introduction

On 11 March 2011, the massive 9.0 magnitude earthquake and the ensuing tsunami devastated northeastern coastal regions in Japan. The Tohoku earthquake, tsunami and the resulting nuclear disaster, which were both "natural" and man-made disasters, prompted a flurry of discourses about Japanese-ness or "Japanese national character." For example, Shintarō Ishihara, Governor of Tokyo, stated on March 14 that the Japanese had been tainted with gayoku or "egoism," and asserted that the tsunami represented tembatsu or "divine punishment" for the egoism of Japanese people although he later retracted his remark (McCurry, 2011). Others claimed that the triple disasters shaped an entirely new Japanese national character. For instance, Hiroki Azuma, one of the most well-known Japanese cultural critics, noted on March 16:

> I have never seen Japanese people thinking about and discussing "the public" this much. Only recently the Japanese people and the government were seen as indecisive and selfish, muddled with complaints and bickering. But now, they are boldly trying to defend the nation together, as if they are a changed people. To borrow an expression from the younger generation here, the Japanese people seem to have completely transformed their kyara (character). Oddly enough, the Japanese are proud to be Japanese now. Of course, it may be argued that this new kyara is not so welcome, as it will likely lead to nationalism. I am seeing such concerns already surfacing on the Web. Nonetheless, I wish to see a ray of hope in this phenomenon. (Azuma, 2011)

The discourse around Japanese national character is broad and continuing to unfold, but there is one source that played a crucial role: social media. Indeed, Anthropologist David H. Slater et al (2012) point out that: "If Vietnam was the first war fully experienced through television, 3/11 was the first natural disaster fully experienced through social media" (p. 94). Not surprisingly, people talked about their personal experiences following the triple disasters, situated them in history, and as a consequence, and discussed how Japanese ought to be by harnessing social media such as Twitter.

Much scholarship has focused on the role of Twitter in the aftermath of natural disasters. Scholars have examined the reliability of Twitter posts as information source, and discussed how Twitter users play a significant role in shaping news and information in the wake of natural disasters. (Acar & Muraki, 2011; Doan et al, 2011; Earle, et al, 2010; Hermida, 2010; Nihon Saiken Initiative, 2012; Mendoza, et al, 2010; Sasaki, et al, 2010). Twitter, however, became somewhat a story-telling resource for its users in the wake of the triple disasters.

This study analyzes how people constructed narratives of their personal experiences by harnessing Twitter, and shows how they contributed to constructing discourses of Japanese national character. In doing so, the present study focuses on investigating a corpus of messages posted to Twitter ("tweets" hereafter) collected and represented by the website titled "prayforjapan.jp." In the immediate aftermath of the triple disaster, Hiroyuki Tsuruda, a Keio University student, gathered and catalogued "inspiring and heart-warming tweets from Japan and messages of support from around the world" on the website (Prayforjapan.jp, 2011). All the uplifting tweets were ultimately translated into at least 12 languages (Prayforjapan.jp, 2011). As such, despite being unedited and raw voices, the content of any messages represented by Pray for Japan is essentially positive, and an analysis of Pray for Japan alone makes it difficult to capture the whole picture of Japanese experiences following the disasters. That said, the collected tweets were ultimately published as a book in April 2011, and it became a bestseller in Japan. Through the collected tweets, people shared a sense of common experiences and consumed beautiful tales of Japanese-ness. Studying Pray for Japan will be a precondition for better understanding of the way in which people harnessed Twitter as a story-telling resource to contribute to constructing Japanese national character in the wake of the triple disasters.

This study of Pray for Japan is significant for a couple of reasons. First, by examining Pray for Japan, I underscore the ability of citizens to construct and mediate Japanese national character collectively in the wake of natural disasters. Undoubtedly, it is not entirely new that people engage in constructing Japanese national character following natural disasters in Japan. For example, Haruno Ogasawara (1999) shows that the 1995 Great Hanshin Earthquake paved the way for people to construct alternative images of Japanese-ness (and Japan) in the stricken area. As illustrated below, however, people tactically harnessed Twitter as a story-telling resource for themselves in the immediate aftermath of the triple disasters, and constructed narratives of Japanese-ness beyond the Tohoku region. As such, the present study of Pray for Japan will illustrate how networked people interacted with each other by harnessing Twitter as a story-telling resource in the wake of the disasters, and show how they contributed to constructing narratives of Japanese-ness in Japan and beyond. Second, the study of Pray for Japan will help reveal whether an entirely new Japanese national character actually emerged after the disasters. In so doing, this study examines tweets represented by Pray for Japan in a historical context in order to analyze to what extent the post-disaster Japanese national character is really new. Therefore, this study examines how Japanese national character was collectively constructed by individual tweets, which were represented by Pray for Japan, and shows what kind of Japanese national character actually emerged in the immediate aftermath of the triple disasters.

In order to elucidate the collectively constructed post-disaster Japanese national character, it is necessary to start with an overview of the concept of national character for this study. The first section of this paper discusses the concept of national character albeit briefly. Once the concept is laid out, drawing on Raymond Williams (2003)'s distinction between television as technology and television as a cultural form, the second section of this paper illustrates Twitter as a technology in which emerging national character is embedded and Twitter as a cultural form. I would argue that while the technological aspect of Twitter might constrain a boundary in which languages of discourses were shaped, Twitter users may potentially reshape the boundary provided by the structure of Twitter. In the third section, drawing on the Discourse-Historical Approach (DHA) proposed by Martin Reisigl and Ruth Wodak (2009), I will examine the specific contents of tweets represented by Pray for Japan, and analyze their discursive strategies involved in the construction of Japanese national character. Finally, I will examine how tweets interacted with each other, and indicate how the meaning of tweets was situated and reproduced by different audiences. Needless to say, there were inter-discursive links between discourses on Japanese national character through Twitter and those represented by other media such as mass media. However, this study focuses primarily on considering the discursive formation of Japanese national character through tweets represented by Pray for Japan alone.

2. National Character as Social Practice

At this point, I will elaborate more precisely the concept of national character. For this purpose, however, it is necessary to briefly review the meaning of the term "national character" so that this study can clarify what Japanese national character means in its context.

Much attention has been invested in studying national character (Benedict, 1989; Clark, 1977; Doi, 2002; Dale, 1986; Mead, 1965; Nakane, 1972; Saeki & Haga, 1987; Watsuji, 1979; Uchida, 2009). Most of the studies, however, assume nations as units of analysis, and treat "all societies and cultures as if they were national societies or cultures and treat[s] the relations between them as inter-national relations" (Neiburg and Goldman, 1998, p. 71). While the theoretical framework of national character studies appears to be challenged in the discussion of trans-nationalization of societies and cultures, Neiberg and Goldman (1998) illustrate why national character research still matters as follows:

> *What must be done is to map out, in its various foci of production and propagation, the mechanisms of constitution and diffusion of the categories related to this notion [national character], showing how apparently self-evident concepts and facts, as well as the most commonplace of words and things come to acquire, throughout history and in social usage, the density that is attributed to them as if it were a second nature (p. 71).*

As such, it is useful to treat national character as "objects and practices" (Neiburg and Goldman, 1998, p. 72), by which national character studies, despite the poverty of their nationalized theoretical framework, may potentially enhance our understanding of societies and cultures. As Neiburg and Goldman (1998) indicated, however, it is necessary to avoid the risk of justifying the nationalized theoretical framework of national character studies.

With that caveat in mind, this study treats national character as objects and practices, and examines how people constructed Japanese national character in the wake of the triple disasters. It should be underlined that the discursive formation of Japanese national character should not be restricted into a national context alone; it cannot be fully captured without any critical look at a trans-national context. As illustrated later, while Japan is certainly a nationally constituted state, Japanese people have actively taken up and reproduced the representation of Japanese national character constructed by "Western" gaze as their own self-image (Yoneyama, 1999). Therefore, this study investigates the discursive formation of Japanese national character both within, and outside of Japan.

Now that the concept of Japanese national character has been discussed, the following section will illustrate how people harnessed Twitter in order to construct narratives of the post-disaster Japanese national character in greater depth. This will allow for the analysis of Pray for Japan.

Tweets as a Story-Telling Resource in the Post-Disaster Japan

Twitter, a popular microblogging service, allows its users to post instant messages via different devices, such as computer, cell phone, and iPad. Tweets are shared by multiple audiences that include those who follow by subscribing to users' feeds, and those who search (Zaooavigna, 2011). One of the striking characteristics of Twitter is that each tweet is constrained to no more than 140 characters in length. Twitter's 140-character limit was originated from text messaging, which has 160-character limit such that Twitter users could use extra 20 character for their individual address (Millian, 2009). As such, Greg Mayer (2010) points out that that the core characteristic of Twitter is its time-binding nature. Given the 140-character limit, its characteristic as "the eternal present continuous" (Mayer, 2010, p. 75) may exclude some discourses that ask for long and substantial discussion.

In this section, I will focus on the role of tweets in shaping narratives of Japanese national character by drawing on Raymond Williams' distinction between media as technology and those as cultural form. In

Television, Williams (2003) examined the relationship between television as technology and television as a cultural form. In so doing, Williams criticized Marshal McLuhan's views of media specificity ("The medium is the message," which means that the characteristic of media constrains the content of discourse (McLuhan, 1964)), and indicated that specific media could be seen as social practices. More specifically, Williams suggested that new media technologies such as Twitter may need to be seen as an effect of a particular social order.

With this view in mind, I would argue that while Twitter's 140-character format might establish a boundary in which the meaning of the triple disasters is shaped, Twitter users might be able to reshape the boundary tactically. More specifically, although discourses through Twitter may be constrained by its real-time and time-binding nature and its word limit, Twitter users might be able to take advantage of freedom provided by Twitter such that they could recreate the nature of its medium specificity. Indeed, danah boyd et al (2010) maintain:

> ...while participants often shorten and otherwise modify tweets to fit into 140 characters, this characteristic of Twitter can also be seen as an advantage. The brevity of messages allows them to be produced, consumed, and shared without a significant amount of effort, allowing a fast-paced conversational environment to emerge.

As such, people tactically harnessed Twitter as a story-telling resource to produce their uplifting experiences following the disasters and, as a consequence, to contribute to the construction of the post-disaster Japanese national character.

A historical analysis of Twitter use might help explain why people tactically harnessed Twitter as a story-telling resource to construct narratives of Japanese national character collectively. Founded in 2006, Twitter started its service for Japanese speakers in 2008. Despite its short history, Twitter has become an extremely popular social medium in Japanese society. While Facebook, one of the most popular social network services, was also introduced to Japan in 2008, Japan is reportedly the only country where the number of Twitter users is larger than that of Facebook users (Yarow, 2012). While Mixi, a Japanese social network service, may have helped prevent Facebook from gaining its popularity, the large number of Twitter users still suggests that Twitter is extremely well-received by Japanese society. According to Tomoya Sasaki (2011), there are at least three reasons for the increasing popularity of Twitter in Japan. Firstly, since Japanese people were used to text-messaging by harnessing cellphones before the advent of Twitter, it was easy for Japanese people to get used to communication via Twitter. Secondly, Japanese people were familiar with posting their personal experiences to weblogs and embraced "the openness of the Internet." And finally, Twitter made it easy for Japanese users to register for its service, and its 140-character limit allowed them to express their experiences easily.

Given the increasing popularity of Twitter, particularly noteworthy about the brief history of Japanese speakers' use of Twitter is the fact that Japanese Twitter usage significantly grew during the 2010 FIFA World Cup (Net Marketing, 2011). Japanese speakers used a hashtag (#) and a keyword to talk about their excitement about games, and cheered up their national soccer team together (Net Marketing, 2011). Indeed, Japanese speakers published about 3383 tweets a second after Japan's victory over Denmark at the soccer event (Van Grove, 2010). This event indicates that despite the short history of Twitter use, these experiences may have paved the way for people to harness Twitter as a story-telling resource by which they talked about their inspiring experiences collectively in order to "cheer up" their stricken country in the wake of the triple disaster.

Now that some of the interplay between Twitter as a technology and Twitter as a cultural form has been discussed, I will take the Discourse-Historical Approach and examine tweets represented by Pray for Japan in the next section.

3. Tweets Represented by Pray for Japan

The Discourse-Historical Approach is derived from Critical-Discourse Analysis (CDA). Wodak and Meyer (2009) have characterized CDA as "being fundamentally interested in analyzing opaque as well as transparent structural relationships of dominance, discrimination, power and control as manifested in language"(p. 20). Similarly, the DHA is an attempt to "demystify the hegemony of specific discourses by deciphering the ideologies that establish, perpetuate or fight dominance" (Reisigl & Wodak, 2009, p. 88). Thus, the DHA has been predominantly concerned about "the language use of those in power who have the means and opportunities to improve conditions" (p. 88). As illustrated later, however, people can now participate in constructing or de-constructing hegemonic discourses by using social media, which may contribute to the renegotiation of the DHA.

The DHA originally examines three critical aspects of discourses: contents or topics, discursive strategies, and linguistic means (Reisigl & Wodak, 2009, p. 93). However, this study focuses exclusively on examining the first two aspects of discourses on Pray for Japan because they are primarily relevant to the analysis of the post-disaster Japanese national character.

4. Dataset

The data analyzed in this study are a corpus of tweets represented by the webpage "Pray for Japan" three months after the 2011 Tohoku earthquake, tsunami, and nuclear crisis. The resulting corpus contained 43 tweets available on the website. So complicated and extended is its discussion of significant events that analysis calls for multiple interventions to read, assemble and assess discourses of emergent national character that emerged within and altered many previous public expectations and disputes. In what follows, I will focus primarily on examining the topics and discursive strategies of tweets represented by Pray for Japan, and show how people contributed to the construction of the post-disaster Japanese national character by using Twitter as a story-telling resource.

Contents and Topics

The main topics of emerging Japanese national character following the disaster can be described as "orderliness" and "decency," which seemed to be perceived as being undisputed Japanese natural habits. Ruth Benedict's *The Chrysanthemum and the Sword* (1989), for example, offers a historical description of Japanese national character as "unprecedentedly polite" and remarks on the "robot-like discipline" of the Japanese; these description can certainly be seen as symbolic resources for re-constructing Japanese national character as orderliness (p. 2). By the same token, similar rhetoric surrounding the 1995 Great Hanshin Earthquake appeared in the discursive formation of national character as decency (Ogasawara, 1999).

The following are examples of emerging Japanese national character as orderliness and decency. It is hardly surprising that all the creators of these examples framed their local experiences or anecdotes as a part of Japanese national character.

> *I recall my late mother's words. "We don't have enough when we fight over things, but we have more than enough when we are willing to share." I am deeply proud of the victims of this disaster who are living by those words, and of Japan. Please stay strong. (@yoshi0miyu, 2011)*

This Twitter user identifies herself as a mother who raised two children in Tokyo. This tweet was reproduced for 2,452 times (yoshi0miyu, 2011). She symbolically identified disaster victims in the disaster-stricken district with the rest of Japan, and thus discursively constructed Japanese national character as orderly and decent. However, there was actually much panic overbuying occurring in Tokyo where this Twitter user lives (the Sankei shinbun, 2011). Given that people essentially tailor their self-representation based on contexts and the audience (Goffman, 1959; Hogan, 2010), it might have been difficult for her to refer to negative events such as panic overbuying in Tokyo area even if she recognized them. Even though she had actually reported negative events by using Twitter, however, her anecdote would never have been represented by Pray for Japan because Pray for Japan collected beautiful tales of Japanese experiences alone. In the end, this anecdote was represented and reproduced as an "official" story on Japanese national character on the website.

> *On my four-hour walk home, I encountered a woman standing out on the sidewalk holding up a sketchbook that read, 'Please feel free to use our bathroom!' She was offering her own bathroom to others who needed it. Japan has got to be the most heartwarming country*

in the world. When I saw that I was so moved that I had to cry.
(@command_s, 2011)

This tweet again exemplifies Japanese national character as one marked by decency, using an anecdote from real life. This Twitter user reported that he was working as a designer in Yokohama, Kanagawa. Although his specific experience was not generalizable to Japanese experience, he also identified his local "heartwarming" experience with Japanese national character.

The owner of a ramen shop was living in an evacuation center because his home was washed away, but his restaurant was spared so he was treating victims to free bowls of noodles. That's how warm people in Japan are... I'm so proud to have been born here.
(@maromaro25, 2011)

This tweet also constructed Japanese national character as decency. This tweet was reproduced for 11 times (maromaro25, 2011).This tweet reported on what that twitter user overheard. This Twitter user identified himself merely as a male who loves to hang around, living in Hiroshima. Although Hiroshima was not affected by the triple disasters, he likewise identified a heartwarming event at the evacuation center with the rest of Japan including Hiroshima. This tweet suggests that discourses about Japanese national character might have been becoming prevalent in regions that were not affected by the disaster.

While Twitter's word limit and real-time nature might have constrained adequately-contextualized and well-thought discourses from the discursive formation of Japanese national character, it should be underlined that people took full advantage of freedom provided by Twitter to report their inspiring experiences and stories. Indeed, Twitter users reproduced tweets so easily that these tweets were likely to be reproduced by multiple audiences and shared as legitimated Japanese national character pretty quickly even if the heroic narratives of the tweets might have been far from the truth. Thus, Twitter users tactically harnessed Twitter as a story-telling resource to talk about their experiences and contributed to the construction of Japanese national character.

Discursive Strategies

In this section, I will investigate how symbols were strategically utilized for the formation of national character as orderliness and decency. According to Wodak and Meyer (2009), there are at least four types of discursive strategies involved in constructing national identities:

1) Constructive strategies (aiming at the construction of national identities)
2) Justificatory strategies (aiming at the conservation and reproduction of national identities or narratives of identity)
3) Transformative strategies (aiming at the change of national identities)
4) Destructive strategies (aiming at the dismantling of national identity) (p. 18)

Not coincidentally, the first three strategies were also employed in constructing Japanese national character following the disaster whereas the fourth strategy does not seem to be applicable for this study (Wodak et al, 1999). In addition to the first three strategies, this paper also examines a historically-rooted Japanese discursive strategy: foreign gaze-invoked strategy.

The following is an example of constructive strategies. Constructive strategies serve to constitute the "we-group" naturally by using the pronoun "we" rather than the term "Japanese."

> *Two old ladies were talking on the train. "The police say we're short on electricity and are telling people to turn out the lights." "Well, we're used to spending time in the dark for the sake of our country. This time, it's not as if bombs are falling from the sky– we're happy to turn the lights off, aren't we?" For a moment there was complete silence on the train, and I tried to hold back my tears. (@tabletalkcafe, 2011)*

This tweet reported on what the Twitter user witnessed. The Twitter user identified himself as an owner of a game center called as "Table Talk Café Day Dream" in Kanda Ward, Tokyo. The two old ladies of the previous tweet were reported to use "we," which symbiotically enhanced a sense of national solidarity among the Japanese, and served as a foundation for constructing national character as orderliness (and resiliency) that seemed self-evident for all generations of Japanese.

Justificatory strategies were also employed in this example. They aim at maintaining and reproducing a preexisting national character by preserving narratives of a nationalized history. In general, historical symbols embedded in narratives of national history tend to evoke heroic narratives that are taken to comfort its society by allowing its nationals to take pride in their national history (Gluck, 2007). Indeed, the author of the previous tweet evoked the trope of Japanese wartime patriotism and seemed to praise Japanese national character as orderliness. In this case, it could be argued that the old ladies strived to "establish continuity with a suitable historic past" (Hobsbawm, 1983, p. 1) by re-contextualizing their local wartime experiences as Japan's national history. Here is another example which utilizes justificatory strategies:

> *The United Nations commented on the disaster: "Japan has long helped people around the world as a major foreign aid benefactor. This time, the UN will do everything it can to assist Japan in its time of need. (@akitosk, 2011)*

This tweet reported on what the Twitter user learned from mass media report. The gender of the actor is not mentioned, but this Twitter user identified herself as a Japanese otaku living in Tokyo. On March 11, Ban Ki-moon, the Secretary General of the United Nations, issued this statement to Japan. The statement was widely reported by Japanese mass media, reproduced by multiple twitter users including this Twitter user, and utilized for the discursive formation of Japanese national character as decency. By emphasizing that Japan contributed to the world "as a major foreign aid benefactor," this tweet contributed to the nationalization of Japan's history in order to construct narratives of Japanese national character.

> *Free Suntory vending machines, free SoftBank WiFi hotspots...people from every corner of society are working together, and inspiring people from around the world to help as well. Since the Hanshin earthquake sixteen years ago, when the government hesitated to accept support from other countries and delayed sending in the Self-*

> *Defense Forces, Japan has undoubtedly become a stronger country.*
> *(@dita_69, 2011)*

This tweet reported on what this Twitter user overheard. This user only reported that he is living in Nagoya. Contrasting the Japanese governmental poor management of the 1995 Great Hanshin earthquake with the private companies' prompt voluntary responses toward the 2011 crisis, he concluded that "Japan has become a stronger county." Rather than viewing the role of governmental actors in managing the 2011 crisis, he focused exclusively on the rescue operations from non-government actors and constructed Japanese national character as decent.

We see within these tweets the third strategies: transformative strategies. They aim at shifting one relatively well-established element of national character to another. Here is an example:

> *I was thinking as I walked home for four long hours from the center*
> *of Tokyo. The streets were overflowing with people, but everybody*
> *walked in silence in orderly lines. Convenience stores and drug*
> *stores, supermarkets and gas stations—they all kept doing their*
> *work. Internet infrastructure withstood the tremors, establishments*
> *everywhere threw open their doors for stuck commuters to stay the*
> *night, and the trains are said to be up and running again throughout*
> *the night. What a country. Who cares what our GDP rank is.*
> *(@resaku, 2011)*

This tweet illustrates how its creator interpreted what he witnessed in Tokyo. It is noteworthy that the Twitter user strived to frame Japan as an orderly country while dismissing the declining status of Japan's economy in the world as irrelevant to the assessment of Japanese national character. Historian Kenneth B. Pyle (2007) argues that one of the recurrent characteristics of the modern Japanese state in relation to the international systems was "a persistent obsession with status and prestige" among the international societies (p. 62). Given that Japan's status as the world's second biggest economy was overtaken by China in 2010, and because the triple disaster devastated the northeastern coastal regions of the entire country, the Twitter user might have needed to redefine Japan as a prestigious country in a different way. Ultimately, the Twitter user appeared to dismiss Japan's declining economic status as irrelevant to Japanese national character as orderliness. More importantly, this newly-defined prestigious national character was reproduced by multiple Twitter users and well shared as a redefined Japanese national character. In the end, this tweet was reproduced for as many as 2,341 times (resaku, 2011).

Finally, I will examine Japan's historically-rooted strategies involved in constructing national character, which could be termed as foreign gaze-invoked strategies. They can be categorized as a part of constructive strategies, but their agents are distinct in some degree. As previously noted, Japanese national character has been constructed by not only Japanese people but also foreign gaze. In other words, Japanese self-representation is shaped by not only how Japanese see themselves, but also how Japanese think they are seen by foreigners. Here is an example:

> *I just got a message from my Korean friend: "You're the only country in the world to have fallen victim to nuclear attacks. You lost the Second World War. Every year there are typhoons. Earthquakes happen. You're ever struck by tsunamis. You're just a tiny-nation, but you wouldn't be Japan if you didn't get up again every time. Stay strong, stay very strong." I can't help but cry. (@copedy, 2011a)*

This tweet reported on a letter the Twitter user received from his Korean friend. The actor did not identify his location. In an argument similar to constructive strategies, the Korean friend was reported to use "you," which also symbiotically enhanced a sense of national solidarity among Japanese people, and constructed national character as orderliness. What is difference from constructive strategies is that this tweet described how Japan was seen by a Korean. As a result, this tweet invoked the Korean gaze and let the Japanese consider how the Japanese ought to behave, with the result that Japanese national character as orderliness was discursively constructed.

Tweet Interaction

The final section briefly investigates how tweets interacted and, as a result, discursively constructed Japanese national character as orderly and decent. Perhaps not surprisingly, an analysis of the tweet interaction shows that there was no substantial dialogue between twitter users. However, it does not mean that there were no interactions between Twitter users to construct Japanese national character. All of the tweets we have examined were reproduced for more than 10 times as "retweets," which suggests that people tactically spread discourses on Japanese national character by harnessing Twitter.

The final section of this study will focus primarily on investigating the previous tweet as a case study for an analysis of tweet interaction. I chose this text because the meaning of the previous tweet appeared to be interpreted slightly differently according to different readers. Moreover, the previous tweet was reproduced for as many as 16,540 times, which indicates that the tweet gained wide attention from Twitter users. At 11:54pm March 11, a Twitter user named "copedy" produced the following tweet:

> *I just got a message from my Korean friend: 'You're the only country in the world to fallen victim to nuclear attacks. You lost the Second World War. Every year there are typhoons. Earthquakes happen. You're ever struck by tsunamis. You're just a tiny-nation, but you wouldn't be Japan if you didn't get up again every time. Stay strong, stay very strong.' I can't help but cry. (copedy, 2011a)*

After the previous tweets, copedy seemed to have many replies from other Twitter users, and at 7:13am on March 12, he tweeted as follows:

> *Thank you very much for many replies to my [previous] tweet on Korean friend. Although I would like to respond to all of your replies if possible, but since there are too many, I would like to express my gratitude [to you]. I told my [Korean] friend that many people were encouraged by his message. (copedy, 2011b)[translated by the author]*

At 8:45am on March 12, however, an 18-year old Japanese high school female student named "yuuukyy" responded to the first tweet that copedy posted as follows:

> *@copedy I retweeted [your tweet on a message from your Korean friend]. Tears flowed from my eye [when I read your tweet]. I thank your Korean friend. I also appreciate your tweeting. Thank you. Let's do our best. (yuuukyy, 2011) [translated by the author]*

She clearly referred to his Korean friend in her response, and thanked the Korean personally. Intriguingly, she thanked his Korean friend first, and then she added her gratitude to copedy. Her response indicates that she perceived the message from his Korean friend as one that is directed to all the Japanese. It could be argued that as a Japanese national, she may have thought that she would have to express her gratitude to the Korean first. In her response, his Korean friend was represented to play an active role in the discursive formation of Japanese national character through the heartwarming tweet. At 8:48am on March 12, copedy replied to the high school student as follows:

> *Thank you very much for your trouble in replying [to my tweet]. I am proud of this [Korean] friend. Although there are still aftershocks ongoing, let's do our best! (copedy, 2011c) [translated by the author]*

Similarly, he clearly acknowledged his Korean friend and stated that he is proud of his Korean friend. His response also suggests that the Korean friend played a significant role in framing Japanese national character quite positively.

However, another Twitter user interpreted copedy's first tweet differently. This twitter user did not identify his or her gender and reported that he or she was a worker for a facility for the physically handicapped in Gunma prefecture. The twitter user, whose pseudonym is "Saboten58," posted the following tweet at 8:52am on March 12:

> *I saw a message from your Korean friend. I cannot stop crying. He is your good friend. Let's do our best together." (Saboten58, 2011) [translated by the author]*

Unlike the previous response posted by the high school student, this twitter user did not express thanks to copedy's Korean friend. Also, this tweet might suggest that Saboten58 perceived the message from copedy's Korean friend as one that was directed only to copedy, not to the whole Japanese society. Therefore, Saboten58 represented copedy's Korean friend merely as copedy's "good friend" with the result that this Twitter user appeared to acknowledge copedy more than his Korean friend. In response to saboten58's reply, copedy posted a tweet at 8:56am on March 12 as follows:

Thank you very much for your trouble in replying [to my tweet].
Although there are still aftershocks ongoing, let's do our best! (copedy,
2011d) [translated by the author]

Conspicuously, copedy did not mention his Korean friend in his reply
to Saboten58 perhaps because Saboten58 did not thank his Korean friend
at all. In other words, the symbol of the foreign gaze was somewhat
marginalized from his response when compared with his response to the
high school student.

Finally, there was one more short response to copedy's first tweet on
March 13. The Twitter user, whose pseudonym is sarukani5133, also did
not identify his or her gender, living in Nagano prefecture. Sarukani5133
posted the following tweet at 4:32am on March 13:

I was touched [by your tweet on a message from your Korean friend].
[The message from your Korean friend is] absolutely right. Let's do
our best.[@sarukani5133 (March 13) translated by the author]

The symbol of copedy's Korean friend completely disappeared in
this response. Sarukani5133 appeared to acknowledge the content of
copedy's message only, but excluded the Korean gaze from his or her own
interpretation of the message. This tweet also indicates that this twitter user
may have appeared to reproduce the representation of Japanese national
character constructed by "Korean" gaze as their own self-image. In response
to this reply, copedy posted almost exactly the same tweet that he sent to
Saboten58 perhaps because both Saboten58 and sarukani5133 did not
express thanks to his Korean friend.

Thus, an analysis of the twitter interaction reveals that the multiple
meanings of copedy's first tweet were situated and reproduced by different
audiences. In this process, Japanese national character as orderliness and
decency was discursively constructed in multiple ways.

5. Conclusion

This chapter has examined how people talked about their experiences following the 2011 Tohoku earthquake, tsunami and nuclear disaster, how they situated them in history, and, as a consequence, how they contributed to the construction of Japanese national character by harnessing Twitter. This research reveals the following key findings:

The first conclusion is that people tactically harnessed Twitter as a story-telling resource to contribute the construction of Japanese national character. While Twitter as technology may have constrained a boundary in which the meaning of their personal experiences was shaped, people tactically harnessed Twitter and made it possible for a fast-paced interaction to emerge in the wake of the triple disasters. This finding suggests that people could recreate the nature of its medium specificity. While much scholarship has focused on examining the role of Twitter after natural disasters for varieties of reasons, more scholarly attention should be paid to the role of Twitter as a story-telling resource in the wake of natural disasters.

The second conclusion is that orderliness and decency were reconstructed as main contents of Japanese national character following the triple disasters. The DHA revealed that the two concepts were not entirely new. This paper also showed that the Japanese twitter users employed four different discursive strategies to construct Japanese national character. While the DHA appears to focus primarily on the language use of powerful people, this finding suggests that now that people can participate in constructing or de-constructing hegemonic discourses of Japanese national character by using social media, the DHA may be also applicable to an analysis of the languages of ordinary citizens.

The third conclusion is that even if there are discursive strategies, the meaning of tweets was actually situated and reproduced differently according to different people. In this process, Japanese national character was discursively constructed and consumed in multiple ways.

Obviously, this study cannot capture the fundamentally complex phenomenon of emergent national character following the triple disasters. As noted, Pray for Japan collected and represented beautiful tales of Japanese experiences alone, and further research would be needed to gain a better perspective of Japanese national character following the triple disasters. However, I hope that this research can contribute to the development of DHA, and can portray at least some aspects of the discursive formation of the post-disaster Japanese national character in a networked era.

Acknowledgements

An earlier version of this paper was presented to the 4th Tokyo Conference on Argumentation on August 12, 2012. I would like to thank Japan Debate Association (JDA) for allowing me to reproduce my work. I would also like to thank Gerald Goodnight for providing feedback.

References

Acar, A., & Muraki, Y. (2011). Twitter for crisis communication: Lessons learned from Japan's tsunami disaster. *International Journal of Web Based Communities, 7*, 392–402.

Azuma, H. (2012, March 16). For a change, proud to be Japanese. *The New York Times*. Retrieved from http://www.nytimes.com/2011/03/17/opinion/17azuma.html

Benedict, R. (1989). *The chrysanthemum and the sword: Patterns of Japanese culture*. Boston, MA: Houghton Mifflin Company.

boyd, d., Golder, G., & Lotan, G. (2010, January). *Tweet, tweet, retweet: Conversational aspects of retweeting on Twitter*. Paper presented at HICCS-43. IEEE, Kauai, HI. Retrieved from http://www.danah.org/papers/TweetTweetRetweet.pdf

Clark, G. (1977*). Nihonjin: Yunikusa no gensen [Japanese: The origin of uniqueness]*. Tokyo, Japan. Saimaru shuppan.

copedy. (2011a, March 11). *Tweet*. Retrieved from https://twitter.com/copedy/status/46222426639568897

copedy. (2011b, March 12). *Tweet.* Retrieved from
https://twitter.com/copedy/status/46613581982208000

copedy. (2011c, March 12). *Tweet.* Retrieved from
https://twitter.com/copedy/status/46589587589566464

copedy. (2011d, March 12). *Tweet.* Retrieved from
https://twitter.com/copedy/status/46615603217313792

Dale, P. N. (1986). *The myth of Japanese uniqueness.* Oxford, UK: Croom
Helm.

Dita_69. (2011, March 13). *Tweet.* Retrieved from
https://twitter.com/dita_69/status/46309373458382849

Doan, S., Vo, B., Collier, N. (2011). *An analysis of Twitter messages in the
2011 Tohoku earthquake.*
Retrieved from http://arxiv.org/abs/1109.1618

Doi, T. (2002). *The anatomy of dependence.* New York, NY: Kodansha
USA.

Earle, P., Guy, M., Buckmaster, R., Ostrum, C., Horvath, S., and
Vaughan, A. (2010). OMG earthquake! Can Twitter improve
earthquake response? *Seismological Research Letters, 81*(2), 246–251.

Gluck, C. (2007). Operations of memory: "Comfort women" and the
World. In S. M. Jager & R. Mitter (Eds.), *Ruptured histories: War,
memory, and the post-Cold War in Asia* (pp. 47–77). Cambridge,
MA: Harvard University Press.

Goffman, E. (1958). *The presentation of self in everyday life.* New York,
NY: Anchor books.

Hermida, A. (2010). From TV to Twitter: How ambient news became
ambient journalism. *Journal of Media and Culture, 13*(2), Retrieved
from http://journal.media-culture.org.au/index.php/mcjournal/
article/viewArticle/220

Hobsbawm, E. (1983). Introduction: Inventing traditions. In
E. Hobsbawm., & T. Ranger. (Eds). *The invention of tradition*
(pp. 1–14). Cambridge, UK: Cambridge University Press.

Hogan, B. (2010). The presentation of self in the age of social media: Distinguishing performances and exhibitions online. *Bulletin of Science, Technology & Society, 30*(6), 377–386.

Maromaro25. (2011, March 14). *Tweet*. Retrieved from https://twitter.com/maromaro25/status/47613447843758080

McCurry, J. (2011, March 15). Tokyo governor apologizes for calling tsunami 'divine punishment': Shintaro Ishihara said tsunami was retribution for 'egoism' of Japanese people. *The Guardian*. Retrieved from http://www.guardian.co.uk/world/2011/mar/15/tokyo-governor-tsunami-punishment

McLuhan, M. (1964). *Understanding media: The extensions of man.* New York, NY: Signet.

Mead, M. (1965). *And keep your powder dry: An anthropologist looks at America.* New York, NY: Morrow Quill.

Mendoza, M., Poblete, B., and Castillo, C. (2010). *Twitter under crisis: Can we trust what we RT?* Retrieved from http://snap.stanford.edu/soma2010/papers/soma2010_11.pdf

Milian, M. (2009, May 3). Why text messages are limited to 160 characters. *The Los Angeles Times*. Retrieved from http://latimesblogs.latimes.com/technology/2009/05/invented-text-messaging.html

Myers, G. (2010). *The discourse of blogs and wikis.* London, UK: Continuum.

Nakane, C. (1972*). Japanese Society.* Berkeley, CA: University of California Press.

Neiburg, F. & Goldman, M. (1998). Anthropology and politics in studies of national character. *Cultural Anthropology 13*(1), 56–81.

Net Marketing. (2011). Nihon no Twitter riyo sarani kasoku, gekkan 2.5 oku tuito ni, W-hai ga kenin [The rapidly developing of Twitter use: the FIFA World Cup helped increase the number of tweets to two hundred and fifty million per month]. *Net Marketing*. Retrieved from http://business.nikkeibp.co.jp/article/nmg/20100706/ 215290/?ST=nmg_page

Nihon Saiken Initiative. (2012*). Fukushima genpatsu jiko dokuritsu kensho iinnkai: Chosa/kensho hokokusho [Independent investigation commission on Fukushima Daiichi nuclear accident: Investigation report].* Tokyo, Japan: Discover 21.

Ogasawara, H. (1999). *Living with natural disasters: Narratives of the Great Kanto and Great Hanshin Earthquakes* (Doctoral dissertation). Retrieved from http://www.proquest.com/en-US/

Pyle, B. K. (2007). *Japan rising: The resurgence of Japanese power and purpose.* New York, NY: Public Affairs.

prayforjapan.jp. (Ed.). (2011). *PRAY FOR JAPAN.* Tokyo, Japan: Kodansha.

Reisigl, M., & Wodak, R. (2009). The discourse-historical approach (DHA). In R. Wodak., & M. Meyer. (Eds). *Methods of critical discourse analysis* (pp. 87–121). Thousand Oaks, CA: Sage.

resaku. (2011, March 11). *Tweet.* Retrieved from https://twitter.com/resaku/status/46249199825715200

saboten58. (2011, March 12). *Tweet.* Retrieved from http://ja.favstar.fm/users/saboten58/recent

Saeki, S., & Haga, T. (1987*). Gaikokujin ni yoru Nihonjin ron no meicho [The excellent books on theories about the Japanese written by foreigners].* Tokyo, Japan: Chuokoron shinsho.

Sarukani5133. (2011, March 13). *Tweet.* Retrieved from https://twitter.com/sarukani5133/status/46896412532813824

Sasaki, T. (2011). Kakudai o tsuzukeru Twitter no shinsai ni okeru katsuyaku to kongo no tenbo [The role of growing Twitter in playing a lively part in the earthquake and its future prospects] *AD Studies, 36*, 20–24. Retrieved from http://www.yhmf.jp/pdf/activity/adstudies/vol_36_01_04.pdf

Sasaki, T., Okazaki, M., & Matsuo, Y., (2010*). Earthquake shakes Twitter users: Real-time event detection by social sensors.* WWW2010, 26–30.

Slater, D.H., Nishimura, K., & Kindstrand, L. (2012). Social media in disaster Japan. In J. Kingston (Ed). *Natural disaster and nuclear crisis in Japan* (pp. 94–108). London, UK: Routledge.

The Sankei Shinbun. (2011). *Tonai de kaidame osamarazu [Panic buying cannot be controlled in Tokyo]*. Retrieved from http://sankei.jp.msn.com/affairs/news/110315/dst11031521260160-n1.htm

Van Grove, J. (2010, June 25). *Twitter sets new record: 3,283 tweets per second.* Retrieved from http://mashable.com/2010/06/25/tps-record/

Uchida, T. (2009). *Nihon henkyo ron [Japan: A nation of outlier]*. Tokyo, Japan: Shinchosha.

Watsuji, T. (1979). *Fudo [Climate and culture]*. Tokyo, Japan: Iwanami shoten.

Williams, R. (2003). *Television: Technology and cultural form*. New York, NY: Routledge.

Wodak, R. (1999). The discursive construction of national identities. *Discourse & Society*, 149–173.

Wodak, R & Meyer, M. (2009). Critical discourse analysis: History, agenda, theory and methodology. In R. Wodak., & M. Meyer. (Eds). *Methods of critical discourse analysis* (pp. 1–33). Thousand Oaks, CA: Sage.

Yarow, J. (2012, January, 6). *Chart of the day: There's only one place in the world where Twitter is bigger than Facebook*. Retrieved from http://www.businessinsider.com/theres-only-one-place-in-the-world-where-twitter-is-bigger-than-facebook-2012-1

Yoneyama, L. (1999). Habits of knowing cultural differences: Chrysanthemum and the sword in the U.S. liberal multiculturalism. *Topoi, 18*, 71–80.

yoshi0miku. (2011, March 15) *Tweet*. Retrieved from https://twitter.com/yoshi0miyu/status/47896309688049664

yuuukyy. (2011, March 12). *Tweet*. Retrieved from http://favstar.fm/users/yuuukyy

Zappavigna, M. (2011). Ambient affiliation: A linguistic perspective on Twitter. *New Media & Society*, 1–19.

XII.   Mad Cow Blues: South Korea, Clay Shirky and the Digital Public Sphere

Jason L. Jarvis

Department of Communication, Georgia State University
jasonleighjarvis@gmail.com

Abstract

New York University Professor Clay Shirky deploys the 2008 beef protests in South Korea as proof of the Internet's democratizing power. I argue that Shirky's analysis misunderstands the causes, context and results of the beef protests. First, he provides a reductionist assessment of the cause of the protests that ignores the role of yellow journalism in the mainstream media, viral rumors and political blunders by Lee, Myung Bak. Second, Shirky does not account for the historical role of beef in nationalist and anti-American protest movements. Finally, Shirky overestimates the democratic results of the protests.

Keywords: South Korea, beef, public sphere, Clay Shirky

1. Introduction

In 2008, nationwide protests in South Korea paralyzed political institutions and dominated the public sphere. Anti-American sentiments were rampant and beef was the touchstone. Food and drink build close bonds in South Korea. Good barbecue is available at all hours of the day or night, and groups of co-workers and friends spend many evenings sharing a meal and a toast or three. The social drama of American beef in South Korea was evident in the culinary public sphere in restaurants across the country that scrambled to label their beef as Australian rather than American. This paper is a comparative history of beef in South Korea set against the description of the 2008 beef protests by digital public sphere scholar Clay Shirky. Shirky analyzes the beef protests in his 2010 book Cognitive Surplus. He also references the crisis in a 2011 Foreign Affairs article on social media and the public sphere. For Shirky, the beef protests are proof of the democratizing power of the internet, and their ability to bring new members of society into the public sphere.

I take issue with the causes, context and results of the protests in Professor Shirky's analysis. First, his account of the causes of the protest is incomplete. Shirky overlooks important factors such as political blunders, rumors, and sensationalist media accounts while identifying social media as the catalyst of the protests. Second, Shirky provides no real context for understanding the conflict over beef. Beef has been a lightning rod for anti-American protesters and democracy activists since the efforts of the United States to liberalize South Korean markets in the 1980s. Moreover, many South Korean citizens do not trust the United States because of the Kwangju massacre during the Carter administration and an American tank that gruesomely killed two young girls in 2002.

Finally, Shirky overstates the success of the protests, remaining silent on the threat that they posed to South Korean democratic institutions. In fact, the beef protests reveal the fissures in South Korea's nascent democracy by highlighting the barriers between the public and the policymaking process (Oh, 2012). South Korea demonstrates how new communication technologies can pose threats to the stability of democratically elected governments. Protest and the enactment of public opposition is not necessarily equivalent to a healthy democracy.

Prior to discussing the causes of the beef protests, I want to correct two factual errors made by Shirky. Initially, the primary location for the protests was City Hall (Si-Chung) not "Cheongyecheon Park" as he asserts in both 2008 and 2011. "Cheon" is Korean for "stream." The park runs for miles from Dongdaemoon (the fashion center of Seoul) to Si-Chung (City Hall). This is because the park is actually a stream that runs through north-central Seoul. Cheongyecheon's restoration required demolition of an elevated superhighway. Reclamation of the stream snarled traffic for years, and was the centerpiece achievement of Lee, Myung Bak's term as mayor of Seoul (Yonhap News, 2008a). Lee would become the focus of beef protests as the newly inaugurated president in 2008.

When Shirky suggests that the protests were so big that they destroyed the grass in Cheongyecheon (2010, p. 32) then it appears that he doesn't understand the local geography. The majority of the park is a sidewalk on both sides of the stream. There is very little grass. If grass was destroyed it was in City Hall, not Cheongyecheon (unless protestors chose to pick the reeds in the reclaimed stream). City Hall is where South Koreans famously massed to watch games and celebrate during the World Cup in 2002. It is a place where protests happen regularly.

Second, Shirky consistently misnames Naver as a social network rather than an internet portal/search engine.

Services based in the United States, such as Facebook, Twitter, Wikipedia, and YouTube, and those based overseas, such as QQ (a Chinese instant-messaging service), WikiLeaks (a repository of leaked documents whose servers are in Sweden), Tuenti (a Spanish social network), and Naver (a Korean one), are among the sites used most for political speech, conversation, and coordination (2011).

The same mistake happens in Cognitive Surplus. Naver is not a walled garden like Facebook or MySpace; rather it is a web portal akin to Yahoo. Naver includes a search engine in addition to news, shopping, and other features. For many Koreans, Naver *is* the internet as the majority of citizens use local search engines rather than foreign competitors such as Google or Yahoo. To suggest that Naver is a "social network" is either wholly incorrect or unintentionally misleading. In fact, the most popular social network in South Korea was/is Cyworld (a network that, to my knowledge, is not run by Naver). I would not dispute that postings on Cyworld and other mainstream/citizen centric digital platforms were widespread for protesters. During the beef crisis, many of my own students and friends shared such posts with me. However, digital media is only one component of the story, and the details presented by Shirky are sloppy at best and hint at a lack of familiarity with South Korea.

2. Causes: Deadly Beef Sensationalism in Korea

Professor Shirky (2010) argues that the mass media were not responsible for the protests. He dismisses suggestions that news reports or the efforts of political opposition groups were essential to the expansion of the protests. Shirky claims that the scale of the protests is significant because they were the largest protests in decades, and they widened the public sphere to include young people in politics, teen girls in particular (Shirky, 2011). Shirky claims that the power of teenage girls to spread information to other fans on the website of boy band DBSK is what radicalized the public.

Shirky apparently misunderstands the complex mix of sensational media accounts, networked rumors and political blunders that ignited a third generation of beef protests. His claims ignore recent history on the Korean peninsula, not to mention historical animosities surrounding America, trade and beef. Protests over American beef are not new, nor were they the first time that young girls joined nationwide, networked political movements. While Boy Band DBSK may have been strident and vocal about the beef issue, their voices echoed others in the mainstream media and were given legitimacy by Lee's miscalculations in responding to early protests.

I do not take issue with the claim that many teenage girls attended the protests. This is true. Shirky's assertion that the crowd was 60–70% teen girls is a claim that I can neither confirm, nor deny. Shirky cites Mimi Ito (2009) who cites a web link that no longer works for this claim. Ito's work is also the foundation of Shirky's claim that the fan website of boy band DBSK was the reason beef protests spun out of control. While Ito focuses on the importance of young people to the protests, it is a stretch to use her conference keynote address about Pokémon to justify claims about the pivotal role of teenagers in the beef protests.

Moreover, Shirky's assertion that the beef protests reflected a unique radicalization of teen girls is false. Contrary to Shirky's claims (2010, p. 37), the beef protests did not introduce teenage girls into the South Korean public sphere. That process began at least 6 years earlier in 2002, when two young women, Shim, Mi-sun and Shin, Hyo-soo, aged fourteen, were killed by an American tank that ran them over on their way home from school (Jung, 2010). The soldiers driving the tank were not tried in South Korean courts because they were on duty, and thus not subject to South Korean law or its legal system. After a trial in an American military court, the tank operators were acquitted of negligent homicide. The verdict confirmed the suspicions of many South Korean citizens that America supports its own interests over justice and the democratic ideals it preaches.

The incident was a public relations nightmare for the United States Forces in Korea, as the bodies of the children were still on the road when photographers arrived. During the autumn of 2002, I passed protesters holding images of Mi-sun and Hyo-soo's death at the entrance to Kyung Hee University every morning as I went to work. The organs of the children gruesomely covered the road adjacent to their flat, lifeless bodies. Photos of the corpses and the gut-strewn pavement populated leaflets, placards, and websites. Candlelight vigils took place across South Korea, and digital message boards were popular locations for organizing and sharing information (Y. Song, 2007). The protests were crucial in helping to elect the late liberal leader Roh, Moo Hyun who ran on a strong Korea/anti-American platform. His unlikely election rode the anti-American wave created by the tank incident, and utilized online news sources to help circumvent traditional media (Y. Song, 2007). Teen/public radicalization during the beef protests reflected a much deeper held set of suspicions linked to perceived American apathy and antipathy toward the value of children's lives.

The key factors driving the 2008 protests were a series of sensationalist news reports about American beef. The biggest offender in the mainstream press was MBC television program PD Notebook. Their program was instrumental in fanning the fears that led to the 2008 protests, particularly among younger people and university students (Beck, 2008). Two substantial mistakes were made in their broadcast. First, the program aired images of "downer" cattle that were unable to walk, falsely claiming that they were cows suffering from mad cow disease. Second, they cited "scientific research" that claimed Korean people were genetically vulnerable to mad cow disease, making them more likely to contract it from infected beef (Gee, 2008; Kirk, 2010).

Kim, Yong-son who authored the study cited by MBC refuted the use of his research, adding that he regularly eats American beef (Salmon, 2008). MBC was ordered to air corrections to their reporting by the Seoul

Southern District Court and was further ordered to apologize publicly by the Korean Communications Commission ("MBC offers apology over US beef report," 2008). The corrections themselves were also the subject of controversy. MBC blamed the reporting errors on translation mistakes by employees. However, translator Jeong, Ji Min disputes this claim, asserting that the translations were correct, but editors and producers intentionally used faulty information in an effort to stoke public reaction and garner ratings (Yonhap News, 2008b).

Scientists' retractions and efforts by the government to spread facts about the safety of beef were unpersuasive to the public, many of whom believe the media reports (Harden, 2008b). PD Notebook was not the only source of rumors. Opposition groups working against the President repeated unfounded charges regularly (Klingner, 2008). Moreover, school children were targeted by mass text messages (Lewis, 2008) providing an alternate explanation for why children and parents were radicalized. A range of half-truths and falsehoods populated the digital public sphere, spread by mobile phone and online forums (J. Lee, 2012). A widely repeated rumor indicated that contaminated beef would be served to school children due to its cheap price (Harden, 2008a). Another rumor claimed that babies would be put at risk by a beef by-product that was an ingredient in diapers ("Seoul tries to set standards for Internet accuracy," 2008). Many Koreans also believed that American ranchers fed bits of dead cow to cattle raised for humans, a practice that was banned in 1997 (Harden, 2008b).

Having abolished the post of Senior Officer for Public Relations upon taking office, President Lee lacked guidance that might have helped him in the early stages of the crisis (Jinsoo Kim & Cho, 2011). President Lee refused to negotiate with protesters (Choe, 2008a). He arrested religious and political leaders supporting the protests ("South Korea cracks down on protesters," 2008). Demonstrators were attacked with water cannons and fire extinguishers (T. J. Lee, 2008). Ultimately, "the government's inept, unprepared and irresponsible responses triggered prolonged media coverage, which, in turn, put the issue at the center of controversy" (J.-N. Kim, Ni, Kim, & Kim, 2012, p. 158). Nineteen public debates about beef appeared on national broadcasters KBS, MBC and SBS (Cho et al., 2012). Lee's violent response to protesters only confirmed leftist framing of Lee as a dictator (J. Lee, 2012). Furthermore, Lee unified opposition to him by simultaneously pushing education reform (a key issue for teachers and parents given the $1 billion/year private education industry), as well as privatization of state funded companies (Choe, 2008b). Protests expanded to include these issues, going beyond beef to encompass unrelated grievances with the President.

The Kim, et al (2012) study argues that the lifting of the ban appeared to be a sudden policy change to the majority of the public. Kim and Cho (2011) argue that the perceived policy shift by President Lee radicalized students and the normally apolitical "stroller moms." They contend that because mothers feel personally responsible for issues of food safety and family health they turned out in droves, with their children, during the protests. In fact, the resumption of imports is an agreement signed by Lee's liberal predecessor Roh, Moo Hyun in 2007 (Klingner, 2008). The problem facing Lee was that he and his party had been bitterly opposed to the deal that Roh negotiated (Cho, Choi, & Park, 2012). Appearing to kowtow to American demands and ignoring public health concerns, Lee apologized on two occasions (Choe, 2008b). The first apology failed because the public felt Lee was trying to appease them without meeting their demands (Harden, 2008a). Lee's cabinet had no choice but to resign (Harden, 2008b).

In sum, Professor Shirky's assertion that the online connections made by teenage girls in chat rooms were the crucial component in the protests reduces the protests to a single cause. The lack of documentation for his claims makes them tenuous in principle. It is also patently incorrect that the beef protests represented a unique moment for networked politics or teen girls in South Korea. The tank incident in 2002 radicalized teenage girls and families more generally, and the tank incident coupled with the election of Roh, Moo Hyun brought online citizen journalism (particularly Oh My News) to the forefront of local politics much earlier in the decade.

There is little doubt that the Lee administration did not effectively manage its message on digital platforms during the beef crisis (Chang & Park, 2012; Cho et al., 2012). At the same time, dozens of public debates and extensive mainstream media coverage focused the nation on the issue. DBSK and teen girls were part of this cultural milieu, but were not the source of the initial reports or the cause of Lee's inept responses. Online blogs spread rumors taken directly from the yellow journalism of mainstream media outlets and text messages spread by Lee's recently defeated opponents in labor unions and liberal political groups. In fact, the immediate causes of the protest worked in tandem with a reservoir of resentment about American beef that Shirky never acknowledges. The political blunders of the newly elected leader ensured that this toxic stew would boil over.

3. Context: A Symbolic History of Beef

Beef has symbolic significance in South Korea for both culinary and political reasons. Beef is an important ingredient (along with seaweed) in "miyeok guk": the soup served to mothers after childbirth. Beef is also the main ingredient in the popular dish bulgogi that is part of South Korea's global branding strategy (Ho & Hong, 2012). Meals are social events in South Korea because food is communal. Diners share common dishes from which an individual takes a personal portion. As the introduction to this chapter noted, barbecue restaurants are common nationwide and critical to community maintenance. The university where I taught, for example, held barbecue dinners for the faculty at the conclusion of each semester.

Shirky's analyses of the 2008 protests do not provide an adequate context for understanding either the culinary symbolism of beef or its relationship to the role of the United States in the modern history of the Korean peninsula. Professor Yoshi Tsurumi (2008) claims that the 60 year occupation of South Korea by the United States laid the foundation for the beef protests, wherein beef became the vehicle for expressing general discontent with America. From 1961 to 1979, Park, Chung-hee ruled South Korea. A military coup in 1979 installed Chun, Doo-hwan, ending Park's regime. American President Jimmy Carter did not oppose the coup, accepting Chun's legitimacy (Shorrock, 1986).

In May of 1980, protests against Chun's declaration of martial law turned violent in Kwangju. American diplomats estimated that 150,000 people were involved in protests against the regime and its arrest of dissident (and eventual Nobel Peace Prize recipient) Kim Dae Jung (Gonzalez, 2005). 20,000 South Korean troops were dispatched to quell the uprising after citizens took control of a local armory and demanded negotiations with the government (Shorrock, 1986). Chun's troops were brutal. Officially 500 citizens were killed in Kwangju, but the numbers are disputed by human rights groups who claim that up to 2000 civilians died (Gonzalez, 2005). The United States denied any role in the event, but later admitted that it had allowed the redeployment of South Korean troops to Kwangju (G.-W. Shin, 1996). The hypocrisy of the Jimmy Carter administration in supporting Chun's attack on protesting citizens laid the foundation for modern anti-Americanism (Jinwung Kim, 1989).

After Kwangju, many Korean citizens saw freedom from America as the first step toward true independence. A key battleground for testing South Korean independence is beef. The first beef protest in South Korea took place in 1985 when hundreds of farmers marched on the American embassy in Seoul to protest liberalization of beef markets (G.-W. Shin, 1996). Students also directly challenged US pressure on South Korea to open markets to food, services, and high tech products (Shorrock, 1986). Farmer antipathy to trade liberalization resonated with student activists who joined forces with them as the 1980s progressed.

Rhetoric now focuses on trade issues to a considerable extent, as some students see that such issues will generate more support for their cause— and far more anti-American sentiment. Korean farmers may not care much about American troops in Korea, but bitterness is growing about American beef and grain that enter the country and depress prices, threatening their survival. (Jinwung Kim, 1989)

Beef resurfaced as an issue in the 1990's during the Uruguay round of the GATT (General Agreement on Tariffs and Trade) trade negotiations (G. Lee & Koh, 2010). The 2008 crisis over beef was directly related to trade as the beef quarantine was a crucial sticking point in the Korea-US Free Trade Agreement negotiations (Rohter, 2008; "US to raise beef issue," 2011). Lee's decision to lift restrictions as a component in negotiations appeared to bow to American pressure. A move that strikes at the heart of nationalist, anti-American sentiment related to Kwangju and the ongoing American occupation of South Korea.

In sum, it is difficult to separate the beef protests from their historical anti-American context. American beef imports have been a salient issue for nationalists and farmers for three decades, suggesting that the protests were not entirely spontaneous, nor rooted in digital communication tools. The historical symbolism of beef is essential to understanding the context that made beef protests so widespread. American beef is a metaphorical vessel for nationalism and anti-American sentiment. The role of anti-Americanism is summarized by an image of an American warship carrying bulls instead of troops and weapons that became a popular poster in South Korea (Ho & Hong, 2012).

4. Results: Democracy and Governance

The ultimate value of the South Korean beef protests for Shirky is that they illustrate the democratic potential of the civic connections made possible by new communication technologies. Shirky claims that the beef protests were a democratic victory because the protests forced Lee to consult the public on major issues (2010, p. 36). While I ultimately agree that the revolutionary potential of the internet lies in its ability to create spaces of civic communication and political communication, I am uncomfortable with the conclusions drawn by Shirky about South Korea.

Seeing the beef protests as a victory for democracy ignores the fact that very little changed after the protests, and that the protests themselves threatened the stability of a recently elected government. On the first day that large supermarket retailers put American beef back on the shelves 50 tons of meat were sold (Harden, 2008b). Despite the vitriol of the protests, consumers quickly moved on and began feasting on cheap American chuck. The public was moved, but toward what end?

Chang and Park's (2012) study shows large growth in blogs during the beef crisis, but also shows that the digital public sphere in Korea is not very diverse. Most bloggers are male, middle class, city dwellers. Additionally, journalists run the most popular blogs. Despite claims to the contrary, Chang and Park's study suggests that the South Korean blogosphere is similar to the homogenized sphere of journalistic discourse that is prevalent in the United States (Hindman, 2008).

From the perspective of democratic governance, the beef protests are troubling. Several months after electing a new President in a landslide victory, the South Korean public turned on their newly elected leader over public health lies mixed with nationalism. In the aftermath of the beef protests, there was no restructuring of the South Korean government, or major changes in its policies toward American beef. While Lee, Myung Bak was shamed into apologizing to the public (twice) the agreement reached with the United States was a voluntary ban by American cattle producers, not consumer safety laws (H. Shin, 2008). Moreover, the KORUS Free Trade Agreement entered into force, meaning that the United States ultimately achieved its goal of opening South Korean markets to its products writ large. American Congressional estimates suggest that the South Korean beef market alone will be worth $1.8 billion annually for American ranchers (Donald, 2011).

It also appears that the extent of the protests has actually hurt the digital public sphere. Since the beef protests, the government has tried to stifle online dissent in two ways: (1) by harassing individual's with influence (such as economic critic Minerva); and (2) through new regulations such as the Cyber Defamation Law (D. Song, 2011). Jennifer Oh contends in a 2012 Asian Survey article that the beef crisis reveals the fragility of a nascent Korean democracy, highlighting the lack of institutional and organizational mechanisms for citizens to engage the policymaking process:

> Korea needs to strengthen its weak mediating institutions— specifically its interest groups and political parties—in order to improve state-society relations. In the absence of systematic ties to the political community through mediating institutions, it is very difficult for actors in Korean civil society to exercise real influence over policies. The protest over U.S. beef imports clearly demonstrated that turning out in large numbers did not necessarily guarantee increased policy leverage. If the Korean government and society continue to engage outside the system in one-sided communication, a strong civil society poses a potential danger to existing democratic institutions. (2012, p. 549)

Oh's analysis demonstrates that free speech is necessary for democracy but it is not sufficient. The beef protests were a significant moment of nationwide venting. They appear in many ways to have been the only real option for citizens outside of an actual coup because institutionally citizens lack access to the halls of policymaking and power.

Rather than being a sign of a healthy society, the beef protests prove South Korea is still a developing democracy, not a nation with responsive institutions. If anything the beef protests sharpened the generational divide between younger liberal citizens and older conservatives who have traditionally been in charge of the political system ("Bush met by dueling protests in Seoul," 2008). DBSK might have gotten more hits on its website, but it is hard to conclude that this was a victory for democratic politics. South Korea is still a country trying to square its Confucian, hierarchical past with an increasingly globalized and rapidly urbanizing population that does not share the life experiences or values of its conservative elders.

5. Conclusion: A Theoretical Grounding for a Civic Public Sphere

A charitable interpretation of what Shirky says about South Korea would extend his analysis to suggest that the civic communication facilitated by the internet was the source of the beef protests. While I take issue with the details of Professor Shirky's analysis of South Korea, I am not entirely hostile to his claims about the role of networked communication and the digital public sphere. Civic linkages are unpredictable and do lay a foundation for political communication. A different version of this argument is advanced (minimally) by Ikegami (2000) and applied to the digital public sphere by Peter Dahlgren (2005a, 2005b) and Ikegami and Hut (2008). However, both Dahlgren and Ikegami arrive at their positions through a critique of Jurgen Habermas, which makes their approaches inconsistent with the work of Shirky.

Shirky (2011) makes references to Habermas in his discussion of the public sphere and then goes on to suggest that the civic linkages created by new communication platforms provide a foundation for revolutions and challenges to authority. I believe that a strong case can be made (and has been made) for the role of civic connections and the revolutionary potential of civic publics. Habermas (1991) however, comes with theoretical baggage that is not helpful to this project.

The move to Habermas is puzzling because it appears to be both unnecessary and anti-strategic for Shirky. It is worth noting that Habermas (2006) himself specifically rejects the value of networked communication for promoting a public sphere in democratic countries. Additionally, Habermas' approach to the public sphere has received substantial (warranted) criticism. A simple (and important) example of such criticism is advanced by Nancy Fraser (1992). Fraser argues that Habermas ignores the inequalities inherent in the public sphere. She advances the concept of the subaltern counterpublic: groups that exist at the margins of the public sphere because they are excluded from public discourse by hegemonic forces.

Other scholars are directly addressing the issues raised by digitalization and the public sphere. Peter Dahlgren (2005a), for example, argues that we are currently witnessing the cyber-transformation of the public sphere through the digital expansion of civic cultures. While supporting Shirky's (2011) claims about the role of civic communication, Dahlgren highlights the flaws in the Habermasian approach to digital communication. Dahlgren (2005b) contends that politics is not simply a given and that "civic culture" is a pre-condition for political action. For Dahlgren (2005b) the public sphere is composed of structures (laws and media institutions), representations (media products, symbols and myths), and interactions (reception and circulation of representations by/between people). Civic linkages and civic cultures set the stage for action by people connected through digital platforms.

A second approach is the work of Eiko Ikegami (Ikegami & Hut, 2008; Ikegami, 2000). She argues that an uncritical application of the Habermasian public sphere to other cultures is inappropriate. Habermas advocates a very Westernized understanding of politics, founded in Western approaches to discussion and debate. The rational-critical public sphere does not account well for difference (which is the source of Fraser's 1992 critique). Ikegami examines the haiku communities of Tokugawa, Japan. She contends that the civic linkages made possible through these spaces allowed citizens to experience alternate worlds. In the process, people made personal connections through creative public space that laid a foundation for later revolution. In 2008, Ikegami and Hut extend this analysis to virtual spaces like Second Life, claiming that similar linkages are forming through virtual communication platforms.

The point I want to make here is that there is too much literature on the public sphere to vaguely reference Habermas and not at least acknowledge potential pitfalls in such an approach. This is particularly true when Habermas himself is skeptical of networked communication and scholars like Dahlgren and Ikegami directly challenge a Habermasian approach to the digital public sphere. I have personally found Professor Shirky's work to be insightful and helpful to me in understanding the social changes caused by digitalization. However, the expansion and development of new communication technologies is an indeterminate process that has case-by-case outcomes. While the beef protests at first blush appear to be democratic, they were rooted in an anti-democratic challenge to a democratically elected leader. This exercise of free speech was dangerous because it threatened the legitimacy of democratically elected leaders who had barely begun implementing policies that were core issues in their campaign.

Anti-Americanism is a critical issue in South Korea. Seoul National University professor Kim, Seong-kon laments the double standards that are endemic in Korean society with respect to the United States (S. Kim, 2008). He notes the lack of nationwide protests over melamine found in Chinese dairy products and a similar apathetic response to Chinese citizens who attacked South Koreans in Seoul during the Olympic torch relays in summer of 2008. Andrew Salmon, writing in the South China Morning Post summarizes the many factors that sparked the protests:

> *Following President Lee, Myung-bak's surprise announcement of the lifting of a five-year ban on US beef imports, a mad cow disease frenzy has been fanned by local farmers, left-wingers, anti-American groups and those opposed to the conservative president, who took office in February. The announcement came during last month's summit with US President George W. Bush, and was followed by the airing of a television documentary alleging that Koreans are particularly vulnerable to mad cow disease - though there is not a single reported case of the disease in the US. The decision also ignited a controversy that has raged through Korean cyberspace, inspired*

street protests and was being debated in the National Assembly.
(2008)

The beef protests were not just a product of the DBSK fan blog. Mass media sensationalism dramatized the danger of mad-cow disease to a population primed to believe that America didn't care about its children. Beef is an old dispute linked to nationalism, anti-Americanism and the survival of South Korean farmers in the face of first world market liberalization. Digital activism, children's activism and candlelight vigils are all South Korean protest forms that repeated themselves during the 2008 protests. This may mean that something unique happened in 2002, or it may simply point to the collateral damage that inevitably flows from decades of military occupation.

While Shirky (2011) laments the fact that so much of the debate about social media has been over examples, this chapter illustrates why it is important to explore those examples in detail. That the digital revolution is important to South Korean society is a truism. South Korea is a testing ground for next generation technology created by indigenous corporate powerhouses such as Samsung and LG. However, modern South Korea is complex and in the midst of social and political transitions. It is a nation shaped by military, economic, cultural, educational and digital flows. Ignoring this complexity is dangerous for scholars (Korean and Western) because it runs the risk of creating reductionist analyses of layered phenomena.

South Korea is a beautiful country that will always be dear to my heart. It is a next generation society struggling with its ancient customs and roots as it continues to grow economically and democratically, making it ripe for study by scholars of new communication technology. Finally, perhaps more than any other nation in Asia, South Korea rewards the intrepid traveler (or scholar) with amazing food. It is a nation always prepared to answer that age-old Americanism: "Where's the beef?" A final word of advice for enjoying Korean barbecue: When you get to the restaurant, (1) make sure to ask if they serve an-chang-sal, (inner rib meat) (2) have some jigae and rice to go with the meat and (3) order a bottle of soju to wash it all down.

References

Asen, R. (2002). Imagining the public sphere. *Philosophy and Rhetoric,* *35*(4), 345–367.

Beck, P. M. (2008, June 30). Mad cows and angry Koreans; They've got a beef with their new president. *The Weekly Standard,* p. Lexis nexis article.

Beef dust up threatens South Korea's global standing. (2008, July 14). *The Nikkei Weekly,* p. Lexis Nexis article. Japan.

Benkler, Y. (2011). Networks of power, degrees of freedom. *International Journal of Communication, 5,* 721–755.

Benkler, Y. (2012, April 4). Hacks of valor. Foreign Affairs. Retrieved April 7, 2012, from http://www.foreignaffairs.com/articles/137382/ yochai-benkler/hacks-of-valor?page=show

Bush met by dueling protests in Seoul. (2008, August 6). The Frontrunner. Australia.

Chang, W., & Park, H. W. (2012). The network structure of the Korean blogosphere. *Journal of Computer-Mediated Communication, 17,* 216–230.

Cho, S. E., Choi, M., & Park, H. W. (2012). Government-civic group conflicts and communication strategy: A text analysis of TV debates on Korea's import of U.S. beef. *Journal of Contemporary Eastern Asia, 11*(1), 1–20.

Choe, S.-H. (2008a, June 10). South Korean cabinet offers to quit after beef protests. *The New York Times.*

Choe, S.-H. (2008b, June 20). Weakened by protests, Lee battles to recover; 2nd apology in Seoul amid nationwide rage over U.S. beef accord. *The International Herald Tribune,* p. 1.

Dahlgren, P. (2005a). The Internet, public spheres, and political communication: Dispersion and deliberation. *Political Communication, 22,* 147–162.

Dahlgren, P. (2005b). The public sphere: Linking the media and civic cultures. In *Media Anthropology* (pp. 318–327). Thousand Oaks, CA, USA: Sage Publications.

Donald, B. (2011). *Pending free trade agreements.* Washington, DC: Congressional Documents and Publications.

Fraser, N. (1992). Rethinking the public sphere: A contribution to the critique of actually existing democracy. In C. Calhoun (Ed.), *Habermas and the Public Sphere* (pp. 109–142). Cambridge, MA: MIT Press.

Gee, M. (2008, June 13). Give Mr. Lee a chance; The supposed sins of South Korea's President don't warrant the scale and passion of recent protests. *The Globe and Mail*, p. A19. Toronto,Canada.

Habermas, J. (1991). *The structural transformation of the public sphere.* (T. Burger & F. Lawrence, Trans.). Cambridge, MA: MIT Press.

Habermas, J. (2006). Political communication in media society: Does democracy still enjoy an epistemic dimension? The impact of normative theory on empirical research. *Communication Theory (10503293), 16*(4), 411–426.

Harden, B. (2008a, June 4). In South Korea, a reversal on U.S. beef imports; Under public pressure as poll ratings fall, new president backs off plan to end ban. *The Washington Post*, p. Lexis Nexis article.

Harden, B. (2008b, December 10). South Koreans have new regards for U.S. beef. *The Washington Post*, p. A20.

Hindman, M. (2008). What is the online public sphere good for? In J. Turow & T. Lokman (Eds.), *The Hyperlinked Society: Questioning Connections in the Digital Age* (pp. 268–288). Michigan, USA: Digital Culture Books.

Ho, M., & Hong, C.-S. (2012). Challenging new conservative regimes in South Korea and Taiwan. *Asian Survey, 52*(4), 643–665.

Ikegami, E. (2000). A sociological theory of publics: Identity and culture as emergent properties in networks. *Social Research, 67*(4), 989–1029.

Ikegami, E., & Hut, P. (2008). Avatars are for real: Virtual communities and public spheres. *Journal of Virtual Worlds Research, 1*(1), 1–19.

Ito, M. (2009, February 24). *Media literacy and social action in a post-Pokemon world.* Presented at the 51st NFAIS Annual Conference, Philadelphia, PA. Retrieved from http://www.itofisher.com/mito/publications/media_literacy.html

Jung, H. J. (2010). The rise and fall of anti-American sentiment in South Korea: Deconstructing hegemonic ideas and threat perception. *Asian Survey, 50*(5), 946–964.

Kim, H. (2008). Micromobilization and Suicide Protest in South Korea, 1970-2004. *Social Research, 75*(2), 543–578.

Kim, J.-N., Ni, L., Kim, S.-H., & Kim, J. R. (2012). What makes people hot? Applying the situational theory of problem solving to hot-issue publics. *Journal of Public Relations Research, 24*(2), 144–164.

Kim, Jinsoo, & Cho, M. (2011). When the "Stroller Moms" take hold of the street: A case study of how social influence made the inactive publics active in anti-U.S. beef protest in Seoul-An sssues processes model perspective. *International Journal of Strategic Communication, 5*(1), 1–25.

Kim, Jinwung. (1989). Recent anti-Americanism in South Korea: The causes. *Asian Survey, 29*(8), 749–763.

Kim, S. (2008, October 1). Where have protesters gone? *The Korea Herald,* p. Lexis Nexis article. Seoul, South Korea.

Kirk, D. (2010, November 11). Bridging the gap on cars and beef; U.S. and South Korean push to end 3-year delay in signing trade accord. *The International Herald Tribune.*

Klingner, B. (2008, June 8). Getting the bulldozer back on track. *The Korea Times,* p. Lexis Nexis article. Seoul, South Korea.

Lee, G., & Koh, H. (2010). Who controls newspapers' political perspectives? Source transparency and affiliations in Korean news articles about US beef imports. *Asian Journal of Communication, 20*(4), 404–422.

Lee, J. (2012). Micro-dynamics of protests: The political and cultural conditions for anti-U.S. beef protests in South Korea. *Sociological Perspectives, 55*(3), 399–420.

Lee, T. J. (2008, June 27). Face-off in Seoul as US beef ban is lifted; Hundreds of activists gater at storage facilities to thwart distribution of frozen beef. *The Straits Times*. Singapore.

Lewis, L. (2008, May 9). Internet geeks trigger panic over "tainted beef" imports. *The Times*, p. 52. London, UK.

MBC offers apology over US beef report. (2008, August 13). *The Korea Times*, p. Lexis Nexis article. Seoul, South Korea.

Oh, J. S. (2012). Strong state and strong civil society in contemporary South Korea: Challenges to democratic governance. *Asian Survey, 52*(3), 528–549.

Rohter, L. (2008, June 15). When a populist stance meets a complex issue. *The New York Times*, p. 17.

Salmon, A. (2008, May 26). Sick with worry; Mad cow disease fears are hampering plans to lift a ban on US beef imports and may sink a trade agreement. *South China Morning Post*, p. 18. Hong Kong.

Seoul tries to set standards for Internet accuracy. (2008, August 4). *The International Herald Tribune*, p. 13.

Shin, G.-W. (1996). South Korean anti-Americanism: A comparative perspective. *Asian Survey, 36*(8), 787–803.

Shin, H. (2008, June 25). South Korea set to restart US beef imports amid signs of more protests. *BBC Monitoring Asia Pacific (Yonhap News)*. Seoul, South Korea.

Shirky, C. (2010). *Cognitive Surplus: How technology makes consumers into collaborators*. New York, NY: Penguin.

Shirky, C. (2011). The political power of social media: Technology, the public sphere and political change. *Foreign Affairs, 90*(1), 28.

Shorrock, T. (1986). The struggle for democracy in South Korea in the 1980s and the rise of anti-Americanism. *Third World Quarterly, 8*(4), 1195–1218.

Song, Y. (2007). Internet news media and issue development: A case study on the roles of independent online news services as agenda-builders for anti-US protests in South Korea. *New Media & Society, 9*(1), 71–92.

South Korea cracks down on protesters. (2008, July 1). *The New York Times*, p. 8.

Squires, C. R. (2002). Rethinking the Black public sphere: An alternative vocabulary for multiple public spheres. *Communication Theory, 12*(4), 446–468.

Tsurumi, Y. (2008, June 22). Lame conclusions about U.S. occupations. *The Japan Times*, p. Lexis Nexis article. Tokyo, Japan.

US to raise beef issue. (2011, May 5). *Korea Times*, Lexis Nexis Article. Seoul, South Korea.

Yonhap News. (2008a, May 6). South Korean protesters pledge to continue anti-US beef vigils. *BBC Monitoring Asia Pacific*.

Yonhap News. (2008b, June 26). South Korean broadcaster accused of biased US beef report. *BBC Monitoring Asia Pacific*.

PART FIVE:
SOUTH ASIA

XIII.   Social Media and Protest —The Indian Spring

David M. Lucas

Department of Communication, Ohio University Southern, Ironton, Ohio
lucasd@ohio.edu

Abstract

India has emerged as a competitive market within the global social media outlets. With a rapid growth rate in communication technology and with a tendency toward early adoption of technology, India's population seems poised to become the single most logged on people in the world.

Social media such as Facebook, Twitter, Google+ and Orkut have become the driving forces behind this tech savvy, logged on population. Indians tweet, give status updates and post online at a remarkable rate by using smart phones, handheld devices and computers. The densely populated cities of India contribute heavily to the total number, but surprisingly, rural areas also swell the sum of Indians logged on during any given hour of the day. Going online has become a national pastime in India.

This chapter provides insights in the various perspectives of the social media in India by noting historical, economic, political, cultural and ethical aspects of the impact of social media in the country. Social media use has penetrated the seams of the fabric of Indian culture and data demonstrate that the culture of India stands at the precipice of a great cultural revolution to be ignited by the influence of social media.

Keywords: Social media revolution, India, communication technology, caste system, communication in India, rhetoric in India, digital revolution in India

1. Introduction

The social media revolution continues throughout the world and the heavily populated country of India poses no exception. In fact, communication serves as a social pastime in India. The culture depends on social exchanges in the marketplace, at home, in the streets, neighborhoods, villages, cities, and throughout the cultural experience of India. Indians thrive on the process of communication. Some might say that they even have a compulsion to communicate: "India is the most linguistically diverse country in the world. Its 28 states, demarcated primarily on a linguistic basis, speak 22 different languages in over 1500 dialects. Contrary to the general notion of lay outsiders, there is no language called Indian. The most widely spoken language is Hindi, although some southern states reject it as the primary official language. As a result, English has become the primary medium of communication across the country especially between Hindi and non-Hindi speakers" (Ilankumaran & Venugopalan, 2012, p. 31)

The idea of communication appears to be sewn into the fabric of Indian life. Deogawanka writes:

> *Communications in India have always been typically endemic to the Indian subcontinent. Beginning with the early era, one comes across these visually appealing yet enduring practices of that period. Whether it is the primitive drawings and heliographic characters found in caves, the carvings of ancient temples and pillars, or the stone tablets that have been the boon to archaeological discoveries, they all represent vibrant stories with messages of their own. In fact, these visual modes of communication may be interpreted as symbolic of the ethos of that period and have traversed across a timeline of centuries. (Deogawanka, n.d.,part 1, para. 2)*

Although India occupies only 2.4% of the world's land area, it supports over 15% of the world's total population. The population has burgeoned to a staggering 1.25 billion (Kemp, 2011, p. 2) and rates only second to China which boasts an even larger population. India's median age stands at 25, making it one of the youngest cultures among the largest economies in the entire world. (Kemp, p. 3) About 70% of the population lives in the 550,000 villages found in the country while the remainder of the people live in the hundreds of towns and cities that comprise the teeming metropolitan areas of India. Throughout its history, India has been invaded by tribes, hordes and armies from the Iranian plateau, Central Asia, Arabia, Afghanistan, and the West. In a testament to their social stamina, flexibility, adaptation and capabilities, the Indians absorbed, assimilated, modified and integrated all of these influences to produce a diverse, remarkable racial and cultural synthesis. ("Background Note: India (04/17/12)," 2012, People section, para. 1)

Religion, caste, and language operate as major determinants of social and political organization in Indian culture. Currently, with more job opportunities in the private sector and positive social changes for upward mobility, the cultural structure of India has begun a quiet social transformation. The government recognizes 18 official languages, but Hindi, the national language, is the most widely spoken. English serves as a national lingua franca. Although about 80% of the people in India are Hindu, the country also accommodates more than 138 million Muslims making it home to one of the world's largest Muslim populations. Other groups include Christians, Sikhs, Jains, Buddhists, and Parsis. ("Background Note: India (04/17/12)," 2012, People section, para. 2)

Jodha argues that "Social communication in India has always been a complex and difficult process. The presence of diverse communities and social groupings based on varying combinations of caste, religion, culture and language, and the hierarchies they represent has determined the flow and denial of information throughout Indian history. While the foundations of a modern Indian nation state are only half a century old, the process of social communication in the subcontinent has always been burdened with all kinds of limitations." (Jodha, 2000, p. 164)

The attempts in communication, however, date back to the beginning of Indian culture some 4500 years ago. To say that India has a long history in communication would be an understatement. For example, Oliver argues that "Oral communication has served even more definitively the social, political, and commercial needs of the Indian people." (Oliver, 1971, p. 22) Thus, the Indian bent on communication arises as a part of the historical, cultural context of Indian existence. The casualness of public and social speaking appealed much more to the ancient Indians than did any formal written rhetoric. Oliver maintains, "The choice to communicate largely through spoken rather than written discourse was a deliberate one." (Oliver, 1971, p. 22). One would be hard pressed to find a culture more primed for social media dissemination than the Indian culture. "In each village there were special locations—such as the blacksmith shop, the portico of a public building, a low wall along the public square, or benches in a park—that were recognized as the 'conversational sitting places.'" (Oliver, 1971, p. 23) Admittedly the oral traditions of India were passed down through oral renditions but this meant that the narratives had to be memorized and passed down through successive generations. The cultural stage was set early on—the impact of social media would appeal to an orally trusting culture.

"India is a developing country with lot of achievements in all the fields of modern day life including that of science & technology, agriculture and industry." (Kaul, 2000, p. 4) Oral communication came first and foremost but from the earliest periods of recorded history, the Indian ancestors also communicated with script, pictographs, and drawings and later began using pigeons to relay messages from one part of the kingdom to another. All of this came in response to a culture that thrived on information exchange.

This tendency toward communication only paved the way for quick acceptance of communication media that enhanced the thriving, personal oral communication. "The 20th century has witnessed the immense impact of communication technologies, from the telegraph, telephone to the spread of sound recording, motion pictures and radio as world-wide phenomena to the emergence of television as a dominant influence in nearly every institution, to the explosion of the Internet at the turn of the new century." Kaul, 2000, p. 5) The digital revolution, then, provides new avenues for the Indians to explore and manipulate into personal avenues for communication. The new inventions provide ready foundations to challenge assumptions that were accepted as socially fundamental and irreversible. This trend allows communication scholars to contribute to the cultural understanding of India, and forecast the shaping of the parameters of the ever-changing technological and academic environment.

In this chapter I present the impact and perceptions of social media in India. I have divided the chapter into six different sections in order to describe the various perspectives concerning social media affecting India.

Within each of the sections along with the various citations, quotations and graphs discovered in the literature I have also included quotes and details from a qualitative research project executed superficially for this work. Using folknography (Lucas, 2006) as the qualitative research method, I facilitated six different focus groups via Skype from the United States in six different Indian institutions of higher education. Primarily, I wanted to discover the perceptions of the students concerning the use of social media in India along with the possible impact and influence that their social media experience might have on their lives. The study included a total of 67 different students with 33 women and 34 men making up the respondents in the focus group sessions. The group included 42 undergraduates and 23 graduate students. The focus groups originated on or nearby six campuses that included: Panjab University in Chandigarh, Chandigarh; University of Pune in Pune, Maharasthra; IAAN School of Mass Communication in New Delhi, Delhi; International Media Institute of India in Noida Gautam Buddh Nagar district of Uttar Pradesh; University of Poona in Pune, Maharasthra and Bharathidasan University in Tiruchirappalli, Tamil Nadu. No students received compensation for participating and all volunteered to respond in the focus group events. I have changed the names of the quoted respondents for confidentiality.

The reason for the inclusion for such a chapter in this book should be somewhat obvious. "India is the world's fastest growing industry in the world in terms of number of wireless connections after China. According to the world telecommunications industry, India will have 1.2 billion mobile subscribers by 2013. Furthermore, projections by several leading global consultancies indicate that the total number of subscribers in India will exceed the total subscriber count in the China by 2013." (Amruth H. R., 2011, para. 1-3) Indians spend numerous hours on the Internet and that participation appears likely to increase. The social media expansion, influence, impact and persuasive potential in India deserve consideration.

2. Social Media in India: A Historical Perspective

In order to understand the prolific expansion of social media in India, we must first reflect on the historical aspects of communication practices of the people of India. Culturally, Indians seek to communicate. They gather in geographic spaces in order to share, communicate and learn. In general, Indians embrace the practice of communication.

Jodha argues that: "The ruling elite in pre-British, pre-print and largely oral India had a history of patronizing the writers, poets, record keepers and others. Nevertheless, it was only through the British Raj, using a variety of social communication forms in their administration, that the print culture, the Macaluyan education system and educational institutions led to the birth of a large reading public and a modern Indian bureaucracy" (Jodha, 2000, p.164-169). Indians sought out information and relayed it in order to function as a community, culture and country. As with many other ancient cultures, India depended greatly on oral narratives and information distributed by wise teachers, religious leaders and informed ones. Both men and women disseminated much of the information needed by the general public. The comparison stops there, however. India developed into a complex culture with gurus, teachers, vocal oral histories and complex dramas, stories and verbal lessons provided by learned and respected individuals. (Oliver, 1971, p. 29–30)

> *An ancient Indian educator, communicator or guru might ask, WHO is the genuine Guru (preceptor)? He who teaches by precept and example, with good conduct, right thinking, loyalty to truth, mental discipline and sense of duty honors his student and vocation. Who is the genuine student? He who learns these does well. These are the qualities that will guarantee happiness here and bliss hereafter. These virtues will effectively countermand the evils that degrade man into a monster. The educational system that brings both teacher and student together, has two aspects, first, the provision of skills and information so that man can live in health and happiness and the second, the understanding of one's inner urges and their sublimation in order to attain lasting peace, equanimity and bliss. The two aspects are not opposed; they are bound irrevocably together. Both teachers*

and students have to recognize this truth. ("Teaching in Ancient India", 1980, para. 1–2).

Later, after the princes and gurus lost domination to the British, the tactics of communication from the Western influences took a foothold in the Indian culture. "Tracing its history we have to go back to communities who listened to rural radio broadcasts in the 1940s, the Indian school of development communication. One distinguishing element of those early programs was that they focused on the use of indigenous languages—Marathi, Gujarati and Kannada. India's earliest organized experiments in development communication were held in the 1960s, sponsored by India's universities and other educational institutions, and by the Bretton Woods-school institutions. Educational institutions that played an important part in this effort include the University of Poona, the Centre for the Study of Developing Societies, Delhi University, the Christian Institute for the Study of Religion and Society and the University of Kerala." (Kaul, 2011, p. 4).

Prior to radio in the rural areas, however, according to Amruth H. R., an electronics engineer from India, the

> *"Postal means of communication was the only form of communication until the year 1850. In 1850 experimental electric telegraph started for first time in India between Calcutta (Kolkata) and Diamond Harbor (southern suburbs of Kolkata, on the banks of the Hooghly River). In 1851, it was opened for the use of the British East India Company. Subsequently construction of telegraph started throughout India." (Amruth H.R., 2011, How Telecommunication started in India, section, para. 1-4)*

Dr. William O'Shaughnessy, who pioneered the telegraph and telephone in India, directed the opening of a separate office for the telegraph service in 1854. Calcutta (Kolkata) was selected for the office site since it was the capital of British India. In early 1881, Oriental Telephone Company Limited of England opened telephone exchanges at Calcutta (Kolkata), Bombay (Mumbai), Madras (Chennai) and Ahmedabad. On the 28th January 1882 the first formal telephone service was established with a total of 93 subscribers. According to Amruth H. R.,

"From the year 1902 India drastically changed from cable telegraph
to wireless telegraph, radio telegraph, radio telephone, trunk dialing.
Later the industry moved to digital microwave, optical fiber, satellite
earth stations. Duri" (Amruth H.R., 2011, How Telecommunication
started in India? section, para. 1-4).

Radio as communication technology continued to dominate, even
after the introduction of television simply because of the availability
of low-cost receivers. Television, however, made remarkable strides
in the metropolitan areas and contributed to language, education and
philosophical dissemination in Indian culture. (Peterson, n. d.)

The roots for the acquisition and transition to social media were sown
in India when the

"First mobile telephone service on non-commercial basis started in
India on 48th Independence Day at country's capital Delhi. The first
cellular call was made in India on July 31st, 1995 over Modi Telstra's
MobileNet GSM network of Kolkata. Later mobile telephone services
are divided into multiple zones known as circles. Competition has
caused prices to drop and calls across India are some of the cheapest
in the world." (Amruth H.R., 2011, para. 14)

In the focus group from Bharathidasan, Chiaravalli laughed when I
asked the question about the historical perspectives of the media in India.
I asked why she was laughing and, apologizing, she said,

"I was not laughing at you or the question. I laughed because the
history of social media in India is still being written. We are only
on the ground floor of consideration. Later, after we move into our
careers, only then we will know the true impact the social media
has had on India. I imagine the impact will be great and I hope it
will be good." (Effects of Social Media in India [Focus Group Notes],
Bharathidasan University, 2012, p. 7).

3. The Rise of Indian Social Media

The Indian population continues to hold newspapers and news print in high regard. The radio as a medium thrives in India as new radio stations enter the market every year. Television broadcasting ranks fourth in comparison to the nations of the world. Yet, as all of these media make notable strides in the large media market of India, in a recent five year span alone, Orkut saw a 500% growth in customers. Today they say social media will make or break a brand in India. (Soravjain, 2011, YouTube Video). How did all of this happen? How did social media become the hot item in Indian communication? The progress and change have been interesting.

Bohra observes,

> *"Nokia has played a pioneering role in the growth of cellular technology in India, starting with the first-ever cellular call a decade ago, made on a Nokia mobile phone over a Nokia- deployed network. Nokia started its India operations in 1995, and presently operates out of offices in New Delhi, Mumbai, Kolkata, Bangalore, Hyderabad and Ahmedabad." (Bohra, 2011, para. 1)*

Tate inquires,

> *"So how has all of this social media usage impacted India? According to a December 16th article by The Economic Times, 70 percent of India's businesses use social media for not only gaining new customers, but for making new hires. The rate of India's use of social media in businesses is only superseded by the U.S. (71%) and China (88%)." (Tate, 2012, para. 5)*

The early players in social media and social networking sites included Orkut, Myspace and others: "While MySpace attracted the majority of media attention in the U.S. and abroad, social network systems were proliferating and growing in popularity worldwide. Friendster gained traction in the Pacific Islands; Orkut became the premier SNS in Brazil before growing rapidly very soon after in India." (Madhavan, 2007; boyd & Ellison, 2007, A Global Phenomenon section, para. 1)

After the year 2010, India's population became the fastest adopter of Facebook accounts in the world. Although boasting one of the largest populations, India's saturation of the social media penetration remains in the lower percentile when compared to other countries such as Brazil. (DMAAWiki, 2011, YouTube Video) In other words, India remains wide open for additional clients, users and social media opportunities.

The outlets of social media have established a great foothold with the young people of India. These digital natives have certainly embraced the conversational, interactive nature of the media. From all six of the focus groups I discovered and constructed the seven reasons why the youth of India love to log on to social media. I discerned these points from the comments made by the youth in the various focus group meetings. The students of India suggested they use social media for

1. Sharing interests, goals and conversation (communication) with friends
2. Finding or making new friends
3. Re-connecting with previous or old friends
4. Making career or business contacts
5. Furthering their own personal development or education
6. Debating various issues or advocating a particular position

(Summary of Focus Groups, Effects of Social Media in India, 2012)

The students all maintained that they did not see social media as a potential threat to their safety, security or well-being. When asked about those in government who might seek to restrict their interaction on the social media, without exception they countered that information and knowledge is power. Social power brings about change. Fahad, one of the male students asserted, "The government should want us to know more about our world. We will soon be the ones running India. We can't make good decisions without knowledge." (Effects of Social Media in India [Focus Group Notes], Pune University, 2012) The students all seemed to agree with Fahad's statement. I would assume that most Indian youth think the same way. The waves of social media seem to be uncontrollably crashing powerfully onto the shores of India's culture. The youth, it appears, seem to be swimming happily in the tide.

4. Social Media in India: A Political Perspective

Indian political powers recognize the potential of social media and the impact possible on campaigns, candidates, opponents and popularity. The social media allow parties and people to interact with the masses and make them participate, thereby enabling more personal communication. In recent elections, almost every candidate and party used social media to promote the desired message out to the masses. For example, the Congress, Bharatiya Janata Party, Samajwadi Party, Bahujan Samaj Party, and most candidates used Twitter, Facebook or some other form of presence in the social media market.

Each party and candidate maintained a website, prolifically issued updates and participated in posting views, political issues and campaign slogans for the social audience consumption. Rahul Gandhi, a pop icon among the youth in India engages almost every social medium available. He socially makes use of networking sites, writes blogs, Tweets, and sends texts in order to share his views on all current issues in India. The same applies in case of Mr. L. K. Advani who avidly writes and posts to his own blog. One popular political analyst in India observed, "This makes us feel that they are within our reach" (Sayed, 2010, Impact of social media on politics section, para. 5). The blog writer goes on to remark,

"Talking about twitter, there is no dearth of politicians on twitter. From famous and well known political bigwigs like Shashi Tharoor who is recognized for his tweets to Narendra Modi and from lesser known politicians like captain Gopinath to Meera Sanyal, Indian politicians have engaged social media." (Sayed, 2010, More on twitter, facebook, blogs section, para. 2) This attitude about various media came from the politicians' desire to stay in touch with as many people as possible. As a matter of fact, most political parties have official twitter accounts for releasing press releases, political campaign action and all other propaganda. This activity, they believe, provides more transparency in interaction with the masses. (Sayed, 2010, More on twitter, facebook, blogs section, para. 2).

All of India's politics have been impacted it appears: "Social media is a means for politicians to appeal to citizens; it makes them seem more personable, and gives them the advantage of keeping in constant contact with their supporters. What it really translates to are more votes and a bigger chance of being elected. Obama's use of social media in the U.S. 2008 presidential election is believed to be one of the determining factors in his successful election. India politicians, specifically the Samajwadi Party and Congress, have also turned to social media for their campaigns; Twitter, Facebook, and YouTube have been their means to get their messages across in the social media world." (Tate, 2012, para. 6)

Most Indian politicians have begun targeting all social networking media: The best example one can offer

> "is that of Rahul Gandhi. He makes his presence felt everywhere. He moves from having interaction with his fans as well as youths who aspire to be like him and serve the country on traveling by local trains in Mumbai!" (Sayed, 2010, More on twitter, facebook, blogs…, para. 3)

The simple fact emerges: Indian politicians seek to affect the populace's thinking by engaging the social media. They recognize the immense potential, power and personal nature offered by social media.

The student Kaamil responded to a question about politics and social media when he said,

> "I know the political powers seek our influence. They reach out on Orkut and Facebook seeking to get us to like them or follow them. In one way I am happy that they want our input. But maybe they just want our vote. In any case, the political forces will need to use the social media because that is where we are." (Effects of Social Media in India [Focus Group Notes], University of Poona, 2012)

The political parties, powers and persuaders all recognize the potential and power of the social media networks. No doubt their use and deployment will only continue. As political powers become savvier on the ways to reach the youth of India the same powers will surely garner more power, resources and political capital for making their desired changes in India.

5. Social Media in India: An Economic Perspective

Much has been written about the vast commercial and marketing opportunities in India primary because of the huge population. Additionally, e-commerce has emerged as a genuine avenue for making many overnight millionaires. Many writers contend that India offers the next bonanza. As communication companies and e-trade expands in India, the profitable predictions hold great promise. Government records demonstrate:

For 2011, India's estimated GDP was $1.843 trillion with 7.8% growth. Services, industry, and agriculture account for 56%, 26%, and 18% of GDP, respectively. India's population is estimated at 1.2 billion and is growing at 1.3% a year. The country is capitalizing on its large numbers of well-educated people skilled in the English language to become a major exporter of software services and software workers, but more than half of the population depends on agriculture for its livelihood. 700 million Indians live on $2 per day or less, but there is a large and growing middle class of more than 50 million Indians with disposable income ranging from 200,000 to 1,000,000 rupees per year ($4,166-$20,833). Estimates are that the middle class will grow tenfold by 2025. ("Background Note: India (04/17/12)," 2012, Economy section, para. 1)

Technology expansion and growth in India continue to push the economy into new highs. "The rapidly growing software sector is boosting service exports and modernizing India's economy. Software exports surpassed $35 billion in FY 2009, while business process outsourcing (BPO) revenues hit $14.8 billion in 2009. Personal computer penetration is 14 per 1,000 persons. The number of cell phone users rose above 300 million in 2010." ("Background Note: India (04/17/12)," 2012, Economy section, para. 6) These trends change the landscape of the business, market and political climate by the sheer power of e-industry. "Facebook and other social media outlets understand the sheer size of India provides a great testing ground for saturation, peak implementation and expansion. "The lessons the company could learn here will apply in other emerging

*markets like Indonesia, Brazil and parts of Africa, executives said. 'As
we think about how to deliver the best possible Facebook experience
to an emerging-market customer, India is probably the best place
to incubate and experiment on different ways we can deliver that
experience,' said Meenal Balar, Facebook's director for international
growth." (Sharma, 2012, para. 4).*

One of the difficulties in gauging the impact of the social media on the
economic status of India rests in the fact that proper, reliable metrics for
studying social media economics remains in flux. Divol, Edelman and
Sarrazin state:

*"We believe there are two interrelated reasons why social media
remains an enigma wrapped in a riddle for many executives,
particularly non marketers. The first is its seemingly nebulous nature.
It's no secret that consumers increasingly go online to discuss products
and brands, seek advice, and offer guidance. Yet it's often difficult
to see where and how to influence these conversations, which take
place across an ever-growing variety of platforms, among diverse and
dispersed communities, and may occur either with lightning speed or
over the course of months. Second, there's no single measure of social
media's financial impact, and many companies find that it's difficult
to justify devoting significant resources—financial or human—to an
activity whose precise effect remains unclear." (Divol, Edelman &
Sarrazin, 2012, para. 2)*

The truth remains that social media offer a personal experience in a mass
media platform. This makes measurement of impact difficult to gauge and
standard methods yet to be designed. The rapid growth of social media
and the technologies that support them have far outpaced the metrics and
accepted measurements to record all of the impact, action and effects. The
word rapid applies in the truest sense.

Regardless as to the difficulty in metrics, entrepreneurs from all over
the globe have settled in India because of the large, youthful buying
audience that has emerged there. "A study showed that a large percentage
of teenagers got news about current events online. A high percentage of
Indian teens also regularly make purchases online for items, like books

and clothes, while others reported that they looked mainly for information related to health, diet and physical fit.

Bina Ararwal, Professor of Development Economics at the University of Manchester, UK believes that the new realities of social media offer great opportunities for small farmers and others to finally cooperate and collaborate in powerful and exciting new ways. (Agarwal, 2012, YouTube Video) It appears that many agree with this assessment of the potential and power of the Internet. For example, Raghu studies economics at the University of Pune. During the focus group I asked about the economy of India in regard to social media. He stated,

> *"See…this is not just about India. This is about the world. We connect with the world through social media. We can order music, listen to speakers or chat with friends. I have friends in the United States. I chat with them. Soon, we will do everything by these (he holds up a smart phone). This is the economics of the new India." (Effects of Social Media in India, Focus Group Notes, page 12).*

It appears that India stands at the threshold of new economic possibilities.

6. Social Media in India: A Cultural Perspective

Shaheen Sayed studies at the University of Mumbai pursuing a masters degree in public relations. Concerning the changing culture in India she wrote,

> *"Lenhart, Madden, MacGill, and Smith state in their book that 'teens use social media platforms for more than simple voice communication. Social media are becoming a primary outlet and expressive written medium via web pages, blogs and more.'" (Sayed, 2010, Use of social media among teens in today's time section, para. 2).*

Beyond the written word, social media also provide a platform for teen expression in visual arts, photographs, music and video sharing sites. This opportunity to produce and share culture, views and expression across all the platforms has contributed to the rapid growth in teen use of social media in India.

More specifically regarding Indian teens, the young people of India spend a staggering amount of their time daily on Facebook. Additionally, Indians have also turned to Twitter, according to a recent survey conducted by McAfee. "On a daily basis, the surveyed Indian teens spend 86 per cent of their time on Facebook followed by 54 per cent time on Twitter." ("Indian teens 'shock' on Facebook, Twitter," 2012, para. 2) Such statistics causes any advertiser with products targeted at teens froth at the mouth. Young people in an emerging market have disposable income and the companies with products directed toward youth eagerly seek to sell. The social media in India offers an immediate channel for that particular audience. The possibilities and potential of the various media will only grow in the coming years. Such immense influence reaches beyond commerce. With the time, energy and attention Indian youth pay to the social media, language, customs, philosophy and thought processes will most certainly be affected. Recent world events demonstrate that both Twitter and Facebook help fuel communication of civil revolution and political change.

There is no doubt that the social media have affected the culture and communities of India. Their reach not only affects the youth but also adults. Facebook and Twitter are the signposts of the Anna Hazare movement along with so many other social, political and commercial events in recent times in India. ("Anna Hazare", 2008, para. 1) Kasturi argues that there remains a lesson to be learned from the social media influence and reach. He states,

> "the fact that it is a means of communication, persuasion and a means of commerce. Seen another way, communication in social media has become interactive, allowing participants to voice their feelings and opinion on the ether while also doing business. This is a phenomenon that will forever change the nature of humankind interactions. Across India, small businessmen, craftsmen and farmers use mobile phones to do their business. (Kasturi, 2012, para. 3-4).

Using Anna Hazare as an example, he asserts, "social media helped in multiplying the sentiments of the urban populations across India who feel that Hazare provides direction for their pent up feelings. People are not only taking to the streets in huge numbers but are taking to Facebook and Twitter to state their case. So those who are at work and cannot go to India Gate can at least tweet their support! Recent events demonstrate that even governments are worried about the rapid spread in the use of social media" (Kasturi, 2012, para. 3-4).

Undoubtedly, however, the major social change that these media could possibly bring about within the culture revolves around the much deliberated social structure in India known as the caste system. For generations, the people of India have been relegated to thousands of castes and caste-like cultural clans. Membership in these hierarchically ordered and strategically named groups is decided by birth. "India's four main castes, or varnas, are subdivided into thousands of specialized subcastes, or jati, with each jati assigned a specific occupation." (Johnson & Karlberg, 2005, p. 13) Caste members are expected to marry within the group, follow all caste rules pertaining to diet, avoid all ritual pollution, and keep many other directives suitable for that particular caste of the Indian culture. "Although elements of the caste system, such as untouchability, were outlawed over 50 years ago by the Indian constitution, caste remains an obvious feature of rural Indian society." (Johnson & Karlberg, 2005, Introduction section, para. 1) The majority of the Indian population is Hindu (80%) which obviously has a big impact on the Indian culture in general. Although officially the caste system is not in place anymore, caste continues to play a big role in societal hierarchy. Especially in more rural areas it still significantly organizes society, but in the upper and middle classes the caste-system seems to be of less importance as income and career increases in influencing the reputation and future of many Indians (Johnson & Karlberg, 2005, p. 3).

Johnson and Karlberg continue:

> *"With the advent of mass media and channels of communication and information the Brahmins, who have traditionally been at the top of the caste system, have been seemingly replaced by those with color television sets in their homes. The next level down seems now to be those with only the access to color TV, followed by black and white TV owners and then those with only access to black and white TVs" (Johnson & Karlberg, 2005, p. 12).*

Caste lines have been increasingly blurred, however, as Indians quest to gain access to information, entertainment and knowledge. Television viewing, especially in the rural areas, has become a communal event and it is not uncommon for TV owners to position their television sets facing an open door; allowing members of other caste groups to sit outside the home and enjoy the shows.

> *"Similarly, in villages where there is one common, government-provided television set, members of the village gather around to watch communally. This is especially the case for religious programs as well as those related to agriculture." ("Associated Content," 2006, Changes in Social Structure section, para. 3)*

The entire process provides new ramifications for the term social media. Television occurs as a social event throughout India on a daily basis. The media serve as a collective force bringing groups together.

The caste community known as Brahmin, which numbers more than 35,000 members, represents what is considered one of the highest ranked castes in India. The caste offers numerous chat rooms and discussion forums on various Internet sites for the caste members to discuss the rules, regulations, requirements and expectations of caste life. Members join forums to debate their religion's history and why cows cannot be eaten. Dalits, on the other hand, remain as one of the lowest ranked caste societies and struggle to gain access to greater opportunity despite the suppression. The Dalits too have discussion forms, blogs and e-sites devoted to their struggle for greater acceptance in Indian cultural life. If indeed Friedman is correct and the world has become more flat in the scope of all things considered, then India will continue to face a flattening of the social structure once so rigidly guided by the caste system. (Friedman, 2005).

Facebook, Orkut, Twitter, Google+ and other social media sites in India take the discussion of the caste system out of the normal venues such as the classroom, coffee shops or newspapers and into the personal spaces and spheres of cyber discussion. Some argue the country's young people no longer need to discuss the caste in public. Instead, they retreat to an anonymous and the socially safer online world to debate and discuss these controversial issues. "Social networking sites are giving youth a platform to discuss caste," said Sunil Gangavane, of Partners for Urban Knowledge,

Action and Research (PUKAR), who is conducting research on how caste identities are reproduced on Orkut. Gangavane said students in Mumbai "rarely discuss caste among themselves." Yet Gangavane said that "online, young people seek out caste-related communities and engage in debates related to those identities." (Ingber, 2010, para. 1-2)

In an extensive survey by the Center for the Advanced Study of India at the University of Pennsylvania, researchers found that Dalits living in concrete homes, not huts made from mud and straw had jumped from 18 percent to 64 percent between 1990 and 2007 in one north Indian district. Ownership of various household goods such as fans, chairs, pressure cookers and bicycles – had skyrocketed over the same period. The study also detailed a weakening of some caste traditions, with, for example, far fewer Dalits being seated separately at non-Dalit weddings. While most Dalits still support themselves as rural laborers, there is also a growing Dalit middle class, many of them civil servants who have benefited from affirmative action laws. (Joy, 2009, para. 1)

Other social advocates agree with this Indian social forecast. "'Caste is losing its grip,' said Chandra Bhan Prasad, a Dalit writer, social scientist and one-time Marxist militant who has become a leading voice urging the Dalit poor to see the virtues of capitalism. In a consumer society, Prasad argues, "wealth can trump caste – at least sometimes. Growing economies also foster urbanization," he states flatly. "This allows low-caste Indians to escape traditional village strictures. Finally, economic growth also means that the traditional merchant castes are not large enough to fill every job. This means other castes also have a chance in the business world," Prasad said. To Prasad, the new millionaires are a way to prove that Dalits can make it in the changing India. "Experts can no longer say that success is not possible because of the caste system," he said. "Here is a list of Dalits who are doing well." (Sullivan, 2011, para.16-20)

Not everyone agrees, however. Some argue that the social media will allow the caste system to operate in India more efficiently and discretely. The social media take the argument off the street and tuck it way onto the Internet. "In a country of nearly 1.2 billion people, there are 54 million Internet users, and Indians use their mobiles for everything. More than 500 million Indians have mobile phones, so in general, this is how social networks are accessed. Facebook and local social networking site Orkut and even Twitter (with a mere 1.5 million users) are widely accessed and the caste debate has led to the creation of hundreds of groups." (Munford, 2010, para. 4).

The ever growing number of discussion forums on these sites only underscore how divided these communities remain. "In a recent example, 3,000 members of a scheduled online community bemoaned how their caste identity had created an unbreakable glass ceiling, while other more venomous comments from higher-caste members accused them of being 'beggars' who used their status to acquire jobs. Comparable, some would say, to the more unpleasant debates about immigration in the UK." (Munford, 2010, para. 5).

Sanjay, An Indian by birth, works as a New Delhi manager of a hotel. He remains in contact with scores of business people, youth advocates and political activist. In an interview he observed,

Indian culture, as we've known it and in generalized terms, is fading in some sense. Impact of globalization enhanced by social media can be seen as affecting the younger generations. International brands of soft drinks, coffee, and mini-skirts have taken over Hindi traditional music, tea and the saree. On the other hand it has revolutionized the communication in new ways and communication forges the new Indian identity also. Over 90% of the Indian male population owns the application ' On t cricket' or mobile owners set Hindi pops as a ring tone. So you can say some parts are gone but some parts of the culture only continue in different ways. (Sanjay, E-mail Interview, December 10, 2012)

The Caste system, for example, remains largely intact and mostly unspoiled by social media. A Brahman (the highest in the social caste) would not add a Magwal (the lowest caste) as a Facebook friend nor vice versa. You can say there may be more understanding between castes but to break the long established norm seems to me nearly impossible.

The social media industry is clearly booming. Its prospects and projected growth will be enormous. Home-grown social media continue to grow at an explosive rate. This prospect of Indian social media remains very appealing to the society. Now people rate a movie star as good by how he or she tweets or interacts with fans on social media. That is exactly how Priyanka Chopra became the best female

star in India. All of this demonstrates the power of social media!"
(Sanjay, E-mail Interview, December 10, 2012)

Professor M.N. Srinivas, India's best known sociologist, agrees with this assertion. He has continued to hold the opinion that caste hierarchy has been somewhat affected by "the impact of new ideas of democracy, equality and individual self-respect. While caste, as a system, is dead or dying, individual castes are thriving" (Srinivas, 2003, p. 132). Others disagree with the Srinivas assessment. Some contend that the end of the caste system in India comes only as a hope or a dream rather than a reality-based possibility. Chandra Bhan Prasad, a leading Dalit intellectual, has indicated that only a few of the government's programs to transform a caste-ridden society have made any noticeable impact on the culture. He asserts that the cultural tradition continues to maintain the grip on the nation and constitutes the greatest paradox of Indian society. (Rajan, n. d.)

To be sure, the speculation will continue. Although no one seems ready to forecast the death of caste or other prejudicial systems or processes in India, most everyone agrees that change continues in India, spurred on by the continued onslaught of the many social media efforts. The information, opportunity to share and desire for change appear too great for the culture of India to remain static. "Let me quote a taxi driver from Mumbai. "The only thing that doesn't change in India is the fact that everything is changing." He checked his cell phone screen as we turned a corner making sure he was following the map app correctly. " (Rajan, Effects of Social Media in India, Poona University, [Focus Group Notes], 2012).

7. Social Media in India: An Ethical Perspective

To first get an understanding of the Indian culture and the ethical considerations to be grasped in regard to the function of social media in the culture, it is useful to look at Hofstede's model in order to understand how the Indian culture might utilize messages from the virtual networks.

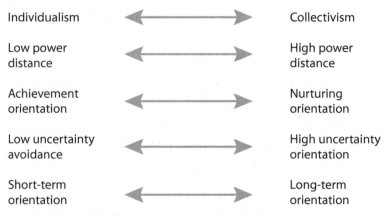

Hofstede's Model of National Culture (Hofstede, Nevijen, Ohayv & Sanders, 1990, p. 286–316)

The graph demonstrates the different dimensions of the social structures (in this case India) and as shown, power distance has the highest score, which means that the level of inequality ranks high in India. Individuality ranks similarly to the world average, indicating that India does not have a very individualistic culture. The masculinity/achievement rankings come in just above the world average, indicating that Indian society continues to demonstrate a more male-dominated social structure. Uncertainty avoidance ranks at a lower rate than the world average, indicating that social media can have a large impact in the Indian society. The graph demonstrates that Indians are open to new ideas. This profile makes the majority of Indians perfect early adapters. As such, Indians may allow outside or new messages affect the traditions, philosophy, cultural norms or ethical standards that may now be in place.

According to David Kenny, community-based societies respond much more readily in adopting social media than individualistic societies. As pointed out in Hofstede's model, the Indian culture is a community-based country, so according to David Kenny, social media can be easily adopted into the Indian culture. There exists a huge potential for social media influence and change in the Indian market. (Kenny, Kashy, & Cook, 2006, p. 406).

This is not to say, however, that the social fabric and ethical considerations have not been tested by the social media influences. Some government officials, religious leaders, education leaders and others have bitterly objected to the tactics and tendencies of those using social media in India. To better understand how Facebook and other social media managers address the ethical, moral and cultural norms affecting a host country's concerns, once again we turn to Facebook. Facebook handlers observe,

> *"The country poses some special cultural challenges. Indian government rules require Internet companies to remove, within 36 hours of being notified, content that falls into a broad range of categories, including anything 'grossly harmful,' 'menacing in nature' or 'ethically objectionable.' That has put Facebook, Google Inc. and Twitter Inc. in the uncomfortable position of being arbiters of free speech. Erring too much on the side of removing things the government deems offensive would carry the risk of alienating users. Facebook has said it only removes content that violates its terms of use or local laws." (Sharma, 2012).*

Hence Facebook, Google, Twitter and other social media concerns perform a balancing act between the users and the minders. Religious beliefs and social stipulations keep the managers on constant alert as to how to best deal with objections, protests, government regulations and their customer concerns.

Not all comes up on the positive side, however, when people assess the moral or ethical impact of social media. Hate speech, discrimination, prejudicial campaigns and persecution have been organized, prompted or motivated via the social media networks. One report suggests,

> *"The online hate campaign targeting people from the northeast has put the spotlight on the power of the social media network in India, which counts more than 60 million users, and how this burgeoning community can be manipulated for insidious propaganda." (IANS, 2012, para. 1).*

In another instance, numerous bogus Twitter accounts and other social media sites went to the chopping block as the Indian government tried to clean up online molestation.

> *"A spokesman for the prime minister's office said the blocking of six fake Twitter accounts attributed to the prime minister has been in*

the works for months and wasn't related to the recent crisis. He said the move was in response to tweets containing hate language and caste insults that readers could easily mistake as the Indian leader's. A dozen Twitter accounts and about 300 websites were blocked, according to news reports." (Magnier, 2012, para. 9).

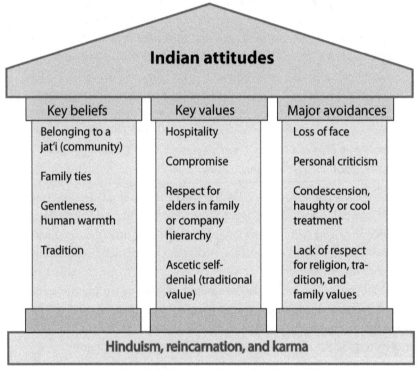

Figure 2: Key Indian beliefs, attitudes and values. ("Summary of Indian Attributes," 2009. para. 2)

In Panjab University, Hansa remained quiet during most of the focus group. Several of my attempts failed to draw her out into the conversation. Finally, when I asked about the traditions of India she stated,

"India must change. I am a woman. The world changes around us. We yearn for change. Women need to assert their humanness and voice their thoughts, feelings and ideas. It is hard, I know. Things have been one way in India for so long. Now times change; India changes.

I will speak out and help to make those changes. I am afraid of what may come to me but I will do this. We must be heard not only in India but, for the sake of all women, around the world." (Effects of Social Media in India [Focus Group Notes], IAAN School of Mass Communication, 2012).

The very basics of Indian traditional values, social frameworks and ethical considerations seem to be laid out on the table of change. No one seems to be able to prophetically announce where the changes will lead but everyone agrees that social media sites are having a profound effect on the behavior, actions and attitudes of Indians, and especially the youth. The alternative may also be true. Indian culture continues to be spread around the globe via these media outlets. The argument continues: Change: Is it good or bad? The answer all depends upon our perspective.

Conclusion

The social media impact appears all around us. Politicians, celebrities, educators, religious leaders and average citizens have moved to the electronic platforms to post observations, their status or the latest photo. India, too, has joined the fray. In fact, some might forecast, India may one day lead the charge in the use of social media. The technologies we use today surely will change many cultures of the world. These advances will change India as well.

Uday Parma and his business associates did an in-depth study of the impact of social media on business and marketing. Consider these remarkable facts:

- *"One in every nine people on Earth is on Facebook.*
- *People spend 700 billion minutes per month on Facebook.*
- *Each Facebook user spends on average 15 hours and 33 minutes a month on the site.*
- *More than 250 million people access Facebook through their mobile devices.*
- *More than 2.5 million websites have integrated with Facebook.*

- *30 billion pieces of content is shared on Facebook each month.*
- *300,000 users helped translate Facebook into 70 languages.*
- *People on Facebook install 20 million 'Apps' every day.*
- *YouTube has 490 million unique users who visit every month (February 2011).*
- *YouTube generates 92 billion page views per month. "*
(Parmar, 2012).

These facts speak volumes as to the change that such activity can bring to a culture. Although these numbers refer to a global audience and participation, I infer that something very similar will continue to occur in India. Parmar, of course, is Indian. His entire study refers to the remarkable impact and opportunities still to come in the Indian market. India will continue to go online.

We have viewed these changes in the Indian reality from different perspectives. This is not an exhaustive review nor was it ever intended to be so. The purpose of this effort rests in the prospect of discussion, dialogue and communication. I firmly believe what Howard Conkey, an attorney from Detroit, once told me. He said, "Every problem has a solution and every conflict has a resolution." Communication offers the key to unlocking the door for solving social problems and discovering resolution to conflict. We know this. We believe this, but, for some reason, we keep turning to armed conflict, firing off rockets or resorting to violent protest. Maybe, as in India's case, change just does not come soon enough for some.

On the other hand, some think that social media becomes an avenue of another addiction. We see on the streets of Delhi and Mumbai people walking, not watching the traffic, their children or the streets scenes, but rather the communication device screen. Has this generation become compulsive communicators? After completing a fairly detailed study on this very concept James McCrosky and Richmond noted,

Although we began this research assuming that there were people who are compulsively driven to communicate and that this compulsion causes them (and probably others around them) problems, we are convinced the original assumption is completely accurate. The research does suggest that some people indeed are compulsive communicators, but the evidence of this being a problem for those people is scant indeed. Whether it is a problem for others remains an open question. Thus, future research should examine both the communication behaviors and orientations of compulsive communicators as well as reactions of other people to these individuals (McCroskey & Richmond, 1995, p. 51)

The application of their research summary is clear. Maybe the compulsion to communicate has gripped this new generation in India with such force that, although it may not be negative for those affected by the compulsion, the new reality may just be more than the traditional social structure can stand. Revolution rages all around us. We all certainly find ourselves surrounded by the blur and whirl of a communication revolution fueled by social media. Where this will all end or take us remains in the not so far future. This we can project: the India we have known will clearly continue to change as the effects of social media progressively and rhythmically impact the social, economic, cultural and values of the second largest country on the planet.

References

About India. (n. d.). India Visa Center. Retrieved December 11, 2912, from https://indiavisa.travisaoutsourcing.com/about-india

Agarwal, B. (2012, November 7). World Economic Forum on India 2012 social media corner. Retrieved December 11, 2012, from http://youtu.be/DwYCEfLdnE0

Amruth, H. R. (2011, May 29). History of Indian telecommunication. TelecomTalk.info, Tracking developments in Indian telecom and mobile phone industry. Retrieved December 11, 2012, from http://telecomtalk.info/history-of-indian-telecommunication/67789

Ancient Indian Culture. (2012, May 22). IndiaNetzone. Retrieved December 11, 2012, from http://www.indianetzone.com/5/ancient_indian_culture.htm

Associated Content (2006, March 29). The impact of the mass media on Indian culture and forms of communication. Retrieved from http://princessratna.blogspot.com/2006/03/impact-of-mass-media-on-indian-culture.html

Background Note: India (04/17/12). (2012, April 17). U.S. Department of State. Retrieved December 11, 2012, from http://www.state.gov/outofdate/bgn/india/200052.htm

Bohra, A. (2011, January). Sales management, Nokia mobile phones in India. Study Mode. Retrieved December 11, 2012, from http://www.studymode.com/essays/Nokia-Mobile-Phones-In-India-552618.html

boyd, d. m., & Ellison, N. B. (2007). Social network sites: Definition, history, and scholarship. *Journal of Computer-Mediated Communication, 13*(1), article 11. http://jcmc.indiana.edu/vol13/issue1/boyd.ellison.html

Deogawanka, S. (n.d.). History of postal communications. Stamps of India. Retrieved December 11, 2012, from http://www. stampsofindia.com/readroom/sdhpc.htm

Divol, R., Edelman, D., & Sarrazin, H. (2012, April 1). Demystifying social media. *McKinsey Quarterly*. Retrieved December 11, 2012, from http://www.mckinseyquarterly.com/Demystifying_social_media_2958

DMAAWiki (2011, November 4) Digital media in India—the social landscape today! Retrieved December 11, 2012, from http://youtu.be/NMVzIKowXwU

Effects of Social Media in India. (2012, October) [Focus Group]. Bharathidasan University. Participants: Students from Bharathidasan University. City, India.

Effects of Social Media in India. (2012, September) [Focus Group]. Pune University. Participants: Students from Pune University. City, India.

Effects of Social Media in India. (2012, September) [Focus Group]. University of Poona. Participants: Students from University of Poona. City, India.

Effects of Social Media in India. (2012, September) [Focus Group]. University of Poona. Participants: Rajan. City, India.

Effects of Social Media in India. (2012, September) [Focus Group]. IAAN School of Mass Communication. Participants: Students from IAAN School of Mass Communication. City, India.

Friedman, T. L. (2005). The world is flat: A brief history of the twenty-first century. New York, NY: Farrar, Straus and Giroux.

Hazare, A.. (2008). Anna Hazare. Retrieved December 11, 2012, from http://www.annahazare.org/

Hofstede, G. (n.d.). Retrieved December 11, 2012, from http://geert-hofstede.com/

Hofstede, G., Nevijen, B., Ohayv, D. D., & Sanders, G. (1990). Measuring Organizational Cultures: A Qualitative and Quantitative Study Across Twenty Cases. *Administrative Science Quarterly, 35*(2), 286–316.

IANS (2012, August 21). Social media becoming double-edged sword. *The Times of India.* Retrieved October 9, 2012, from http://articles.timesofindia.indiatimes.com/2012-08-21/social-media/33302561_1_social-media-india-pages-twitter

Indian teens 'shock' on Facebook, Twitter. (2012, November 22). The Indian Express. Retrieved December 11, 2012, from http://www.indianexpress.com/news/indian-teens-shock-on-facebook-twitter/1034799

Ingber, H. (2010, January 21). Facebook, Orkut and the caste system. Global Post. Retrieved December 11, 2012, from http://www.globalpost.com/dispatch/india/100108/social-media-castes?page=0,1

Ilankumaran, M., & Venugopalan, P. (2012). The Transition of English as a Language for Communication from Gutless Past to Glorious Present. *Research Access e-Journal, 1*(1), 31. Retrieved December 11, 2012, from http://www.researchaccess.in/PDFS/6.%20M.%20Ilankumaran%20&%20P.pdf

Jodha, V. S. (2000). Social communication in India: A minority view. *Asia Pacific Media Educator, 1*(9). Retrieved April 11, 2012, from http://ro.uow.edu.au/cgi/viewcontent.cgi?article=1145&context =apme

Johnson, K., & Karlberg, M. (2005). Rethinking power and caste in rural India. *The International Scope Review, 7*(12). Retrieved December 11, 2012, from http://myweb.wwu.edu/karlberg/articles/ Power&Caste.pdf

Joy, S. K. (2009, December 2). Study claiming liberalization helped Dalits stoke debate. Live Mint & The Wall Street Journal. Retrieved December 11, 2012, from http://www.livemint.com/Politics/ xDYX8Wq2MWChm9r99iEPfP/Study-claiming-liberalization-helped-Dalits-stokes-debate.html

Kasturi, B. (2012, January 8). The impact of social media. The Sunday India. Retrieved December 11, 2012, from http://www. thesundayindian.com/men/story/the-impact-of-social-media-/31/27616/

Kaul, V. (2011). Development communication in India: Prospect, issues and trends. *Global Media Journal - Indian Edition, 2*(2). Retrieved December 11, 2012, from http://www.caluniv.ac.in/Global%20 mdia%20journal/Winter%20Issue%20December%202011%20 Commentaries/C-2%20Kaul.pdf

Kemp, S. (2011, April). Digital, mobile and social media in India. Retrieved December 11, 2012 from http://www.slideshare.net/ eskimon/digital-mobile-and-social-media-in-india-april-2011

Kenny, D. A., Kashy, D. A., & Cook, W. L. (2006). Dyadic data analysis. New York, NY: Guilford Press.

Lucas, D. M. (2006). The handbook of folknography: a qualitative research method for giving voice. Boston, MA: Pearson Custom Publishing.

Lucas, D. M. (n.d.). The method of folknography. Folknography. Retrieved December 11, 2012, from http://www.folknography.com

Madhavan, N. (2007, July 6). India gets more net cool. Hindustan Times. Retrieved July 30, 2007 from http://www.hindustantimes.com/business-news/ColumnsBusiness/India-gets-more-Net-cool/Article1-235066.aspx

Magnier, M. (2012, August 23). India limits social media after civil unrest. Los Angeles Times. Retrieved October 16, 2012, from http://articles.latimes.com/2012/aug/23/world/la-fg-india-twitter-20120824

McCroskey, J. C., & Richmond, V. P. (1995). Correlates of compulsive communication: Quantitative and qualitative characteristics. *Communication Quarterly, 43*(1), 39–52. Retrieved December 11, 2012, from http://www.jamescmccroskey.com/publications/160.pdf

Munford, M. (2010, April 2). How Indians are using Facebook to fight the caste system. The Telegraph. Retrieved December 11, 2012, from http://blogs.telegraph.co.uk/news/montymunford1/100032530 /how-indians-are-using-facebook-to-fight-the-caste-system/

Oliver, R. T. (1971). *Communication and culture in ancient India and China* (1st ed.). Syracuse, N.Y.: Syracuse University Press

Parmar, U. (2012, January 18). The great Indian social media experiment, assessing how far along the journey Indian corporations are. Presentation at AMCF India Leadership Event, New Delhi, India.

Peterson, A. (2004). Early Radio in India. Radio Heritage Foundation. Retrieved February 20, 2013, from http://www.radioheritage.net/Story23.asp

Prasad, C. B., & Babu, S. D. (2009, June 6). Six Dalit paradoxes. *The Economic and Political Weekly*.

Rajan, V. (n.d.) 'DALITS' And the Caste system of India, some explorations and conjectures. TRANSCEND Research Institute,. Retrieved December 11, 2012, from http://www.transcend.org/tri/downloads/The_Caste_System_in_India.pdf

Sanjay. [last name consealed[(2012, December 10). Email interview.

Sayed, S. (2010, April 3). Use of social media among teens in today's time. Retrieved from http://socialmediainpolitics.blogspot.com/

Sayed, S. (2010, May 8). Impact of social media on politics. Retrieved from http://socialmediainpolitics.blogspot.com/

Sharma, A. (2012, October 20). India, a new Facebook testing ground. The Wall Street Journal. Retrieved December 11, 2012, from http://online.wsj.com/article/SB10000872396390443749204578048384116646940.html

Social media and Indian teenagers. (2011, April 22). alivenow. Retrieved December 11, 2012, from http://blog.alivenow.in/2011/04/social-media-and-indian-teenagers.html/

Social media revolution, India, communication technology, caste system, communication in India. Retrieved from: http://www.chillibreeze.com/articles/Indian-communication.asp

Soravjain (2011, February 10). Social media revolution in India. Retrieved December 11, 2012, from http://youtu.be/wJsQegdSiZc

Srinivas, M.N., (2003, February 1). An obituary of caste as a system. *The Economic and Political Weekly, 38*(5).

Sullivan, T. (2011, December 22). India: caste system faces challenges. The Huffington Post. Retrieved December 11, 2012, from http://www.huffingtonpost.com/2011/12/22/india-caste-system_n_1165874. html

Summary of Indian attributes. (n. d.) Retrieved December 11, 2012, from http://comm215.wetpaint.com/page/India%3A+Cultural+Issues

Tate, A. (2012, March 7). Social media's impact on India. Little About. Retrieved December 11, 2012, from http://www.littleabout.com/India/social-media-impact-india/98947/

Teaching in Ancient India. (1980). Aum Sri Sai Ram. Retrieved December 11, 2012, from www.sssbpt.info/ssspeaks/volume14/sss14-50.pdf

The Indian way of communication—Cross Cultural tips. (n. d.). Ciri, N.
(ed.) *Chilli Breeze*. Retrieved December 11, 2012, from
http://www.chillibreeze.com/articles/Indian-communication.asp

XIV. When Freedom Tweets: Social Media Invigorate India's Psyche of Free Speech

Debashis "Deb" Aikat

School of Journalism and Communication,
University of North Carolina at Chapel Hill
da@unc.edu

Abstract

By situating the role of social media in a larger intellectual context of intercultural communication, this chapter delineates the state of social media in India at the confluence of conflict, culture and censorship.

Based on a meta-analysis of classic cases, theories and concepts, this chapter theorizes that social media has facilitated new-found freedom in India's democratic society and invigorated India's psyche of free speech. The research reported in this chapter incorporates multidisciplinary perspectives to analyze India's social media in four parts. The first part features the state of India's burgeoning media landscape and enunciates how social media enrich India's media milieu and democratic society. The second part elucidates the power and peril of India's social media by focusing on its role in fostering intercultural communication. The third part delineates how social media have invigorated India's psyche of freedom and traces the evolution of free speech in contemporary India. The fourth and final part theorizes that restrictions on India's social media chill free speech because media freedom enhances intercultural communication. The chapter epilogue proposes future research directions by exploring theoretically-grounded implications that advance the role of social media in India's democratic society.

Keywords: Social media in India, intercultural communication in India, freedom of expression in India, restrictions on social media in India, free speech in India's social media

Where the clear stream of reason
has not lost its way into the dreary desert sand of dead habit;
Where the mind is led forward by thee into ever-widening thought
and action
— Into that heaven of freedom, my Father, let my country awake.

From India's first Nobel laureate Rabindranath Tagore's
1901 poem "Where the mind is without fear" in the *Gitanjali*
[English subtitle: Song Offerings] (Tagore, 1914, p. 27–28, poem 35).

This quotation enunciates India's first Nobel laureate and poet Rabindranath Tagore's vision of the indomitable spirit of freedom in 19th century India under British Rule. Tagore envisioned that "the clear stream of reason" and "ever-widening thought and action" would awaken India into a "heaven of freedom" (Tagore, 1914, p. 28). Tagore's vision was fulfilled in 1947 when India attained independence from British Rule after an arduous freedom movement that culminated in a keystone victory (Basham, 1995; Narayan & Meherally, 2006, Thapar, 1966; SarDesai, 2008)

More than 110 years later, India's social media seem to have conjured and revived Tagore's vision of freedom. Enraged by the Indian government's restrictive interpretation of social media, India's Internet enthusiasts have galvanized themselves through "thought and action" to invigorate a psyche of freedom in their democratic society.

1. India's Social Media Transform Free Speech

Besides enabling its users to instantaneously communicate and engage with friends, foes and family, India's social media milieu seems awakened by a spirit of free speech that evokes inspiring intimations of justice, freedom, equality, liberty and related democratic values that are both timely and timeless for freedom of expression and intercultural communication researchers (Jain, Prosser, & Miller, 2010; Prosser, 1973). India's free press and social media have helped sustain Indian democratic traditions in sharp contrast to some neighboring nations such as Pakistan, Burma (Myanmar) and Bangladesh where military dictators have stifled the press and democratic values.

As the world's second-most populous nation with over 1.2 billion people, India is home to people from different religious, social, ethnic, and educational backgrounds. Besides facilitating instant communication among friends, foes and family, social media enable unacquainted people in India to communicate with each other (Berlatsky, 2013; Islam & Ehsan, 2013). In a nation fragmented by local languages and cultural differences, India offers new theoretical paradigms that explicate how social media are redefining the interplay between culture and communication. Complex modes of intercultural communication encompass communication problems and accomplishments affecting India's diverse population (Schneider & Gräf, 2011; Behnke, 2010; Toch, 2012; Ruff & Schwartau, 2010; Rosen, Dabney, Hamilton, & Seay, 2009; Jain, 1975).

India's media form part of the communication processes that emerge from a complex political terrain (Bel, Brouwer, Das, Parthasarathi, & Poitevin, 2005). As the most populous democracy in the world, India continues to face free speech challenges and related intercultural communication problems (McIntyre-Mills, 2000). Some of these problems have been more pronounced since 2007 when India's social media drastically altered the nation's classic two-way cross-cultural interaction of ideas and issues that foster intercultural communication (Deibert, 2012; Mintz, 2012; Mendelson, 2012). India's social media have empowered and engaged people to protest social ills such as gender intolerance, jingoism and created awareness about them. Women in India often complain about increasing abuse and insult online and in the public sphere, which is primarily male-dominated. The 2009 Pink Chaddi campaign gained renown as a brilliant example of a democratic protest transcending the offline and online media divide. In February 2009, around Valentine's Day, the irreverently named "Consortium of Pubgoing, Loose Forward Women" launched a Facebook page requesting women to send pink *chaddis* (Hindi colloquial for underwear) as a 'Valentine's gift' to a Hindu chauvinist group that opposed women's freedom. Millions of supporters joined the protest organized on Facebook to strike back against moral policing by religious conservatives. The campaign attained the attention of international media that highlighted the protests, which ridiculed bigots engaged in moral policing. India's social media were also abuzz in 2013 in response to public outrage over a fatal December 2012 gang rape and beating of a young woman on a bus in New Delhi, India's capital city. Social media messages influenced the passing of India's historic anti-rape law. India approved in April 2013 the Criminal Law (Amendment) Bill-2013, which provides for life term and even death sentence for rape convicts besides stringent punishment for offences like acid attacks, stalking and voyeurism.

Such events illustrate the immense potential of India's social media for both disruptive and constructive innovation in other facets of life such as business, local, state and federal governance, education, healthcare, entertainment, media and communications and civic life. (See Figure 1: India's Social Media Profile: India's Internet users spend a quarter of their time online using social media).

2. Research Preamble and Epistemological Objectives

India provides a captivating context to study the role of India's social media at the confluence of conflict, culture and censorship. By conceptualizing free speech in social media within a larger intellectual context of intercultural communication, this chapter reports research that incorporates multidisciplinary perspectives on the role of social media in India's democratic society.

A commitment to free speech and democratic ideals has sustained the freedom of India's social media. India is now witnessing an exciting transformation of the social and the symbolic (Bel et al., 2007; Seneviratne & Singarayar, 2006). Drawing upon meta-analyses of the role of social media in a democratic society, this chapter delineates the state of social media in India at the convergence of conflict, culture and censorship. Based on analysis of classic cases, theoretical articulations and conceptual constructs, this chapter presents the state of India's social media in four

India's Social Media Profile

India's internet users devote 25% of their time online to social media and another 23% to email (comScore, 2013). The growth of mobile phone usage in India has led to an active social network beyond the Internet

← *The Indian government's social media sites feature the national emblem of four Asiatic lions, symbolizing power, courage, pride, and confidence. The emblem is adapted from the Lion Capital built by Indian Emperor Ashoka in about 250 BCE. India's national motto of Satyameva Jayate ("Truth Alone Triumphs") appears at the bottom of the emblem.*

India's
Internet Domain

❖ 1.21 billion people in India (2011 census).

❖ India has the third largest number of internet subscribers, at 164.81 million, after China and the US, in March 2013 (TRAI, 2013).

Low Internet
Penetration

❖ India's Internet penetration is low (12.6%) and ranks 164 among 192 nations.

❖ 75% of India's Internet users were younger than 35, compared to 50% worldwide, in March 2013 (comScore, 2013).

Rise of Mobile
Phone Users

❖ India's sparse count of 15 million broadband users contrasts with the rising number of 873 million mobile users, in June 2013 (TRAI, 2013, September 5). India ranked second only to China's 1.19 billion mobile phones in July 2013.

❖ Nearly 87% of India's Internet users accessed the Internet through mobile phones in March 2013 (TRAI, 2013, August 1).

Government
Surveillance

❖ The Indian government ranked second only to the U.S. government in information requests about users of Facebook, Microsoft and Google in 2012 and 2013.

Figure 1: India's Social Media Profile (© Debashis Aikat 2014)

parts. The first part enunciates how social media enrich India's media milieu by tracing the evolution of India's burgeoning media landscape as a 20th century phenomenon and its surging significance in the 21st century digital era. The second part elucidates social media as a force of intercultural communication in India with particular emphasis on the interplay of theory, concept and practice relating to the power and peril of social media for intercultural communication. The third part delineates how social media have invigorated India's psyche of free speech and traces the evolution of free speech in contemporary India. The fourth and final part theorizes that India's social media crackdown chills free speech because media freedom enhances intercultural communication. The chapter epilogue proposes needed research directions by exploring theoretically-grounded implications that advance the role of social media in India's democratic society.

The research reported in this chapter focused on India's social media through three epistemological objectives, as outlined below:

- *Research Objective 1*: Explore theoretical perspectives on the role of social media by analyzing how social media enrich India's burgeoning media landscape.
- *Research Objective 2*: Explicate theoretical and intercultural communication concepts that enunciate the role of social media in India's democratic society.
- *Research Objective 3:* Identify the theoretical themes and conceptual constructs that foster intercultural communication in relation to India's psyche of free speech.

These epistemological objectives construed a comprehensive four-step research method that enhanced the methodology of prior studies of communication concepts (Aikat & Remund, 2012; Scollon, Scollon, & Jones, 2012; Dallmayr, 2002; Prosser, 1985). This chapter also identifies key theoretical themes of India's social media, based on multi-pronged analyses of fundamental principles and patterns (Ali, 1999; Sastry, 2005; Gopalan, 1998; Russell, 2011; Sitaram & Prosser, 1998; Jahanbegloo & Thapar, 2008).

2.1. Research Method

The emergence of communication technologies and the subsequent growth of social media have spawned significant intercultural communication subgenres such as media, politics, technology, culture and community (Gojkov, 2011; St.Amant & Kelsey, 2012). Intercultural communication subgenres connote multidisciplinary dimensions that encompass social sciences, arts and sciences, humanities, law, ethics, information science and communication (Remund & Aikat, 2012; Balnaves, Donald, & Shoesmith, 2009; Prosser, 1972; Prosser, 1978a). Researchers of diverse intercultural communication subgenres enunciate and explicate the state of contemporary media in India (St.Amant & Sapienza, 2011; Hershock, Stepaniants, & Ames, 2003). Such research efforts enabled us to formulate the four sequential methodological steps.

The first methodological step involved searches for scholarly works (such as books, research papers and articles) that conceptualize intercultural communication, social media and free speech in India. These searches yielded a substantive body of published research that delineated scholarly characterizations of intercultural communication, social media and free speech in India (Glasser, 2013; Ravi, 2013; St.Amant, 2007). The body of published research facilitated the second step of further analysis of the "sensitized concepts" that are central to intercultural communication, social media and free speech in India. Sensitized concepts are "taxonomical systems that discover an integrating scheme within the data themselves" and facilitate analytical focus in qualitative research (Christians & Carey, 1989, p. 370). The third methodological step entailed use of sensitized concepts to identify the respective multidisciplinary connections among diverse theories and concepts relating to intercultural communication, social media and free speech in India. These sensitized concepts enabled this research study to explicate and explore the concepts, causes and consequences of conflict, culture and censorship, based on significant research works in intercultural communication (Venkateswaran, 1999; Hershock, Stepaniants, & Ames, 2003; Prosser & Sitaram, 1999; Jain et al., 2010; Donahue & Prosser, 1996; Sitaram & Prosser, 2000; Cady, Mogdis, & Tidwell, 1984). In the fourth and the final step, we conducted comprehensive analyses of statistical data and related trends that inform emerging trends in India's entertainment and media industry, changes in census data, India's economic growth, and other updated information from primary sources such as government reports (TRAI, 2013a), ranked indices (Transparency International, 2012; Freedom House, 2013a; Reporters Without Borders, 2013) and reports from international agencies (Freedom House, 2013b).

The culture of communication in India involves both modest and vociferous expressions of interaction, negotiations, and even conflicts

(Bel et al., 2010; Sen, 2003; Merino, 2013). This research method facilitated the articulation of theoretical constructs and concepts that explicate and enunciate the theory and practice of intercultural communication, social media and free speech within India's burgeoning media landscape (Jarvis, 2007; Alexander, 2011). This research method also enabled insightful reviews of the rich historiography of intercultural communication and the state of media and free speech in India and enabled the author to refine cross-disciplinary perspectives, as identified in prior studies of intercultural communication (Martin & Wilson, 1997; Prosser, 1973; Holledge & Tompkins, 2000; Fischer & Merrill, 1976; Hooker, 2011), social media (Aikat & Remund, 2012; boyd and Ellison, 2007) and free speech in India (Freedom Forum, 1999; Thapar, Champakalakshmi, & Gopal, 1996; Kaur & Mazzarella, 2009; Morris & Waisbord, 2001; Rares, E., Fenger, L., Rosenmeier, L., Ehlers, L. N., & Carl, S. M., 2006; Varennes, 1996; Fischer & Merrill, 1970; Sides, 2006). Through this research method we identified related theoretical constructs that advance the role of social media in India's democratic society (Price, Verhulst, & Morgan, 2013) and the impact of social media (Price, et al., 2013; Fortner & Fackler, 2010). Subsequent analyses of published research works helped us broaden the communication perspectives that contribute to intercultural communication, social media and free speech in India.

We accomplished the first step by searching for archival data in 32 multidisciplinary English language article databases that encompass humanities and social sciences disciplines, international and India studies, and the sciences. We restricted searches to relevant texts in English language and publication period of May 2002 through July 2013, a span of more than 10 years that may have witnessed the genesis and growth of research into intercultural communication, social media and free speech in contemporary India. The search in English language article databases for scholarly resources relating to the theoretical and conceptual evolution of intercultural communication, social media and free speech in India respectively in these multidisciplinary databases facilitated individual, collective and meta searches into database records that index, abstract and curate academic, trade publications, general-interest and scholarly journals, popular and academic journal articles, content of books, dissertations and theses.

By both design and intent, the four-step research method enabled robust, retrospective and specific searches of scholarly literature, including peer-reviewed papers, theses, books, preprints, abstracts and technical reports from broad areas of research. This method also yielded a list of several seminal works that contributed to the theoretical constructs and core concepts that are reported in subsequent sections of this chapter.

3. Social Media Enrich India's Media Milieu

India's media, comprising both traditional and contemporary media, empower, educate, and entertain a surging 1.2 billion population, which is roughly one-sixth of the world's people. With greater diversity than the continent of Europe, India is still one nation (Thapar, 1978). India is the seventh-largest country by area and the second-most populous country after China.

As one of the world's most ancient surviving civilizations, India's origins date back to 70,000-50,000 BCE, when humans first migrated to India (Wood, 1988; Thapar, 2003). India's rich legacy in art, culture and learning has thrived with unbroken continuity to modern times (Thapar, 2000; Thapar, 1992; Thapar & Spear, 1965; Monier-Williams, 1875). Market-based economic reforms in 1991 facilitated India's growth into the fastest-growing major economies for more than two decades (Friedman, 2005). India suffered a sharp economic downturn in August 2013.

A vibrant economy has reinvigorated Indian media with increased advertising spending, rising international investment, growing income levels, and a surge in consumer spending. India's newspaper market is among the largest in the world (Rothermund, 2008; Cohen, 2002; Shekhawat, 2007; Panagariya, 2008l; Alchediak, 2009).

The prosperous times for the Indian media may be attributed to several factors such as government's liberal reforms inviting foreign investment in media, a traditional print media market devoid of free content online due to low Internet penetration, a rising literacy rate, sophisticated print and broadcast technologies, increased purchasing power of the middle class, rise in advertising and consumerism, growing popularity of infotainment, and round-the-clock media content on television and the Internet. Figure 2 provides details about it.

Social Media Transform India's Democratic Society

← *India's tricolor flag signifies the secular and democratic spirit of India. The saffron color denotes renunciation or disinterestedness. The white band denotes the path of truth. The lower green band symbolizes prosperity, vibrancy and life. The Ashok Chakra (wheel) represents progress and the dynamism of a peaceful change. The 24 spokes of the wheel represents the 24 hours of a day.*

Although less than 12% of India's 753 million voters are active on social media, more than 72% use mobile phones to communicate. The people of India have effectively adopted social media for the pursuit of equality, entertainment and empowerment.

Engage
Audience

❖ India's social media enable users to instantaneously communicate and engage with friends and family.

Empower
Civil Society

❖ Indians have embraced social media to voice their opinions, exercise their free speech rights and fight for freedom.

Entertain on
Demand

❖ Indians access social media for entertainment, news and information.

Educate at
Low Cost

❖ Social media provide valuable education at low cost for both the rich and the poor.

Engineer
Consent

❖ Savvy organizations use social media to advocate for change and market products and services.

Enlighten the
Electorate

❖ India's politicians intensified their social media campaigns for the 2014 general elections.

Figure 2: Empowering democracy: Social media have transformed India's democratic society. (© Debashis Aikat 2014)

3.1: India's Social Media Exert Influence in Local and Global Realms

Social media have re-defined life and liberty in India in less than 10 years. India witnessed the advent of social media in 2004, when budding groups of Internet users in India collaborated with expatriate Indians to create social networking relationships. By 2007, social media emerged in India as a significant trend, albeit limited to a nascent group of social media users.

Compared to the superlative growth of India's print and broadcast media, the state of India's social media remains rudimentary. India's Internet penetration of 13% is low when compared to 80% in the US and 43% in China (World Bank, 2013b). Most analysts believe that better access, widespread use of Internet content and infrastructural improvements to India's digital ecosystem will improve India's Internet penetration (IBEF, 2013b). The sparse count of 15 million broadband users in India may be attributed to the high price of broadband access. India's broadband subscriber base is expanding with a yearly growth of 9% in broadband subscribers from March 2012 to March 2013, according to TRAI data of May 2013 (TRAI, 2013b). Industry analysts have demanded that broadband data transfer should be raised to more than 5 Megabits per second (the US plan is to give every household 100 Mbps connectivity). They also feel broadband costs must come down sharply, by slashing or removing all government levies and instituting real competition among service providers.

Industry observers also have cited India's low Internet penetration to predict a "golden period of the Internet sector between 2013 to 2018 with incredible growth opportunity and secular growth adoption for e-commerce, Internet advertising, social media, search, online content, and services relating to e-commerce and Internet advertising" (Aggarwal, 2013).

India's social media users in June 2013 numbered 66 million, which is less than 6% of its population (IAMAI, 2013). Despite such low penetration, India's social media are characterized by the strength for its online users. With more than 170 million Internet users, India now has the third largest Internet population in the world after China (at 575 million) and the US (at 275 million) (Aggarwal, 2013). India is also emerging as the third largest

Internet market and its e-commerce business is likely to reach revenues of $736 millionin 2015 up from $221 million in 2013 (IBEF, 2013b).

India's Facebook users soared to 82 million in June 2013, up 5% from 78 million a year ago (Facebook, 2013a). Industry estimates posit that user growth of Facebook will be fueled by emerging markets such as India while growth slows in mature markets like the United States, the U.K., Canada and western Europe. Facebook reported in May 2013 that its user base in India was up 50% and it increased its monthly active users (MAUs) to 1.11 billion worldwide (Facebook, 2013b). Facebook defines MAUs as registered Facebook users who logged in and visited Facebook through the website or a mobile device or took an action to share content or activity with their Facebook friends or connections via a third-party website that is integrated with Facebook, in the 30 days before measurement (Facebook, 2013a). MAUs are a measure of the size of its global active user community. India was among the few nations contributing to Facebook's global growth in the first quarter of 2013 with 78 million MAUs, an increase of 50% compared to the same period in 2012 (Facebook, 2013a).

A rising number of active Internet users fuel social media use in India. In August 1995, India began full-scale Internet service for public access through the Videsh Sanchar Nigam, India's overseas communications agency. That led to rapid diffusion of Internet communication nationwide. According to the United States based Freedom House, "Internet access is largely unrestricted, although some states have passed legislation that requires Internet cafés to register with the state government and maintain user registries. Under Indian Internet crime law, the burden is on website operators to demonstrate their innocence. Potentially inflammatory books, films, and Internet sites are occasionally banned or censored." (Freedom House, 2013a)

The Internet and Mobile Association of India (IAMAI) and its market research collaborators observed in March 2013 the emergence of India's social media as a distinct digital entity. It noted that users "matured" into using social media for customer engagement as opposed to just connecting with family and friends (IAMAI, 2013). According to the IAMAI report, Indian Internet users in September 2012 were spending 30 minutes on social media on weekdays, compared to 29 minutes during weekends. Facebook was the most used social media website, followed by Google+,

LinkedIn and Twitter (IAMAI, 2013). Google hosted 90% of Internet searches in India and its sites (like YouTube, Google+) ranked first in unique visitors. Facebook was second, followed by the sites of Yahoo, Microsoft and Wikimedia (comScore, 2013).

India's social media marketplace has experienced recent changes. While Google-owned Orkut lost users in India, Linkedin and Twitter gained consumers, followed by Pinterest and Tumbler (comScore, 2013). India's online population remains skewed at 39% women, which is lower than the worldwide average of 47%. The heavy users are men under 35 and women between 35 and 44 (comScore, 2013). India's social media users seem to prefer international social media entities such as Facebook and Twitter over homegrown social media sites such as Big Adda and BharatStudent, which are simplified clones of their Western counterparts. Nearly 75% of India's Internet users were younger than 35, compared to 50% worldwide, in March 2013 (comScore, 2013). Younger users also dominated the social media penetration in India. The highest proportion of social media users were 'young men' (84%) and 'college going students' (82%) (IAMAI, 2013).

3.2. More Users Access Social Media Through Mobile Phone

Social media usage is also fast catching up with mobile Internet users. Nearly 77% of the users use mobile for social media. Email, social media, search, app access, chat and instant messaging are used every day by those accessing Internet through mobile (IAMAI, 2013). According to the IAMAI report, social media rank only after e-mail in terms of usage. Entertainment, gaming, utility and texting were the other top activities of urban active Internet users (IAMAI, 2013).

This trend of more users accessing social media through mobile phones is widespread in other parts of Asia where the boom in wireless and mobile technologies is remaking the media sector in the world today (Rao & Mendoza, 2005; Kim, 2012).

India ranks second after China in the number of mobile phones in use with 867 million mobile phone subscribers and an overall mobile phone penetration of 70.42% (TRAI, 2012). In a short span of five years, India doubled its mobile phone subscriber base that is also the world's fastest growing mobile phone market. Most Indians access social media through mobile phones. According to data from the Telecom Regulatory Authority of India (TRAI), India's mobile teledensity—the number of mobile phone subscriptions for every 100 individuals—was 139 (60%) in urban areas compared to 41 (40%) in rural areas in June 2013 (TRAI, 2013). This urban-rural divide existed in March 2013, when India's urban teledensity was consistently over three times higher than the teledensity of 40 in the rural areas (TRAI 2013).

Compared to traditional landline phones, mobile phones have emerged as the dominant mode for telephony in rural areas, where fewer people own phones and it is easy to link distant villages with cost-efficient installation of mobile infrastructure. Mobile phones also provide similar flexibility and convenience to the urban consumer.

Increasing penetration of mobiles and wireless connections have led to rapid growth of the Internet in India. As a result, digital advertising showed impressive growth of 41%, with earnings surging from $948 million to $ 1327 million in 2012 (IBEF, 2013b). The 2013 mobile advertisement market is estimated at $45 million in India. It is expected to grow 43 per cent to $69 million in 2014, driven by affordable smartphones and tablets (IBEF, 2013b). The growth of India's mobile subscribers and Internet users attains increased attention since the world's largest social networking site, Facebook, reported in May 2013 that more users in India and other emerging markets were accessing their site on their mobiles or handheld devices in the first quarter of 2013 (Facebook, 2013a).

Mobile devices have also emerged as a major medium for advertising and content delivery. Every three out of four users in the country are expected to access the Internet through a mobile phone by 2015. The ad spending on mobile phones is estimated to cumulatively earn more than $651 million, according to industry observers (IBEF, 2013b). India has experienced since 2011 a significant shift in the usage of communication technologies such as tablet PCs and Fablets (an intermediate between a smart-phone and a tablet) among youth, with a compounded annual growth rate of 59% (IBEF, 2013b).

3. 3. Social Media Compete With and Complement Traditional Media

India's social media have enriched the burgeoning media landscape which encompasses a mix of the traditional and contemporary media. The traditional media that dominate India's media industry comprise media entities that are owned and operated by a rising number of multigenerational family entrepreneurs. For instance, most major newspapers in India are owned by local families with decades-long ties to their community and have grown with succeeding generations. In its traditional mode, Indian journalism operated in a hierarchical mode where print and broadcast content catered to a passive audience. In its contemporary mode, social media have enabled journalism in India to be more decentralized, democratic and participatory.

The widespread growth of the Internet in urban India has led to a spurt in online journalism comprising news websites, blogs, wikis, and some crowd-sourced citizen journalism that has permeated the national consciousness. India's burgeoning blogging community, comprising millions of blogs, covers topics like politics, social issues, Bollywood celebrities, Indian culture, and technology trends. Mirroring the success and influence of India's local language media, Indian bloggers represent the rich diversity of regional languages and local issues. A significant number of Indian bloggers communicate in English to reach an audience both in India and abroad.

Since 2000, online journalism in India has exposed a range of issues such as political corruption, misuse of state funds and match-fixing in professional cricket, India's national pastime. A significant section of the Indian online news audience regularly accesses websites of mainstream media, Twitter, photo and video sharing sites, wikis, blogs for breaking news, images and commentary. During the November 2008 terrorist attacks in Mumbai, more than nine million people in India and abroad accessed the website of The Times of India, India's largest English-language newspaper. Page views on the Times of India website saw a fourfold increase from 4.5 million on November 27, 2008, the day after the attacks, to more than 17 million the next day. This was a two-fold increase over the Times of India's nearly 8 million readers who browse the newspaper in its traditional paper version. Breaking news of the terrorist attacks prominently featured on blogs and Twitter messages.

3. 4. India's Burgeoning Print Media

As an emerging medium for news information and entertainment, India's social media compete with and complement the nation's print and broadcast media and serve a significant section of its growing population. India's Internet penetration is low (13%) and ranks 164 among 192 nations. In addition, few people have access to computers and such low digital penetration of the Internet has enabled newspapers in India to summarily subdue the influence of the Internet era.

More people read a newspaper in India every day when compared to the United States, Europe, and other parts of the developed world. Newspaper circulation, however, has declined due to social and technological changes such as the availability of news on the Internet. Print media in the U.S. and Europe are reeling under declining revenues, forced to make widespread job cuts and often being dismissed as past their prime. On the other hand, in some developing countries, circulation is surging as these factors are more than canceled out by rising incomes, population, customized content that caters to a localized audience and rising literacy. In many Asian countries such as China and India, newspapers are thriving and expanding.

Despite a newspaper downturn worldwide, India's print media remain buoyant and have been arguably experiencing its most successful run in terms of profits, circulation and journalism. The rise of India's print media can be attributed to rising literacy, growing purchasing power of the middle class and population growth. Also due to low penetration of the Internet outside large urban centers, newspapers in India enjoy rising circulation. India may be among the few countries that may experience sparse effects of digital penetration because Internet penetration is still nascent and migration to the Internet is, at best, modest.

With little direct competition from the fledgling Internet media and low Internet penetration, India's print media's revenue and profit have soared. India's print media continue to grow by over 5.5% compared to the previous year, according to data compiled by India's Ministry of Information and Broadcasting (IBEF, 2013b; RNI, 2012). India was home to

86,754 registered print publications in 2012, comprising 11,304 newspapers and 75,450 periodicals in more than 124 languages and dialects and every publishing day more than 370 million copies (RNI, 2012) are printed, which amounts to more than three print media copies per person for India's 1.27 billion estimated population in 2013 (RNI, 2012). The Paris-based World Association of Newspapers' list of "World's 100 Largest Newspapers" features 17 Indian newspapers, including three English dailies, seven Hindi publications, and seven regional language publications (World Bank, 2013a). All of these newspapers publish and maintain an active presence online including social media. Most of these newspapers publish color broadsheet editions printed simultaneously in several cities and maintain websites for their domestic and international readers (WAN-IFRA, 2013b). Multinational media publishers and private entrepreneurs have increased their investments in India's print media since 2002 when the Indian government eased a 1955 ban on foreign investment in magazines and newspapers.

3. 5. The Rise of India's Broadcast Media

Social media messages often react to the content and context of India's broadcast media. India's television market is the world's third largest after China and the USA. India's broadcasting and cable TV services sector has consistently expanded since the early 1990s (TRAI, 2012). Over 686 active television channels feature news and entertainment programs in English and 22 national languages (TRAI, 2013b). Of the 247 million television households, nearly 61% (150 million homes) are served by cable TV systems, direct-to-home (DTH) services, Internet Protocol television (IPTV) services and Doordarshan, the state-run terrestrial TV network, which covers about 92% of India's population through a network of 1415 terrestrial transmitters (TRAI, 2012).

Even as 46 million registered DTH subscribers and around half a million Internet Protocol Television (IPTV) subscribers. IPTV is a digital television service delivered through an Internet network infrastructure. IPTV provides viewers with a new visual digital experience enhanced by myriad value-added interactive services that meld infotainment and e-commerce. With the imminent convergence of information, communication and entertainment media, India plans to implement IPTV. Such plans may lead to an augmented demand for broadband connectivity in India.

Since its emergence in the early 1990s, the pay television services sector, has chalked an average growth of 34% in 20 years, with 168 registered pay television channels (TRAI, 2012). The pay television universe comprised 168 pay channels (out of 831 registered TV channels) in 2012, 94 million cable TV subscribers including nearly one million subscribers for services using a conditional access system, which is a digital mode of transmitting TV channels through a set-top box (TRAI, 2012).

Social media provide a more interactive experience than traditional television. However, a large segment of the population enjoys television. India's state-owned public service television network, Doordarshan (meaning "View from Afar"), is one of the largest terrestrial television networks in the world (Chatterji, 1991). Faced with competition from private channels, Doordarshan has augmented its programs with sports, news and entertainment content and introduced a satellite television service with no subscription fees. Doordarshan's direct-to-home television service reaches 93% of India's population through 35 channels beamed from 67 studio centers and a network of 1415 terrestrial transmitters (TRAI, 2012). While a significant part of the Doordarshan's television content is entertainment, its news channel reaches 49% of the Indian population, according to Doordarshan data. Doordarshan remains the most widely available network, especially in rural areas, where a majority of the population lives.

Radio broadcasting started in India with the Radio Club of Bombay's first broadcast in 1923. This was followed by regular Broadcasting Services in 1927 with two privately-owned transmitters at Bombay and Calcutta. The Indian Government took over the transmitters in 1930 under the aegis of Indian Broadcasting Service, re-named All India Radio in 1936 and Akashvani (meaning the "Voice from the Sky") after 1957. India's radio industry has grown rapidly as part government reforms that began in 2005. India's private frequency modulation (FM) radio industry accounts for nearly 4% of the country's total advertising market with more than 252 private FM stations operating in 86 cities. The FM radio sector is projected to garner $423 million in revenue by 2016 within three years of the third phase of FM radio. This will allow for 839 radio channels in 227 cities. The FM radio sector is anticipated to earn revenues of $258 million with 245 private FM stations (IBEF, 2013b). These services act as a useful supplement to the radio services of All India Radio.

India's social media lack the growing rural reach of radio. The state-owned All India Radio served 99% of the population and 92% of the geographical area with 385 broadcasting stations and 237 broadcasting centers in 2012. AIR originates programming in 23 languages and 146 dialects. The privately-owned radio industry, which is entirely dependent on advertisement revenues, registered a growth of around 15% in 2011, according to TRAI data (TRAI, 2012). Indian radio industry accomplished a 5% growth and a record revenue of $282 million in 2012 and are estimated to further expand by 7% in 2013 (IBEF, 2013b).

3. 6. The Digital Future of India's Media and Entertainment Industry

India's social media compete with print and broadcast media in the entertainment space. With about 12% growth in 2012 and $6.8 billion revenue, television dominated India's media and entertainment industry landscape followed by the print media (IBEF, 2013b). Advertising expenditure across media expanded by 9% to $6.0 billion in 2012; wherein print continued to be the largest beneficiary, accounting for 46% of the advertising pie at $ 2.8 billion (IBEF, 2013b).

India's media and entertainment industry has experienced rapid growth in profits as digital technologies transform India's entertainment, information and news content. Launch of advanced media devices has facilitated access of the same content on a variety of media platforms. This has led to the emergence of new business models and revenue streams, not only for content providers, but for a variety of new players joining the new media ecosystem (IBEF, 2013b).

With an estimated 12% growth in 2013, the Indian media and entertainment industry has emerged as among the fastest growing sectors of the Indian economy (IBEF, 2013b). The Indian film industry, the largest in the world, grew by 21% accounting for $2.1 billion revenues in 2012 (IBEF, 2013b). Indian animation industry is also undergoing rapid transformation. While the industry is poised to grab greater outsourcing pie from global players, it is also prepared to move up the value chain and play a better role in the overall animation and gaming ecosystem. Indian studios are now becoming more advanced and look to create their own intellectual property through innovative business models. This is in sharp contrast to the earlier years when India conducted only post-production work and other outsourced tasks from Hollywood studios (IBEF, 2013b).

4. Social Media Foster Intercultural Communication in India

India's burgeoning mass-mediated public sphere serves the political, economic and social interest of the nation (Moraes, Howe, & Galbraith, 1974; Firth & Hand, 2001; Lamb, 1966). As Stuart Hall observes "the mass media are more and more responsible for providing the basis on which groups and classes construct an 'image' of the lives, meanings, practices and values [that] can be coherently grasped as a 'whole'" (Hall, 1979).

India's social media contribute to a social construction of media identity, the relationship of media and culture, and the formation of ideology. A key concept is Antonio Gramsci's notion of hegemony – the process whereby a cultural "common sense" is produced. This has been described and defined by Graeme Turner (Turner, 1990). Gramsci considered the press a "prominent and dynamic part" of how ideological hegemony is achieved, when ideology is defined – as it is here – as a set of ideas and beliefs that reproduce a particular social order (Gramsci, 1985).

India's social media contribute to the construction of what Hall refers to as "social knowledge" or "social imagery" within a mass-mediated cultural sphere (Goodwin & Jasper 2012; Sowers & Toensing, 2012; Emden, 2012; Fortner & Fackler, 2010). Like traditional print and broadcast media, social media are not only a mere carrier of ideology; rather, media shape people's very idea of themselves and the world (Golding and Murdock, 1979). In 1922, Walter Lippman famously referred to stereotypes as "pictures in our heads" (Lippman, 1922). His comment presaged several decades of research on how perceptions of stigmatized social groups are represented in the mind.

4. 1. Technology Fosters Intercultural Communication

The rapid spread of computer-mediated communication, such as wireless connectivity, robust mobile communication, incessant media content digitally accessible to audiences from anywhere at any time, and ubiquitous social media, has great potential for altering intercultural communication (Haynes, 2002; Dyson, L. E., Hendriks, & Grant, 2007; Freedman, 2009). For instance, Internet telephony, which enables voice communication over the public Internet instead of the public switched telephone network, has radically transformed how people of different cultures recognize, perceive and interact with one another (Tayler & Mariner, 2012). Such tools may also foster intercultural communication to address development needs (Ishida, 2010; Magnan, 2008; Ess & Sudweeks, 2001; Packer, 2002).

4.2. The Power and Peril of Social Media for Intercultural Communication

All technologies come with mixed blessings and the 21st century media revolution reflects that dictum (Creekmur & Sidel, 2007; Forest, 2007; Mohammed, 2011; Ahern, 2011; Hofstede, 2001). While communication technology has transformed society (Kline, Burstein, De, & Berger, 2005; Castells, 2004), such changes have prompted researchers to posit a range of insights such as how the Internet generation "challenges and destroys" (Jarvis, 2009), the "promise and peril" of big data (Bollier, 2010), more "public sharing" (Jarvis, 2011), the Internet's effect on "our brains" (Carr, 2010), "culture, loss, and identity" (Kelty, 2005; Kelly, 2009), the Internet as "killing our culture" (Tankard & Bray, 2011; Keen, 2007) and the "persistence of ignorance" (Mohammed, 2012). These perspectives illustrate the boon and bane of this media revolution (Thomas & Nain, 2004; Jarvis, 2009; Jarvis, 2011; Ahern, 2011; Kovach & Rosenstiel, 2010; Kline et al., 2005; Gillmor, 2004; Kelty, 2008).

Social media, like all technology, are ethically neutral, though generally their applications are not (Feher, 2007; Chomsky, Mitchell, & Schoeffel, 2002; Costigan & Perry, 2012). Technology is neither good nor bad; nor is it neutral. Technology's interaction with the social ecology is such that technical developments frequently have environmental, social, and human consequences that go far beyond the immediate purposes of the technical devices and practices themselves. (Kranzberg 1986, p. 545)

4. 3. Social Media as a Force of Intercultural Communication in India

In several sectors of India's society, social media have democratized and decentralized decision-making and, therefore, redefine the intercultural communication that fosters such mediation. Effective intercultural communication seeks to establish and understand how people from different cultures behave, think or act (Orbe, Flores, & Allen, 2008; McIntyre-Mills, 2000). Researchers posit theories, enunciate strategies and develop tools to create a better intercultural communication environment by motivating people to overcome differences in language, technology and values to appreciate different cultures (Pager & Candeub, 2012; Gudykunst, 2005). With their multifarious powers of customization and communication, social media have emerged as a powerful tool for intercultural communication in India.

Indian democracy seems to be on the cusp of a social media revolution as Indian politicians intensify their social media campaigns for the 2014 general elections. Although less than 12% of India's 753 million voters are active on social media, more than 72% use mobile phones to communicate. The people of India have effectively adopted social media for the pursuit of equality, entertainment and empowerment. Pollsters estimate that social media will have a significant impact on more than 175 constituencies and influence public opinion in India.

Social media enhance intercultural communication in India's multicultural society (Mohanty, 2012; Aram, 2008). With their diverse audience, social media cater to India's complex combination of distinct doctrines, violent sectarianism, extreme views, gender and class inequality and a striking coexistence of the traditional and modern thought (Freedom

Forum, 1999). In his 2005 book *The Argumentative Indian*, Nobel prize-winning economist Amartya Sen argues the need to understand contemporary India in the light of its long argumentative tradition. Sen posits the understanding and use of this rich argumentative tradition are critically important, Sen argues, for the success of India's democracy, the defense of its secular politics, the removal of inequalities related to class, caste, gender and community, and the pursuit of sub-continental peace are mandatory (Sen, 2005).

As a medium of intercultural communication, social media foster a vibrant exchange of meaningful and unambiguous information across cultural boundaries, in a way that preserves mutual respect and minimizes antagonism (Lent & Fitzsimmons, 2013; Mandiberg, 2012; Partridge, 2011). Contending that India's long argumentative tradition is vital for the success of its democracy and secular politics, Sen posited that India's rich history of heterodox doctrines and public discourse, cultural legacy has fostered diverse religious communities (such as Hindu, Muslim, Christian, Buddhist, Jain, Jewish, Parsee, Sikh and Baha'i), as well as a venerable line of atheist and materialist thought, while nurturing classic thinking in science and mathematics, and embracing theories of governance (Sen, 2005).

Social media's multifarious content and context also nurture India's diverse culture, which is a complex mix of symbols, beliefs, attitudes, values, expectations, and norms of behavior sustained by its postcolonial identity and multicultural values. Besides fostering such intercultural diversity, India's social media bridge the urban and rural divide. Nearly 34% of India's social media users lived in top eight cities (Mumbai, Delhi, Kolkata, Chennai, Bangalore, Hyderabad, Ahmedabad and Pune), while 35% of users comprised residents of towns with less than half a million people (IAMAI, 2013). Thus, the remaining segment of 31% comprises other user segments including users from rural areas (IAMAI, 2013). Nearly 74% of all active Internet users in urban India use social media. Social media users in urban India soared to 62 million in December 2012. Such growth is estimated to lead to increased social media use also in rural areas due to growing literacy and increased use of mobile devices (IAMAI, 2013).

4. 4. Social Media Reflect Striking Contrasts in Contemporary India

Social media were conceptualized to serve diverse demographic segments (Aaker, Smith, & Adler, 2010; Solomon, 2011; Qualman, 2009; Mansfield, 2012). India's social media cater to a privileged segment of the Indian population. But that has not stopped a small but influential group of users in India from expressing through social media their concern about India's many problems.

The chasm has widened between the rich and poor in India where the rich get richer. India was home to 55 billionaires (defined as assets in US dollars) with a total net worth of $194 billion (Bhat & D'Souza, 2013). In striking contrast to such opulence, poverty is widespread in India. Every third Indian lives below the poverty line and the nation is also estimated to have a third of the world's poor (World Bank, 2000). In 2010, the World Bank reported that 33% of all Indian people fall below the international poverty line of $1.25 per day (PPP) while 69% live on less than $2 per day (World Bank, 2013a). In addition, India faces problems such as overpopulation, environmental degradation, government and business corruption, economic inequities, an extensive underground black market economy, ethnic conflict, a bigoted caste system, gender discrimination, race and religious riots, terrorism, poverty and neglect of children (Baird & Ferro, 2003; Engineer, 2004; Akbar, 1988; Thapar, 1977; Akbar, 1985; Akbar, 2003; Sahai, 1997; Lal, 1995). These problems have long been a staple of news coverage in India and now the people of India vociferously discuss and debate these issues through social media messages.

Despite impressive gains steered by sweeping economic reforms (and some deregulation) since 1991 and by growing international investment, India suffers from an infrastructure deficit such as inadequate electric power and water supply, and a woeful lack of well-maintained roads, sea ports and efficient distribution channels to attain manufacturing prowess (Tharoor, 2006; Tharoor, 1998). Several developmental and industrial projects are delayed or simply abandoned due to lack of adequate resources (Naipaul, 2003; Naipaul, 1991). Despite a widening digital divide, modern communication systems in Indian cities co-exist with abysmal connectivity in the remote villages, where more than 70% of India's population lives (Rao, 2003)

In developing nations like India, a sizable segment of the Indian population is illiterate and impoverished (Prasad, 2005; Heitzman, J. & Worden, 1995). More than one-fourth (26%, 2011 Census) of India's population cannot read or write but they are avid audiences of radio, and television. Many of the others consume multimedia programs, and Internet content including social media. India's urban elite uses social media to make friends and to influence the media agenda. According to the 2011 census, India's literacy rate is 82% for males and 65% for females, which adds up to an overall literacy rate of 74%.

Despite such daunting economic and social challenges, India's social media are thriving with diversity of content, excellence in intercultural communication and a deep commitment to free speech. Exciting changes in interactive content, phenomenal growth in mobile telephony, widespread Internet connectivity and burgeoning print media characterize India's constantly evolving media landscape. India's social media have enriched and re-shaped this media mix with a plethora of media choices that empower its users to participate and protest.

Social media spurred India's anti-corruption revolution that redefined the nation's public sphere. Corruption has dogged Indian society for decades. India ranked 94th out of 176 nations in 2012 in Transparency International's Corruption Perception Index (Transparency International, 2012). India scored 36 out of 100 on a scale from 0 (highly corrupt) to 100 (very clean) which is a result of an average of 10 studies including World Bank's Country Performance and Institutional Assessment and Global Insight Country Risk Ratings (Transparency International, 2012). India is ranked below neighboring countries like Sri Lanka and China, while Afghanistan, Iran, Nepal, Pakistan and Bangladesh fared much worse than India when it came to corruption in public sector undertakings. Sri Lanka, which is slowly limping back to normalcy after a three-decade civil war, is ranked at 79 while China is ranked at 80.

India was ranked 72 among 180 countries for the first time in 2007 and since then the country's rankings have been showing a decline. While India was placed at 87 in 2010, the position was 95 in 2011. Recent attempts to address political corruption, through legislation and activism, have been driven by domestic and international pressure to counter the negative effects of graft on government efficiency and economic performance (Freedom House, 2013a).

Social media constituted a key aspect of the anti-corruption movement that mobilized millions in India in 2011. With its global audience, social media brought international focus to anti-corruption movements, which ranked high in Time magazine's "top 10 news stories in the world in 2011" list that included the Arab Spring and the killing of Osama bin Laden.

Social media contributed significantly to the popular perception of its anti-corruption revolution in 2011 through 2012. Social media imparted a visual representation of revolutionary protests to transform India's public sphere (Rajagopal, 2009; Ninan, 2007). India's anti-corruption revolution began in April 2011 as a protest movement to establish stringent legislation and enforcement against corruption. It gained momentum when anti-corruption activist Anna Hazare began a hunger strike, which is reminiscent of protests by Mahatma Gandhi, who engaged in several famous hunger strikes to protest British rule of India. Describing Hazare as an "activist with a Gandhian air," Time magazine reported: "In a year with more than its share of protests worldwide, perhaps the most striking act of dissent took place in India, where the country's ruling coalition took flak for a host of corruption cases implicating a number of leading politicians" (Tharoor, 2011).

Protests are hardly new to India where Mahama Gandhi successfully adopted non-violence to resist British colonial rule. However, India's anti-corruption protests in 2011 and 2012 attained historical relevance. The protests, which were initially aimed to alleviate corruption in the Indian government through a legislation called the Jan Lokpal Bill, thrived on the power of a nationwide revolution. For instance, although the 2011 protests did not lead to stringent legislation and enforcement against endemic political corruption, it led to widespread opposition against corruption. As a result, the people and the press in India have revealed corrupt practices in public life, exposed misuse of public funds and called for repatriation of black money in Swiss and other foreign banks among other forms of illicit wealth.

India's social media contributed to the anti-corruption revolution that was marked by significant trends such as a rapid transmutation of a colonial public sphere, the resurgence of a national psyche, the emergence of mass consumerism in a digital milieu. globalization and the pains, the struggles, the humiliations, and the glories of a revolutionary public protest that has gained widespread support from expatriate Indians, immigrants of Indian origin and the Indian diaspora that constitutes an important, and in some respects unique, force in India's globalized culture (Rajagopal, 2009; Ninan, 2007).

As a nation of vibrant media markets, India provides fascinating insights into the popular perception and visual ramifications of its anti-corruption revolution. The revolutionary protests transformed the public sphere. India's social media and public protests contributed to widespread consent for the India's Jan Lokpal Bill (Citizen's ombudsman Bill), which proposed improvements to the Lokpal and Lokayukta Bill 2011, which was passed by Lok Sabha (House of the People), the lower house of the Parliament of India, in December 2011. The Jan Lokpal Bill is a draft anti-corruption bill proposed by prominent civil society activists seeking the appointment of a Jan Lokpal, an independent body that would investigate corruption cases and complete within a year the investigation and trials for such cases. As the Freedom House observed: "Recent attempts to address political corruption, through legislation and activism, have been driven by domestic and international pressure to counter the negative effects of graft on government efficiency and economic performance (Freedom House, 2013a).

4.5. Indian Leaders Try to Curb, Control and Censor Media

The rapid growth of social media has spawned free speech concerns (Sponder, 2012; Brockman, 2011; Handley & Chapman, 2011). The people of India cherish their freedom, especially on social media. Some government officials repeatedly reprimand and investigate social media users for "offensive" content. Restrictions on India's social media chill free speech and activists oppose "draconian" sections of India's Information Technology Act 2000 that limits Internet freedom. The Act requires Internet companies to remove "disparaging" or "blasphemous" content if they receive a complaint from an "affected person".

Despite its rich legacy of media freedom, India faltered in response to free speech issues in the digital domain. The Indian government has been feuding with technology giants like Facebook, Google, Microsoft, Yahoo! and YouTube over free speech. "Which Internet will India choose?" asked Google's Executive Chairman Eric Schmidt in a Times of India article on March 19, 2013. Schmidt observed, "Only about two billion of the world's seven billion people have an Internet connection, and I believe the remaining five billion will get one in the next decade. Almost one billion of them will come online in India…. Now is the moment for India to decide what kind of Internet it wants for them: an open Internet that benefits all or a highly regulated one that inhibits innovation" (Schmidt, 2013).

The Indian government ranked second only to the U.S. government in information requests on users of Facebook, Microsoft and Google in 2012 and 2013. While the Indian government has justified such information requests as essential to maintain law and order, critiques accuse the Indian government of needless surveillance and Internet censorship.

Anonymous India, an Indian spin-off of the international hackers' collective Anonymous, protested on June 9, 2012 against Internet censorship in 19 Indian cities, after some Internet Service Providers (ISPs), blocked file-sharing sites in India. Anonymous India protesters wore the stylized mask of the English revolutionary Guy Fawkes, spawned by the graphic novel and popularized by the 2006 movie V for Vendetta. The use of the stylized Guy Fawkes mask for modern protests originates to the 2011 Occupy Wall Street and similar protests around the world.

The June 2012 protesters displayed signs that stated: "We Are Against Internet Censorship." They were protesting in response to a court order in March 2012 directed at ISPs to prevent a newly released local movies from being offered in a pirated version online. Some ISPs went ahead and blocked some file-sharing sites altogether, rather than the offending web source

As part of its June 2012 protests, Anonymous India brought down the website of the state-owned phone service, Mahanagar Telephone Nigam Limited (MTNL) by a Distributed Denial of Service attack. On a Twitter feed set up for its India campaign, with the handle @opindia_revenge, Anonymous India tweeted: "MTNL, your website's been down for too long. Sad news for an ISP." Such attacks elicited no official reaction by the government. But Indian Computer Emergency Response Team (ICERT), India's national agency monitoring computer security incidents, acknowledged that the attacks took place.

Anonymous gained high profile in India in 2011, when it attacked the website of the Indian army. It quickly reversed its decision in October 2011 to attack the site and kept a low profile after drawing protests from some of its own members. Several people criticized Anonymous after it announced that it had hacked the Indian army's site. Social media users criticized the organization with words such as "I won't support hacking the page of Indian Army. SAD," said one user on "Anonymous' Operation India page" on Facebook. "Why Indian army? What do they have to do with this? This is not Pakistan," said another user on the Facebook page. Anonymous stated that the attack on the Indian army site had not led to any loss of data for the army, but the attack was intended to send a message to the Indian government about corruption. It also posted videos of its demands on YouTube. Anonymous India's checkered record of protests against censorship illustrates the complex nature of India's public sphere. Indians have vociferously protested attempts to curb Internet freedom because they believe free speech helps to advance civil society in the long run, while helping to prevent abuses of power in the short term (See Figure 3: Social Media Tribulations: Restrictions on India's social media chill free speech).

4.6. The Complexity of Social Media Overwhelms Administrators

Social media empower people with participatory tools of activism. (Bryfonski, 2012; Haerens & Zott, 2013; Foth, 2011; Kanter & Fine, 2010) Since the rise of the Internet in the early 1990s, India's networked population has grown from the low millions to nearing a billion. Over the same period, social media have transformed India's multicultural civil society by redefining the collective role of change agents such as opinion leaders, urban citizens, social activists, nongovernmental organizations, telecommunications firms, government officials. For instance, social media have fostered easy exchange of intercultural communication and information between the tech-savvy opinion leader and the inadequately equipped farmer in the rural heartlands through tripartite collaboration involving the local government, telecommunications firms and nongovernmental organizations.

India's Trials and Tribulations with Social Media

The people of India cherish their freedom, especially on social media. Although the Indian government does not filter or censor the Internet, some government officials repeatedly reprimand and investigate social media users for "offensive" content.

Government Crackdown

❖ Activists oppose "draconian" sections of India's Information Technology Act 2000, which limits Internet freedom.

Free Speech Feuds

❖ The Indian government has been feuding with technology giants like Facebook, Google, Microsoft, Yahoo! and YouTube over free speech.

Rumors in Social Media

❖ India's largely technophobic government was caught unaware in August 2012 when insidious rumors, spread via mobile phones and social media, disseminated bigotry and malice.

Piracy of Content

❖ India continues to be a major hub for unabated piracy of media content.

Religious Tension

❖ Mischievous messages on India's social media have often aggravated ethnic and religious tensions, especially among Hindus and Muslims.

Fake User Accounts

❖ In response to complaints, Twitter blocked in August 2012 six fake accounts which misrepresented and impersonated India's prime minister.

Figure 3: Social Media Tribulations: Restrictions on India's social media chill free speech. (© Debashis Aikat 2014)

The power of social media overwhelms India's administrators. India's government officials seem oblivious to the power of social media. A case in point is the state-run National Portal of India. Although it seeks to "provide comprehensive, accurate, reliable and one stop source of information about India and its various facets" (India NIC, 2013), it provides sparse resources on social media. Social media seem to be missing the National Portal of India's objective "to provide a single window access to the information and services being provided by the Indian Government for citizens and other stakeholders" (India NIC, 2013). A primary reason for this omission may be that the government officials hosting the portal do not consider social media as a credible source of information although several government agencies use social media entities such as YouTube, Twitter and blogs to spread their message.

The Indian government's social media mavens have also assigned a low priority to the presence of their head of state, the prime minister's profile on Twitter. In response to widespread complaints, Twitter blocked in August 2012 six fake accounts which misrepresented and impersonated India's prime minister. This occurred in a year when two-thirds of all world leaders were significantly communicating on Twitter, as reported by the Twiplomacy study of 2012 (Lüfkens et al., 2012a).

As the Twiplomacy study pointed out lapses in the Indian Prime Minister's use of Twitter as a networking tool it stated:

> "The Prime Minister of India is the latest of the G20 leaders to embrace Twitter in late January 2012. Manmohan Singh has tried, so far unsuccessfully, to connect with his peers in Moscow, London and Washington on Twitter" (Lüfkens et al., 2012a).

However, the Twitter account of the Prime Minister of India could have functioned better, as this excerpt from the Twiplomacy study indicates:

> The Twitter account, run by the office of the Indian Prime Minister is quite active with an average of almost 5 tweets a day. The account was started in an effort to inform people about the work done by his office and is managed by his communications team. It is clear that the main purpose of the account is to disseminate information, as the tweets are mainly government news and announcements, quotes from statements made by the prime minister, messages to the people

from the prime minister and what is "happening now" at the Prime Minister's Office. Engagement on the account is extremely limited. Only 1% of his tweets are @replies and 5% retweets. However, the account is considered a great source of information as almost 95% of the tweets have been retweeted. The most popular tweet sent by the Prime Minister is a message of sorrow after the brutal assault and murder that took place in late 2012 in New Delhi: "While she may have lost her battle for life, it is up to us all to ensure that her death will not have been in vain." The account is mutually following only the Prime Minister of Singapore (Lüfkens et al., 2012a).

Despite its professed status as a technology power house, India did not feature in the "Top 25 most connected World Leaders on Twitter" list" of Twiplomacy report, which was based on a global study of world leaders on Twitter (Lüfkens et al., 2012a). The study found Twitter accounts in two-thirds of the 193 UN member countries. However, 45% of the 264 accounts analyzed were personal accounts of heads of state and government and only 30 world leaders tweet themselves and very few on a regular basis, the study concluded (Lüfkens et al., 2012a).

The Twiplomacy study reported that India's Twitter presence was devoid of direct interaction with other world leaders and was among half of world leader accounts analyzed that don't follow any of their peers. Nearly 25% of world leaders and governments follow President Barack Obama and the White House, but @BarackObama and the @WhiteHouse established mutual Twitter relations with only three other world leaders: Norway's Jens Stoltenberg, the UK Prime Minister and Russia's Dmitry Medvedev (Lüfkens et al., 2012a). India was also not among the governments using Twitter for automated news feed from their website or Facebook page (Lüfkens et al., 2012a). The Twiplomacy study reported that the 264 government accounts analyzed cumulatively attracted more than 5 million followers (Lüfkens et al., 2012a).

India was not among the nine nations out of 193 country accounts that were officially managed by their government or tourism organizations (Lüfkens et al., 2012b). The study found that Twitter handles such as @GreatBritain, @Israel, and @Sweden were government-run and were successful in promoting their countries on Twitter either as part of a country promotion campaign, or an exercise in people's diplomacy (Lüfkens et al., 2012b).

India was not among the nine countries with "an official twitter account" (Lüfkens et al., 2012b). The Twitter handle @India was among the 67 Twitter "personal accounts" used by their owners for "private use" and not always with the intention of promoting the country. As the "Country Promotion" section of the Twiplomacy reports stated: "Interestingly the @India account is owned by an Indian person living in Guangzhou, China. The account owner shares pictures from his daily life and has made it clear that his Twitter handle is not for sale" (Lüfkens et al., 2012b). However, India's YouTube (http://www.youtube.com/India) channel has been officially run by India's Ministry of Tourism. The Ministry promotes tourism in India through its brand "Incredible India," that has gained renown because of its aggressive social media marketing. Such examples illustrate the opportunities of public diplomacy through social media. It also indicates India government's lack of understanding of social media as an emerging medium of global reach and impact. India's government officials were caught unaware in August 2012 when insidious rumors, spread by mobile phones and social media, disseminated bigotry and malice. Mischievous messages on India's social media have often aggravated ethnic and religious tension, especially among Hindus and Muslims. Sharp differences over communal, caste and regional issues continue to haunt Indian politics, sometimes threatening its long-standing democratic and secular ethos (Thapar, Mukhia, & Chandra, 1969; Thapar, 1977).

Such instances have prompted India's technophobic government leaders to find ways to limit social media and the Internet access. In December 2011, India's minister for communications and information technology Kapil Sibal sought to evolve guidelines to ensure that blasphemous content on the Internet or television was not allowed, because Internet and social networking sites such as Google, Microsoft, Twitter, Yahoo, and Facebook allegedly failed to respond to and cooperate with the Indian government's request to keep "objectionable" content off their sites. The move followed posts about some senior Congress party leaders, including party president Sonia Gandhi. In response to countrywide protests, the Indian minister later withdrew his move saying the Indian government did not believe in censorship.

As Google's Schmidt responded,

> *"If people in power are overly pessimistic about the Internet, their pessimism will be self-fulfilling. In seeking to control all of it, including the good parts that are working well, they'll stop good Indians from doing great things. Instead, they should focus on giving every Indian the best shot at using the Internet to make his or her country even better" (Schmidt, 2013).*

Recent government initiatives in social media indicate promise. Acknowledging the social media realities of a new India, Gujarat chief minister Narendra Modi was among the first government leaders to interact with the public on a Google+ hangout in August 2012. India's finance minister P. Chidambaram hosted March 4, 2013, an interactive session on the Federal Financial Budget for the year 2013–2014 and Planning Commission deputy chairman Montek Singh Ahluwalia interacted on March 15, 2013, with the public on the 12th Five Year Plan. Other developments also indicate promise. The Indian Army, the largest component of India's Armed force, started its Twitter communication in March 2013 and launched in May 2013 its Official Indian Army Facebook Page that attracted several "likes." India's Ministry of Information and Broadcasting launched in 2013 the "MyIndia Initiative—Digital Volunteer Programme," which is "aimed at people who are keen to use their personal social presence on different social media platforms to talk about Government schemes and programmes" (India I&B Ministry, 2013a). Deeply "rooted in the ideals of Participative Governance," the program seeks to help "the Government of India achieve a real time engagement with people leading to a personalized interaction with the target groups" (India I&B Ministry, 2013a). However, the initiative has evoked a lukewarm response (India I&B Ministry, 2013b).

5. Social Media Invigorate India's Psyche of Free Speech

Social media have transformed India's democratic society. India's social media have broadened and deepened India's democracy by acting as a bridge between the government and the governed. The people of India have effectively adopted social media for the pursuit of equality, entertainment and empowerment. India's social media have galvanized civil society to campaign more vigorously for institutional reforms and greater government accountability by melding multiple aspects of effective intercultural communication to act as an inexorable watchdog of democracy.

Independent watchdog organizations annually evaluate India's free speech record as a democracy. India dropped nine places to 140 in the list of 179 countries in the 2013 World Press Freedom Index, which its authors, Reporters Without Borders, said was the lowest for the "world's biggest democracy" since 2002 (Reporters Without Borders, 2013). "In Asia, India (140th, minus 9) is at its lowest since 2002 because of increasing impunity for violence against journalists and because Internet censorship continues to grow," Reporters Without Borders stated (Reporters Without Borders, 2013). Reporters Without Borders, registered in France, is a non-profit organization which defends the freedom to be informed and to inform others throughout the world.

Concerned over "a general decline in freedom of information in South Asia," the Reporters Without Borders pointed out that the Indian subcontinent experienced the sharpest deterioration in free speech in news and information in 2012. According to the report, in almost all parts of the world, influential countries, including India, that are regarded as "regional models" have fallen in the index (Reporters Without Borders, 2013).

The United States-based Freedom House rated India as "Free in Freedom in the World 2013" and "Partly Free" in Freedom of the Press 2013 and "Partly Free" in Freedom on the Net 2012 (Freedom House, 2013b). However, the Freedom House criticized the Indian government for restricting foreign funding for non-governmental organizations (NGOs). Freedom House stated that such restrictions were a "blow to civil society in India" (Freedom House, 2013b).

The Freedom House stated: "Despite this vibrant media landscape, journalists continue to face a number of constraints. The government has used security laws, criminal defamation legislation, hate-speech laws, and contempt-of-court charges to curb critical voices (Freedom House, 2013b). According to the United States-based Freedom House,

"*In September 2012, cartoonist Aseem Trivedi was arrested in Mumbai on charges of sedition for a set of cartoons that lampooned government corruption, though the charges were dropped in October. In November, two women were arrested for expressing dissent on the social-networking site Facebook regarding public mourning after the death of a prominent politician in Maharashtra*" *(Freedom House, 2013b).*

Indians have embraced social media to voice their opinions, exercise their free speech rights and fight for freedom. In its best role, India's social media have acted as an important source, albeit dubious, for news and information, a crowd-sourced critic of the government, a vibrant voice of the people, a vociferous critic of corruption and other socially endemic problems, an intellectual interpreter of events; and a forum for public expression of censure and praise. Thus, India's social media have not only influenced democracy but helped preserve it.

5.1. India's Rich Legacy of Free Speech

The confrontation between the Indian government and free speech activists escalated in April 2011 over restrictive regulations on social media. Social media have changed life and liberty in India. Activists oppose "draconian" sections of India's Information Technology Act 2000 that limits Internet freedom and they filed public interest litigations to challenge anti-freedom laws in the Supreme Court, among other courts. The protesters engaged the people by enunciating the harmful effects of the Internet regulation.

The quest for free speech in contemporary India dates back to the 18th century after Britain's East India Company emerged as rulers of India. India's first newspaper appeared under fortuitous circumstances in the 1760s when the East India Company's Indian empire grew to paramount power (Barns, 1940). Despite its business and imperial power, the Indian empire was devoid of newspapers in Calcutta, the seat of British colonial rule for decades and second only to London in population. In 1780, James Augustus Hicky, an expatriate Irishman, published India's first English newspaper, the Bengal Gazette or the Calcutta General Advertiser. Hicky quickly realized that truly distinguished newspapers should serve society, even at the risk of official displeasure. His newspaper made interesting reading with its ample dose of scurrilous reporting, risqué advertisements reflecting low morality in society, and scandalous accounts of the misdeeds of British administrators. In 1781, British rulers charged him with libel. He was harassed, attacked, and jailed. Undaunted, Hicky continued to edit his newspaper from prison, though his publication did not survive long and Hicky died a pauper in 1802.

The early 19th century saw the birth of several newspapers, both in English and regional Indian languages. In 1818, the Baptist missionaries of Serampore published a Bengali newspaper, Samachar Darpan (The Mirror of Truth) and the English periodical, The Friend of India, which were self-proclaimed organs of Christian thought and doctrine. Ram Mohan Roy, the Indian leader and social reformer, published in 1821 the Bengali newspaper, Sambad Kaumudi (Moon of Reason), which propagated the radical Western Hindu viewpoint. By 1822, there were six Bengali papers in and around the Calcutta area with circulations of 400 to 800 copies and widespread influence among readers. In 1823, when the British tried to censor the Calcutta press, Roy, as founder and editor of India's earliest newspapers, organized a protest designating freedom of speech and religion as natural rights for the people. Founded in July 1822, the Gujarati publication, Bombay Samachar, has been the oldest continuously published newspaper in India (SarDesai, 2008).

The newspaper emerged as a powerful social and political force during the freedom movement in India (Besant, 1915; Borden, 1989; Ion, 1997). The British rulers enacted in 1878 the Vernacular Press Act to repress "seditious propaganda" in regional language newspapers. Lord Lytton, the British viceroy, denounced vernacular newspapers as "mischievous scribblers preaching open sedition" to end the British Raj. Faced with severe criticism and protest, the British rulers repealed the Act in 1882 (Natarajan, 1954-55). In 1880, Bal Gangadhar Tilak, a social reformer and nationalist, founded the Marathi daily Kesari (Lion), which attracted widespread readership for its opposition to British rule. British officials jailed Tilak in 1897 for his writings.

Fewer than two decades later, Mahatma Gandhi, the architect of India's freedom from British rule, played a prominent role as editor of three newspapers—Young India, Harijan (meaning "child of God," coined as a euphemism for Untouchables by Gandhi in 1931) and Navajivan, (New Life)—which became major vehicles for Gandhian thought and action. As an outstanding 20th century leader, Gandhi authored a prodigious number of words. Through his newspaper columns, he assiduously propagated his ideas as a prophet of non-violence and Satyagraha (the firmness of truth). This empowered members of the meek Indian masses to fight against seemingly invincible British rule (Vadgama, 1997; Thapar-Björkert, 2006). In 1938, Gandhi's lieutenant Jawaharlal Nehru founded the English newspaper, National Herald, and its sister Urdu publication Qaumi Awaz ("Voice of the Community") to uphold such national values as secularism and non-alignment. Nehru, who became the first prime minister of independent India in 1947, gained renown for his political acumen and scholarship.

India gained independence from British rule in 1947. India's founding fathers cherished free speech. Deriving freedoms from Western liberalism, the Indian Constitution provides for "the right to freedom of speech and expression," but stipulates the government can restrict those rights under some circumstances, such as maintenance of public order, state security, and public morality. In 1975, under controversial circumstances of political instability, India declared a "State of Emergency" to restore the "security of India threatened by internal disturbances" (Government of India, 1977). During the 21-month "State of Emergency" (1975-77), Prime Minister Indira Gandhi imposed restrictions on the media, curtailed civil liberties, suspended elections, and resorted to severe misuse of power (Grover & Ranjana, 1997). Opposition leaders and journalists were jailed. However, the press in India survived the "State of Emergency" to report Indira Gandhi's defeat in the 1977 general elections. Unshackled from draconian excesses of the Emergency, people called for institutional reforms and greater government accountability (Tully & Masani, 1988; Anant & D'Harnoncourt, 1997; Ryan, 1977). This led to a massive increase in the number of newspapers and magazines, contributing to a media boom.

In 2005, India introduced the Right to Information Act that authorizes citizens to request information from a "public authority," which has been stipulated to reply "expeditiously or within 30 days." The act also requires public authorities to computerize their records for wide dissemination and to proactively publish certain categories of information. With the crusading zeal of a perpetual adversary, the Indian media campaigned and influenced public demands for this right with fervent calls for a free flow of information.

Freedom House has commended India for the role of the 2005 Right to Information Act to "improve transparency and expose corrupt activities" (Freedom House, 2013a). But the organization expressed concern that, "while this legislation has had clear positive effects, over a dozen right to information activists have reportedly been killed since late 2009 (Freedom House, 2013, May 1).

In Asian nations like China and India cultural attitudes toward media freedom are often distinctly different (Price, Verhulst, & Morgan, 2013). The power of social media derives from diverse aspects such as "Urban informatics, social media, ubiquitous computing, and mobile technology to support citizen engagement" (Foth, 2011), "networked nonprofits" drive change by connecting with social media (Kanter & Fine, 2010), through real-world social media engagement (Fouts, 2009) They negotiate the needs of a media ecosystem where the fittest survive and thrive, as social media change work, life, and the future (Blossom, 2009). Non-Western models that transcend the international supranational economic and political groupings are redefining free speech in India (Price et al., 2013). That has led to India's somewhat checkered record of freedom.

6. Lessons Learned in Free Speech and Social Media

In conclusion, social media have enhanced India's media and communications landscape by facilitating a more participatory networked population to gaining greater access to information, more opportunities to engage in civil society, and cultivate collective action. In the birthplace of nonviolence, India's activists convened public protests using online and traditional tools. Thousands of social media users started online petitions as a public space to register their protest. Some protesters relied on the global reach of social media to influence public opinion worldwide and gain media attention. Dissenters adopted crowdsourcing and other participatory activities, online and offline, to fight for free speech

Activists Embraced Six Strategies to Foster Free Speech in India

The confrontation between the Indian government and free speech activists escalated in April 2011 over restrictive regulations of social media.

← *A 1972 commemorative postage stamp released on the 25ᵗʰ anniversary of India's independence depicts the people celebrating Independence Day by holding high the Indian flag in front of the Indian Parliament.*

Lobby the
Leaders

❖ In the birthplace of nonviolence, India's activists convened public protests using online and traditional tools.

Engage the
People

❖ The protesters engaged the people by enunciating the harmful effects of Internet regulation.

Protest
Online

❖ Thousands of social media users started online petitions, using the internet as a public space to register their protest.

Solicit Global
Support

❖ Protesters relied on the global reach of social media to influence public opinion worldwide.

Seek Justice
in Court

❖ Activists filed public interest litigations to challenge anti-freedom laws in the Supreme Court, as well as lower courts.

Crowdsource
Complaints

❖ Dissenters adopted participatory activities, online and offline, to fight for free speech.

Figure 4: Nonviolent Protest: India's activists embraced six strategies to foster free speech in social media. (© Debashis Aikat 2014)

6. 1. Social Media Crackdown Chills Free Speech in India.

The exponential growth of India's social media has led to an explosion of communications surveillance. So, government officials have a propensity or an aggressive urge to know and control when, where, and with whom a citizen is communicating. In sharp contrast to such surveillance attempts, India's constitution guarantees freedom of expression for its citizens. The right to freedom of expression is an essential requirement for democracy because needless interference with citizens ' privacy can both directly and indirectly limit the free development and exchange of ideas for the young and the old (PII, 1981).

The India government's attempted crackdown in 2012 on free speech in social media and the Internet was criticized as a failed effort to squelch dissent and chill free speech. Such crackdown chills free speech because restrictions on social media and the Internet communication dissuade people from their freedom to express their opinion.

In a legal context, the government's threat of legal sanction imparts a chilling effect that inhibits and discourages legitimate exercise of a constitutional right. Such chilling effect curtails and suppresses the right to free speech. A chilling effect may be caused by legal actions such as the passing of a law, the decision of a court, or the threat of a lawsuit; any legal action that would cause people to hesitate to exercise a legitimate right (freedom of speech or otherwise) for fear of legal repercussions. When that fear is brought about by the threat of a libel lawsuit, it is called libel chill.

India's multi-party democracy has long considered its free flow of information as a force to sustain democracy. India's government also appreciates that democracy, freedom of information and free speech are fundamental contributions to the fulfillment of human aspirations. Faced with vast capabilities in a digital age, India government's crackdown attempt highlights journalism's essential role in democracy.

6. 2. Media Freedom Enhances Intercultural Communication

The crackdown of India's social media prompted demands to the Indian government to respect its commitment to media freedom. It also provides a significant opportunity for social media users to realize the importance of ethical practices that contribute to media freedom. For instance, the ethical contours of social media communication in India have not been outlined even as India's social media have reshaped civil society, politics and the public sphere. An increasing number of politicians and political parties use social media platforms and have misused social media messages to spread rumors under the guise of free speech.

Throughout its rich legacy as a multi-party democracy, India has promoted socio-economic policies to advance and support independent and pluralistic media. The Indian government seems committed, in both letter and spirit, to the belief that independent, pluralistic and free media are essential to effective intercultural communication that nurtures democracy in a nation. Social media complicate that paradigm because of its amorphous roles in serving as medium of personal communication and mass dissemination of information. For instance the widespread connotation of an independent press refers to a media organization that is independent from governmental, political or centralized economic control or from control of materials and infrastructure essential for the production and dissemination of newspapers, magazines and periodicals. Similarly, a pluralistic press is contingent upon the absence of monopolies of any kind and the existence of the greatest possible number of newspapers, magazines and periodicals reflecting the widest possible range of opinion within the community. In striking contrast to such traditional media models, social media encompass and extend the independence and pluralistic role of media to magnanimous proportions such as global dissemination at minimal cost.

6.3. Limitations, Caveats and Directions for Future Research

Some caveats and limitations relate to some research decisions and, therefore, temper the conclusions and the results of the research reported in this chapter. This research study examined 32 multidisciplinary English language article databases that encompass humanities and social sciences disciplines, international and foreign areas studies, and the sciences. Future research projects that are based on research publication databases may yield works in languages other than English, which was beyond the purview of this study. Further, we examined only sensitized concepts of intercultural communication relating to free speech and the role of social media in India. It would be worthwhile to compare the results of this study with other sensitized concepts in languages other than English. The research analysis for this current study was restricted to the content of relevant works in English language and publication period of May 2002 through July 2013, a time period of more than 10 years. It may be pertinent to explore the dimensions of intercultural communication relating to free speech, if any, in other time periods such future years.

7. Epilogue: When Freedom Tweets

Social media have decentralized and deepened democracy by acting as a bridge between the government and the people. To this end, social media have galvanized civil society by motivating citizens to campaign more vigorously for institutional reforms and greater government accountability by melding multiple democratic roles as an inexorable watchdog of democracy.

Technology giants such as Google have propounded open access to the Internet for India, As Google's Schmidt observed, "The past 10 years show that the safest economic, social and political bet is on openness. Where there is a free and open Web, where there is unbridled technological progress, where information can be disseminated and consumed freely, society flourishes" (Schmidt, 2013).

In its worst role, India's social media have been misused for propaganda and rumors. In its best role, the India's social media have served society as a reliable source for news and information, a credible critic of the government, an active adversary, an investigator of corruption, an intellectual interpreter of events, and a forum for public expression of censure and praise. Thus, Indian social media have not only influenced democracy but helped preserve it.

Five Key Attributes of India's Social Media Revolution

← *Many social media users display this iconic postage stamp to support free speech. The stamp depicts the Hindi words 'Jai Hind' (Long Live India) at the top right, and on the left, 15 Aug. 1947, the date of India's independence from British rule. When it was issued on November 21, 1947, this stamp was among the first three postage stamps of independent India.*

Since their emergence in 2004, social media have re-defined life and liberty in India, the world's largest and most populous democracy.

Facebook's
Mobile Users

❖ India's Facebook users soared to 82 million in June 2013, up 5% from 78 million a year ago (Facebook, 2013, July 24).

❖ Nearly 76% of India's users accessed Facebook through their mobile devices rather than through other digital devices (Facebook, 2013, July 24).

Google Tops
Unique Visits

❖ Google hosted 90% of Internet searches in India and its sites (like YouTube, Google+) ranked first in unique visitors. Facebook followed, along with sites like Yahoo, Microsoft and Wikimedia (comScore, 2013).

Social Media
Marketplace

❖ While Orkut lost users in India, Linkedin and Twitter gained consumers, as did Pinterest and Tumbler (comScore, 2013).

Urban Rural
Teledensity

❖ Most Indians access social media through mobile phones. The teledensity of mobile phones numbered 139 (60%) in urban areas compared to 41 (40%) in rural areas in June 2013 (TRAI, 2013).

Gender Ratio
Skewed

❖ India's online population remains skewed at 39% women, which is lower than the worldwide average of 47%. The heaviest users are Men under 35 and women between 35 and 44 (comScore, 2013).

Figure 5: Internet Revolution: Social media have re-defined life and liberty in India. (© Debashis Aikat 2014)

With a theoretical conceptualization of intercultural communication, the chapter has delineated the state of social media in India and incorporated research that presents theoretical perspectives on the role of social media in India's democratic society. Based on a meta-analysis research method within the larger intellectual context of intercultural communication, this chapter theorizes that a commitment to free speech sustains social media's new found freedom in India's democratic society. This chapter concludes that social media have invigorated India's psyche of free speech amidst a confluence of conflict, culture and censorship.

By identifying theoretically-grounded implications of free speech, this chapter explicates how India's legacy of free speech has protected the freedom of expression for millions of India's citizens—regardless of religion, education or income. India's rising number of active Internet users and their communication on social media have disseminated among the people of India important issues and ideas that they need to understand the world.

India's social media entities constitute a medium without gatekeepers and, therefore, subject to wanton distortion and serious discussion. To that end, India's social media has filled a widening gap in the media milieu by engaging its audience with discourse about social problems such as corruption, among other mediated information that traditional media invariably overlook. India's social media have, therefore, enhanced intercultural communication by fostering free speech through media content.

By theorizing intercultural communication and social media at the threshold of research about technology, media and culture, it may be useful to revisit the public controversy and concern about truth in social media and free speech in India to learn from the past, perceive the present and prepare for the future. It may also be useful to conduct research that may compare and contrast, in greater detail, the power and peril of social media as an artifact of free speech in India and how it feeds the news agenda of the traditional media such as newspapers, radio, and television.

As an innovation in intercultural communication, India's social media have significantly contributed to the evolution and proliferation of information in India's multicultural society. As communication channels continue to flourish, fragment and demassify India's media repertoire, India's social media have transformed their role in India's democratic society with sustaining changes such as mutating from media persuasion to building relationships, redefining models that stereotype intercultural communication, and fostering freedom of expression with intercultural communication strategies that are constantly challenged, tested, and refined.

We hope this chapter will inform and inspire other researchers to focus on the role of social media as an essential element of intercultural communication and free speech in India. Other researchers may replicate this study to appraise the role of social media in India's democratic society as a research paradigm to explore cultural and critical perspectives that abate or advance intercultural communication and free speech in other nations. Such research replications highlight the importance of the intercultural communication, social media and free speech as research paradigms that inspired academic researchers and professionals to explore the surging significance of social media in the 21st century and beyond.

As a contemporary medium for intercultural communication and free speech, India's social media complement print, broadcast and other traditional media to fulfill a joint mandate of providing a voice for marginalized communities, diverse cultural groups, and other segments of society. India's social media's deeply engaging, informative, and analytical messages have galvanized its people to reshape the role of media in India's democratic society.

Acknowledgment

The author gratefully acknowledges his debt to Dr. Michael Prosser, Dr. Uli Spalthoff, and Professor Cui Litang for leading this book project and thanks four anonymous reviewers and Ms. Jacqueline Yvonne Borrett for their critiques to earlier versions of this research project; Mr. Mark Staines, Ms. Charnelle Williams, Ms. Divya Aikat and Mr. Vikram Aikat for research help; and Dr. Jay Aikat for research feedback and ideas to enhance this study.

References

Aaker, J. L., Smith, A., & Adler, C. (2010). *The dragonfly effect: Quick, effective, and powerful ways to use social media to drive social change*. San Francisco, CA: Jossey-Bass.

Aggarwal, S. (2013, February 1). 2013 India Internet outlook. Techcircle. in [Web log post] Retrieved from: http://techcircle.vccircle .com/2013/02/01/2013-india-Internet-outlook/

Ahern, C. A. (2011). *Beyond individual differences: Organizing processes, information overload, and classroom learning*. New York, NY: Springer.

Aikat, D. D. & Remund, D. (2012) Of Time magazine, 24/7 media, and data deluge: The evolution of information overload theories and concepts. In J. B. Strother, J. M. Ulijn & Z. Fazal (Eds.), *Information overload: An international challenge to professional engineers and technical communicators* (pp. 15–38). IEEE Professional Communication Society, Hoboken, NJ: John Wiley & Sons and IEEE Press. DOI:10.1002/9781118360491.ch2

Akbar, M. J. (1985). *India: The siege within*. Harmondsworth, England: Penguin Books.

Akbar, M. J. (1988). *Riot after riot: Reports on caste and communal violence in India*. New Delhi, India: Penguin Books.

Akbar, M. J. (2003). *The shade of swords: Jihad and the conflict between Islam and Christianity*. London, UK: Routledge.

Alchediak, J., (2009). *India: Asian giant*. New York, NY: Insight Media

Alexander, B. (2011). *The new digital storytelling: Creating narratives with new media*. Santa Barbara, CA: Praeger.

Ali, D. (1999). *Invoking the past: The uses of history in South Asia*. New Delhi, India: Oxford University Press.

Anant, V., & D'Harnoncourt, A. (1997). *India: A celebration of independence, 1947–1997*. New York, NY: Aperture.

Aram, I. A. (2008). *Media, technology, and society*. Chennai: United Evangelical Lutheran Churches in India/Indian Society for Promoting Christian Knowledge.

Baird, M., & Ferro, M., (2003). *India sustaining reform, reducing poverty*. New Delhi, India: Oxford University Press.

Balnaves, M., Donald, S., & Shoesmith, B. (2009). *Media theories and approaches: A global perspective*. Basingstoke, UK: Palgrave Macmillan.

Barns, M. (1940). *The Indian press: A history of the growth of public opinion in India*. London, UK: G. Allen & Unwin.

Basham, A. L. (1975). *A Cultural history of India*. Oxford, UK: Clarendon Press.

Behnke, P. (Ed.) (2010). *Social media and politics: Online social networking and political communication in Asia*. Singapore: Konrad-Adenauer-Stiftung.

Bel, B., Brouwer, J., Das, B., Parthasarathi, V., & Poitevin, G. (2005). *Media and mediation*. New Delhi, India: Sage Publications.

Bel, B., Brouwer, J., Das, B., Parthasarathi, V., & Poitevin, G. (2007). *The social and the symbolic*. New Delhi, India: Sage Publications.

Bel, B., Brouwer, J., Das, B., Parthasarathi, V., & Poitevin, G. (2010). *Communication, Culture and Confrontation*. New Delhi, India: Sage Publications.

Berlatsky, N. (2013). *Social networking*. Detroit, MI: Greenhaven Press.

Besant, A. W. (1915). *India: A nation: A plea for Indian self-government*. London, UK: T.C. & E.C. Jack.

Bhat, S. & D'Souza, N. (2013, April 5). Forbes Billionaires 2013: Where India Inc. Stands. Forbes India Magazine. *Retrieved* from: http://forbesindia.com/article/special/forbes-billionaires-2013-where-india-inc-stands/34947/1

Blossom, J. (2009). *Content nation: Surviving and thriving as social media changes our work, our lives, and our future.* Indianapolis, IN: Wiley Technology.

Bollier, D. (2010). *The promise and peril of big data.* Washington, DC: Aspen Institute, Communications and Society Program, Aspen Institute Roundtable on Information Technology.

Borden, C. M., (1989). *Contemporary Indian tradition: Voices on culture, nature, and the challenge of change.* Washington, DC: Smithsonian Institution Press.

boyd, d. & Ellison, N. B. (2007). Social Network Sites: Definition, History and Scholarship. *Journal of Computer-Mediated Communication, 13*(1)

Brockman, J. (2011). *Is the Internet changing the way you think? The net's impact on our minds and future.* New York, NY: Harper Perennial.

Bryfonski, D. (2012). *The global impact of social media.* Detroit, MI: Greenhaven Press.

Cady, R., Mogdis, F., & Tidwell, K. (1984). *Major power interactions with less developed countries, 1959–1965.* Ann Arbor, MI: University of Michigan Institute for Social Research.

Carr, N. G. (2010). *The shallows: What the Internet is doing to our brains.* New York, NY: W.W. Norton.

Castells, M. (Ed.) (2004). *The network society: A cross-cultural perspective.* Cheltenham, UK: Edward Elgar

Chatterji, P. C. (1991). *Broadcasting in India.* New Delhi, India: Sage Publications.

Chomsky, N., Mitchell, P. R., & Schoeffel, J. (2002). *Understanding power: The indispensable Chomsky.* New York, NY: New Press.

Christians, C. G., & Carey, J. W. (1989). The logic and aims of qualitative research. In G. H. Stempel III, & B. H. Westley (Eds.), *Research methods in mass communication* (2nd ed., 354–374). Englewood Cliffs, NJ: Prentice-Hall.

Cohen, S. P. (2002). *India: Emerging power.* Washington, DC: Brookings Institution.

comScore (2013, August 22). 2013 India digital future in focus. Retrieved from: http://www.comscore.com/india2013

Costigan, S. S., & Perry, J. (Eds.) (2012). *Cyberspaces and global affairs.* Farnham, UK: Ashgate.

Creekmur, C. K., & Sidel, M. (2007). *Cinema, law and the state in Asia.* Basingstoke, UK: Palgrave Macmillan.

Dallmayr, F. R. (2002). *Dialogue among civilizations: Some exemplary voices.* New York, NY: Palgrave Macmillan.

Deibert, R. (2012). *Access contested: Security, identity, and resistance in Asian cyberspace.* Cambridge, MA: MIT Press.

Donahue, R. T., & Prosser, M. H. (1996). *Diplomatic discourse: International conflict at the United Nations; Addresses and analysis.* Norwood, NJ: Ablex.

Dyson, L. E., Hendriks, M. A. N., & Grant, S. (Eds.) (2007). *Information technology and indigenous people.* Hershey, PA: Information Science Publishing.

Emden, C. (2012). *Changing perceptions of the public sphere.* New York, NY: Berghahn Books.

Engineer, A. (2004). *Communal riots after independence : A comprehensive account.* Delhi, India: Shipra.

Ess, C., & Sudweeks, F. (2001). *Culture, technology, communication: Towards an intercultural global village.* Albany, NY: State University of New York Press.

Facebook. (2013a, May 1). Facebook Reports First Quarter 2013 Results [Press release]. Retrieved from http://investor.fb.com/releasedetail.cfm?ReleaseID=761090

Facebook. (2013b, July 24). Facebook Reports Second Quarter 2013 Results [Press release]. Retrieved from http://investor.fb.com/releasedetail.cfm?ReleaseID=780093

Feher, M. (2007). *Nongovernmental politics.* New York, NY: Zone Books.

Firth, K., & Hand, F. (2001). *India: Fifty years after independence.* Leeds, England: Peepal Tree Press.

Fischer, H. D., & Merrill, J. C. (1970). *International communication: Media, channels, functions.* New York, NY: Hastings House.

Fischer, H. D., & Merrill, J. C. (1976). *International and intercultural communication.* New York, NY: Hastings House.

Forest, J. J. F. (2007). *Countering terrorism and insurgency in the 21st century: International perspectives.* Westport, CT: Praeger Security International.

Fortner, R. S., & Fackler, M. (Eds.) (2010). *Ethics & evil in the public sphere: Media, universal values and global development: Essays in honor of Clifford G. Christians.* Cresskill, NJ: Hampton Press.

Foth, M. (2011). *From social butterfly to engaged citizen: Urban informatics, social media, ubiquitous computing, and mobile technology to support citizen engagement.* Cambridge, MA: MIT Press.

Fouts, J. (2009). *Social media success! Practical advice and real-world examples for social media engagement.* Cupertino, CA: Happy About. info.

Freedman, L. (2009). *The offensive art: Political satire and its censorship around the world from Beerbohm to Borat.* Westport, CT: Praeger.

Freedom Forum. (1999). *Media at the millennium:* India. Arlington, VA: Freedom Forum. Retrieved from http://www.freedomforum.org/publications/international/MediaForum/1999/asia/indiaforum.pdf

Freedom House (2013a, May 1). Freedom of the Press 2013. Retrieved from: http://www.freedomhouse.org/report/freedom-world/2013/india

Freedom House (2013b, May 20). Restrictions on NGOs Threaten Civil Society in India, the World's Largest Democracy [news release). Retrieved from: http://www.freedomhouse.org/report/freedom-press/freedom-press-2013

Friedman, T. L. (2005). *The world is flat : A brief history of the twenty-first century.* New York, NY: Farrar, Straus and Giroux.

Gillmor, D. (2004). *We the media: Grassroots journalism by the people, for the people.* Sebastopol, CA: O'Reilly.

Glasser, C. J. (2013). *International libel and privacy handbook: A global reference for journalists, publishers, webmasters, and lawyers.* Hoboken, NJ: Bloomberg Press.

Gojkov, G. (2011). Education as a factor of intercultural communication. *CEPS Journal 1*(2), 87–104.

Golding, P. & Murdock, G. (1979). Ideology and the Mass Media: The Question of Determination. In M. Barrett, P. Corrigan, A. Kuhn & J. Wolff (Eds.) *Ideology and Cultural Production.* New York, NY: St. Martin's Press.

Goodwin, J. & Jasper, J. M. (2012). *Contention in context : Political opportunities and the emergence of protest.* Stanford, CA: Stanford University Press.

Gopalan, S. (1998). *India and human rights.* New Delhi, India: Lok Sabha Secretariat.

Government of India (1977, August). White paper on misuse of mass media during the internal emergency. New Delhi, India: Controller of Publications.

Gramsci, A. (1985). *Selections from Cultural Writings.* D. Forgacs, G. Nowell-Smith and T. W. Boelhower (Eds.). London, UK: Lawrence and Wishart.

Grover, V., & Ranjana, A. (1997). *India: Fifty years of independence.* New Delhi, India: Deep & Deep.

Gudykunst, W. B. (Ed.) (2005). *Theorizing about intercultural communication.* Thousand Oaks, CA: Sage.

Haerens, M., & Zott, L. M. (2013). *The Arab spring.* Detroit, MI: Greenhaven Press.

Hall, S. 1979. *Culture, the Media, and the 'Ideological Effect'*. In *Mass Communication and Society,* edited by J. Curran, M. Gurevitch and J. Woollacott. Wesbury Park, CA: Sage Publications.

Handley, A., & Chapman, C. C. (2011). *Content rules: How to create killer blogs, podcasts, videos, ebooks, webinars (and more) that engage customers and ignite your business.* Hoboken, NJ: Wiley.

Haynes, J. D. (Ed.) (2002). *Internet management issues: A global perspective.* Hershey, PA.: Idea Group Publishing.

Heitzman, J. & Worden, R. L (1995). *India: A country study.* Washington, DC: Library of Congress. Retrieved from http://lcweb2.loc.gov/frd/cs/intoc.html

Hershock, P. D., Stepaniants, M. T., & Ames, R. T. (2003). *Technology and cultural values: On the edge of the third millennium.* East-West Philosophers' Conference. Honolulu, HI: University of Hawaii Press.

Hofstede, G. H. (2001). *Culture's consequences: Comparing values, behaviors, institutions, and organizations across nations.* Thousand Oaks, CA: Sage Publications.

Holledge, J., & Tompkins, J. (2000). *Women's intercultural performance.* London, UK: Routledge.

Hooker, R. D. (2011). *First with the truth: Synchronized communications in the counterinsurgency fight.* Arlington, VA: Institute of Land Warfare, Association of the United States Army.

IAMAI (2013, March 12). Internet & Mobile Association of India report on social media in India—2012 Retrieved from: http://www.iamai.in/rsh_pay.aspx?rid=0B2QPqlHSwM=

IBEF (2013a). India Brand Equity Foundation. Retrieved from http://www.ibef.org

IBEF (2013b). India Brand Equity Foundation Media and Entertainment Industry. Retrieved from http://www.ibef.org/industry/media-entertainment-india.aspx

India I&B Ministry (2013a, February 7). MyIndia initiative - digital volunteer programme. Retrieved from: http://inbministry.blogspot.com/2013/02/myindia-initiative-digital-volunteer.html

India I&B Ministry (2013b, June 14). Contributions from Digital Volunteers. Retrieved from: http://inbministry.blogspot.com/p/contributions-from-digital-volunteers.html

India NIC (2013). National Informatics Centre National Portal of India. Retrieved from http://india.gov.in/

Ion, E. (1997). *India: 50 years of independence.* London, UK: Lloyd's List.

Ishida, T. (Ed.) (2010). *Culture and computing: Computing and communication for crosscultural interaction.* Berlin, Germany: Springer.

Islam, M. M., & Ehsan, M. (Eds.) (2013). *From government to e-governance: Public administration in the digital age.* Hershey, PA: Information Science Reference.

Jahanbegloo, R., & Thapar, R. (2008). I*ndia revisited: Conversations on contemporary India.* New Delhi, India: Oxford University Press.

Jain, D. (1975). *Indian women.* New Delhi, India: Publications Division, Ministry of Information and Broadcasting, Government of India.

Jain, N. C., Prosser, M. H., & Miller, M. H., (Eds.) (1974). *Intercultural communication: Proceedings.* New York, NY: Speech Communication Association.

Jarvis, J. (2009). *What would Google do?* New York, NY: Collins Business.

Jarvis, J. (2011). *Public parts : How sharing in the digital age improves the way we work and live.* New York, NY: Simon & Schuster.

Jarvis, P. (2007). *Globalisation, lifelong learning and the learning society: Sociological perspectives.* London, UK: Routledge.

Kanter, B., & Fine, A. H. (2010). *The networked nonprofit: Connecting with social media to drive change.* San Francisco, CA: Jossey-Bass.

Kaur, R., & Mazzarella, W. (2009). *Censorship in South Asia: Cultural regulation from sedition to seduction.* Bloomington, IN: Indiana University Press.

Keen, A. (2007). *The cult of the amateur: How today's Internet is killing our culture.* New York, NY: Doubleday/Currency.

Kelty, C. (2005). Geeks, social imaginaries, and recursive publics. *Cultural Anthropology, 20*(2), 185–214 doi: 10.1525/can.2005.20.2.185

Kelty, C. M. (2008). *Two bits: The cultural significance of free software.* Durham, NC: Duke University Press.

Kelly, U. A. (2009). *Migration and education in a multicultural world : Culture, loss, and identity* (1st ed.). New York, NY: Palgrave Macmillan.

Kim, Y. (2012). *Women and the media in Asia: The precarious self.* Basingstoke, UK: Palgrave Macmillan.

Kline, D., Burstein, D., De, K. A. J., & Berger, P. (2005). *Blog! How the newest media revolution is changing politics, business, and culture.* New York, NY: CDS Books.

Kovach, B., & Rosenstiel, T. (2010). *Blur: How to know what's true in the age of information overload.* New York, NY: Bloomsbury.

Kranzberg, M. (1986). Technology and history: Kranzberg's laws. *Technology and Culture, 27*(3), 544–560.

Lal, A. (1995). *India: Enough is enough.* New Delhi, India: Virgo Publications.

Lamb, B. P. (1966). *India: A world in transition.* New York, NY: F.A. Praeger.

Lent, J. A., & Fitzsimmons, L. (2013). *Asian popular culture: New, hybrid, and alternate media.* Lanham, MD: Lexington Books.

Lippman, W. (1922). *Public opinion.* New York, NY: Macmillan.

Lüfkens, M. et al, (2012a, July). Twiplomacy study of world leaders: Mutual relations on Twitter (Burson-Marsteller's #Twiplomacy study published online on July 26, 2012). Retrieved from http://twiplomacy.com/twiplomacy-study-2012/

Lüfkens, M. et al, (2012b, November). Country Promotion on Twitter (Burson-Marsteller's #Twiplomacy study published online on November 15, 2012) Retrieved from http://twiplomacy.com/country-promotion/

Magnan, S. S. (2008). *Mediating discourse online.* Amsterdam, The Netherlands: John Benjamins Publishing.

Mainwaring, S. (2011). *We first: How brands and consumers use social media to build a better world.* New York, NY: Palgrave Macmillan.

Mandiberg, M. (Ed.) (2012) *The social media reader.* New York, NY: NYU Press

Mansfield, H. (2012). *Social media for social good: A how-to guide for nonprofits.* New York, NY: McGraw-Hill.

Martin, E., & Wilson, G. B. (1997). *Hong Kong speaks: Free expression while becoming China.* Hong Kong: Hong Kong Baptist University.

Matsuura, K. (2009). *Changing world, new challenges: Selected speeches 2007-2008.* Paris, France: UNESCO.

Matynia, E. (2009). *Performative democracy.* Boulder, CO: Paradigm Publishers.

McIntyre-Mills, J. J. (2000). *Global citizenship and social movements: Creating transcultural webs of meaning for the new millennium.* Amsterdam, The Netherlands: Harwood Academic.

Mendelson, B. J. (2012). *Social media is bullshit.* New York, NY: St. Martin's Press.

Merino, N. (2013). *Civil liberties.* Detroit, MI: Greenhaven Press.

Mintz, A. P. (2012). *Web of deceit: Misinformation and manipulation in the age of social media.* Medford, NJ: CyberAge Books.

Mohammed, S. N. (2011). *Communication and the globalization of culture: Beyond tradition and borders.* Lanham, MD: Lexington Books.

Mohammed, S. N. (2012). *The (dis)information age: The persistence of ignorance.* New York, NY: Peter Lang.

Mohanty, N. (2012). *Radicalism in Islam: Resurgence and ramifications.* Lanham, MD: University Press of America.

Monier-Williams, M. (1875). *Indian wisdom or examples of the religious, philosophical, and ethical doctrines of the Hindūs with a brief history of the chief departments of Sanskrit literature, and some account of the past and present condition of India, moral and intellectual.* London, UK: W.H. Allen & Company Retrieved from babel.hathitrust.org/cgi/pt?id=mdp.39015047654432

Moraes, F. R., Howe, E., & Galbraith, J. K. (1974). *India.* New York, NY: McGraw-Hill.

Morris, N., & Waisbord, S. R. (2001). *Media and globalization: Why the state matters.* Lanham, MD: Rowman & Littlefield.

Naipaul, V. S. (1991). *India: A million mutinies now.* London, UK: Vintage.

Naipaul, V. S. (2003). *India: A wounded civilization.* New York, NY: Vintage Books.

Narayan, J., & Meherally, Y. (2006). *India: Struggle for freedom, political, social and economic.* Gurgaon, India: Hope India Publications.

Natarajan, J. (1954-55). *History of Indian journalism: Part II of the report of the Press Commission.* New Delhi, India: Publications Division, Ministry of Information and Broadcasting.

Ninan, S. (2007). *Headlines from the heartland : Reinventing the Hindi public sphere.* Los Angeles, CA: Sage Publications.

Orbe, M. P., Flores, L. A., & Allen, B. J. (Eds.) (2008). *Intercultural communication in a transnational world.* Washington, DC: National Communication Association.

Packer, C. A. A. (2002). *Using human rights to change tradition: Traditional practices harmful to women's reproductive health in Sub-Saharan Africa.* Antwerp, Belgium: Intersentia.

Pager, S. A., & Candeub, A. (2012). *Transnational culture in the Internet age.* Cheltenham, England: Edward Elgar.

Panagariya, A. (2008). *India: The emerging giant.* New York, NY: Oxford University Press.

Partridge, K. (2011). *Social networking.* New York, NY: H.W. Wilson.

PII (1981). Press Institute of India report on the status of journalism & communication education in India. New Delhi, India: University Grants Commission.

Prasad, C. S. (2005). *India: Economic policies and performance, 1947–48 to 2004–05: Year-wise economic review of the Indian economy since independence.* Delhi, India: New Century.

Price, M. E., Verhulst, S., & Morgan, L. (Eds.) (2013). *Routledge handbook of media law.* Abingdon, UK: Routledge.

Prosser, M. H. (Ed.) (1972). *Intercommunication among nations and peoples.* New York, NY: Harper & Row.

Prosser, M. H. (1973). *Major books on intercultural communication.* Pittsburgh, PA: Intercultural Communications Network of the Regional Council for International Education.

Prosser, M. H. (1978). *The cultural dialogue: An introduction to intercultural communication.* Boston, MA: Houghton Mifflin.

Prosser, M. H. (1978b). *USIA intercultural communication course: 1977 proceedings.* Washington, DC: International Communication Agency.

Prosser, M. H., & Sitaram, K. S. (Eds.) (1999). *Civic discourse: Intercultural, international, and global media.* Stamford, CT: Ablex.

Qualman, E. (2009). *Socialnomics: How social media transforms the way we live and do business.* Hoboken, NJ: Wiley.

Rajagopal, A. (2009). *The Indian public sphere : readings in media history.* New Delhi, India: Oxford University Press.

Rao, M. (Ed.) (2003). *News media and new media : The Asia-Pacific Internet handbook, episode V.* Singapore: Eastern Universities Press.

Rao, M., & Mendoza, L. (Eds.) (2005). *Asia unplugged: The wireless and mobile media boom in the Asia-Pacific.* Thousand Oaks, CA: Response Books.

Rares, E., Fenger, L., Rosenmeier, L., Ehlers, L. N., & Carl, S. M., (2006). *In between freedom and equality.* København, Denmark: Copenhagen Business School Institut for Interkulturel Kommunikation

Ravi, B. K. (2013). New media order for a safe South Asia. Academic *Research International 4*(2) March 2013. Retrieved from http://www. savap.org.pk/journals/ARInt./Vol.4%282%29/2013%284.2-13%29. pdf, 143-156

Remund, D. & Aikat, D. D. (2012) Drowning in data: A review of information overload within organizations and the viability of strategic communication principles. In J. B. Strother, J. M. Ulijn & Z. Fazal (Eds.), *Information overload: An international challenge to professional engineers and technical communicators* (pp. 231–246). IEEE Professional Communication Society, Hoboken, NJ: John Wiley & Sons and IEEE Press. DOI:10.1002/9781118360491.ch11

Reporters Without Borders (2013, January 31). 2013 World Press Freedom Index. Retrieved from: http://en.rsf.org/press-freedom-index-2013,1054.html

RNI (2012, December 28). Ministry of Information & Broadcasting: Press in India: 2011-12 annual report of the office of the Registrar of Newspapers for India. *Retrieved* from: http://inbministry.blogspot. com/2012/12/press-in-india-2011-12.html

Rosen, L., Dabney, L. M., Hamilton, L., & Seay, G. L. (2009). Communicating across culture: Edmund Wilson: A life in literature: The Lee Hamilton commentaries: In *Congress, first impressions matter. The Lee Hamilton commentaries in the U.S.* [sound recording] Washington: Woodrow Wilson International Center for Scholars.

Rothermund, D. (2008). *India : The rise of an Asian giant.* New Haven, CT: Yale University Press.

Ruff, L., & Schwartau, W. (2010). *#Privacy tweet: Addressing privacy concerns in the day of social media.* Cupertino, CA: THINKaha.

Russell, M. A. (2011). *Mining the social web.* Sebastopol, CA: O'Reilly.

Ryan, N. (1977). *India: Nationalism and independence.* Kuala Lumpur: Longman.

Sahai, S. B. (1997). *India: Twilight at midday (Untold story of a sick society).* New Delhi, India: Gyan Publications.

SarDesai, D. R. (2008). *India: The definitive history.* Boulder, CO: Westview Press.

Sastry, T. (2005). *India and human rights : Reflections.* New Delhi, India: Concept.

Schmidt, E. (2013, March 19). Which Internet will India choose? The Times of India. *Retrieved from:* http://articles.timesofindia. indiatimes.com/2013-03-19/edit-page/37843053_1_open-Internet-indian-engineers-innovation

Schneider, N. C., & Gräf, B. (2011). *Social dynamics 2.0: Researching change in times of social media and convergence: Case studies from Egypt, Lebanon, Iran, India, Malaysia and Indonesia.* Berlin, Germany: Frank & Timme.

Scollon, R., Scollon, S. W., & Jones, R. H. (2012). *Intercultural communication: A discourse approach.* Chichester, UK: Wiley-Blackwell.

Sen, A. (2005). *The argumentative Indian : Writings on Indian history, culture and identity.* London, UK: Allen Lane.

Sen, G., (2003). *India, a national culture?* New Delhi, India: Sage Publications.

Seneviratne, K., & Singarayar, S (Eds.) (2006). *Asia's march towards freedom of expression and development.* Singapore: Asian Media Information and Communication Centre (AMIC) and School of Communication and Information, Nanyang Technological University.

Shekhawat, B. S. (2007). *Vision of vibrant India.* New Delhi, India: Ocean Books.

Sides, C. H. (2006). *Freedom of information in a post 9-11 world.* Amityville, NY: Baywood Company.

Sitaram, K. S., & Prosser, M. H. (Eds.) (1998). *Civic discourse: Multiculturalism, cultural diversity, and global communication.* Stamford, CT: Ablex.

Solomon, L. (2011). *Doing social media so it matters: A librarian's guide.* Chicago: American Library Association.

Sowers, J. L. & Toensing, C. (2012). *The journey to Tahrir: Revolution, protest, and social change in Egypt.* London & New York, NY: Verso.

Sponder, M. (2012) *Social media analytics: Effective tools for building, interpreting, and using metrics.* New York, NY: McGraw-Hill

St.Amant, K. & Kelsey, S. (Eds.) (2012). *Computer-mediated communication across cultures: International interactions in online environments.* Hershey, PA: IGI Global.

St.Amant, K. & Olaniran, B. (Eds.) (2011). *Globalization and the digital divide.* Amherst, NY: Cambria

St.Amant, K. & Sapienza, F. (Eds.). (2011). *Culture, communication, and cyberspace: Rethinking technical communication for international online environments.* Amityville, NY: Baywood Publishing Company.

St.Amant, K. (Ed.) (2007). *Linguistic and cultural online communication issues in the global age.* Hershey, PA: Information Science Reference.

Tagore, R. (1914). *Gitanjali (Song offerings)*. London: Macmillan. Retrieved from http://storage.lib.uchicago.edu.libproxy.lib.unc.edu/ pres/2007/pres2007-0239.pdf

Tankard, R. M., & Bray, A. (Eds.) (2011). *Big Porn Inc: Exposing the harms of the global pornography industry*. North Melbourne, Australia: Spinifex Press.

Tayler, L., & Mariner, J. (2012). *In the name of security: Counterterrorism laws worldwide since September 11*. New York, NY: Human Rights Watch.

Thapar, R. (1966). *A history of India*. Harmondsworth, England: Penguin Books.

Thapar, R. (1977). *Tribe, caste, and religion in India*. Delhi, India: Macmillan Company of India.

Thapar, R. (1978). *Ancient Indian social history: Some interpretations*. New Delhi, India: Orient Longman.

Thapar, R. (1978). *Change and conflict in India*. Delhi, India: Macmillan.

Thapar, R. (1992). *Interpreting early India*. Delhi, India: Oxford University Press.

Thapar, R. (2000). *Cultural pasts: Essays in early Indian history*. New Delhi, India: Oxford University Press.

Thapar, R. (2000). *History and beyond*. New Delhi, India: Oxford University Press.

Thapar, R. (2003). *Early India: From the origins to AD 1300*. Berkeley, CA: University of California Press.

Thapar, R., & Spear, T. G. P. (1965). *A history of India*. Baltimore, MD: Penguin Books.

Thapar, R., Champakalakshmi, R., & Gopal, S. (1996). *Tradition, dissent and ideology: Essays in honour of Romila Thapar*. Delhi, India: Oxford University Press.

Thapar, R., Mukhia, H., & Chandra, B. (1969). *Communalism and the writing of Indian history*. Delhi, India: People's House.

Thapar-Björkert, S. (2006). *Women in the Indian national movement: Unseen faces and unheard voices, 1930–42.* New Delhi, India: Sage Publications.

Tharoor, I (2011) Anna Hazare's Hunger Fasts Rock India, Time Magazine Dec. 07, 2011 Retrieved online http://www.time.com/time/specials/packages/article/0,28804,2101344_2101368_2101650,00.html

Tharoor, S. (1998). *India: From midnight to the millennium.* New York, NY: HarperPerennial.

Tharoor, S. (2006). *India: From midnight to the millennium and beyond.* New York, NY: Arcade

Thomas, P., & Nain, Z. (Eds.) (2004). *Who owns the media? Global trends and local resistances.* London, UK: Zed Books.

Toch, H. (2012). *Cop watch: Spectators, social media, and police reform.* Washington, DC: American Psychological Association.

TRAI (2012). The 2011-12 Annual report of Telecom Regulatory Authority of India. *Retrieved from:* http://www.trai.gov.in/WriteReadData/Miscelleneus/Document/201301150318386780062Annual%20Report%20English%202012.pdf

TRAI (2013a, May 29). *Highlights on telecom subscription data as on 31st March 2013.* Telecom Regulatory Authority of India press release number 38/2013. [Press release]. *Retrieved from:* http://www.trai.gov.in/WriteReadData/PressRealease/Document/PR-TSD-Mar13.pdf

TRAI (2013b, August 1). The Indian Telecom Services Performance Indicators, January–March, 2013. *Retrieved from:* http://www.trai.gov.in/WriteReadData/WhatsNew/Documents/Indicator%20Reports%20-01082013.pdf

TRAI (2013c, September 5). Highlights on Telecom Subscription Data as on 30th June 2013 [Press release]. *Retrieved from:* http://www.trai.gov.in/WriteReadData/WhatsNew/Documents/PR-65-TSD-June13.pdf

Transparency International (2012, December 5). Corruption Perceptions Index 2012. Retrieved from: http://cpi.transparency.org/cpi2012/results/

Tully, M., & Masani, Z. (1988). *India: Forty years of independence.* New York, NY: G. Braziller.

Turner, G. (1990). *British Cultural Studies. pp. 66–67, 210–15.* New York, NY and London, UK: Routledge.

Vadgama, K. (1997). *India: British-Indian campaigns in Britain for Indian reforms, justice & freedom, 1831–1947.* London, UK: Banyan Tree.

Varennes, F. (1996). *Language, minorities and human rights.* The Hague: Martinus Nijhoff Publishers.

Venkateswaran, K. S. (1999). India. In S. Coliver, P. Hoffman, J. Fitzpatrick, & S. Bowen (Eds.) *Secrecy and Liberty: National Security, Freedom of Expression and Access to Information,* (pp. 321--331). The Netherlands Martinus Nijhoff

WAN-IFRA (2013a). Just Published: Trends in Newsrooms 2013 [Press release]. Retrieved from http://www.wan-ifra.org/press-releases/2013/06/04/just-published-trends-in-newsrooms-2013

WAN-IFRA (2013b). World Association of Newspapers and News Publishers World press trends. Darmstadt, Germany: World Association of Newspapers (WAN-IFRA).

Wood, S. H. (1988). *India: From the Raj to independence.* Basingstoke: Macmillan Education.

World Bank. (1997). *India: Achievements and challenges in reducing poverty.* Washington, DC: World Bank.

World Bank. (2000). India: Reducing poverty, accelerating development. Retrieved from http://www-wds.worldbank.org/servlet/WDSContentServer/WDSP/IB/2000/03/21/000094946_00022505304120/Rendered/PDF/multi_page.pdf

World Bank (2013a). World Bank Poverty & Equity Data, India. *Retrieved* from: http://povertydata.worldbank.org/poverty/country/IND

World Bank (2013b, June 14). Internet users (per 100 people). Retrieved from: http://data.worldbank.org/indicator/IT.NET.USER.P2

XV.   Community Broadcasting as a Predecessor of Social Media in Sri Lanka

Pradeep N' Weerasinghe

Department of Mass Media, University of Columbo,
Wewala, Horana, Sri Lanka
pradeep@spc.cmb.ac.lk

Abstract

Online media play a decisive role in the contemporary world in order to strengthen the democracy which provides a platform for the Sri Lankan community to speak out their own accent and to relatively interact and engage in civic activism. This study has explored the involvement of online media during the continuous strike and the protest campaign among university academics (FUTA), school teachers, opposition political parties, labor unions, students' federations, artists and intellectuals for ninety nine days in the year 2012 for the purpose of increasing the government's expenditure up to 6% from GDP for Education in Sri Lanka. This struggle was considerably and purposefully neglected by the mainstream media owned by the government and the private business sector.

Consequently, the activists of *6% GDP for Education Movement* decided to utilize online media in order to build up a fostering unity, interrelation, interactivity and co-operation among sister unions of FUTA and the activists in other related unions for the purpose of promoting the imminent discussions and critical analysis of the education system in Sri Lanka. Data collection of this study was mainly done through emails, blogs and websites by triangulating them with data taken from in-depths interviews. It was found that online media such as e-mails were of innermost importance to build up the co-operation among sister unions of FUTA and their members, to organize subversive activities, to distribute reports, to write articles and reports on trends and threats as regards the struggle while the online media developed a platform for the activists to express themselves principally.

Keywords: broadcasting, online media, activism, education, Sri Lanka

1. Introduction

This study is an investigation of the functions of mass media in the human development and democracy with a particular focus on Community Broadcasting in Sri Lanka. In relation to human development and democracy, the media play a crucial role as a Facilitator; a Watch-Dog; an Agenda-Setter and a Gate-Keeper. To understand this relationship, this study employed media functionalist and empowerment theories. Theorists of media and development have pointed out the Community Radio as an ideal medium for citizen empowerment at grass-roots level. This concept of Community Radio is echoed by the founders of the Sri Lankan Community Radio within the experience gained in the last three decades. The study is based on the data collected from case studies of three Community Radio stations. The study concludes that Community Radio could be used as a tool to minimize the distance between citizens, human development and democratic processes.

Convergence of Empowerment and Community Broadcasting

Many findings (Melkote & Steeves, 2001; Skuse, 2001; United Nations Development Programme (UNDP), 2006; Vuuren, 2006; World Bank, 2003) indicate the media can play a crucial role in empowering grass root communities. UNDP (2006) further identified the particular importance of radio in communication for empowerment strategies and for achieving the Millennium Development Goals, "because its reach, accessibility to the poor and increasingly interactive character" (p. 1). Theorists of media and development practitioners saw Community Radio, as an ideal medium for participatory democracy and citizen empowerment, for articulating grass-roots information and communication needs and demands in the development process (Bresnahan, 2007; UNDP, 2006). Meanwhile, investigating the Australian Community Broadcasting sector, Vuuren (2006) recognizes that Community Radio Stations are best understood and evaluated from the perspectives of community development and citizen empowerment functions. The World Bank (2003) has identified a broader development arena of community empowerment through grass-roots media. The community radio initiative provides an opportunity to create and effectively utilize spaces for community mobilization. "Strengthening local institutions for public voice and community mobilization becomes essential for the promotion of both empowerment and social accountability" (World Bank, 2003, p. 1).

Through participatory media, grass-roots members of civil society become producers, and not merely receivers, of information and opinion, and are able to articulate for themselves their social vision and demands (Bresnahan, 2007; Dragon, 2001; Rodriguez, 2001; Vreg, 1995).

> "Community Radio is a prime example of such participatory media and serves to empower not only the participants in the production but the community in which the station is embedded" (Bresnahan, 2007, p.213).

Sirivardana (2004) found that, at present, citizen empowerment has been identified as a basic strategy for the participation of the beneficiaries for the grass-roots level development projects in Sri Lanka. This article tests the combined concept of Empowerment with Community Broadcasting ideals. The study explores Sri Lankan Community Radio in the broader context of Empowerment. Jayaratne, Jayawardena, Guneratne & Silva, focusing on Sri Lanka, suggest:

> Good governance and sustainable development require the informed involvement of communities and individual citizens in public policy. Community broadcasters have proven to be a key of facilitating informed involvement of local and rural communities in public policy processes. They can enhance local capacity and empower the poor to be proactive in social policy, budget making and other public affairs. They are an important foundation upon which local stakeholders

and international partners may establish effective development and
poverty-reducing initiatives. (2007, p.2).

At times, this conception of Community Radio is echoed by the founders of the Sri Lankan Community Radio within the experience gained in the last two decades. These explorations provide insights in developing a better application model of Community Radio in the Sri Lankan context. International concern has acknowledged the Sri Lankan Community Radio model as one of the best models, which is in line with human development (Librero, 2004; Melkote & Steeves, 2001; Valbuena, 1988). However, there seem to be a lot of unidentified opportunities and realities, which are to be explored. Although the Community Radios, a part of public service broadcasting, were established about 25 years ago, most of Sri Lankan literature on media studies has neglected the significance of the role of Community Radio in citizen empowerment.

Community Broadcasting in Sri Lanka

Sri Lanka pioneered community broadcasting with the creation of the Mahaweli Community Radio project in South Asia. David (1986) suggests that "the establishment of the Mahaweli Community Radio in 1981 could be regarded as a turning point in Sri Lankan rural-broadcasting because its approach and working procedure were quite novel" (p. 10). CPA (2005) notes that "with its beginnings in 1981 as Mahaweli Community Radio (MCR), the government made effort to assist hundreds of thousands of people in the process of resettlement and readjustment which resulted from the Mahaweli Development Project" (p. 13). Policy planners of the project identified there was a role for mass media to assist to settlers facing challenges. The objective of the community radio project "is to accelerate and facilitate socio-economic improvement of the new settlers in the Mahaweli development plan through rapid, timely and relevant sharing of settlers' experience using the medium of radio" (as cited in UNESCO report, 1983, p. 5).

Meanwhile David (1986) suggested that "the theoretical base of Sri Lankan community radio is development communication" (p. 4). "Mahaweli community radio (MCR) was rolled out as a channel of two-way communication; it was expected to use MCR as a means of facilitating the flow of information and ideas to and from the community. Furthermore another expectation was that the MCR broadcasts conceptualized, designed and produced with active participation of Mahaweli settlers would eventually lead to attitude and behavior change on the part of the Mahaweli settlers as well as the Mahaweli officers" (Karunanayake, 1990, pp. 235–236). "The development approach of Mahaweli Community Radio is to support the development of rural communities by motivating the villagers to take active part in the development process" (UNESCO, 1983, p. 6).

Funds for the MCR were given by the Danish International Development Agency (DANIDA) and consultation was offered by UNESCO. The first part of MCR commenced in 1981 under the Sri Lanka Broadcasting Corporation (SLBC). After few years of experimental programmes, the MCR project expanded establishing small community radio stations focusing on particular sectors of the Mahaweli project, namely "Giradurukotte" (1985), "Mahailluppalama" (1987), and "Kothmale" (1989). The latest initiative "Uva Community Radio" is operating outside the Mahaweli development project which was established in 2003 under a pilot development project of UNDP titled "Area Based Equity Programme."

2. Methodology

The study considered three basic cases related to Community Radio applications in Sri Lanka as:
- Giradurukotte Community Radio Station (GCR)
- Kothmale Community Radio Station (KCR)
- Uva Community Radio Station (UCR)

Accordingly, it was expected to derive three cases of community broadcasting applications and evaluate them, as with the direction of the study. This procedure, resulted in a qualitative study of the possibility of using community radio stations as a facilitator of citizen empowerment in the process of human development. The three cases mentioned above were chosen by considering their contribution of empowerment functions. The researcher has selected these three-radio stations based on the following criteria: Radio's role as a facilitator for (a) Integrating folk media and old media for empowerment; (b) Integrating old media and new media for empowerment; (c) Citizen mobilization for empowerment. Accordingly, the case of Giradurukotte Community Radio station was selected to investigate Radio's role as a facilitator for integration of folk media and old media for empowerment. The Kothmale Community Radio station was selected based on integrating old media and new media for empowerment, and the Uva Community Radio station was selected based on citizen mobilization for empowerment. Further review of literature, findings of a pilot study that was carried out during the 2004–2005 period, and the researcher's own practical experiences and knowledge in the community radio sector in Sri Lanka guided the selection of cases. This case study has been developed through in-depth interviews, document analyses, participatory observations, and focus group discussions.

3. Discussion

Integrating Old Media and Folk Media for Empowerment: The Case of Giradurukotte Community Radio (GCR)

In the following section, the essay will present and analyze the findings for the GCR. It is based on various sources in order to get data, as the GCR station started in 1985 and is inactive by now. Data have been collected mostly through the interviews held with the pioneer community broadcasters and volunteers who were involved in the GCR station as well as their diaries, field note books, announcer's log books etc. Further research reports as well as published and unpublished documents were used as the source of data for this investigation.

GCR was established in 1985 under the Mahaweli Community Radio project. The Giradurukotte was located in system C of Mahaweli development programme . Twenty five thousand families who lived in the area were covered by the GCR. David's (1986) study found that the majority of settlers (83%) were farmers. The rest lived by running small enterprises and fishing in reservoirs in the area. 12% of the settlers have not gained formal education. 35% of them had primary education. 54% of settlers had secondary education. Almost in all houses there was a radio receiver set. 72% of the population read newspapers. Television receiver sets existed in 450 houses. About 98% of them listened to the GCR programme in order to get useful information for day-to-day living.

Programming

The daily broadcasting duration of GCR was 3 hours per day. The programmes were broadcast from 17.00 pm to 20.00 pm. "GCR programmes were being treated as programmes which the whole family can listen to. 81% listened with the entire family. 9.5% listened as a group. The popular place for group listening was the tea kiosk" (David, 1986, p. 23). Principal GCR's method of programme production was a community based team production instead of individual. The process of producing programmes commenced with a short visit of a producer to a village. The producer who goes to a village to build a basic connection with the village leaders. Then he meets the rest of the villagers in the public places, at the farms and even on the roads and discusses with them. "Although these discussions tend to be long drawn out, they are not discouraged as they help settlers to come out with their problems without any reservations" (Valbuena, 1988, p. 7). During this visit villagers' communicative needs and development issues were identified. Finally a date and place to produce radio programmes was planned with the villagers. On the due date GCR production team moved into the village equipped with mobile broadcast equipments. Then the production team camped out there for four days mixed freely with villagers, speaking the local dialect and trying to live as typical villagers. The purpose was to observe and become familiar with villagers. They went to the temples, community center or tea kiosk to build up a dialogue with villagers about their concerns and interests. "This approach results in the villagers being the focal point in the production process" (Karunanayake, 1990, p. 236). The villagers who met on the road or anywhere in the village are invited to a common place in the evening by the GCR radio progamme producers. The villagers who gathered at a common place were asked to plan a radio programme. Under the guidance of radio producers, the programme is planned by discussing their problems and suggesting the alternative solutions. The title of the programme, format and content are decided by the villagers. The participants of the programme were also villagers. Programme recording or live broadcasting are done at the same time or on the following day. If the programme was recorded, at end of the recording it was played to villagers, and then gets their comments and approval to broadcast it. Villagers have titled it as "Game Api" (We in the village). As a result of this process the villagers have been empowered as broadcasters. Their voice could be heard within the public sphere.

In addition to the above villagers' programmes, health, educational, entertainment and news programmes are broadcast daily by the GCR. Most of these programmes were targeted to give solution to the farmers' day-to-day problems. David (1986) has described GCR programmes in four ways:

- Providing news and information
- Providing agricultural knowledge
- Social control
- Solve problems

Use of Program Format for Community Empowerment

There was a special identity in the format of GCR programmes. These formats were identified by the community. They often have selected a folk media format to present their own problems and solutions through the radio medium. Balit showed:

> *Indigenous media have been successfully adopted to promote issues of relevance to marginal groups. Popular theater, puppet show, music and dance have been used, for instance in health care, to discuss family size, female genital mutilation, teenage pregnancies, HIV/AIDS, and unsettling life styles. Traditional forms of communication can also integrated with other media such as radio television. (2004, p. 9).*

Folk media are a medium of communication created by the villagers to fulfill their communicative needs. These have lasted for a long time among villagers. These formats and contents were easy for them to understand as they were created by themselves for their needs. Folk media were very close to the villagers. The significant features of folk media were its multiple, wonderful, flexible and alternative way. Artists who present folk media can be found within the villagers. GCR experience has shown that the folk media can be used to present the modern messages. The following folk media formats were identified by the villagers to present their own radio programmes through the GCR station:

- "Kavikolaya": (Barcarole. Singing newly created poems. It is a form of folk media in verse satirizing the foibles of people in society).
- "Virudu": (A Bard. Singing newly created narrative songs while playing a small drum).
- "Sokari": (A folk drama).
- "Kopi Kade": (Coffee café in the village).
- "Rabanpada": (Rhythmical singing while playing a traditional drum).
- "Gamsabawa": (A traditional village forum for decision making in the village).
- "Avidda Paya": (A proverb).
- "Gami Katawa": (Folk story telling).
- "Kaviyata Kaviya": (A traditional poem singing debate in the village level which was used in the entertainment ceremonies).
- "Street drama": (Informal folk drama which was played on the street).
- "Dinapotha": (Diary).
- "Ayubowewa": (May you live long. A drama based on a traditional devil-exorcism dance ritual to help cure the sick by warding off evil spirits. Central to this ritual is a conversation between the dancer and the drummer. Following the format of this witty dialogue, Ayubowewa attempts to cure social ills by correcting bad health and agricultural practices (Valbuena, 1988, p. 9).
- "Katha Baha": (Evening talk).
- "Keth Ratawa": (Field Patterns).
- "Thawalama": (A kind of pageant).
- "Game Api": (A cultural show).

Through the GCR programme the folk media format was integrated with the radio medium as a traditional media. Since the magnetic nature of the folk media and accessibility of the radio medium, the GCR programmes became not only attractive to the audience but also succeeded in influencing them. Figure 1 illustrates the operational scenario of the GCR in the empowerment process.

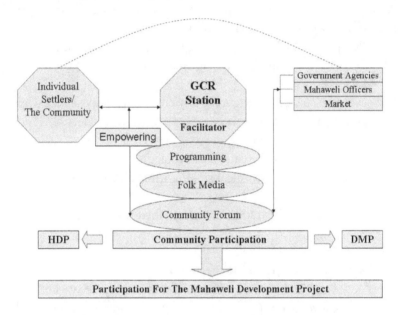

Figure: 1. The Role of the GCR Station in the Empowerment Process. GCR= Giradradurukotte Community Radio, HDP= Human Development Process, DMP = Democratic Process

4. Findings: Evidences of Empowerment

Evidence: 1

"Kavikolaya" became the most popular programme among the GCR programmes. "The "Kavikolaya" was the most popular programme as 33.5%

of the respondents stated that this was the most preferred programme" (David, 1986, p. 39). On the other hand, "Kavikolaya" played the role of social controller and watch dog function of mass media. The problems accusations, social injustice, and pains of a person were written in a "Kavikolaya" and broadcast from the GCR station. Sarcasm, entertainment, sadness, happiness and fables are included in a "Kavikolaya". Any person could write a "Kavikolaya" on facts of an incident and send it to the GCR station. It was reproduced to suit the "Kavikolaya" format and then it was broadcast without being censored. The "Kavikolakaraya" (the narrator/artist/presenter) who presented the "Kavikolaya" was a villager.

Most of the incidents which occurred in the area are highlighted by a "Kavikolaya". "The incidents highlighted are associated with deviant behavior" (David, 1986.p. 39). The way how she was affected by the smoking and drinking of alcohol of her husband, a member of the family or a neighbor once became the topic of "Kavikolaya". Or, a bias, an injustice, a deceit, corruption or inefficiency of government officers' became the topic of "Kavikolaya". The significance of "Kavikolaya" is that the incident once highlighted is followed up in the next "Kavikolaya" programme. Both the feedback and impact after "Kavikolaya" were broadcast and the response of the targeted person was presented in the next "Kavikolaya" programme. Most of the people were afraid of "Kavikolaya" and abstained from anti-social activities as "Kavikolaya" could have brought them a status of incompatibility with the society. Thus, in the marginalized villages the powerless and voiceless were empowered through the "Kavikolaya" programme.

A producer of the GCR station, Karunanayake, was once sick and admitted to Kandy hospital. The patient who was next to his bed did not know that Weerasinghe Karunanayake was an employer of GCR station. Then the nurse who was in-charge of that ward came with another patient who was relative of her and asked the patient who was next to Karunanayake's bed to give his bed to the patient who came with her. He had to obey her order. After giving the bed he came to Karunanayake and said that "I will write a "Kavikolaya" for the GCR station about this injust incident as soon as I go home". This experience shows the potential of empowering people integrating the radio medium and the folk media format.

Evidence 2

Once, diarrhea spread in the Meegahakiula area. A production crew of the GCR station went there to produce a programme. It was identified by the health officers that the reason was refusal to use healthy toilets. The villagers did not have a habit of using sanitary toilets. Even through they were given material to build sanitary toilets they were not interested in it. The villagers decided to produce a radio programme to solve this problem. They have chosen "Rabanpada" (drum poem) as the format of the programme. The villagers created a new drum poems for this purpose. The contents of drum poems indicated the reasons of spreading diarrhea and suggestions to prevent it. They played these drum poems by using a big drum. It was recorded and broadcast by GCR. The message reached villages successfully and they mobilized to prevent diarrhea.

Evidence 3

One day in the evening when the GCR programme was going on air, a villager visited the radio station. He accompanied a kid. The kid was crying at that time. The villager mentioned that his wife has gone to live with another person and the kid was crying for missing his mother. Both of them were asked to come to the live on air studio. The announcer asked them to say what they had to say. They asked her to come back. It went on air lively. The following evening the villager came to the radio station with his wife and kid. He mentioned that his wife had listened to GCR channel and returned. This incident shows that people had an opportunity to solve even individual problems through community radio.

Evidence 4

When farmers lost their cattle or even their identity card they used to come to the community radio station. They were allowed to present their request in the live broadcast. Then listeners helped them to find their identity card or cattle. The GCR station was used to share their massages. For example it was used to convey funeral notices. Government officers used it to convey messages to farmers about meetings. The messenger's role of GCR gained successful outcomes.

Evidence 5

Very often settlers could not find a solution for their day-today problems. As these problems remained unsolved for a long period of time it had become an obstacle for them to reach the aim of the Mahaweli development programme. Most of their problems needed an immediate solution. On the other hand there was a big gap between the settlers and the Mahaweli project authorities. The GCR station introduced a programme called "ask from Mr. Pathirana" to fill this gap. Traditionally when a villager faced a problem, he used to ask for a solution from village leaders, elder citizens, indigenous medical advisers and religious leaders. This programme has followed this format. The GCR station invited the authorized officers of the area to come to a settlers' village. Then settlers are allowed to present their problems to relevant officers. The officers had to propose a solution for the problems. The questions and answers have been broadcast live from the village or recorded and broadcast later. When early announcements were broadcast with information about this programme the settlers who lived in other villages would send their problem to the GCR station in writing. These problems also were presented to the officers by the moderator of the programme. As a result of the "Ask from Mr. Pathirana" programme, settlers were empowered not only to question authorities but also they were empowered to express their ideas, opinions and suggestions directly to the authorities. The solutions given by the authorities during this programme were followed up in the next programmes. Therefore the authorities were not in a position in avoiding the problems of settlers. Most problems presented by the settlers were based on common facilities, irregular activities, and ineffectiveness of officers. As David (1986) observed "it brings social power to the settlers and also helps the administration to have an insight into the settlers' problems at grass-roots level. It also affords a certain extent of control over the official and functions as a fuse valve to the settlers' grievances" (p. 43).

Evidence 6

Kalyani Manike (a young woman) worked as a volunteer producer at GCR station. She belonged to a settler's family. According to her experience, the settlers did not have a habit of saving, which has a negative influence on improving their living condition. She had planned a project to make a habit of saving within the settlers. Women from settlers' family were selected for this purpose. She believed that women can be influenced easier than men in these matters. First she discussed with a bank in the area about distributing tills free among the settlers. She informed her idea through a radio programme and distributed the tills among farmers' wives. She asked to put the change money into the till after shopping at the Sunday fair and to keep records in a note book. She examined these record books at times and announced the amount that each woman served during the radio programme. At end of the period of three months she asked women to come to the GCR station with their tills. She invited the bank officers too on this occasion. Accordingly bank accounts were opened with the money from the tills. An instant loan was offered to the women who had served most. By using this loan they were led to find new ways of income generation. As a result of this the rest of the women were also motivated to save. This is one of the best examples for empowering women individually.

Evidence 7

Gamage, a producer who was involved with the GCR station reveals his experience:

> *"One day early in the morning in 1992 when I was at the radio station the leader of the farmers, Gunathilaka came to the radio station. He complained to the radio station that the farmers are not in position to sell their paddy harvest and asked radio station to find solution for this problem. Gunathilaka's complaint was that the government had imposed a fix price and given money to paddy marketing board to buy rice from the farmers. But the paddy marketing board did not do so. Even the whole sale dealers did not buy because of fix price. Gamage has recorded Gunathilaka's story and broadcast it. While the programme was going on air, the problem*

*was presented to the high officers of the agricultural ministry. It was
investigated by the ministry. Then it was found that the area officer in
charge of the paddy marketing board had purchased rice from whole
sale dealers for fix price with money given to office to buy rice from
farmers. Then the officer was interdicted and the money was sent
again to buy rice from the farmers. The entire process of incidents
was followed up by GCR programmes."*

The "Kathabaha" (evening talk) format was chosen for the programme.
Gamage's experience shows that the farmers are empowered to solve this
problem as a result of GCR's involvements.

Evidence 8

The ritual "Thovil" was traditionally used by the villagers to prevent
themselves from illnesses. It is a drama based on a traditional devil-
exorcism dance ritual to help cure the sick by warding off evil spirits.
Central to this ritual is a conversation between a supporter, the drummer
and the patient. Malaria spread widely in these villages. Once, the villagers
have chosen "Thovil" format in order to raise awareness of malaria. One
night they gathered at a common place in the village and played a "Thovil".
The witty dialogue between the drummer and supporter sent the message
about the way to prevent malaria. At the end of the drama the villagers
were asked to comment on the received message. "What is the message
presented?", "Can the suggested things be followed?", and "What are the
alternative suggestions?" Such questions were asked. As a result of these
interviews, it was able to get a feedback on the programme. The villagers
have titled this programme as "Ayubowewa" (May you live long). The entire
process went live on air from the village.

Evidence 9

The villagers have had the habit of story-telling and listening for a long
period of time. Because of the simple narrative nature, story-telling became
popular among villagers. This format was chosen by the community radio
producers to deliver the agricultural messages. The agriculture officer of

the area, who comes daily to the farm or the radio station, presented the agricultural information as a narrator by using the story telling format. He did not forget to include poems, dialogues and idioms which are popular among villagers, when it was necessary. Finally, the agriculture officer Wijerathna Banda who presented this programme became popular among the farmers.

Evidence 10

One day Sunil and Kolitha, the community radio producers visited a village, "Kolama". The Kolama villagers belonged to low caste. As a result of their low cast they were marginalized. They were shunned by neighboring villagers. Sunil and Kolitha came to know that the majority of the villagers were not legally married; as a result, they had to face many problems daily. Inability of their children being admitted to school, inability of getting jobs and inability of allotting their property were the foremost problems for them. Sunil and Kolitha discussed this matter with government officers. Then they decided to organize a marriage ceremony for these villagers to get married legally. All the legally unmarried villagers were invited to the ceremony and asked to register their marriage. At this ceremony about seventy couples got married legally. Sunil and Kolitha had chosen dairy format to broadcast this process. Thus, this entire process went on air through the radio dairy programme.

Evidence 11

Nachachadoova is an old colony that belonged to the Mahaweli project. Community radio producers visited this village. When they arrived they came to know that the farmers had abandoned their farming and used to spend their days in an indeterminate life style. The reason was they were addicted to illegal liquor and gambling. Consequently, their living condition was bad. Radio producers went to a place of gambling. They interviewed the persons who were defeated. Then radio producers went to their houses and interviewed their wives and children. Finally a radio programme was produced with them by using recorded interviews. Then the villagers were allowed to listen to this recorded radio programme.

After that, another programme was produced and it was included with the opinions of villagers on previous programme. Finally they produced series of programmes on this problem and broadcast them. After the broadcasting of these programmes series, there was a dismay in the minds of the villagers about their evil life style. Then little by little they gave up gambling and drinking liquor and returned to farming.

Evidence 12

Once, a community radio producer visited a house in Nachachadoova. At that time the house holder was quarrelling with his family members. He was drunk. All the sounds came out of that house were recorded by the radio producer. Then he interviewed the husband, wife and children about this incident. Then he managed to produce a radio programme with them. Then they were allowed to listen to it. The husband was ashamed of his life style and behavior. Then he promised to the members of his family that he would avoid this life style.

Evidence 13

It was national housing year, 1987. Community radio producer, Harischandra stated that they decided to commence a housing project with the participation of the community:

> *"We selected 'Rajanganaya' area, which was not included to the Mahaweli programme for this project. Twenty five families had lived in temporary houses for a long period of time with scant facilities. They neither had their own interest to build permanent houses for them nor did any organization come to assist".*

The Community radio motivated and mobilized them to build their own houses. "You can do it" was the theme of the project. Harischandra explained that

> *"firstly a community organization of Rajanganaya villagers was formed. Then the members of radio clubs which already had been established in the Mahaweli zone were integrated with this village organization. The needed labour was supplied by voluntary*

radio clubs. The necessary raw material was supplied by various organizations and donors of the area. The government gave technical assistance".

After building the houses, a house gardening project commenced and a sweet meals factory was build in the village targeting income generation of villagers. The community radio programme facilitated to coordinate the project. "Finally, by using the radio medium, we were able to mobilize and empower the community to build their own houses. The microphone was the only tool which we used for this", Harischandra added.

Evidence 14

Villagers had a habit to chat about daily events in the coffee shop. It was rather a tradition of the villagers to chat with each other while buying goods or having a cup of coffee. This format was chosen to present the news and current affairs programme of GCR. Perera has produced the "Coffee Kade" (Coffee Café) programme for a long period. According to Perera, the Coffee Kade programme was presented as a drama format. The characters of various persons who live in the village and who gathered to the coffee café were included in the drama. Perera said:

"In the café they shared the news which they heard from radio or on the street or in the town. Some times they read the newspapers. Then they commented, argued and presented their opinion on the news. The effects of that news for their life were discussed. The style of presenting news has become magnetic to the villagers because news was presented by a person they were familiar with and it was presented in the local dialect".

5. Integrating Old Media and New Media for Citizen Empowerment: The Case of Kothmale Community Radio (KCR)

In the following section the article will present and analyze the findings of the KCR. Data have been collected mostly fromwebsites, recorded radio programmes, announcers' log books, listeners' letters and early research documents. Besides these, in-depth interviews were used to explore stories, experiences and understandings on citizen empowerment.

KCR was established in 1989 under the Mahaweli Community Radio project. The Kothmale was the second largest dam project under the Mahaweli development programme. According to the experience of KCR station manager, Wijesinghe, this radio station was the only source of information for the people of many villages nearby. The space between the people who do have access to information and those who do not have in the society is called *Digital Divide*. In January 2001, an international seminar was held at Kothmale, Sri Lanka on integrating new and traditional information and communication technologies for community development. At the seminar, Jayaweera has pointed out factors which cause Digital Divide as shown in figure 2.

In order to minimize the Digital Divide, integration of Internet and radio was made by the KCR Internet Radio project. "The aim of the KCR Internet project was to explore the possibilities to use community radio, a traditional medium, as an effective interface between the Internet and the rural communities, thus empowering the marginalized rural communities to take advantage of new communication technologies" (Including The Excluded, 2001, p. 3). The KCR role was to provide a knowledge infrastructure. The KCR experience shows the potential of the community radio station for giving opportunity to the marginalized community to access to information from the Internet by overcoming language barriers.

The impact of the Digital Divide is shown in Figure 2, Figure 3 shows the potential of using the radio medium and Internet to minimize the Digital Divide.

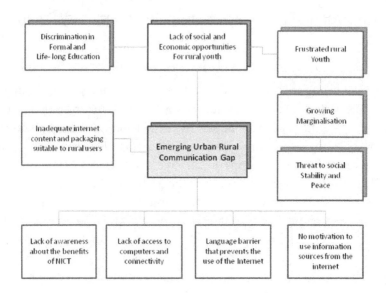

Figure 2: Emerging Urban Rural Gap—Digital Divide
Source: Jayaweera (2001): Seminar on integrating new and
traditional communication technologies; Kothmale.

6. Operationalization

Under the KCR Internet project, six computer terminals, a scanner machine, a digital camera and Internet facility were provided for the KCR station. This multi-media center was connected with two libraries in two sub-urban cities, Gampola and Nawalapitiya. Multimedia facilities were provided to these libraries, too. Community members were given an opportunity to access these facilities for free. The KCR radio programmes, which had already become popular, have facilitated to raise awareness about the Internet among community members subsequently. The community got the service of volunteers in all three multi media centers.

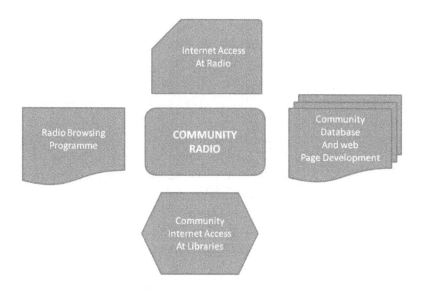

Figure 3: Bridging the Gap by Combining New and Old Media
Source: Jayaweera (2001). Seminar on integrating new and
traditional communication technologies; Kothmale

The professionals in the area such as lawyers, doctors and teachers worked as volunteers in these centers. In addition to that Tanya Notley, the Australian volunteer assumed the main role of this project. The function of the volunteers was to raise awareness of the Internet among the community members who come to the multimedia centers and were guided to use the Internet and interpret information from it. "The advantage is that the community radio provides the requested information in local language making Internet information accessible to those who do not understand the English language" (Including The Excluded, 2001, p. 3). Meanwhile, every weekday the KCR station broadcasts an one-hour live radio browsing programme. The programme was presented by the volunteers. The community members before requested needed information by mail. Sometimes, the volunteers have visited villagers and learned wich information they needed. Then the information was retrieved from the Internet, and volunteers presented it through the radio browsing programme. The Internet browsing programme has raised awareness among community members on benefits and information sources of new information technology. On the other hand, the community who did not have access to computer and Internet got an access from this project. Further, the villagers who had lost the opportunity to access to new technology benefits because of language barriers have got an opportunity to overcome this by means of the community radio. Twenty to twenty-five community members have used the Internet facility at the multimedia center of the community radio centre and ten to fifteen of community members have used Gampola and Nawalapitiya multimedia centers daily. Most of them have requested news from international television channels and information on job opportunities, school projects, new technology, life style, wild life and business opportunities.

7. Finding Evidences of Empowerment

Many evidences of citizen empowerment were identified. Some of those evidences had been identified in the previous research. Evidences of the community using the Internet for a variety of purposes are as follows:

Evidence 1

Kothmale is a hilly area and it suffered frequently from natural disasters. Weather is wet in this area throughout the year. Earth slips are abundant because of this. Many lives and properties have lost. In order to make people ready to face natural disasters, a disaster communication unit was established by KCR. The station manager Wijesinghe explained

> "We have developed a data base by consulting department of meteorology and the disaster management experts. Undergone area of earth slip was identified and mapped. How is area protected from the natural disaster? Communication details of the villagers such as telephone numbers have collected to communicate with them during a natural disaster situation. In addition to that the public places such

as temples where there is the public speaking system, can be used to warn about the incoming danger have been identified. Now we can link people, officers and institutes immediately in the emergency situation. Now we have ability to coordinate relief aid and to give expert advice with the Internet and radio". Thus, the villagers were empowered by the KCR Internet project to face disasters and prevent them."

Evidence 2

The volunteers who worked with the KCR Internet project were more than 500. The majority of them were ordinary people. Most of them did not have a permanent income. Their lives were vagrant. They did not have a plan to face life. They spent the days in desperation. After joining the KCR project their life was completely changed. They have improved the skills of radio programme production and broadcasting. They are trained on using IT and Internet. The skills of leadership, organizing and public relations were developed by working with the community. Currently, the majority of volunteers are working in the IT sectors in the country. Some of them have attached to leading companies as broadcasters, technicians and computer programmers. Some of them are working in the non-government organizations. Sriyapali and Sunil Shantha who worked as KCR volunteers expressed that their lives were completely changed because of KCR. Meanwhile station manager Wijesinghe stated that he was content of having the opportunity to empower the volunteers to win their lives. When the KCR Internet project was established, the villagers were isolated and generally shunned by their better-off neighboring society. Relationships among villagers themselves were limited. With commencement of this project they were able to develop relationships with each other and the outside. The KCR Internet project has become a window to the world for Kothmale villagers. Through that they have given voice. "Kothmale has shown that ordinary people, even very young kids, can learn to browse the web, they can make their own websites, they can search and obtain the information they need for their lives. Even for human rights. When people know they can shout on the Internet when their rights are violated, they are encouraged to assert their rights" (David, as cited in Arnaldo, 2000, p. 7).

Evidence 3

The experience of the initial step of the KCR Internet project has revealed that arousing awareness in the village community through the established multimedia centers and making access to the Internet faced limits. Success was limited by the fact that all villages were situated remotely so people had to spend much time to come to the multimedia centers as the transport facilities of these areas were very poor. Most of the time the villagers were extremely busy as they were occupied with agricultural works as well as daily earning occupations. Further multimedia centers, as an accustomed place to the villagers, improve accessibility by remote villagers. As an alternative for this problem the "e-TukTuk" project was commenced with the idea to mobilize the multimedia centre, going to the location where the villagers live.

In Sri Lanka the only profitable and popular option of the people, those who have not got any public transport facility, was three-wheels (The vehicle is an Indian-built 4-stroke auto rickshaw). In order to implement the second step of the KCR Internet project, the community broadcasters have chosen an Internet centre and broadcasting unit installed in a three-wheel. "There is a shelf for the laptop, and space to mount a CDMA (code division multiple access) phone, scanner, camera, and battery operated printer. "Even in the most remote villages of Kothmale, with the e-Tuk-Tuk one can access the Internet, scan and upload documents, downloads files, print them and take digital photographs" (Venniyoor (2004),p. 91). The volunteers have gone to rural villages by the e-TukTuk three-wheeler daily for outside broadcast. Then Internet browsing programmes were presented live from the three-wheeler in the neighboring villages. The villagers were informed about arrival of the mobile three-wheel unit prior by using KCR programmes, public notice and interpersonal communication channels. At the village, villagers were allowed to watch a video which included the successive stories of Internet use for citizen empowerment. After that they were allowed to express their comments on those stories. Then a discussion was commenced with villagers about the information technology and its benefits. This discussion was focused on raising awareness about information technology. After that villagers were given basic skills of using the computer and Internet. Finally they were given necessary information from the Internet by using the e-TukTuk mobile unit. Here the volunteers were facilitated to overcome language and technical barriers. This process went on air live from the village. As a result of this the villagers in the other areas were motivated to use information and communication technologies. This process was followed up by KCR programmes continually. Steve Buckley, the president of AMMARC stated "With this eTukTuk, it seems to me you've got a great vehicle both in the physical and the symbolic sense, to go out to the communities and the neighborhoods and to let people speak through their community radio station. I think this is a trend that is going to catch on" (Venniyoor, 2004, p. 90).

The KCR experiences reveal that modern technology has the ability of fulfilling the needs of grass-roots communities. The strengths of community radio were influenced by that. The experience of the KCR Internet project indicates that grass-roots community can be empowered by integrating information technology and radio medium.

8. Citizen Mobilization for Empowerment: The Case of Uva Community Radio (UCR)

In the following sections the essay will present and analyze the findings of the UCR. Participatory observation was the key research method that was used for examining Uva Community Radio in the citizen empowerment context. The researcher carried out fieldwork from January 2001 to January 2008 in the Uva province in Sri Lanka. Focus group discussions were held in three places in the Badulla District of the Uva province, namely Palagolla, Kottegoda and Katawala, and Nitula in Monaragala District. Besides these, the researcher has conducted in-depth interviews with community broadcasters, volunteers and listeners of UCR station, government and non-government policy makers and development practitioners who work with people at grass-roots level, village leaders, and representatives of village level volunteer organizations, beneficiaries of grass-roots level human development projects and randomly selected citizens.

The Uva Community Radio was established in the Uva province in Sri Lanka between 2001 and 2003 under the ABGEP project. Jayaratne, Jayawardena, Guneratne and Silva suggest:

> *"The community radio component was conceived as a tool to facilitate peoples' participation in developing planning, implementation and evaluation. Previous development programmes had lacked community participation in development and therefore had failed to advance community aspirations, to reflect community opinion on contextually significant issues, and to maximize community income."* (2007, p. 35).

9. Finding Evidences of Empowerment and Mobilization of the Community

When the founders of the Uva Community Radio station (a broadcast manager from Sri Lanka Broadcasting Corporation (SLBC) and a consultant from UNESCO) arrived at the Uva province, purchasing of technical equipment for the proposed community radio station had been started under the UNDP/ABGEP project. The Uva provincial council had activated governmental funds for the construction of the radio station building. In addition to that, the Uva provincial council was preparing to recruit a group of communicators in order to fulfill human resources for the proposed community radio station. The Uva community radio station founders who observed this situation realized thatthe nature of this preparation showed characteristics of a commercial radio station. The community who represented the key shareholders and beneficiaries of the radio station was not involved in the initial planning process of the UCR. Thus, it had merely become an officers' task. The community members of the Uva province were almost not aware of the community radio, which was on its way to be established. Additionally, the community members did not feel the necessity of a community radio station. Although the ABGEP project members recognized the aim of UCR was to nurture community participation in the development process in the Uva province, no attention was drawn towards suitable mechanisms for community involvement of the proposed community radio station. The officers of the provincial council and council members who had already been engaged in the commencing process did not have a clear idea about the concept of community broadcasting. Therefore, this was the initial task of the founders of the Uva community radio.

Thus, it was decided to encourage wide community participation in this radio station. At the same time, they tried to suit the basic objectives of the ABGEP project. Accordingly, this community radio station was conceptualized as "programmed, managed and owned by the community". The next task was to identify a suitable mechanism to mobilize the community to apply this concept. The target group of the UCR included 1.8 million people. They spread over a vast area. The first attention was drawn towards a method of reaching this target audience. Accordingly, the founders invited a meeting in the "Rideepana" village, which was organized by the Uva Community Center, a non-governmental organization. About thirty villagers attended this meeting. Through a discussion held there, it became obvious that the participants were an elite group among the villagers. Additionally, there was no acceptance of the activities of non-governmental organizations among villagers. Finally, the attention was drawn to look into whether there would be a possibility of getting the assistance of government village officers who were already working with the village community. Therefore, the founders invited three community meetings organized by these village officers. The community participation in these meetings was very poor. Again, due to later observations, village officers were not accepted by the community. There was an idea in the minds of the grass-roots community that these officers with power were corrupted, partial and inefficient. Through this initial observation, the founders realized that the organizations and officers established in the area who already had connections with the community were not suitable for the task of mobilizing them for the proposed community radio station.

Then it was discussed whether the communicators, who had been recruited for the affairs of the community radio station by the provincial could be used to mobilize the community. Finally, a group of forty young people was selected as communicators. First they were given training on theoretical and practical aspects of community mobilizing, community broadcasting and social marketing. Then they were given the responsibility to mobilize the community in their native places. It was successful to create awareness in their native area. The first community meeting organized by communicators was held in a small village school in 'Bibila'. In this meeting, community radio founders and all communicators participated. During the gathering, it was expected to provide practical experience about their future activities of communicators. Almost hundred of community participants attended this first meeting. It seemed that different community groups in the area were represented. First, the community participants of this meeting were divided into small groups. Afterwards they were asked to list the radio programmes which they listen to and the reasons for that. Additionally they had to identify available opportunities of participation and weaknesses of these radio programmes. Furthermore, they tagged advantages and programmes, which they would like to broadcast, if a radio station was established in the area they live in. Finally, they were allowed to present the facts listed by them in front of the whole community. This presentations and discussions were focused on peoples' media needs and the necessity of a community radio by the community radio founders. At the end of the meeting, community participants had realized that the government and the business class own the mainstream media in the country, but none of these would fulfill the needs of the community or give an opportunity for community voices. This led to the explanation of the proposed community radio station. Community participants decided to meet again to discuss their role in the proposed community radio station.

Accordingly, about 150 participants gathered again after two weeks. At this gathering, they agreed on forming a community organization which should be involved in the project of the new radio station. Community members were suggested to select a core group from the participants to run this proposed community organization. However it was observed that the selected core group consisted of elite members of the community. Thus, there were no ordinary community members among them. Therefore, criteria for selecting the core group were suggested by the community radio founders and were agreed by the community members. According to these criteria, a core group was selected. The chosen ones were neither political activists, nor holding any office bearer in a volunteer organization, and representing various professions and had both genders.

This community organization was named "Knowledge Society". Following this first Knowledge Society model, about 178 Knowledge Societies have been established in the Uva Province by the Communicators of the Uva Community Radio station by 2003. In each Knowledge Society, a volunteer group was also established. The same training, which had been given to the communicators, was given to these volunteer groups. Accordingly, 4500 volunteers were trained. The task of producing programmes for the proposed community radio was assigned to these volunteers. A special training of newsgathering and news presenting for the community radio was given to 800 volunteers.

After these Knowledge Societies had been established, with participation of core groups of Knowledge Societies, two district conferences were held. The first conference took place at the "Badulla" district and about 1000 Knowledge Society representatives participated in it. 450 attended the second conference held at "Monaragala" district. The way of involvement of community members for the proposed community radio stations' programmes, its management structure and it's ownership at these conferences were widely discussed. Finally, the district and provincial Knowledge Society Federation was established. At the end of the conferences, it was realized that the community participatory mechanism for ownership, management and programming of the proposed community radio station had been gained through these Knowledge Society network. CPA notes:

> *Approximately one fourth of these knowledge society members have received basic training on the concepts of community radio and radio journalism. All programs are planned and scheduled with the involvement of the 'Gnana Samaja' (Knowledge Societies) via radio 'facilitators' who visit the societies in order to discuss potential stories, production mechanism and scheduling details. The societies are also a given 30–minute slot in order to broadcast their own programming with no editorial interventions made by the station. (2005, p. 15).*

Empowering Communicators

The way of selecting communicators (facilitators) and volunteers to work in the UCR and the manner they were trained were directly affecting the role of UCR. In the beginning, the communicators, who had been recruited for the affairs of the community radio by the provincial council were given the task of mobilizing the community. 927 young people of the area had applied for this communicator post. As a result, the authorities of the provincial council explained they agreed to select the facilitators suitable to the concept of community broadcasting. Accordingly, the criteria for the selecting process were suggested which included ethnic, gender and personal skills. It was also recommended to choose representatives from various localities of the area. Although the necessity of various professions as a selection criterion was pointed out, the authorities of the provincial council did not agree on that, because they thought that it would not be practical. Finally, a group of forty young people was selected as communicators. It was decided to firstly mobilize and empower these communicators. First they were given training on theoretical and practical aspects of community mobilizing, community broadcasting and social marketing. Then they were given the responsibility to mobilize the community in their native places. It was successful to create awareness in their native area. In addition to that, 400 volunteers have been trained in the same way. A special training approach was used in order to train these communicators and volunteers. It was similar to the training approach developed in Ghana for community radio workers and took its name from 'Kente', which is the name for traditional hand woven cloth of the Ashanti people. Batti explains:

> *The kente approach is based on the belief that community radio is a different kind of radio and represents a different theoretical and operational model from public and commercial radio. This implies that community radio requires a new kind of "professional" —a community worker with a specific set of values, skills, and standards that are focused on community empowerment. Thus, the training of community workers is woven into the culture of the community and the process of empowerment. It is a practical hands-on approach that integrates theory (development communication,*

communication, culture, management) with experience and the practice of broadcasting as it applies to community radio, but context-based. (2004, p.10)

The volunteers and communicators working in UCR were trained in several steps. All the workers, belonging to different ethnic groups, were given accommodation together at the same place and made to participate together in the same training sessions when they were trained. Most probably, prior to this project, journalists belonged to multi-ethnic groups who communicate in different languages were trained separately. Moreover, if they work together in the same media institution later, the possibility to understand the relationship between them was limited. A vast gap or rather a "separation" of ethnic and culture among them could be seen. Because of this, the radio programmes they produced and presented were biased to their own ethnic group with some special productions and these programs included some nasty contents in the minds of listeners from other ethnic groups. The training approach of UCR expected to avoid this plight. After this training programme, the communicators and volunteers who work in UCR said that they were able to listen to the opinions of other ethnic groups to respect their traditions and prospects while working with them. Further they pointed out there was not any partiality of building of the evil concepts in their programmes. "Though we as Tamils, Sinhala and Muslims live together in this area, the majority of us who were trained together did not know the culture, opinion and beliefs of other ethnic groups and even did not talk with them until accommodated with others in the training workshop". "We had a great fear of the 'language'. Therefore, we had a shy of the way of this training programme. However, at the end of the training programme, we found a method to communicate with each other. At the end of the programme we understood the similarity of the problems, actions, feelings, and concepts of all three ethnic groups in our area except for the language gap," (Personal interviews, 2006, at Bandarawela). During this training programme the participants belonging to different ethnic groups were allowed to involve in the activities as a single group or team and when they were free from the training programme they were encouraged to organize activities together. Through this, an environment was created for the trainees to motivate them for intercultural communication. As a result of this process, this young communicators group firstly was empowered to mobilize community members for UCR and accordingly they established 178 Knowledge Societies across the Uva province. Secondly they have been empowered as trainers and they have trained more than 1400 volunteer communicators. Finally they were trained as broadcasters to run the Uva Community Radio station.

The Outcomes of Mobilization of the Community

The obtaining of community participation in the Uva development process and the strengthening of the democratic activities of the area through member mobilization occurred as a result of the Knowledge Societies. The grass-roots level citizens so far marginalized by provincial development activities and the political process were empowered by this mobilization. The majority of the participants and the leaders in these knowledge societies were young men and women and ladies. During this study it was observed that in the Sri Lankan society women were a marginalized lot whose involvement in the decision making process was limited. This is clearly reflected not only in social activities but also in the home affairs. The woman in the Sri Lankan society leads a domestic role while the man dominates in the outside world. The male domination in Sri Lankan society is basically formed by ethical and religious influences. As a result, a woman in Sri Lankan society is treated as an ornament or as a character that provides domestic functions and requirements of the children and the husband. They have no voice in either mass media or social activities. But, today in the knowledge societies established by the community radio the leadership is held by females. Hence, the females can now be directly involved in the social activities and participate in the decision making process. The Uva community radio has provided a voice for the voiceless. Thus by the mobilization of women, the knowledge societies have successfully empowered them.

At focus group discussions of this study (at Palagolla, 18.08.2007; at Katawala, 11.08.2007; at Kottegoda, 20.02.2007; at Nitula, 22.02. 2007) it was found that both young men and women of Uva so far had no opportunities to participate in development activities of the region. They were a marginalized group in the social and political activities. They had no voice in the mainstream media. One of the causes for the youth insurgencies in 1971 and 1988 is identified as the marginalization of these youth in the society. The Uva province is one of the principal areas where the views of the youth predominated in 1971 and 1988 youth insurgencies. The majority of the office bearers and active members of the Knowledge Societies established by the Uva Community radio are male and female youth. By this they found a forum to actively participate not only in the development process but also in the political arena. They planned to make use of the radio air time allocated for the knowledge societies to fulfill their unmet needs. The majority of the volunteers who were trained on broadcasting with community mobilization were the young girls and boys of the province.

Accordingly, the Knowledge Societies established to cover the whole province created an environment by which the community could contribute actively to the development process and the democratic activities of the province. The success of the Knowledge Societies can be attributed to the absence of political, economic, religious and officialdom interference. The community of Uva was empowered as a result of being mobilized by knowledge societies. Once established, they prepared programmes to use the air time of the Uva community radio as a tool for their empowerment.

Though the community lost the direct participation in ownership and management of the Uva community radio they had the opportunity to participate in its programmes. This is a result of the MOU signed between SLBC and UPC. Both parties agreeing to implement the programme guidelines had already been prepared by the community. Accordingly, the community had the opportunity to utilize the 30 minutes air time allocated by the Uva community radio to each Knowledge Society to achieve their unmet daily needs. Hence the Knowledge Societies were able to produce and broadcast their programmes without any undue influence and restrictions.

Programming

The programme objectives of the community radio were:
- Increase democratization
- Strengthen dynamic civil society

- Support community participation in the development process in the Uva province

Accordingly, the UCR structured radio programme formats to promote democracy, active involvement of communities in the development process and allowed communities to set up their own development agendas. Finally UCR has exercised the use of radio to empower communities living at grass-roots level in the Uva province. At present the programme schedules, formats and contents of the Uva community radio are prepared in conformity with the above objectives. Thus the UCR is pioneering a new type of media experience in Sri Lanka.

The Communicators (Community facilitators) in the Uva community radio station use their own bicycle or the public transport to go from village to village and estate to estate. On these visits they meet the members of the Knowledge Societies. They discuss with them their problems and alternative suggestions and record their programmes. In addition they record their long ignored folklore and music. Then they analyze the issues, complaints and grievances revealed through the programmes produced by the knowledge societies and forward them to the relevant and responsible officers and politicians. Later along with responses of the relevant authorities these programmes go on air. In the programmes of the following week a follow up action will be taken. The progress and the follow-up of the issues will continue both by the radio station and the Knowledge Society until a satisfactory decision is reached. The programmes produced by the knowledge society members will include family and community conflicts, poor governance and service delivery at central, provincial, local government and non-governmental levels.

The members of the 178 Knowledge Societies established by the Uva community radio contribute to the planning, production and presentation of programmes. Each knowledge society consists of at least 50 members. 1400 volunteers selected from among the members of the knowledge societies have been given training in radio broadcasting, production of radio programmes, presentation and news gathering. They were trained by the communicators of the Uva community radio. They are also provided opportunity to produce the programmes in their own village and the Uva community radio supplies the radio programme production equipment and mobile broadcasting units to present live broadcasts from their villages.

UCR is concerned about raising the living standards of the community of the area and has provided the opportunity to use the radio medium for this purpose. UCR encourages planning and communicating dialogue with and among grass-roots levels as well as bureaucracy and political leaders. It provides a voice to voiceless marginalized groups to communicate by allocating space for public dialogue, debate on the day-to-day issues that affect them. UCR also provides a channel to communicate information on development issues with developed entrepreneurs and authorities. In addition, the UCR has established a forum for the members of knowledge societies to converse and openly discuss and question the decisions taken by them with the members and people's representatives whom they have voted and sent to the various assemblies.

10. Conclusion

According to GCR experiences, the influential factors on community empowerment have been the programme production method and programme formats. The GCR programme production method is primarily based as a mechanism to find solutions to development issues in the daily life in the target community. On the other hand, an environment suited for active democratic practices has been created by the programme production method. The GCR acted as a bridge between community members and authority. The strategy used was the utilization of the folk media of the villagers as radio formats. By integrating radio medium with folk media, individuals and community groups were empowered. What was done by KCR was, to integrate radio as an old medium and Internet as a new medium. This project has brought about great changes in the lives of individuals in this area. Those who lack social power and social capital have been empowered by this project. Small-scale businessmen, farmers, manufactures were able to use new technology and production methods. A once isolated community has now been connected to the outer world through Internet. The UCR provides evidence as to how citizens could be empowered through mobilization. This analysis presents evidence as to how the radio medium can facilitate in the dialogue between the government and citizens in a democratic society, and how citizens can be mobilized towards this goal. It is discussed how people get involved in the democratic process through mobilization of citizens. Here, the community uses the radio medium as a tool to express their views and problems to the authorities. Sometimes, the radio medium acts as a mechanism to create a dialogue between the government and the community and also between citizens. The radio medium is thus used as a forum or bridge for such purposes. The second role played by the UCR is to act as a mechanism to get the participation of the beneficiaries for the development activities. That is to get the contribution of the community for identifying development needs of the area, making decisions on them, planning to action, implementation and the monitoring process. In doing so, the UCR plays different roles at different times, such as an organizer, facilitator, a bridge or forum. Sometimes it acts as a watchdog of society. GCR, KCR and UCR experiences indicate that the radio medium can contribute towards participation of citizens in democratic and development processes. Through mobilization of their community, they can be made owners of the community radio. The UCR case reveals that citizens can contribute to democratic and development processes when they are empowered by making them the real owners of community radios. The study concludes that Community Radio could be used as a tool to minimize the gap between citizens, human development and democratic processes.

References

Arnaldo, C. (2000). *Assessment of technical proposals to establish Uva Community Radio [No. Project SRL/97/101]*. Kuala Lumpur, Sri Lanka: UNESCO.

Balit, S. (2004). *Communication for isolated and marginalized groups: Blending the Old and the New. Rome*, Italy: FAO.

Bresnahan, R. (2007). Community radio and social activism in Chile 1990–2007: Changes for grass-roots voices during the transition to democracy. *Journal of Radio Studies, 14*(2), 221–233.

Center for Policy Alternative (2005). *Study of media in Sri Lanka.* Colombo, Sri Lanka: CPA.

David, M. J. R. (1986). *An evaluative study on the impact of a settlement based community radio. SLBC.* Colombo, Sri Lanka.

Dagron, G. (2001). *Making waves—Stories of participatory communication for social change.* New York, NY: Rockefeller Foundation.

Jayaratne, T., Jayawardena, K. P. P., Guneratne, J. de Almeida & Silva, S.. (2007). Legal challenges and practical constraints: A comprehensive study of "Community Radio" in Sri Lanka. *Law & Society Trust, 18*(241), 1–62.

Jayaweera, W. (2001: January). Integrating modern and traditional information and communication technologies for community development. Paper presented at the International Seminar on ICT, Kothmal, Sri Lanka.

Karunanayeke, N. (1990). Sixty six years broadcasting in Sri Lanka. Colombo, Sri Lanka: Centre for Media and Policy Studies.

Librero, F. (2004). *Community broadcasting; Concept and practice in the Philippines.* AMIC. Singapore.

Melkote, Si. (2005). Viewpoint: Public service broadcasting in the age of globalization, *Media Asia, 32*(2), 67–68.

Melkote, S. R. & Steeves, H. L. (2001). *Communication for development in the third world: Theory and practice for empowerment.* London, UK: Sage.

Rodriguez, C. (2001). *Fissures in the mediascape: An international study of citizens' media.* Creskill, NJ: Hampton Press.

Shansak, A. (1995*). Empowering women in rural development: A collaborative action research project in Northern Thailand.* Unpublished Doctoral thesis. School of Agriculture and Rural Development, University of Western Sydney.

Sirivardana, S. (2004). Innovative practice amidst positive potential for paradigm shift: The case of Sri Lanka. In P. Wignaraja and S. Sirivardana (Eds.) *Pro-poor growth and governance in South Asia* (pp. 224–304). London, UK: Sage.

Skuse, A. (2001*). Information communication technologies, poverty and empowerment*. Social Development Department. London, UK: Department for International Development.

UNDP (2003). *Final TOR outcome evaluation. Draft Terms of Reference of Outcome Evaluation*. Colombo, Sri Lanka: UNDP.

UNDP (2006). *Communication for empowerment: Developing media strategies in support of vulnerable groups*. Colombo, Sri Lanka: UNDP.

UNESCO (1983). *Mahaweli community radio: Project findings and recommendations;*. Restricted Terminal Report [FIT/510/ SRL70FMR/COM/DCS/83/218(FIT)]. Paris, France: UNESCO.

UNESCO (2001). Kothmale FM community radio. Including the excluded: The Kothmale experience.

UNESCO (2006). *Communication for development: Achieving the millennium development goals: Draft proposal for the 10th interagency round table on communication for development.* Paris, France: UNESCO.

Valbuena, V. (1988). *Mahaweli community radio project; An evaluation.* AMIC: Singapore.

Venniyoor, S. (2006). On air, in the hills. *Frontline, 23*(13), 90.

Vreg, F. (1995). Political, national, and media crisis. In D. Paletz, K. Jakubowicz & P. Novosel (Eds.), *Glasnost and after: Media and change in Central and Eastern Europe* (pp. 49–61). Creskill, NJ: Hampton Press.

Vuuren, K. (2004). *Community participation in Australian community broadcasting: A comparative study of rural, regional and remote radio.* Unpublished Doctoral thesis. School of Arts, Media and Culture, University of Griffith.

Vuuren, K. (2006). Community broadcasting and the enclosure of the public sphere. *Media Culture & Society, 28* (3), 379–392.

World Bank (2003). Social accountability and public voice through community radio programming. *Social Development Notes* (No. 76). New York, NY: World Bank.

PART SIX:
SOUTH EAST ASIA

XVI. Content Analysis of Interactions between Global Brands and Their Publics on Global and Thai Facebook Brand Pages

Pitchpatu Waiyachote

School of Journalism and Mass Communication,
The University of North Carolina at Chapel Hill
pwaiyachote@gmail.com

Abstract

The increasing presence of brands and Facebook globally and locally leads this study to examine how brands and their publics interact with each other on Facebook brand pages. A content analysis of Facebook postings (n = 8,878) on official global and Thai brand pages of 18 top global brands during one week was conducted. These postings were a combination of initial posts and responding comments generated by the global brands and their publics. Communication content posted on Facebook brand pages was analyzed to understand the objectives of the brands and their publics for using brand pages. The findings revealed that the global brands and their publics used Facebook brand pages to communicate with each other. More specifically, the global brands and their publics primarily used the global Facebook brand pages to maintain relationships with each other because the most frequently posted content was relational content. On the local Facebook brand pages, the global brands were likely to generate promotional content to distribute product or service information, whereas their publics were likely to post relational content. The findings also showed that the types of industry (IT vs. non-IT brands) accounted for differences in types of posted content. In addition to communication content, this study focused on an international public relations strategy applied to local Facebook brand pages. This study confirmed that a glocalization strategy was being practiced by the top global brands. It means that the global brands provided both global and local information regarding the brands, products, or services, as well as special events to their local publics.

Keywords: Public relations, social media, Facebook, global brands, Thailand, communication content, glocalization

1. Introduction

The phrase "Follow us on Facebook" is often seen or heard in advertisements, as many brands encourage consumers to click "like" on their brands' or products' Facebook pages to become their "fans." Consequently, several studies have recently examined how social media, including Facebook, have contributed to public relations as communication tools between not only for-profit corporations but also not-for-profit organizations and their publics. These studies mostly found that social media have been used to provide information as well as to develop relationships with their online publics (e.g., Bortree & Seltzer, 2009; Rybalko & Seltzer, 2010; Briones, Kuch, Liu, & Jin, 2011).

This is not surprising because relationships are a core construct of public relations (Ledingham, 2003). The concept of public relations emphasizes "building mutually beneficial relationships between organizations and their publics," according to the Public Relations Society of America (2011). Therefore, social media that offer two-way communication are recommended tools because of their spontaneity and ability to reach a wide range of stakeholders (Semple, 2009). While most public relations studies have put an emphasis on how organizations use social media strategically to develop relationships with their publics, little is known about how the publics use social media to communicate with organizations. To better understand a process of strategic communication with the goal of building mutual relationships, public relations researchers should also pay attention to how publics use social media to reach organizations. Because brands embrace a presence on Facebook, this study examined how Facebook is used to develop mutual relationships between top global brands and their publics.

Furthermore, brand presence on Facebook has spread across the world. Thus, this study also explored how relationship-building strategies using Facebook have been adopted or adapted in other markets. With the presence of many top global brands in the market, Southeast Asia is a local market of over half a billion people, with a combined domestic product in excess of US$1.1 trillion and total trade of over US$1.4 trillion (Bhasin, 2010). Thailand could be a representative of this local market because the number of Facebook users in Thailand has increased rapidly in 2011 (Socialbakers.com). Although Facebook users account for only 18% of the country's population, social media users have high purchasing power, according to the Economic Intelligence Center (2011), a research unit of Siam Commercial Bank. Thus, these social media users are more likely to be consumers of global brands.

This study adds insights in implementing Facebook pages for public relations purposes and fills a research gap in terms of how consumers use Facebook to connect with brands. Brands and communication practitioners will better understand publics from their postings on Facebook. The overall goal of the study is to examine how top global brands and their publics communicate with each other on Facebook. More specifically, this study is designed to explore types of communication content generated by the top global brands and their publics on global and local Facebook brand pages. This study also aims to examine communication strategies—whether globalization, localization, or glocalization—that the top global brands use to communicate with their local publics in Thailand on Facebook.

2. Literature Review

Relationship Management

According to Ledingham and Bruning (1998), important dimensions of healthy organization-public relationships consist of trust, openness, involvement, investment, and commitment. As online communication has become an effective way of communication, Hallahan (2008) introduced five major concepts that measure the building of an organization-public relationship in an online environment. These five concepts are commitment, trust, control mutuality, communality, and satisfaction. These concepts were developed based on Kent and Taylor's (1998) dialogic principles, and they are related to Ledingham and Bruning's (1998) organization-public relationship dimensions.

Commitment is the concept that examines how committed organizations are to online engagement. Being committed can be demonstrated through resources invested in establishing relationships and efforts to communicate with the publics (Hallahan, 2008). In terms of marketing or consumer relations, brand loyalty can represent the publics' commitment toward an organization or a brand (Morgan & Hunt, 1994).

Trust is given to another party when one is confident and willing to disclose oneself to the other party (Grunig & Huang, 2000). Trust involves a feeling that an organization is believable, reliable, and consistent (Thomlison, 2000). To gain trust, an organization must open itself up to its publics by transparent communications and providing information regarding its business openly and honestly, whether it is positive or negative (Bruning & Ledingham, 2000). Trust is also related to a criterion and is significant in influencing perceptions of satisfaction toward the organization (Bruning & Ledingham, 2000). Disclosure or openness by the publics to an organization can be measured by counting suggestions, complaints, inquiries, and other contacts made by publics including media (Grunig & Huang, 2000). Trust can encourage consumers to seek, share, and pass information to others (Chu & Kim, 2010).

Control mutuality in the online communication context refers to the interactivity that occurs between an organization and its publics; meanwhile, communality refers to the degree to which an organization and its publics share common values, beliefs, and interests with each other (Hallahan, 2008). Satisfaction is an indicator that an organization-public relationship positively meets the publics' needs and surpasses their expectations (Hallahan, 2008). According to Grunig and Huang (2000), satisfaction involves affection and emotion. Satisfaction is perceived as a significant outcome of the effective maintenance of a relationship (e.g., Bruning & Ledingham, 2000; Grunig & Huang, 2000).

Managing Relationships with Communication Content

To understand how organizations use social media to establish relationships and communicate with their publics, scholars analyze communication content disseminated through media. For example, Waters, Burnett, Lamm, and Lucas (2009) explored how nonprofit organizations adopted social media to build and maintain relationships with their publics. They found that many nonprofit organizations have their online presence through social media in addition to websites. However, Waters et al. suggest that nonprofit organizations should have used social media to their fullest extent to take advantage of the two-way communication feature to build and maintain relationships with their publics. They summarized three important concepts when using social media strategically. First is disclosure. Practitioners should disclose information openly through social media. Second is usefulness. Waters et al. found that a lot of organizations include their history and mission statement on social media profile pages; however, they should have regularly posted news releases and links to an official website for more useful information. The content should not be limited in the form of text. It could include images and video files. The third key concept is interactivity. Waters et al. recommended posting a calendar of volunteer opportunities to engage online audiences with an offline environment.

Ahuja and Medury (2010) examined the ability of an organization to use its corporate blog to stimulate consumer engagement by posting content and encouraging consumers to provide comments. They analyzed 100 blog posts across 10 Fortune 500 corporate blogs and found 27 different types of posts. Then a factor analysis was conducted to categorize 27 types of posts into three main types of content typologies: organizational, promotional, and relational. The results showed that relational content was able to generate greater volumes of consumer engagement, which was measured in terms of the number of consumer comments, than other types of content. Furthermore, Ahuja and Medury (2010) examined relationships between the number of posts by the organization and the number of comments.

They found a positive correlation between the number of organization posts and the volume of consumer comments.

Similar to the goal of Ahuja and Medury's study, Waters et al. (2009) examined how Facebook, in particular, was used to engage and cultivate relationships between nonprofit organizations and their stakeholders. A content analysis of 275 randomly sampled nonprofit organization profiles on Facebook was conducted. Based on relationship development strategies, the study closely examined the presence of items representing organizational disclosure, information dissemination, and involvement. The study revealed that disclosure was the most often used strategy. In addition, the study found that message boards, video files, and fundraising were used differently, depending on the type of nonprofit organization.

Another recent example is a content analysis of 1,760 wall comments on health organizations' Facebook pages (Park, Rodgers, & Stemmle, 2011). The analysis was conducted to examine how health organizations used Facebook to manage their brand for advertising purposes. Overall, health organizations used Facebook strategically for health advertising and promotions as well as image management. However, nonprofit health organizations did not take full advantage of interactive features or other social media channels, such as YouTube, Twitter, etc., which can be integrated with Facebook strategies. In contrast, health care institutions incorporated a wide range of social media channels, including Twitter, YouTube, and Flickr, more frequently than other health organizations. Similar to Waters et al. (2009), the study of Park et al. (2011) indicated that the use of Facebook and other social media tactics varied by the type of organizations.

While several studies have focused on how social media have been used by organizations, only a few studies have explored how publics use social media to communicate with organizations. Fernandes, Giurcanu, Bowers, and Neely (2010), for instance, examined the political involvement of college students through their conversations regarding the 2008 presidential election on student Facebook groups supporting the 2008 presidential candidates, John McCain and Barack Obama. A content analysis of nine Facebook groups from seven universities located in swing states was conducted to examine what topics the students were talking about on the walls. College students focused mostly on praising the candidate whom they supported rather than criticizing him or his opponents. Additionally, the overall tone of the wall posts on these Facebook groups was positive rather than negative, with the focus on supporting the group's candidate.

Glocalization

In addition, this current study aims to examine the use of Facebook brand pages to communicate with local publics through the lens of glocalization. According to Svenssen (2001), "the glocal strategy" concept comprises local, international, multinational, and global strategy approaches (p. 15). It differs from a global strategy approach because it explicitly recognizes the importance of local adaptation and tailoring in the marketplace of business activities. He also argues that glocalization means "the standardization versus the adaptation, and the homogenization versus the tailoring, of companies' business activities are optimized" (Svenssen, 2001, p. 15). Similarly, Maynard and Yan (2004) explain that glocalization integrates both globalization and localization perspectives by tailoring a global standard in terms of products along with marketing and communication processes to a certain degree to meet local preferences.

Glocalization can be applied to management, marketing, and communication. For example, Hong Kong Disneyland had faced business challenges since it started operating in 2005. A year later, management executives decided to tailor their business strategies to meet the local Chinese context. Several adaptations were made, including a communication strategy, especially the use of languages. Cast members (staff) at the theme park speak both English and local dialects that are commonly spoken in Hong Kong and mainland China. Brochures describing Disney's shows and rides are printed in traditional and simplified Chinese characters, as well as in Japanese and English. After the glocalization principle was executed, both park attendance and revenues have increased (Matusitz, 2011).

In addition to Disney, other global brands have also applied the glocal approach to their communication strategies in a local market. A content analysis of the Chinese websites of the 100 top global brands revealed that the glocal strategy was presented on Chinese web pages of the top global brands (Maynard & Yan, 2004). These top brands showed a high level of localization on their websites by integrating local characteristics in terms of culture, politics, and economy into their branding strategies. For example, on Coca-Cola's Chinese website, the brand featured its sponsorship of the top Chinese women soccer players. The study found that postings of local events such as the 2003 SARS epidemic as well as awards given by the Chinese government and local community were the two most significant predictors of localization. At the same time, these brands also provided Chinese consumers with links to the websites of their headquarters. "This approach positioned the brand as local, but with a global reach" (Maynard & Yan, 2004, p. 290).

The literature review has provided a good indication that social media have become important communication- and relationship-building tools for practitioners and the publics. It has also revealed that the type of organization accounts for the different ways practitioners use social media. Therefore, the following research questions were addressed:

RQ1: What is the relationship between types of industry and types of communication content that brands generate on Facebook brand pages?

RQ2: What is the relationship between types of industry and types of communication content that the publics generate on Facebook brand pages?

The type of industry served as an independent variable. An industry referred to the production of an economic good or service. Brands that manufacture or offer computers, software, and electronic goods or services were grouped together as the group of IT brands. The rest were grouped as the group of non-IT brands. The types of communication content by brands and those by their publics were the dependent variables in RQ1 and RQ2, respectively.

Additionally, one of the previous studies emphasized the ability of communication content to stimulate public engagement through social media. Among other types of content, relational content was able to generate the greatest volume of consumer interaction on corporate blogs (Ahuja & Medury, 2010). Thus, the first hypothesis examines the relevancy of the effectiveness of a specific type of relational content on Facebook brand pages. Thus, an independent variable was the percentage of each type of communication content posted by brands, while a dependent variable was the proportion of feedback. On a Facebook brand page, the publics can generate content to communicate with the given brand. In this study, public interaction on Facebook brand pages is communication created by the publics on Facebook brand pages. Feedback, in particular, is operationalized as a positive experience in using products or services, which is considered the most positive public interaction. Both initial postings and responding comments in the form of text, images, and video clips are included.

H1: Relational content posted by the brands attracts the highest proportion of feedback on global and local Facebook brand pages when compared with other types of content.

The second hypothesis was based on Maynard and Yan's (2004) research regarding the concept of glocalization, which integrates perspectives of both globalization and localization to meet local preferences. The study found that the glocalized strategy was applied to Chinese websites of global brands. Consequently, this hypothesis speculated that the glocalization strategy would be implemented on Facebook, which is also an online outlet. The type of industry served as an independent variable, and the glocalization strategy served as a dependent variable.

H2: Top global brands across industries apply the glocalization strategy to their local Facebook brand pages.

3. Method

A content analysis was conducted to explore how the top global brands and their publics used Facebook to interact with each other. The population of content in this study was postings by the top global brands and their publics on Facebook brand pages. This study used a multistage sampling process. Based on the list of the top global brands reported by Interbrand, 18 of the top 50 brands were selected purposively because they offer a global brand page in English and a parallel local brand page in a Thai language. The unit of analysis was a comment posting on a wall of a Facebook page. The unit of analysis was the same as the coding unit. The group of comment postings generated during seven consecutive days (from February 21 to 27, 2012) constituted the sampling unit. Most of these global brands post content daily on their brand page. Many brands also have a weekly posting pattern on their brand page. For example, a trivia question is posted every Friday. Therefore, the cluster of postings over one week was selected. Prior to the analysis, the researcher monitored and captured screenshots of Facebook postings by the 18 global brands and their publics during the selected week on global and Thai brand pages.

For RQ1, RQ2, and H1, each posting by the 18 global brands and their publics was coded for the type of industry and the type of communication content. The global brands were classified into two types: IT brands (offering computer, software, and electronic products: Microsoft, Intel, HP, Nokia, Samsung, Canon, Sony, and Dell) and non-IT brands (offering other types of products and services: McDonald's, Mercedes-Benz, Gillette, Pepsi, Nike, Nescafé, Ikea, L'Oréal, Citi, and Ford). The type of communication content was categorized into three types based on communication objectives of communication content. Organizational content is content that aims to enhance brand image. Organizational content is operationalized as postings/responses on brand activities regarding corporate social responsibility, employee experiences, business plans, financial growth, brand achievements, and recognitions.

Promotional content is content that mainly provides the publics with information about a product (or a service) and passively persuades the publics to embrace the product. Promotional content is operationalized as postings/responses regarding product features, prices, promotional campaigns, and new product launches.

Relational content is content that aims to develop and maintain relationships with the publics (Ahuja & Medury, 2010). Relational content is operationalized as postings/responses that deal with consumer praises, feedback, complaints, or controversies about the brand, product, or service. In addition, this includes trivia questions, information about the brand's relationship development activities with the publics (such as a sports day), and general topics.

Although the conceptual definitions of the content types were initially defined from a brand's perspective, it is also relevant to define content generated by the publics according to the communication purposes. When publics-generated content is concerned with a brand's overall image, strategy, and performance, it is organizational content. If the publics specifically inquire or provide comments regarding product information, it is considered promotional content. Content responding to the brands' relational content as well as content focusing on the positive and negative sides of consumer experience are considered relational content. The level of measurement of the type of industry and the type of communication content is nominal. Public interaction is operationalized as the number of wall postings, including initial and responding comments, by the publics, and its level of measurement as ratio.

Additionally, the content from Thai brand pages was coded for the communication strategy to examine whether the content is glocalized. If both globalization and localization approaches are present on Facebook brand pages, meaning that global as well as local content are posted, those brand pages would be considered to employ the glocalization strategy. Globalization is operationalized as wall postings about brands, products, employees, customers, campaigns, and activities in a global context—global/U.S. public figures, international organizations, the U.S. government, and global communities. Localization is operationalized as wall postings about brands, products, employees, customers, campaigns, and activities in a local context—local public figures, local organizations, and the local government.

There were two coders who are competent in English and Thai, one being the researcher, for this study. The second coder was trained by the researcher to analyze the Facebook postings by using a protocol and a coding sheet. The researcher directed the second coder to the global and Thai Facebook brand pages of the top global brands. Once she became familiar with the page layout and unit of analysis, she was trained to use the content analysis protocol to deal with the content. Then the researcher and the second coder practiced coding some content together. Questions or disagreements were discussed. When the second coder became comfortable with the procedure, both coders practiced coding more content independently. Results were compared. Since there were major differences in the results, the second coder was trained again before coding the actual data independently. The content used during the practice was not included in the content samples for reliability testing. The second coder coded content samples from all (18 x 2) 36 Facebook brand pages for reliability testing. Within each brand page, one out of seven-day clusters was randomly selected. One cluster contains all postings posted within one day, such as a cluster of postings on February 21 on Microsoft's global brand page. Therefore, the second coder coded a total of 36 sampling clusters (or about 14% of the content). Krippendorff's alpha was computed for intercoder reliability with a minimal acceptable level of reliability of .80. Intercoder reliability ranges from .81 to 1.00.

4. Results

A total of 8,878 Facebook postings were coded. About half of them (57%) were postings on official global pages. Proportionally, there were more postings by the brands on the Thai brand pages (20%) than those posted by the brands on the global brand pages (10%). On the other hand, there were slightly fewer postings by local publics on the Thai brand pages (80%) than postings by global publics on the global brand pages (90%).

	Global		Local		Total
	IT	Non-IT	IT	Non-IT	
Brands	243	270	437	305	1,255
Publics	2,795	1,738	1,535	1,555	7,623
Total	3,938	2,008	1,972	1,860	8,878

Table 1: Number of postings

On the global brand pages, the brands were most likely to generate relational content (68%), followed by promotional and organizational content. Similarly, global publics mostly posted relational content (75%), followed by promotional content, other content, and organizational content.

On the local brand pages, the brands mainly posted promotional content (57%) and relational content, whereas the Thai publics posted relational content (59%), promotional content, and other content.

Relational content, in particular, was classified into seven types, including feedback, complaint, suggestion, conversation, trivia, event, and other relational content.

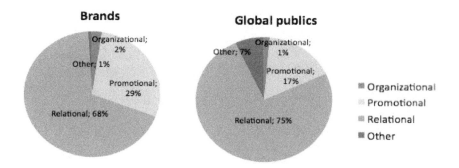

Figure 1: Types of content generated by the brands and their global publics on the global brand pages

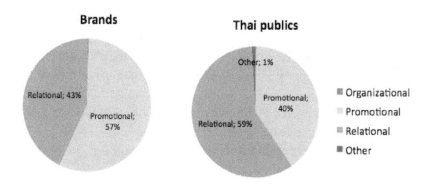

Figure 2: Types of content generated by the brands and their Thai publics on the Thai brand pages

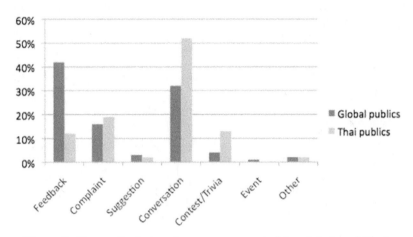

Figure 3: Types of relational content generated by global and Thai publics on the global and Thai brand pages, respectively

RQ1 asked what the relationship between types of industry and types of communication content that the brands generated on Facebook brand pages was. A z-test was used to examine whether there was a difference in distributing communication content by IT and non-IT brands. On the global pages, all types of posted communication content except organizational content differed significantly by the type of industry. IT brands posted promotional content more than non-IT brands did ($z = 4.04$, $p < .001$). However, IT brands posted relational and other content less than non-IT brands did ($z = -3.98$, $p < .001$ and $z = -8.21$, $p < .001$, respectively). The type of industry did not account for differences in generating organizational content ($z = 0$, $p =$ ns).

On the local pages, organizational, promotional, and relational content posted by the brands differed significantly by the type of industry. (There was no posting in the other content category.) IT brands posted organizational content less than non-IT brands did ($z = -5.82$, $p < .001$). Promotional content was posted more on IT brands' Facebook pages than on non-IT brands' pages ($z = 6.64$, $p < .001$). As for relational content, IT brands posted such content less than non-IT brands did ($z = -6.34$, $p < .001$). On both global and local pages, IT brands were most likely to distribute content relating to their products, while non-IT brands were most likely to post relational content.

RQ2 asked what the relationship between types of industry and types of communication content that the publics generated on Facebook brand pages was. Similar to RQ1, a z-test was used to examine whether there was a difference in communication content posted by the publics of IT and non-IT brands. On the global pages, all types of posted communication content except organizational content differed significantly by the type of industry. IT brands' publics posted more promotional content than non-IT brands' publics did ($z = 8.44$, $p < .001$). The publics of IT brands, on the other hand, posted less relational content than those of non-IT brands did ($z = -5.41$, $p < .001$). The publics of IT brands also posted less other type of content than the publics of non-IT brands' publics did ($z = -2.53$, $p < .05$). The type of industry did not account for differences in posting organizational content ($z = -0.28$, $p = $ ns).

On the local brand pages, promotional and relational content posted by the publics differed significantly by the type of industry. IT brands' publics posted more promotional content than non-IT brands' publics did ($z = 19.94$, $p < .001$) but posted less relational content than non-IT brands' publics did ($z = -19.85$, $p < .001$). However, the type of industry did not account for differences in neither posting organizational content ($z = 0$, $p = $ ns) nor other content ($z = 0$, $p = $ ns). On both global and local pages, IT brands' publics were most likely to post content regarding products and services, while non-IT brands' publics were most likely to post relational content.

H1 predicted that relational content posted by the brands would attract the highest proportion of feedback by the publics on both global and local brand pages when compared with other types of content. The hypothesis was not supported. First, the actual numbers of three types of postings by the brands and feedback posted by their publics on both global and local brand pages were adjusted into percentages. Then these percentages were used in a regression that was run to examine the relationship between feedback postings on the global brand pages as the dependent variable and the types of brand content as the predictors. The regression equation for the global brand pages was not significant ($p > .05$). The other regression was also run to find the same relationship on the local brand pages. The regression equation for the local brand pages was not significant either (p > .05).

H2 hypothesized that the top global brands across industries would apply the glocalization strategy to their local Thai Facebook brand pages, and it was supported. The global brands used both globalized and localized elements on the local brand pages, meaning that the glocalization strategy was implemented. However, there were significant differences in using some elements according to the type of industry. A Pearson's chi-square test was conducted to examine the relationship between the type of industry and languages as well as globalized and localized items used on the local brand pages. There could be more than one item appearing in each initial posting by the brand.

In terms of languages, both IT and non-IT brands mainly used the Thai language to communicate with the local publics. However, the use of languages differed significantly by the type of industry ($\chi 2$ (df = 3, N = 202) = 13.14, p < .05). Globalized and localized items that were used consisted of a link to a brand's global website, a link to another international website, product availability in a global market, a global event, a global public figure, a global cooperative partner, a link to a brand's local website, a link to another local website, product availability in a local market, a local event, a local public figure, and a local cooperative partner. The use of four among these items differed significantly by the type of industry. The non-IT brands featured global public figures more than the IT brands did ($\chi 2$ (df = 1, N = 202) = 9.20, p < .05). On the other hand, the IT brands used local public figures more than the non-IT brands did ($\chi 2$ (df = 1, N = 202) = 5.85, p < .05). The IT brands posted links to their local websites more often than the non-IT brands did ($\chi 2$ (df = 1, N = 202) = 18.43, p < .05). As for showing cooperative relationships with local partners, Facebook postings of the IT brands contained these relationships less than those of the non-IT brands ($\chi 2$ (df = 1, N = 202) = 14.63, p < .05). Table 9 displays percentages of the uses of the globalized and localized items. The items that were not used by both IT and non-IT brands included relationships with the U.S. and Thai governments, global and local awards, as well as global and local community service.

5. Discussion

This study revealed that the global brands and their publics used official Facebook brand pages to communicate with each other. Similar to several previous studies (e.g., Bortree & Seltzer, 2009; Rybalko & Seltzer, 2010; Briones et al, 2011), this study has confirmed that Facebook is used mostly as a communication channel to develop relationships between the brands and their publics. On the official global brand pages, these 18 brands posted content that aimed primarily at developing and maintaining relationships with their publics. The non-IT brands, in particular, were more likely to post more relational content than IT brands. For example, Nike posted a trivia question regarding a soccer player almost every day. Most IT and non-IT brands were more likely to respond to feedback and complaints posted by their publics on the brand pages. Similar to the brands, the publics also used Facebook brand pages as a communication board where they expressed their positive and negative experience in using products or services. In addition, the publics also generated and responded to general conversation topics that were on these official global brand pages. The publics of the non-IT brands posted relational content more than those of the IT brands.

Distributing or exchanging information regarding products or services was the secondary objective for both the brands and their global publics to use Facebook brand pages. The IT brands, which regularly introduce their new or upgraded products, posted promotional content to provide product information more often than the non-IT brands. Similarly, the IT brands' consumers also posted content dealing with products more than non-IT brands' consumer did. These promotional content provided product functions, prices, availability, etc.

These global brands used their official Thai brand pages slightly differently. There were postings about products or services more than postings that directly aimed at cultivating relationships with the publics. Thus, it implied that the global brands, especially the IT brands, used Facebook brand pages to distribute information about their products or services to local consumers. The main objective of the brands using Facebook brand pages did not match that of their publics. Their local publics primarily posted relational content, especially conversations, on the Thai brand pages. When exploring the types of content by industry, the local publics of the IT brands posted more promotional content but less relational content than those of the non-IT brands. Postings that contained organizational content appeared infrequently on both global and local brand pages. When they did appear, it was about employment opportunities and insights from brand executives.

Although relational content seemed to be posted often by both the brands and their publics, it did not attract the highest proportion of feedback, which is the most positive form of public interaction on Facebook brand pages. There may be other important factors that influence the publics to post positive comments about the brands. This could be explored in a future study.

Overall, in terms of relationship management, this study revealed several relationship outcomes that indicate the quality of an organization-public relationship. Control mutuality, which refers to the interactivity, could be seen on Facebook brand pages. Questions or feedback regarding products could represent another dimension of the relationship, which is communality. At least it showed that brands and their publics shared a common interest in branded products. Trust was revealed to some extent as well. As most brands kept posting information about their products and activities, the publics were willing to respond. Some share positive experience with the brands on Facebook, while others made suggestions or complained. Although this study was not designed to measure satisfaction, monitoring the publics' comments on Facebook brand pages was one way to learn whether a brand effectively serves their publics' expectations. However, consumer satisfaction should be assessed thoroughly with well-developed measures if brands intend to measure satisfaction. Furthermore, most of these selected global brands demonstrated their commitment developing and maintaining relationships with their publics through communications on Facebook. Most brands were likely to keep their publics engaged in online communications by posting promotional and relational content. Particularly, global brands that responded to comments, both positive and negative, posted by the publics were seen as more committed to online engagement than brands that did not do so.

Furthermore, this study revealed that these global brands applied the glocalization approach to the way they used their local Facebook brand pages. In other words, these brands utilized or posted both global and local information on their local brand pages. For example, the IT brands, such as Microsoft, used local public figures to help promote their promotional activity. The non-IT brands—such as Nike, Mercedes-Benz, and Ford—featured global public figures on their brand pages more often than the IT brands did. However, the IT brands provided a URL link to their official Thai website more often than the non-IT brands did. This could be because they provided the link so that their consumers could learn more information about their products, especially about how to upgrade cell phones and other IT gadgets. The findings showed that the global brands made an effort to demonstrate themselves as global brands, but they did it in a way that was appropriate to the local Thai market.

One implication for this study for public relations practitioners is that Facebook serves as an efficient means to globally and locally communicate and develop mutual relationships between an organization and its publics. The brands' publics, especially those who are current customers, wanted to benefit from the existing brand pages. They shared their positive and negative experience of being the brands' customers. They also asked questions, made suggestions, and engaged in conversations. Therefore, it is important that the brands keep monitoring their brand pages and posting regularly. Furthermore, it is crucial that the brands provide responding comments to the publics' postings to acknowledge that their voices were heard. These tactics should be helpful for building and maintaining healthy relationships with both global and local publics.

A limitation of this study is that it collected the postings that were posted during one week, which might be considered a short period of time. In terms of exploring how Facebook brand pages were used locally, this study used only Thailand as a representative. In the future, the scope for a study to observe patterns of the use of brand pages should be broadened in terms of a range of time and geographical areas. Based on the mismatch between the brands' and their local publics' objectives of using Facebook brand pages, there is a potential to conduct a follow-up study on the publics' perceptions and satisfaction toward the brands. In addition, future study may specifically observe whether relational content posted by the publics across cultures are different.

6. Conclusion

In conclusion, many top global brands employed Facebook to reach global and local publics. A Facebook brand page seemed to serve as a public relations tool when it is developed for the global public, whereas a Facebook brand page seemed to be used mainly for marketing purposes at the local level, particularly in Thailand. However, both global and local brand pages could attract participation from the publics in the form of postings. The most frequently posted content by both global and local publics was relational content, followed by promotional and organizational content. As the top global brands have made efforts to build and maintain relationships with their publics through Facebook, their publics are also willing to connect with these brands on Facebook as well.

References

Ahuja, V., & Medury, Y. (2010). Corporate blogs as e-CRM tools – Building consumer engagement through content management. *Journal of Database Marketing & Customer Strategy Management, 17*(2), 91–105. doi:10.1057/dbm.2010.8

Bhasin, B. B. (2010). *Doing business in the ASEAN countries.* New York, NY: Business Expert.

Bortree, D., & Seltzer, T. (2009). Dialogic strategies and outcomes: An analysis of environmental advocacy groups' Facebook profiles. *Public Relations Review, 35*(3), 317–319. doi:10.1016/j. pubrev.2009.05.002

Chu, S., & Kim, Y. (2011). Determinants of consumer engagement in electronic word-of-mouth (eWOM) in social network sites. *International Journal of Advertising: The Quarterly Review of Marketing Communications, 30*(1), 47–75. Doi:10.2501/IJA-30-1-047-075

Economic Intelligence Center. (2011, July–August) *How should businesses adapt to the social media era?* Retrieved from http://www.scb.co.th/eic/en/scb_eic_insight.shtml

Fernandes, J., Giurcanu, M., Bowers, K. W., & Neely, J. C. (2010). The writing on the wall: A content analysis of college students' Facebook groups for the 2008 presidential election. *Mass Communication & Society, 13*(5), 653–675. doi:10.1080/15205436.2010.516865

Grunig, J. E., & Huang, Y. H. (2000). From organizational effectiveness to relationship indicators: Antecedents of relationship, public relations strategies, and relationship outcomes. In J. A. Ledingham & S. D. Bruning (Eds.), *Public relations as relationship management: A relational approach to the study and practice of public relations* (pp. 23–54). Mahwah, NJ: Lawrence Erlbaum Associates.

Hallahan, K. (2008). Organizational-public relationships in cyberspace. In T. Hansen-Horn & B. D. Neff (Eds.), *Public relations: From theory to practice* (pp. 46–73). Boston, MA: Allyn & Bacon.

Ledingham, J. A., & Bruning, S. D. (1998). Relationship management in public relations: Dimensions of an organization-public relationship. *Public Relations Review, 24*(1), 55.

Ledingham, J. A. (2003). Explicating relationship management as a general theory of public relations. *Journal of Public Relations Research, 15*(2), 181–198. Retrieved from EBSCOhost.

Matusitz, J. (2011). Disney's successful adaptation in Hong Kong: A glocalization perspective. *Asia Pacific Journal of Management, 28*(4), 667–681. doi:10.1007/s10490-009-9179-7

Maynard, M., & Yan, T. (2004). Between global and glocal: content analysis of the Chinese websites of the 100 top global brands. *Public Relations Review, 30*(3), 285–291. doi:10.1016/j.pubrev.2004.04.003

Morgan, R. M. & Hunt, S. D. (1994) The commitment-trust theory of relationship marketing. *Journal of Marketing, 58*(3), 20–38.

Park, H., Rodgers, S., & Stemmle, J. (2011). Health organizations' use of Facebook for health advertising and promotion. *Journal of Interactive Advertising, 12*(1), 62–77.

Public Relations Society of America. (2011). *What is public relations?* Retrieved from http://www.prsa.org/AboutPRSA/ PublicRelationsDefined/

Rybalko, S., & Seltzer, T. (2010). Dialogic communication in 140 characters or less: How Fortune 500 companies engage stakeholders using Twitter. *Public Relations Review, 36*(4), 336–341. doi:10.1016/j. pubrev.2010.08.004

Semple, E. (2009) Update your crisis comm plan with social media, *Strategic Communication Management, 13*(5), 7. Retrieved from Communication & Mass Media Complete database.

Socialbakers. (2011). *Facebook statistics by country.* Retrieved from http://www.socialbakers.com/facebook-statistics/

Svenssen, G. (2001). "Glocalization" of business activities: a "glocal strategy" approach. *Management Decision, 39*(1), 6.

Thomlison, T. D. (2000). An interpersonal primer with implications for public relations. In J. A. Ledingham & S. D. Bruning (Eds.), *Public relations as relationship management: A relational approach to the study and practice of public relations* (pp. 177–204). Mahwah, NJ: Lawrence Erlbaum Associates.

Waters, R. D., Burnett, E., Lamm, A., & Lucas, J. (2009). Engaging stakeholders through social networking: How nonprofit organizations are using Facebook. *Public Relations Review, 35*(2), 102–106. doi:10.1016/j.pubrev.2009.01.006

XVII.   The Transition from the Traditional to the New Social Media Network in Malaysia

Fong Peng Chew

Faculty of Education, University of Malaya, Kuala Lumpur, Malaysia
Corresponding author: fpchew@um.edu.my

Fatt Hee Tie

Faculty of Law, University of Malaya, Kuala Lumpur, Malaysia
tiefh@um.edu.my

Abstract

With the advent of the Internet era, the new social media networks have brought a tremendous change to people's lives. Compared to the traditional media, the new media network with the ability to store large amounts of information, and its mode of transmission that has immediacy and interactivity can present information in text, images, sound, video, and other means of communication. Despite the many advantages, the rapid development of the new social media network does not affect the dominance of the traditional media in Malaysia. The discussion consists of five sections. Firstly, it examines the new media platforms that have emerged and the status of online media users in Malaysia as compared to other countries in Asia. Secondly, it analyzes the use of traditional and online newspapers. Thirdly, it discusses the present status of broadcasts and webcasts. Fourthly, the discussion focuses on the traditional television and network television. Finally, it examines the status of the traditional media and the new network media. The analysis from the social, legal, and cultural perspectives is derived from various reports.

Keywords: Traditional media, new media network, investment influence

1. Introduction

With the advent of the Internet age, whether it is from Web1.0 to Web2.0, or to the "Fifth Media", the 'new social media' have a significant influence on education, the economy, and the lives of many individuals. The new mode of transmission and exchange of information and knowledge via the new media networks have made a profound impact on all individuals. In order to meet the changing needs and demand of the consumers, the new media networks have also become more sophisticated and complex in nature. Most of the major newspapers and magazines have already established their online version.

On January 17, 1996, the newspaper Malaysia Doot (Utusan Malaysia) created its own online version to disseminate the latest news and other information. It established Malaysia's first online version of a newspaper. With the development of the Multimedia Super Corridor project by the government, more newspapers, magazines, and even government agencies have also established their own websites. Following Malaysia Doot (Utusan Malaysia), a number of newspapers have set up an online news website. These include the The Star, New Straits Times, Daily News (Berita Harian), Le Monde (Kosmo), Daily Sin Chew (Sin Chew Jit Poh) and Nanyang Siang Pau.

The traditional form of radio and television broadcasts and transmission has also undergone change. In order to provide news and other information on a twenty-four-hour basis, the radio and television stations have established their own individual online presence. In the cyber space that is seamless and borderless, this strategy is effective in helping to overcome the limitations of space and time. On December 27, 1995, the former Prime Minister Mahathir Muhammad, launched the government's Radio Television Malaysia Net. The online radio and television allows the audience to enjoy continuous Internet radio and television services (Ramli Mohamed & Adnan Hussein, 2006). Today, the Radio Television

Malaysia Net website in Malaysia continues to improve the quality of its content. Besides audio data, the website offers videos. In addition, it has also introduced a variety of "guest" content. These include "blogs", "podcasts", and "shoot-offs." The main purpose of these measures is to enrich the quality of service provided by the mass media.

2. New Media Platforms in Malaysia

Table 1 shows the use of the Internet, population data, penetration rate, and Facebook users in Asia. According to the Internet World Stats survey, in 2000, Malaysia had only 3.7 million Internet users; reaching 17.7 million Internet users in 2012, an increase of 478% in 12 years. In June 2012, the Internet penetration rate was 61%. Among the other developing countries in Asia, Malaysia's Internet penetration is among the highest ones. In comparison, the Indonesian Internet penetration rate was 22%, the Philippines penetration rate was 32%, and India featured only 11%. In China, with the largest number of Internet users in the world, the Internet penetration was 40%.

Among Internet users, Facebook is the most visited site in Malaysia (76%). Henceforth social media are responsible for one-third of web traffic in Malaysia. In April 2012, Facebook had a total of 900 million active users. There are more than 3.5 billion pieces of content (web links, news stories, blog posts, etc.) shared each week on Facebook. Up till date, there are 12,747,100 Facebook users in Malaysia, ranking number 18 among all countries. This also means that 49% of the Malaysian population is on Facebook.

There are 340 million tweets every day. Twitter has a total of more than 22 million daily unique visitors. Around 55% of Twitter users access the platform via their mobile. On the other hand, Pinterest hit 10 million monthly unique visitors, enjoying faster growth than any independent site in history. Pinterest is projected to account for 40% of social media driven purchases in the second quarter of 2012 (Facebook 60%). YouTube handles 10% of the Internet's traffic worldwide and has 4 billion views per day. Google+ is the second-most used social network for sharing multimedia content from a mobile device (10%) (22 Facts that You Must Know about Social Media in Malaysia, 2012).

When the Internet was introduced to Malaysia in 1995, only about one in a thousand Malaysians had Internet access. The number of Internet subscribers in Malaysia is expected to rise as it moves further towards advanced information, communications and multimedia services (Internet World Stats, 2012). Malaysian netizens spend on average 20 hours per week using the Internet (We are socials guide to social digital and mobile in Malaysia, 2011).

Figure 1 shows the amount of time that Malaysians spent online. Generally, Malaysians spent about 20 hours online a week. On the other hand, Singaporeans spent the highest amount of time online per week whereas Indonesia is the lowest.

(continued on page 572)

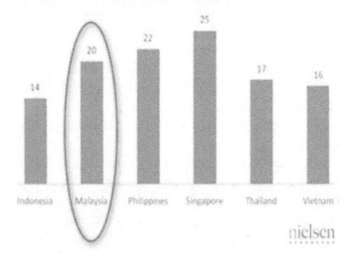

Figure 1: Time Spent Online by Malaysians
(Source: Nielsen Report 2011)

	Population (2012, estim.)	Internet Users (2000)	Internet Users (June 2012)	Penetration (% of Population)	User share (% of Asia)	Facebook Users (Sept. 2012)
Afghanistan	30,419,928	1,000	1,520,996	5 %	0.1 %	331,720
Armenia	2,970,495	30,000	1,800,000	61 %	0.2 %	335,480
Azerbaijan	9,493,600	12,000	4,746,800	50.0 %	0.4 %	896,980
Bangladesh	161,083,804	100,000	8,054,190	5.0 %	0.7 %	2,987,820
Bhutan	716,896	500	150,548	21.0 %	0.0 %	79,060
Brunei Darussalem	408,786	30,000	318,900	78.0 %	0.0 %	253,140
Cambodia	14,952,665	6,000	662,840	4.4 %	0.1 %	662,840
China *	1,343,239,923	22,500,000	538,000,000	40.1 %	50.0 %	611,640
Georgia	4,570,934	20,000	1,300,000	28.4 %	0.1 %	829,260
Hong Kong *	7,153,519	2,283,000	5,329,372	74.5 %	0.5 %	4,037,620
India	1,205,073,612	5,000,000	137,000,000	11.4 %	11.4 %	56,698,300
Indonesia	248,645,008	2,000,000	55,000,000	22.1 %	5.1 %	47,539,220
Japan	127,368,088	47,080,000	101,228,736	79.5 %	9.4 %	15,691,380
Kazakhstan	17,522,010	70,000	7,884,905	45.0 %	0.7 %	596,080

Table 1: Asia Population Data, Internet Use, and Facebook Statistics (* China figures do not include SAR Hong Kong, SAR Macao nor Taiwan, which are reported separately for statistical purposes.)

	Population (2012, estim.)	Internet Users (2000)	Internet Users (June 2012)	Penetration (% of Population)	User share (% of Asia)	Facebook Users (Sept. 2012)
Korea, North	24,589,122	--	--	--	--	n/a
Korea, South	48,860,500	19,040,000	40,329,660	82.5 %	3.7 %	9,434,920
Kyrgystan	5,496,737	51,600	2,194,400	39.9 %	0.2 %	91,460
Laos	6,586,266	6,000	592,764	9.0 %	0.1 %	224,720
Macao *	578,025	60,000	366,510	63.4 %	0.0 %	210,720
Malaysia	29,179,952	3,700,000	17,723,000	60.7 %	1.6 %	13,078,320
Maldives	394,451	6,000	134,860	34.2 %	0.0 %	134,860
Mongolia	3,179,997	30,000	635,999	20.0 %	0.1 %	438,940
Myanmar	54,584,650	1,000	534,930	1.0 %	0.0 %	n/a
Nepal	29,890,686	50,000	2,690,162	9.0 %	0.2 %	1,828,700
Pakistan	190,291,129	133,900	29,128,970	15.3 %	2.7 %	7,227,780
Philippines	103,775,002	2,000,000	33,600,000	32.4 %	3.1 %	29,657,780
Singapore	5,353,494	1,200,000	4,015,121	75.0 %	0.4 %	2,869,300
Sri Lanka	21,481,334	121,500	3,222,200	15.0 %	0.3 %	1,395,660

Table 1 (continued)

	Population (2012, estim.)	Internet Users (2000)	Internet Users (June 2012)	Penetration (% of Population)	User share (% of Asia)	Facebook Users (Sept. 2012)
Taiwan	23,234,936	6,260,000	17,530,000	75.4 %	1.6 %	12,242,200
Tajikistan	7,768,385	2,000	1,012,220	13.0 %	0.1 %	39,460
Thailand	67,091,089	2,300,000	20,100,000	30.0 %	1.9 %	16,834,140
Timor-Leste	1,143,667	0	10,293	0.9 %	0.0 %	n/a
Turkmenistan	5,054,828	2,000	252,741	5.0 %	0.0 %	8,200
Uzbekistan	28,394,180	7,500	8,575,042	30.2 %	0.8 %	145,260
Vietnam	91,519,289	200,000	31,034,900	33.9 %	2.9 %	7,876,200
TOTAL ASIA	3,922,066,987	114,304,000	1,076,681,059	27.5 %	100.0 %	235,989,160

Table 1 (continued)

Notes to Table 1: The demographic (population) numbers are based mainly on data contained in Census Bureau. The usage numbers come from various sources, mainly from data published by Nielsen Online, ITU, and other trustworthy sources.

Source Internet World Stats 2012, http://www.internetworldstats.com/.

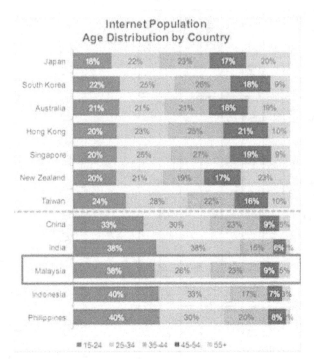

Figure 2: Internet Population Age Distribution by Country (Source: Com.Score Inc., 2011)

	Share of total online minutes
Social Networking	32%
Entertainment	12%
Portals	11%
Instant Messenger	5%
email (web-based only)	4%

Table 2: Top Online Categories by Share of Total Minutes in Malaysia (August 2011, visitors age 15+, home/work locations). Source: Com.Score, 2011

Table 2 shows that the majority of the Internet users in Malaysia are between the ages of 15 and 24 (38%), followed by those aged 25–34 (26%), 35–44 (23%), 45–54 (9%), and 55+ (5%). In 2011, about 46 percent of the users are males compared to 54 percent of female users (Asia Digital Marketing Year Book 2011).

TM net, a subsidiary of Telekom Malaysia is Malaysia's largest Internet service provider. While there are currently more than 10 Internet service providers in Malaysia, Telekom Malaysia owns a virtual monopoly of the broadband market due to their ownership of the nation's last mile connections.

There has been a rise in the use of social media both by customers and businesses. In Malaysia, social networking accounts for one third of all time spent online, where 78% of Malaysian Internet users spend their time on Facebook and 51% on YouTube. In comparison, the total minutes spent on web-based email on the other hand has seen a decrease in recent years. This has been attributed to the increasing number of young users that is driving email usage down. Web-based email has been replaced by communicating via wall posts, messages, tweets etc. This could also be due to the increase in mobile email users.

The British Broadcasting Corporation has coverage of the findings from a TNS report which suggest Malaysians are, on average, the world's biggest users of social networks with more friends than any other country in the world. The report found social networks users in Malaysia have, on average, 233 friends, with fellow Asian country Japan at the bottom of the list with an average of just 29 friends, while China is similarly low with an average of just 69 friends on social networks. As well as having the most friends, Malaysians are also the heaviest users of social networking sites, spending an average of nine hours per week on them. The study found that consumers are now spending more time on social networking sites than using e-mail. This is fueled in part by the rise in mobile net access. In rapid growth markets, users are embracing these new channels in much more active ways. The digital world is transforming how they live, develop and interact (Russel, 2010).

Social media affecting more and more aspects of life attracts more Malaysians and leads to more frequent use. The spread of the new media networks is instant, unlike traditional media which are limited by the publishing and broadcast cycle. New media networks can spread to the audience immediately, and information is updated 24 hours. Second, the large amount of information network installation and widespread use of the information of the new media is another strength that overshadows the traditional media. The latter are limited by broadcast time and regional restrictions (Mohd Safar Hashim, 2003: 90).

In addition, the new network media are compatible with text, pictures, sound, video, and other means of communication. They are able to provide information in a more attractive and effective manner rather than the single expression of the traditional media (Ramli Mohamed & Adnan Hussein, 2006, p. 4). Finally, the new network media interactive capabilities promote a more personalized service and foster stronger community public relations. These advantages make new network media more competitive. They have become a great threat to traditional media in many countries. They have caused a decline in newspaper circulation, and a decrease in advertising revenue. However, Malaysia's traditional media have adopted some measures to face the threat. The traditional media have successfully integrated new elements into the new media and, gradually build a dynamic and healthy medium ecological balance.

3. Traditional Newspapers versus Online Newspapers

The Printing Presses and Publications Act of 1984 requires all publications in Malaysia to obtain licenses from the Minister for Home Affairs. However, the license can be revoked at any time. The minister's decision is final, and there is no judicial review available. The United Malay National Organization (UMNO), Malaysia's dominant ruling political party, and its allies in the ruling National Front coalition directly own or control all major newspapers, radio and television stations. Dissemination of alternative news and opinions to the public is difficult. In 1987, the government halted the production of four newspapers as they reported some criticisms related to the government's policies. As a result, the Malaysian press is extremely careful when dealing with Malaysia's government's policies.

To date, there are more than 80 daily and weekly newspapers in various languages such as Malay, English, Chinese and Tamil (the size of the segment of each newspaper language is also in this order). Though the government advocates freedom of speech and a free press, it is said to restrict the flow of information in practice. Certain issues such as citizenship for non-Malays and the extraordinary position of the Malays in the social order are considered sensitive and citizens must refrain from discussing these issues. The media generally practice self-censorship and often provide optimistic and noncritical reports of governmental activities.

At present, the international standards that judge the influence of a newspaper consist of three aspects: spread speed, active reading rate, and reading circulation rate. As in other countries, newspaper circulation in Malaysia faces tremendous challenges due to competition posed by developments in information technology and online news websites. Readers have access to other alternative news media that provide a critical analysis of contemporary development.

In contrast, some experts disagreed with the above theories. These include Sohu CEO, Charles Zhang; China News general administration deputy director Shi Feng, Yu Guoming; and even Rupert Murdoch, the owner of the world's largest media group. They stated that the newspaper industry's difficulties are only temporary. Newspapers should merge and integrate to increase its strong competitiveness to face the challenge (The Global Market of Newspaper Industry Development, 2011).

When newspapers around the world are facing a sharp contraction in circulation, Malaysia newspaper circulation has been in a state of growth. Towards the end of 2008, the Media Specialist Association (MSA) published a report on the Malaysian newspaper circulation. The report showed that from 1988 to 2008, total newspaper circulation in West Malaysia has been on the upward trend overall (see Figure 3).

In 2009, the Omnicom Media Group (OMG) survey report showed that the Malaysian newspaper's average daily circulation was 4.8 million copies. According to the findings of a study released by the Omnicom Media Group in 2010, newspapers still maintain their advertisement revenue at the level of 57% from 2003 to 2010, despite the challenge from new online media. Since the study commenced in 2000, the OMG researchers found that there has been an increase of the circulation of newspapers in

Malaysia. The country is unique compared to other countries that showed a decline in the circulation of newspapers.

The total newspaper circulation is generally on the rise since 1998. The actual figure for 2008 would have being higher if data from newspapers such as Nanyang, Malay Mail and Weekend Mail are included. The statistics seems to show that the newsprint is "not dead yet" in this part of the world and it will co-exist nicely with online media. In fact, the growth in newspaper circulation has been steady all these years, partly contributed by the increase in the population and the development of a knowledge society. The growth of newspaper circulation in the country is encouraging, as the average daily net circulation crossed 2.8 million copies for the year ended June 30, 2008. This represented an increase of 12% from 2.5 million recorded on July 1, 2005 to June 30, 2008.

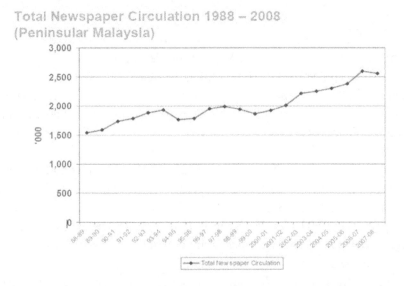

Figure 3: Total Newspaper Circulation 1988-2008 (Peninsular Malaysia).
Source: Malaysia Crunch, 2009

According to The Audit Bureau of Circulations Malaysia, as of the end of June 2010, the total newspaper circulation is Malaysia was around 4.5 million. Selangor state, where the capital of Kuala Lumpur is located, accounts for 40%, or 1.8 million copies. Malay language newspapers were most purchased at close to 40%, followed by Chinese and English dailies at around 20% each. However, the traditional media in Malaysia are facing a growing threat from online news platforms. According to the Audit Bureau of Circulations Malaysia, the average daily newspaper circulation in the country dipped one percentage point, about 50,000 copies, as compared to the previous year. The table below reflects circulation figures for the period ending 30 June 2010.

Daily Newspaper	Language	Circulation
Sin Chew Daily	Chinese	382,578
The Star	English	286,409
The Sun	English	300,550
Utusan Malaysia	Malay	170,558
Berita Harian	Malay	160,597
Harian Metro	Malay	378,354
New Straits Times	English	109,341
Weekend Circulation	Language	Circulation
New Sunday Times	English	129,554
Metro Ahad Was	Malay	431,418
The Sunday Star	English	295,552

Table 3: Circulation of Malaysia Newspaper in Mid-year of 2010 (Source: The ABC Report, 2010)

The study found that adults over the age of 30 spend more time than young people in reading newspapers in Malaysia. They read newspapers every day for 50 minutes on the average, the adolescent reading a newspaper only 30 minutes. The average adult's daily online time was around 3 hours and 19 minutes, while the 20 to 29 year-old youth daily averages spend more than four hours on the network (Mohd Safar Hasim, 2003).

In a study by Nielsen (2010) on the 30-day network activities, the findings showed that 34% of the Internet users in Malaysia read the local newspaper online. Social networking activities remained the most important activities among the Internet users (71%). Therefore, in general, the demands of Internet users in Malaysia are entertainment and socializing. The time spent by young Internet users to read online newspapers is less than the adults. Adults over the age of 30 tend to access news information more frequently.

The development of the online services is rapid, but the status of Malaysia's traditional newspapers is still stable. This is due to the relatively liberal media environment in the country and the public reading habits. While the mainstream media are under the ruling party's influence, the opposition parties are free to publish their own newspapers such as The Rocket, Suara Keadilan (Sound of Justice) and Harakah. The content of the above publications are more realistic than online information and a stable concept has been instilled in the Malaysian education system, particularly in the citation in academic papers and books. Therefore, compared to online information, Malaysians are more confident of the authenticity of the paper publications.

The brand strength of the traditional newspapers, the use of modern technology, and the creation of the online edition of authoritative newspapers have combined to change the "net user" into a "reader". It is capable of forming a stable reading group as the traditional newspapers are able to maintain their credibility and enhance interaction among their readers. According to Mohd Yahya and Noor Ismawati Jaafar (2009), online visits to the network at Utusan Malaysia from 2005 to 2008 presented increasing growth rates of 8%, 16% and 36% over the years. Obviously the online edition of the newspaper is changing the reading habits of the public. It showed the newspaper authoritative's information while at the same time, it is quick, cheap, interactive, and content-rich. It has less limitations and its uniquenessis able to attract more readers.

Besides that, Malaysian government is trying to defend the role and influence of the traditional media. It stated that news carried by the traditional media, such as television, still plays a crucial and interpretative role that audiences cannot do without despite the pervasiveness of the Internet. It suggests that the 'Internet and new media competed for people's time and left questions and doubts in the users' minds about the content, interests and sources, and that rumors and sensationalized stories and even outright lies were being spewed out in the name of news' (Digital Media in Malaysia, 2012).

According to Table 7, the Nielsen study found that the radio has a large group of loyal listeners. Every week, there are 1.55 million listeners in total. Nine out of ten listeners are aged 10 years and above. The study also found that the average listening duration increased by 5% to 22 hours a week.

3. Traditional Broadcasters versus Webcasts

Unlike the newspaper, the traditional broadcast and network broadcast only occur from the perspectives of technicality and changes in the carrier mode. Listening to the radio is no longer confined to the radio. As long as there is a computer and network, people can listen to the radio at home, in the office and even in the library. Some websites also save recordings of past programs, and provide later access to audience who missed the program.

Everyday 2.05 million listeners listen to the radio for at least 15 minutes. The study showed that the top three radio stations are the stations that used the Malay language. A weekly average of about 4.22 million listeners listens to the Sinar radio while the ERA Radio has 4.15 million listeners. In third place is Hotfm, which have an audience of 3.55 million. The ranking in Table 4 showed that the top 10 radio stations play pop music. Therefore, Malaysian radio listeners like to listen to music as a form of entertainment. In Malaysia crackdown against piracy of intellectual property rights protection by the authorities is relatively strong. However, most of the local site pop songs cannot be downloaded directly. An online music box that is similar to Baidu does not exist.

In 2010, Yahoo Synovate Co., Ltd.'s survey of network usage trends in Malaysia showed that almost 51% of Internet users upload and download songs from Youtube. Although YouTube has become the main channel to download and upload audio and video materials, the content in the website is mainly in the form of micro-video. Those who want to download free

Malaysia local songs in mp4 format face many difficulties. Even though there is a web page to download songs, it is slow to do so.

Position	Station	Listeners Weekly	Share of Listenship
1	SINAR	4.22 Million	24.6%
2	ERA	4.15 Million	24.3%
3	Hotfm	3.55 Million	20.7%
4	THR	3.64 Million	19.3%
5	MY fm	2.03 Million	11.9%
6	Suria Fm	1.88 Million	11.0%
7	hitz.fm	1.57 Million	9.2%
8	988	1.55 Million	9.0%
9	Klasic Nasional	1.26 Million	7.4%
10	Muzikfm	1.08 Million	6.3%

Table 4: The top radio stations in Malaysia
Source: Nielsen Radio Audience Measurement, 2010

By eliminating the need to find and download music channels, the music moderator is always in a lively conversation broadcast with today's most popular songs. Some music stations also operate a VOD system where listeners can send text messages or phone calls and choose the songs that they want to hear. This interaction aims to strengthen the sense of audience participation. In Malaysia, there has been an increase of listeners at two radio stations, the Hot FM and the Fly FM stations. From 2006 to 2011, Hot FM recorded a 37% increase in listeners whereas Fly Fm recorded a 30% increase in listenership (Media Prima Annual Report 2011). The increase in listeners showed that Malaysians prefer the traditional media as a source of entertainment rather than the new media network.

4. Traditional TV versus Network TV

Three different groups owned the television stations in Malaysia, namely the government television, the semi-government television, and the private television stations. Malaysia's state-run television stations (Radio Television Malaysia, RTM) consists of two channels, TV1 and TV2. It broadcasts news, talk shows, children's programs, documentaries, entertainment, drama and other related programs. The semi-government Bergama TV, provides network television. The private television stations consists of four free wireless television (TV3, NTV7, 8TV, TV9), and three subscription televisions (FineTV, Astro, DETV). It is worth mentioning that the above four private television stations now are controlled by Media Prima Limited Malaysia (Media Prima Berhad, MPB).

Media Prima Co., Ltd. is the largest media group in Malaysia. It owns 100% of the equity of the domestic private television channels and has a 43% stake of The New Straits Times Group company. As a leader in the television industry, the programs attracted 54% of the audience in Malaysia. However, the group's annual report showed that its two free television viewership shares are at different degrees of decline. TV3's share declined from 35% in 2005 to 28% in 2010 whereas NTV7 fell from 8% in 2005 to 5% in 2010. On the other hand, market shares of the other two other televisions, TV9 and TV8 increased after several years of decline. Nevertheless, all the television channels experienced growth. Even if the viewership shares are down, the absolute value of the four television shares remained high, and the worst at 5%, the highest TV3 reached 28%, which is much higher than the other national and foreign television program shares (Media Prima Annual Report 2010).

In 2010, the top American television program market share in the United States was 5.3%, whereas the program "American Idol" reached 7%. In China, the top-rated program "Happy Camp" has a 7% rating. On the other hand,, the other two programs "You Are the One" and "Happy Girl" have a 2–3% rating even though both are popular programs.

In Malaysia, the viewership shares of television programs are high as the number of television stations is small. In 2010, Chinese TV (DETV) became Malaysia's first network television (IPTV). The DETV broadcasts mainly Chinese television programs. As the audience consists of local

Chinese (25% of the total population), it does not have much appeal for the two other ethnic audiences, the Malays and the Indians. The development of Malaysia's network television is still at an infant stage. Currently the most competitive service is YouTube.

In recent years, more young people are watching video online. However, in a 2011 survey by Nielsen, 83% of Malaysians spent on average 10 hours and 6 minutes daily watching television. However, almost 42% of Malaysians used the Internet and other non-official sources to watch the television. In comparison, a report showed that in the United Kingdom and United States adults spent 28 hours per person per week watching television (Nation Master, 2011). Overall, Malaysians spend less time watching television than the Americans and British. Malaysians prefer to watch major sports events or important news event live on television. This is to avoid the slow Internet speed. In 2010, RTM telecasted the World Soccer tournament to about 4 million people. In 2010, RTM's live telecast of the Suzuki Cup football finals in Southeast Asia brought about 2.8 million viewers (RTM Sasar Empat Juta Penonton Piala Dunia FIFA 2010, 2010), In 2011, NTV7 broadcast the British royal wedding live between Prince William and Catherine Middleton, and attracted 2.30 million viewers across the country.

5. Traditional Media and the New Network Media Status Quo

Notwithstanding the challenges of the new media, whether online newspapers, magazines, radio or television, the traditional media in Malaysia remain a powerful influence. In other words, the mainstream media remain the 'mainstay for engagement' in Malaysia. There is a close relationship between the power of influence and the brand of the product. The media provide quality products and services to strengthen its branding and promote loyalty among its customers. The network media may avoid the stringent audit of the traditional media. However, the online media have limited human and financial resources. They face a number of challenges especially when they insist on independent practices. An example is that of the Independent News Online May 19, 2011, which is a popular online private news site among young people. As a result of the financial crisis, the sponsors of the site stopped its investment in the company. The news site shut down due to a lack of funds. In contrast, the traditional media are either controlled by the ruling political party or monopolized by entrepreneurs. They are financially strong and possess tremendous human and financial resources, plus experience in operation and management.

The semi-government owned corporation, Media Prima, owns four terrestrial television stations, (including market leader TV3), three radio stations and some other newspapers. Two other government-owned channels are used to reach out to the 'rural and civil service' audiences. Radio is a powerful voice in the country, reaching nine out of ten Malaysians. AMP Radio is the key player. In addition, the entrepreneur Tiong Hiew King owns five major Chinese newspapers, namely, "Sin Chew Daily", "China Daily", "Nanyang Siang Pau" and "Guangming Daily". Although freedom of the press is limited, these newspapers continue to attract a wide audience because they provide better information and services. The online media create a healthy media ecology as they are able to inject vitality, but the fragility and instability of the brand has long remained a challenge.

The influence of the traditional media is being rapidly deconstructed by the popularity of socio-political bloggers and online news sites, such as 'Malaysiakini', 'Malaysia Today', 'The Malaysian Insider' and 'The Nut Graph'. Earlier, the government had promised to ensure that it does not restrict the freedom of the network media as it seeks to attract more foreign investment. However, the online news website 'Malaysia Today' editor had been detained under the anti-terrorist security laws, before being released two months later, for writing on a corruption scandal and the murder of a foreigner. He was the first Malaysian blogger to be charged under the Sedition Act 1948. The threat of being charged for a criminal offence gives rise to tension between the authorities and the country's blogosphere.

Blog content that identifies the actual author under the real-name system is more transparent, honest, convincing and realistic from the public's perspectives. The real-name system is able to attract the attention of the authorities when the influential blog discusses some sensitive topics. In the

Malaysia-ASEAN Blog Forum, the present Prime Minister expressed that Malaysia would never filter and review network content. He welcomed the "Democratic Network Blog" and also advises the bloggers to tell the truth to avoid legal action. Generally, the healthy development of the network media not only relies on the government's open policy, but also depends on the media literacy and individual values of the Internet users.

Consequently, the Ministry of Information, Communication and Culture supported Malaysia Social Media Week (MSMW) 2012, an inaugural event with the objective to engage people with ideas through communication platforms. One of the topics that the MSMW 2012 discussed are the emerging trends in social and mobile media. It was delivered through interactive conferences and videos that were streamed online (Malaysia Social Media Week, 2013). Some of the audiences that the MSMW 2012 targeted are the C-level executives, journalists, bloggers, marketing managers, social media strategists, and students. The platform enables and connects like-minded people into a community that makes the sharing of ideas possible.

The functionality of the media also determines the size of the force of its impact. Malaysians use the traditional media as the primary means to access information as they are deemed to be authoritative, and reliable, Television and radio continue to be a major source of information to a large group of individuals as it is convenient and easy to own. About 55% of the population uses the Internet. However, the penetration rate of computers and networks is less than that of radio and television. In the villages and towns, almost every household has a television. Families who own a computer are not much less.

Malaysians have the habit of having morning and afternoon tea. During tea time, office workers can be seen sipping coffee while reading the newspaper or watching television at the roadside stalls. Indeed, to turn on the television or radio is more convenient than starting the computer to read the news. Housewives tend to listen to the radio or watch television more than the office workers. A survey showed that the main purposes of browsing the Internet among Malaysians are for entertainment, to play computer games and to socialize. The implementation of the Multimedia Super Corridor project has promoted the development of the new media in Malaysia, whether newspaper network or online radio and online television. To some extent, the new media have provided the Malaysian public with enriched entertainment, a high degree of openness and greater freedom of expression.

The limitations of the network of new media in online audiovisual and download function also weakened its audience appeal. In Malaysia, due to copyright protection, the vast majority of local Websites provide fee-based services to download a song or video. The audience must select the correct fees package which has a certain amount of risk before enjoying the service. The free online on-demand and download YouTube website is not owned by local Malaysians. As a result, the video contents are varied but dispersed. In addition, due to the time limit upload video on YouTube, some Malaysian movies are cut into several fragments to upload. As a result, more people are willing to spend RM7–15 in the cinema to enjoy a stunning visual experience unlike the fragmented video that is available online. In the last two years, Malaysia's state-run television began its official website to provide online television programs on demand. A number of private television stations also provide free TV shows-on-demand service via the website www.tonton.com.my. This formed the start of Malaysia's local network TV shows on demand.

Currently, advertising in the media is still biased in favor of the traditional media. The traditional media's advertising revenue accounted for 95% of the total amount of advertising revenue. However, heavy capital investment is needed to take advantage of the new network media to promote public relations. Studies have shown that the new media have a lot of potential since network advertisement spending increased two times. The media itself needs promotion and new packaging to attract more audiences and expand their market share.

6. Conclusion

The traditional media in Malaysia remain strong. Its integration with new media is the development trend of the Malaysian media in the future. The traditional media must improve its content if they want to maintain their competitiveness and to attract more users. They must implement media product optimization strategies to strengthen their brand. They also must meet the needs of the users, personalize their services, and enhance interactivity between the media and the general public. The new network media has broken the monopoly of the traditional media. The new media allow greater freedom of expression and allow extensive and frequent interaction among members in the society. They will form a new media ecological balance.

References

22 facts that you must know about social media in Malaysia 2012 (2012). Downloaded from http://www.entrepreneurs.my/22-facts-that-you-must-know-about-social-media-in-malaysia/

Administration training center of the state administration of radio, flm and television. *The ASEAN development overview on radio and television* (2008). Beijing, China: China Radio and Television Press.

Asia Digital Marketing Association (2011). *Asia digital marketing year book 2011*. Downloaded from http://www.asiadma.com.

Audit Bureau of Circulation (2010). *The ABC report: Circulation figure for the period ending 30 June, 2010.*

Cohen, N. (2012, April 24). The Breakfast Meeting: Grilling for James Murdoch, and Facebook Tops 900 Million Users. *The New York Times.*

Com.Score. Inc. (2011, October 17). *Social networking accounts for one third of all tme spent online in Malaysia.* Downloaded from http://www.comscore.com/fre/Insights/Press_Releases/2011/10/Social_Networking_Accounts_for_One_Third_of_All_Time_Spent_Online_in_Malaysia

Digital media in Malaysia (2012). Downloaded from https://wiki.smu.edu.sg/digitalmediaasia/Digital_Media_in_Malaysia

Internet world stats (2012). *Internet usage statistics: The Internet big picture.* Downloaded from http://www.internetworldstats.com/stats3.htm # asia

Malaysia Crunch (2009). *An observation on newsprint circulation. 2009.* Downloaded from http://www.malaysiacrunch.com/2009/06/observation-on-newsprint-circulation.html

Malaysia social media week (2013). Downloaded from http://socialmediaweek.com.my/

Media Prima Berhad (2010). *Media prima annual report 2010.*

Media Prima Berhad (2011). *Media prima annual report 2011.*

Mohd Y. M. A, & Sudhaman, A. (2010: March 12). Malaysia is rapidly becoming the poster-child for the transformative power of social media. 12 March, Downloaded from www.prweek.com. A. (2010: March 12). Malaysia is rapidly becoming the poster-child for the transformative power of social media. 12 March, Downloaded from www.prweek.com. & Noor Ismawati Jaafar. 2009. "Online newspaper in Malaysia: A perliminary study", *Malaysian Journal of Media Studies, 11*(1), pp.83-94.http://www.marketing-interactive.com/news/17417

Nation Master (2011). *Media statistic: Television viewing by country.* Downloaded from http://www.nationmaster.com/graph/med_tel_vie-media-television-viewing

Nguyen, J. (2010). *The state of social networks in Asia Pacific, with a focus on Malaysia. 2010.* Downloaded from http://www.comscore.com/Press_Events/Presentations_Whitepapers/2010/The_State_of_Social_Networks_in_Asia_Pacific_with_a_Focus_on_Malaysia/%28language%29/eng-US

Nielsen (2011). *Nielsen Report 2011*: The digital media habits and attitudes of Southeast Asian consumers. Downloaded from http: //www.my.nielsen.com/news/20110413.shtml

Nielsen radio audience measurement (2012). Downloaded from http://www.nielsen.com/us/en/measurement/radio-measurement.html

Ramli M. & Adnan H. (2006). The media in Malaysia: Aspirations, choices and realities. *Kajian Malaysia, 24*(1 & 2), pp. 1-7.

RTM Sasar Empat Juta Penonton Piala Dunia FIFA (2010: February 28). *Star, 28.*

Russel, J. (2010: October 11). Is Malaysia world's biggest social network addict? *UTC.*

Sudhaman, A. (2010: March 12). Malaysia is rapidly becoming the poster-child for the transformative power of social media. Downloaded from www.prweek.com.

Synovate (2010). *Websites for Malaysia network usage yrends.* Downloaded from http://www.statmyweb.com/s/website-for-malaysia

We are social's. Guide to social, digital, and mobile in Malaysia (2011: December). Downloaded from http://www.slideshare.net/wearesocialsg/we-are-socials-guide-to-social-digital-and-mobile-in-malaysia-dec-2011

PART SEVEN:
THE PACIFIC RIM

XVIII.   Australian Social Media Trends

John Harrison

School of Journalism and Communication,
The University of Queensland, Brisbane, Australia
j.harrison@uq.edu.au

Sean Rintel

School of Journalism and Communication,
The University of Queensland, Brisbane, Australia
s.rintel@uq.edu.au

Elizabeth Mitchell

School of Journalism and Communication,
The University of Queensland, Brisbane, Australia
Corresponding author: ek.mitchell@uq.edu.au

Abstract

The vast distances Australians must negotiate to connect their small, highly urbanized population both nationally and internationally have long created the incentive for invention, innovation and the early adoption of communication technologies. Important also in any reflection in relation to Australia's socio-technological evolution is this country's location as a modern, developed, predominately western nation perched in the south-east of the Asian landmass. The Australian continent's seven million square kilometers are geographically, and increasingly economically, politically and culturally, part of Asia. Forty percent of Australians were born overseas and almost one third of overseas-born Australians were born in Asia (Australian Bureau of Statistics, 2013). At the end of 2012, Australia's population was approaching 23 million with about half that number—12.2 million—Internet subscribers. Broadband subscribers accounted for 98% of subscriptions; the split between private and public (business or government) use was 76% and 24% respectively. After exploring some of the central characteristics and tensions of the social media landscape in Australia, the authors illustrate issues and trends in social media usage in Australia and conclude with a discussion of salient policy issues, including challenges around the evolution of digital infrastructure, media law and copyright.

Keywords: Social media, Australia, social networks, social business, online communication, Internet, national broadband network, regulation, copyright, Twitter

1. Introduction

Increasingly more present in the lives of every Australian, the rise of social media in Australia has been rapid, unrelenting and invigorating. We have, as a nation, been left breathless at the pace, the intensity and the drama that continues to unfold, co-created by many voices across an ever-increasing array of platforms. Take, for example, the case of Australian television presenter Charlotte Dawson, who was admitted to a psychiatric hospital after being attacked by trolls on Twitter (Hornery & Hall, 2012). Another example comes from the much-loved world of cricket; coach Mickey Arthur closed his Twitter account after being abused by fans unhappy with the sacking of four players before the Third Test against India (Badel, 2013). Also from sport, a promising Australian rugby league star, Josh Dugan, lost a lucrative $2 million, three-year contract after an unsavoury social media rant on Instagram (Garry, 2013). Finally and perhaps most notably, former Australian Prime Minister Kevin Rudd has the most-followed Twitter account in the country (1.2 million). When Rudd made a third run for the leadership of the country and was rejected, the drama played out across social and traditional media platforms around the nation (Vonow, 2013). Social media in Australia are in their adolescence, and we are watching their maturation with interest and not a little trepidation.

This chapter describes and explores some of the central characteristics and tensions of the social media landscape in Australia. We begin by outlining key trends in social media usage by individuals, businesses, and institutions. We elaborate some of the more interesting emergent issues using five vignettes and conclude with details of the most salient policy issues, ranging from infrastructure to media law and copyright.

Social media, in the context of the discussion that follows, are online communication platforms with three distinct features: The first feature is that human social networks are technologically manifested through bounded systems in which users (a) construct public, semi-public, or private profiles, (b) accept or articulate a list of other users with whom they share a connection, and (c) view and traverse their lists of connections and those made by others (see also boyd and Ellison's (2007) definition of social network sites). Secondly, social media involves some element of user-generated content: multi-media products generated by individual users or by an aggregation of users. Generation of content covers both original content from a user and content posted by a user but from another source. Thirdly, user-generated content is shared, searchable, and can be responded to, across one or many technologically-articulated human social networks.

2. Internet Connectivity in Australia

With Australia's population approaching 23 million, at the end of December 31, 2012 there were 12.2 million Internet subscribers in this nation. Of the 98% who were broadband, 76% were households, and 24% were classified as business and government. As for mobile use, at 31 December 2012, there were 17.4 million subscribers with Internet access connections via a mobile handset in Australia, an increase of 7% over the six month period from 30 June 2012 (ABS, 2012a). Between June 2011 and May 2012, the take-up of smartphones doubled, increasing from 25%

of the adult population at June 2011 to 49% at May 2012 (Australian Communications and Media Authority, 2013).

Age Profiles of Internet Users

Previous research, both in Australia (Sum, Mathews, Hughes & Campbell, 2008) and internationally (Czaja & Lee, 2007), has shown that older people are least likely to be connected to the Internet. As at mid-2012, Sensis reported that 100% of those in the demographic bands 14 to 19, 20 to 29, and 30 to 39 all had access to the Internet; while 99% of those aged 40 to 49 and 50 to 54 had access, and that of those aged 65 and over 93% had access. Thus Internet access in Australia is all but universal. There are data to suggest that urban dwellers have more intense patterns of use, as have younger people, those with higher incomes, and those with higher levels of education (Sensis, 2012, p. 10).

Time and Activity Online

Research by the Roy Morgan organisation conducted in the first half of 2012 found that online messaging and interaction (not including e-mail) accounted for the largest proportion of time spent online, some 13 minutes each day, and three times the amount of time spent on second most frequent activity – search (Roy Morgan Research, 2013).

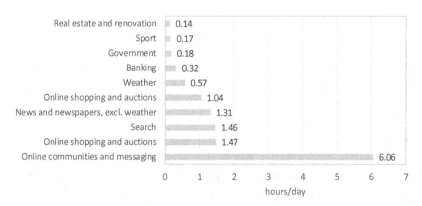

Figure 1: Hours spent online per month by Australians (as of 2012)

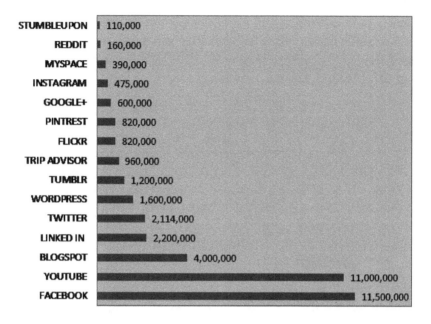

Figure 2: Active users of top 15 social media sites in Australia (as of August 2012)

Significant gender differences have also emerged in the types of activities undertaken online, with news and newspapers ranking at number five for women at number two for men; e-mail at number two for women and number four for men, and online shopping and auctions at number four for women and number six for men (Roy Morgan, 2013). Figure 2 describes the penetration of social media in Australia as at August 2012, from both fixed and mobile accounts, the latest data available from AdCorp (2013).

3. The Social Media Landscape in Australia

The two biggest sites by usage are Facebook, with the number of Facebook accounts equal to 50% of the Australian population, and

YouTube. Facebook has 11.5 million user accounts; YouTube 11 million. More recent data from Social Media News (2013) suggest that in 2013 the number of Facebook accounts fell away slightly in the first quarter of 2013, although growth between 2011 and 2012 was 1 million new accounts. YouTube growth has also plateaued in 2013 after year-on-year growth from 2011 to 2013 of about 1 million accounts.

Facebook

The average Australian accesses Facebook 20 times a week, with men on average 21.6 times and women 19.8 times. There are substantial differences in Facebook usage by age, which reflect lower uptake of social media by older persons, as indicated in Figure 3 (Sensis, 2012, p. 19).

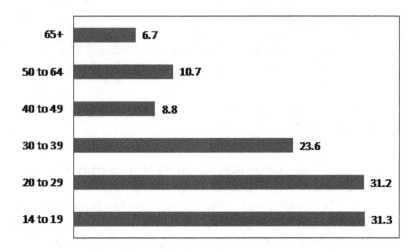

Figure 3: Average weekly use of Australian's use of Facebook in age ranges (as of 2012)

Australian Facebook users reportedly spend an average of 18 minutes each time they access the site (Sensis, 2012, p. 20). Australians use Facebook in many of the same ways as users from all cultures (mostly interacting with friends and family by sharing personal images and statuses), but they seem to be especially keen on sharing image macro-style memes (Rintel, 2013) on Facebook groups. All Australian cities have many pages and groups devoted to sharing image macros commenting on varied aspects of social life. Three categories are especially common: city pages/groups about the behaviour of residents from certain suburbs; university and school pages/ groups about internal or external issues; and public transport pages about bus or train services. While there are often culturally-insensitive posts on such pages/groups, an overtly racist indigenous Facebook meme group received strong public outcry was removed after online petitions (Sykes, 2012).

YouTube

There are several common threads in four of the top five YouTube accounts: they are young; they are comedic; they are metropolitan (from either Sydney or Melbourne), and three of the four are of Asian descent. With the possible exception of Natalie Tran, none have a profile in mainstream media, but their YouTube presence is linked extensively with other popular social media platforms, such as Facebook, Twitter and Tumblr. The data in Figure 4 come from Social Blade (2013), a social media tracking site.

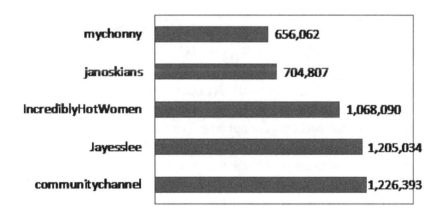

Figure 4; Top five Australian YouTube accounts (as of 2013)

Natalie Tran's video blogs styled Community Channel have made her an Internet celebrity. The daughter of a refugee family from Vietnam, Sydney-based Tran (born 1986) began posting in 2006, and to date has nearly 300 two to three minute observational and frequently self-deprecating posts. Tran has successfully monetised her site, and has been able to cross over into mainstream media such as the Sydney Morning Herald and The Project on Network 10.

Korean-born Sydney-raised pop duo, Janice and Sonia Lee, popular in Thailand, Singapore, and Hong Kong, and the second most popular You Tube account in Australia, have no mainstream media profile. SBS World News was the only Australian media outlet to run a story about the twins, in the past two years, despite coverage in The Bangkok Post, The Straits Times and The South China Morning Post. The Lees are members of the New Life Community Church in Rydalmere, which they describe as "charismatic Presbyterian", one of some 150 diasporic Korean churches in Sydney (Park, 2012). IncrediblyHotWomen is a YouTube channel which features heavily pixelted excerpts of soft core porn films.

Janoskians—an acronym for Just Another Name Of Silly Kids In Another Nation—are a group of Melbourne-based teenage street comedians. Using social media to showcase their activities—grotesque to some, appealing to others—has propelled them to Internet fame that evolved into real life when the group embarked on a tour of the United Kingdom in early 2013. The visit caused chaos at Heathrow, London's major airport, when the efforts of 1,200 waiting fans to see their idols were thwarted by authorities claiming health and safety concerns (Saunders, 2013). Approximately ten thousand fans were then reported as descending upon London's Hyde Park after the group tweeted their location (Coster, Dennehy, Epstein & Te Koha, 2013). The moral of the tale is that pot of international fame is now waiting at the end of the social media rainbow for those with the talent and the mix of digital savvy, talent and good luck to build a following.

Another social media celebrity in the Australian milieu is John Luc (born 1991), known online as mychonny. A Melbourne-based Australian of Vietnamese-Chinese descent, John Luc joined You Tube in 2008. Luc runs several channels which focus in a comedic fashion on his Asian heritage and his Australian context. Luc has five you tube channels "Mychonny" "Yourchonny" "chonnyday" "Chonnygame" and "KPopchonny" and his website sells games and merchandise.

Blogspot and Wordpress

Google-owned Blogspot, currently the number three social media site in Australia, is facing increased competition from WordPress. Blogspot has dropped from 4.7 million users in 2011 to 3 million in 2013 while WordPress has jumped from 1,600,000 accounts in 2012 to 2.9 million in the first quarter of 2013 (Social Media News, 2013a). On these figures, WordPress would have a 12.5% share of the Australian population, and as the art of blogging becomes more sophisticated, it seems that bloggers are turning to a platform that gives them greater options—WordPress.

LinkedIn

The two sources we have consulted for statistics on the size of social media sites in Australia Social Media News and AdCorp have substantially different data on LinkedIn. In 2012, LinkedIn had 2.2 million accounts, according to Social Media News and AdCorp. In the first quarter of 2013, the number of LinkedIn accounts grew, but the rate of that growth is contested. According to Social Media News, the growth was 500, 000 to 2.75 million. In contrast, AdCorp (2013) puts the figure at 3.7 million accounts. Irrespective of which figure is accurate, LinkedIn is growing quickly in Australia, as concerns about privacy move consumers to distinguish personal social media sites such as Facebook and their professional sites such as LinkedIn. Other factors that may have influenced this growth include a much softer employment market in 2012 that saw many more professionals on the job market.

Twitter

The high public profile of Twitter probably reflects its widespread use in discourse across the public sphere, especially among journalists, politicians and pundits. While Twitter grew from an estimated 1.8 million accounts in 2011 to 2.1 million in 2013, it is a controversial medium. Press gallery veteran Dennis Shanahan of Rupert Murdoch's The Australian newspaper has heavily criticized Twitter's accuracy, self-serving usage for self-promotion, it's arrogance and predisposition to invite hostility (Shanahan, 2013).

While the social value of Twitter is contended, the fact that Twitter is a self-promoting tool for politicians, celebrities and pundits is uncontested. Four of those in the top ten Twitter list in Australia are musicians, another is an actor, and two are sportsmen. However, the most followed Twitter account in Australia in April 2013 was former Prime Minister, Kevin Rudd (see Figure 5).

Musician David King, the Wollongong-based musician whose group the Contagious (@the_contagious) features 14-year-old singer Annalivia follows Kevin Rudd at number two; actress and model Jasmine Curtis-Smith (@jascurtissmith) is number three. A large gap emerges between the top three, who have more than a million followers, and the rest of the field, which begins with just over half a million followers (see Figure 5). Rugby union player Quade Cooper (@QuadeCooper) and Australian cricket captain Michael Clarke (@MClareke23) are number four and number seven respectively. The digital media strategist for evangelical international aid and development agency World Vision, Alistair Cameron (@alicam), and Mark Ferris, (@suburbview) a first-time buyer who was frustrated as he was unable to locate properties quickly and efficiently on the Internet, and who launched his real estate search engine in 2006, are number five and six respectively.

Melbourne-based band Cut Copy (@cutcopy) formed in 2001 by Dan Whitford, a DJ and graphic designer is number eight; Fawaz Adam Ibrahim, (@itsfuzzwuzz), 19-year-old Australian singer-songwriter is number nine, and Hillsong singer and worship leader Darlene Zscheh (@DarleneZscheh) rounds out the top ten. Hillsong is a Sydney-based Pentecostal mega-church. The dominance of musicians on the Australian top ten list bears out the acuity of Twitter launching its own digital music service in April 2013.

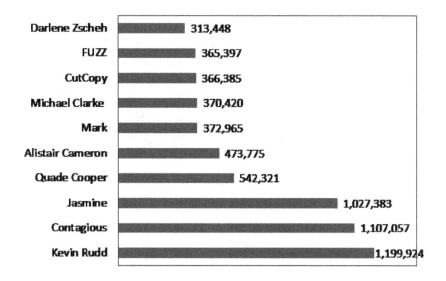

Figure 5: Most followed Australian Twitter accounts (as of April 2013)

Former Australian Prime Minister, Kevin Rudd (@KRuddMP), completely dominates the social media landscape in politics. In contrast, the current Prime Minister, Julia Gillard, has 371,264 followers on Twitter; Opposition Leader Tony Abbott 115,975; the Opposition's shadow minister for the digital economy, Malcolm Turnbull has 159,980 followers. The government Minister for Communications, Broadband and the Digital Economy, Senator Stephen Conroy does not tweet.

Taking a wider view, the rise of Twitter has made it possible for Axel Bruns and colleagues to create the Australian Twitter News Index, which provides weekly snapshots of how mainstream news outlet stories are retweeted and commented upon. Bruns (2012) contends that this index provide a more accurate sense of how Australians are meaningfully engaging with Australian news content than traditional circulation figures.

Tumblr and Pinterest

Tumblr, (founded 2007) probably because of its ease of use, has grown from 1 million users in 2011 to 2.6 million users in 2013. It has a high level of popularity with young people, whereas Pinterest (released in 2011) is popular among women, and related lifestyle interests such as weddings, fashion, cooking and design. Estimates of the number of users of Pinterest vary from 640,000 (Social Media News, 2013), to 1.2 million (AdCorp, 2013).

Instagram and Flickr

The popularity of photo sharing sites Instagram (established 2010) and Flickr (founded 2006) have both shown a decline from 2012 to 2013, and current subscriptions to both are calculated variously. Social Media News (2013) suggests that Instagram declined from 1,283,500 users in 2012 to 1,083,924 in 2013. In contrast, Ad Corp (2012, 2013) suggests the platform only had 425,000 users in 2012 but 834,202 in 2013. Flickr, which celebrates its 10th anniversary in 2014, has either plateaued, or is in decline, with Social Media News (2011, 2013) showing 1.3 million users in 2011, down to 850,000 in 2013. Ad Corp (2013) figures show Flickr users at 924,045 in 2013.

In assessing the currency of social media sites, and the popularity of various users, it needs to be recognised that these data are simply a snapshot in time, and the advent of new devices, new platforms, and new applications can change the landscape quickly. We should not forget the lesson of MySpace, which once dominated social media, but is now down to less than 390,000 users in Australia. In 2007, the application had a reported 3 million users in Australia (Haynes, 2007).

Business and Social Media

As at 30 June 2011 (the latest reliable data available) 91.2% of Australian businesses had Internet access (ABS, 2012b). However, less than half of Australian businesses had any online presence, including a social media page. According to the Department of Broadband, Communications and the Digital Economy (DBCDE), there is a significant gap between micro and big businesses, with just 33.2 % of micro businesses having a web presence compared to 97.3 % of big businesses (DBCDE, 2012). Those least likely to have an online presence are businesses in agriculture, forestry and fishing (13.0 %), transport, postal and warehousing (21.6 %) and construction (31.9 %) (DBCDE, 2012).

In this environment, Australian business, particularly in the business-to-business category, has been slow to commit to social media. Even the uptake of the "social business" tools has been largely limited to global professional services firms and digital natives. This in spite of the availability of intranet-embedded enterprise social platforms such as Microsoft SharePoint™ which supports Yammer™, which is generally used as an organisation-specific micro blogging tool for employees.

Companies venturing into social media outside of intranets have done so with mixed results. In June 2012 industry research conducted by Sensis, in conjunction with the Australian Interactive Media Industry Association (AIMA) reported that 27% of small business, 34% of medium businesses and 79% of large businesses claim to have a social media presence, with the prevalence of social media in businesses having increased steadily in the past year (Sensis, 2012) Facebook was the dominant form of social media presence for business with Twitter and LinkedIn also playing important parts across business size. Large businesses also are reported to use Google+, Youtube and blogs (Sensis, 2012).

It is important to note that growth is, however, happening quickly. Between 2011 and 2012, the proportion of small to medium enterprises (SMEs) with a social media presence increased from 14% to 27%, with smaller but significant increases also recorded for medium and larger businesses (Sensis, 2012). The investment made by business in social media that is not internally focused and private, generally is positioned as a marketing expense or an investment in stakeholder relationship-building or issues management. The AIMA Sensis report concluded:

> *The most common use of social media across all there business categories is to invite online comments, ratings or reviews. Not far behind, use for two-way communication with clients or contacts is the next most common usage category ahead of providing incentives via social media. Some 34% of small, 27% of medium and 35% of*

large businesses who engage in social media offer incentives. Most commonly these are discounts, giveaways or coupons (Sensis, 2012, p. 47).

The AIMA Sensis report drew the following conclusions about social media use by business:

- Average social media spends by business are increasing with small and medium businesses almost doubling the proportion of the marketing budget devoted to social media between 2011 and 2012.
- Large businesses were likely to have social media policies for staff, and the majority had social media training. While small businesses mostly update their social media weekly, large businesses are more likely to be doing it on a daily basis (Sensis, 2012).
- A quarter of small businesses have no strategy to drive traffic to their sites and simply put links on their social media sites to their website. The most popular method across all business sizes was to put links to social media on the business website. A quarter of large businesses reported paying for advertising on other websites to drive traffic to their sites (Sensis, 2012).
- Businesses are "still focused on establishing, maintaining and updating their social media presence rather than driving people to it" (Sensis, 2012).

The conclusion to be drawn from this is that many businesses do not understand that the basic principle of Web 2.0 is "interactivity" (Berners-Lee et al., 2001), or that from a risk perspective, they see little commercial advantage in engagement and many legal and other constraints given the laws and regulations to which public companies must adhere. There is some anecdotal evidence that resources companies—coal and gas companies in particular—whose activities generate controversy on environmental and social issues, see little benefit in, or opportunity for social media engagement. Such Web 1.0 models of behaviour may change for listed companies when regulatory authorities in Australia follow the example of the Securities and Exchange Commission and deem social media posts as an acceptable form of continuous disclosure (Holzer & Bensinger, 2013).

4. Australian Social Media Stories

The following five vignettes of social media in Australia show the interaction between social media users and the wider public sphere. Exemplified within are the universal issues that have emerged with social media, including online anonymity, cyber-bullying, and the shifting balance of power between traditional, legacy media and online media. Social media have compelled the attention of scholars, regulatory authorities, media, politicians, business, other influencers and an engaged public; while their goals and perspectives vary, the importance of social media is accepted by all.

The Qantas Pyjama Folly of 2011–Think Before You Tweet

Some large Australian corporations have proved less than adept in their use of social media for promotional purposes. One of the nation's most iconic, internationally recognised companies, Qantas, had a particularly high profile social media crisis in 2011, receiving an ignominious #epicfail accolade in November 2011 for asking on Twitter: What is your dream luxury inflight experience? (Be creative!) Answer must include #QantasLuxury. The prize was a pair of Qantas pyjamas, and a "luxury amenity kit".

While unremarkable in consumer campaign circles, Qantas issued the invitation on Twitter in the month following a major industrial dispute with employees. The dispute grounded the airline's entire fleet with little or no notice to passengers, leaving them stranded across the globe. Within 60 minutes of the original tweet, more than 50 tweets a minute were posted. The vast majority were uncomplimentary, and the hashtag began trending on Twitter (Wood, 2011). One of the most instructive tweets said: "Somewhere in Qantas HQ a middle-aged manager is yelling at a Gen Y social media 'expert' to make it stop" (Quoted in Glance, 2011).

Parodies based on the 2004 film Downfall have become an Internet meme and Qantas soon joined the list, with the role of Hitler channelling Qantas Chief Executive Officer, Alan Joyce (see YouTube at https://www.youtube.com/watch?v=QTCwPlWzZnQ))

Traditional and non-traditional news media followed the social media disaster story with glee, selecting some tweets for publication in news media reports published on digital and other platforms. Selected notable tweets (quoted in Glance, 2011) were:

> *"Getting from A to B without the plane being grounded or an engine catching fire. #qantasluxury".*

> *"#qantasluxury is chartering a Greyhound bus and arriving at your destination days before your grounded Qantas flight".*

> *"#QantasLuxury is grounding the fleet so I can fly with @VirginAtlantic instead."*

In the rush to rebuild customer relationships using Twitter, Qantas overlooked the timing and context of the conversations being evoked. While "message testing" isn't part of the culture and conventions of social media, the Qantas misstep provides a rationale for applying some traditional rigour to using a social medium to advance business relationships.

Charlotte Dawson and the Trolls

The 2012 case of Australian television personality, Charlotte Dawson, highlighted some of the darker and more anti-social consequences of social media. At times a moderately controversial television host and fashion commentator, Dawson became the target of a campaign of online abuse—trolling—after she retweeted the offensive comment of one troll (Moses & Hornery, 2012). The Oxford English Dictionary defines a "troll" as "Computing slang…(for) A person who posts deliberately erroneous or antagonistic messages to a newsgroup or similar forum with the intention of eliciting a hostile or corrective response. Also: a message of this type."

Dawson's intention was to discourage trolling by outing the offender in some way. Instead, Dawson's reaction precipitated a barrage of abuse from the trolls—from the mildly offensive to the utterly disgusting—and this drew a counter-reaction from many of Dawson's mostly young, female followers. The intensity and ugliness of that discourse around Dawson attracted widespread mainstream media attention. This attention increased when the embattled and emotionally battered Dawson attempted suicide.

Dawson's suicide attempt and the online campaign of abuse that had preceded, and continued to rage on, has triggered a wider debate in the mainstream media about the nature of trolling and the online culture that fosters bullying, harassment and intimidation. Speculation about how to arrest bad online behavior is countered with arguments around what public figures should and should not expect in terms of privacy. The actions Dawson took to expose the identity of her Twitter abusers seemed to incite a much wider reaction from the trolls, who claimed that, unlike the trolls, Dawson's public persona made her fair game.

The ugly episode was explored by commentators online and offline. Bernard Keane, a journalist with the online news site Crikey, ventured that Charlotte Dawson may have been another arbitrary victim of an ongoing online war between competing online communities (Keane, 2012). He contended that she was selected merely because of her media profile with many participants in the attack having had no idea who she actually was (Keane, 2012). Another widely discussed aspect of the Dawson case was perception of this attack as enthusiastically anti-female (Keane, 2012). At the time of writing Charlotte Dawson was continuing her career and she involved with Community Brave, an anti-cyber bullying initiative.

Destroy the Joint

One of Australia's highest rating broadcasters, Alan Jones, is also one of the country's most divisive and controversial figures (Masters, 2007). Known for his politically and socially conservative views, Jones' role as a popular Sydney breakfast radio host provides him with a national platform to shape and shock public discourse. In September 2012, Jones claimed on-air that women in Australia were "destroying the joint." His rant singled out the female Australian Prime Minister, Julia Gillard—a favourite target— as well as Sydney's Mayor, Clover Moore and former Victorian Police Chief, Christine Nixon (Farr, 2012). Rather than explode with insults at the broadcaster, women such as Sydney ad and media personality, Jane Caro, and surgeon Jill Tomlinson started the hashtag #destroythejoint, triggering an avalanche of satirical and potent tweets (Tuohy, 2012). The witty Twitter hashtag trended for four days. Jones triggered an outpouring of humour and created another reason for like-minded Australians, women and men, to reshape the discourse around women and leadership. At the time of writing there were over 27,000 likes on the Destroy the Joint community Facebook page.

The community's Facebook page states that: "This page is for people who are sick of the sexism dished out to women in Australia, whether they be our Prime Minister or any other woman…. We're not out to destroy the joint - that was someone else's description. We're rebuilding it with good humour and optimism," (Destroy the Joint, 2012).

Jones' comments had a commercial impact. Pressure on the brands advertising with Jones' show was applied by "Destroy the Joint" participants and sympathisers. The efforts produced results when many withdrew their advertising. The radio station's management then suspended advertising "in a bid to change the narrative in which Jones was being abandoned in a highly visible (well, audible) way by his supporters," (Angyal 2012).

Jill Meagher and the Scales of Justice

When the young, beautiful and married ABC employee, Jill Meagher, disappeared on her very short journey home one evening in Melbourne, one of her distraught husband's first actions was to post a message on Facebook. He asked Jill's friend if she knew what may have become of his wife. There started a short and ultimately tragic search for the brutally murdered young woman which was dramatically supported by the anguished outreach of family and friends who used social media platforms like Facebook and Twitter.In the aftermath, police and Meagher's family applauded the role social media had played in the successful investigation of the circumstances of Jill's death and the identification of her alleged killer (Posetti, 2012).

The next chapter of this story has given rise to an important and unresolved conflict between the Australian legal system and the conventions and culture of social media. The very outpouring of grief over Meagher's death and anger at her alleged killer has, at times, threatened the prosecution of the accused. The principle of sub judice governs publication in the state in which a case is to be prosecuted. Broadcast, print and online media in this country are required by law to restrict publication of any material about a person under arrest that could be prejudicial to a fair trial or facing charges (Posetti, 2012). The laws have long been part of the bounded and organisationally-tethered world of traditional media. The risks of "trial by social media," which have been the subject of discussion among Australian journalists, law and media academics for some time, have been richly illustrated by the Meagher case.

The anger directed at Meagher's accused murderer precipitated his legal team's successful bid to suppress media coverage of the case. Traditional media argue that their silence would be irrelevant given the ubiquity of social media attention to the case. While the social media chatter continued, calls were made by the courts, police, and even Meagher's grieving husband for more restraint in the frenzy of online outrage. One of Australia's foremost media law experts, Mark Polden, reiterated on the news site Crikey, that commentary around the case would have potentially dire consequences for the administration of justice (Knott, 2012). Of social media commentary, Polden said. "Individuals need to ask themselves: does what I'm doing have the potential to interfere with a fair trial? Could my sense of moral outrage lead to someone not being able to get a fair hearing?" (Knott, 2012).

Subsequently, one of Australia's best known outrage specialists, the controversial broadcaster Derryn Hinch, was charged with contempt by breaching a Supreme Court suppression order. Hinch—known in Australia as "the Human Headline—used his blog to post other details of the case (Russell, 2013). In the wake of the Meagher case, the Attorney General in the state of Victoria has set up a working group comprising academics, journalists, lawyers, lawmakers and social media company representatives in an effort to navigate this complex but fascinating territory (Posetti, 2012).

The Rise of the Fifth Estate: Greg Jericho and Grog's Gamut

The traditional rationale for the mass media has been to keep those in power accountable. This is known as the Fourth Estate theory of the press, which draws from Thomas Carlyle's famous aphorism about the reporting of the House of Commons (Carlyle, 1850). In the Australian context, such a role for the media has been championed by academic and current ABC board member, Julieanne Schultz (1998) in her Reviving the fourth estate: democracy, accountability and the media. However, social media do not compete with legacy media, but critique it.

One such critical commentator was Greg Jericho, a Canberra public servant who blogged and tweeted anonymously as Grog's Gamut, until outed by a journalist then at The Australian, James Massola. As Jericho watched both Commonwealth and State politics, especially the 2010 national election, he grew increasingly discontented with the vapid quality of Australian political journalism. He began to use his blog to launch scathing attacks on the mainstream media, including one excoriating post:

> *Here's a note to all the news directors around the country: Do you want to save some money? Well then bring home your journalists following Tony Abbott and Julia Gillard, because they are not doing anything of any worth except having a round-the-country twitter and booze tour.*
> *It is a sad thing to say but we could lose 95 percent of the journalists following both leaders and the nation would be none the poorer for it. In fact we would probably be better off because it would leave the 5 percent who have some intelligence and are not there to run their own narrative a chance to ask some decent questions of the leaders. Some questions which might actually reveal who would be the better leader of this country. (Grog's Gamut, 2010).*

Massola (2010) rationalised his outing of Jericho on the grounds that Jericho's posts demonstrated an ostensible bias against the politically conservative Opposition, which was unconscionable, and a breach of the Australian Public Service (APS) Code of Conduct, given his employment as a Commonwealth public servant, even though he blogged anonymously (Massola, 2010). There is a widely held alternative view that Jericho was outed because of his uncompromising views on contemporary journalism practice and news management, and was even payback by a vexed News Ltd. Jericho subsequently resigned from the APS, and wrote a book about his experience. In broad terms, he makes the case for political blogging, and the 'fifth estate', as he styles it, to be a corrective to the corporatist, and even corrupt, transactional nature of contemporary mainstream journalistic practice. In particular, he argues through the use of case studies from recent Australian federal politics, for the function of Twitter in enabling real time reporting of events (Jericho, 2013). His observations about Australian political blogging being left-leaning and male dominated are astute.

5. Public Policy and Social Media

Infrastructure: The National Broadband Network

Social media, as part of the digital economy, rely on broadband infrastructure, both terrestrial and wireless. Increasing commercial and consumer demand for faster broadband download speeds is a challenge for governments who have to set the policy parameters, foster the construction of the required infrastructure, regulate both its provision and ultimate content, and also for the commercial service providers. Even more so, given the size of the Australian land mass (7.692 million km2) is almost as large as the land area of the United States (9.83 million km2), and the relatively small population of Australia (23 million) compared with some 315 million people in the United States.

The incumbent ALP government's solution has been the creation of the National Broadband Network, (NBN) a publicly funded, nation-building project designed to provide future-oriented fast broadband access (100Mbps), principally by way of fibre to the premises (FTTP) at an estimated, but contested, cost of approximately $40 billion (AUD). It is funded through government bonds sold at around 4% but returning 7% on the investment, such that the NBN should pay for itself by 2034 and then be an asset fully-owned by the Australian people (Smith, 2012).

The NBN will be a monopoly provider wholesaling to broadband retailers. Established in 2009, the NBN proposes to reach 93% of Australia's population with FTTP over the decade long roll out, with the remaining remote customer provided with fixed wireless and satellite services. At the time of writing, the NBN is significantly behind its projected target of having nearly one third of a million households connected. The actual number of connections at the time of writing is approximately 200,000 (ABC News Online, 2013).

Until recently, the NBN has been a sharp point of difference between the social democratic ALP government and their conservative Liberal National Party (LNP) coalition opposition, who at the 2010 national election opposed the NBN as proposed by the government, and was properly critical of the failure to provide a transparent cost benefit analysis of the project, and for rejecting a market driven solution, and for budget overreach. In this they were joined in a vociferous campaign by the Rupert Murdoch-owned national Australian newspaper, The Australian. Given the NBN rollout is now underway, the opposition have opted for a cheaper but technologically more limited fibre to the node (FTTN) plan, as opposed to the government's FTTP plan (Le May, 2013). One strong proponent of the government model, and opponent of the opposition plan, is Nick Ross, a technology journalist at the tax-payer funded national broadcaster, the ABC (Ross, 2013). Both the ABC (MediaWatch, 2013) and The Australian (Maddern, 2013) have reported that Ross has been reminded by ABC management of his obligations towards fair and balanced reporting on such issues. In the political blogosphere, however, there are suggestions that this is designed to cap criticism of the opposition's plan, and to foster the interests of Murdoch's pay-tv interests (Cummings 2013a; 2013b). Murdoch's News Ltd owns 50% of Foxtel, Australia's monopoly pay tv provider. The other 50% is owned by Telstra, Australia's dominant telco.

6. Regulation of Social Media

Regulation of electronic media in Australia is the responsibility of the Australian Communications and Media Authority (ACMA). The extent to which this includes social media, as we have defined it is, at the time of writing, unclear. The regulatory model, styled "co-regulation", involves the various industry groups, working with ACMA to develop codes of practice which are then endorsed and enforced by the regulator. The codes fall into four groups: radio, television, telecommunications, and Internet service providers. While the regulation of telecommunications is principally about customer service standards for telcos, the regulation of ISPs is principally about the regulation of online pornography.

In relation to online content, as distinct from social media, ACMA has the following functions: It investigates complaints about online content, including online gambling services; it encourages the development codes of practice for Internet Service Providers, and online content providers, and it has an advocacy role in relation to Internet safety. So, for example it has consistently commissioned and promoted research on solutions to cyber bullying (ACMA, 2010).

"Serious Bloggers" and the Australian Press Council

The Australian Press Council is the self-regulatory body of the print media and it embodies the public interest versus profit contradiction (2012). It was established in 1976 with two main aims: to help preserve the traditional freedom of the press within Australia and to ensure that the free press acts responsibly and ethically. The Press Council has long been criticised as being ineffective, lacking teeth, and a captive of the publisher members who fund it, "the publisher's poodle" (Hirst & Harrison, 2006, pp. 170–71). The Press Council was re-energised with the appointment of Professor Julian Disney as chair in 2009. Prior to the announcement of the Finkelstein Inquiry, the Press Council was seeking to extend its reach to cover what Julian Disney described as "serious bloggers", and online news sites not affiliated with current publisher members, (Jackson, 2010; Chessell, 2012). In May 2012 Disney announced that four online-only publishers had joined the APC. They were Private Media, the publisher of Crikey, and other online publications, Focal Attractions, publisher of the Mumbrella website, and two other niche online publications one in banking and one in cinema, (APC, 2012).

The Convergence Review (2012)

Recognising that the existing media policy framework, based as it was around the Broadcasting Services Act 1992 as amended, was a victim of what Hirst and Harrison (2006, p. 265ff) describe as the techno-legal time gap, the Australian government in 2010 established a three person enquiry "to review the current policy framework for the production and delivery of media content and communications services" (DBCDE, 2012, p 110). The Convergence Review attempted to establish how to regulate the future standards, conduct, and technical aspects of communication media, with all its differing platforms. In essence, the Convergence Review proposed a single regulator for all media platforms, but the stance on regulation was inconsistent, especially with regard to user-generated content in social media (Rintel, 2012)

The Convergence Review recognised that industry regulation of user-generated content was likely better than government regulation, but also notes the problem of limited accountability. Its report identified that some hosts of user-generated material are "only scrutinised if users complain" meaning they have "limited accountability for their content" (p. 40). The report approvingly cites a 2008 investigation by the UK House of Commons Culture, Media and Sport Committee on Harmful Content on the Internet and in Video Games (House of Commons, 2008, p. 3) which concluded:

> *It is not standard practice for staff employed by social networking sites or video sharing sites to preview content before it can be viewed by consumers. Some firms do not even undertake routine review of material uploaded, claiming that the volumes involved make it impractical. We were not persuaded by this argument, and we recommend that proactive review of content should be standard practice for sites hosting user-generated content.*

To engage in "proactive review" of content would create circumstance akin to those which led to global protests against the Stop Online Piracy Act (SOPA) introduced into the US Congress in late 2011 which proposed active monitoring of copyright violation (Goodman, 2012). In that case a digital blackout by a number of online service providers saw the proposed legislation discontinued.

In the report of the Convergence Review, the nature of a "proactive review of content" was not directly defined, potentially opening the door to very wide monitoring and other requirements. The Review was most concerned about preventing the viewing of inappropriate content, especially by children, and thus strays into tacit approval of schemes to restrict access to material deemed inappropriate, and while it does not recommend revisiting the controversial and failed Cleanfeed ISP filtering system (Falconer, 2012) nor does it argue strongly against it.

Copyright Review 2013

The issues before Convergence Review have also became enmeshed with the Australian Law Reform Commission (ALRC) review of copyright, currently in progress with a final report due late 2013 (ALRC, 2012). The Convergence Review, for its part, treated the positive fair use of images, video, or audio from copyright sources mixed into/mashed-up in user images, videos, or audio (central issues of what convergence actually materially involve) as beyond its scope:

> *The Convergence Review proposes that the issue of retransmission be examined as part of this ALRC review. The Review also proposes that in investigating content-related competition issues, the regulator should have regard to copyright implications and be able to refer any resulting copyright issues to the relevant minister for further consideration by the government," (DBCBE, 2012, p. 33).*

This failure to take a position on the definition of "fair use" is a missed opportunity, and means the Copyright Review will not be able to treat the Convergence Review as a source of alignment between notions of convergence with those of personal fair use.

The Copyright Review Issues Paper appears to have a more sophisticated approach to the issues of user-generated, and user-appropriated, content than the Convergence Review. It poses nuanced questions surrounding "copying for private use" (ALRC, 2012, pp. 28–32), "online use for social, private or domestic purposes" (ALRC, 2012, pp. 33–35), and, most importantly, "transformative use" (ALRC, 2012, pp. 36–40), which acknowledges that "copyright materials being used in transformative and collaborative ways—for example, in 'sampling', 'remixes' and 'mashups'" (ALRC, 2012, p. 39). These are critical uses of online digital materials, especially given that Australians, in common with people around the world, often use copyright materials in the creation of image macros and other memes in order to comment on current social issues (Rintel, 2013).

However, most troubling in the copyright discussion paper is the failure to refer to various international trade agreements that Australia is in the process of negotiating or signing, such as the Trans-Pacific Partnership (TPP). The Trans Pacific Partnership is essentially a multi-lateral trade agreement between Australia, Canada, Malaysia, Mexico, Peru, the USA and Vietnam which builds on an existing trade agreement between Brunei Darussalam, Chile, New Zealand and Singapore. This, along with the Anti-Counterfeiting Trade Agreement (ACTA) will harmonise copyright laws across trading regions. The processes surrounding the TPP, in particular, are not transparent (Anderson, 2012) and the issue has received little mainstream media attention in Australia.

The EFF's leaked copy of the US draft TPP chapter on intellectual property (Electronic Frontier Foundation, nd) does not contain the words "fair", "share", or other synonyms that might indicate an interest in the free flow of ideas, let alone concepts such as "transformative use". On the other hand, words such as "trademark", "copyright", "patent", all of which treat ideas as property to be jealously guarded, are very prominent. In short, property rights and infringement provisions are created for corporations and governments, but few to no positive rights are created for individuals or the flow of ideas, with the consequent implications for users of social media.

The Copyright Review's terms of reference require it to account for "Australia's international obligations" (ALRC 201, p. 3), but Professor Jill McKeough, the ALRC Commissioner, made it clear in various briefings about the Review that the Attorney-General (2012) advised that these agreements were not to be dealt with. While this does allow a commendable 'clean slate' approach to the issues, it further obfuscates the effects of trade agreements on social media use in Australia

The Finkelstein Inquiry

While the Convergence Review was under way, The News of the World scandal broke, and in September 2011, at the prompting of their coalition partners, The Greens, the Gillard government and in particular the Minister for Broadband, Communications and the Digital Economy, Senator Stephen Conroy, opted for a short, sharp inquiry into the print media, to be headed by retired Federal Court judge Ray Finkelstein QC (Conroy, 2011). Finkelstein's terms of reference were inter alia to examine:

a. The effectiveness of the current media codes of practice in Australia, particularly in light of technological change that is leading to the migration of print media to digital and online platforms.

b. The impact of this technological change on the business model (of) traditional media organisations... in the changed media environment.

c. Ways of substantially strengthening the independence and effectiveness of the Australian Press Council, including in relation to online publications, and with particular reference to the handling of complaints (Finkelstein, 2012, p. 13).

While ostensibly examining "technological change that is leading to the migration of print media to digital and online platforms", and the regulation of online publications, the Finkelstein Inquiry was, as argued elsewhere (Harrison, 2013, pp. 65–70), an investigation motivated by a political desire to get square with News Ltd, which had been consistently critical of the government. It was deeply flawed in both process and outcomes.

Regulatory Reform Legislation Fails

In March 2013 an abortive attempt was made by the national government to bring coherence to the media regulation framework through an overarching Public Interest Media Advocate. This followed the two reviews of media policy discussed above: a broad review around convergence, and a shorter, sharper and more controversial review of print media, and their online offshoots (Harrison, 2013). The first, Convergence Review was an attempt to rationalise the regulation of legacy media and the so-called "new" media (Harrison, 2013).

The attempt failed because the ruling party was unable to secure crossbench support for the changes on the floor of the Parliament. Vociferous opposition to the changes was led by newspaper publishers, who argued that the proposed new regime represented unprecedented government interference in the freedom of the press.

Projecting forward to the likelihood of a change of government in Australia after September 14, 2013, and the ascension of Malcolm Turnbull as Minister for Communications, Broadband and the Digital Economy, News Ltd commentator Mark Day observed:

> *Conroy's bills paid little heed to the fact that media regulation in Australia is past its use-by date. Most of it dates from 1992 when the Internet was in its infancy, mobile phones were like bricks and had none of the computing and communication power of smartphones, pay television was a lobbyist's territory and the media world was divided neatly into print, radio and TV.*
>
> *Conroy's bills are gone, thankfully, but the problem of outmoded regulation remains. Conroy tackled none of this. Turnbull must. He must also address the recommendations of the Convergence Review, also largely ignored by Conroy, who chose to cherry-pick one part of the CR's recommendations on ownership control provisions (Day, 2013, p. 23).*

Subsequently, ACMA announced that it would look at "what content benchmarks media audiences are looking to safeguard as delivery platforms change," release a discussion paper on Regulatory strategies for a network economy and society, examining digital content identity and reputation; and undertake further research on both privacy protection and financial risk associated with mobile phone applications, cloud computing and new wireless technologies such as Near Field Communications (Chapman, 2013; Bodey, 2013). The net effect of these initiatives is that changes to the regulation of online media, and any flow on effect to social media in particular, will progress by way of regulation rather than legislation.

Underlying much of the public discussion about regulatory reform is the expectation that there will be a change of government after the scheduled national election in September 2013, and the policy framework will be tempered by the incoming conservative government's commitment not only to the free market, but also to freedom of expression.

7. Social Media, Surveillance and National Security

The rise in volume, and complexity, and the globalised interconnection of social media data represents a huge challenge for national security and law enforcement agencies, which in July 2012 were successful in having the national Parliament's Joint Committee on Intelligence and Security begin an inquiry into telecommunications interception and security reform (House of Representatives, 2012). This was accompanied by a discussion paper from the Attorney-General (2012) which argued there were national security implications around the combination of mobile, distributed, and social network services (pp. 18–19). Social networking and cloud computing were specifically named as two forms of current telecommunication architecture undreamed of in the 'post and POTS (Plain Old Telephone Service)' era of the 1970s, when interception legislation was last overhauled. The inability to legally intercept data moving over such architectures was argued to create "vulnerabilities in the interception regime that are capable of being manipulated by criminals" (p. 27). There were some 236 responses to the proposals, both supportive (law enforcement and intelligence agencies and allied groups) and resistant (primarily civil society privacy associations). Although expected to report in March 2013, the inquiry is still in progress as of the time of writing.

The balance between the need for improved interception and security measures versus proportional safeguards for human rights, privacy, along with minimising impact on business, became a point of contention. One of the most salient points of debate was that regard to a proposal for mandatory data retention.

The AG's Discussion Paper noted the point in the Terms of Reference that interception and security could be improved if Internet Service Providers were required to meet a mandatory two-year data retention of all customers' meta-data (all information about a communication object bar its specific content). However, the details were limited to repeating the point from the Terms of Reference (p. 10, 13), limited treatment as a reasonable requirement (p. 25), very limited definitions (p. 58), and only a brief reference to balance in terms of being subject to existing privacy laws (p. 55).

Into this proposal, Electronic Frontiers Australia (EFA), a non-profit group advocating digital freedom, access and privacy, rejected projected reforms as "an unprecedented programme of mass surveillance that would invade the privacy of all Australians in the name of catching a tiny minority of serious wrong-doers", (EFA, p. 11). EFA argued:

Central to many of the services that Australians deliberately sign-up for—e.g. Facebook, Twitter, Pinterest, Apple iCloud, etc.—is the concept of sharing across networks. In surveillance of a target's activities in such services, shared friends or media objects connect target and non-target individuals such that following one surveillance target inescapably involves collateral surveillance necessarily breaching the privacy of non-targets… and that the Government should not take advantage of this fact to breach individual privacy in the name of national security. (p. 11).

EFA also pointed out that government agencies did not have a particularly good track record on data security, an issue that would need considerable scrutiny given the 'honeypot' nature of masses of data on Australian citizens.

8. A Final Thought

The rhetoric of 'The Asian Century' has again returned to Australia's political discourse (Camilleri, Martin & Michael, 2013), but the geographic reality remains unchanged. Lying south-east of the Asian landmass, the Australian continent of 7.692 million square kilometers, with a population of over 22 million, is part of Asia. Forty percent of Australians were born overseas, according to the 2011 Census of Population and Housing. Almost one third of those were born in Asia (ABS, 2013). China, Japan, the United States and the Republic of Korea were the nation's top four trading partners in 2011, with over 70 % of Australia's trade with member countries of the

Asia-Pacific Economic Cooperation (APEC) group (Department of Foreign Affairs and Trade, 2012. p. 5).

Perhaps because of vast distances between Australian cities and between Australia and the rest of the world, Australians have long been early adopters of emerging communication technologies, but as Malcolm Turnbull said in his 2012 Alfred Deakin Lecture, commemorating one of Australia's early prime ministers:

> *While the hardware and software of the Internet are indispensable, the scarcest and most valuable resource has never been technology, but technological imagination (Turnbull, 2012).*

The real challenge for social media in "The Asian Century", then, will be to leverage our technological imagination to foster harmonious social ties in a lingustically and culturally diverse region.

Acknowledgements

The authors acknowledge the assistance of John Buencamino, Courtney McKean, and Amber Marshall in researching this chapter.

References

Adcorp. (2012, August). Retrieved from: http://www.adcorp.com.au/news-blog/social-media-statistics-august-2012,-australia-new

Adcorp. (2013, March). Retrieved from: http://www.adcorp.com.au/Social-Media-Statistics-Mar-2013-Aust-NZ

Anderson, N. (2012, February 2). Beyond ACTA: next secret copyright agreement negotiated this week—in Hollywood. *Ars Technica*. Retrieved from: http://arstechnica.com/tech-policy/2012/02/beyond-acta-next-secret-copyright-agreement-negotiated-this-weekin-hollywood/

Angyal, C. (2012, December 11). How to destroy the joint. Retrieved from: http://www.dailylife.com.au/news-and-views/news-features/how-to-destroy-the-joint-20121210-2b51b.html

Attorney-General's Department (2012). Equipping Australia against emerging and evolving threats. A Discussion Paper. Retrieved from: http://www.aph.gov.au/Parliamentary_Business/Committees/House_of_Representatives_Committees?url=pjcis/nsl2012/index.htm

Australian Broadcasting Corporation (ABC) News Online. (2013, March 21). NBN rollout to fall well short of initial target. Retrieved from: http://www.abc.net.au/news/2013-03-21/nbn-figures/4587008

Australian Bureau of Statistics (ABS). (2012a). 8153.0 - Internet Activity, Australia. Canberra ACT. Retrieved from: http://www.abs.gov.au/ausstats/abs@.nsf/mf/8153.0

Australian Bureau of Statistics (ABS). (2012b). 8166.0 - Summary of IT Use and Innovation in Australian Business, 2010-11, Canberra ACT. Retrieved from http://www.abs.gov.au/AUSSTATS/abs@.nsf/Lookup/8166.0Main+Features12010-11?OpenDocument

Australian Bureau of Statistics (ABS) (2013). 2071.0 - Reflecting a Nation: Stories from the 2011 Census, 2012–2013. Cultural Diversity in Australia. Retrieved from: http://www.abs.gov.au/ausstats/abs@.nsf/Lookup/2071.0main+features902012-2013

Australian Communication and Media Authority (ACMA) (2010). Cybersmart parents. Connecting parents to cybersafety resources. Retrieved from: http://www.acma.gov.au/webwr/_assets/main/lib310665/cybersmart%20parents_connecting%20parents%20to%20cybersafety%20resources.pdf

Australian Communications and Media Authority (ACMA). (2013). Smartphones and tablets. Take-up and use in Australia. *Communications report 2011–12 series. Report 3.* Retrieved from: http://www.acma.gov.au/WEB/STANDARD/pc=PC_600063

Australian Law Reform Commission (ALRC). (2012). Copyright and the Digital Economy. http://www.alrc.gov.au/sites/default/files/pdfs/publications/whole_ip_424.pdf

Australian Press Council (APC). (2012, May 24). Online-only members join the Press Council. Media Release. Retrieved from: http://www.presscouncil.org.au/document-search/online-only-members-media-release-24-may-2012/?LocatorGroupID=662&LocatorFormID=677&FromSearch=1

Badel, P. (2013, March 19). Australian coach Mickey Arthur quits Twitter. *The Daily Telegraph.*

Berners-Lee, T., Hendler, J., & Lassila, O. (2001). The Semantic Web. *Scientific American, 284*(5), 28–37.

Bodey, M. (2013, April 13). Bid to untangle media codes. *The Australian.* p. 8.

boyd, d. m. & Ellison, N. B. (2007), Social Network Sites: Definition, History, and Scholarship. *Journal of Computer-Mediated Communication, 13*, 210–230.

Bruns, A. (2012, July 18). How to measure influence: using Twitter to rate Australian news sites. *The Conversation (Online).* Retrieved from: http://theconversation.com/how-to-measure-influence-using-twitter-to-rate-australian-news-sites-8123

Camilleri, J. A., Martin, A., & Michael, M. S. (2013). Courting the Dragon: Australia's Emerging Dialogue with China. *Asian Politics & Policy, 5*(1), 1–25.

Carlyle, T. (Ed.). (1850). *The New Downing Street.* Chapman and Hall: London.

Chapman, C. (2013, April 10). Speech to CommsDay Congress. Retrieved from: http://www.acma.gov.au/WEB/STANDARD/pc=PC_600195

Chessell, J. (2012, September 15). Press Council happy, but wants more funds. *The Australian.* Retrieved from: http://www.theaustralian. com.au/media/press-council-happy-but-wants-more-funds/story-e6frg996-1226137270508

Conroy, S. (2011, September 14). Government announces independent media inquiry. Media Release. Retrieved from: http://www.minister. dbcde.gov.au/media/media_releases/2011/254/

Coster, A., Dennehy, L., Epstein, J. and Te Koha, N. (2013 March 26). Boys a big hit in UK. *Herald Sun,* p. 18.

Cummings, K. (2013a, February 27). Why Murdoch's media is gunning for your NBN. Australians For Honest Politics. Blog. Retrieved from: http://australiansforhonestpolitics.wordpress. com/2013/02/27/why-are-pay-tv-providers-and-news-limited-so-afraid-of-the-nbn-final-words-for-a-dying-beast/ ;

Cummings, K. (2013b, March 12). Nick Ross, the ABC and what lies beneath The Australian's lies. *Independent Australia.* Blog. Retrieved from: http://www.independentaustralia.net/2013/politics/nick-ross-the-abc-and-what-lies-beneath-the-australians-lies/).

Czaja, S. J., & Lee, C. C. (2007). The impact of aging on access to technology. *Universal Access in the Information Society, 5*(4), 341–349.

Day, M. (2013, March 25). Conroy's NBN is Turnbull's hope. *The Australian,* p. 23.

Department of Broadband, Communications and the Digital Economy (DBCDE). (2012). Convergence Review Final Report. Canberra: ACT. Retrieved from: http://www.dbcde.gov.au/digital_economy/ convergence_review#report

Department of Foreign Affairs and Trade (DFAT). (2012). Trade at a glance 2012. Canberra: ACT. Retrieved from: http://www.dfat.gov. au/publications/trade/trade-at-a-glance-2012.html

Destroy the Joint. (2012, October 9). Posting Guidelines for Destroy The Joint. Retrieved from: http://www.facebook.com/notes/destroy-the-joint/posting-guidelines-for-destroy-the-joint/431928773521539

Electronic Frontiers Australia. (2012, August 10). Submission No 121 Inquiry into potential reforms of National Security Legislation. Retrieved from: http://www.aph.gov.au/Parliamentary_Business/ Committees/House_of_Representatives_Committees?url=pjcis/ nsl2012/subs/sub121.pdf)).

Electronic Frontier Foundation. (nd). Transpacific Partnership Agreement. Retrieved from https://www.eff.org/issues/tpp

Falconer, J. (2012, November 9). Finally, Australia's controversial mandatory ISP filtering is off the table. *The Next Web.* Retrieved from: http://thenextweb.com/au/2012/11/09/finally-australias-controversial-mandatory-isp-filtering-is-off-the-table/),

Farr, M. (2012, August 31). ALAN JONES: Women are 'destroying the joint'. *News.com.* Retrieved from: http://www.heraldsun.com.au/ ipad/alan-jones-women-are-destroying-the-joint/story-fnbzs1v0-1226462423804

Finkelstein, R. (2012). Report of the independent inquiry into the media and media regulation. Department of Broadband, Communications and the Digital Economy. Retrieved from: http://www.dbcde.gov.au/ digital_economy/independent_media_inquiry/

Garry, C. (2013, March 31). Josh Dugan's NRL career in tatters after latest social media outburst. *The Daily Telegraph.* Retrieved from: http://www.dailytelegraph.com.au/sport/nrl/josh-dugan-launches-vile-social-media-attack-on-fans/story-e6frexnr-1226609810233

Glance, D. (2011, November 23). #QantasLuxury: a Qantas social media disaster in pyjamas. *The Conversation.* Retrieved from: http:// theconversation.com/qantasluxury-a-qantas-social-media-disaster-in-pyjamas-4421

Goodman, A. (2012, January 18). The SOPA blackout protest makes history. *The Guardian.* Retrieved from: http://www.guardian.co.uk/ commentisfree/cifamerica/2012/jan/18/sopa-blackout-protest-makes-history).

Grog's Gamut. (2010, July 30). Election 2010: Day 14 (or waste and mismanagement – the media). Retrieved from: http://grogsgamut. blogspot.com.au/2010/07/election-2010-day-14-or-waste-and.html

Harrison, J. (2013). The world of news since the end of the News Of The World: Journalism ethics and the spirit of capitalism, in Cohen, S., (et al.). *Ethics, values and civil society: Research in ethical issues in organizations, 9*, 57–79.

Haynes, R. (2007, November 14). Video boost for MySpace. *The Daily Telegraph*, p. 37.

Hirst, M., & Harrison, J. (2007). *Communication and new media: From broadcast to narrowcast.* Melbourne: Oxford University Press.

Holland, J. (2012). Fragmented youth: Social capital in biographical context in young people's lives. *Assessing social capital: Concept, policy and practice, 1*(1), 163-177.

Holzer, J. & Bensinger, G. (2013, April 4) US regulators embrace Twitter for market news. *The Wall Street Journal.* Retrieved from: http:// www.theaustralian.com.au/business/wall-street-journal/us-regulators-embrace-twitter-for-market-news/story-fnay3ubk-1226612019104

Hornery, A., and Hall, B. (2012, August 31). Twitter torment: TV personality taken to hospital after abusive online attacks. *The Sydney Morning Herald*, p. 3.

House of Commons. Culture, Media and Sport Committee. (2008). Harmful Content on the Internet and in Video Games. Tenth Report of Session 2007–08. Retrieved from: http://www.publications. parliament.uk/pa/cm200708/cmselect/cmcumeds/353/353.pdf

House of Representatives. Joint Parliamentary Committee on Intelligence and Security. (2012). Inquiry into potential reforms of National Security Legislation. Retrieved from: http://www.aph.gov. au/Parliamentary_Business/Committees/House_of_Representatives_Committees?url=pjcis/nsl2012/index.htm

Jackson, S. (2010, December 6). Bloggers urged to join press council. *The Australian*. Retrieved from: http://theaustralian. newspaperdirect.com/epaper/viewer.aspx

Jericho, G. (2013). The Rise of the Fifth Estate: Social Media and Blogging in Australian Politics. Scribe Publications Pty Limited.

Keane, B. (2012, September 3). Celeb tweeter just collateral damage in online war. *Crikey*. Retrieved from: http://www.crikey.com. au/2012/09/03/celeb-tweeter-just-collateral-damage-in-online-war/

Massola, J. (2010, September 27). Controversial political blogger unmasked as a federal public servant. *The Australian*. Retrieved from:: http://www.theaustralian.com.au/media/controversial-political-blogger-unmasked-as-a-federal-public-servant/story-e6frg996-1225929679443

Masters, C. (2007). *Jonestown: The Power and Myth of Alan Jones*. Sydney: Allen & Unwin.

MediaWatch ABC TV (2013 March 11) "The difference between advocacy and analysis" Episode 6. Retrieved from: http://www.abc. net.au/mediawatch/transcripts/s3713148.htm).

Moses, A., & Hornery, A. (2012, August 31), Expert says Dawson broke the first rule of social media: don't feed the trolls. *Sydney Morning Herald*. Retrieved from: http://www.smh.com.au/technology/ technology-news/expert-says-dawson-broke-the-first-rule-of-social-media-dont-feed-the-trolls-20120831-254b6. html#ixzz2RkiYtG96

Park, A. (2012, June 21). Korean: Emerging communities. *SBS World News Headline Stories*.

Posetti, J. (2012, October 11). 'Trial by Social Media' in Australia Prompts Clash Over Accused Murderer. Retrieved from: http:// www.pbs.org/mediashift/2012/10/trial-by-social-media-in-australia-prompts-clash-over-accused-murderer285.html

Rintel, S. (2013). Crisis memes: The importance of templatability to Internet culture and freedom of expression. *Australasian Journal of Popular Culture*, 2(2): 253-271. DOI: 10.1386/ajpc.2.2.253_1

Rintel, S. (May 2, 2012). Convergence Review: a bet each way on user-generated content. *The Conversation*. Retrieved from: https://theconversation.com/convergence-review-a-bet-each-way-on-user-generated-content-6766)

Ross, N. (2013, February 21). The vast differences between the NBN and the Coalition's alternative. *ABC Online – Technology and Games*. Retrieved from: http://www.abc.net.au/technology/articles/2013/02/21/3695094.htm)

Roy Morgan Research. (2013). Social networking dominates the Internet. Retrieved from: http://www.roymorgan.com/news/press-releases/2013/1933/

Russell, M. (2013, April 9). Hinch to face contempt charge on Meagher case. *The Age*. Retrieved from: http://www.theage.com.au/victoria/hinch-to-face-contempt-charge-on-meagher-case-20130409-2hi31.html#ixzz2R46hkbi4

Saunders, L (2013, February 22). "They're not there for you!" Retrieved from: http://www.dailymail.co.uk/tvshowbiz/article-2283038/The-Janoskians-cause-havoc-arrive-Heathrow-Airport-mob-1-200-fans.html#ixzz2QzkueSXb

Schultz, J. (1998). *Reviving the fourth estate: democracy, accountability and the media*. Cambridge University Press.

Sensis. (2012). Yellow Social Media Report. Retrieved from: http://about.sensis.com.au/IgnitionSuite/uploads/docs/FinalYellow_SocialMediaReport_digital_screen.pdf

Shanahan, D. (2013, April 1) Don't let facts get in way of promoting the twittersphere . *The Australian*. Retrieved from: http://www.theaustralian.com.au/opinion/columnists/dont-let-facts-get-in-way-of-promoting-the-twittersphere/story-e6frg75f-1226609931385

Smith, M. (2012 August 9). NBN's outlook for the long-term is positive. *Australian Financial Review*. Retrieved from: http://www.afr.com/p/national/nbn_outlook_for_the_long_term_is_bCDFVpkXlT8FrLctGVzOAM).

Social Blade. (2013). Top 100 YouTubers in Australia, YouTube Stats Powered By Social Blade. Retrieved from: http://SocialBlade.com/youtube/top/100AU last visited 1 April 2013.

Social Media News. (2011, August). Retrieved from: http://www.socialmedianews.com.au/social-media-statistics-australia-august-2011/

Social Media News. (2013, March). Retrieved from: http://www.socialmedianews.com.au/social-media-statistics/

Sum, S., Mathews, R. M., Hughes, I., & Campbell, A. (2008). Internet use and loneliness in older adults. CyberPsychology & Behavior, 11(2), 208–211.

Sykes, E. (2012, August 9). Racist Facebook page deactivated after outcry. *ABC News Online*. Retrieved from: http://www.abc.net.au/local/stories/2012/08/08/3563446.htm

Tuohy, W. (2012, September 1). Witty Twitter women 'destroy the joint'. Retrieved from: http://blogs.news.com.au/heraldsun/theperch/index.php/heraldsun/comments/witty_twitter_women_destroy_the_joint/

Turnbull, M. (2012). Free at last! Or freedom lost? Liberty in the Digital Age: 2012 Alfred Deakin Lecture. Retrieved from: http://www.malcolmturnbull.com.au/media/speeches/free-at-last-or-freedom-lost-liberty-in-the-digital-age-2012-alfred-deakin-lecture/

Vonow, B. (2013 March 25) Rudd relaxed despite a lack of power for Passion Week. *The Courier Mail*, p. 6.

Wood, A. (2011, November 22). Qantas makes hash of tweet campaign. The Sydney Morning Herald. Retrieved from: http://www.smh.com.au/travel/travel-news/qantas-makes-hash-of-tweet-campaign-20111122-1nsa4.html

XIX.   We Are All in the Same Waka: Key Concepts of Indigeneous Maori Culture in the Contemporary New Zealand World View

Olga V. Nikolaeva

Department of Philology, Far Eastern Federal University,
Vladivostock, Russia
onikolaeva2009@yandex.ru

Abstract

The present paper deals with the issue of the New Zealand gradual cognitive transition from two separate worldviews (western and indigenous) to an integrated national bicultural worldview. The interaction of western mainstream and indigenous Maori worldviews in New Zealand has been studied on the material of the contemporary Internet-based mass and social media discourse. From the lingua-cognitive analysis standpoint inter-linguistic English-Maori interaction in the New Zealand media discourse can be considered a shortcut to exploring inter-cognitive western-indigenous interaction in the contemporary New Zealand worldview.

The New Zealand worldview of the recent decades has been incorporating more and more concepts of indigenous Maori culture. One of the key Maori concepts adopted by the mainstream worldview is waka (Maori canoe, and also tribe or group of related tribes). In the traditional tribal culture the concept of waka was of a great political significance, and even today Maori tribes trace their lineages to the several ancestral canoe waka in which Polynesian migrants arrived in Aotearoa / New Zealand. The object of this research is to reveal the ways of adaptation of the indigenous concept waka to the bicultural mental realm of contemporary New Zealand. The adoption of the Maori concept waka by the New Zealand worldview symbolically represents the ongoing process of cognitive integration of the nation.

Keywords: worldview, worldview interaction, New Zealand, indigenous Maori culture, inter-cognitive contacts

1. Introduction: We Are in the Same Waka–Bicultural New Zealand Worldview via Internet Media Discourse

For two centuries of contacts between indigenous population and European settlers, New Zealand had been the country with the dominant western cultural profile and hence western worldview. The history of Maori–European interaction had witnessed the turbulent periods of contradictions, violent clashes, mutual alienation and Maori isolation, and later the imperative attempts at Maori integration into the mainstream western community. The supposed unilateral assimilation of Maori however is disputable, for it appears the shifts of identity have affected both Maori and non-Maori. According to the Auckland Regional Council (2006) in the 21st century "New Zealand's future world view may be flavoured by the unique identity of Maori" (p. 7–3). It was stated in the report that "non-Maori New Zealanders may begin to appropriate or at least adopt Maori cultural images and perhaps values as a representation of their identity" (p. 7–3).

However the process of adoption of Maori cultural images by the mainstream New Zealand worldview is already under way. Linguistically, cognitively, and culturally the European mainstream in New Zealand has found itself influenced by Maori. It is primarily manifested by the growing number of Maori loan words in the New Zealand English vocabulary and discourse. According to John Macalister (2007 a) "the average New Zealand English speaker's Maori word vocabulary (other than proper names) at 40–50 words (Gordon & Deverson, 1998) have been too conservative and should be revised upwards, to the 80–90 word range" (p. 35). Scholars investigating the frequency of spoken or written Maori words in the New

Zealand English discourse have estimated the proportion to be six Maori loan words per every thousand English words (Kennedy and Yamazaki, 1999; Macalister, 1999, p. 41; Macalister, 2007b, p. 493).

The adoption of Maori loan words is the most conspicuous way of indicating the incorporation of Maori cultural concepts into the mainstream New Zealand worldview. Among the other, probably less obvious, options are semantic loans, i.e. new meanings added to already existing English words, loan translations or calques, and hybrids containing a Maori element and an element from English (Macalister, 2007b, p. 494–495).

All these lexical and semantic means mark the process of the nativization or indigenization of the English language, which in its turn is a manifestation of a new identity (Schneider, 2003, Schneider, 2007). The use of Maori loan words, according to J. Macalister (2007b), since the early history of post-European settlement has been the means of expression of an emerging New Zealand identity (p. 501). The Auckland Regional Council (2006) reports that "New Zealand's "Maori-ness" gives the country a unique identity in a crowded global market for cultural images and identities" (p. 7-3).

Linguistic research of Maori loan words in New Zealand English (Macalister, 1999, 2007a, Macalister, 2007b, Kennedy, 2001) made it clear that behind the direct lexical or semantic borrowing there is a much deeper process of cognitive appropriation of Maori cultural concepts. The ways of their assimilation to the mainstream New Zealand worldview however has yet to be described and the degree of their cognitive adaptation to be estimated. Hypothetically Maori loan concepts while influencing the New Zealand mainstream worldview do not stay intact either. They may slightly or largely modify on impact with the mainstream values. So, on the one hand, the current state of the mainstream New Zealand worldview may undoubtedly be described as transitional, due to the growing number of adopted concepts from indigenous Maori culture. On the other hand, it is still unknown to exactly what extent Maori-ness has influenced mainstream cultural values of non-Maori (Auckland Regional Council, 2006, p. 7-3).

For this research I have selected one of the key Maori concepts currently entering the mainstream New Zealand worldview—waka (Maori canoe, and also tribe or group of related tribes). In the Maori culture the concept waka has always been of crucial importance. Even today Maori tribes trace their lineages to the several ancestral waka in which Polynesian migrants arrived in Aotearoa / New Zealand. In the traditional tribal culture waka was also of a great political significance. I assume that the cognitive techniques of how the concept waka is being incorporated into the New Zealand worldview symbolically represent the ongoing process of cognitive integration of the whole nation.

Based on the prior linguistic studies my research focuses on cognitive aspects of Maori cultural concept acquisition by the New Zealand mainstream worldview. Inter-linguistic English-Maori interaction in the New Zealand discourse can be considered a way of exploring inter-cognitive western-indigenous interaction in the contemporary New Zealand worldview. To investigate the issue I have been applying the cognitive discourse analysis hypothesizing that contemporary New Zealand Internet-based mass and social media discourse is a shortcut to the contemporary New Zealand worldview.

I found it timely and appropriate for my research to extend the boundaries of the social media definition to include social interaction currently available in other forms of Internet-based media, involving author's and readers' opinions. The possibilities of blogging, leaving commentaries, discussions and debates in the contemporary public mass media made the distinction between mass and social forms of media blurred (Lüders, 2006; Croteau et al, 2012). Marika Lüders (2006) points out that implementation of digital and network technology is making an individual a potential mass communicator: "interpersonal conversations regularly take place in generally accessible environments. Similarly, mass media increasingly develop arenas where readers/users can express themselves" (Lüders, 2006). For example the "readers of newspaper websites can provide instant feedback on a story" (Croteau et al, 2012, p. 289).

Scholars studying forms of communication and forms of media (Croteau et al, 2012) state that "the Internet blurs the distinction between individual and mass audiences, and replaces the one-to-many model of traditional mass media with the possibility of a many-to-many web of communication" (p. 288). For the reasons above in the present paper I used "new" media (Croteau et al, 2012, 289) forms of Internet-based communication, including the one-to-many model with possibility of many-to-many, or one-to-one conversations.

2. Methods

Materials

The New Zealand English discourse was studied on the material of the mainstream New Zealand newspapers The New Zealand Herald, The Listener, The Dominion Post, The Wanganui Chronicle, The Waikato Times, microblogs, forums and commentaries which the newspaper articles were followed by, as well as the other New Zealand Internet-based blogs, forums, and websites. I made no distinction of the authors' ethnicity, because I studied the national New Zealand identity and the national New Zealand worldview, and it was crucial for me to see the extent to which an average New Zealander is capable of comprehending and applying Maori concepts in public and social interaction.

From the above-mentioned sources using random sampling I selected the fragments of discourse, in which the word waka was used. On the second stage out of those examples I chose the fragments where the word waka was used metaphorically as well as the contexts where it had a more generic meaning (canoe, or boat, but not only Maori canoe).

Since pre-European Maori culture was oral I found it appropriate to analyze the traditional Maori values on the material of folklore (myths, prayers or incantations (karakia), saying and proverbs) early gathered, recorded and published by the Europeans.

Procedure

To explore the degree of cognitive adaptation of the Maori concept waka to the mainstream New Zealand worldview I tried to reveal whether and in what ways the mental image of waka in the contemporary New Zealand discourse was identical to or different from that of the traditional Maori discourse. The initial step was the analytical study of values conceived in the traditional Maori concept waka (as an input) further compared with the values conceived in the contemporary concept waka (as an outcome).

To trace Maori values associated with the indigenous concept waka (canoe/tribe) I studied traditional Maori myths and incantations, sayings and proverbs. I applied analytical content-processing approach to the folklore texts in which the word waka was used and semantic analysis of the lexeme waka in those texts. The values revealed that way provided the ground for waka being one of the key concepts in the traditional Maori worldview.

I also analyzed the metaphorical usage of the word waka in Maori sayings and proverbs because recurrent metaphors reveal the cultural preferences of the society, showing the culture-shaped cognitive mechanisms by which people express and explain their worldview. Metaphors can be seen as cognitive models of human categorization of the world (Lakoff, 1987), and mental images arising in human mind in the process of perception of various phenomena. After that I classified all the metaphorical situations thematically to discover the spectrum of events perceived by Maori with the image of waka.

Then I studied the New Zealand English media discourse to analyze the contemporary concept waka and the values associated with it applying the content-processing approach to the fragments of mass and social media texts. By means of semantic analysis I investigated the usage of the word waka (direct, metaphorical, or generalized) in each fragment.

Identification of a more generic meaning of the word waka was necessary because generalization manifests a new stage of integration of a Maori concept into the mainstream New Zealand worldview showing that the concept is no more restricted only to the discourse about Maori.

I studied the metaphorical usage of the word waka in the New Zealand English discourse and then compared it with the metaphors from the Maori discourse to see the similarity and difference of employing the cognitive model waka by traditional Maori and contemporary New Zealand communities. Specific metaphorical usage of the word waka in the New Zealand English discourse different from Maori metaphors was supposed to manifest the highest stage of integration of the concept proving its being a new cognitive tool with which the new national identity perceived the surrounding reality.

So, from the comparison of direct meanings of the word waka in Maori and New Zealand English, as well as indirect metaphorical meanings arising from the discourse I drew the conclusion about the persistence of Maori values into the mainstream New Zealand worldview, their partial or complete substitution by Pakeha or national New Zealand values.

3. Results

The study of the contemporary New Zealand media discourse provided evidence that the Maori concept of waka has become one of the cognitive tools affecting communicative behavior of New Zealanders and thus marking their bicultural identity. The New Zealand worldview is currently affected by three indigenous facets of the Maori concept waka: waka as a Maori canoe, waka as a tribe/group of related tribes, waka as a land, country.

These facets of the traditional Maori concept waka are the source areas for multitude of metaphorical usage of the concept in various spheres of the contemporary media communication. The target areas of the waka-metaphor in New Zealand mass and social media are numerous and diverse. The image of waka is involved in scenarios which can be generally classified into the categories as in Table 1.

Thematically these scenarios can be realized within various domains. However, the sample fragments of media discourse (Table 1), made me think that the concept waka is extremely elaborate in either social or political spheres.

For example, the mental image of waka is increasingly employed by New Zealanders to express and explain the new trends of the contemporary New Zealand social, economic and political situation. One of them is the complex in-country social trend towards acknowledgement of both cultures (indigenous Maori and western Pakeha) to be native to New Zealand, and hence striving for integration of two native cultures into the one bicultural national whole. The distinctive New Zealand perception of the trend may be illustrated with the fragment from *The New Zealand Herald* article:

> *... co-operation involves two parties. If Maori want continuing support and sympathy for their needs and aspirations, they need to bring Pakeha into the waka by acknowledging they are not settlers or strangers anymore but, vide Michael King, indigenous people, too. (Temple, New book on treaty takes political line)*

Scenarios	Examples from New Zealand media discourse
crises or turbulent situation	"If you have a waka and it hits some rough water, there is no need to put a hole in it and sink it." (Gamble, 2003, June 07)
competition, rivalry	"in the turbulent waters of iwi politics, one waka has consistently managed to surge ahead." (Stokes, 2004, June 19)
changing views, disloyalty	"During her term, she became known as the 'waka jumper' after quitting the Alliance - for which she had entered the House as a list MP" ('Waka jumper' MP Alamein Kopu dies, aged 68, 2011, December 6)
useless and point-less activity	"paddling a waka up a waterfall" (Armstrong, Consigning Maori to History) "paddling a waka with a toothpick" (Manhire, 2012, October 26)
team work	"You do not go on the waka alone; it takes many paddlers to make the waters shift." (The University of Auckland website). "Well, we're all on the same waka," he says, smiling. "It's a struggling gig and we all work hard so it makes sense to work together." (Jones, 2010, October 02)
timely actions	"iwi and hapu began assessing the need to catch the waka before it gets too far out from shore" (James, 2008, May 06).

success and failure	"paddle our waka to excellence" (Grant, Back to school for another sharp learning curve) "My waka's certainly going to be in the backwaters, but, hey, I put myself there. Whether I've got the power, the strength, to paddle my waka anywhere else, time will tell." (Derek, 2010, June 15)
belonging to the same social group	"I welcome scientists and academics to join us in making social change for the good of our country, but there will be no room on this waka for bias." (Scientist debunks 'warrior gene', 2009, September 12) "If you don't want to paddle, get out of the waka!" (Hopkins, 2010, February 12)
leadership	"Hone Edwards, head commissioner of programming for the Maori Television Service, has been appointed as a Kaihautu, the name given to a person traditionally in charge of steering a waka in the right direction." ($180,000 guiding hand? 2003, August 15)

Table 1: Scenarios in which the waka image is currently employed

The phrase "bring Pakeha into the waka" in this example metaphorically appeals to the traditional Maori value of a waka as a common property. The Maori saying "he waka eke noa" implies that the canoe waka belongs to no one in particular, as it is the canoe on which everyone may embark (Brougham, 2007, p. 24). So, the reference is made that in the traditional Maori worldview waka was what Annette Weiner (1992) called an inalienable possession, everyone of the tribe was allowed to embark the waka, no matter who actually built the canoe.

In the current fragment of the newspaper article waka is presented as a symbol of the shared home country New Zealand, which should be perceived from the author's standpoint, like a Maori canoe, the common property belonging to all New Zealanders, regardless of their ethnicity. Cooperation between Maori and Pakeha facing lots of social and cultural contradictions is not perceived as an easy path. The waka image in the fragment above enjoys dubious reputation and may be interpreted as either a step forward in the direction of reconciliation, or a psychological means of achieving Pakeha goals. My point is that the waka image in this context hits both targets. It is definitely the step in the direction of nation integration for the only reason that recurrent metaphorical usage of Maori concepts was almost impossible in the mainstream New Zealand English discourse of previous centuries.

The phrase "bring Pakeha into the waka" in the current article however refers to one more facet of the traditional Maori concept waka. In the Maori worldview waka is not only a canoe, but also a tribe. All Maori tribes are believed to be descendants of the crews of the ancestral waka, in which Polynesians arrived in Aotearoa / New Zealand. So, the other underlying idea of the phrase bring Pakeha into the waka is that Maori should admit Pakeha to their waka/tribe, where tribe symbolically represents the indigenous Maori community.

The author of the article in attempt to produce the desirable effect alludes to the prototypical events with the waka image which mentally send back to the Maori traditional worldview. The Maori traditional values are strongly appealed to but in a new situation they are however subdued and serve mainly as a cultural background against which either Pakeha or mainstream New Zealand values are profiling.

The contemporary New Zealand worldview features the further development of the Maori concept waka as a symbol of integration and unity of the bicultural nation. The symbolic nature of the concept waka in the New Zealand worldview, its indigenousness to New Zealand was expressed by Karl du Fresne (2012): "Abraham Lincoln famously said that a house divided against itself could not stand. To translate that into New Zealand terms, we are all in the same waka and should be paddling together".

The material under study provides enough evidence of the fact that the image of waka has become the symbol of striving for integrity of the nation, the cognitive tool which is recurrently employed by New Zealanders in the perception of wholeness and unity of the bicultural country.

The other modern trend currently expressed with the help of the waka image concerns the ways of how New Zealanders see the country's political role and economic place in the world. The obvious economic and political drift of New Zealand towards Oceania and Asia is accompanied with the mental drift closer to the Pacific Rim. Once portraying itself as the Britain of the South contemporary New Zealand is shifting economically, politically and mentally towards the nearer center of gravitation.

The changing mental view of the country from Europe-oriented to Pacific-oriented may probably be traced in the image of New Zealand as Gondwana Waka, presented by Wellington based Samoan artist Sheyne Tuffery in his collection of artworks (Tay, 2006, Jule 19). According to the theory of the Continental Drift (McLauchlan, 2004) Gondwana is believed to have been a giant southern supercontinent which broke into pieces to become lands and territories of the Southern Hemisphere. New Zealand being a part of Gondwana shares a lot of common features with the other countries of the Pacific.

The example revealed the persistence of the indigenous mythological facet of the concept waka, according to which a land, a country had been presented as a Big Canoe. Maori myths and legends featured waka as a cognitive model, a metaphorical means of perception of the land where people lived, a familiar and bright image with which Maori used to explain the origin of the land. The waka as a land cognitive model of the traditional Maori worldview may be traced in one of the mythological names of the South Island: Te Waka a Maui – "Polynesian Demi-God Maui's Canoe".

The name Gondwana Waka though appeals to the mythological values of the traditional Maori worldview, i.e. strong spiritual relation to the ancestral land Hawaiki (East Polynesia), from which Maori are believed to arrive in Aoteraroa / New Zealand, however calls for scientific awareness of the Gondwana continent theory.The author of the phrase Gondwana Waka is evidently biased in favor of Polynesian traditional values but these values are no more independent in the contemporary national New Zealand worldview, they are cultural implications of newly defined mainstream values.

The economic and political relations of New Zealand with the other countries of the Pacific Rim and Asia are recurrently perceived using the image of waka. The fragment of The New Zealand Herald article "if we want to have any chance of hitching our waka to their rickshaw we need to become more nimble, more flexible, more competitive" (Key Urges NZ to Follow Singapore's Example, 2006, April 29) is a brilliant metaphorical description of New Zealand's relations with Singapore. The phrase hitching our waka to their rickshaw highlights a new symbolic facet of the concept waka, manifesting its capability of representing the whole country New Zealand in the world, though the traditional Maori values are only slightly, not more than symbolically, hinted at.

Judging by the contemporary usage of the concept waka in the New Zealand mass and social media discourse I can make the conclusion that the national New Zealand worldview is currently influenced by the Maori worldview on the level of what W. von Humboldt (1988) called the mode of presentation of reality (p. 60). The conceptual fabric of the mainstream New Zealand worldview is gaining conspicuous indigenous coloration. On the other hand, though the Maori traditional values are strongly appealed to, sometimes even favored, or at least symbolically hinted at in all the cases, they however never prevail in this discourse, playing the subsidiary role of a cultural background against which either Pakeha or mainstream New Zealand values stand out.

3. Discussion

Worldview

The notion of worldview has recently become indispensable for describing a culture, or peoples' identity, or peoples' mindset. D. K. Naugle (2002) studied the history of the concept worldview and classified contemporary theoretical approaches to the notion in religious, philosophical and disciplinary contexts.

The term worldview corresponds to German Weltanschauung which was used in the works of German philosophers I. Kant, G. W. F. Hegel, W. von Humboldt. I. Kant employed the term Weltanschauung in the sense of perception of the world, and G. W. F. Hegel used it as a general theory of the universe (either individual or national) related to religion and philosophy (Naugle, 2002, p. 70). Wilhelm von Humboldt developed a linguistic philosophy approach to a worldview. According to Humboldt a characteristic worldview resides in every language and "every language contains the whole conceptual fabric and mode of presentation of a portion of mankind" (Humboldt, 1988, p. 60). Creation of concepts is done with the aid of language. Language therefore provides the nation with an inventory of concepts and serves as a tool which people use to develop their thoughts and ideas about the world, i.e. worldview. Humboldt point out that "to learn a foreign language should therefore be to acquire a new standpoint in the world-view" (p. 60).

James W. Underhill notes that the term worldview being a calque of German Weltanschauung in fact corresponds to two German terms Weltanschauung and Weltansicht (Underhill, 2009). The scholar considering Humboldt's concept of a worldview and Humboldt's philosophy of worldview-language relations points out that in contemporary English the term worldview does not distinguish the difference which existed between German Weltansicht and Weltanschauung (p. 19). Therefore it can currently convey the meanings of both: a network of concepts which language opens to us to interpret the world, and the way the capacity given to us by the language "allows us to go on to formulate different concepts and beliefs systems concerning the world in which we live" (p. 19).

Robert Redfield (1952) introduced the notion of a worldview as a means of cultural identification of a people: "By 'world-view' is here meant that outlook upon the universe that is characteristic of a people" (p. 30). The scholar points out that by using the term, we may "describe the people's way of life in terms of all the customs and institutions which distinguish it" (p. 30), as well as we may "seek the most fundamental and persistent values of a people and describe them in terms of these values" (p. 30). Similarly Barre Toelken defines worldview as "the manner in which a culture sees and expresses its relation to the world around it" (1996, p. 263).

In this paper I adhere to the integrated cognitive-cultural definition of worldview: as the conceptual mode in which an ethnic or a cultural group, or a nation perceives the surrounding reality and expresses its attitude to the world.

I would argue that a worldview is a purely linguistic picture of the world. Language and "a language-entrenched interpretation of reality", as in Bartmiński (2009), is not the only visible presentation of a worldview, for a worldview may be expressed either verbally or non-verbally (clothes, arts, food, behavior etc.).

However the most conspicuous ways of its non-verbal manifestation often become the subject of verbal communication and the hot issues of public debates or interpersonal discussion in mass and social media. For this reason I focus on discourse, i.e. a verbal expression of a worldview as the universal code of a worldview manifestation.

The Concept of Waka in the Traditional Maori Worldview

In the minds of traditional Maori the image of waka related not only to the key means of transportation (a canoe), but also to three components of the triad "man – community – universe". Since Polynesians migrated to Aotearoa / New Zealand waka had become a spiritual means connecting people to their ancestors and their ancestral land Hawaiki, and that equaled to spiritual connection to heavens and the whole universe.

A man was perceived as a member of the tribal community descended from one of the first ancestral waka, and that was why in the Maori traditional worldview the concept of waka got associated with a tribe, or a group of related tribes. New land was also perceived with the image of waka (Te Waka a Maui – The South Island). Waka had become a means of physical and spiritual exploration of the universe, and the image of waka mentally bound together a man, a community, and the universe into one spiritual whole.

In traditional Maori incantations (karakia) waka featured divine origin, and was the object of worship. The following text is the fragment of the chant of the chief of Aotea canoe, which was one of the ancestral waka. The chant has been passed down from one generation to the next for already six centuries (The Maori: Yesterday and To-day, 2007, p. 202). In the chant the path of the canoe (and hence the canoe) was described as being sacred, and as being the child of the great Maori god Tane, who had separated Earth and Sky to let light to the World:

E tapu tena te ara,
Ka totohe te ara
O Tane-matohe-nuku,
Te ara o Tane-matohe-rangi

(Translation)
Before us lies our ocean-way,
The path of the sacred canoe, the child
Of Tane, who severed Earth from Sky.
(The Maori: Yesterday and To-day, 2007, p. 202)

Waka was pictured as a spiritual medium between people and the heavens where their ancestors were believed to be dwelling:

Tena te waka,
Ka tau ki Tipua-o-te-Rangi,
Ki Tawhito-o-te-Rangi,
Nga turanga whetu o Rehua.

(Translation)
Now the course of the canoe rests
On the Sacred Place of Heaven,
The dwelling of the Ancient Ones
Beneath the star-god Rehua's eye.
(The Maori: Yesterday and To-day, 2007, pp. 201-202)

Waka was also perceived as a savior, and was believed to save people during the storms. Waka as well as its parts (e.g. paddle or bailer) were often personified, and had their own proper names:

Ko Aotea te waka,
Ko Turi tangata ki runga,
Ko te Roku-o-whiti te hoe.

(Translation)
Aotea is the Canoe,
Turi is the man on board,
The Roku-o-whiti is the Paddle.
(The Maori: Yesterday and To-day, 2007, pp. 201-202)

In traditional Maori incantations waka was treasure, a cherished possession. In the fragment of the Chant of Takitimu the word kura (Maori: treasure, precious possession, the object of great value) is repeated four times:

> *E ka rere te rere i te waka,*
> *E kutangitangi, e kutangitangi;*
> *E kura tiwaka taua,*
> *E kura tiwaka taua!*
> *E kura wawawa wai,*
> *E kura wawawa wai-i-i!*

> *(Translation)*
> *How the canoe flies!*
> *How fine the paddles sound*
> *All together!*
> *My grand canoe,*
> *My treasured canoe,*
> *A treasure of the waters!*
> *(The Chant of Takitimu, 2007, p. 164)*

The research of Maori sayings and proverbs has provided the whole set of waka conceptual facets. Metaphorical usage of waka can be classified into several categories: waka was an ideal standard of reference to might and force either physical or spiritual, waka was the perception model of life and death, waka was the mental measure of human abilities, and human relations, waka was the image of perception of success or failure, waka was the model of description of a tribe (great, dead, broken etc.), waka was an embodiment of unity and united efforts, waka was the symbol of common property.

For example, in the traditional Maori worldview waka served as an ideal sample of reference to might and force, either human or tribal, either physical or spiritual. This can be illustrated by the Maori saying "He nui maunga e kore e taea te whakaneke, he nui ngaru moana ma te ihu o te waka e wahi" (Brougham, 2007, p. 107), which is translated as "a great mountain cannot be moved, but a giant wave can be broken by the canoe's prow" (Brougham, 2007, p. 107). In this saying the idea of might is transmitted through the image of the bow of a canoe (ihu). The bow of a waka sweeping away everything on the path was perceived as a standard of might of a war party on its march as in the saying: "He maroro kokoti ihu waka" (p. 102) translated as "a flying-fish that cuts across the bow of a canoe" (p. 102). In the following saying the might of a great tribe is expressed by the image of a hull (takere) of a large canoe (waka nui): "E kore e ngaro, he takere waka nui. We will never be lost, we are hull of a great canoe" (p. 113).

The other category of metaphorical usage of the lexeme waka in traditional Maori sayings concerns "life" and "death" domains. In the traditional Maori worldview the image of a floating canoe was the perception model of life and the image of a leaking or overturned canoe, or a canoe dragged ashore symbolized death. The Maori saying "He iti wai kowhao waka e tahuri te waka" (Grove & Mead, 2001, p. 78) translated as "a little water seeping through a lashing hole may swamp a canoe" (p. 78), displays the image of an overturned canoe (tahuri – turn over). In the following Maori saying death is associated with a leak and an open hole in the bottom of the canoe:

> *Mate i te tamaiti he aurukowhao, mate i te whaea he takerehaia.*
> *Death of a child is like a leak in a canoe, but the death of a mother is like an open rent in the bottom of the canoe. (Brougham, 2007, p. 33)*

No wonder that in contemporary Maori the word takerehāia means not only "open damage to the bottom (of a canoe), dangerous leak" (Te Aka Maori-English, English-Māori Dictionary and Index, 2005), but also calamity, disaster, catastrophe, tragedy.

The death of the whole tribe was perceived with the image of a ruined waka as in the saying: "Ka mate taku waka" (Brougham, 2007, p. 121) which could be interpreted as "my canoe is ruined. My tribe is done for and has no possibility of surviving" (Grove & Mead, 2001, p. 169). The Maori word mate (Maori: death, be dead) used together with the lexeme waka symbolically represents defeat and resignation equal to death.

The idea of collective cooperation, united efforts and consolidated actions is another metaphorical facet of the concept waka in the traditional Maori worldview: "Kaua e rangiruatia te ha o te hoe; e kore to tatou waka e u ki uta" (do not lift the paddle out of unison or our canoe will never reach the shore).

So, the image of waka in the traditional Maori worldview was of a spiritual nature, it was something bestowed upon people by the heavens. Spiritual character of the waka made it a universal cognitive standard with which Maori used to perceive a great number of things and events of human life.

The Concept of Waka in the Contemporary New Zealand Worldview

The estimation of the concept waka degree of integration into the mainstream New Zealand worldview was based on the semantic analysis of the word waka in the New Zealand English media discourse. The usage of the word waka currently falls into three major categories: direct, generic and metaphorical.

The following example illustrates the word waka in its direct sense (as a Maori canoe): "Southland history buffs and Maori are celebrating a rare find after part of a waka, or Maori canoe, was dug from the sand near" (Harding, Historic waka dug up in Southland). Such usage restricts the discourse contents to the Maori culture coverage and cannot serve as a valuable proof of full incorporation of the concept waka into the New Zealand mainstream worldview. The concept of such status can be described as a loan concept, denoting a Maori cultural realia. In the mainstream worldview it may occupy an isolated place, having almost no or minimal links to the other cognitive domains.

The second category refers to the examples in which the word waka has a more generic meaning (as a canoe, boat, but not only Maori canoe). The examples show that the concept waka has surpassed the boundaries of the discourse about Maori culture. The concept with a strong Maori cultural flavor may effectively substitute the similar concepts of a canoe or a boat or a vessel in the New Zealand mainstream worldview. The concept waka in such discourse represents the New Zealand bi-culture rather than the Maori mono-culture: "A New Zealand waka and whaling ship will be on London's famous River Thames in a celebration fit for a queen" (Hill, 2012, May 27). The concept is employed in the bicultural realm of New Zealand today to express a new national identity. Such generalization manifests a deeper integration of a Maori concept into the mainstream New Zealand worldview.

In other cases however generalization goes in combination with metaphorical meaning of the word waka. That is exactly what (generalization and metaphor) can be found in Prime Minster John Key's words: "We are sailing in one waka with a strong commitment" (Ferguson, 2009, January 24).

The metaphorical usage of the word waka manifests the third and the highest stage of integration of the loan concept into the mainstream worldview. Since most metaphorical examples thematically refer to social and political domains, let us consider the most conspicuous political and social facets of the concept waka in the mainstream New Zealand worldview.

Waka as a Symbol of Unity of the Nation

The New Zealand nation being relatively young and historically bicultural is in great need of concepts capable of conveying the idea of national unity and integration. New Zealanders are groping for the appropriate means of representation of their emerging national identity. A greater proportion of New Zealanders according to Auckland Regional Council (2006) claim Maori heritage today (pp. 3-7). Since the European population of the country is seeking the status of indigenousness equal to tangata whenua (Maori: people of the land, i.e. Maori), in their self-representation Pakeha tend to outsource in the Maori culture. Probably for this reason the contemporary mainstream worldview has recently introduced an option of metaphorical representation of the country as a waka. Let us consider the fragment from the Frogblog media:

> *We've moved a long way towards settling the Maori grievances since then, and we still have a long way to go. The rush the settlements movement of last election season has mercifully waned, left behind with Don Brash, no doubt. I for one would like to see all the treaty settlements sorted, but not rushed through and half baked. That can only lead to more tears for New Zealand. As the proverb says: He iti wai kowhao waka e tahuri te waka. 'A little water seeping through a lashing hole may swamp a canoe'. Equivalent to 'for want of a nail*

....' Let's take our time and rebuild the waka properly with all parties on board. (Bastion Point 30 Years On, 2008, May 25)

Arguing about the ways of settlement of The Treaty of Waitangi claims the author of the current fragment refers to the Maori saying in which the word waka/canoe symbolizes New Zealand as a country and as a nation. The author appeals to the image of a canoe that may be overturned because of a trifling thing, i.e. in this context – an unreasonable action, and in the final sentence the author employs the image of a waka in need of proper rebuilding so that it could take all parties on board. The symbol of a waka clearly conveys the author's point, for, as it was stated in the previous section, the idea of unity and united efforts was inherent in the Maori concept waka.

The bloggers are persistent in the use of the waka image representing the New Zealand multicultural society: "I like the waka analogy better than the sheep dip analogy, even though a bit of tar could fix the problem in either case" (Bastion Point 30 Years On, posted May 26, 2008). However they are concerned about the sense in which the word waka is used, whether it is only a Maori waka, or a New Zealand waka on which everyone (Maori and non-Maori) may embark:

Amiam: Is that the waka that shows that we are all immigrants? That our diverse immigrant DNA is mixing more and more as time goes on and that all born New Zealanders are Tangata Whenua? New Zealand is the waka and it's the Greens mission to be its guardian for all the future Kiwi. (Bastion Point 30 Years On, posted May 26, 2008)

Content-processing analysis of the mainstream New Zealand mass and social media discourse shows that cooperation between Maori, Pakeha and other ethnic groups is not perceived as an easy path, there are a lot of social and cultural contradictions. The reasoning however is always in favor of cooperation. A Maori saying with the image of waka, or a sentence or a phrase with the lexeme waka often go as a final resumé of the paragraph proving that waka is a symbol of integration and unity of the nation:

We know there are big divides between Maori and Pakeha but at least they talk and argue with each other. What worries me is that the problems the Asian community has with the wider community

and vice versa are kept separate from each other. It is hard to be one
people rowing the same waka if we don't even talk to one another.
Perhaps we can make a start. (Tan, Good neighbours are people who
speak face to face)

The discourse under study presents various samples of phrases and
sentences containing the word waka expressing the trend of striving for
integrity of the multicultural country: "travelling together in one waka",
"only together can we paddle our waka to excellence", "paddle our national
waka over the falls", "we are all on the same waka", "take the waka in the
same direction", "we are sailing in one waka", and others.

Waka as a Tool of Creating the Country Image in the World

The image of waka has made its way to the national New Zealand
worldview and is currently surpassing the country's borders to become
the symbol of the nation not only at home but also for the rest of the
world. As Ngarimu Blair put it, waka can be "a vessel to promote NZ
business and culture at major trade shows and events around the world"
(Newswire, 2012, February). Māori Affairs Minister Dr Pita Sharples
expressed figuratively that waka would take New Zealand to the world
guaranteeing uniqueness of New Zealand national identity (Finlayson,
2012, March 08). The Ministry of Pacific Islands Affairs chief executive
Colin Tukuitonga thinks that perhaps a waka on the national flag can
be "a representation of the country with the biggest Pacific population"
(Tapaleao, 2010, February 11).

Transmitting the image of their country to the rest of the world, New
Zealanders use Maori sayings based on metaphorical interpretation of
scenarios involving waka. The following example is the fragment of New
Zealand Permanent Representative to the United Nations Jim McClay's
speech:

Maori have a saying, "He nui maunga e kore e taea te whakaneke,
he nui ngaru moana ma te ihu o te waka e wahi" - a great mountain
cannot be moved, but a giant wave can be broken by the canoe's prow.
Although the challenges faced by the United Nations might seem
overwhelming, they can be addressed, they can be overcome; even

*the giant wave of the world's many problems can be broken by the
canoe's prow. And that is what the United Nations is all about; and
it also happens to be what New Zealand is all about. (Jim McClay's
speech in full, 2010, August 27)*

In Maori the canoe's prow (te ihu o te waka) which can break the giant
wave is a figurative interpretation of great might and force, either physical
or spiritual. The example shows that contemporary New Zealanders
welcome the waka imagery to express the country's strong political
standpoint in the United Nations.

To host the Rugby World Cup a giant plastic waka-shaped pavilion
on Auckland's waterfront was funded by the government. "Govt says
waka ' important for NZ image" was one of the article titles (Govt says
waka ' important for NZ image, 2011, April 06). The event became a hot
issue in the New Zealand mass and social media. The opinions diverged
on spending $2 million on the project, plastic material of the projected
waka, $20 for entry, etc.: "A plastic waka – a perfect symbol to represent
their plastic "culture"…but with $2 million up for grabs, everything that is
otherwise so precious can be prostituted to line their pockets" (The Plastic
Waka, 2011, April 06); " The plastic Waka will symbolise our struggle
against the Pakeha colonialist oppressors and that will be $20 for entry
thanks" (The Plastic Waka, 2011, April 06).

The debates over the project however do not concern the image of waka
itself, and no one seems to be opposed to the waka symbol of New Zealand
during the international sport event Rugby World Cup. As Ngarimu Blair
told ONE News TV, the waka "will be used for many years all over the
world to promote New Zealand" (TV NZ ONE News, 2011, October 13).
Mr. Blair thinks that "the waka is a symbol of how we all got here, whether
you're Maori or Pacific or Asian or Pakeha" (TV NZ ONE News, 2011,
October 13).

The media examples show that in the New Zealand national worldview
the concept of waka has become a tool of creating the image of the country
in the world. The word waka is used in such discourse generically in
reference to New Zealand rather than only to Maori culture: "Two New
Zealand waka are due to arrive at Easter Island tomorrow after an epic

three-month voyage across the Pacific using only traditional navigation techniques" (De Graaf, 2012, December 4).

Waka as a Model of Perception of Changing Views and Disloyalty

Allegiance to waka (canoe, ancestral canoe, tribe) has always been natural in the Maori concept of waka. The crews of the first waka had spiritual links with the vessel, and the Maori tribes up to now have secured their loyalty to the ancestral waka. Contemporary social media examples show that a bicultural worldview urges New Zealanders to employ the waka image for colorful description of political allegiance. The word waka is used as a synonym to a political party, the phrases waka-jumper or waka-hopper describe a MP politician, who left one political party to join another during his term in Parliament: "During her term, she became known as the "waka jumper" after quitting the Alliance - for which she had entered the House as a list MP" ('Waka jumper' MP Alamein Kopu dies, aged 68, 2011, December 6).

The image of waka is preferred for perception of political issues because it implies a direction in which the action is done: "Brash speaks of 'dangerous drift towards racial separatism', yet this is exactly the direction in which he is paddling his waka" (Tamihere, National damned by vision of unreal world). So, if the shift of political views is becoming obvious, the waka image is capable of showing in what exact direction it occurs.

The metaphorical scenarios of the political issue representation include the sequence of scenes with waka as in the abstract from the Kiwiblog (2012, October 18) below:

> *Chardonnay Guy. I'd always picked John Tamihere as a potential waka jumper, not that he's in the Labour waka to begin with, having been pushed out and currently being repelled with a three metre barge pole as he tries to reboard. That is, if he doesn't decide to swim off in the general direction of the National Party and inflict himself on the blue team instead. If Jones keeps his nose clean and commits no more major gaffes, he should be back in Labour's senior parliamentary echelon, particularly if there's a narrow loss to National in 2014.* (Could Shane waka jump to NZ First, 2012, October 18)

In this fragment the events with the waka image are transmitted by means of such verbal phrases as: push someone out (of the waka); repell someone with a three metre barge pole (from the waka); try to reboard (the waka); swim off in the general direction (of the waka).

It is interesting that in contemporary New Zealand discourse the waka-jumping scene is becoming typical of other acts of "disloyalty" not only political:

In a policy review sent to schools for feedback, it suggests tighter checks to make sure a student's course genuinely matches his or her career intentions. The change appears to be aimed at "waka jumpers" - students who typically get a visa to study for a diploma of information technology at a top school, then switch to a quick and easy certificate in horticulture at a dodgy one as soon as they arrive. (Laxon, 2010, November 13)

A lot of phrases in the contemporary New Zealand media discourse, such as waka-jumper, jump the waka, waka-jumping legislation, waka-jumping accusations, waka-jumping act, waka-jumping charges, waka-hopper, waka-hopping, waka-hopping law and others have proved the waka image to be a unique New Zealand cognitive tool of perception of changing views and disloyalty.

4. Conclusion

The survey of the New Zealand media discourse has shown that the traditional Maori concept waka is often appealed to by New Zealanders and is widely employed in various spheres of communication. The research has revealed diverse metaphorical facets of the waka concept in the contemporary New Zealand English discourse. The comparison of the concept waka direct and metaphorical usage in the traditional Maori discourse and in the New Zealand media discourse yielded the ways of adaptation of the indigenous concept waka to the bicultural mental realm of contemporary New Zealand:

- using the Maori values conceived in the traditional concept waka as a cultural background for profiling newly defined national values;

- creation of new scenarios where the waka image is employed;
- symbolization of the concept waka;
- using the concept waka as an expression of a new bicultural identity.

The techniques of adaptation of the Maori concept waka by the New Zealand worldview symbolically represent the ongoing process of cognitive integration of the nation.

References

Amstrong, J. (n.d.). Consigning Maori to history. Retrieved December 12, 2012, from *The New Zealand Herald* website, http://www.nzherald.co.nz/nz/news/article.cfm?c_id=1&objectid=3546587

Auckland Regional Council. (2006). *Forces Shaping the 21st Century: World Views.* Retrieved from www.arc.govt.nz/.../World%20views.pdf

Bartmiński, J. (2009, October). *Linguistic worldview as a problem of cognitive ethnolinguistics.* A paper presented at the annual meeting of the Slavic CognitiveLinguistics Association(SCLA), Praha. Retrieved from http://www.rastko.rs/rastko/delo/13731

Bastion point 30 years on. (2008, May 25). Retrieved from *The Frogblog: Hopping along the corridors of power,* http://blog.greens.org.nz/2008/05/25/bastion-point-30-years-on

Brougham, A.E. & Reed, A.W. (2007). *Book of Maori proverbs.* Auckland, New Zealand: Reed Publishing (NZ).

Could Shane waka jump to NZ first. (2012, October 18). *The Kiwiblog.* Retrieved from http://www.kiwiblog.co.nz/2012/10/could_shane_waka_jump_to_nz_first.html/

Croteau, D., Hoynes, W. & Milan, S. (2012). Media technology and social change. In D. Croteau, W. Hoynes & S. Milan (Eds.), *Media/society: Industries, images, and audiences* (pp. 285–321). (4nd ed.). Los Angeles, CA: SAGE Publications.

De Graaf, P. (2012: December 4). NZ waka due to end epic voyage across Pacific. *The New Zealand Herald*. Retrieved from http://www.nzherald.co.nz/nz/news/article.cfm?c_id=1&objectid=10851825

Derek, Ch. (2010: June 15). Young Audrey Rising stars to replace shamed trio. *The New Zealand Herald*. Retrieved from http://www.nzherald.co.nz/nz-government/news/article.cfm?c_id=144&objectid=10651965

Du Fresne, K. (2012, July 17). Are we one people, or what? Retrieved from stuff.co.nzwebsite http://www.stuff.co.nz/dominion-post/comment/columnists/karl-du-fresne/7288022/Karl-du-Fresne-Are-we-one-people-or-what

Ferguson, L. (2009, January 24) We're all in the same waka,' says Key. *The Wanganui Chronicle*. Retrieved from http://www.wanganuichronicle.co.nz/news/were-all-in-the-same-waka-says-key/1001281

Finlayson, H. Ch. (2012, March 08). Waka will sail Thames for diamond Jubilee. *National: The National Party website*. Retrieved from http://www.national.org.nz/Article.aspx?articleId=38072

Gamble, W. (2003, June 07). Maori broadcasting weaves tangled web. *The New Zealand Herald*. Retrieved from http://www.nzherald.co.nz/nz/news/article.cfm?c_id=1&objectid=3506166

Govt says waka ' important for NZ image. (2011, April 06). Retrieved from 3news.co.nzwebsite, http://www.3news.co.nz/Govt-says-waka-important-for-NZ-image/tabid/419/articleID/205785/Default.aspx

Grant, F. (n.d.). Back to school for another sharp learning curve. Retrieved December 12, 2012, from *The New Zealand Herald* website, http://www.nzherald.co.nz/lifestyle/news/article.cfm?c_id=6&objectid=10374686

Grove, N. & Mead, H. M. (2001). *Nga Pepeha a Nga Tipuna: Sayings of the ancestors*. Wellington, New Zealand: Victoria University Press.

Harding, E. (n.d.). Historic waka dug up in Southland. Retrieved November 21, 2012, from stuff.co.nz website, http://www.stuff.co.nz/the-press/news/6165516/Historic-waka-dug-up-in-Southland

Hill, M. (2012, May 27). *Waka whaler and royal wow*. Retrieved from stuff.co.nz website, http://www.stuff.co.nz/world/europe/6996145/Waka-whaler-add-royal-wow

Hopkins, J. (2010, February 12). Parliament's back and off to a roaring standstill. *The New Zealand Herald*. Retrieved from http://www.nzherald.co.nz/opinion/news/article.cfm?c_id=466&objectid=10625577

Humboldt, W. von (1988). On Language: On the diversity of human language construction and its influence on the mental development of the human species. In M. Losonsky (Ed.), *Trans. P, Heath. Intro.* H. Aarsleff, Cambridge, UK: CUP.

Jim McClay's speech in full. (2010: August 27). *The New Zealand Herald*. Retrieved fromhttp://www.nzherald.co.nz/nz/news/article.cfm?c_id=1&objectid=10669052

Jones, A. (2010, October 02). Rotorua: Feeling the big squeeze. *The New Zealand Herald*. Retrieved from http://www.nzherald.co.nz/travel/news/article.cfm?c_id=7&objectid=10677423

Kennedy, G. (2001). Lexical borrowing from Maori in New Zealand English. In B. Moore (Ed.). *Who's centric now? The present tate of post-colonial Englishes* (pp. 59–81). Melbourne, AUSTRALIA: Oxford University Press.

Kennedy, G. & Yamazaki, Sh. (1999). The influence of Maori on the New Zealand English lexicon. In J. M. Kirk (Ed.). *Corpora galore: Analyses and techniques in describing English* (pp. 33–44). Amsterdam, The Netherlands: Rodopi.

Key urges NZ to follow Singapore's example. (2006, April 29). *The NewZealand Herald*. Retrieved from http://www.nzherald.co.nz/nz/news/article.cfm?c_id=1&objectid=10379540

James, C. (2008, May 06). Where exactly are Cullen's treaty deals leading us? *TheNew Zealand Herald*. Retrieved from http://www.nzherald.co.nz/nzgovernment/news/article.cfm?c_id=144&objectid=10508071

Lakoff, G. (1987*). Women, fire and dangerous things: What categories reveal about the mind.*Chicago, IL: University of Chicago Press.

Laxon, A. (2010, November 13). Failure is not an option with pass-for-cash scams. *The New Zealand Herald*. Retrieved fromhttp://www.nzherald.co.nz/nz/news/article.cfm?c_id=1&objectid=10687329

Lüders, M. (2006). Converging forms of communication? Interpersonal and mass mediated expressions in digital environments. Retrieved fromhttp://www.academia.edu/406076/Converging_forms_of_communication_interpersonal_and mass_mediated_expressions_In_digital_eEnvironments/

Macalister, J. (1999). Trends in New Zealand: Some observations on the presence of Maori words in the lexicon. *New Zealand English Journal, 13*, 38–49.

Macalister, J. (2007a). Revisiting Weka and Waiata: Familiarity with Maori words among older speakers of New Zealand English. *New Zealand English Journal, 21*, 34–43.

Macalister, J. (2007b). Weka or Woodhen? Nativization through lexical choice in New Zealand English. *World Englishes, 26* (4), 492–506.

Manhire, T. (2012, October 26). Population growth? Open the doors and let 'em in. *The New Zealand Herald*. Retrieved from http://www.nzherald.co.nz/nz/news/article.cfm?c_id=1&objectid=10844542

McLauchlan, G. A. (2004). *Short history of New Zealand*. Auckland, New Zealand: Penguin Books.

Naugle, D. K. (2002). *Worldview: The history of a concept*. Grand Rapids, MI: Eerdmans Publishing Co.

Newswire. (2012, February). The Whitireia Journalism School website. Retrieved from http://www.newswire.co.nz/2012/02/waka-maori-future-showpiece-for-brand-new-zealand

Redfield, R. (1952). The primitive world view. *Proceedings of the American Philosophical Society, 96* (1), 30–36.

Schneider, E. W. (2003). The dynamics of new Englishes: From identity construction to dialect birth. *Language, 79* (2), 233–281.

Schneider, E. W. (2007). *Postcolonial English: Varieties around the world.* New York, NY: Cambridge University Press.

Scientist debunks 'warrior gene'. (2009, September 12). Retrieved from *The New Zealand Herald* website, http://www.nzherald.co.nz/nz/news/article.cfm?c_id=1&objectid=10596821

Stokes, J. (2004, June 19). Ngai Tahu - a house divided against itself. *The New Zealand Herald.* Retrieved from http://www.nzherald.co.nz/nz/news/article.cfm?c_id=1&objectid=3573509

Tamihere, J. National damned by vision of unreal world. (n.d.). Retrieved December 12, 2012, from *The New Zealand Herald* website,http://www.nzherald.co.nz/nz/news/article.cfm?c_id=1&objectid=3545961

Tan, L. (n.d.). Good neighbours are people who speak face to face. Retrieved December12, 2012, from *The New Zealand Herald* website http://www.nzherald.co.nz/nz/news/article.cfm?c_id=1&objectid=10383909

Tapaleao, V. (2010, February 11). Flag debate: Give it a Pacific look, say Islanders. *The NewZealand Herald.* Retrieved from http://www.nzherald.co.nz/nz/news/article.cfm?c_id=1&objectid=10625417

Tay, K. (2006, Jule 19). Samoa inspires flights of fancy. *The New Zealand Herald.* Retrieved from http://www.nzherald.co.nz/lifestyle/news/article.cfm?c_id=6&objectid=10391857

Te Aka Maori-English, English-Māori dictionary and index. (2005). Auckland, New Zealand: Longman: Pearson. Retrieved from http://www.maoridictionary.co.nz

Temple, Ph. (n.d.). New book on treaty takes political line. Retrieved December 12, 2012, from *The New Zealand Herald* website, http://www.nzherald.co.nz/nz/news/article.cfm?c_id=1&objectid=3575919

The Chant of Takitimu. (2007). In J. Cowan, *New Zealand electronic text centre* (p. 164). Wellington, New Zealand. Retrieved from http://nzetc.victoria.ac.nz/tm/scholarly/tei-CowYest-t1-body-d1-d12-d3.html

The Maori: yesterday and to-day. (2007). In J. Cowan, *New Zealand electronic text centre* (pp. 201–202). Wellington, New Zealand. Retrieved from http://nzetc.victoria.ac.nz/tm/scholarly/tei-CowYest-t1-body-d1-d17-d1.html

The Plastic Waka. (2011, April 06). *The Kiwiblog*. Retrieved from http://www.kiwiblog.co.nz/2011/04/the_plastic_waka.html

The University of Auckland. (n.d.). Retrieved December 12, 2012, from The University of Auckland Career Service website,http://www.auckland.ac.nz/webdav/site/central/shared/for/current-students/career-planning/university-careers-service/career-planning-and-researching/career-role-models/docs/Lynette%20Stewart%20.pdf

TV NZ ONE News. (2011: October 13). Retrieved from http://tvnz.co.nz/national-news/controversial-plastic-waka-open-4463483

Toelken, B. (1996). *Dynamics of folklore*. Logan, Utah: Utah State University Press.

Underhill, J.W. (2009). *Humboldt, worldview and language*. Edinburgh, UK: Edinburgh University Press.

'Waka jumper' MP Alamein Kopu dies, aged 68. (2011, December 6). Retrieved from *The New Zealand Herald* website, http://www.nzherald.co.nz/nz/news/article.cfm?c_id=1&objectid=10771201

Weiner, A. (1992). *Inalienable possessions: The paradox of keeping while giving*. Berkeley, CA:University of California Press.

Epilogue

Michael H. Prosser

University of Virginia, Charlottesville, Virginia,
and Shanghai International Studies University
prossermichael@gmail.com

UNESCO Professor Emeritus at the University of Tampere, Finland, Tapio Varis argued in 1999 that the rapid development of information technology was profoundly changing the economic and cultural systems around the world, thus creating a new type of world culture, with three dimensions, the religious, the aesthetic, and the economic, postulating that:

> *Two issues will dominate the future of communication for some time to come: first, the exponential increase in the quantity of information and communication in the emerging global information society and second, knowledge is becoming the most important resource in a global information economy.... Now different forms of communication and technologies integrate and converge with a speed that hardly anyone has the time or ability to assess all of the consequences, real possibilities, or problems.... From the point of view of the human being, one of the main questions could well be defining of one's own individual and social identity in the rapidly changing media and communication environment where time and space are claimed to have lost their traditional meanings—in McLuhan's words: 'space has vanished and time has ceased to exist"(pp. 5–7).*

In my and K. S. Sitaram's 1999 book, Civic Discourse: Intercultural, International, and Global Media, we included in Section I: Overview: Cyberspace, Cybernetics, and Cyber power, the following author's essays, Tapio Varis, James Brant McOmber, Mark W. Anderson and Charles Kingsley, Sorin Matei, David J. Schafer, Wei Wu, and Chris Stephenson (*See "authors' essays" below).

Following the publication of this book, in my series, "Civic Discourse for the Third Millennium", three additional books were published relating to the digital age: Leo Gher and Hussein Y. Amin's coedited Civic Discourse and Digital Age Communications in the Middle East (2000); Lara Lengel's Culture @nd technology in the new Europe: Civic discourse in transformation in post-communist nations (2000), and Richard Holt's Dialogue in the Internet (2002).

Lara Lengel wisely writes:

> Lack of lived experience in regions outside the technology-advanced "West" has left many researchers with broad assumptions about global connectivity and how the Internet affords an opportunity for open and equal dialogue between "West" and "East," "North" and "South."
>
> In the "East" and the "South," however, such an open and equal dialogue is a problematic concept, as many lines of communication are anything but open. Access to and negotiations with technology in the "East" and "South" requires careful examination (2000, xv).

Although that period, in terms of the advancement of the global digital revolution, now seems quite distant, Lengel has made a good argument for our continuing serious analytical study of social media in the second decade of the twenty-first century, especially in underrepresented regions in the "South" and "East." One of the most recent books on social media is Jose van Dijck's The Culture of Connectivity: A Critical History of Social Media (2013), which claims to study "the rise of social media, providing both a historical and a critical analysis of the emergence of major platforms in the context of a rapidly changing ecosystem of a connective media" offering "an analytical prism that can be used to view techno-cultural as well as socio-economic aspects of this transformation as well as to examine shared ideological principles between major social media platforms" (2013).

Still another recent and important book is Al Gore's "The Future: Six Drivers of Global Change" (2013). He devotes much of Chapter 2: "The Global Mind" to the concept of technology and the "world brain":

The supercomputers and software in use have all been designed by human beings, but as Marshal McLuhan once said, "We shape our tools, and thereafter, our tools shape us." Since the global Internet and the billions of intelligent devices and machines connected to it—the Global Mind—

represent what is far and away the most powerful tool that human beings have ever used, it should not be surprising that it is beginning to reshape the way we think in ways both trivial and profound—but sweeping and ubiquitous....

It should not surprise us, then, that the Digital Revolution, which is sweeping the world much faster and more powerfully than the Print Revolution did in its time, is ushering in with it another wave of new societal, cultural, political, and commercial patterns that are beginning to make our world, new yet again" (pp. 46, 52).

Gore stresses, as do many of the authors in Social Media in Asia, the outstanding pace of digital development:

> "The number of people worldwide connected to the Internet doubled between 2005 and 2010 and in 2012 reached 2.4 billion users globally. By 2015, there will be as many mobile devices as there are people in the world. The number of mobile-only Internet users is expected to increase 56-fold over the next five years. Aggregate information flow using smartphones is projected to increase 47-fold over the same period.... More than 5 billion of the 7 billion people in the world now have access to mobile phones" (2013, pp. 53-54).

All of this phenomenal digital global growth has led, Gore contends, to the rise of "Big data: one of the exciting frontiers in information science" (p. 55). He notes that: "Virtually all human endeavors that routinely produce large amounts of data will soon be profoundly affected by the use of Big Data techniques... To put it another way, just as psychologists and philosophers search for deep meanings in the operations of the human subconscious, cutting-edge supercomputers are now divining meaningful patterns in the enormous volumes of data collected on a continuous basis" (p. 56).

Gore concludes this chapter by saying:

> "The world system as a whole is breaking out of an old enduring pattern that has been in place since the emergence of the system based on nation-states. No one doubts that nations will continue as the primary units of account where governance is concerned. But the dominant information system now being used by the world as a whole—the Global Mind—has an inherent unifying imperative,

just as the printing press helped unify nations in the era in which they were born. And the decisions now confronting the world as a whole cannot be made by any single nation or small group of nations" (p. 89).

As we explored scholarly studies of social media regionally and globally, it became apparent that there was no individual book which studied the role of social media in the increasingly important cultural and geographical region of Asia. Thus it became an obvious consideration to bring together a diverse set of authors, including many whose initial localities were in the "East" to jointly study this phenomenon. It is with great mutual satisfaction, both for us as coeditors, and for the included authors, that Social Media in Asia has qualitatively and quantitatively assessed many digital trends, with cross-cultural studies, individual analysis and case studies in Central Asia, East Asia, Northeast Asia, South Asia, Southeastern Asia, and the Pacific Rim. The studies which are included suggest that we have introduced a rather broad stroke, and more studies on the fast rising developments in social media for the region will be welcomed.

*Authors' essays included in Prosser, M.H. & Sitaram, K.S. (Eds.) (1999). Civic discourse: Intercultural, international, and global media. Stamford, CT: Ablex:

Anderson, M.W. & Kingsley, C, Finding resources for the study of multiculturalism.

Kingsley, C., Interactive multimedia and multiculturalism: An exploratory study.

Matei, S., Virtual community as rhetorical vision and its American roots.

McOmber, J. B., The ideology of technology on the World Wide Web: The "Blue Ribbon Campaign" in a global context.

Schaefer, D.J., Communicating in cyberspace: Internet users and a Canadian publications ban.

Stephenson, C., The text of new relationships: Building deaf community in E-space.

Varis, T., Values and the limits of the global media in the age of cyberspace.

Wei Wu, Cyberspace and cultural identity—A case study of cybercommunity of Chinese in the United States.

References

Gher, L.A. & Amin, H. Y. (2000). *Civic discourse and digital age communications in the Middle East.* Stamford, CT: Ablex.

Gore, A. (2013). *The future: Six drivers of global change.* New York, NY: Random House.

Holt, R. (2004). *Dialogue in the Internet.* Westport, CT: Ablex.

Lengel, L. (Ed.) (2000). *Culture @nd technology in the new Europe: Civic discourse in transformation in post-communist nations.* Stamford, CT: Ablex.

Prosser, M.H. & Sitaram, K.S. (Eds.) (1999). *Civic discourse: Intercultural, international, and global media.* Stamford, CT: Ablex.

Van Dijck, J. (2013). *The culture of connectivity: A critical history of social media.* Oxford: Oxford University Press.

Varis, T. (1999). Values and the Limits of the global media in the age of cyberspace, in M.H. Prosser and K.S. Sitaram, *Civic discourse: Intercultural, international, and global media.* Stamford, CT: Ablex.

Authors' Biographies

ABE, YASUHITO

Yasuhito Abe is a PhD student at the Annenberg School for Communication and Journalism at University of Southern California. He received his B.A. and M.A. in Journalism and Mass Communication Studies from Doshisha University in Kyoto, Japan where he authored several theses on the political role of mass media in Japanese foreign policy. He then moved to the United States and earned his second M.A. in East Asian Languages and Cultures from Columbia. Prior to entering the University of Southern California, he worked for the anti-terrorism unit of Radio Press Inc, the news-monitoring agency affiliated with the Ministry of Foreign Affairs of Japan. His primary research interest concerns new media and science communication. In particular, his interest involves the changing media environment and contemporary democracy in relation to the Fukushima nuclear crisis in Japan and beyond. He is also interested in the political role of social media in diplomacy.

ADAMS, TYRONE L.

Tyrone Leeman Adams (Ph.D. and M.S. in Communication, Florida State; B.A. in Communication Studies, University of Florida) is Vice Dean of the Jeddah College of Advertising, Jeddah, Saudi Arabia. He was a Professor of Communication at the University of Louisiana at Lafayette from August 1998 to May 2013, and an Assistant Professor of Speech Communication at the University of Arkansas at Monticello from August 1993 to May 1998. He has been a Visiting Professor at the University of Iowa (1997), Oxford University (1998), Southern Methodist University (2000) and most recently the Kazakhstan Institute of Management, Economics, and Strategic Research (KIMEP) during the 2011-2012 academic year. While at KIMEP, he served as the Dean of General Studies and Vice President of Academic Affairs, while on a Fulbright Senior Scholar Assignment for the U.S. Department of State. He has a son named Alex (16) and a daughter named Cecilia (11).

AIKAT, DEBASHIS "DEB"

 A former journalist, Debashis "Deb" Aikat has been a faculty member since 1995 in the School of Journalism and Mass Communication at the University of North Carolina at Chapel Hill, which is classified as a leading research university by the Carnegie Foundation. An award-winning researcher and teacher, Aikat theorizes social media, international communication and the news media. His research interests range across the mass media. His research has been published in book chapters and refereed journals. The Scripps Howard Foundation recognized him as the inaugural winner of the "National Journalism Teacher of the Year award" (2003) and the IRTS named him the Coltrin Communications Professor of the Year (1997). Aikat graduated with distinction, attaining first rank in M. A. Journalism in 1990, from the University of Calcutta, India, where he also earned a B.A. with honors in English literature in 1984. Aikat earned a Ph.D. from Ohio University and a Certificate in American Political Culture from New York University. He worked as a journalist in India for the Ananda Bazar Patrika's *The Telegraph* newspaper from 1984 through 1992. He also reported for the BBC World Service. He lives in Chapel Hill, North Carolina, USA.

BROWN, WILLIAM J.

William J. Brown is Professor and Research Fellow in the School of Communication and the Arts at Regent University in Virginia Beach, Virginia. He received a Bachelor of Science Degree in Environmental Science from Purdue University, a Masters Degree in Communication Management from the Annenberg School of Communication at the University of Southern California in Los Angeles, and a Masters and Doctorate in Communication, also from the University of Southern California. His academic research interests include international media influence, social influence through heroes and celebrities, and the use of entertainment-education for social change. He has published extensively in academic journals and has contributed book chapters in the field of communication during the past 20 years. Dr. Brown has conducted research in more than 35 nations, including federally funded research projects in Africa. He has taught at the University of Southern California, the University of Hawaii, the University of the Nations, and Regent University. He has served as a Fulbright Specialist to the Netherlands in 2009 and to Norway in 2011. Dr. Brown lived in Hong Kong for five years and has a continuing interest in Asian media and development.

CHEN HUAN

Huan Chen, Ph.D., is an assistant professor of communication at Pennsylvania State University at Erie, The Behrend College. She received a B.A. in advertising and a M.A. in communication from Wuhan University in China. In 2005, she relocated to the U.S.A., where she earned her second M.A. in advertising from the University of Florida and a Ph.D. in communication and information from the University of Tennessee. Her research interests include international and cross-cultural advertising, new media and advertising, and integrated marketing communication.

CHEN SZU-WEI

Szu-Wei Chen (Ph.D., University of Missouri-Columbia) is an Assistant Professor of New Media and Communication at I-Shou University, Kaohsiung, Taiwan. Dr. Chen is interested in how transformation in digital technology affects human communication. Specifically, his research interests center on human interactions in the computer-mediated environment, and he explores topics such as media and health, gender, social advertising and marketing as well as globalization and intercultural differences and the impacts. Dr. Chen has received multiple research and outstanding teaching awards.

CHANG, HUI-CHING

Hui-ching Chang (Ph.D., University of Illinois at Urbana-Champaign, 1994) is Associate Professor of Communication at the University of Illinois at Chicago. Her research focuses on intercultural communication, especially relationship issues. More recently, she has explored Taiwanese national identity as constituted through various communicative practices. Her publications have appeared in Discourse Studies, Research on Language and Social Interaction, Journal of Language and Social Psychology, Journal of Asian Pacific Communication, and International and Intercultural Communication Annuals. She is the author of *Clever, Creative, Modest: The Chinese Language Practice* (2010).

CHEW, FONG PENG:

Fong Peng Chew is a senior lecturer at the Faculty of Education, University of Malaya. Her area of specialization is in language, literature study and education. She has published four books on Malay language and literature, 40 articles in national and international journals, and some translation works.

COUPER, JOHN

John L. Couper (Ph.D. Communication, University of Missouri-Columbia; B.A. Communication, Pittsburg State University) has been Associate Professor of Journalism and Mass Communication at KIMEP University (Almaty, Kazakhstan) since 2009. He was previously a Visiting Professor at American University of Central Asia (Bishkek, Kyrgyzstan) in 2008 and 2004 - 2006, Assistant Professor at Idaho State University in 2006 - 2008, and Assistant Professor at Pittsburg State University (1999 - 2004). He served as Chair of the Department of Journalism and Mass Communication at KIMEP 2010–2012. His research focus is psychological and political factors of mass media. He is also a consultant in media and communication training, curriculum development, and research.

CUI LITANG

Cui Litang, M.A., is a professional instructor of EFL/ESL, Beijing Language and Culture University-certified teacher of Chinese as a foreign language (BLCU, Yangzhou University, Green River Community College, USA and Global LT, USA), and a lecturer of a selective course in mass communication (Getting to Know Mass Communication, SICFL, Shanghai). He has served in translations (*Vengeance*, Beijing Publishing House, 1990), textbook development (*Contemporary Business English*, East China Normal University Publishing House, 2007), web development ("Let's Learn Chinese the E-way!": http://www.chinesenow.biz) and podcasting on YouTube and Flickr, with over 27 years of teaching/consultant experiences at colleges, universities and organizations in China and the USA.

As a visiting scholar at Green River Community College, he has been honored as a cultural ambassador and rewarded with an honorary membership of Green River Community College Humanities Division for his excellent services. He has received an honor for his contribution in instructions at Shanghai Industry & Commerce Foreign Language College. His writings such as "A Map Without Boundaries: William Gibson's Neuromancer-Cyberpunk Novel Reexamined"(2005), "The Communication Convention and Functions of English Discourse Marker in Speech Communication"(2005) and recently as a contributing author for "Communicating Interculturally " (Professor Li Mengyu, Ph.D., and Professor Michael H. Prosser, Ph.D., Beijing, China, Higher Education Press, 2012) reflect his research interest in linguistics and media.

DONG, DALE

Dale Dong is a currently working on her accelerated Pre-Pharmacy program at University of the Pacific. She is expected to receive her doctorate of pharmacy in 2018 with a minor in communication. Her interests in doing communication research led her to become the only high school oral presenter at the Stanford Undergraduate Psychology Conference in May 2012. She and her colleagues presented a research paper on intercultural competence, self-esteem and shyness at the third International Intercultural Communication Conference in Shanghai, China, in December 2012. She presented a research poster on emotional intelligence, self-esteem and communication apprehension at the 2nd National Collegiate Undergraduate Conference at Harvard University, January 23–25, 2013. She has strong interests in working on the impact of the Internet and social media on health information seeking and pharmacy education.

DONG QINGWEN

Qingwen Dong (Ph.D. Communication, Washington State University) is a Professor and Chair of the Department of Communication at University of the Pacific in Stockton, California, where he teaches communication research methods, intercultural communication and a graduate seminar on mass communication. He is author or coauthor of more than 40 research papers that have appeared in scholarly journals and communication publications. He has presented more than 70 communication research papers at international and national communication conferences. He was the University Eberhardt Teacher/ Scholar Award Recipient in 2007. In 2009, he received the Faculty Mentor Award from University of the Pacific and he was also the Faculty Research Award recipient of the University in 2011.

FRASER, BENSON P.

 Ben Fraser is an Associate Professor in the School of Communication and the Arts at Regent University. He received his B.A. in Religion and Psychology at Southern California College, a Masters of Divinity in Theology at Fuller Theological Seminary, a Masters Degree in Psychology at Pepperdine University, a Masters Degree in Communication at California State University, Fullerton, and a Ph.D. in Communication at the University of Washington. His academic interests include intercultural and international communication, celebrities, and the nature and effects of indirect communication. Dr. Fraser specializes in conducting focus group and ethnographic research, having conducted such studies in more than a dozen nations. He is currently producing teaching materials for documenting cultural changes among the Maasai in Africa, where he has led development projects for the past decade. Dr. Fraser leads Friends for Africa Development, a non-profit educational and development organization. Dr. Fraser has taught courses at the University of Washington, University of the Pacific, Azusa Pacific University, Norfolk State University, and Regent University.

GU, XIAOTING

 Xiaoting Gu was born in Shanghai, China. Since a young age, she has shown a high interest in literature and the arts. In the past several years, Gu's enthusiasm has driven her to learn and practice in the related realms. She received a B.A. degree in advertising from Shanghai Normal University. With a growing interest in communication, she continued her study at University of the Pacific in Stockton, California and obtained a M.A. degree in communication, emphasizing media and public relations. Gu is especially interested in research on social media and intercultural communication. Her bicultural background gives her many insights in those topics.

After graduation, she worked as the marketing manager of a law firm. In her spare time, she enjoys landscape photography, painting, traveling, and engaging in pro bono work.

HARRISON, JOHN

 John Harrison brings several decades of professional practice in journalism and communication to his scholarship in social media and digital communication. He has worked in print, radio and television as a journalist, editor and producer, and has won awards for his work in journalism. Recognized for his innovative teaching practice, John collaborates in teaching and research with colleagues in science, medicine and engineering. His most recent contributions to the media and communication disciplines include the 2011 book co-authored with Allan Bonsall, *Brand aid: Brand power at the heart of your business* and the 2012 chapter "*Knowledge and its integrity within a knowledge economy*" in Ethics in Social Research (with co-author David Rooney).

HASLETT, BETH BONNIWELL

Beth Bonniwell Haslett (Ph.D., University of Minnesota) is a professor in the Department of Communication at the University of Delaware. Her research and teaching interests span intercultural and organizational communication, and focus on issues of face, cross-cultural communication and the social impact of information and communication technologies. Her recent book, *Communicating and Organizing in Context: The theory of Structurational Interaction* (2012), integrates the work of Giddens and Goffman. Professor Haslett is particularly interested in applying this new theoretical perspective to cross-cultural interaction, social presence and social media.

HOLT, RICHARD

Rich Holt (Ph.D., University of Illinois at Urbana-Champaign, 1994) is an Associate Professor of Communication at Northern Illinois University. His research focuses on organizational communication across cultural boundaries, and new media in organizational settings. His published work includes *Dialogue on the Internet* (Praeger, 2004), and contributions to scholarly journals, including *Critical Studies in Mass Communication, Current Anthropology, and Mediation Quarterly.*

JARVIS, JASON L.

Jason Leigh Jarvis is completing his Ph.D. in Public Communication at Georgia State University. He earned his M.A. in Communication from Wake Forest University and holds a B.A.b in Religion from Emory University. Jason's academic interests include Visual Communication, the Public Sphere, and International Communication. His dissertation research is on transnational image politics and the digital public sphere.

Prior to entering Georgia State University, Jason spent seven years living in Seoul, South Korea teaching at both the Korea Development Institute School of Public Policy and Management and Kyung Hee University. During his time in Asia, Jason founded the Asian Debate Institute and the North East Asian Open Debate Championship. He also conducted training sessions and helped organize debate competitions in South Korea, Japan, China, the Philippines, Singapore, Malaysia, India, Australia, Thailand, Bangladesh, Slovenia and Iraq.

KIUCHI, YUYA

 Yuya Kiuchi is an assistant professor in the Department of Writing, Rhetoric, and American Cultures at Michigan State University. He is the author of *Struggles for Equal Voice: The History of African American Media Democracy in Community Access Television* (SUNY Press, 2012), and a co-author of *Packaging Baseball: How Marketing Embellishes the Cultural Experience* (McFarland, 2012). He has also translated *Barack Obama's Dreams from My Father* into Japanese. He has also published on African American cultural history, trans-Pacific African American Studies, and other topics. Dr. Kiuchi teaches classes on African American History and Studies, transnational American Studies, and Science, Technology, and Society Studies. He is currently working on social media policy recommendations for public school systems and intercollegiate athletic departments.

LEBEDKO, MARIA

 Maria Lebedko is Doctor of Philology, Full Professor, and honorary researcher of the Russian Federation, teaching intercultural communication (international program), old languages to post-graduate students and "Interaction of language and culture" at Far Eastern Federal University. She serves as an editorial board member of three professional journals and co-editor of

the book *Critical Cultural Awareness* (forthcoming 2013), and a reviewer for *Intercultural Communication Studies.*

She has published articles, books, chapters, databases and dictionaries. The books are *Culture Bumps: Avoiding Misunderstandings in Cross-cultural Communication; Time as a Cognitive Dominant of Culture: Comparing Russian and American Conceptospheres*; plus a chapter in the book *Language Representation of Russia Image in Mass-media Discources of East and West,* as well as dictionaries: *American Quilt: A Reference Book on American Culture* (in collaboration with I. Zhukova); and *Dictionary of Intercultural Communication Terms,* M. Lebedko & Z. Proshina Eds. (in Russian, in collaboration), and several textbooks including the latest, *Practicing Intercultural Communication.* She is an Advisory Board member for the International Association for Communication Studies, and a member of several international professional associations.

LUCAS, DAVID M.

Dr. David M. Lucas identified the qualitative method of research known as folknography. He has directed folknographic research projects in Costa Rica, Mexico, Australia, Vietnam, and the United States. He teaches communication studies at Ohio University. Dr. Lucas teaches a course called Rhetoric and Social Media in which he guides students' investigation in social media. He engages this expertise to guide the participation in this work. He has taught internationally in Hong Kong, Japan, Mexico and Spain.

Dr. Lucas has led hundreds of undergraduate students in numerous field study projects over the years. The projects have led to several discoveries. For example, under his guidance, students found a previously uncharted African American burial site where victims of the American pandemic known as the Spanish Flu were interned with no headstones or burial records. This project made international news with CNN. Additionally, Lucas and one of his undergraduate research teams found a sanctuary in Southern Ohio for refugees of American slave trade traveling the Underground Railroad during the early 1800's known as Window Rock. Along with his research and writing, Dr. Lucas travels throughout the

US and the world as a motivational speaker, guest lecturer and corporate trainer.

MITCHELL, ELIZABETH

Elizabeth Mitchell (Dougall), a Senior Lecturer in the School of Journalism and Communication, joined the University of Queensland in 2013 from an executive role with one of Australia's largest strategic communication and stakeholder engagement consulting firms where she led the corporate communication, marketing communication and training practices. Her work as a researcher and practitioner focuses on social risk, strategic issues management and stakeholder activism. She has published more than 30 articles and conference papers (as Elizabeth Dougall), related to the public opinion environment co-created by stakeholders, including communities, media, activists and government and how issues are compelled and contested by stakeholders which emerge and persist over time. The role of the media in shaping the issues marketplace. Implications for organisations pursuing, contending and arbitrating issues of contention in the public sphere, in particular, those issues that put at risk the social license to operate are of interest to her. Elizabeth teaches undergraduate and post graduate courses in the public relations discipline.

NIKOLAEVA, OLGA V.

Olga V. Nikolaeva is a Doctor of Philology at the Far Eastern Federal University, Vladivostok, Russia. She accomplished her doctoral thesis on the issues of ethnic worldview interaction in multilingual and multicultural communities studied from the cognitive linguistics perspective. Dr. Nikolaeva is the author of two books and a series of publications devoted to theoretical and practical aspects of inter-cognitive, intercultural, and inter-linguistic contacts. One of her recent works is the book on the cognitive approach to the issues of bi- and multiculturalism in New Zealand, *Kuda Dreifuet Waka?* (2010) [*Where is the Waka Drifting to?*

*The New Zealand Culture in the Dynamics of Ethnic Worldview Interactions].
Culture* and an area chair for the Popular Culture Association.

NURMAKOV, ADIL

Adil Nurmakov, Ph.D. is a political science and social media expert. His professional experience started in 2002 with providing political and media consultancy services in Russia and Kazakhstan. His clients included political parties, public figures and businesses. Adil has also been among the first Kazakh bloggers to cover social and political issues and has gained a considerable following for his articles and analysis of current issues.

In 2007 he founded a 'Competitiveness Research Center', an independent research NGO. Since 2011, he works as an Associate Professor at the Journalism Department in the International IT University. Adil is also regularly invited to speak about social media and web-activism at a variety of training and youth events (Democracy school, Central Asia youth camps and other).

In 2012, Adil has founded BlogBasta.kz, a civil initiative for the urban educated youth of Kazakhstan, aimed at increasing citizen awareness and political participation via online and offline activities.

N'WEERASINGHE, PRADEEP

Dr. Pradeep N' Weerasinghe is a Senior Lecturer in Mass Media Studies at the Department of Mass Media Studies, University of Colombo (UCMB), Sri Lanka. Prior to joining UCMB, between1993 and 2003, he served as a broadcast journalist and programme manager to Sri Lanka National Broadcasting Corporation. He was a media expert at China Radio and Television International in Beijing. His primary research focuses on public service and community broadcasting, communication for citizen empowerment, new media applications and contemporary South Asian media practices.

PROSSER, MICHAEL H.

Michael H. Prosser (Ph.D., University of Illinois) is a founder of the academic field of intercultural communication. He has taught long term at the University of Buffalo, Indiana University, University of Virginia, University of Swaziland, Rochester Institute of Technology, Yangzhou University, Beijing Language and Culture University, Shanghai International Studies University, and Ocean University of China and has had various visiting or adjunct professorships in Canada and the US.

He is the editor/coeditor or author/coauthor of 17 published or forthcoming books, among which the most recent ones are: Donahue and Prosser (1997), *Diplomatic Discourse: International Conflict at the United Nations;* Sitaram and Prosser, (Coeds) (1998), *Civic Discourse: Multiculturalism, Cultural Diversity and Global Communication;* Prosser and Sitaram (Coeds) (1999), *Civic Discourse: Intercultural, International, and Global Media;* Kulich and Prosser, (Coeds) (2007), *Intercultural Perspectives on Chinese Communication;* Kulich, Prosser and Weng (Coeds) (2012), *Value Frameworks at the Theoretical Crossroads of Culture;* Kulich, Prosser, and Weng (Coeds) (forthcoming), *Value Dimensions and Their Dynamics across Cultures;* Li and Prosser (2012), *Communicating Interculturally;* Prosser, Sharifzadeh, and Zhang, Coeds. (2013), *Finding Cross-Cultural Common Ground.* From 1998 to 2004, he was the series editor for 17 books on intercultural and international topics for "Civic Discourse for the Third Millennium" for Ablex/Praeger/Greenwood Publishing Group.

Former President of the International Society for Intercultural Education, Training, and Research (1984-1986), he received the Ball State University's Outstanding Alumnus Award in 1978, an International Communication Association Award in 1978, SIETAR International's World Citizen Award (1986) and Senior Interculturalist Award (1990); he has been honored with special recognition awards by the China Association for Intercultural Communication in 2009 and 2011. He is a Fellow of the International Academy for Intercultural Research, and he received an Academy Award in 2013, and he is listed in the Marquis *Who's Who in American Education, Who's Who in America; Who's Who in Asia;* and *Who's Who in the World.*

RINTEL, SEAN

Sean Rintel received his B.A. (Hons 1) and M.A. in English from The University of Queensland in 1995 and 2000, respectively, and Ph.D. in sociology with a specialization in communication from the University at Albany, SUNY, in 2010. He is currently a lecturer in strategic communication in the School of Journalism and Communication at The University of Queensland, Brisbane, Australia. His research focuses on how the affordances and constraints of communication technologies interact with language, social action and culture.

TIE FATT HEE

Fatt Hee Tie is a professor at the Faculty of Law, University of Malaya. His specialization is in education law, educational leadership and management. He has published 4 books on law in education and leadership in education, and 50 articles in national and international journals. Culture and an area chair for the Popular Culture Association.

WAIYACHOTE, PITCHPATU

Pitchpatu Waiyachote is a doctoral student at the School of Journalism and Mass Communication at the University of North Carolina, Chapel Hill, USA. She earned a bachelor's degree in public relations with minors in journalism and marketing from Indiana State University and a master degree's in journalism from West Virginia University. Prior to pursuing her doctoral degree, she had worked as a public relations associate at Hill & Knowlton

Thailand for a few years. Her responsibilities included day-to-day servicing and developing public relations plans and activities for multinational and Thai clients. With clients in various industries, including logistics and automotive, she had opportunities to be involved in several public relations functions, such as media relations, corporate communication, and marketing communication.

Based on her academic and professional background, she is interested in the use of social media in strategic communication, international public relations as well as crisis communication. Her dissertation will focus on a sense of brand community on Facebook pages of global brands in different cultures. After graduation, she will join the faculty of Communication Arts at the University of the Thai Chamber of Commerce in Thailand.

WU YUN

Yun Wu graduated from University of the Pacific, Stockton in 2012. When pursuing the Master's degree in communication, she found her research interests particularly within online social media and their interactions with consumers and society. She and her colleagues have been working on various social media related questions which are feasible and believed to carry social importance. She and her friend, Xiaoting Gu presented their paper *The Impact of Culture and Gender on Chinese Young Adults in Using Social Networking Site* at the 2011 International Communication Association conference in Boston, Massachusetts. Wu's research interests range from the motivational perspective to using social media, to intercultural and gender differences in the consumption of new media.

Index

Other books from Dignity Press:

Arctic Queen
The Pearl

Evelin Lindner
A Dignity Economy

Howard Richards
The Nurturing of Time Future

Howard Richards and Joanna Swanger
Gandhi and the Future of Economics

Ada Aharoni
Rare Flower

Pierre-Amal Kana
Afghanistan – Le rêve pashtoun et la voie de la paix

Kenday Samuel Kamara
Online Collaborative Learning

Dignity Press
World Dignity University Press

Victoria Fontan
Decolonizing Peace

Deepak Tripathi
A Journey Through Turbulence

Francisco Cardoso Gomes de Matos
Dignity - A Multidimensional View

Helmut E. W. Starrach
Augustinus - Ein liebendes und ruheloses Herz

Michael H. Prosser, Mansoureh Sharifzadeh, Zhang Shengyong
Finding Cross-Cultural Common Ground

Li Mengyu, Michael H. Prosser
Chinese Communicating Interculturally

Please visit www.dignitypress.org for more information

 **Dignity Press**
World Dignity University Press

www.ingramcontent.com/pod-product-compliance
Lightning Source LLC
LaVergne TN
LVHW022332060326
832902LV00022B/3989